RECORDS

I0347929

OF THE

COURT OF ASSISTANTS

OF THE

COLONY

OF THE

MASSACHUSETTS BAY

1630–1692

PRINTED UNDER THE SUPERVISION OF

JOHN NOBLE

CLERK OF THE SUPREME JUDICIAL COURT

VOL. I.

SOUTHERN HISTORICAL PRESS
INC.
Book Publishers

Southern Historical Press, Inc.
Greenville, South Carolina

This volume was reproduced
from a personal copy located in
the Publishers private library

Please direct all correspondence and book orders to:
SOUTHERN HISTORICAL PRESS, Inc.
1071 Park West Blvd.
Greenville, SC 29611

Published 1901 by:
The County of Suffolk, MA
ISBN #978-1-63914-654-3
Printed in the United States of America

PREFACE.

UNDER the orders of the Board of Aldermen of the City of Boston, acting as County Commissioners of the County of Suffolk, passed 22d December, 1890, and 8th June, 1896, and approved by the Mayor, the Clerk of the Supreme Judicial Court was authorized to prepare, publish, and distribute all the Records of Courts held by the Governor and Assistants for the Colony of the Massachusetts Bay from 1630 to 1692, and known as the Records of the Court of Assistants. In accordance therewith this volume is now issued, covering the period from 1673 to 1692.

Although chronologically the record of the last twenty years of the Court of Assistants, it has been entitled Volume I., inasmuch as the original manuscript book from which it is printed is the only complete volume of its records now extant, and all that has preserved the specific form of an original record of the Court; while the remainder of its records, so far as they have been recovered or reproduced and are to be printed hereafter, is made up of various material drawn from various sources.

This single, original volume of records is now in the office of the Clerk of the Supreme Judicial Court. It is bound in vellum and is in a state of almost perfect preservation, although somewhat worn and battered by the use of more than two hundred years. The greater part of it is in the handwriting of Edward Rawson, whose peculiar chirography and methods have required especial care in the work of transcribing. It gives a complete record of the Court from 3d March, 1673, to 22d April, 1686, and from 24th December, 1689, till the early part of the year 1692. It is designated by an original entry on the parchment cover as the Secconde Booke of Reccords Begunne the 3d of March 1673.

The earlier original records of the Court, except as hereinafter stated, are lost. The existence of a first book of records at different times in the seventeenth century is proved by copies found upon file made before 1673 and certified by Edward Rawson, Secretary, as taken "out of the Courts book of records," and is also further shown by the title entered upon the parchment cover of the volume just described. When or how the book disappeared is unknown, but it has been missing from a time beyond living memory, and even tradition has lost sight of it. All search for any trace of it has thus far been fruitless.

The volume now issued has been printed with as exact an adherence to the original as possible, and is a reproduction of it in every particular, so far as the difference between print and manuscript will allow. In its preparation, I have been favored with the assistance of William P. Upham, Esquire, which in every stage of the work has been invaluable, and to whose patience, accuracy, research, and knowledge the fullest acknowledgment is due.

Excepting the inter-charter period, there have been but three Courts established for the trial of causes, which have had supreme jurisdiction in judicial matters, during the whole period covered by the history of the Colony of the Massachusetts Bay, by that of the Province, and by that of the Commonwealth of Massachusetts, — namely, the Court of Assistants, under the Charter of the Governor and Company of the Massachusetts Bay in New England, granted in 1629; the Superior Court of

Judicature, under the Province Charter of 1692; and the Supreme Judicial Court, since the adoption of the Constitution in 1780.

During the early years of the Colony of the Massachusetts Bay, the powers and duties of the Governor and the Assistants sitting as a Court of Assistants for the trial of causes, civil and criminal, were not distinguished from the powers and duties of the same magistrates acting in the executive and legislative capacities under the Charter. From 1629 to 1641 their proceedings as Magistrates acting as a Court are entered in the same book, intermixed with the records of the General Court, — the whole forming the first volume of the Massachusetts Records, now in the State Archives.

The Court, as such, was as old as the Colony itself. The first record, which is headed with the formal title, "At a Court of Assistants," is that of the 18th of May, 1629. Its records, beginning on this side of the water with its first sitting, 23 August, 1630, and from that time on for some years, show the exercise by it of all the functions of government, — executive, legislative, and judicial.

The first record of the General Court appears under the date of 19 October, 1630, and thereafter, down to May, 1634, it met only four times, while more than thirty Courts of Assistants appear to have been held, their records occupying six-sevenths of the original pages of the record. The powers and functions of the Court sitting as a judicial tribunal appear to a certain extent in the records, — in such, at least, as have been preserved. They are also indicated by the laws relating to the inferior Courts; the act of March, 1635–6, providing for these inferior Courts in the four counties to be "kept eṽy quarter" to "trie all civill causes, whereof the debt or damage shall not exceede X^{l}, & all Criminal Causes not concerning life, member, or banishm^{t}," with a right of "appeale to the nexte greate Quarter Court;" that of September, 1639, establishing "Speciall Courts" to be held quarterly by "such of the Magistrats as shall reside in or near to Boston, or any 5, 4, or 3, of them, the Governo^{r} or Deputie to bee one," with substantially the powers of the County Courts; and by other acts establishing the Strangers' Court and other small Courts. Such Courts, though the Magistrates sat in them, were wholly distinct from the regular Courts of Assistants.

All Acts referring to the Court of Assistants merely recognize its existence and jurisdiction, and fix its terms of sitting: that of March, 1635–6, provides that "There shalbe foure greate Quarter Courts kept yearely att Boston, by the Govr, & the rest of the Magistrates," fixing its terms; and that of October, 1649, reduces this number from four to two.

In the Laws of 1660 and those of 1672, the Chapter on Courts prescribes the terms of sitting, and states the powers of the Court of Assistants as follows: —

> For the better administration of justice, & easing of the country of unnecessary charges and travaile, — It is Ordered by this Court and the Authority thereof, that there be two Courts of Assistants yearely kept at Boston by the Governour, Deputie Governour, and the rest of the Magistrates, on the first Tuesday of the first month, and on the first Tuesday of the seventh month, to heare and determine all and onely actions of appeale from inferiour Courts; all Causes of Divorce, all Capital and Criminal causes, extending to life, member or banishment. And that justice be not deferred, nor the Country needlessly charged, It shall be lawful for the Governour, or in his absence the Deputie Governour, (as they shall judge necessary), to call a Court of Assistants for the tryal of any Malefactour in Capital Causes.

This jurisdiction, thus recognized, appears to have existed in fact, uninterruptedly, from the beginning of the Colony.

The separation of the functions, — executive, legislative, and judicial, which resulted in the Court of Assistants becoming a purely judicial body, took place gradually.

The legislative function seems to have been surrendered by agreement amongst the Magistrates and Freemen at the General Court in May, 1634; while the executive function continued to be exercised by it occasionally for some years. It was not till 1650 that the Magistrates, sitting as a Council, had a separate record.

In its modes of procedure, the Court seems to have been governed by the general principles of the Common Law which the Colonists had brought with them from England; by the habits of legal practice which they had acquired as Englishmen, — some of them by special training; by the limitation in the Charter that no laws should be made repugnant to the laws of England, — as they construed that limitation; and by the guide of those only other sources of law which they recognized, — the Mosaic Code as interpreted by themselves, and the enactments of the General Court from time to time, with the advice, sometimes, of the Elders of the Churches.

From time to time, as it appears by the Colonial records, committees were appointed to make a draught of laws: 6 May, 1635, "of such Lawes as they shall judge needefull for the well ordering of this plantačon;" 25 May, 1636, "of lawes agreeable to the word of God, wch may be the Fundamentalls of this Comonwealth;" while "in the meane tyme the Magistrates and their associates shall ꝑcede in the Courts to heare & determine all causes according to the lawes nowe established, & where there is noe lawe, then as neere the lawe of God as they can;" — and so on at different times thereafter. Meantime the Magistrates seemed inclined to let laws "arise *pro re nata* upon occasions," and thus be founded more upon accepted customs and practice than upon special enactments. In this connection the following extract from Winthrop's History of New England, (November, 1639), throws light upon the policy pursued by the founders of Massachusetts, and perhaps explains why no formal establishment of, and commission to, the Courts of Assistants was ever made: —

"The people had long desired a body of laws, and thought their condition very unsafe, while so much power rested in the discretion of magistrates. Divers attempts had been made at former courts, and the matter referred to some of the magistrates and some of the elders; but still it came to no effect; for, being committed to the care of many, whatsoever was done by some, was still disliked or neglected by others. At last it was referred to Mr. Cotton and Mr. Nathaniel Warde, etc., and each of them framed a model, which was presented to this general court, and by them committed to the governour and deputy and some others to consider of, and so prepare it for the court in the 3d month next. Two great reasons there were, which caused most of the magistrates and some of the elders not to be very forward in this matter. One was, want of sufficient experience of the nature and disposition of the people, considered with the condition of the country and other circumstances, which made them conceive that such laws would be fittest for us which should arise pro re nata upon occasions, etc., and so the laws of England and other states grew, and therefore the fundamental laws of England are called customs, consuetudines.

"2. For that it would professedly transgress the limits of our charter, which provide we shall make no laws repugnant to the laws of England, and that we were assured we must do. But to raise up laws by practice and custom had been no transgression; as in our church discipline, and in matters of marriage, to make a law that marriages should not be solemnized by ministers, is repugnant to the laws of England; but to bring it to a custom by practice for the magistrates to perform it, is no law made repugnant, etc. At length (to satisfy the people) it proceeded, and the two models were digested with divers alterations and additions, and abbreviated and sent to every town, to be considered of first by the magistrates and elders, and then to be published by the constables to all the people, that if any man should think fit, that anything therein ought to be altered, he might acquaint some of the deputies therewith against the next court." (i.322.)

In further illustration of this subject I quote from a letter of William Pynchon to John Winthrop, some years later. This alludes also to the dealings of the Courts with private rights and controversies. In such matters the Court of Assistants would have had original jurisdiction in certain cases, and in others appellate jurisdiction.

"Springefeild this 9 of the 1 m. 1646.

. . . .

"But how soeuer, their endeuors cannot but haue an ill construction; yet I thinke the Courte both of magistrates & deputies, should not turne of[f] all the particulars wherein they desyre a reformation, without making a right vse of so much of their position as doth iustly cale for reformation: for as we had the happinesse to be bredd & borne vnder such lawes for ciuill gouernment as I conceiue no nation hath better, so it should be our care, in thankefulnesse both to God & that state, to preserue & adhere to what euer lawes or customes they haue, except those that be contrary to God, & therein we must obey God & not man, & yet we haue liberty from the pattent to make what soeuer by lawes may tend to the good of this place: & I cannot but apprehend that your spirit lies this way, for I remember at oure first comminge, as soone as euer the people were diuided into seuerall plantations, you did presently nominate a conestable for each plantation, as the most common officers of the king's peace, & gaue them their oath in true substance as the conestables take it in England: likewise all controuersies about meum & tuum were tryed by juries, after the manner of England, & after a while grand juries were appointed, for further inquiry into such matter as might tend to the king's peace; & still thes courses, I thinke, are contin[ued,] & thes courses are the best courses that this Commonwealth can take, if they ha[ue] free liberty to alter: as Fortescue in commendation of the lawes of England [to] my satisfaction doth shew. He giues good reasons for the necessary vse of juries for all tryalls, shewing that it is consonant to the word of God, & preferrs it far aboue the course of justice in France, which is also of high respect." (4 Massachusetts Historical Collections, vi., 381.)

Codifications of the laws appear in the Body of Liberties in 1641, and in the Colonial Laws of 1660 and 1672. There was also a code of laws established in 1649, but no copy thereof is known to be in existence.

At the time when this volume begins (1673) the Court had become a purely judicial body, the Court of highest original jurisdiction in causes civil and criminal, and with a wide appellate jurisdiction, — a tribunal invested with all the attributes of a Court, equipped with all the necessary legal machinery for the due administration and execution of its powers and duties, and as such following established and recognized modes of practice and procedure. Its Bench was the Magistrates, a body characterized not so much by profound legal learning or judicial distinction, as by plain sense, a rugged idea of justice, integrity, and a standing derived from eminent public service in various capacities.

Volume I. of the Records of the Court of Assistants, now published, covers, as already stated, the period from 1673 to 1692.

Volume II., now in preparation, and to be issued as soon as possible, will contain, in three Parts, a restoration of such portions of the earlier records of the Court as can be recovered.

Part I. will contain those portions of the first volume of the Records of Massachusetts in the State Archives which relate specially to the jurisdiction and proceedings of the Court of Assistants. This matter has already been included in Volume I. of the Records of the Governor and Company of the Massachusetts Bay in New England, 1628–1641, edited by Dr. Nathaniel B. Shurtleff. In the forthcoming volume the text will follow the originals in the State Archives with strict adherence in every point, and be an exact reproduction in print.

Part II. will comprise a copy of a portion of the records of the Court of Assistants, extending from 28th October, 1641, to the 5th March, 1643–4, recently discovered in the Barlow Manuscript copy, or duplicate, of the records of the Colony of the Massachusetts Bay, which was bought for the Boston Public Library in 1890, and published in that year, by order of the City Council of Boston, by William H. Whitmore, Record Commissioner, in his Bibliographical Sketch of the Laws of the Massachusetts Colony. In printing these records there will be the same exact adherence to the original manuscript and the same strict conformity with it as in Part I.

These earlier records are not, however, as has been often assumed, the complete record of the doings of the Court, as such, during those periods. With scarcely an exception, such records as have thus come down to us in consecutive order contain only criminal matters or matters of public concern; there is no reference to any dealing by the Court with civil matters, like suits between individuals or questions of property, where the Court had, and often exercised, unquestioned jurisdiction. It is clear, that at the outset no record whatever of such last-mentioned proceedings was kept. Carrying out a suggestion of Lechford, made in 1639, the General Court, at its session in September of that year, enacted: —

"Whereas many iudgments have bene given in o^{r} Courts, whereof no records are kept of the evidence & reasons whereupon the verdit & iudgment did passe, the records whereof being duely entered & kept would bee of good vse for president to posterity, & a releife to such as shall have just cause to have their causes reheard & reveiwed, it is therefore by this Court ordered & decreed that henceforward every iudgment, wth all the evidence, bee recorded in a booke, to bee kept to posterity." (Massachusetts Colony Records, i.275.)

At the same time, provision was made for a record of probate proceedings and of births, marriages, and deaths. That such a book of records was in existence in 1643, and at times thereafter, is evident from certified copies in the Early Court Files.

A considerable collection of material showing the exercise of this civil jurisdiction during these periods, and making a more or less complete record of what was done, has been gathered, and will be presented in the next volume, to which further consideration of the matter is deferred.

In Part III., it will be attempted, so far as accessible material allows, to fill the gap between 1643 and 1673, a period of thirty years during which no continuous or consecutive record is to be found, and to reproduce the doings of the Court, so far as may be possible, by a careful and thorough investigation which has been made in every quarter where anything bearing upon the matter was likely to be found. It is designed to give all copies of its records during this period between 1643 and 1673, which could be found either in the Suffolk Court Files, where many have been preserved, in the State Archives, among the files of courts in any of the other older counties of the Commonwealth, or in any record office within or without the Commonwealth, or that could be obtained from contemporaneous history, or any other authoritative source, — all to be brought together and arranged chronologically.

If the execution of this plan shall be successfully carried out, it is hoped that a very considerable accumulation of matter for the study of the origin, development, and methods of procedure of this Colonial Court of ultimate resort and supreme jurisdiction, — the predecessor of the Superior Court of Judicature and of the Supreme Judicial Court — will be presented in one view and form which may be of value in its relation to the history of the Commonwealth and to the history of its jurisprudence.

JOHN NOBLE.

SUPREME JUDICIAL COURT,
OFFICE OF THE CLERK,
BOSTON, 1 July, 1901.

COURT OF ASSISTANTS.

RECORD 1673–1692.

FROM THE ORIGINAL BOOK OF RECORDS IN THE CLERK'S OFFICE OF THE SUPREME JUDICIAL COURT.

EXPLANATION OF MARKS AND CHARACTERS.

MARKS.

A mark over a letter indicates an omission of one or more letters.

A caret ‸ indicates one or more words omitted in the original.

Brackets [ ] indicate words or letters in the original which are illegible or doubtful or apparently erroneous.

Parallels ‖ ‖ enclose words interlined in the original.

CHARACTERS.

ff signifies ff or F.

n̄ " ner, nor, or no.

ꝑ " par or per.

ꝓ " por or pro.

ꝑ " Per.

ū " ver.

&c " &c. (etc.)

[illegible] Court of Assistants held at Boston in New England the 3d of march 1673

John Bonner plaintiffe agt John Heyman & the rest of the Jury wth him defendts in an action of Appeale from the verdict of the Jury in September last on Attaint. After the Jurys verdict the Attachmt Reasons of Appeale & evidences in that case was read wth ye said Heyman & Jury wth him Answer committed to the Jury and are on file wth the records of this Court the Jury brought in theire verdict they found a speciall verdict i.e. If the law doth Impower a Jury of twelve men to give damage according to what they Judge Rationally might be sustained by the party complaining then wee find for the defendants but if the law doth not allow the Jury that power or liberty then wee find for the now plaintiffe. The magists declared on perusall of ye verdict for the defendants Costs of Courts five pounds three shillings & sixpence.

[illegible] Clarke plaintiffe against Joseph Bartlet defendant in an action of [appe]ale from the Judgment of the County Court at Cambridge in october last [illegible]ing his bond to be forfeited &c

Clarke plaintiff agt Joseph Bartlet defendant in an action of Appeale [from] the Judgment of the County Court in Cambridge in october last &c

Clarke plaintiff agt Joseph Bartlet defendant in an action of Appeale [illegible] of the County Court in Cambridge in october last [illegible]

present
Jno Leve[illegible]
Sam Sy[illegible]
Simon [illegible]
Daniel [illegible]
Daniel [illegible]
Richard [illegible]
Thomas [illegible]
Wm Haw[illegible]
Edward [illegible]
Wm Sta[illegible]
Thomas [illegible]

persons [illegible]
service of [illegible]
and that [illegible]
Capt Jno [illegible]
Edmund [illegible]
Hugh Dr[illegible]
Abel Por[illegible]
Robt Wal[illegible]
Wm Daw[illegible]

Clarke plaintiff agt Joseph [illegible] in an action of Appeale
the Judgment of the County Court in Cambridg in october last
[illegible] the Attachment, Court Judgment, reasons of Appeale & Answ[ers]
evidences in the case produced being read & heard in these 4 actions
plaintiff & deffendant Agreed & Consented in open Court one wth another
the meritt of the whole case that should have binn heard & tryed at the
Court of Assistants in September should now be heard & as it fell so
costs & damages should be and so the case was Committed to the Jury
brought in their verdict they found for the plaintiff on the
meritt of the case reversion of the former Judgment & costs of
two pounds fourteen shillings & eight pence. Elen. 1st Jur.

[illegible] Gibbs plaintiffe agt the Judgment or sentence of the County Court
[illegible] in January last in reference to Henry Ashtons Complaint. Elen
the Courts Sentence Complaint & reasons of Appeale were read Committed to
[the jury] with the evidences in the case produced which are on file with the Records
[of this] Court the Jury brought in their verdict they found the Confirmation
[of the] former County Courts Judgment & costs of Courts [illegible] Elen. 2d Jur.
[illegible] Gibbs plaintiff agt Henry Ashton deffendt in an action of Appeale from the
[illegible] of the last County Court in Boston as to the action of review: After the Attachment
[illegible] reasons of Appeale evidences in [illegible]

Henry …
Joseph Ta…
Randall N…
Richard …
James Hyn…
Jonas Cla…
Thomas …

persons ret…
the Jury for …
of Attaint

Mr. Wm Ma…
John …
John Heyw…
Edward …
Barth…
Robert …
Samuel …
Jno Whitney
Richard …
Peter Tuff…
Joseph Hom…
Tho: …
Tho …

Records of the Court of Assistants, 1673.
Engraved from the original for the County of Suffolk.

COURT OF ASSISTANTS

[S]ECCOND BOOKE OF RECCO[RDS]

BEGUNNE THE 3D OF MARCH, 1673.

[*The title given above is written on the parchment cover. The first six leaves of the book are blank.*]

[1] 1673:

Att a Court of Assistants held at Boston in New England the 3d of march 1673

John Bonner plaintiffe agt John Heyman & the rest of the Jury wth him deffendts in an action of Appeale from the virdict of the Jury in Septembe^r last on Attajnt =

Affter the Jurys virdict the Attachmt Reasons of Appeale & euidences in that case was Read wth ye sajd Heyman & ye Jurys wth him Ansr Comitted to this Jury and are on file wth the reccords of this Court the Jury brought in their virdict they found a speciall virdict i e If the Law doeth Impower a Jury of twelve men to give damage according to what they Judge Rationally might be susteyned by the party Complayning then wee finde for the deffendants: but if the Lawe doth not allow the Jury that power or liberty then wee finde for the now plaintiffe. = The magists declared on pervsall of ys virdict ffor the deffendants. Costs of Courts five pounds three shillings & sixpence. =

present*
Jno Leueret [Esqr]
Sam. Symonds Esqr
Simon Bradstreet
Daniel Gookin
Daniel Dennison
Richard Russell
Thomas Danforth
Wm Hauthorne
Edward Tyng
Wm Staughton
Thomas Clarke
— — — —
persons returned [for] service of the Gr[ ] and that were swo[rne]
Capt Jno Allen
Edmund Jackson [S]
Hugh Drury
Abel Porter
Robt Walker
Wm Dawes
Griffin Crafts
Robert Willjams
Henry Bright
Joseph Taintor
Randall Nicholls
Richard Withington
James Mynott
Jonas Clarke
Thomas ffox
— — — —

John Clarke plantiffe against Joseph Bartlet deffendant in an action of Appeale from the Judg-

---

* The edge of the first leaf is much worn.

ment of the County Court at Cambridge in octobe^r^ last declaring his bond to be forfeited =

John Clarke plantiff ag^t^ Joseph Bartlet deffendant in an action of Appeale from the Judgment of the County Court in Cambridge in octobe^r^ last: ℘r =

Hugh Clarke plantiff ag^t^ Joseph Bartlet deffendant in an action of Appeale from the Judgment of the County Court in Cambridg in octobe^r^ last declaring his bond to be forfeited ℘r 1673:

Hugh Clarke plantiff ag^t^ Joseph Bartlet deffendant in an action of Appeale from the Judgment of the County Court in Cambridg in octobe^r^ last [as] aboue The Attachments Courts Judgments Reasons of Appeale^s^ & Ans^rs^ wth the euidences in the Case^s^ produced being read & heard in these 4 actions both plaintiffs & deffendant Agred & Consented in open Court one wth another that the merrit of the whole Case that should haue binn heard & trjed at the last Court of Assistants in Septembe^r^ should now be heard & as it fell so the Costs & Damages should be and so the Case was Comitted to the Jury who brought in their virdict they found for the plantiff^s^ on the whole merrit of the Case reuersion of the forme^r^ Judgment & Costs of Courts five pounds fowerteen shillings & eight pence = = 1st Jur. =

Benjamin Gibbs plaintiffe ag^t^ the Judgment or sentence of the County Court in Boston in January last in refferenc to Henry Ashtons Complaint = After the Courts Sentence Complaint & reasons of Appeale were read Comitted to the Jury wth the euidences in y^t^ Case produced wch are on file wth the Reccords of this Court the Jury brought in their virdict they found the Confirmation of the forme^r^ County Courts Judgment & Costs of Courts — 2^d^ Jur.

Benjamin Gibbs plaintiff ag^t^ Henry Ashton deffend^t^ in an action of Appeale from the Judgment of the last County Court in Boston as to the action of Revejw: After the Attachm^t^ Courts Judgment Reasons of Appeale & euidences in the Case produced were read Comitted to the Jury and are on file wth ye Reccords of this Court the Jury brought in their virdict

persons return^d^ to s[erve on] ye Jury for y^e^ trjall of [ ] of Attaint & sworne
Mr Wm Manning
John ffreake
John Heyward
Edward Shippen
Bartholmew Cheiv[ers]
Robert Seavor
Samuel Gary
J^no^ Whitney Se[n^r^]
Richard Louden
Peter Tuffts
Joseph Homes
Tim^o^: ffoster
Tho Langhor[ne]

John Bonner plaintiff agt [illegible] defendant

Appeale from the Judgment of the County Court [illegible]
this attachment Court Judgment Reasons of appeale [illegible]
case produced were read Committed to the Jury & are [illegible] on file
the Honors of this Court the Jury brought in their verdict they found for
the deffendant Confirmation of the former Judgment [illegible]
Costs seventeen shillings & six pence [illegible]

Joseph Cooke plaintiff agt Thomas Skinner deffendant [illegible]
Appeale from the Judgment or sentence of the County Court [illegible]
in Boston after the attachment Court Judgment reasons of appeale
evidences in the case produced were read committed to the Jury which are
on file with the Records of this Court the Jury brought in their verdict
they found for the deffendant Confirmation of the former Judgment & [illegible]
Costs of Court [illegible]

Emanuel Bowly plaintiff on Appeale from the Judgment of the [illegible]
of the County Court held at [illegible] in [illegible] the [illegible]
Called the plaintiff & [illegible] himself to the Bench after the [illegible]
had therefore heard the case & perused the County Court sentence Reasons
of Appeale evidences therein produced declared they found [illegible]

and that he stand committed to Cambridge prison till the same be performed

Joseph Rock administrator to the Estate of ye late John Coggan himselfe plaintiff agt Thomas Clarke defendant in an action of appeale from the Judgment of the last County Court in Boston relating to give possession After the Attachment Courts Judgment reasons of Appeale & evidences in ye case produced were read comitted to the Jury & remayn on file wth the records of this Court in a matter of law & so belonging to the Bench to determine the magistrates found for the defendant costs of Courts thirteen shillings & sixpence

Adam Winthrop in an action of appeale from the Judgment of the County Court in Boston relating to the sd Clarks refusall to pay [illegible] Covenant this action being called & answered [illegible] The magistrates found for the defendant costs of Courts thirteen shillings & sixe pence

Thomas Pattyn Attourney to Jno Pattyn plaintiff agt Jno [illegible] in an action of Appeale from the Judgment of the last County Court [illegible] Attachment Courts Judgment reasons of Appeale [illegible] produced were read comitted to the Jury & [illegible]

[illegible]

they found for the plaintiffe ffower pounds [&] Costs [ ] eight shillings & fower pence.

Daniel Tur[ell]
Richard Sha[rpe]
[ ]

[2]

1673

[George Woo]d-ward
[Daniel Da]uison
[Jacob He]wens
[Thomas] Pearse
[Hump]hry Warren
— — — —

John Bonner plaintiffe ag^t Henry Ashton deffendant in an action of Appeale from the Judgment of the County Court last in Boston = After the Attachment Courts Judgment Reasons of Appeale and euidences in the case produced were read Comitted to the Jury & are remayning on file wth the Records of this Court the Jury brought in their virdict they found for the deffendant Confirmation of the forme^r Judgment & Costs of Courts : seventeen shillings & sixe pence ‖ besids y^e 12^s [ ] in all 29.6^d‖ = 1st Jur.

[ ] Returned to serve [on the] Jury for trjalls [Appeales of] life limbe &
[& swor]ne were =
[John] Woodmansey
[Dani]el Turell
[Rich]ard Sharpe
[ ]ge May
[Samuel] Gary
[George] Mayo
[Gregor]y Cooke
[George] Wood-ward
[Daniel] Dauison
[Jaco]b Hewens
[T]homas Pearse
[J]ohn Watson
— — — —

Joseph Lowle plaintiffe ag^t Thomas Skinner defendant in an action of Appeale from the Judgment or Sentenc of the County Court last in Boston = After the Attachment Courts Judgment reasons of Appeale & euidences in the Case produced were read Comitted to the Jury and are on file wth the Reccords of this Court the Jury brought in their virdict they found for the deffend^t Confirmation of the forme^r Judgment & Costs of Courts = 1st Jur.

[Pers]ons Returned to serve [on the] 2^d Jury for tryalls [ ] Appeales for life limbe &
[&] sworne were
[John] Winsley
[John] Heyward
[Edw]ard Shippen
[Ba]rtholmew Cheivers
[Robe]rt Seavor
[Jo]hn Whitney Senr
[Robert] Herrington
[Ric]h. Louden
[Peter] Tuffts
[Jos]eph Homes
[Tim^o:] ffoster
[Tho.] Langhorne

Benanuel Bowe^{r}s plantiff on Appeale from the Judgment or sentence of the County Court held at charls Towne in december last the Accon was Called the plantiff Referred himself to the Bench. Afte[r] the magists had therefore heard the Case & pervsed the Courts Sentence Reasons of Appeale & euidences therein produced declared they found Confirmation of the former Judgment fiue pounds mony & costs of Courts and that he stands Comitted to Cambridge prison till the sentence be performed = 1st Jury

exec. Iss^d out 12 Sep: 1674
[Rock]e ag^t Clarke

Joseph Rocke administrator to the estate of y^e late John Coggan & [Mar]tha his wife plantiff ag^t Thomas Clarke deffendant in an action of Appeale from the Judgment of the last County Court in Boston relating to his denying to give possession &c = After the Attachment Courts Judgment Reasons of Appeale & euidences in y^e Case produced were read Comitted to the Jury & Remayne on file wth the Reccords of this Court it being a point of law & so belonging to the Bench to determine the magists declared for the deffendant Costs of Courts: thirteen shillings & sixe pence

I[dem] vsus Idem exec. Issued out [12] March 74

Idem vsus Idem: in an action of Appeale from the Judgment of the last County Court in Boston relating to the sajd Clarks refusall to pay Rent according to his Couenant this accon being Called &c and as the other The magists declared for the deffendant Costs of Courts thirteen shillings & sixe penc =

[Pattyn] ag^t Winsley

Thomas Pattyn Atturney to Jno Pattyn plantiff ag^t Jno Winsley defendt in an action of Appeale from the Judgment of the last County Court in Boston After the Attachment Courts Judgment Reasons of Appeale & othe^r euidences in the case produced were read comitted to the Jury & remajne on file wth the Reccords of this Court the Jury brought in their virdict they found for the deffendant Confirmation of the former Judgment & Costs of Courts twenty [shillings] pence =

[3] 1673.

Pattyn ag^t. Dyer

Thomas Pattyn Atturney to John Pattyn plantiff ag^t Giles Dyer Deffend^t in an Accon of Appeale from the Judgment of the last County Court in Boston After the Attachment Courts Judgment reasons of Appeale & euidences in the case produced were read Comitted to the Jury & remajne on file wth the Reccords of this Court the Jury brought in their virdict they found for the Deffendant confirmation of the forme^r Judgment & Costs of Courts fifty one shillings & sixpence = 1st Jur.

Cheeckly ag^t w^ms ꝑ Abig Atkinson

Anthony Cheeckly Atturney to Theode^r Atkinson sen in behalf of his Daughter Abigaile Atkinson plantiff against John willjams deffend^t in an action of Appeale from the Judgment of the last County Court in Boston after the Attachment Courts Judgment reasons of Appeale & euidences in the case presented were Read Comitted to the Jury & remajne on file wth the

Reccords of this Court the Jury brought in their virdict they found a speciall virdict i e That In Case this deed of Gift from Theode^r^ Atkinson sen̄ to his children be authentick & good in law: then wee finde for the plantiffe that he haue the houses & lands sued for but if not Authentick &c then wee finde for y^e^ deffendant Costs of Courts. The magistrates finde for y^e^ deffendant costs of Courts thirty fiue shillings = 2^d^ Jur

Ludden & Stuart appea[ ] from sentenc of y^e^ Cou[Cou]

Joseph Ludden & James stuart plantiffs on Appeale from the Judgment or sentence of the last County Court in Boston relating to the thirty pounds the Jury found against them for An W^m^s & Robert Pigget &c After the Attachm^t^ Courts Judgment or sentenc wth y^e^ Reasons of Appeale & euidences in the case produced were read Comitted to the Jury & are on file wth y^e^ Reccords of this Court the Jury brought in their virdict they found for the plantiff^s^ reuersion of the former Judgment = 1st Jur.

Dudson &c ag^t^ Darvall

Joseph Dudson Richard wharton & John ffaireweather plaintiffe against Wm Darvall defendant in an action of Appeale from the Judgmen^t^ of the last County Court in Boston = the action was Called the plantiffs made default by their non Appearanc when Called the Case was nonsuited =

Thayer ag^t^ Rose

Richard Thayer plantiff ag^t^ Roger Rose deffendant in an action of Appeale from the Judgment of the County Court in Boston in octobe^r^ last = After the Attachment Courts Judgment Reasons of Appeale & euidences in the case produced were read Comitted to the Jury and remajne on file wth the Reccords of this Court the Jury brought in their virdict they found for the Deffendant Costs of Courts thirty fowe^r^ shillings = 2^d^ Jur.

Martyn ag^t^ winsly

Georg Martyn & susannah his wife plaintiff ag^t^ Nathaniel Winsly & mary his wife defend^ts^ in an action of Appeale from the Judgment of the last County Court at Hampton this Accon was called y^e^ deffend^t^ objecting y^e^ plantiff had no^t^ signed the Reasons of Appeale yet the Deffendant yeilded on the plantiff^s^ promise to pay the deffend^t^ costs of this Court to this day & so Hampton Costs wch was donn & so the Case proceeded after the Attachment Courts Judgment Reasons of Appeale & euidences in the Case produced were read Com̄itted to ye Jury & are on file wth the Reccords of this Court The Jury brought in their virdict they found for the plantiff there being no legall prooffe of Richard North's will that the estate the sajd North left be left to the disposall of the County Court there in Norfolk as the law prouides & Costs of Courts five pounds one shilling & six penc

[4] 1673

Pike agt Gove
2d Jur.

Major Robt Pike plantiffe against Edward Goue deffendant in an action of Appeale from the Judgment of the County Court at Hampton = After the Attachment Courts Judgment Reasons of Appeale & euidences in the Case produced were read Comitted to the Jury & are on file wth the Reccords of this Court the Jury brought in their virdict they found for the ~~deffendant Confirmation~~ || plantiffe Reuersion || of the former Judgment & one shilling damage & Costs of Courts sixe pounds seuen shillings = 1st Jur * =

miles Agt Heyden

Experience miles plantiff agt Ebenezar Heyden deffendant in an action of appeale from the Judgment of the Comissioners Court in Boston in december last = After the Attachment Courts Judgment reasons of Appeale & euidences in the Case produced were read Comitted to the Jury & are remayning on file the Jury brought in their verdict they found for the deffendant confirmation of the former Judgment & Costs of Courts = twenty three shillings & sixe penc

2d Jur.

Winsly Agt Martyn

Nathaniel Winsly plantiffe agt George Martyn deffendt in an accon of Appeale from the Judgment of the last County Court at Hampton After the Attachmt Courts Judgment reasons of appeale & euidences in the case produced were read Comitted to the Jury and are remayning on file wth the Reccords of this Court the Jury brought in their virdict they found for the plantiffe reuersion of the former Judgment & Costs of Courts = three pounds [fower] & 2d

2d Jury

Roby & Boulter agt Evins

Henry Roby & Nathaniel Boulter plantiffe agt Robert Evins deffendt in an accōn of Appeale from the Judgment of the County Court at Hampton After the Attachment Courts Judgment reasons of Appeale & euidences in the Case produced were read Comitted to the Jury & are

* Probably an error for "2d Jur."

remayning on file wth the Reccords of this Court the Jury brought in their virdict they found for the deffend^t^ Confirmation of the forme^r^ Judgment & Costs of Courts

2^d^ Jur =

Henry Roby & Jno stanion plantiff ag^t^ Edward Colcord deffendt in an action of Appeale from the Judgment of the County Court at Hampton = After the Attachment Courts Judgment Reasons of Appeale & euidences in the Case produced were read Comitted to the Jury & are on file wth the Reccords of this Court the Jury brought in their virdict they found for the plantiffe^s^ Reuersion of the former Judgment & Costs of Courts fower pounds ten ^ & ten penc

Roby & Stanion ag^t^ Boulter* 1st Jury

Edw. Colcord p^r^tending all y^e^ Copies were not sent sd he could say nothing =

Jno Teudo^r^ Assignee of Joseph Dell Assigne of Jno Smith plaintiff ag^t^ Wm Aglin deffend^t^ in an action of Appeale from the Judgment of the Comissione^r^s Court in Boston in January last After y^e^ Attachm^t^ Courts Judgment Reasons of Appeale & euidences in the Case produced were read Comitted to the Jury & are on file wth the Reccords of this Court the Jury brought in their virdict they found for y^e^ defend^t^ Confirmation of the former Judgment & Costs of Courts = fowrteen shillings

Tudo^r^ ag^t^ Aglin 1st Jur =

John Ryde^r^ plantiffe ag^t^ John Sharp deffendant in an action of Appeale from the Judgment of the County Court in Boston January last After the Attachm^t^ Courts Judgment Reasons of Appeale & euidences in the Case produced were Read Comitted to the Jury & are on file wth the Reccords of this Court the Jury brought in their virdict they found for y^e^ plantiff reuersion of the forme^r^ Judgment & Costs of Courts

Ryder ag^t^ Sharpe 2^d^ Jur =

[5] 1673.

John Samborne & Edward Colcord Atturney^s^ for & on behalfe of the Toune of Hampton plantiffs ag^t^ ‖Daniel‖ Tilton deffendant in an action of Appeale from the Judgment of the County Court at Hampton = After the Attachment Courts Judgment Reasons of Appeale & euidences in the Case produced were read Comitted to the Jury & are remayning on file wth the Reccords of this Court the Jury brought in their virdict

Samborn & Colcord Ag^t^ Tylton. 2^d^ Jur. =

* Error of the Secretary for "Colcord."

they found for the plantiffe reuersion of the former Judgment ‖forty shillings damage ‖ & Costs of Courts foure ‖(4)‖ pounds 4s 6d.

Goue agt ffouler
2d Jur.

Edward Goue plantiffe as Assignee to phillip Greely agt Samuel ffouler deffendant in an Accōn of Appeale from the Judgment of the County Court at Hampton = After the Attachment Courts Judgment reasons of Appeale & euidences in the Case produced were read Comitted to the Jury & are on file wth the Reccords of this Court the Jury brought in their virdict they found for the deffendant Confirmation of the former Judgment & Costs of Courts = fiuety fiue shillings & six penc

Peck agt Lauton
2d Jur.

Thomas Pecke plantiff agt Henry Lauton deffendt in an action of Appeale from the Judgment of the County Court in octobe last in Boston — After the Attachment Courts Judgmt Reasons of Appeale & euidences in the Case produced were read Comitted to the Jury & remajne on file wth the Reccords of this Court the Jury brought in their virdict they found for the deffendant Costs of Courts =

Godfry agt Clark
2d Jur

John Godfrey plantiff agt Edward Clarke marshall Gen̄ Deputy deffendt in an action of Appeale from the Judgment of the County Court at Ipswich. After the Attachment Courts Judgment Reasons of Appeale & euidences in the Case produced were read Comitted to the Jury & are on file wth the Reccords of this Court the Jury brought in their virdict they found for the deffendant Costs of Courts = three pounds seuen shillings & 4d =

Collecot agt Pinchon
2d Jur

Richard Collecot plantiffe agt Jno Pinchon Jun̄ Assignee of John Pinchon Senr Esqr deffendt in an action of Appeale from the Judgment of ye last County Court in Boston = After ye Attachmt Courts Judgment Reasons of Appeale & euidences in the Case produced were read Comitted to ye Jury and are on file wth the Reccords of this Court the Jury brought in their virdict they found for ye deffendant Confirmation of ye former Judgment & Costs of Courts =

Knight agt Bratle

Richard Knight shopkeepr plant agt Tho Bratle Atturney to Jno Cutt of Portsmouth defendt in an action of Appeale from the Judgmt of the last County Court in Boston

After the Attachment Courts Judgm[t] Reasons of Appeale & euidences in the Case produced were read Comitted to the Jury and are on file wth the Reccords of this Court the Jury brought in their virdict they found for the defend[t] Confirmation of the former Judgment & Costs of Courts = three pounds sixteen shillings =

[6] 1673

Keyne ag[t] Piper 1st Jur

John Kejne plantiff ag[t] Nathaniel Piper defendant in an action of Appeale from the Judgment of the County Court at Ipswich = After the Attachment Courts Judgment Reasons of Appeale & euidences in the Case produced were read Comitted to the Jury and are on file wth the Reccords of this Court the Jury brought in their virdict they found for the plantiff the abatement of fiuety shillings of the forme[r] Judgment & the Costs of this Court = wch in all came to fiue pounds one shillings * & six penc to be deducted out of y[e] form[r] Judgm[t] & costs wch was eleven pounds nine shillings =

Smiths Judgm[t] reŭest 1st Jur=

Joseph Smith plaintiff on Appeale from the Judgment of the County Court at Boston = After the Courts Judgment Reasons of Appeale and euidences in the Case produced were read Comitted to the Jury and are on file the Jury brought in their virdict they found for the Appellant reuersion of the forme[r] Judgment =

Batt ag[t] Seuerans 1st Jur execution Issued out 5 Dec 74, for 3[li] 15[s] 10 Costs & dd to mr norman y[t] was his Atturney & came in his name for it =

Timothy Batt plantiffe ag[t] Joseph Seuerans deffendant in an action of Appeal from the Judgment of the County Court at Hampton After the Attachment Courts Judgment Reasons of Appeale and euidences in the Case produced were read Comitted to the Jury and are on file wth the Reccords of this Court the Jury brought in their virdict they found for the plantiff reuersion of the forme[r] Judgment & Costs of Courts three pounds fiueteen shillings & ten pence =

Jonathan Shoare plantiff ag[t] Tmothy Yale deffendant in an action of Appeale from the Judgment of the County Court in Boston octobe[r] last After the Attachment was Read this Case was dismist on both partjes Appearing in Court & owning that they were Agreed =

---

* Error in the record for "shilling."

Ruth Reads sentence.

Ruth Read being Comitted to prison & brought to the barr to Answer for that hauing binn aboue fowe' yeares in England absent from hir husband and bringing wth hir a child of About two yeares old Affirming that she received it at Brandford in England that Augustin Lyndon who chandging his name to John Rogers & hirselfe by the name of Rebeckah Rogers as she also Affirmed betweene whom seuerall letters wickedly (as if man & wife ^ had passed between them which are on file, and that John Rogers told hir the childs name was John Rogers, and most Impudently returning to these parts Imposing the sajd child on hir husband Wm Read The Court sentenct the sajd Ruth Read that named hirself Rebeckah Rogers if found in this Colony two month^s after this date that shee stands in the markett place on a stoole for one hower wth a paper on hir breast wth y^s Inscription THVS I STAND FOR MY ADVLTEROVS AND WHORISH CARRIAGE and that on a lecture day nex^t after the lecture and then be seuerely whipt wth thirty stripes =

11 M^rch 1673

[7] 1673

Benja Goads Indictm^t

Benjamin Goad being found Guilty of Bestiallity by y^e Grand Jury = was Brought to the barr and was Indicted by the name of Benjam̃i Goad of Roxbury in New England for that he not hauing the feare of God before his eyes being instigated by the the Divill did on the seventh day of february last past in the Afternoone the sun being two howe^rs high Comitt the vnnatural & horrid act of Beastiallitje on a mare in the highway or field Contrary to the peace of ou^r Soueraigne Lord the King his Croune & Dignitie the lawes of God and of this Jurisdiction = to wch Indictm̃ent holding vp his hand at the barr he pleaded not Guilty sajd he would be trjed by God & the Countrje making no exception ag^t any of the Jury the case proceeded and after the euidences in the Case produced ag^t him were read Comitted to the Jury & are on file wth the Reccords of this Court the Jury brought in their virdict i e a speciall virdict If the prisoners confession ag^t himself vpon his first app^rhention & examination before his trjall togethe^r wth one euidence be sufficient to a legall conviction, then wee find him Guilty according to Indictment, othe^rwise no^t legally guilty of the fact but of a most horrid attempt of Beastiallity, wch wee leaue to the determination of the Honored Court — The magis^ts on the pervsall of this virdict they declared they found him Capitolly

his Sentenc

Guilty The Goūne[r] proceeded to sentenc him i e That yo[w] shall * returne from y[s] place (y[e] barr) to the place from whence yo[w] † Came & from thence to the place of execution & there hang till yow be dead = And that the mare yow abused before your execution in yo[r] sight shall be knockt on y[e] head. =

It was also Ordered that the sajd Prisoner Condemmed to dye should be executed on the fifth day next Come fortnight being the seccond day of April next after the lecture & y[t] the Secretary Issue out his warrants seasonably to the marshall Generall to see & order the same as in other cases wch was donn Accordingly as by y[e] m[r]shalls Return on file = On Courts Adjo[r]m[t] 13 m[rch] his execution

In the Case of Anna Edmunds Complajned on by Samuell Bennet & his wife on suspition of witchcraft After the Court had heard all the euidences produced against her the Court declared that they saw no Ground to fix any charge against her & so dismist hir The Court also Ordered that Samuel Bennet defray and pay the charges of the wittnesses in y[e] case = thirty shillings & ffees : Anna Edmond[s] Accus[d] dischardgd =

In the Case of John & Samuel Bennet bound ouer to this Court that the sajd John & Sarah Bennet & Elljnor squire shall Appeare before this Court to Answer for the great neglect of Alice wilson & the son of the sajd Alice wch might occasion their deaths and for burying the child in an obscure and clandestine manner in the Garden of the sajd Samuel Bennet The Court hauing considered of the euidences in the case produced Ordered that the sajd John Bennet & Samuell in behalf of his wife &c shall sattisfy & pay the Constables bill of charges by him layd out for phisick diet &c on y[e] sajd Alice the sume of forty sixe shillings & six penc & y[e] sd W[m] Edmonds & Anna Edmonds their witnesses & charges wch comes to : thirty two shillings & ffees of Court = Ju[o] & Sam Bennet find &c = Samuel Townsend execution Issued out for 46 : 6 : & dd to m[r] [fl]oyd —

[8] 1673

In Answer to y[e] order of the Generall Court october 1673 relating to the Inhabitants of y[e] East- 7 m[rch] 73 p[r]sent y[e] Goūnor

* "He should" changed to "yo[w] shall." † "He" changed to "yo[w]."

Dep^t Gov̄
m^r Tresurer
m^r Danforth
m^r Tynge
m^r Clarke

ward Kenebecke &c The Gov̄no^r & magis^ts present Ordered That Thomas Humphrys be constable at Kennebeck for this yeare Robert Gamon Constable of Capenawagen & Damerills Coue John Dillon constable of monhegin and Edward Arrowsmith constable for Pemaquid also for y^e yeare =

Ans^r to Aluin Childs peticōn

In Ans^r to the peticōn of Aluin child in behalf of his Correspondents m^rchants in Lexbon * concerned in y^e ship Antonio & Goods &c The Court ordered that the secretary Issue out warrant for majo^r Nicholas Shapleigh to Come & appeare before this Court now sitting ye 11th Instant at nine of ye clocke.

Georg Cole & other Quakers Admonisht &c

At this Court the Constable of Boston made his returne of his warant that he on the Lords day last in time of publick excercise found in the house of Nicholas moulder certeine Quake^rs as Georg Cole speaking to them y^t were present as Nicho moulder & christian his wife steven Hussey Dauid ffogg John Somes Joshua Buffam Ann Gillam martha Amy Elipl[am] stratten & Hester Dew contrary to our law The Court sent for them they Appeared It being declard to them y^t their meeting was contrary to our Lawe &c the Court ordered them as the law directs to be all admonish^t the Gov̄no^r Admonish^t them Accordingly & they were told the law would be too hard for them & ^ must if they fell into ye like transgression expect ye execution thereof

Chardge ag^t Nicholas Shapleigh

m^r Isac Addington was Appointed to Implead maj^r shapleigh & draw vp a charg ag^t him majo^r Nicholas Shapleigh being sum̄oned to Appeare at this Court this 11th Instant at nine of ye clocke in the morning to Ans^r what should be layd aganst him as relating to the Criminall part of his bond Given into this court at the tjme he was Called three times but Appeared not his sue^rty^s Appearing Alleadged the badnes of the weather affirming they had sent the warrant & expected him howerly: in the afternoone he made his Appearance and desired the liberty of his triall by a Jury & entred his Action m^r Isack Addington also Appeared & presented a charge against him which was publickly read after wch the sajd Nicholas Shapleigh Owned and confessed that the mentioned seaman w^m ffforrest Alexand^r wilson &c ~~the mentioned seamen~~ were in his warehouse and that out of foollish pitty to them he suffered them to

* Error in the record for "Lisbon."

be there that he was su'prised &c: After ye Declaration & euidences & pleas in the Case produced were read Comitted to the Jury and are on file wth the Reccords of this Court the Jury brought in their virdict they found the sajd Nicholas shapleigh convicted of the three first articles exhibbited against him & vehemently suspitious of being Guilty of the fowerth = Nicholas Shapleigh being Con. victed by the virdict of the Jury yt vnder the pretence of buying
1stly Did receive & Conceale Goods pirattically & ffelloniously obteyned by wm fforrest & his Complices in the ship Antonio of Lizborne amounting to one hundred pounds or vpwards yeilding no valluable Consideration for the same =
2ly And that he did clandestinly enterteyne Conceale & hide away in his ware house wm fforrest Allexander wilson & John Smith Capitall offenders hauing

[9] 1673

their hands in ffelloniously & pirattically seizing & possessing themselues of the ship Antonjo and Goods on the high seas dispossessing the right master merchant & othe'rs exposing them to the hazard of their liues (and that after to his knowledge) the sajd persons were detected for the same & pu'rsued by Authority in order to their Apprhention =
3ly And that he the sajd shapleigh did harbour majnteyne & order provissions for the sustenance of the sajd persons, during their concealment = all wch the Jury found him Guilty of

And further by the virdict of ye Jury rendred vnder vehement suspition of being Guilty of Prouiding ordering working an escape for, and in the night privately conveying away the aboue sajd three offendrs by all wch endeavoring to obstruct the free course of Justice against such Capitoll offendors and thereby making himself an Abetter of them all wch hath occasioned great expense & charge to the Country to prosecute & bring such high offendors to their due tryall The Court to beare their due testimony against such high offences doe sentenc yow the sajd Nicholas shapleigh to pay as a fine to the Country fiue hundred pounds in mony standing Comitted till the sentenc be prformed =

Nicho Shapleighs censure = find 500 li &c

In Ansr to ye peticon of mr wm Darvall & mr. Isack melines It being put to the Question whither y're case should come to a tryall here in a Court of Admiralty. It was resolued on ye negative =

at ye Adjormt [1]3th mrch 1673. Ansr to mr Darvalls peticon no hearing

Nich Shapleighs peticon & fine abated

In Answer to the petiĉon of Nicholas Shapleigh humbly desiring this Court to favo[r] him w[th] y[e] Abatement of a considerable part of his fine & Alteration of the speciæ: his estate not being able to beare it The Court declares that on the petitioners payment of three hundred pounds to the Tresure[r] of the Country he shall be dischardgd =

Benja Goad libe[r]ty to goe to Roxbury er =

In Ans[r] to y[e] peticon of Benja Goad y[e] Court Grants his request libe[r]ty to Goe to meeting on y[e] lds day at Roxbury y[e] m[r]shall Genll or his deputy taking effectuall cours for his return to prison y[e] same day.

This Court was Adjourned to the 14[th] Instant at eight of the clock in y[e] morning

14 of march 1673

The Court being mett The Gou̅no[r] declared that It was Agreed that the prisone[r] Condemned Benjamin Goad should be executed on the nex[t] fifth day fortnight being the second day of Aprill next presently after the lecture and that the secretary Issue out his warrant seasonably to the marshall Gen̄erall to see & order the same as in othe[r] cases = wch was donn Accordingly =

The Court adjourned themselves to the 23[d] of march 1673.

Ans[r] to m[r] Darvalls peticon & y[e]ir Case to be heard 10 Ap[r] 74.

At wc[h] time the Court mett and In Ans[r] to the peticon of m[r] w[m] Darvall and m[r] Isaac Melines ordered theire Case to be heard on fryday fortnight being the 10[th] of Aprill at nine of the clocke and that the Secretary Give notice to all the magis[ts] and partjes Concerned to Attend at y[t] time =

Letters to the seuerall magis[ts] to give them notice as to y[e] Courts adjourm[t] was sent accordingly & notice Giuen to the partjes Concerned.

from 3[d] March 1673

Amy wellen the Indictment being found ag[t] hir by the Grand jury was brought to y[e] barr Refusing to object ‖ ag[t] ‖ any of y[e] jury of trialls holding vp hir hand at y[e] barr was Indicted by y[e] name of Amy Wellen wife to Richard wellen for not hauing the feare of God before hir eyes did sometime[s] the last spring being w[t]hin a twelve moneth being instigated by y[e] divill comitt

Adultery wth Jno Glandfeild of black point in the house of willjam Buttyn * of black point Contrary to ye peace of our Soueraigne Lord his Croune & dignity the lawes of God & of this jurisdiction to wch Indictment she pleaded not guilty & put hirself on trjall by God & the Country After y^{e} Indictment & euidences in the Case produced ag^{t} the prisoner at the barr were read Comitted to the Jury & are on file wth the Reccords of this Cour^{t} The Jury found hir not Guilty = & so she was dismist =

The Grand Jury finding the like bill ag^{t} Jno Glandfeild of black point he was alike tried for Comitting adultery wth Amy Wellen mutatis mutan[dis] & on hearing of all y^{e} euidences the Jury found him not Guilty as above & he was [also] dismist †

[10] 1674

Att the Adjournm^{t} of the Court of Assistants from the 23^{d} march 1673 to the 10th of Aprill 1674.

p^{r}esent
Jno Lev̄et Esqr Gov̄n^{r}
Sam Symonds Esqr Dep^{t} Gov̄.
Daniel Gookin, Tho Danforth, Edw. Tyng, Wm Staughton, Tho: Clarke . . . } Esq^{rs}

The Court mett at the time The Court enjoyned John Lowell on his bonds to Appeare before ye next County Court of Boston in Aprill to Ans^{r} to what shall there be layd to his charge in relation to his holding a Correspondency wth the Dutch & ye like m^{r} messmake^{r} if he be sent for.

Att this Court m^{r} melynes & m^{r} Darvall y^{t} were attending on this Court for their tryall hauing deliuered in their Complaints agt m^{r} Dudsson m^{r} wharton m^{r} Paige and m^{r} faireweather both partjes were Called after much debate This Court Referr^{d} the hearing of this case to the twenty eighth of may next at nine of the clock in the morning & y^{t} the ship be not sent away hence till the case be heard = to wch time they Adjourned themselues =

Att y^{e} Adjournment of the Court of Assistants held at Boston 28th may 1674. this Court Adjournd themselues from day to day to y^{e} 6th June 1674. when mett declard &c

present
Jno Lev̄et Esqr Gov̄
Saml Symonds Esqr dep^{t} Gov̄.
Symon Bradstreet
Dani Gookin.
Dani Dennison
Symon Willard
Rich. Russell

The Court hauing heard & Considered the request of Joseph Dudson & Company pleading the

* Or Battyn.

† These last two paragraphs appear to have been written by the Secretary at a later date and in a blank space left at the foot of the page.

29 3mo 74
Tho. Danforth
Wm Hathorn
Jno Pinchon
Edw. Tyng
Wm Staughton
6 June 74
Thomas Clarke
. . . .

benefit of the law of this Comonweale for the Judication of the ship expectation whereof Isaack Melynes was Comander by them lately seized at Nantucket & brought into this Jurisdiction It appearing on the hearing of the pleas & euidences presented in the case that the ship was by them first carrjed into plimouth Jurisdiction where on their request to the Gouernment there for Judication the sajd Dudson & Company gaue bond in a thousand pounds sterling that after the ship was fitted in Boston then to give notice to the sajd meljnes & Company of the Port to which he Intended to carry the sajd ship for trjall &c and when there Arrived before the Gouno^r of the place or court of Admiralty there Constituted, to render a Just account of the Goods and that so those Concerned may haue oppertunity to recouer their respective rights & Interests. = This Court Considering the premisses doe not Judg meet to give the sajd Dudson & Company Judication of the sajd vessell; but doe refferr them to the obse^rvance of their bonds given to the Goument of Pljmouth Colony =

memd. ye Gounor & all yo magist[] declard & ordred ye secretary to Return all ye papers to ye part[] each their oune = vide day booke =

[11] 1674

In Ans^r to the petition of Nicholas Shapleigh The Court ordered that on the peticon^rs giving such sufficient ‖ & satisfactory ‖ security his engagement of his house & land so farr as it respects The Country as to the criminall part shall be dischardged =

present
Jno Leuet Esqr Gou
Sam Symonds Esqr
Dept Gou:
Symon Bradstreet
Daniel Gookin
Daniel Denison
Symon willard
Richard Russell
Thomas Danforth
Wm Hauthorne
Jno Pinchon
Edward Tyng
Wm Staughton
} Esq^rs
. . . .
persons returnd to se^rve on ye Grand Jury & sworne were
. . . .

Att A Court of Assistants held at Boston ye 1st of September 1674 =

2d Jur

Edward Goue plantiffe against majo^r Robe^rt Pike deffendant in an accon of Appeale from the Judgment of the last County Court at Salisbury = After the Attachment Courts Judgment Reasons of Appeale & euidences in the case produced were read Comitted to the Jury & are remayning on file wth the Reccords of this Court the Jury Brought in their virdict they found for the deffendant Confirmation of the forme^r Judgment & costs of Courts = ‖ forty two shillings & two pence costs granted 14s p ye Court march 80/1 maj^{r} [affirming] y^{e} 1st execution was granted another dated the 23 octobe^{r} 82 ||

John Sands plaintiff ag^{t} Capt Edward Hutchinson deffendant in an action of Appeale from the Judgment of the last County Court sitting in Boston = After the Attachment Courts Judgment reasons of Appeale & euidences in the Case produced were read Com̄itted to the Jury & are remayning on file wth the Reccords of this Court the Jury brought in their virdict they found for the plantiff Reuersion of the former Judgment and forty-two shillings dam̄age & costs of courts fowe^{r} pounds fowe^{r}teen shillings & sixpenc

James chase plantiff ag^{t} m^{r} John Wheelewright as ffeoffee in trust to the wife and children of the late Robert Nanny deffendant in an action of Appeale from the Judgment of the last County Court at Salisbury The Accon was Called The plantiffe by his Atturney Appearing Ready to prosecute It being Affirmed the Ac̄con was Agreed The Court Allowed y^{e} plantiff to wthdraw his Accon =

Joseph Rocke Adminstrator to the estate of y^{e} late m^{r} Jno & m^{rs} martha Coggan plantiff against Anthony stoddard Guardian to Thomas Robbinson = Deffendt in an action of Appeale from the Judgment of the last County Court in Boston = After the Attachment Courts Judgment reasons of Appeale & euidences in the case produced were read Com̄itted to the Jury & are remayning on file with the Reccords of this Court the Jury brought in their virdict they found for the plantiff reuersion of the former Judgment & Costs of Courts. =

Benjamin Gibbs plantiff against John Bonner & James Euerell Deffendants in an action of Appeale from the Judgment of the last County Court in Boston = After the Attachment Courts Judgment Reasons of Appeale & euidences in the case produced were read Com̄itted to the Jury & are remayning on file wth the Reccords of this Court the Jury brought in their virdict they found for the Deffendant costs of Courts thirty fower shillings & eight pence

Left Joshua Scottow
John Blake
Symon Lynde
w^{m} Taylor
Jno Conney
Jno Coolidge
Ellis Baron
Robt williams
Thomas Weld
Jno Pelton sen̄.
Timothy Mather
Eljas Rowe
Rich Sprague
Justinian Holding
Jno ffuller

— — — —

persons returnd to serve on ye 1st Jury for trjalls of Appeales life & & sworne were

— — — —

m^{r} Anthony Cheeckley
Joseph Tounsend
Benjamin Batten
Jno Noyce
Isaack Newell
Nathaniell Brewer
Tho Tollman Jun̄
Israell How
Jno Phillips
w^{m} Goddard
James Bernard
Pyam Blower
Jno Goue.

— — — —

[12] 1674

persons Returnd to serve on ye 2d Jury for trjalls of Appealls lifee/r sworne were

— — — —

Mr Richard Knight
Joseph Swett
Ephrajm Turner
Tho. Dewer
Jno watson
Robt Pepper
Obadiah Hawes
Zekary Long
Wm Bond.
Joseph Taintor
Tho Broune
Wm Barrat

— — — —

2d Jur Zackariah Crispe plantiffe agt Jno Joanes deffendant in an action of Appeale from the Judgment of the last County Court in Boston = After the Attachment Courts Judgment Reasons of Appeale & euidences in the case produced were read Comitted to the Jury and are remajning on file wth the Reccords of this Court the Jury brought in their virdict i e. a speciall virdict:

[*blank*]

The magists on pervsall of this virdict they declard for the deffendant & costs of courts

1st Jur Benjamin Gibbs plaintiff agt Jno Bonner & James Euerell deffendts in an accon of Appeale from the Judgment of the last County Court in Boston & was on Reveyw. After the Attachment Courts Judgment Reasons of Appeale and euidences in the case produced were read Comitted to the Jury and are remajning on file wth the Reccords of this Court the Jury brought in their virdict they found for the deffendant costs of Courts = thirty fowr shillings & six pence

2d Jur
Sevy agt Deering Thomas Sevy plaintiff against Henry Deering deffendt in an action of Appeale from the Judgment of the last County Court in Portsmouth = After the Attachmt Courts Judgment Reasons of Appeale & euidences in the Case produced were read Comitted to the Jury and are on file wth the Reccords of this Court the Jury brought in their virdict they found for the plantiff Reuersion of the former Judgment & costs of Courts = fforty sixe shillings & six pence

Colcord agt Redman
2d Jur. Edward Colcord plaintiffe against Jno Redman deffendant in a action of Appeale from the Judgment of the last County Court at Salisbury: the Case was called plaintiff & deffendant Appearing This Case propperly belonging to the Court to determine The magists after hearing the parties & euidences wth the

Reasons & Courts Judgment determined for the plantiff libe^r^ty to Reveyw & Costs of Courts

2^d^ Jur
Colcord ag^t^ Palmer exec Issued out 11 M^r^ch 74 dd to m^r^ Norton of piscata[gr] for 52^s^ = mony

Edward Colcord plaintiff ag^t^ X^t^ophe^r^ Palmer deffendant in an Action of Appeale from the Judgment of the last County Court at Salisbury. After the Attachment Courts Judgment Reasons of Appeale & euidences in the Case produced were read Comitted to the Jury & are remayning on file wth the Reccords of ye Court the Jury brought in their virdict they found for the deffendant Confirmation of the former Judgment & Costs of Courts

Redman ag^t^ Hampton
2^d^ Jur

Jno Redman Atturney to w^m^ Bacon & Thomas Cannida plantiff against the Towne of Hampton or their Atturney Deffend^t^ in an Action of Appeale from the Judgment of the County Court at Salisbury — After the Attachment Courts Judgment Reasons of Appeale and euidences in the Case produced were read Comitted to the Jury and are Remayning on file wth the Reccords of this Court the Jury brought in their virdict they found for the deffend^t^ Confirmation of the former Judgment & Costs of Courts three pounds nine shillings & eight pence. =

Exec. Issued out for 3·9 : 8 : 5th 7 : mõ 1674 : E R S.

2^d^ Jur
Sandford ag^t^ Putman

Robt Sandford plantiff ag^t^ Nathaniel Putman deffend^t^ in an action of Appeale from the Judgment of the last County Court in Salem After the Attachment Courts Judgment Reasons of Appeale & Euidences in the case produced were Read Com̃itted to the Jury and are remayning on file wth the Reccords of this Court the Jury brought in their virdict they found for the plantiff reuersion of the former Judgment & costs of Courts

Ord^r^ ab^t^ Isaac Griffin

Isaac Griffyn Apprentice to Roge^r^ Rose making Complaint to ye Court that his sajd master had not ꝑformd his couenants wth him to his great damage the Court vejwed the Indenture & vpon hearing both partjes It was consent^d^ to by the sajd Rose that vpon the payment of three pounds mony to him by the sajd Griffyn he would release to him the remayning time of his Indenture Prouided that he be acquitted & secured from any further demand from the sajd Griffyn wch ye Gou^r^no^r^ & magists^ts^ approved of & ordered that they Give discharg[e] each to ye other past by y^e^ [Court] E R S. Rog^r^ Rose [ed] in Court he had Rec^d^ 3li mony of s^d^ Griffyn

[13] 1674

Batt agt Harris
1st Jur.

Paul Batt plantiff agt Jno Harris deffendt in an Action of Appeale from the Comissioners Court in Boston After the Attachment Courts Judgment Reasons of Appeale & euidences in the case produced were read Comitted to the Jury and are remayning on file wth the Reccords of this Court the Jury brought in their virdict they found for the plantiff reuersion of the former Judgment & Costs of Courts twenty sixe shillings =

Bartlet agt James: Legg [&c]
1st Jur.

Robert Bartlet plantiff agt Erasmus James John Legg James Dennis and Nathaniel walton deffendts or either of them in behalfe of the Comons at marblehead in an Action of Appeale from the Judgment of the County Court last at Ipswich, — After the Attachment Courts Judgment Reasons of Appeale & euidences in the Case produced were read comitted to the Jury and are remayning on file wth the Reccords of this Court the Jury brought in their virdict they found for the plantiff Reuersion of the former Judgment & Costs of Courts = execution of charges was suspended in both Cases till ye Adjourmt & Genll Court.

Lattimore vsus Idem
1st Jury

Xtopher Lattimore plantiff against Erasmus James Jno Legg &c as before in Bartlets case = After the Attachment Courts Judgment Reasons of Appeale & euidences in the Case produced were read Comitted to the Jury & are on file wth the Records of this Court the Jury brought in their virdict they found for the plantiff reuersion of the former Judgment & Costs of Courts. This Case & the other was by Consent || & desire || of parties refferred to the hearing & determination of the selectmen of Salem wth mr Thomas Laughton of Lynn and for that end major Hathorne is to Appoint time and place of meeting and all partjes concerned are to Attend the meetings & Giue in their pleas Accordingly and that their determination be returned under at least the major pte of their hands into the next Generall Court for their settlement thereof

Courts ordr in both cases

Bishop agt white

Samuell Bishop plantiffe agt George White Deffendt in an action of Appeale from the Judgment of the County Court at Ipswich Tho Bishop Appearing in Court & hauing Appealled in behalfe of his brother Samuel Bishop Vndertook in Court to sattisfy all dam̃ages that shall be recouered &c After the attachm̃t Courts Judgm^t Reasons of Appeale & euidences in the case produced were read Com̃itted to the Jury and are remayning on file wth the Reccords of this Court the Jury brought in their virdict they found for y^e plantiffe reũsion of the former Judgment as it is chanceried and three pounds fiueteen shillings Additionall dam̃ages & Costs of Courts = Three pounds & eleven shillings The deffend^t desiring a chancery the plantiff Gonn & not to be found The Court ordered a respit of y^e execution till the 9 of october next to wch time this Court Adjournd themselues = [* & chanceried the dam̃age Additionall to 40^s only]

exec Issued out 5th novemb^r 74 for 40^s dam̃ & (3^li 11^s costs in mony:) E R S

9 octob^r 1674

Jno Gold plantiff ag^t Thomas Bishop deffendant in an Action of Appeale from the Judgment of the County Court at Ipswich = After the Attachm^t Courts Judg^t Reasons of Appeale & euidences in the Case produced were read Comitted to the Jury & are remayning on file wth the Reccords of this Court the Jury brought in their virdict they found for the deffendant confirmation of the fformer Judg^t & costs of Courts.

Gold ag^t Bishop
Judg^t 25. 13^s. 4
Costs 2 13 8
28. 7 0

exec. Issued out 10 Sep^tr

In Ans^r to a motion of w^m Leathe^rland in prison vpon execution libe^rty is Granted him wth his keeper to goe to the Ordinances of christ in Boston as also to vissit his sick wife wth his keeper he not lying out of of y^e prison at any time one night = The like libe^rty is Granted to Henry Lauton as to willjam Leathe^rland as to the 1st parte =

Ans^r to w^m Leath^r. lands motion his & Henry Lautons Liberty =

[14] 1674

Tho Atkins plaintiff ag^t Ann Joy widdow defendant in an action of Appeale from the Judgment of [*blank*] Court in Boston the ^

Atkins ag^t Joy

This Accõn was wth drawne by Consent of partjes & allowance of the Court.

Tom Indian being presented by the Grand Inquest & left to tryall was brought to the barr & there holding vp his hand was Indicted by the name of

Jurymen sworn as to To † tryall of Tom Indian || & his || Indictmt

* This with the marginal date added later by the Secretary.

† The Secretary evidently neglected to cancel the "To."

mr. Rich Knight
Joseph Taintor
Ephraim Turner
Tho [*blank*]
Jno watson
Zackary Long
wot biompanow natow
Sho Shannough
Ahauton
James Aasanemeset

his Sentence

Tom Indian for that yow not hauing the feare of God before yor eyes & being Instigated by the Divill did on or about the 15th of June last Comitt a rape on the body of Sarah the wife of John Jempson an Indian forcing hir to vnlawfull Copulation wth you Contrary to the peace of our Soueraigne Lord the King his Crowne and dignity the lawes of God & of this Jurisdiction To wch he pleaded not Guilty sajd he would be tryed by God & ye Country: a Jury of twelve men six English & six Indians against none of which he Objected who being Impanneld & sworne After the euidences produced against him were read Comitted to the Jury & remajne on file wth the Reccords of this Court the Jury brought in their virdict they found Tom Indian Guilty according to Indictment It being voated by the magists that the sajd Tom the Indian being found Guilty according to Indictment that he should dy for his offence And accordingly after the Gouernor had Askt him why he being found Guilty sentenc of Death should not be pronounct agt him The Goūnor proceeded & declared that he should Goe from the barr to the prison from whence he came & from thence to the place of execution & there hang till he be dead =

Warrt Issued out Accordgly 10: Sept 74 =

Joseph Blanchard
Georg Grimes
bonds to Appear at County Court at Cambridge =

Joseph Blandchard sonn to George Blandchard & George Grimes being bound ouer to this Court to Ansr what should be layd to their charge in relation to Coyning of base mony or putting it Away = After the Court had heard what they Could say for themselues The Court ordered them to be bound in twenty pounds apeece to ye Tresurer of ye Country on Condicon that they Appeare before the next County Court at Cambridg to Ansr what should be lajd agt them in such respect and Accordingly the sajd Joseph Blandchard & George Grimes each for himself acknowledged himsef respectively bound in twenty pounds apeece to Richard Russell Esqr Tresurer of the Country on this Condicon that they shall & will Appeare at the next County Court in Cambridg to Ansr what should be layd agt them or either of them in such respect as above sajd =

Majo‍r ‖ Genͬ ‖ Daniel Dennison took his oath as major Generall in open Court =

Att A meeting of the Gou̅no^r & Council Assembled in Boston 4 Sep^t 1674 A Day of publick Thanksgiving was Appointed wch was sent to the presse & printed =

Day of thanksgiuing 24 Sep^t 1674

[15] 1674

This Court was Adjourned to the 9th of octobe^r next at eight of the clocke in the morning =

The Court of Assistants on their Adjournment mett at the time 9th october 74 : = This Court Adjournd themselues from day to day the Generall Court being sitting to the 21th Instant octobe^r 1674 then sitting as a Court of Admiralty. Att this Court Jonas Clarke Jun̅ m^r of the Catch Hopewell entred his libell against Richard Starr & Joseph Tounesend requiring sattisfaction for his sajd Catch to this day according to charter party — After all the euidences & pleas made in the Case by both plantiffe & deffendant & the Charte^r-party & all Read & Considered of The Court found for the plantiff and ordered the Deffendant to pay vnto the plantiffe ninety pounds mony damage & costs of this Court forty shillings wth the officers fees five shillings and that the ouno^rs of the sajd Catch to haue the freight home. =

present Jno Leueret Esqr Gou̅
Sam Symonds Esqr dept Go[u]
Symon Bradstreet
Daniel Gookin
Daniel Dennison
Symon Willard
Richd Russell
Thomas Danforth Esqr[]
Wm Hathorne
John Pynchon
Edward Tyng
Wm Staughton
Thomas Clarke
. . . .

Courts Judgm^t in Jonas Clarks Case ag^t [Jos *] Starr &c

John Weaver marriner & master of the ship Richard & mary of swansey being in prison was sent for and on hearing of all the euidences & pleas in the case produced he being Convicted of notorious lying falsswearing and profanes together with his wilfull neglecting his duty that the sajd ship was lost and sunck in merrimack Riuer on the 5th of September last his endeavoring by his false oath to haue procured the Seale of the Colony giving in false Information to the publick Notary to draw vp his protest to saue himself pretending his great losses of an estate therein which appeared not The Court on the whole ^ proceeded to censure the sajd John Weauer for his sajd lying & false swearing to be whipt with twenty stripes severely layd on or pay the sume of ten pounds in mony

Courts Judgment ag^t Jno Weauer.

* Error in the record for "Richard."

together with the charges of the Court the sume of five pounds mony together with the charges of the witnesses and prosecution wth the officers ffees y^{e} eight wittnesses were allowed twelve shilling apeece mony they discharging what they haue expended on y^{e} Country^{s} account here & there =

Courts Judgm^{t} ag^{t} Edw Thomas one of y^{e} marrine^{r}s belonging to ship Rich^{d} & Mary of Suansey =

The Court also proceeded to censure Edward Thomas one of the marriners now in prison for his false oath to be whipt wth ten stripes seuerely layd one or pay the sume of forty shillings dischardging the office^{r}s ffees standing Comitted till y^{e} sentence be performed —

Ans^{r} to Edw Colcord pet'n

In Ans^{r} to the petition of Edward Colcord The Court ordered that the Tresurer sattisfy & pay vnto the sajd Colcord the some of forty shillings more out of majo^{r} shapleighs fine when he Receives it =

[16] 1674

p^{r}sent
Jno Leueret Esqr Go$\bar{u}$
Sam Symonds Esqr dep^{t} Go$\bar{u}$
Symon Bradstreet
Daniel Gookin
Daniel Dennison
Richd Russell
Thomas Danforth
Wm Hauthorn
Edward Tyng
Wm Staughton
Thomas Clarke } Esq^{r}s
persons Returnd to serve on the Grand Jury & sworne: were
— — — —
m^{r} christopher Clarke
Joshua Tyd
Joseph Lynde
Richrd Bennet
Thomas Smith
Abell porter
Silvester Evely
John Wells
Edward Morrice
Amiel Weekes
Enock Wisewall
Jonas Clarke
Samuel Andrews

Att a Court of Assistants held at Boston 2^{d} of march 1674

1st Jur m^{r} Joseph Belknap & Richard wharton Atturney^{s} to & in behalfe of Nicholas Rice plaintiffe in an Acc$\bar{o}$n of Appeale from the virdict of the Jury & Courts Judgment in the County Court at Boston in January last ag^{t} m^{r} Jno Oxenbridge James Allen Anthony stoddard & Humphry Davy trustee^{s} & executo^{r}s to the last will & Testament of Richard Bellingham Esqr deceased = After the Courts Judgment reasons of Appeale and evidences in the Case produced were read Comitted to the Jury & remajne on file wth the Reccords of this Court the Jury brought in their verdict they found for the plantiffs A reuersion of the former Judgment & Costs of Courts three pounds twelve shillings & ten pence : =

2^{d} Jur Joseph Tounsend plantiff ag^{t} Elias parkeman deffendant in an action of Appeale from the virdict of the Jury & County Courts Judgment at Boston in october last After the Courts Judgment Attachment Reasons of Appeale & euidences in the Case produced were read Comitted to the Jury & remajne on file wth the reccords of this Court the Jury brought in their virdict they found for the deffendant the Confirmation of the former virdict of the County Court at Boston & Costs of Courts.

exec. for 12. 9. 6 Issued out 9 June 75 w[th] 5[s] E R S. addi: costs

Richd Beers
Henry Bright

they brought in their p[r]sentm[ts] & Indictm[ts] ag[t] Rob[rt] Driver & Anna Negro : =

Jurymen Returnd to serve on the 1[st] Jury of tryalls for Appeales & for life limb & banishment = sworne

m[r] W[m] Hilton
Tho. Lord
W[m] Dauis
Samuel Gore
Thomas Edwards
Thomas Walker
Habbacuck Glouer
Jn[o] Minot *
Roge[r] Wellington
Nathaniel Coulidg
Jn[o] Barnard
Joseph Beamis

persons Returnd to serve on y[e] 2[d] Jury of Trjalls &c at y[s] Court sworne

m[r] w[m] maning
Daniel Dauison
Edw wilson
Jabez Tatman †
Barnard Trot
Jn[o] Scarlet
Henry Kemble
David Copp
Jn[o] Pason
James Bird
W[m] Boardman sen̄
James White =

W[m] Broune sen̄. of Salem merchant plantiff ag[t] willjam Lethe[r]land deffendant in an Accon of Appeale from the virdict of the Jury & County Courts Judgment at Boston in octobe[r] last = After the Attachment virdict of the Jury Reasons of Appeale & euidences in the case produced were read Comitted to the Jury & remajne on file with the Reccords of this Court the Jury brought in their virdict they found for the plantiff the reuersion of the former Judgment & Costs of Courts forty eight shillings =

Thomas Newman plantiff in an accon of Appeale from the virdict of the Jury & County Courts Judgment in octobe[r] last against Jn[o] Smith merchant Atturney to George Smith merchant = After the virdict of the Jury Attachment Reasons of Appeale & euidences in the case produced were read Comitted to the Jury &c the plantiff & deffendant Appearing in Court (by Consent the plaintiff w[th]drew the accon) : putting their differences relating to the sajd accon to Arbitration i e to the fynall Award of Capt Samuel Scarlet m[r] Peter lydget and m[r] John Richards or the majo[r] pte of them giving it in writting vnde[r] their hands by the first of Aprill || next || bearing the charges of law already expended each for himself & Acknowledged themselues bound in eight ‡ hundred pounds each to other to stand to Abide by & performe the sajd Award so Given. × × & this was thus donn in open Court 5 march 1674 m[r] Richards to Appoint time & place of meeting || & each pty Concerned accordingly to Attend their

* Or Mynor. † Or Tolman. ‡ This word changed from six to eight.

Concernes ‖ × × = as Attests Edw. Rawson secre^t^. all y^e^ papers in y^e^ case to be delivered vp to the ‖ partjes for the ‖ Arbitrators =

Wm Rawson plantiff ‖ ag^t^ Habbacuk Glouer ‖ in an Accon of Appeale from the virdict of the Jury & Judgmt of the County Court in Boston in octobe^r^ last After the Accon was Called both partjes Appeared & they both declaring they were Agreed the plantiffe wth the Courts Consent wi^th^drew his Accon =

[17] 1674

Bozoone Allen ag^t^ Jennet Whiple

Bozoone Allen plaintiff ag^t^ m^r^s Jennet whiple defendant in an Accon of Appeale from the Judgment of the last County Court at Ipswich. After the Attachment County Court of Ipswich Judgment reasons of Appeale & euidences in the case produced were read Comitted to the Jury and are remayning on file wth the Reccords of this Court the Jury brought in their virdict they found for the plantiffe — reuersion of the former Judgment & Costs of Courts seven pounds & ten pence. =

Rich^d^ & Return Wayte ag^t^ Jennet Whiple =

Richard wayte & return wayte plantiffs ag^t^ Jennet whiple execcutrix to Thomas Dickinson^s^ last will deffend^t^ in an action of Appeale from the virdict of the Jury & County Courts Judgm^t^ at Ipswich = After the Attachm^ts^ Courts Judgment Reasons of Appeale & euidences in the Case produced were read Comitted to the Jury & are remayning on file wth the Reccords of this Court the Jury brought in their virdict reuersion of the former Judgm^t^ & Costs of Courts = fowe^r^ pounds eleven shillings =

Rawson ag^t^ Billing

Wm Rawson plantiffe ag^t^ Roger Billing deffend^t^ in an Accon of Appeale from the virdict of the Jury & County Courts Judgm^t^ in Boston in January last After the Attachm^t^ Courts Judgmen^t^ Reasons of Appeale & euidences in the case produced were read Comitted to the Jury & are remayning on file wth the Reccords of this Court the Jury brought in their virdict they found for the deffendant Confirmation of the former Judgm^t^ wth Costs of Courts nineteen shillings & one penny =

Taintor &c ag^t^ chenree *

Joseph Tainto^r^ & Jno whittacre Atturney^s^ to m^r^s martha Ayres widdow plant ag^t^ John Chenery

* Intended for "Chenery."

deffend^t in an action of Appeale from the virdict of the Jury & County Court^s Judgm^t at Cambridge After the Attachment Courts Judgm^t reasons of Appeale & euidences in the Case were produced & Read Comitted to the Jury & are remayning on file wth the Reccords of this Court the Jury brought in theire virdict they found for the deffendant Confirmation of the former Judgment & Costs of Courts = fifty sixe shillings one penny.

Samuel Legg plantiff ag^t Thomas Dauis deffend^t in an action of Appeale from the virdict of y^e Jury & County Courts Judgm^t in Boston october 1674 After the Attachment Courts Judgment Reasons of Appeale & euidences in the Case produced were read Comitted to the Jury & are remayning on file wth the Reccords of this Court the Jury brought in their virdict they found for the deffendant Confirmation of the former Judgment & Costs of Courts forty fowe^r shillings & eight pence = Legg Ag^t Dauis

Samuell Rouland plaintiff ag^t Jno Hobbs defend^t in an action of Appeale from the Judgment of the last County Court at Salem After the Attachm^t Courts Judgment Reasons of Appeale & euidences in ^ case produced were read Comitted to the Jury and are remayning on file wth the Reccords of this Court the Jury brought in their virdict they found for the deffendant Confirmation of the former Judgment wth Costs of Courts fiuety fiue shillings & fowe^r pence = Rouland ag^t Hobbs 5^li to be p^d in S[ec^ry]

[18] 1674

Ensigne John Gold & Tho Baker plantiffs ag^t Nathaniel Putman deffend^t ‖ in behalfe of the owno^rs of the Iron workes ‖ &c in an Accõn of Appeale from the virdict of the Jury & County Courts Judgment at Ipswich in septembe^r last After the Attachment Courts Judgment Reasons of Appeale & euidences in the Case produced were read Comitted to the Jury & are on file wth the Reccords of this Court the Jury brought in their virdict they found That where trespas is sued for and prooved and no sume of dam̃ages prooved yet if Costs of Court may be Given to the plantiffe then they found for the deffendant ‖ a ‖ Confirmation of the former Judgment and Costs of Courts if not wee finde for the plantiffe Costs of Courts = The Court on Consideration of this virdict reuers the former Judgm^t & find for the present plaintiff^s Costs of Courts fiue pounds seuen shillings Gold & Bake^r ag^t Putman

& two pence to be p[d] not in mony but in other pay as the Custome of that Court allowes =

Gifford ag[t] Hathorne

John Gifford plantiffe ag[t] John Hathorne deffend[t] in an action of Appeale from the virdict of the Jury & County Courts Judgment at Ipswich in Septembe[r] last = After the Attachment Courts Judgmen[t] Reasons of Appeale & euidences in the Case produced were read Comitted to the Jury and are remayning on file wth the Reccords of this Court the Jury brought in their virdict they found for the plantiffe ‖ a ‖ reuersion of fforme[r] Judgment and Costs of Courts = fifty one shilling & fowe[r] pence =

Hutchinson ag[t] Payne

Eliakim Hutchinson plantiff ag[t] John Payne deffendant in an action of Appeale from the virdict of the Jury & County Courts Judgm[t] in Boston in January last After the Attachment Courts Judgment Reasons of Appeale and euidences in the Case produced were read Comitted to the Jury and are remayning on file w[th] the Reccords of this Court the Jury brought in their virdict i e they found a speciall virdict i e. If the Collateral contract or Agreement betwixt m[r] Eljakim Hutchinson m[r] olliuer purchis & m[r] John Payne bearing date the thirtjeth of Janua[r]y 1667: not prooved broaken doth according to law cut of or make voyd m[r] John Paynes obligation to sajd m[r] Hutchinson bearing date the 28[th] of Decembe[r] 1664 then wee finde for the now deffendant the Confirmation of the Judgment of the County Court at Boston & Costs of Courts But if m[r] John Paynes first obligation standeth in force according to Law then wee finde for the now Plantiffe the reuersion of the former Judgment of the Court Appealled from wth one hundred sixty nine pounds twelve shillings money according to obligation by bill & Costs of Courts The Court or Bench on Consideration of this virdict declared they found for the deffend[t].

Paul Batt plantiff ag[t] John Harris deffend[t] in an Action of Appeale from the virdict of the Jury & County Courts Judgment at Boston in January last After the Attachm[t] Courts Judgment Reasons of Appeale & euidences in the Case produced were read Comitted to the Jury & are remayning on file wth the Reccords of this Court the Jury brought in their virdict they found for the deffendant a Confirmation of the form[r] Judgment i e fiueteene shillings mony & Costs of Courts: twenty fowe[r] shillings & fowe[r] pence =

[19] 1674

Robert Orchard as sue^r^ty & Atturney to John Shakeley & Peter Jacobson plantiff ag^t^ Richard midlecot & John Willjams Atturneys to Samuel winslow deffend^t^ in an action of Appeale from the virdict of the Jury & County Courts Judgment in octobe^r^ last the Accon was Called both partjes Appearing & the Case Agreed betweene them: The Court allowed the plantiff libe^r^ty to w^th^draw his accon wch he did =

orchard &c ag^t^ winslow &c

Samuel mighill ‖ & Elisabeth his wife ‖ plantiff ag^t^ Jacob Toppan &c deffendant in an action of Appeale from the virdict of the Jury & County Courts Judgm^t^ in Septembe^r^ last the Case was called the deffend^t^ Appeared not the Case proceeded & After the Attachment Courts Judgment Reasons of Appeale & euidences in the Case produced were read comitted to the Jury and are on file wth the Reccords of this Court the Jury brought in theire virdict they found for the plantiff a Reuersion of the former Judgment & fiue pounds eight shillings damage wth Costs of Courts =

mighill ag^t^ Toppan

Bozoone Allen was called before the Court to Ans^r^ for his reflections declared in his Reasons of Appeale ag^t^ one of the magistrates & County Court at Ipswich from whenc he Appealled for which the Court fined him tenn pounds =

Bozoon Allen fined 10li

In Ans^r^ to the peticon of Bozoone Allen having Given in his Acknowledgm^t^ of his offenc the Court sees cause to remitt the fine to forty shillings =

on his Peticon his fine remitted to 40^s^.

Anna Negro servant to m^rs^ Rebeckah Lynde widdow of charlsToune being Comitted to Prison for hauing a Bastard & being vnder sore suspition of making it away &c in orde^r^ to furthe^r^ tryall The Grand Jury found a bill of indictment ag^t^ hir: she was brought to the Barr & there holding vp hir hand pleaded not Guilty put hirself on God & the Country for hir tryall thô she had liberty yet objected not ag^t^ any of the Jewry: was Indicted by the name of Anna Negro as aboue for not hauing the feare of God before hir eyes & being Instigated by the Divil did about the 14th of December last maliciously & wilfully murder an Infant child then borne of hir owne body Contrary to the peace of our Soueraigne

Anna Negro Indictm^t^ & sentence

Lord the King his Croune & dignity and the lawes of this Jurisdiction the Jury went out & brought in their virdict they found the sajd Anna Negro Guilty of hauing a Bastard child & privately conveyed it away. The Court Considering of this virdict sentenct the sajd Anna Negro to stand on the Gallowes wth a Roape fastened about hir necke to the Galloues for one hower and thence to be tyed to & whip^{t} at the Carts Tayle to the prison wth thirty stripes & so comitted to the prison there to lye for one moneth and then to be Conveyed by the marshall Generall to charlsTowne & there on the lecture day to be alike tyed to & whipt wth thirty stripes & then on hir m^{rs} paying the charges of the tryall & prison she is dischardged =

Robe^{r}t Driver scotch man being Comitted to prison (hauing fled for murdering his m^{r}: Robe^{r}t willjams of Piscataqua fisherman) in order to his tryall was brought to the Barr the Grand jury hauing presented him & Indicted him he holding vp his hand at the barr pleaded not Guilty put himself on his triall by God and the Country hauing his liberty to object against any of the Jury Impannelled he objecting not was Indicted by the name of Robert Driver late Apprentice & servant to the late Robert Willjams for not having the ffeare of God before his eyes & being

[20] 1674

Drive^{rs} Indictm^{t} & sentenc of Death =

Instigated by the Divil in or about the 10th of february last together wth Nicholas favo^{r} * then yor fellow servant did maliciously and wth wicked hands murder your † then master Robe^{r}t willjams or did abett Consent vnto, & Conceale the sajd murderers & villanous Act Contrary to the peace of our Soueraigne Lord the King his Croune & Dignity the lawes of God & this Jurisdiction = he hauing pleaded not Guilty: Afte^{r} the Jury had pervsed their euidenc they brought in their virdict they found him Guilty
The Court vnanimously Agreed that sentenc of Death should be pronounct ag^{t} him accordingly. The Goṽno^{r} proceed. yow Robert Driuer hauing binn found Guilty as aboue are to Goe from henc to y^{e} place from whenc yow Came & from thence to the place of execution & there to hang by y^{e} neck till yow be dead. God haue mercy on thy Soule =

mary Sande^{r}s at liberty to marry &c =

In Ans^{r} to the peticon of mary Sande^{r}s humbly desiring a legall divorcement from hir husband w^{m}

* Or fævo^{r}.

† "Their" changed to "your."

Sande^rs who is marrjed to another woman in London The Court on pervsall of the euidences Daniel webb stephen Swasy & phillip English Judged it meet to declare the peticone^r to be at liberty from hir former husband w^m Sande^rs =

Ans^r to mary Hawkins peticōn

In Ans^r to the petition of mary Haukins humbly Imploring the Courts favou^r to remitt to hir hir seccond punishment This Court Judgeth it meet wth the Consent of the County Court to Grant hir request & remitts her seccond punishment ordering the keeper of the prison to dismiss hir from the prison & set hir at libe^rty =

majo^r Thomas Clarke is Appointed wth the secretary to allow of the bills of Costs this Court.

mary Parsons presented & Indicted for witchcraft =

The Grand Jury was Called againe and they pervsing seuerall euidences sent doune from the County Court at North Hampton relating to mary Parsons the wife of Joseph Parson^ they presenting an Indictment against hir on suspicion of witchcraft leaving hir to further trjall The Court Ordered hir Comittment to the prison in Boston there to remaine & be kept in orde^r to hir furthe^r tryall

Paul Batts admonicōn =

Paul Batt was Called for to Ans^r for his reflections declared in his reasons of Appeale. the sajd Paul Bat presenting his peticōn declaring his hopes for the future to be better Advised The Court past his offenc by ordering him to be Admonisht wch was donn :

Ans^r to Eze: ffoggs peticōn

In Ans^r to the peticon of Ezekiel ffogg in relation to some libe^rty &c The Court declares that when the peticōne^r hath honestly payd his debts he may be at his libe^rty altogether =

Courts Adjourn^t & order to send for y^e wittnesses ag^t mary Parsons =

This Court is Adjourned to the 13th of may next at 10 of the clock in the morning It is ordered that the Secretary Issue out his warrants for such & so many of the wittnesses as once wth in a moneth m^r Danforth m^r Tinge & majo^r Clark shall wth the Secret. on their pervsall determine to be necessary and that a letter be writt to majo^r Pynchon to Accomodate y^t Affaire Relating to mary Parsons

In Ans^{r} to Capt Hutchinsons petiĉon Jno Sands his execution ag^{t} him is respitted till the 15th of May next =

[21]

1674

present
Jno Leueret Esqr Goũ.
Symon Brads^{t}reet
Daniel Gookin
Richard Russell
Tho Danforth
Edw. Tyng
Wm Staughton
Tho: Clarke
} Esq^{r}s

— — — —

persons Returnd to serve on the Grand Jury & sworne =

— — — —

Left Richard Beers
Henry Allen
Peter Bracket
John Phillips
Robe^{r}t Sande^{r}s
Jacob Elljot
Jonas clarke
Samuel Andrews
Henry Bright
John Boules
Robe^{r}t Willjams
Samuel Clap
Enock Wisewall
Jno Penticost
w^{m} Johnson

— — — —

persons Returnd to serve on the Jury of tryalls for life & death were sworne —

— — — —

m^{r} w^{m} Bartholmew
Humphry Hodges
Richd wooddey
Wm Ingram
Rich'd medlecott
Jno Greene
Zack Hicks
Jno Barnard
Nath: Coolidge
Abra: How
Phillip Curtes
Amiel weeks

— — — —

Att A speciall Court of Assistants Called by the Gou^{r}n^{r} & magistrates in Boston in order to the tryall of Nicholas ffaevo^{r} 11th March 1674.

The Grand Jury on pervsall of Nicholas faevo^{r}s examination presented & Indicted him for murder leaving him to further tryall =

He was brought to the barr & was Indicted by the name of Nicholas faevo^{r} for not hauing the feare of God before his eyes and being Instigated by the Divil in or about the 10th of february last he the sajd Nicholas ffaevo^{r} together wth his then fellow servant Robe^{r}t Driver did maliciously & wth wicked hands murder their then master Robe^{r}t willjams, or did Abett Consent unto & conceale the sajd murdere^{r}s & villainous act, contrary to the peace of our Soueraigne Lord the king his Croune & dignity & the lawes of God, & of this Jurisdiction=he holding vp his hand all y^{e} while pleaded not Guilty put himself on his trjall by God & the Country — The Jury on consideration of the euidence brought in their virdict they found him Guilty = And accordingly the Gouerno^{r} pronounc^{t} sentenc agt him yow Nicholas ffaevo^{r} hauing binn found Guilty of murde^{r} according to yor Indictmẽnt are to Goe from hence to the place from whence yow Came ‖ & from thenc ‖ to the place of execution & there to hang by the neck till yow be dead: God haue Mercy on thy soule: =

Edward Naylor being Complayned on for Intruding into his late wiues Katherin Nanny^{s} Company &c. The Court on hearing what was lajd to the sajd Naylors charge doe Judge & declare his bond to be forfeited and doe order the Secretary to put the sajd Bond in suite = And that he stands Comitted till he dischardg his bond. =

This Court ordered the executions of the sajd Robe^r^t Drive^r^ & Nicholas ffaevo^r^ to be on the 5th day next after the lecture & that the Secretary Issue out his warrants Accordingly and that Anna Negro haue hir sentenc then executed on hir as to y^e^ 1st p^t^e

Att A Court of Assistants on Adjournment held at Boston 13th of may 1675

present
Jno Leṽert Esqr Goṽ
Sam. Symonds Esqr dep^t^ Gou
Symon Bradstreet
Daniel Gookin
Daniel Dennison
Symon Willard
Richd Russell
Tho Danforth
Wm Hathorn
Jno Pinchon
Edwd Tyng
Wm Stoughton
Tho Clarke
} Esq^rs^

Att this Court Mary Parsons the wife of Joseph Parsons of Northampton in the County of Hampshire in the Colony of the Massachusetts being presented & Indicted by the Grand Jury was also Indicted by the name of Mary Parsons the wife of Joseph Parsons for not hauing the feare of God before hir eyes and being Instigated by the divill hath at one or other of the times mentioned in the euidences now before ye Court entred into familliarity wth the divill and Comitted seuerall acts of witchcraft on the person or persons of one or more as in the sajd euidences relating thereto refference being thereto had Amply doeth and may appeare and all this Contrary to the peace of our Soueraigne Lord the king his Croune and dignity the lawes of God and of this Jurisdiction = After the Indictment

[22] 1675

and Euidences in the Case were Read the prisone^r^ at the barr holding vp hir hand & pleading not Guilty putting hirself on hir triall, the Jury brought in their virdict they found hir not Guilty = & so she was dischardged =

The names of y^e^ Jury of tryalls for life & death sworne were
— — — —
Mr Joseph Cooke
Hugh Drury
Tho Dure*
Theode^r^ Atkinson señ
Sam: Mayrs
Benj Gamlin
Wm Symes
Jno Heyman
Nath fiske sen^r^
Henry Spring
Richd Hall
Samuel Paul
— — — —
Beckfords death May 14 (75)

By virtue of a warrant wee whose names are herevnder written being warned by ye Constable of Boston to serve as a Jury of Inquest to make diligent Search & Inquiry after the Cause of the death of a youth named Christopher Bickford we find the sajd youth in his face to be much bruised & two of his fingers on his right hand hurt and that the sajd youth by Information of the master & seamen which belonged to the sajd ship he Came ouer in was missing euer since tuesday last betweene betweene † six &

* Or Durd.

† Repeated in the record.

eight of the clocke at night & Judge or Conceive a fall from the ship or som blow or blowes on his face wth falling from the ship into the waters to be y[e] Cause of his death = Subscribed Seth Perry Rich[d] way Jn[o] W[ms] Rich[d] wooddje Ephraim Turner Tho. Bingly Jn[o] marrion Jn[o] morse W[m] ‖ [Seŵick] ‖ W. Wright Jn[o] Lake Edward Ellis Jn[o] Buttolph Benja Thirston. The Jurors subscribed attested to the trueth of this virdict vpon their oaths before me Dani Dennison

present
Jn[o] Leueret Esq[r] Goŵ
Sam Symonds Esq[r] dept Goŵ
Symon Bradstreet, Daniel Gookin, Daniel Dennison, Rich[d] Russell, Tho Danforth, W[m] Hathorn, John Pinchon, Edw. Tyng, W[m] Stoughton, Tho Clarke — Esq[rs]
— — — —

Att A Court of Admiralty or Court of Assistants Called by the Gou[r]no[r] & Assembled in Boston 17[th] of May 1675

m[r] Humphry Warren of Boston merchant in behalfe of m[r]s Elisabeth ffreake relict of the late m[r] John ffreake merchant ‖ & m[r] Sam Shrimpton m[r]cht ‖ preffering their libell Against Peter Rodrjego as also ag[t] Cornelius Andreson John Roads & Company. The Court on a full and due pervsall of the aboue mentioned libell & hearing of all partjes Concerned w[th] the euidences produced doe Judge it meete to declare & Graunt ajudication of the vessells & Goods taken & brought in by Cap[t] Samuel Mosely to Humphry Warren in behalfe of the late m[r] John ffreake & Elisabeth his relict & m[r] Samuel Shrimpton for theire Reparation for their vessell & Goods taken from them by the sajd Rodriego Roads & Company and the sajd warren and shrimpton are to pay the chardges of the Court & prosecution of the Case for y[e] hearing of the Case seven pounds mony besides the office[r]s ffees & charges. =

The Court declard that the sajd Peter Rodriego Cornellius Andreson Jn[o] Roads Peter Grant Randall Judson Rich[d] ffowler &c to be lawfull prisoners Remanding them to prison Againe and Referred them to further Tryall. =

The Council Act of 15[th] febr 1674 comissionating y[e] Aboue mentioned Cap[t] Sam Mosely to fetch in the aboue mention[ed] Rodriegoe & Company in Ans[r] to m[r] Jn[o] ffreaks peticon & mosely ^ Instruction are on y[e] Courts file. =

[23] 1675

p[r]sent
Jn[o] Leueret Esq[r] Goŵ.
Sam Symond Esq[r] dep[t] Go.

Att A Court of Assistants held at Boston y[e] 24[th] of may 1675 & called by y[e] Court for trjall of the prisone[r]s =

Peeter Rodrjego Dutchman being presented & Indicted by the Grand Jury was Indicted by the name of Peeter Rodrjego for that he not hauing the feare of God before his eyes he wth othe^r^ his Complices sometimes in the moneth^s^ of Novembe^r^ Decembe^r^ & January last by force of Armes did vpon the sea^s^ pyrattically & ffelloniously seize & take seuerall smale English vessells (and theire Companyes) belonging to his Maj^t^ys subjects of this Colony & made prize of theire Goods & in particcular the barcque Phillip & her goods belonging to the late m^r^ John ffreake of Boston Georg maning being master then of hir wounding the sajd maning & his mate Contrary to the peace of our Soueraigne Lord the King his Croune & dignity the lawes of God & of this Jurisdiction. — to wch Indictm^t^ ye prisone^r^ at the barr pleaded not Guilty put himself on triall by God & the Country — saying he had no exception ag^t^ any of ye Jury : the Case proceeded and after the Indictment & euidences in the Case were Read Comitted to the Jury & are on file wth the Reccords of this Court the Jury brought in thr virdict they found him Guilty according to the aboue written Indictment and Accordingly had sentenc of death pronnounc^t^ ag^t^ him by ye Gou̅. to be Carrjed from hence to the place from whence he came & thence to the place of execution & there to hang till he be dead

Symon Bradstreet
Symon willard
Richd Russell
Tho Danforth
Wm Hathorn
Edw. Tyng
w^m^ Stoughton
} Esqr

— — — —

Grand Jurymen Returnd to serve At y^e^ Court & Sworne were =

— — — —

m^r^ Jno sherman —
Rich^d^ wellington
Richd Baker
Tho. Russell
Jno Long
Symon Lynd
Jno woodmansey
Jn^o^than Bolston
Habbacuck Glouer
Jno Bateman
Jonas clarke
ffrancis Moore
Tho: Hastings
Jno Bowles
Tho weld

— — — —

Jury men Returnd to Serv[e] on the Jury of tryalls
m^r^ John Checkly
Jno Bird
Benj: Bale
Benj: Moore
Benj: Gillam
Samuel Goffe
Tho Longhorne
Tho ffa[ning]
Tho Hastings
Jno Stone
Edw. B[rjdge]
Daniel Brewer

— — — —

And on his peticon the Court Gaue him opp^r^tunity to peticon the Gen̅^ll^ Court for his life = In like manner

Cornelius Andreson Dutchman was brought out of Prison to the barr & Indicted by the name of Cornelius Andreson for not hauing the feare of God before his eyes he together wth other his Complices sometimes in the moneth^s^ of November Decembe^r^ & January last past did vpon the seas by force of Armes Pyrattically & ffelloniously seize and take seuerall smale English vessells (wth theire Companyes ^ belonging to his maj^ty^ subjects of this Colony making prize of their Goods and in particcular the vessell & Goods that belonged to Edward Hylliard & w^m waldron Contrary to the peace of our Soueraigne Lord the King his Croune & dignity the lawes of God & of this Jurisdiction = in like manner he put himself on God & the Country for his tryall: and After the Indictment & euidences in the Case produced against him were Read Comitted to the Jury & are on file wth the Reccords of this Court the Jury brought in their virdict they found him not Guilty &c on sending out Againe they brought in they found him Guilty of Theft or Robbery by taking from willjam waldron & Edward Hylliard fowerteen moose skins two packs of Beaver & seuen martin skins

Andresons Case

And In Answer to his humble peticon & Acknowledgment of his Evills. wch he owned in open Court was pardoned =

order for T^r: to pay w^m Kent 45: 6:

It is ordered y^t y^e Tresurer pay m^r Kent forty fiue shillings sixe pence & is for a dinner for y^e magists at a Court of Admiralty Aprill 9 (74) — —

[24] 1675

Jno Roads Peter Grant &c the Rest of the prisone^rs were Called into the open Court & had the Grand Jury^s presentment & Indictments ag^t them Read as Pyrates but the euidences not being viva voce they were by the Court Remanded to prison ye Court adjourning till the 3^d 5th day of June being ye 17th day at nine of ye clock ye wittnesses to be sent for

Jno Roads objected ag^t ye forem Jno Checkly so Benja Gillam was ffo^rman in the rest

present
Jno Leueret Esqr Gou
Sam Symonds Esqr dep^t Go:
Symon Bradstreet
Daniel Gookin
Daniel Dennison
Symon Willard
Richd Russell
Tho Danforth
Edwd Tyng
Wm Stoughton
Thomas Clarke
— — — —
Jurymen Impaneld & sworne were for ye Triall of these 6
— — — —
Capt Benja Gillam
Jno Bird
Benj: Bale

Att A Court of Assistants on Adjournment held at Boston 17th June 1675 Jno Roads was brought to the barr & holding vp his hand was Indicted by the name of John Roads late of Boston for that he not having the feare of God before his eyes & ~~being Instigated by the Divill~~ he wth othe^rs his Complices sometimes in the mon^ths of November December & January last past did by force of Armes vpon the seas Pyrattically & ffelloniously seize & take seuerall Smale English vessells & theire Companjes belonging to his Maj^ty subjects of this Colony and made prize of their Goods & in particcular the barcque Phillip & her Goods belonging to the late m^r John ffreake of Boston George maning being

Roads Indictm^t

then master of hir wounding the sajd maning & his mate Contrary to the peace of our Soueraigne Lord the King his Croune & dignity the lawes of God & of this Jurisdiccon to wch he pleaded not Guilty put himself on God & the Country for his trjall after ye Indictment & euidences produced agt him were read Comitted to the Jury & are on file wth the Reccords of ys Court the Jury brought in their virdict they found him Guilty according to Indictment and accordingly ye next day had sentenc of Death pronounct agt him: yt he should Goe from the barr to ye place from whenc he Came & thenc to the place of execution & there hang till he be dead. =

Wm Whitwell
Richd Knight
Sam Goffe
Tho Longhorne
Edwd Bridge
Daniel Brewer
John Holbrook
Jno Swett
Jno Davenport
— — — —

Sentenc

Richd ffouler was brought to the barr & holding his hand there vp ^ was indicted by the name of Richard ffowler Englishman for that he not hauing the feare of God before his eyes he wth others his Complices sometimes in the moneths of November december & January last past did by force of Armes vpon the seas pyrattically & felloniously seize & take seuerall smale vessells & their Companyes belonging to his majtys subjects of this Colony making prize of theire Goods and in particcular the barcque Phillip & her Goods belonging to the late mr John ffreake of Boston George maning being then master of her wounding the sajd maning & his mate Contrary to the peace of our Soueraigne Lord the King his Croune & dignity the lawes of God & of this Jurisdiction: = This case as Jno Roads being Comitted to the Jury &c the Jury brought in their virdict they found him Guilty according to Indictment = ye sentenc of death in like manner was pronounct agt him:

ffoulers Indictmt & sentenc

Peeter Grant was also brought to the barr where holding vp his hand was Indicted by the name of Peeter Grant scotch man for not hauing the feare of God before his eyes he wth others his Complices sometimes in the months of Novembe december & January last past

[25] 1675

did vpon the seas by force of Armes pirattically & ffelloniously seize & take seuerall smale English vessells (wth theire Companyes ^ belonging to his majtys subjects of this Colony making prize of theire Goods and in particcular the barcque Phillip & her Goods belonging to the late mr John ffreake of Boston George

Grants Indictmt

maning being then master of hir wounding the sajd master & his mate Contrary to the peace of our Soueraigne Lord the King his Croune & dignity & the law^{s} of this Jurisdic̃on to wch Indictment he pleaded not Guilty & put himself on God & the Country for his tryall = & **& sentenc** being Comitted to the Jury they brought in their virdict they found him Guilty & accordingly sentenc of death was pronounct ag^{t} him as ag^{t} Jno Roads

Randolph Judson was brought to the barr & Indicted by the name of Randolph Judson Englishman for not hauing the feare of God before his eyes & ~~being Instigated by the Divil~~ wth others his Com- **Judsons Indictm^{t}** plices, sometimes in the months of Novembe^{r} Decemb^{r} & January last past did by force of Armes vpon the seas pirattically & felloniously seize & take seuerall English vessells (and theire Companjes) belonging to his maj^{ty} subjects of this Colony and made prize of theire Goods and in particular the barcque Phillip & her Goods belonging to the late m^{r} John ffreake of Boston George maning being then master of her wounding the sajd maning & his mate Contrary to the peace of our Soueraigne Lord the King his Croune & dignity & the laws of this Jurisdiction: to wch Indictment he also pleaded not Guilty put himself on God & the Country for his trjall & **& Sentenc** being comitted to the Jury they brought in their virdict they found him Guilty according to Indictment &c and accordinghly he had y^{e} sentenc of death pronounct ag^{t} him: = as Jno Roads had

Jno willjams was brought to the barr and was Indicted by the name of John willjams Englishman for that he not hauing the feare of God before his eyes wth others his Complices some times in the months of Nouember December & January last past did vpon the seas by force of Armes pirattically & ffelloniously seize & take seuerall smale English vessells wth their Compãyes belonging to his Maj^{ty} subjects of this Colony making prize of their Goods and in particular the barcque Phillip & her Goods belonging to the late m^{r} John ffreake of Boston **Wm Indictm^{t} & freedom** George maning being then master of her wounding the sajd maning & his mate Contrary to the peace of our Soueraigne Lord the King his Croune & dignity & the lawes of this Jurisdiction. to wch Indictment ye prisone^{r} pleaded not Guilty & put himself on God & the Country for his trjall wch Indictm^{t} & euidences comitted to the Jury the Jury brought in their virdict they found him not Guilty

[26] 1675

John Thomas was brought to the barr and was Indicted by the name of John Thomas for not having the feare of God before his Eyes he together wth other his Complices sometimes in the mon^ths^ of Nouembe^r^ Decembe^r^ & January last past did vpon the seas by force of Armes piratticcally & ffelloniously seize and take seuerall smale English vessells (wth their Companyes) belonging to his Maj^tys^ subjects of this Colony making prize of their Goods and in particular the barcque phillip & hir Goods belonging to the late m^r^ John ffreake of Boston Georg maning being then master of hir wounding the sajd maning & his mate Contrary to the peace of our Soueraigne Lord the King his Croune & dignity & y^e^ laws of this Jurisdiction = to which Indictment y^e^ prisoner pleaded not Guilt[y] & put himself on God & the Country for his triall (wch Indictm^t^ & euidences was Comitted to the Jury that brought in their virdict they found him not guilty

John Thomas Indictm^t^

ffreed

It is ordered that John Roads Randall Judson Peter Grant & Richard ffouler being Condemned to suffer Death the time Appointed for their execution shall be on y^e^ 5th day next Come seven night being the first day of July presently after the lecture and warrants Issued out accordingly =

At A Court of Assistants or Admiralty held at Boston the 17th of June 1675

Vpon the Complaint of willjam measure of lyme in New England merchant exhibbited vnto this Court by his libell against Robe^r^t Haughton of Boston marriner & master of the Catch Hopewell This Court having heard & considered the pleas & euidences in the Case doe order & decree that Robert Haughton shall deliuer unto Wm Measure all his Apparrell and other Goods in his posession and pay & duely sattisfy unto the sajd measure or his Assignes the some of two hundred & ten pounds in lawfull money of New England And It is further ordered & decreed that the sajd Wm Measure shall pay all the seamens wages & Catch hire and victualls untill hir Arrivall in New England and the sajd master is to receive what freight is due for any Goods brought in the sajd Catch from Berbadoes to Boston & pay the Costs of the action in money the summe of sixe pounds thirteen shillings and officers fees and this to be a fynall Issue of the case =
E R S.

[27] 1675

Bacon: Parsons & agt Jno Bull.

ye Courts Decree therevpon

Whereas John Bacon willjam Parsons Robt Brounsford Abraham Sanford Andrew Couzens & Nicholas Smith marriners exhibited to this Court theire libell & Complaint against John Bull master of the ship Prouidence of ljme declaring that they were shipped by Walter Tucker (one of the Owno'rs of the sajd shipp) for a voyage from Lyme to virginea and from thence to ljme againe the Port of their discharge, and accordingly coming to virginia they could not obteyne Tobacco sufficient to load the vessell to Content of the master and Jno Smith merchant of the sajd ship wherevpon they the sajd master & merchant resolved for new England the Complaynants Complying therein being desirous to further the Concernes of the owno'rs and are now come to Boston || where they Ap'rhend their wages to be due it being || the second deliuering Port but the master denying the payment thereof, they doe Craue the Justice of this Court, that their wages may be pajd them or that the master be ordered to Giue them security for the payment thereof in England on demand; and also that they may be freed from the sd ship; or haue security for their wages for the time to come till they come to the Port of their right discharge =

The aboue named partjes appearing before this Court and hauing had libe'rty to present their full plea & euidence in the Case wch haue binn duely considered It is heereby Ordered & decreed that John Bull master of the sajd ship Providence shall Giue to the aboue named John Bacon wm Parsons Robe'rt Brounesford Abraham Sanford, Andrew Cuzens and Nicholas Smith a Cirtifficat vnder his hand legally Attested declaring the time they haue served in the sajd ship in pursuance of their Contract wth their ouno'rs & Implojers and that their wages is due vnto this time wch being Accordingly performed by the sajd master then the sajd seamen are Ordered to proceed on their voyage on the same Conditions that they were first shipped vpon the Costs of this Court || to || be payd by the sajd John Bull i e forty six shillings: Cirtifficate was Giuen & signed by ye sd Jno B[ou]ll & owned in Court & is on file =

Whereas Isaak Rand mate of the ship John & mary of London, Robe'rt Kemp Carpenter, Henry Butte'rfield Gunner John Smart Quartermaster Wm Lock chirurgeon moses Patrick Robert Dauis & James King all marriners of the sajd ship Exhibited a libell & Complaint against John Smith me^r^chant and part Owno^r^ of the ship John & Mary late of London Josiah Hare late Cōmand^r^ This Court hauing heard & Considered the pleas & euidences in the Case doe order & decree that John Smith shall forthwith sattisfy unto the sajd persons before named in mony the sume of seventy nine pounds sixe shillings & six pence that is to say sixty one pounds sixe shillings & sixpenc for wages each man his proportion and for saluage of Goods eighteen pounds i e to Isack Rand sixteen pounds five shilling to Robt Kemp fiueteene pounds two shillings & six pence to Henry Butterfield nine pounds sixteen shillings to John Smart nine pounds two shillings & six pence To w^m^ Lock chirurgeon eleven pounds seven shillings & six penc To Robt Dauis six pounds sixteen shillings to moses Patrick six pounds seventeen shillings & to James King fower pounds in all seventy nine pounds six shilling & six penc and the sajd John Smith is to pay y^e^ Costs of Court & office^r^s fees five pound fowe^r^ shillings. =

[28] 1675

Att a Court of Admirality or Court of Assistants held at Boston 6th August 1675 =

p^r^sent y^e^ Gōūno^r^
Mr Bradstreet
Capt Gookin
Major Dennison
Rich. Russell
Tho. Danforth
Edw Ting
Wm Stoughton
Tho. Clarke
Esq^rs^

Courts order & decree in Moore & May^s^ Case Execution Issued out for y^e^ Costs =

In the Case of Thomas Moore mast^r^ in behalfe of himself & the rest of the Owno^rs^ of the Pink Supply plaintiff by his libell & complant exhibitted to this Court ag^t^ w^m^ may now master of the sajd Pinke defend^t^ the Court hauing duely heard & Considered the plea^s^ & euidences in the Case doe find for y^e^ deffendt and order & decree y^t^ the plantiff pay the Costs of Court in all fifty nine shillings =

Courts order & decree in phillip owen Charls frost &c Newton & Gordons Case

The Court hauing Considered the Complaint or libell of Phillip owen charls ffrost John Bell Arthur Richards & w^m^ maxfeild mariners of the ship George of London Derry ag^t^ Charls Newton part owno^r^ & James Gordon Agent & facto^r^ for Jarvice Ba[r]ty the other owno^r^ of the sajd ship doeth order and decree that the sajd Newton & James Gordon shall before the eleventh of this Instant August Giue security to the secretary or Clarke of this Court to the value of one hundred pounds that they shall sayle wth the sajd ship George from this port directly to London Derry in Ireland or otherwise to pay unto the sajd Phillip Owen & Company as aboue their wages to this day the some of fiuety pounds three shillings sixe penc mony being fowe[r] month and a halfe ending August the 7th inst to be divided amongst them according to their seuerall pro * proportions and In Case the deffendants shall pay the plantiffs their wages then the sajd Plantiffs are ordered to Continue in their service in the sajd ship Prouided their voyages be only to lawfull Ports and that they be not kept out aboue one yeare from their first setting forth from London Derry and that the defend[ts] pay the Costs of this Court & officers ffees which came to forty eight shillings besids y[e] seamens Costs =

Thomas Mitchell & Edward Vring being bound ouer to this Court to Ans[r] for their seuerall misdemeano[r]s in their being & seeming concurrance w[th] John Roads & the rest of the Pyrates were Called and Appearing The Court hauing heard & considered their pleas & euidences presented doe sentence the sajd Thomas michell to make & pay treble sattisfaction to m[r] George munjoy for the fowe[r] sheepe stolne i e nine pounds twelve shillings & that both the said mitchell & vrin be whipt w[th] twenty stripes a peece & dischardgeing their fees standing Comitted till this sentence be performed

Courts sentenc of vrin & mitchell

[29] 1675

Vppon a Complaint of Robe[r]t Haughton of Boston marriner master of the late Catch called the Hopewell exhibbited to this Court by his libell against willjam measure merchant in an Action of the Case for breach of charter party. This Court hauing heard & considered the pleas & euidences in the Case doe order & decree that the plantiff pay the deffendant his Costs of Court & the office[r]s ffees:

Vpon a Complaint of Robert Haughton of Boston marriner master of the Catch Hopewell plaintiffe by his libell exhibbited to this Court against w[m] measure merchant deffendant in an Action of Revejw of the Judgment & decree of this Court in June last The Court having heard & Considered the pleas & euidences & Refferred it to Audito[r]s who haue made their returne wch this Court Approoves of and doe order and decree that the defendant pay unto the plaintiffe one hundred fiuety fowe[r] pounds fowe[r]teen shillings & one penny and his Costs of this Court & office[r]s fees : =

Execution Issued out y[e] 18[th] Inst

this Court is dissolued

* The Secretary evidently neglected to cancel the "pro."

Att A Court of Admiralty or Court of Assistants held at Boston the 30th of August 1675

In the Action brought before this Court between Jno Toton of Rochell chirurgeon by his libell Complayning against Thomas Patten of Boston merchant as to his wages as Pylot for fower monthe certeine after fiue pounds ℘ moneth and for fower barrells of Brandy and for one eighth part of the Cargoe. = After the Court had heard & Considered the euidences produced doe Judge order and decree that the sajd Thomas Patten sattisfy & pay vnto John Toton for his Pilotage fiueteen pounds money [he having received five pounds in france] † and for what is vnpayd him for his Brandy thirteen pounds fowerteen shillings in money and for his owne eighth part of the Cargoe one hundred and ten pounds in all one hundred thirty eight pounds ^ twelve shillings & fower pence Costs of this Court and office's ffees six pounds twelve shillings & fower pence and for mr Baylys concernes ‡ the Court sees no Cause to medle wth that =

This Court is dissolued

present
the Govnr
dept Govnor
Symon Bradstreet
Daniel Gookin
Daniel Denison
^wm Hauthorn *
Rich. Russell
^Tho. Danforth
Edw Tyng
wm Stoughton
Tho Clarke
} Esqrs.
— — — —

Courts decree in Totons Case

Execution Issued out the 9th Septemb 1675 : & returnd

[30] 1675

Att a Court of Assistants held at Boston 7th September 1675

The Grand Jury brought in their Indictments & presentments

1st Ju. Henry Dow plant Atturney & in behalfe of the Toune of Hampton agt Nathaniel Boulter || Atturney to Jno Huggens || defendant After the Attachment Courts Judgment Reasons of Appeale & euidences in the Case were Read Comitted to the Jury & are on file wth the Reccords of this Court the Jury brought in their Virdict Confirmation of the Judgmt of Salisbury Court the land in Controuersie & Costs of Courts. =

present
Jno Levet Esq Govr
Sam Symonds Esqr Dept Gov
Symon Bradstreet
Daniel Gookin
Daniel Dennison
Richd Russell
Tho. Danforth
Wm Hathorn
Edward Tyng
wm Stoughton
Thomas Clarke
} Esqrs
— — — —

persons Returnd to serve on ye Grand Jury & Sworne
— — — —
mr wm Parkes
wm Needom
Samuel Sendall
John Conney

* The two carets are in the original and probably indicate that Hauthorn's name should come after Danforth's. † In brackets in the original. ‡ Written over the word "demands."

ffrancis Douse
Giles Pason
Jn° Smith
Timothy mather
Joseph Lynd
Jn° Heyman
Jonas Clarke
Tho ffox
Jn° Coolidge
Eli[z] Baron
— — — —
persons to serve on ye Jury of trialls for life & death Appeales & Returnd & sworn 1st Jur were
— — — —
Left Elisha Hutchinson
Samuel walker
Thomas moore
Zeckaryah Long
Jn° Knight
Nicholas Clap
Timothy Tyleston
Jno Hennoway
Richd Norcrosse
Robert Herrington
wm Dixon
Noah wisewall
— — — —
Jno Thaxter in som Cases insteed of Ric: Norcross
— — — —

2d Jur Elisabeth Smith widdow relict of francis Smith plant agt wm Hudson defendt in an Accon of Appeale from the Judgment of the County Court in Boston in Aprill last After the Attachment Courts Judgment Reasons of Appeale & euidences in the Case produced were read Comitted to the Jury & are on file wth the Reccords of this Court the Jury brought in their virdict the Jury finds for ye plantiff Reuersion of the former Judgmt & Costs of Courts twenty sixe shillings

Exec. Issued out 20 Sept 77

Edward Richards plantiff agt Left Thomas Putman deffendant in an Accon of Appeale from the Judgment of the County Court at Salem after ye Attachmt Courts Judgment Reasons of Appeale and euidences in the Case produced were read Comitted to the Jury and are on file wth the Reccords of this Court the Jury brought in their virdict they found for the plantiff Reuersion of the former Judgmt & Costs of Courts

Richd Dumer plaintiff agt Capt wm Gerrish Joseph Hills Jn° Knight & Sam P[lum]er deffendants in an Accon of Appeale from the Judgment of the County Court at Salem After the Attachmt Courts Judgmt Reasons of Appeale & euidences in the Case produced were read Comitted to the Jury & are on file the Jury brought in their virdict they found for the plantiff reuertion of the former Judgment & Costs of Courts three pounds.

Joshua Atwater plantiff in an action of Appeale from the Judgmt of the County Court at Boston agt Jn°than Balston deffendant after the Attachment Courts Judgment Reasons of Appeale & euidences in the Case produced were read Comitted to ye Jury the plantiff wthdrew his Accon wth ye Courts Consent & ye deffendts

Robert Sandford plantiff against Nathaniel Putman deffendant in an action of Appeale from the Judgment of the County Court at Salem After the Attachment Courts Judgment Reasons of Appeale & euidences in the Case produced were read Comitted to the Jury & are on file wth the Reccords of this Cour[t] the Jury finds for the plaintiff reuersion of the former Judgment and finde the brooke the bounds of Sandfords land as farr as that ‖ wch ‖ was Skeltons land lyes ag^t^ it & the land in Controuersy to be Sandfords = wth Costs of Courts fiue pounds two shillings & fowe^r^ pence

Execution Issued out 4th Octo^b^ 75

[31] 1675

Sampson Sheaffe plaintiff on Appeale from the Judgment of the County Court at Boston in Aprill last ag^t^ Rich Collecot Assignee of Left Richard Cooke in behalf of Rebeckah Hunkin defendant After the Attachment Courts Judgment Reasons of Appeale & euidences in the case produced were read Comitted to the Jury and are on file wth the Reccords of this Court the Jury brought in their virdict they found for the plantiff reuersion of the forme^r^ Judgment & Costs of Courts =

The name of those returned to serve on y^e^ 2^d^ Jury for trialls of Appeales & for life limbe & banshm^t^ & sworne were

— — — —

m^r^ Jno ffrost
w^m^ Harris
James Blake
Peter lyon
Sam Stone
Jno Spring
Gregory Cooke
Georg Woodward
Jno Holbrooke
Nathani Homes
Rich. Martyn
Giles fifeild =

— — — —

Jacob Jesson in Stones Roome in Ben Gibbs Case &c

— — — —

Jno Gold plaintiffe ag^t^ Nathaniel Putman in an Action of Revejw on Appeale from the Judgment of the County Court at Salem after the Judgment Reasons of Appeale & euidences produced were read Comitted to the Jury & are on file the Jury brought in their virdict (the Attachm^t^ of Ipswich Court last not being produced & found) they found for ye deffend^t^ Costs of Courts

Jno woodmannsey plantiff ag^t^ Tho Joy deffendt in an action of Apeale from the Judgment of the County Court at Boston After the Attachment Courts Judgment Reasons of Appeale & euidences in the Case produced were read Comitted to the Jury & are on file wth the Reccords of this Court the Jury brought in their virdict they found for the deffendant Confirmation of the forme^r^ Judgment & Costs of Courts = m^r^ woodmansey in open Court ‖ declared that he Attainted the Jury & declared he doubted not but he would ‖ ~~in Reff[eranc] to Errors he sajd he would~~ proove = ‖ error ag^t^ the Jurors ‖ and the sajd Jno woodmansey acknowledged himself bound in fiue hundred pounds to the Treasurer of the Country & to his successors &c and w^m^ Rawson and Timothy Batt his sue^r^tyes alike acknowledged themselues heires executo^r^s &c

Woodmancy ag^t^ Joy

bound in two hundred & fiuety pounds a peece to the sajd Tresurer of the Country Richd Russell Esqr & to his successors on Condition that the sajd John woodmansey shall prosecute his Attaindure at the next Court of Assistants to effect according to law. = as Attests Edw. Rawson Secrety.

Garlands judgmt reu'st — Jno Garland & Elisabeth his wife plantiffe on Appeale from the Judgment of the County Court last at Salisbury After the Courts Judgment Reasons of Appeale & euidences in the Case produced were read Comitted to the Jury and are on file wth the Reccords of this Court the Jury brought in their virdict they found for the plantiff reuersion of the former Judgment =

wainwright agt Pickering — ffrancis waynwright plantiff against Jno Pickering deffendant in an action of Appeale from the Judgment of the County Court held at Douer ffrancis wajnwright being three times called both he & ye deffendt made their default (It being sd they were Agreed):

Smith agt Rand exec. Issued out — Jno Smith merchant plantiff agt Isaack Rand & Company deffendts in an Accon of Appeale from the Judgment of the County Court at Boston. After the Attachmt Courts Judgment Reasons of Appeale & euidences in the Case produced were read Comitted to the Jury & are on file they brought in their virdict they found for the deffendant Confirmation of the former Judgment & Costs of Courts fower pound & two penc

Patridg agt wainwright — Nehemiah Patridge plaintiff agt ffrancis waynwright defendt in an Accon of Appeale from the Judgment of the county Court at Douer After the Attachment Courts Judgment Reasons of Appeale & euidences in the Case produced were ~~read comitted to the Jury & are on file wth the~~ the plaintiff & deffendant being three times Called made their default

[32] 1675

1st Jur: Harris agt chick &c — Thomas Harris plaintiffe agt Richd Chick defendant as Atturney to George Greeneoway in an action of Appeale from the Judgment of the Comissioners Court In Boston After the Attachment Courts Judgment Reasons of Appeale and euidences in the Case produced were read Comitted to the Jury & are on file wth the Reccords of this Court the Jury brought in their virdict they found for the plantiff Reuision of the form^r Judgment & Costs of Courts

Andrew Clark plaintiffe against John Nicholls deffendt in an action of Appeale from the Judgment of the County Court in Boston in Aprill last After the Attachment Courts Judgment Reasons of Appeale & euidences in the Case produced were read Comitted to the Jury & are on file wth the Reccords of this Court the Jury brought in their virdict they found for the deffendant Confirmation of the forme^r Judgment and Costs of Courts forty one shillings & six penc

1st Jur Clark ag^t Nicholls Execution Issued out

Anthony Cheecкley plaintiff ag^t Jabez Salter deffendt in an action of Appeale from the Judgment of the County Court in Aprill last after the Courts Judgm^t Attachm^t Reasons of Appeale & euidences in the case produced were read Comitted to the Jury & are on file wth the Reccords of this Court the Jury brought in their virdict they found for the deffendant Confirmation of the former Judgment & Costs of Court

1st J: Cheeckly ag^t Salter Execution Issued out 4th of october 1675

Tho. Bishop plantiffe against John Gold deffnd^t In an action of Appeale from the Judgment of the County Court at Salem After the Attachment Courts Judgment Reasons of Appeale & euidences in the Case produced were read Comitted to the Jury & are on file wth the Reccords of this Court the Jury brought in their virdict they found for the deffendant Confirmation of the form^r Judgment & Costs of Courts three pounds thirteen shilling & five pence.

2d Jur Bishop ag^t Gold Execution Issued out for ye bill of sale & 3 13 5 Costs 14 December 1683

Samuel Bishop plaintiffe ag^t Jno Gold deffendant in an action of Appeale from the Judgments of the County Court at Salem After the Attachment Courts Judgment Reasons of Appeale & euidences in the Case produced were Read Comitted to the Jury & are on file wth the Reccords of this Court the Jury brought in their virdict they found for the plaintiffe reuersion of the former Judgment & Costs of Courts three pounds fower shilling & six pence

Samuell Bishop ag^t Gold Tho Bishop his Atturney engag^d for y^e [charges?]

Wells agt Batt

Tho wells plaintiff against Timothy Batt defendant in an action of Appeale from the Judgment of the County Court at Boston After the Attachment Courts Judgment Reasons of Appeale & euidences in the Case produced were Read Comitted to the Jury & are on file wth the Reccords of this Court the Jury brought in their virdict they found for the defendant Confirmation of the former Judgm[t] & Costs of Courts twenty six shillings & sixe penc

[33] 1675

Hudson agt Levt Judgt 102. 7. 2d vide County Courts Judgt

Capt w[m] Hudson plaintiff ag[t] Hudson Leueret defendt in an action of Appeale from the Judgment of the last County Court in Boston after the Attachm[t] Courts Judgment Reasons of Appeale & euidences in the Case produced were read comitted to the Jury & are on file the Jury brought in their virdict they found for the deffendant Confirmation of the former Judgement & Costs of Court forty-three shillings & 10[d]

Wharton agt Joy

Richard wharton plaintiffe ag[t] Joseph Joy Assignee of Tho Joy defend[t] in an Accon of Appeale from the Judgment of the County Court at Boston after the Attachment Courts Judgment Reasons of Appeale & euidences in the case produced were read Comitted to the Jury & are on file wth the Reccords of this Court the Jury brought in their virdict they found for the plaintiff reuersion of the form[r] Judgm[t] & Costs of Court fiuety-two shillings & a penny :

Grenleafe agt Gilbert Execution Issued out abt 30th Sept 1675

Enock Greenleafe plaintiffe ag[t] John Gilbert deffend[t] in an action of Appeale from the Judgment of the County Cour[t] in Boston in Aprill last After the Attachment Courts Judgment Reasons of Appeale & euidences in the Case produced were read Comitted to the Jury & are on file wth the Reccords of this Court the Jury brought in their virdict they found for the plaintiffe reuersion of the form[r] Judgment & Costs of Court twenty eight shillings & sixe pence =

Gifford agt Hathorne

Jn[o] Gifford plaintiff ag[t] Jn[o] Hathorne deffendant in an action of Appeale from the Judgment of the County Court at Ipswich. After the Attachment Courts Judgment Reasons of Appeale & euidences in the Case produced were read Comitted to the Jury & are on file wth the Reccords of this

Court the Jury brought in their virdict they found for y[e] deffendant Confirmation of the former Judgmen[t] & costs of Courts

John Gifford plaintiff ag[t] John Hathorne deffendant in an action of Appeale from the Judgment of the County Court at Ipswich After the Attachment Courts Judgment Reasons of Appeale & euidences in the Case produced were read Comitted to the Jury & are on file wth the Reccords of this Court the Jury brought in their virdict they found for the plaintiff Reuersion of the former Judgment & Costs of Courts = forty two shillings and eight pence

Gifford ag[t] Hathorne executi: Issued out 12 July 76 : =

John Gifford plaintiffe against John Hathorne deffendant in an action of Appeale from the Judgment of the County Court at Ipswich After the Attachment Courts Judgment Reasons of Appeale & evidences in the Case produced were read Comitted to the Jury & are on file w[th] the Reccords of this Court the Jury brought in their virdict they found for the plantiff Reuersion of the forme[r] Judgment & Costs of Courts = three pounds fowe[r]teen shillings & six pence

|| in behalf of his wife || Gifford ag[t] Hathorne || in 3[d] action of Battery = || Executi Issued out 12 July 76

Jn[o] Gifford plaintiff ag[t] Jn[o] Hathorne deffendant in an action of Appeale from the Judgment of the County Court at Ipswich After the Attachment Courts Judgment Reasons of Appeale & euidences in the Case produced were read Comitted to the Jury & are on file wth the Reccords of this Court the Jury brought in their virdict they found for the plantiff reuersion of the forme[r] Judgment & Costs of Courts three pounds eight shillings

|| in behalf of his wife || Gifford ag[t] Hathorn || in y[e] Action of slander || Exec. Issued out 12 July 76 for 3[li]: 8[s]:

Benjamin Gibbs plantiff ag[t] Rouland Gideon &: *Baruch deffend[t] in an action of Appeale from the Judgment of the County Court in Boston After the Attachment Courts Judgment Reasons of Appeale & euidences in the Case produced were Read Comitted to the Jury and are on file wth the Reccords of this Court the Jury brought in their virdict they found for the deffendant confirmati† of the fforme[r] Judgment & Costs of Courts

Gibbs ag[t] Gideon execution Issued out but sattisfied w[thout]

* This space left blank in the original. † Intended for "confirmation."

[34] 1675

Leūet agt Briggs

Hudson Leueret plantiffe against Abraham Briggs ‖ Assignee of Jno Gifford ‖ deffendt in an Action of Appeale from the Judgment of the County Court at Boston After the Attachment Courts Judgment Reasons of Appeale & euidences in the case produced were read Comitted to the Jury & are on file wth the Reccords of this Court the Jury brought in their virdict they found for the plantiff forty seuen shillings abated of the former Judgmt & Costs of Courts =

Gibbs agt whetcombe

Benja: Gibbs plaintiff agt Josiah whetcombe Assignee of Joseph watters defendt in an action of Appeale from the Judgment of the County Court at Boston After the Attachment Courts Judgment Reasons of Appeale & euidences in the Case produced were read Comitted to ye Jury who were seu'll times sent out =^

Courts sentenc & Jugt agt Samuell Guile

Samuel Guile of Hauerill being Comitted to Prison in order to his tryall for Comitting a Rape was presented & Indicted by the Grand Jury ^ was brought from the prison to the barr where holding vp his hand was Indicted by the name of Samuel Guile for not hauing the feare of God before his eyes & being Instigated by the divill did on or about the 25th day of December last in the woods violently & forcibly seize on & Comitt a rape on the body of Mary Ash the wife of John Ash of Amesbury Contrary to the peace of our Soueraigne Lord the King his Croune & dignity the lawes of God & of this Jurisdiction = to which he pleaded not Guilty and put himself on God & the Country = After the Indictment & euidences were Read Comitted to the Jury & are on file wth the Reccords of this Court the Jury brought in yeir virdict they found the prisoner at the barr Guilty & he accordingly had sentenc pronounct agt him yow Sam Guile are to Goe from hence to ye place from whence yow came & thence to ye place of execution & there ‖ be ‖ hangd till yow be dead &c wch was accordingly donn 16 october 1675. =

Costs to ye wittnesses 6. 18

Sixe pounds eighteen shillings allowed for ye Tresurer to pay newbery men as witnesses out of the estate of sajd Guile in his power as also out of ye same estate to pay unto Mary Ash fiue pounds =

Recompenc to Mary Ash 5li

Dorothy Jones being Comitted to prison in order to hir tryall was brought ^ the barr & being presented and Indicted by the Grand Jury holding vp hir hand at the barr was Indicted by the name of Dorothy Jo[a]nes for not having the feare of God before hir eyes & being instigated by the diuill did murder the late Edward Leuis a lodger in hir house some times in January or february last Contrary to the peace of our Soueraigne Lord the King his Croune & dignity the lawes of God & of this Jurisdiction the Jury after perusall of ye Indictment & euidences in the Case produced brought in their virdict they found hir not Guilty

Dorothy Jones Indictmt

Maurice Bret being in like manner Comitted to Prison was brought to the barr & holding vp his hand was Indicted by the name of maurice Brett of Boston for not hauiug the feare of God before his eyes & being instigated by the Divill did in the house of morgan Jones or elswhere murder the late Edward Leuis a lodger in the house in or about January or february last Contrary to the peace of our Soueraigne Lord the King his Croune & dignity the lawes of God & this Jurisdiction = after ye Indictment & euidences were Comitted to ye Jury &c the Jury brought in their virdict they found ye prisoner at the barr not Guilty

Maurice Brets Inditmt

At this Court obadiah Walkr was bound ou & Acknowledgd himself bound in fiue hundred pound & mr Hezekiah Vsher & Arthur mason acknowledgd themselues bound in two hundred & fiuety ^

[35] 1675

Zeckariah Crispe being Also Comitted to the prison as Jones & Bret was brought to the barr was Indicted by the name of Zekariah Crispe of Groaten for not hauing the feare of God before his eyes & being Insticated by the Divil did in the house of the late morgan Jones or elswhere in Boston murder the late Edward Leuis a lodger in the house in or about January or february last contrary to the peace of our Soueraign Lord the King his Croune & dignity the lawes of God & of this Jurisdiction. the Indictmt & euidence alike Comitted to ye Jury who brought in their virdict they found the prisoner not Guilty. =

Zeckariah Crispe Indictment =

This Court was Adjourned to 21 Instant =

present
Jnº Leueret Esqr Gou
Sam Symonds Esqr dept Gou
Symon Bradstreet
Richd Russell
majr wm Hathorne
Edward Tyng
wm Stoughton
Thomas Clarke
— — — —

Att A Court of Admiralty or Court of Asistants held at Boston 13th of septemb 1675

In the Case betweene mathew Johnson & Henry Tickner plaintiff in behalfe of the owno'rs of the ship Doue agt Robert Cannon deffendant brought to this Court by their peticon & libell against the sajd Cannon The Court having heard & considered the case & euidences produced doe order and decree that the said Robert Cannon shall forthwith deliuer the sajd ship Doue with all hir tackle Apparrell & Appurtenances together wth all the Cargoe belonging to the sajd Ouno'rs vnto the sajd Mathew Johnson & Henry Tickner and also pay them in mony two hundred & eight pounds vpon receipt whereof they shall Giue unto the sajd Robert Cannon a receipt and discharge for the same And that the sajd mathew Johnson & Henry Tickner shall pay & sattisfy the sajd Cannon his wages after the Rate of sixe pounds mony ꝑ moneth to this day and also secure him the sajd Cannon from the seamens wages that is due to be pajd them = the Sajd Cannon paying the charges of this Court fiue pounds & officers ffees wth costs of Court in all seuen pounds fiueteen shillings & sixe pence

The Court ordered the dept Gouno'r & majo'r Hauthorne should pay as a fine fiue shillings apeec for their departing the Court wthout leaue

Also mr Ting was fined twelue penc for his Absenc from ye Court after dinner

The Court was Adjournd to the 21th Instant Septembe'r 1675 at wch time A Grand Jury was to be sumoned in order to the trjall of seuerall Indians sent doune from marlborough & Lancaster by Capt mosely being vehemently suspected to haue a hand in ye murder of those at Nashaway

present
Jnº Leuet Esqr Gou
Sam Symonds Esqr dept Gou
Symon Bradstreet
Dani Gookin
Dani Dennison
Richd Russell
Tho Danforth
wm Hathorne

Att An Adjournement of ye Court of Assistants held at Boston ‖ & 18 Sept 75 thenc adjournd [to ?] ‖ 21 : September 1675

Att this Court Capt moselys lette'r and Account was Read wth the euidences produced agt * Indians he tooke at marlborow & were trjed according ^ their seuall Indictments

* This space left blank in the original.

Edwd Tyng
Wm Stoughton
Tho clarke
— — — —

John Indian was Indicted by the name of Jno Indian belonging to marlborow for that he not having the feare of God before his eyes & being instigated by the divil did wth seuerall Indians at Lancaster at or about the 23 of August last murder or was Confœderat wth seuerall Indians as an Abbettor or Concealer of the murther of the Inhabitants of the ^ Lancaster wth one of this Colonjes souldjers named wm ffagg * contrary to the peace of our Soueraigne Lord the King his Croune & dignity the lawes of God & of this Jurisdiction the prisonr was brought to ye barr pleaded not Guilty put himself on tryall by God & the Country the pleas & euidences were Comitted to ye Jury who brought in their virdict they found ye prisoner at the barr not Guilty according to Indictment

persons Returnd to serve on ye ||Grand|| Jury were sworne on leafe

[36]

Grand Jury
Mr John Saffyn
Jno Tappin
Wm Ingram
Jno Trumble
Tho Jenner
Jonas Clarke
Pyam Blowers
Richard Hall
Tho Lake
Symon Stone
Samuel Starnes
Isaack Johnson
John Weld
— — — —
ye Jury for Trialls were as in Sepr Court
Mr Jno ffrost
Wm Harris &c
— — — —

— Joseph Spoonhaut Indian was alike Indicted = put himself on like tryall pleas & euidences in the case produced Comitted to ye Jury who brought in their virdict they found him Guilty of Confœderacy And if Samuel Scriptures testimony of the prisonrs owning of ye fact be one legal euidenc they found him Guilty of murder = The Court ordered him to be sent away =

Litle Jno Indian yt Came as a messengr from † being prooved to be a murderer of the English in ye warr was Condemnd to be hangd & was executed accordingly =

— Revp Indian of sd marlborow was Alike Indicted put himself one like tryall &c = the Jury brought in their virdict they found him not Guilty

— mampaus nackosut Indian was alike Indicted put himself on like tryall &c the Jury brought in their virdict they found him not Guilty

— James Aliass Acompanut Indian was alike Indicted put himself on like tryall &c the Jury brought in their virdict they found him not Guilty

* Flagg? See Bodge's "Hist. of King Philip's War," p. 352.
† Blank in the original.

— John Alias Anusquenu^{t} Indian was alike Indicted put himself on like trjall ℘ the Jury brought in their virdict they found him not Guilty =

— Peter aljas Paguskmēut Indian was alike Indicted put himself on like tryall ℘ the Jury brought in their virdict they found him not Guilty

— muckscumpey Indian was alike Indicted put himself on like tryall ℘ the Jury brought in their virdict they they found him not Guilty

— Jno Alia^{s} Mucksumquenut Indian was Alike indicted put himself on like tryall ℘ the Jury brought in theire virdict they found him not Guilty.

— Thomas Alia^{s} mumucksuncasusucquate^{r} Indian was alike Indicted put himself on like tryall ℘ the Jury found him not Guilty =

— James nanapatu was alike Indicted pleaded alike not Guilty put himself on tryall on the bench: who pervsing the euidences produced ag^{t} him (by Capt ffishe^{r} & Left way Appointed Atturney^{s} by y^{e} Court on behalf of the Country to Implead him & the Rest) saw Cause to acquitt & dischardg him

Dauid Indian & Phillip^{s} man was ordered to be sent away by the Treasurer of the Country =

The Court ordered old Jethro Indian for his abusive speeches to be whipt And that he & the rest of the Indians aboue named Acquitted by y^{e} Jury shall be dischardged & sent for y^{t} end by Jno Watson to Cambridg Prison & warrant Issued out to Jno Watson to Conduct the sajd Indians to the keep^{r} of the prison at Cambridge and from him to take & Conduct them to natick to waban the Rule^{r} of natick by him to be releast only whipping or Causing Jethro to be whipt wth thirty stripes for his wicked speeches vttered by him in m^{r} willurds yard at Groaton for wch he is Convicted

In the Case of Jno ffoster accidentally dischardging gun[s] at foules on y^{e} neck thereby wounding Samuel fflacks son so as he djed the Court sentenct him to pay the fathe^{r} of the boy tenn pounds and to pay tenn more as a like fine to the Country. wch was declard and on his humble peticon the Court saw Cause to Remit five pounds of the Country^s fine =

[37] 1675

The Court Judged it meet to ffine Jacob Jesson the sume of tenn pounds mony for his Contemptuous Carriage in the Court in obstructing the eleven of the Jury dissenting from them from tjme to tjme & not Giving the Court a sattisfactory Reason =

Mr Jacob Jesson find ten pounds for obstructing ye Jury er

Att A Court of Admirality or Court of Asistants held at Boston 1st of october 1675

present
Jno Leueret Esqr Gou:
Symon Bradstreet, Daniel Gookin, Rich. Russell, Edward Ting, wm Stoughton, Thomas clarke — Esqrs

The Court on pervsall of the libell of mr Thomas Russell & mr Jno Phillips plaintiffs against mr John Patten as he is Agent factor or Assignee of Jno Bayly merchant finding the plaintiffs haue missed it as to their missing * it as to theire returne nothing Appeared to be secured the Court Ordered the plaintiffs to pay ye chardg of the Court & office^rs ffees. ye deffendnt making default by not appearing when called The Court on ye Requests of the plaintiffs doe Judge meet to grant them another Court of Admiralty to be held in Boston on the seccond day next fowe^rth Instant. =

Att A Court of Admiralty or Court of Assistants held at Boston 4th octobe^r 1675

present
Jno Leueret Esqr Gou.
Symon Bradstreet, Dani: Gookin, Richd Russell, Tho Danforth, Edw Tyng, Thomas Clarke — Esqrs

The Court after the due pervsall of the libell & Complant of Thomas Russell & Jno Phillips of charls-Toune merchants Complayning of & Aganst Jno Patten merchant as he is Agent factor partner or Assignee of Jno Bayly of Rochell in ffrance merchant together wth the euidences in the Case produced doe find for the deffendt and doe order & decree that the plaintiffs pay the sajd Costs chardg of this Court & office^rs ffees =

Att A Court of Assistants or Court of Admiralty Called by the Gou̅no^r & Council & held at Boston the nineteenth of November 1675 =

present
Jno Leueret Esq Gou
Symon Bradstreet, Daniel Gookin, Richd Russell, Tho. Danforth, Edwd Tyng, Tho: Clarke — Esqrs

In the Case brought to this Court by John Grafton exhibbitting his libell & Complaint against Lawrenc Zackariah s[hi]ce a dutchman master of

* "it as to their missing" appears to be superfluous.

a Catch now called the Hopewell formerly the nightingall the said s[hi]ce Appeared & denyd that he was master of the sajd Catch and that he would stand to the Tryall of the Case Affirming that he Could & would produce Judication for hir and in open Court owned the sajd Catch forme^r^ly to belong to the sajd John Grafton and was then Called the Nightingale so the Case proceeded And after the euidences produced the sajd * w^m^ Demeire declaring that his originall Judication was in his Fathers Custody at New Yorke and desired that he might haue time allowed him to produce it on Consideration whereof The Court declared that no ffynall decree should passe about it till the next Court of Assistants being the 1st tuesday in march next to be held at Boston that he had his request Granted him any time betweene this & that to produce his Judication to the sajd Court Giving sufficient bond wth sue^r^tjes to the Treasurer of the Country to the double value the sajd Catch shall be vallued at Jointly & seuerally that he shall then appeare and

persons Returnd to serve on ye Grand Jury & sworne were
m^r^ Tho Brattle
Joseph Cooke
Jonah Clarke
Richd woddy
Abell Porter
Theophilus ffrary
Sam: Shrimpton
Jno Peirpoint
Hugh Clarke
Jno Edy
Tho Hastings
Richd Leeds
w^m^ Pond
Edw Carrington
w^m^ Johnson

persons Returnd & servd on the Jury of tryalls
Left Richard way
John Greene
Tho Parke
Nath Dauenport
James Brayden
Tho Berry
John Stebbins
John Newell

abide by, & Respond the Judgment & decree of that Court of Admiralty relateing to the sajd Catch and the Case to Continue to that time. =

maurice Brett was Indicted by the name of Maurice Brett now of Boston for not hauing the feare of God before his eyes being instigated by the divil did on the † day of † last Comitt Adultery wth mary Gibbs contrary to the peace of our Soueraigne Lord the king his Crowne & dignitye the lawes of God & of this Jurisdicõn To wch Indictment he pleaded not guilty put himself on trjall on God & the Country After the Indictment & euidences in the Case produced were read Comitted to the Jury the Jury brought In their virdict they found him not legally Guilty but Guilty of very filthy carriage & The Court Considering the Case sentenct him to goe from hence to ye prison & thence to be Carrjed to the Gallows & there wth a Roape about his necke to stand half an hower & thenc tjed to the Carts tajle & whipt

* Wm Demeire not mentioned before in the record. † Blank in the original.

seuerely wth thirty ‖ nine ‖ stripes and that he be banished this Jurisdiction & kept in prison till he be sent away paying the prison chardges ^ he is dischardged

Nath Coolidge
Jno B[ruscō]
Richd Leadbetter
obadiah Hawes
John Smith

Mary Gibbs the wife of * Gibbs of Boston for y^e^ same fact was alike Indicted ꝑ and found ^ had the like sentenc banishment excepted =

John weave^r^ was Called & none Appearing to prosecute him for wounding Cole paying the keepe^r^s due^s^ was dischardged

Georg Robbins & Jno Largin being both Indicted & not found Guilty of killing y^e^ Indians were bound ouer to the next County Court at Cambridg in Aprill next to Ans^r^ for their wounding of the Indians vnder the Courts protection Giving their oune bonds so to doe All the euidences in yr Case Returned to that Court =

In the Case of maurice Brett for his Contemptuous Carriage Confronting the sentenc of this Court was sentenct to stand in the pillory on y^e^ morrow at one of y^e^ clock his eare nayld to ye pillory & after an howrs standing there to be cut of & to pay twenty shilling for his swearing or be whipt wth ten stripes

Jn^o^than Crispe & John Barrat in ffforty pounds apeece wth their sue^r^tjes in 20^li^ apeece Capt Sam Addams solomon Keys to the Tresurer of y^e^ Country that they shall appeare Attend the Court & Abide their Judgment at y^e^ Courts Adjo^r^nm^t^

Jno Parke^r^ was alike bound in forty pounds wth James Conv̄s & Tho Parker his surtyes to the Tresurer of the Country on Condicōn that he also abide the order & sentence of the Court ꝑ =

In Ans^r^ to the Humble petition of maurice Brett Humbly beseeching y^e^ Courts favo^r^ ꝑ the Court Remitted y^t^ ꝑt of y^e^ sentenc of nayling & Cutting of his eare

This Court is Adjourned till the 30th Instant at nine of y^e^ clocke & thence to the 4th december 1675

---

* This space left blank in the original.

The Court mett at ye time = 4 Dec, 75

Jn° Parker Jonathan Crispe & Jn° Barrat The Court orde^rs yo^w to Repaire home & to Appeare at the Randevous at dedham wednesday next at eleven of the clocke euery way fitted & Compleatly Armed and furnished with clothes and to march forth wth the forces. —

[39] 1675

present
The Gou̅no^r
m^r Bradstreet
Capt Gookin
m^r Russell
m^r Danforth
m^r Ting
m^r Tho Clarke
— — — —

Att A Court of Admiralty or Court of Assistants Called & held at Boston 16 Dec̃ 1675

In the Case brought to this Court by the libell & Complaint of Nicholas Skinner master of the ship Doue in behalfe of himself & Company against the sajd ship Doue nicholas moulde^r p^t ouno^r of the sajd ship & James Loyd his Assignee deffend^t for wages for himself sajd Skinner & Company & expences layd out on sajd ship = This Court finds for the plaintiffe and orde^rs & decrees that the deffendant pay unto the plaintiff the sume of two hundred sixteene pounds nine shillings & fowe^r pence damage in mony & costs of this Court three pounds sixteen shillings =

In the Case of James Elson master of the ship Blessing in behalfe of himself & his ouno^rs of sajd ship plaintiffe against m^r Richard wharton deffend^t brought to this Court by his libell & Complaint The Court duely Considering the pleas & euidences in the Case produced doe orde^r & decree the plaintiff to pay the deffendant the Costs of this Court = fowe^rteen shillings

This Court is dissolued

present
Jn° Leueret Esqr Gou̅
Sam Symonds Esqr dep^t Go
Symon Bradstreet
Daniel Gookin
Daniel Dennison
Symon Willard
Rich. Russell
Tho Danforth
Edwd Tyng
w^m stoughton
Tho Clarke
} Esq^rs
— — — —
persons Returnd to serve on ye Grand Jury =
— — — —

Att A Court of Assistants held at Boston the 7th of march 1675/6.

at this Court w^m Demeire appeared by his ffather Nicholas Demeire as did John Grafton by his Atturney Anthony checkly according to the Court of Admiralty in Nouembe^r last Adjourn^t and after the euidences in the Case produced were Read & pervsed the Court declared they found for the Deffend^t m^r Demeir originally Costs of Court fowe^r pounds seventeen shillings & sixepence

In the Case of Attaynt depending betwixt m^r John

Woodmansey plaintiffe and mr John ffrost foreman in behalfe of ye Jury of Appeales deffendant after the Courts Judgment Reasons of Appeale & euidences in the Case produced were Read Comitted to ye Jury & are on file the Jury brought in their virdict they found for the plaintiff allowing full damage or Costs of Court to the originall suite as the law for Attaints prouides and Gaue in their Reason because we find one hundred forty seuen pounds seven shillings and eight penc of Tho Joys charge given him for which thers no prooffe but his oune oath 2 ly because the Jury Attainted haue Given the sajd Joy three hundred forty fower pounds seventeen shillings & eight penc which is not only more debt then is legally prooved but obleidged to be pajd in prouissions a species not sued for & for the two hundred thirty seuen pounds fiueteen shillings which is plainly due by mr woodmancys acknowledgment it concernes not this Jury it being a distinct Case from that Comitted to us wee being only obleidged to Attend that Case that mr woodmansey is bound to prosecute which is the Jurys Atteint not the debt to Tho Joy = Thomas Broughton foreman of ye Jury

wm Parks
Tho weld
wm Johnson
wm Dady
Rich. Robbins
John Greene
Henry Bright
Elliz Barron
Jer. ffitch
Joseph How
Tho watkins
Edwd Grant
Theoder Atkinson
Richd Leeds
Wm Sumner
— — — —
no work Appearing they were dismist

[40] 1675

James Elson master of the ship blessing plantiff agt mr Richd wharton & mr Thomas Bendish deffendts in an Accon of Appeale from the Jurys ~~& Courts Judgment~~ || virdict || in the last County Court in January last &c after the Courts Judgment Reasons of Appeale & euidences in the Case produced were read Comitted to the Jury & are on file wth the Reccords of this Court the Jury brought in their virdict they found for the deffendant Confirmation of the former Judgment & Costs of Courts

persons Returnd to serve on the Jury for trjalls of Appeales &c sworne were =
— — — —
1st
mr Thomas Broughton
~~Phillip Searle~~
Joseph Wise
Nath: Seavor
Sam Douse
Walter Hastings
Tho Langhorne
Tho fflagg
Wm Gibson
Nath Blage
Anthony Heywood
Nath Byfeild
James ffoster
— — — —
person Returnd to serve on ye seccond Jury & sworne were
— — — —
mr John Phillips

Wm Cogswell plaintiff against John Cogswell in an Accon of Appeale from the virdict of ye Jury & County Courts Judgment at Ipswich After the Courts Judgment Reasons of Appeale & euidences in the Case produced were read Comitted to the Jury & are on file wth the Reccords of this Court the Jury brought in their virdict they found for the deffendant Confirmation

Phillip Searle
Jno Chandler
Tho Chadwell
Richd Ecles
Andrew Boardman
Jno Sawin
Nath Thayer
phesant Eastwick
Steven Burton
Nath Clap
James Taylor
— — — —

of the former Judgment & Costs of Courts and also the sajd plantiffe Giue a Just & legall accompt to the deffendant as sued for at or before the sixteenth of June next ensuing vpon the pœnalty of the sume of three hundred pounds = costs fiuety fower shillings & two pence

Samuel & margaret Bishop execcutor & execcutrix to the late Thomas Bishop plaintiff against ffrancis wainewright deffendt in an action of Appeale from the Judgment at ye last County Court at Ipswich = After the Courts Judgment Reasons of Appeale & euidences in the Case produced were read Comitted to the Jury & are on file wth the Reccords of this Court the Jury brought in their virdict they found for the deffendant Confirmation of the former Judgment & Costs of Courts thirty seuen shillings one penny

exec Issued out & Returnd on file in ye Case

Richard wooddy plaintiff in an action of Appeale Agt John Harrison sen deffendt from the Courts Judgment in January last in Boston. After the Courts Judgment Reasons of Appeale & euidences in the Case produced were Read Comitted to the Jury and are Remayning on file with the Reccords of this Court the Jury brought in their virdict they found for the plaintiff A reuersall of the former Judgment wth two shillings damage and Costs of Courts fiue pounds & three pence and the Highway sued for to be as formerly

James ffoord being bound ouer to this Court to Ansr for his driving ~~ouer~~ a Cart ouer Abigaile King that the child died After the Court had duely Considered the Case sentenct him to pay the fine of fiue pounds to the Country & fiue pounds mony to Its father Samuel King:

[41] 1675

Richard Scott was Called the evidenc agt him wth his letter wch he denyed refferd himself for trjall to the Bench was Comitted to prison there to lye till the Court took further order =

Richard Scott was called being at the barr the wittnessed his * letter to major Savage was also produced & Read wherein many vntruths & seuerall reproachfull were written & on enquiry mr scott declared that Ezekiel ffogg wrote it er

* This word appears to be superfluous.

Rich[d] Scott in two hundred pounds Anthony cheeckly & James whetcombe in one hundred pounds a peece as his sue[r]tjes acknowledged themselues bound respectively to the Tresure[r] of the Country on this Condition that he the sajd Richard Scott shall attend the Court from tjme to tjme & Abide the Sentence of the Court this done in open Court

14 m[r]ch 75/6

The Court on a full hearing what Richard Scott Could say Considering his offence sentenct him the sume of one hundred pounds to majo[r] Gookin whom he had so vilely reproacht & vnworthily and that he pay a fine to the Country fiuety pounds and to be bound to his Good behauiour himself in twenty pounds and two sue[r]tjes in tenn pounds apeece standing Comitted till this sentence be pformed

Ezekiel ffogg being Called who not only abused Richard scott in indicting and writing such a scurrillows letter putting a superscription vpon it whereby Authority was abuse[d] The Court sentenct ^ to pay as a fine to the Country fiue pounds mony standing Comitted till the sentence be performed —

prsent	
Jn[o] Leu̅et Esq[r] Go̅u	
Symon Bra[d]street	Esq[rs]
Daniel Gookin	
Symon willard	
Rich[d] Russell	
Tho. Danforth	
Edw[d] Ting	
w[m] Staughton	
Tho Clarke	

Att A Court of Assistants or Admiralty held at Boston 29 m[r]ch 1676.

Jonathan Woodman plaintiff against m[r] Bartholmew stratten Elisha Hutchinson for himself & for Elisha Sandford John Poole & mary the administratrix of Henry Kembles estate deffendants ouno[r]s of the ship Salamande[r], built by the plaintiffe for w[th]holding his payment for the sajd ship: The Court hauing heard and Considered the plea[s] and euidences in the case produced doe find for the plaintiffe damages one hundred eighty five pounds in the specie & manne[r] following viz[t] from Bartholmew stratten for one eighth part twenty three pounds two shillings & sixepence Elisha Hutchinson one quarter pte forty sixe pounds fiue shillings payable in Goods at merchants price and for Elisha sandford for one quarter part which he vndertooke for forty sixe pounds fiue shillings halfe in mony and halfe in Goods; John Poole for one quarter pte forty sixe pounds fiue shillings halfe in mony and halfe in goods at merchants price Mary Administratrix of the sajd Henry Kemble for one eighth part twenty-three pounds two shillings & sixe pence halfe mony halfe Goods at the merchants price this whole sume of one hundred eighty fiue pounds to be pajd to the plaintiffe in full of the Hull of the sajd ship Sallamander

[42] 1676

wth Costs of Court seuen pounds tenn shillings & two pence — And the worke of the builde[r] left vnfinished is abated by the Court and not recconed in the some aboue sajd. =

Jonathan woodman Appearing in Court The Court demanded of him whether he had had his ship surveyed as the law directs wch was Read he sajd he had no[t] pretending to Ignorance of the law & hauing some shipwrights vejwing it thought it was sufficient The Court declared that they Imposed the fine of tenn pounds on him for* his wages according to law to be pajd to the treasurer

Courts order as to officers ffees at Court of Admiralty

The Court ordered the marshall to be allowed halfe a croune which ^ pajd in Court & fowe[r] shillings for serving fowe[r] warrants =

As also the Secretary[s] ffees for receiving entring the libell action and recording it fiue shillings and for warrants as the marshall = one shilling

21th July 1676

In Ans[r] to the peticon of & motion of Thomas Lynde & Capt Hamond[s] motion a Court of Admiralty is Granted by the Gou̅no[r] & magistrate^ to be held at Boston 26 Instant at two of the clock in y[e] Afternoone as Attests Edward Rawson secret[y]

present
y[e] Gou̅no[r]
dep[t] Gou̅
m[r] Danforth
m[r] Ting
m[r] Stoughton
m[r] Clarke
m[r] Dudley

Att A Court of Admiralty held at Boston 26 of July 1676

Attachment & seuerall sumons for witnesses Issued out &c

Thomas Lynde master of the Catch Pellican by his libell complayning in behalfe of him self & owno[r]s plaintiff against Daniel Dauisson of charlsToune merchant deffendant for that he the sajd Daniel Dauison hath neglected to pay vnto the sajd plantiffe the sume of forty one pounds money for y[e] hire of the sajd Catch for sixe month[s] twenty fiue dayes as p charter pty he was bound to pay as also

* Evidently an error in the record for "from."

for not paying the some of sixty sixe pounds three shillings & two penc mony for the seamens wages in all one hundred & six pounds two shillings* After the libell w[th] the sumons & Attachment & euidences in the Case produced || were Read || & duely Considered || of || the Court orde[r]s & decrees that the sajd Daniell Dauison deffendant pay unto the sajd Tho Linde plantiffe the some of one hundred & sixe pounds three shillings two pence* mony w[th] Costs of Court in mony three pounds nine shillings =

[43] 1676

the Gov̄no[r]
dep[t] Gov̄no[r]
m[r] Danforth
m[r] Tyng
m[r] Stoughton
m[r] Clarke
m[r] Dudley

on the motion of m[r] Richard Lord & m[r] Jn[o] Blackleach a Court of Admiralty was Granted to be held in Boston the 31 of y[s] Instant July 1676

Attachment [& sev̄ll] sumons Issued out after they had entred thei[r] libell

Att A Court of Admiralty called & held at Boston the 31th July 1676

Richard Lord & John Blackleach merchants plaintiff[s] by their libell exhibbited to this Cour[t] Against Richard wharton & Company defendants for breach of charter party After the libell & euidences in the Case produced were read & duely Considered of the Court declares that they ordered & decreed that the plaintiffs pay unto the deffendant Costs of Court

22th August
By y[e] Gov̄n[r] & magists

on the motion of charls Hodsdal pylot of Ship nevis facto[r] & Bartholmew Hoope[r] w[th] Georg Keith an ~~Admirall~~ || Admiralty || Court was Granted to be held at Boston the 28 of August Instant

||Attachments & sumons Issued out after their libells were entred||

p[r]sent
y[e] Gov̄no[r]
dep[t] Gov̄
m[r] Danforth
m[r] Tyng
m[r] Stoughton
m[r] Clarke
m[r] Dudley

Att a Court of Admiralty held at Boston 28[th] August 1676.

In the Case of charls Hodsdall Pylot by his libell Complayning against Sam: Dauis master of ship nevis facto[r] & sajd ship for refusing to pay him his wages for his se[r]vice donn in the said ship as Pylot fiue pounds p̱ moneth from the 22[th] february last to the 30[th] of July last After the libell & euidences in the Case produced were read & duely Considered The Court ordered & decreed that the sajd Sam.

* There is evidently an error in the record here.

Dauis master & sajd ship make good y^e^ payment of twenty sixe pounds fiue shillings to the sajd Charls Hodsdale pylot in mony as his damage & Costs of Court forty one shilling =

In y^e^ Case of Bartholmew Hooper Carpenter of ship neuis facto^r^ by his s^d^ libell Complayning ag^t^ Samuel Dauis master of sajd ship for refusing to pay him his wages for worke donne in sajd ship as Carpenter ‖ after ^ 54^s^ ꝑ month from 25 octob^r^ to 30th July ‖ after the libell & euidences in the Case produced were read & duely Considered the Court found ffor the plantiff twenty fowe^r^ pounds fiueteen shillings mony & orde^r^s & decrees that the sajd Dauis & sd ship pay the sajd Bartholmew Hooper y^e^ plantiff y^e^ sd sume wth Costs of Court forty one shillings. =

George Keith by his libell exhibited to this Court Plaintiffe against Samuel Dauis master of the ship nevis facto^r^ deffendant Complayning against the sajd Dauis as maste^r^ for Refusing to deliuer him his logwood put aboard him after the libell & euidences in the Case produced were duely read & Considered the Court found for the plaintiffe his logwood being fiue hundred thirty sixe sticks marked as by the boatswaynes Receipt once w^th^in three dayes or els pay the plaintiffe two hundred pounds in mony & Costs of Court three pounds fiue shillings =

[44] 1676

Mrs Lydget plantiff ag^t^ Jno Poole =

In the Case of m^r^s Elisabeth Lydget executrix to the last will & testament of m^r^ Peter Lydget deceased in the behalfe of hirself & the rest of the ouno^rs^ of the Catch Content by hir libell exhibbited to this Court plaintiffe against John Poole merchant & w^m^ Trott marriner deffendants for not paying freight for the sajd Catch nor deliuering the sajd Catch as ꝑ Charter ꝑty they were bound after the libell Attachment & euidences in the Case produced were read & duely Considered The Court doth Giue Judgment for the plaintiffe the forfeiture of the bond of fiue hundred pounds Given for performanc of Charte^r^ ꝑty respitting execution to the nex^t^ Court of Admiralty after two month^s^ in which time the deffendant may present his plea for chancery of his bond & Costs of Cour^t^ = vide fol 65 =

present
The Gou^r^no^r^
Dep^t^ Gou^r^n^r^

Att a Court of Assistants held at Boston the 5th of Septembe^r^ 1676 Jno Ruggles plantiff against

James Hudson deffendant in an action of Appeale from the Judgment of the Commissione^r^s Court After the Attachment Courts Judgment Reasons of Appeale and euidences in the Case produced were read Comitted to the Jury & are Remayning on file the Jury brought in their virdict they found for the plaintiffe reuersion of the forme^r Judgment & Costs of Courts twenty sixe shillings & Eight penc

Exec Issud out 12 8 mo 76

Symon Bradstreet, Daniel Dennison, Tho Danforth, Wm Hathorne, Jno Pynchon, Edwd Tyng, Wm Stoughton, Thomas Clarke, Joseph Dudley — Esq^rs^

— — — —

persons to serve on ye Grand Jury & sworn were —

— — — —

m^r^ Richard Collecott
Richard way
Jno vyall sen
Benja Negus
Jno Blake
Tho Dewe^r^ sen
Giles Pason
Robert willjams
Tho Hastings
Joseph Beamis
Laurenc Douse
w^m^ ffoster
Richd Hall
Ralph Haughton
Jno Stone
Walter Hastings

— — — —

1st Andrew NewComb plaintiff on Appeale from the Judgment of the County Court in Boston in Aprill last After the Courts Judgment Reasons of Appeale & euidences in the Case produced were read Co͞mitted to the July & Remajne on file wth the Reccords of this Court the Jury brought in their virdict they found the Confirmation of the forme^r^ Judgm^t^ & costs of Courts:

2 Ju: Wm Rauson plaintiffe against Habbacuck Glouer John Glouer & Pelatiah Glouer deffendant in an Acc͞on of Appeale from the Judgm^t^ of the ‖·last ‖ County Court in Boston After the Courts Judgment Attachm^t^ Reasons of Appeale and euidences in the Case produced were read Comitted to the Jury & Remajne on file wth the Reccords of this Court the Jury Brought in their virdict they found for the deffendant Confirmation of the former Judgment & Costs of Courts

2^d^ Wm Rauson plaintiffe against Abraham Briggs defendant in an Acc͞on of Appeale from the Judgment of the last County Court in Boston After the Attachment Courts Judgment Reasons of Appeale & euidences in the Case produced were read Comitted to the Jury and are remayning on file wth the Reccords of this Court the Jury brought in their virdict they found for the deffendant Confirmation of the former Judgment and costs of Courts =

persons Returnd to serve on the Jury of trjalls & sworne =

— — — —

[1st]
m^r^ John Hubbard
Richd Bulkley
Sam Rugles:

[45] 1676

Jno Gifford plaintiff ag^t^ Abraham Briggs deffendant in an action of ^ from the Judgment of the County

Tobias Dauis
Thom: ffegg
Jno Morse

Sam Peirce
Zackary Johnson
Tho Welch
Roger Billing
James Bird
Nicholas Bolton
— — — —
persons Returnd to serve on the second Jury & sworne = *
— — — —

Court in Boston After the Attachm^t^ Courts Judgment Reasons of Appeale & euidences of the Case produced were read Comitted to the Jury & Remajne on file wth the Reccords of this Court they brought in their virdict they found for the deffendant Confirmation of the former Judgm^t^ & Costs of Courts =

Jno Conney & Samuel Sendall plaintiffs ag^t^ the Judgment or sentence of m^r^ Anthony Stoddard, Comissioner in Boston the sentence & Reasons of Appeale being Read and Comitted to the Jury & Remajne on file the Jury brought in their virdict they found for the Appellant Reuersion of the former Judgmen^t^ ~~& Costs of Courts~~

Jno Alden plaintiffe ‖ ag^t^ majo^r^ Thomas Clark deffend^t^ ‖ in an Action of Appeale from the Judgment of the County Court in July last in Boston After the Courts Judgm^t^ Attachm^t^ Reasons of Appeale & euidences in the Case produced were read Comitted to ye Jury & are Remayning on file wth the Reccords of this Court the Jury brought in their virdict they found for the defendant Confirmation of the forme^r^ Judgm^t^ & Costs of Courts :

Wm Cogswell plaintiffe in an action of Appeale against John Cogswell deffend^t^ ffrom the Judgment of the County Court at Salem last After the Attachment Courts Judgment Reasons of Appeale & euidences in the Case produced were Read Comitted to the Jury & Remajne on file wth the Reccords of this Court the Jury brought in a speciall virdict i e If the Judgment of the Court of Assistants was a legall foundation for a process for the present deffendant wee find for the deffendant Confirmation of the forme^r^ Judgment & Costs of Courts if not wee finde for the plaintiffe & reuerse the forme^r^ Judgment & Costs of Courts The Court finds for the plaintiffe & Reuerse the former Judgment & grants Costs of Courts

Jonathan Heynes plaintiffe against Peter Toppan deffendant in an action of Appeale from the Judgment of the County Court at Ipswich. After the Attachment Courts Judgment Reasons of Appeale & euidences in the Case produced were read Comitted to the Jury and are on file wth the Reccords of this Court the Jury brought in their virdict

* The names of the second jury are not given.

they found for the plaintiffe Reuersion of the forme^r Judgment & Costs of Courts =

Walter Barefoote plaintiffe against w^m shackford deffendant in an action of Appeale from the Judgment of the County Court at portsmouth After the Courts Judgment Reasons of Appeale & euidences in the Case produced were Read Comitted to the Jury & are on file wth the Reccords of this Court the Jury brought in their virdict they found for the deffendant Confirmation of the forme^r Judgm^t & Costs of Courts —

m^r Jno Joyliffe majo^r Tho Sauage m^r Humphry Davy m^r Anthony Stoddard Capt Tho Bratle Capt Tho Clarke Capt John Richards chosen by the freemen of Boston for this yeare were Allowed & Approoved of by the Court =

[46] 1676

Edward Tyng Esqr plaintiffe against Joseph Dauis deffendant in an action of Appeale from the Judgment of the Comissione^rs Court in Boston After the Attachment Courts Judgment Reasons of Appeale & othe^r euidences in the Case produced were read Com̃itted to the Jury & Remayne on file wth the Reccords of this Court the Jury brought in their virdict they found for the plaintiffe Reuersion of the forme^r Judgmen^t & three pounds in siluer according to bill & Costs of Courts 18^s 6^d

3 actions of Tho woodbridge ag^t w^m Gerrish w^th-draune by Consent & Referd to Arbitration =

Thomas Woodbridge plaintiffe ag^t w^m Gerrish sen̄ defendant in an action of Appeale from the Judgment of the County Court at Salem last as to deffamation = After the Attachment Courts Judgment Reasons of Appeale & euidences in the Case produced were Read Comitted to the Jury on motion made of Compromising this & two othe^r Acc̄ons of Appeale of the sajd woodbridge ag^t the sajd Gerrish on Revejw on Account & on Revejw from the sajd Court the partjes Consenting thereunto & nominating their arbitrato^rs in p^t making it knowne y^t both parties pitched on the Honor^d Gou̅no^r to be y^r vmpire hauing entred bond each to othe^r to stand to the Award they wth drew their Accons & ye Court ordered all their pape^rs dd in Reasons of Appeale &c to be deliuered vp to them in orde^r therevnto wch was donn accordingly.

2^d Jur woodbridge ag^t winslow

Thomas Woodbridge Atturney to Thomas Sexton plaintiff against Nathā winslow deffendant in an Accon of Appeale from the Judgment of the County Court at Hampton. After the Attachment Courts Judgment Reasons of Appeale & euidences in the Case produced were read Comitted to the Jury and are Remayning on file wth the Reccords of this Court the Jury brought in their virdict they found for the deffendant Confirmation of the former Judgment & Costs of Courts

2^d Jury Shoare ag^t Gibbs

Sampson shoare plaintiff against Benjamin Gibbs deffendant in an action of Appeale from the Judgment of the County Court in Boston in Aprill last After the Courts Judgment Reasons of Appeale & euidences in the Case produced were Read Comitted to the Jury & are on file wth the Reccords of this Court the Jury brought in their virdict they found for the deffendant Confirmation of the forme^r Judgment & Costs of Courts =

Gilman ag^t foulesham

Moses Gilman plaintiffe against John foulsham sen̄ deffendt in an action of Appeale from the Judgment of the County Court at Hampton = After the Attachment Courts Judgment Reasons of Appeale & euidences in the case produced were read Comitted to the Jury and are Remayning on file wth the Reccords of this Court the Jury brought in their virdict they found for the deffendant Costs of Courts.

Cox &c ꝑ ffog ag^t wms.
— — — —

Thomas Cox & Phillip read sue^rtjes for Ezekiell ffog plaintiff ag^t John willjams deffend^t in an Action of Appeale from the Judgment of the County Court in Boston in Aprill last After the Courts Judgment Reasons of Appeale & euidences in the Case produced were Read Comitted to the Jury & are Remayning on file wth the Reccords of this Court the Jury brought in their virdict they found for the deffendant Confirmation of the former Judgment & Costs of Courts

[47] 1676

Sheaffe ag^t Hawkins

Charles oughtred Atturney to Sampson Sheaffe plantiffe ag^t Thomas Hawkins deffendant = After the Courts Judgment Reasons of Appeale and euidences in the Case pro-

duced were read Comitted to the Jury and are on file wth the Records of this Court the Jury brought in their virdict they found for the plaintiff Reuersion of the former Judgment & Costs of Courts =
|| 27[s] [& y[s]] Courts Costs ||

Jn[o] Pickering plaintiff ag[t] charles ffrost in an action of Appeale from the Judgment of the County Court held at Portsmouth after the Courts Judgment Reasons of Appeale & other euidences in the Case produced were read Comitted to the Jury and are on file wth the Reccords of this Court the Jury brought in their virdict they found for the deffendant Confirmation of the former Judgm[t] & Costs of Courts.

pickering ag[t] ffrost

Edward Cowell plaintiff against Nathaniel Elkin defend[t] in an action of Appeale from the Judgment of the County Court in Boston. this Accõn was wth draune by Consent of partjes. =

Cowell ag[t] Elkin

Jno Bennet plaintiffe against Samuel Addams deffendant in an action of Appeale from the Judgment of the County Court in Boston After the Courts Judgment Reasons of Appeale and euidences in the Case produced were read Comitted to the Jury and are on file wth the Reccords of this Court the Jury brought in their virdict they found for the plaintiff Reuersion of the former Judgment & Costs of Courts twenty eight shillings & ten pence =

Bennet ag[t] Addams

Jn[o] Bennet plaintiff ag[t] widdow * Gridley || deffend[t] || after the Courts Judgm[t] Reasons of Appeale & euidences in the Case produced were read Comitted to the Jury & are Remajning on file w[th] the Reccords of this Court the Jury brought in their virdict they found for the deffendant Confirmation of the former Judgment & Costs of Courts = twenty ~~eight~~ || one || shilling & ten penc

Bennet ag[t] Gridley

Rich[d] wharton sue[r]ty to Richard Smith plaintiff ag[t] Obadiah Swift Tho Bird & Jn[o] Clarke deffend[ts] in an action of Appeale from the Judgm[t] of the County Court in Boston er this Accõn by Consent of partjes was w[th] draune. =

wharton ag[t] Swift

* This space left blank in the original.

The Jurys were dismist
The Court is Adjourned to the 13th Instant

present the Gou͠no͞r
Dept Gou͠no͞r
mr Bradstreet
mr Danl Dennison
mr Danforth
mr Hauthorne
mr Pinchon
mr Tyng
mr Stoughton
mr Clarke
mr Dudley
— — — —

The Court mett at ye time 13th septemb'r 1676

Thomas Dauis late Resident in Boston was Indicted by the name of Thomas Dauis for not hauing the feare of God before his eyes & being Instigated by the divil about the begining of June last did Co͞mitt Adultery wth Elisabeth Browne Contrary to the peace of our Soueraigne Lord the king his Croune & dignity the lawes of God and of this Jurisdiction the laues of God & of this Jurisdiction * to wch Indictment the prisonr at the barr pleaded not Guilty put himself on hir † tryall by God & the Country After the Indictment & euidence in the Case produced were read Comitted to the Jury & are on file wth the Reccords of this Court the Jury brought in their virdict they found him not Guilty legally according to Indictment but found him Guilty of very suspitious acts leading to Adultery = The Court on Con[si]deration of this virdict proceeded to sentence him to Goe from henc to the place of execution and thenc by the marshall Generall &c to be Carrjed to the Gallows on the next Fiuth day after the lecture & there to stand on the Gallows wth a Roape

The names of the Jury men Returnd to serve on tryalls of life limbe &c sworne [were]

[48] 1676

1st Jury
mr Jnothan Balston
Richard Bulkley
Jnothan Bridgham
John Harris
Richard Whitney
Symon Coolidge
Joseph child
Jno Morse
Tho Welch
wm wright (Sam Peirse)
Tho flegg
Zackariah Johnson
— — — —

about your necke one hower & tjed to the Gallows and thenc at the Carts tajle to to be seuerely whipt not exceeding thirty nine stripes to the prison & there to lye till the next lecture day at Charls Toune & carried then thithr & be there alike seuerely whipt not exceeding thirty stripes & discharging yor prison ffees to be dischardged =

Elisabeth Broune the wife of Wm Broune of Charls Toune was alike Indicted by the name of Elisabeth Broune for not hauing the feare of God before hir eyes & being instigated by the Divil about the begining of June last did Comitt adultery wth Thomas Dauis Contrary to the peace of our Soueraigne Lord the King his Croune & dignitje the lawes of God

2d Jury mens names yt were Returnd to serve on trjalls of life &c & sworne were =
— — — —

* Repetition of eight words in the record. † Evidently an error in the record for "his."

& of this Jurisdiction the prisoner at the barr pleaded not Guilty put hirself on God & the Country for hir triall after the libell & euidences in the Case produced were read Comitted to ye Jury and ^ on file Remajning wth the Reccords of this Court the Jury brought in their virdict they find hir not legally Guilty according to Indictment but doe find hir Guilty of Prostituting hir body to him to Comitt Adultery The Court pe-rvsing this sentence do order yow to Goe from hence to the place from whenc yow Came & thenc on the next lecture day by the marshall Genll to be Conducted to the Gallows & by the executioner to haue a Rope tied about your neck to ye Gallows & so there to stand one hower & thenc to be tyed to the Carts tayle & seuerely whipped not exceeding thirty nine stripes to the prison & thr left till the next lecture day at CharlsToune & then Carrjed ouer & be there alike seuerely whipt wth thirty stripes & discharging yor prison ffees yow are dischardged =

mr Roger Billing
Left Hugh Drury [in foremns]
Nath. ffrothingham
James Bird
Nicholas Bolton
Timo Tileston
Tho Toleman
Roger Su[mn]er
Humphry Bradshaw
Tho ffoster
Jnothan Remington
Rich Ell[e]s
noah wisewall
in R[emin]gton steed objected agt by Dan Hoa[re] & Wilder

Stephen Goble of Concord thow art Indicted by the name of Steeven Gobl for not having the feare of God before thy eyes & being Instigated by the divill wth other thy Complices at or on the seuenth of August last at or neere Hurtleberry Hill in the woods in the precincts of Concord or neere thereabouts did murder & kill three Indian weomen & three Indian children Contrary to the peace of our Soueraigne Lord the king his Croune & dignity the lawes of God and of this Jurisdiction. After the libell & euidences in the Case produced were Read Comitted to the Jury ^ are Remayning on file wth the Reccords of this Court the Jury brought in their virdict i e they found him Guilty. = And Accordingly sentenc of Death was pronounct agt him that he should Goe from henc to ye place from whence he came & thenc to the Gallows and thr be hangd till thou beest dead.

Daniel Goble of Concord thou art Indicted by the name of Daniel Goble In the County of Midlesex in New England for that thow not hauing the feare of God before thy Eyes & being Instigated by the divil wth other thy Accomplices at or on the seventh of August last at or nere Hurtlebury Hill in the woods in the precincts of Concord or neere thereabouts did murder and kill three Indian weomen and three Indian children Contrary to the peace

Daniel Gobles Indictmt

of our Soueraigne Lord the king his Croune & dignity the law of God and of this Jurisdiction = to which Indictmen[t] the prisone[r] at the barr pleaded not Guilty & put himself on his triall by God and the Country: After the Indictment & euidences in the Case produced were Read Comitted to the Jury and are Remayning on file wth the reccords of y[s] Court the Jury brought in their virdict the[y] found him Guilty = And accordingly had sentenc of Death pronounct ag[t] him by the Gou̅no[r] yow shall Goe from hence to the place ~~of exec~~ from whenc yow Came & from thence to y[e] place of execution & there be hang[d] till yow be dead: & y[e] Lord be mercifull to thy soule.

[49] 1676

Nath wilder's Indictm̅

Nathaniel wilde[r] of Concord in the County of midlesex in New England thou art Indicted by the name of Nathaniel wilder for not hauing the feare of God before thy eyes being Instigated by the Diuil wth othe[r] thy acomplices at or on the sevent[h] of August last at or neere to Hurtlebury Hill in the woods in the precincts of Concord or neere thereunto did murde[r] & kill three Indian woemen and three Indian children Contrary to the peace of ou[r] Soueraigne Lord the king his Croune & dignitje the lawes of God and of this Jurisdiction = to wch Indictment the prisoner at the barr pleaded not Guilty and put himself on his tryall of God & the Country after the Indictment & euidences in the case produced were Reade and are Remayning on file wth the Reccords of this Court the Jury brought in their virdict they found him Guilty: And accordingly had sentenc of death pronounced Against him as the other = to be Returnd from hence to the place from whence he Came & thence to the place of execution there to be hang[d] till thou beest dead =

Daniel Hoares Indictment

Daniel Hoare of Concord in the County of midlesex in New England thou art Indicted by the name of Daniel Hoare for not hauing the feare of God before thy eyes and being Instigated by the Divil with othe[r] thy Accomplices at or vpon the seventh day of August last at or nere Hurtleberry Hill in the woods in the p[r]ecincts of Concord or neere thereunto did murde[r] & kill three Indian weomen and three Indian children contrary to the peace of ou[r] Soueraigne Lord the king his Croune and dignity the lawes of God and of this Jurisdic̄con to which Indictment the prisone[r] at the barr pleaded not Guilty and put himself on his tryall of * God & the Country After

* Written over the word "by."

the Indictment & euidences produced in the Case were read Comitted to the Jury and are Remayning on file wth the Reccords of this Court the Jury brought in their virdict they found him Guilty = And Accordingly || he || had sentenc of Death pronounct aganst him to be Returned from hence to y^e^ place from whence he Came and from thence to the place of execution there to be hangd till thow beest dead =

Benjamin Symons of wooborne in the County of midlesex in New England being brought to the barr was Indicted by the name of Benjamin Symonds for that he not having ^ feare of God before his eyes & being Instigated by the divil on the fifth of July last in the woods in the precincts of sajd wooborne did Comitt a Rape on the body of Elizabeth Peirce & that forcibly Contrary to the peace of ou^r^ Soueraigne Lord the King his Croune & dignity the lawes of God & of this Jurisdiction to wch Indictment the prisone^r^ at the barr pleaded not Guilty & put himself on his tryall by God & the Country After the Indictment & euidences in the Case produced were read Comitted to the Jury^ brought in their virdict they found him not guilty according to Indictment but || Guilty || of Attempting of a Rape on the body of Elizabeth Peir[c]e = The Court bound ouer the s^d^ Symons to y^r^ Ans^r^ for this at the nex^t^ County Court at charlsToune & the s^d^ Benja Symonds in 20^li^ & Jno Howard of Concord & Joseph Symons in ten pounds apeec as his suertjes acknowledged themselues respectively bound in s^d^ somes to y^e^ Tresurer of y^e^ County of midlesex on Condicon y^t^ sajd Benja Symons shall appeare Accordingly before the next County Court in midlesex to Ans^r^ w^t^ shall be layd to his charg for his fornication

[50] 1676

or his forcibly abusing Elizabeth Peirce. = ɐr

Peter Cole of charlsToune was Indicted by the name of Peter Cole for|| y^t^ he || not hauing the feare of God before his eyes & being Instigated by the Divil did on or about the first of July last Comitt Adultery on the body of Sarah Bucknam wife to John Bucknam of Boston contrary to the peace of our Soueraigne Lord the king his Croune and dignity the lawes of God & of this Jurisdiction = to wch Indictment y^e^ prisone^r^ at the barr pleaded not Guilty & declared he would be tryed by God & y^e^ Country: After the Indictment & euidences in the case produced were read Comitted to the Jury & are on file wth the Reccords of this Court the Jury brought in their

Coles Indictm^t^ & censure

virdict they found him not Guilty according to Indictment but Guilty of vnlawfull & vncivil Accompanying wth the sajd Sarah Bucknam wife to Jno Bucknam being in bed $togethe^{r}$ The Court $sentenc^{t}$ him to goe from henc to y^{e} place whenc he Came & thence on the nex^{t} fifth day after lecture by the marshall Generall & his $orde^{r}$ to be Carried to the $Gallow^{s}$ & there stand wth a $halte^{r}$ throune ouer y^{e} $Gallow^{es}$ to stand on $howe^{r}$ & then tooke doune & tyed to the $Cart^{s}$ tajle & be seuerely whipt wth thirty nine stripes & paying his prison ffees was dischardged

Sarah Bu[ck]nams Indict^{t} & sensur as aboue

Sarah Bucknam was alike Indicted as sajd Cole mutatis mutandis & being found by the Jury as aboue not Guilty according to Indictment but Guilty of like vncivill Accompanying wth Peeter Cole being in bed together had the like sentenc $p^{r}onounc^{t}$ ag^{t} hir =

Basto negro^{s} Indictment

Basto Negro slaue to $Robe^{r}t$ Cox of Boston was Indicted by the name of Basto negro for that he not hauing the feare of God before his eyes & being Instigated by the Divill vpon the 14th of Aprill last or thereabouts did Comitt a Rape vpon the body of martha Cox daughter to his sajd master being a child about three yeares old contrary to the peace of ou^{r} Soueraigne Lord the King his Croune & dignity the law^{s} of God & of this Jurisdiction To wch Indictment he pleaded not Guilty: After y^{e} $euidenc^{s}$ ag^{t} him were read Comitted to the Jury & are on file wth the Reccords of this Court the Jury brought in their virdict they found him Guilty according to Indictment = & Accordingly had the sentenc of Death pronounced ag^{t} him i e That he should Goe from the barr to y^{e} place from whenc he Came & thenc to the place of execution & there hang till he be dead =

Jack negro Indictm^{t}

Jack negro $se^{r}vant$ to m^{r} Jno faireweather of Boston was Indicted by the name of Jack negro for that he not hauing the feare of God before his eyes & being Instigated by the Divill did on the beginning of Aprill last Comitt Beastiality wth a Cow contrary to the peace of our Soueraigne Lord the King his Croune & dignity the law^{s} of God & of this Jurisdiction To wch Indictment he pleaded not Guilty after the Jury had ꝑvsed the Euidences wch are on file wth the Reccords of this Court they brought in $y^{e}re$ Virdict they found him not Guilty.

[*One leaf missing.*]

[53] 1676

Capt Thomas Daniel & Left Wm Vaughan plaintiffe by theire libell & complaint exhibitted to this Court against mr walter ThornHull deffendant wch is manifested in two Attachments now given into this Court against the said ThornHull who in open Court Consented to give Answer thereunto and abide the decree of this Court therein The plaintiffs declaring they had & did lett fall their Attachments as to the Courts of Portsmouth & Douer in June next and so the action at this Court proceeded And after their libell was read wth the euidences in the Case produced & the Court had heard & Considered the pleas & Answers The Court doe order determine & decree that the deffendant pay vnto the plaintiff the sume of twenty pounds damage in mony for his breach of promise and not standing to his Agreement & Costs of Court seven pounds seven shillings

Att this Court mr Dauid Anderson entred his libell & complaint against Robert orchard searcher deffendant for his Illegall & undue seazing of certein Raccoone skinns &c aboard his ship after the libell and euidences in ye Case produced were read &c The Court declared and ordered that the plaintiff pay the defendant Costs of Court =

In Ansr to ye peticon of Henry Lauton the keeper securing the peticoner the keeper* is permitted ^ Goe to the meeting as is desired =
E R S

At ye Adjournment of ye Court of Assistants or Admiralty in Boston 9th october 1676;

In the Case of Benjamin Gibbs plaintiffe by his libell exhibbited to this Court against Henry Wheeler master of the ship Recouery for Refusing to deliuer him the sajd shipp according to charter party & for his damage susteyned thereby After the libell wth the euidences in the Case produced were read & duely Considered of The Court doth order & decree that the deffendt proceed in the Intended voyage according to charter party mutually Agreed vpon and pay damages to the plaintiff twelue pounds in mony to be defaulcated out of his payment that shall Arise due by charter pty & Costs of Court three pounds & ten pence =

The Court Adjournd to the 12th of october 1676:

* Probably an error of the record for "petitioner."

The Court mett and hauing heard what Caleb Indian & Calumbine Indian^{s} could say for themselues hauing binn open & murderous ennemyes why sentenc of death should not passe ag^{t} them The Court proceeded and sentenct them forthwith to be Carrjed by the marshall Generall to the place of execution & see that they hang till they be dead =

[54] 1676

present
The Go$\overline{u}$no^{r}
Dept Go$\overline{u}$
Symon Bradstreet, Tho. Danforth, Wm Hathorn, John Pynchon, Edw Tyng, Wm Stoughton, Tho Clarke, Joseph Dudley — Esq^{rs}
— — — —

Att A Court of Assistants or Admiralty held at Boston 23 octobe^{r} 1676

Tho moore master of the Ship Phoenix plaintiffe in behalfe of himself & owno^{r}s by his libell exhibbited to this Court against m^{r} Abraham Bartholmew & m^{r} Jacob Jesson his Agent deffendant after the Court had heard the libell & both plaintiff & deffendants pleas & euidences in the Case produced the Court declares they Giue Judgment for the plaintiff & orde^{r} & decree that the Deffendant pay unto the plaintiffe thirty one pounds damage in mony & Costs of Court fiue pounds fowe^{r} shillings the deffendant hauing prooved payment of twenty pounds at Bilbou & by m^{r} Rucke seventy sixe pounds seventeen shillings =

Samuel Dauis master of the ship neuis factor plaintiffe ag^{t} the sajd shipp for his owne & seamens wages & his expences on hir as by his libell & Complaint exhibbited to this Court After the Court had heard the plantiffs plea^{s} & euidences in the Case produced the Court declares they found for the plaintiff and orde^{r}s and decrees that the sajd shipp & hir Appurtenances belonging to Richard Hall & hir earnings dischardge the sajd plaintiffs Account Given in & allowed two hundred & forty pounds eighteen shillings & ten pence in mony for his & his seamen^{s} wages & his expences & Costs of Court three pound eleven shilling & sixepenc. = y^{e} wages of Edw: willjams Edw Benjamin and James Haukins marrin^{r}s wages excepted & Abated for two month^{s} left behind amounting to eight pounds thirteen shillings

Att A Court of Admiralty or Court of Asistants held at Boston 26 octo^{br} 76 Henry wheeler master of the ship recouery plaintiffe in behalfe of himself & owno^{r}s by his libell & Complaint exhibbitted to this Court against Capt Benjamin Gibbs deffendant for breach of his promise in refusing to give security to value of seuen hundred pounds ⁊c for performance of charter ꝑty as by the lybell may appeare After the Court had heard the plaintiff & deffendants pleas wth the euidences in the Case the Court declared that they found for ye plaintiffe that the deffendt deliuer vp his Counterꝑt of the charter party wth the first date of it & give seven hundred pounds security that the plaintiffe may proceed vpon the voyage Giving the plaintiff his Costs fower pounds seuen shillings =

[55]

Att A Court of Assistants or Admiralty held at Boston 5th march 1676

present the Gou Dept Governor Symon Bradstreet, Daniel Dennison, Wm Hauthorn, Edw. Ting, Tho Clarke, Joseph Dudley Esqrs — — — —

Jno Dauenport marriner master of the barcque Endeavor by his libell & Complaint exhibbited to this Court plaintiff against Nicholas Paige merchant deffendant for his dispossessing him as master of sajd vessell & Refusing to pay him his monethly wages to value of thirteen pounds seuen shillings or thereabouts as ꝑ Attachmt & libell ⁊c The Court after pervsall of the libell Attachment sumons & euidences in the case produced they declared they Gaue Judgment for the deffendant Costs of Court — —

Att A Court of Assistants held at Boston the 6th of march 1676.

present the Gou Dept Gou Symon Bradstreet, Daniell Dennison, Tho Danforth, Wm Hathorne, Edwd Tyng, Thomas Clarke, Joseph Dudley Esqrs — — — —

The Grand Jury was Impanneld made their presentments & was dismist.

Isaack waldron plaintiff on Appeal from the Judgment or sentence of the last County Court in Boston in Janry. — After the Courts Judgment reasons of Appeale & euidences in the Case produced were read Comitted to the Jury the Jury brought in their virdict they found for the defendts Confirmation of the former Judgment & Costs of Courts: nine pounds & tenn penc = & to Jno ffloyd Constable sixe shillings. —

Benjamin Gibbs plaintiffs * against John Sweete ‖⁊c‖ deffendants in an Acon of Appeale from the Judgment of the County Court in Boston in october last: After the Attachment Courts Judgment Reasons of

persons to serve on the Grand Jury Impaneld & sworne were — — — —

* Error of the record for "plaintiff."

mr Wm Barthol-mew
Moses Pajne
John Blake
ffrancis Johnson
John Tappin
wm Lakin
Jno Biscoe
Robert Seavor
Wm Gary
James Russell
Jno Heyman
Wm Manning
Richd Robbins
Wm Pond
Samuell Weekes

Appeale & euidences in the Case produced were read Comitted to the Jury and are on file wth the euidences * of this Court the Jury brought in their virdict they found for the plaintiffe Reuersion of the forme' Judgmt & Costs of Court:

Joell Jenkins plaintiff against Isaack Waldron deffendt in an Accon of Appeale from the Judgment of the last County Court in Boston in Janūy After the Attachment Courts Judgment Reasons of Appeale & euidences in the Case produced were Read Comitted to the Jury & are on file wth the Reccords of this Court the Jury brought in their virdict they found for the deffendant Confirmation of the forme' Judgment & Costs of Courts

Capt Thomas marshall plaintiff agt Isaack waldron deffendt in an action of Appeale ffrom the Judgment of the last County Court in January in Boston After the Attachment Courts Judgments Reasons of Appeale & euidences in the Case produced were Read Comitted to the Jury and are on file wth the Reccords of this Court the Jury brought in their virdict they found for the deffendant Confirmation of the forme' Judgment & Costs of Courts thirty sixe shillings and eight pence fil. 3/8

persons Returnd on ye service of 1st Jury of trjals for Appeales & for life ljmbe & banishmt & were sworne were

Barnard Capen tooke the oath of a freeman in open Court

[56] 1676

mr Symon Lynde
John Balston
Sam Hoffe
Robt Herrington
James Barnard
Jno watson
Suball seavor
Peter frathingham
Tho white
Jno ffuller
~~Jno spring~~
[Cleomen]maxfeild
Barnard Capen
filing 1:2

Wm Basset plaintiff agt Isaack waldron deffendt in an action of Appeale from the Judgmt of the County Court last in January in Boston After the Attachment Courts Judgment Reasons of Appeale & euidences in the Case produced were Read Comitted to the Jury & are on file wth the Reccords of this Court the Jury brought in their virdict they found for the deffendant Confirmation of the forme' Judgmt & Costs of Courts twenty seuen shillings & 4d. =

* The Secretary evidently wrote this word by mistake instead of the word "records."

Benjamin Muzey plaintiff ag[t] Isaack waldron deffend[t] in an Accō of Appeale from the Judgment of the last County Court in Janūy in Boston After the Attachment Courts Judgm[t] Reasons of Appeale & euidences in the Case produced were read Comitted to the Jury & are on file wth the Reccords of this Court the Jury brought in their virdict they found for the plaintiff reuersion of the former Judgment & Costs of Courts forty two shillings & tenn penc.

2[d] Jury Persons Returned to serve on y[e] Jury of Tryalls for Appeales life limbe & banishment sworne

— — — —

Capt Joshua Scottow
Jn[o] Lowell
James Greene
Tho: Walker
Jn[o]than Broune
Isack Newell
Jn[o] Crafts
Tim[o] Symms
Tho olliuer
Tho Laughorne
Samuel Robbinson
John Toleman
fil: 2:

— — — —

W[m] Edmonds plaintiff against Isack waldron deffend[t] in an Accōn of Appeale from the Judgment of the County Court last in January in Boston. = After the Attachment Courts Judgment Reasons of Appeale & euidences in the Case produced were read Comitted to the Jury & are remayning on file w[th] the Reccords of this Court the Jury brought in their virdict they found for the defend[t] Confirmation of the forme[r] Judgment & Costs of Courts twenty seven shillings.

fil: 2

Endicot ag[t] Alford

Jn[o] Endecot & Tho Scottow Execcuto[r]s in trust to the estate of the late Andrew shepheard plaintiffe ag[t] Benjamin Alford Atturney to John sweeting deffend[t] in an Action of Appeale from the Judgm[t] of the County Cour[t] in Boston in octobe[r] last = After the Attachment Courts Judgment Reasons of Appeale & euidences in the Case produced were Read Comitted to the Jury & are Remayning on this Courts file of Reccords the Jury brought in theire virdict they found for the plaintiff Reuersion of the former Judgm[t] & Costs of Courts twenty eight shillings =

obbinson ag[t] Gilbert

Exec Issued out 15[th] m[r]ch 167$\frac{8}{9}$

W[m] Obbinson plaintiffe against John Gilbert deffendant in an action of Appeale from the Judgment of the County Court in Boston in octobe[r] last After the Court[s] Judgment Reasons of Appeale & euidences in the Case produced were Read Comitted to the Jury & are on file w[th] the Reccords of this Court the Jury brought in their virdict they finds for the deffendant that the plaintiffe w[th]in eight dayes shall deliuer unto him his leather which was propperly his and fower pounds for damage thereof w[th] ten shillings more for damage for his Goods & prouissions & Costs of Courts And in default thereof that the plaintiffe pay vnto the deffendant twenty pounds in mony: w[th] Costs of Courts Reuersing of the former Judgm[t] fiuety seven shillings & 6[d]: —

6 Constables sworn in Court 12[th] m[r]ch 76

m[r] Jn[o] Parmiter Leiu[t] Edw[d] willis m[r] John Saffyn m[r] Anthony Steward * m[r] Anthony Howard m[r] Samuel Jacklin & m[r] Ephrajme ^ † were chosen Constables for y[e] Toune of Boston for y[e] yeere ensuing = & tooke their oath in open Court

[57] 1676

Perry ag[t] Deane

Seth Perry plaintiff ag[t] Thomas Deane deffendant in an action of Appeale from the Judgment of the last County Court in Boston. — The plaintiff & deffend[t] Appearing in Court & declaring they had agreed & the plaintiffe desiring libe[r]ty to w[th]draw his Action the Court Approoved thereof & it was accordingly w[th]draune =

He[r]bert ag[t] Clarke

Jn[o] Herbe[r]t plaintiffe ag[t] Mathew Clarke & Company deffendt in an action of Appeale from the Judgment of the last County Court in Boston — this action as aboue was w[th]draune =

Thompson ag[t] Emery

Ben: Thomson Acknowledged y[t] he tooke not Adminstration to Jn[o] Godfrys estate & Renounceth y[e] Adminstration

Benjamin Thompson plaintiff ag[t] Jn[o] Emmery deffendant in an action of Appeale from the Judgment of the County Court at Ipswich = After the Attachment Courts Judgment Reasons of Appeale & euidences in the case produced were Read Comitted to the Jury and are on file w[th] the Reccords of this Court the Jury brought in their virdict they found for the plaintiff Reuersion of y[e] former Judgment & Costs of Courts 28[s] =

Pease ag[t] way

Jn[o] Pease plaintiffe against Richard Way Atturney to m[r]s ffreake deffend[t] in An action of Appeale from the Judgm[t] of the County Court in Boston the parties Appearing in Court & declaring it that they were Agreed the plaintiff w[th]drew his Accon as Aboue =

---

* This name (Anthony Stoward) was entered by mistake of the Secretary. He probably intended to cancel it. The other six names agree with the Boston record. See 7[th] Report, Record Com[rs], p. 107.

† "Savage" on the Boston Record.

Poole agt oughtred

Jn° Poole plaintiff against Charles oughtred deffendt in an Accon of Appeale from the Judgment of the County Court in Boston = the parties Appearing in Court & being Agreed the plaintiff wthdrew his action as aboue =

Greely agt Younge executi Issued out 9 mrch 76/7

Phillip Greely plaintiffe against Jn° young deffendant in an Action of Appeale from the Judgment of the County Court at Sallisbury After the Attachment Courts Judgment Reasons of Appeale & euidences in the Case produced were Read Comitted to the Jury and are on file wth the Reccords of this Court the Jury brought in their virdict they found a speciall verdict i e In Case the law title Appeales sect: 1: doe not barr nor Impede the Plaintiffe for whom the Action was found in the Court he Appeales from then wee finde for the plaintiffe the Confirmation of the former Judgment of Court i e tenn pounds more wth Costs of Court: But In Case the aforesajd law Barrs his Appeale then wee finde for the deffendant Costs of Courts The Court Affirmes to the 1st pt that the plaintiff might Appeale & so finds for the plantiff as aboue = Costs seven pounds fower shillings & nine penc ‖ at 35s p [m̃l] boards ‖

wooddey agt speere

Isaack wooddey plaintiffe agt George Speere deffendant in an action of Appeale from the Judgment of the Comissioners Court in Boston After the Attachment Courts Judgment Reasons of Appeale & euidences in the Case produced were Read Comitted to the Jury & are on file wth the Reccords of this Court the Jury brought in their virdict they found for the deffendt Confirmation of the former Judgment & Costs of Courts thirty three shillings & 4d — —

Colcord agt Drake 1 Ac execution Issued out 12 of march 76. 3:18:6d

Edwd Colcord plaintiffe agt Abraham Drake deffendt in An action of Appeale from the Judgmt of the County Court After ye Attachm̃t Courts Judgment Reasons of Appeale & euidences in the Case produced were Read Com̃itted to ye Jury & Are on file wth the Reccords of this Court the Jury brought in their virdict on the question whither a marshall levying execution on person & estate & afterwards letting ye person Goe free deteyning only ye estat ^ the Resolution was on the Affirmative being in the fiery * thereof & found for ye deffendant Costs of Courts three pounds eighteen shillings & sixe pence :=

* fieri?

[58] 1677

Colcord ag^{t} Drake

Edward Colcord plaintiff ag^{t} Abraham Drake deffend^{t} in an Action of Appeale from the Judgment of the Salisbury Court After the Attachment Courts Judgment Reasons of Appeale & euidences in the Case produced were read Comitted to the Jury and are Remayning on file the Jury brought in their virdict they found for the deffendant Confirmation of the former Judgment & Costs of Courts fowe^{r} pounds fowe^{r} shillings & fowe^{r} pence =

Ring ag^{t} Worcester

Robe^{r}t Ring plaintiffe against Samuel worcester deffend^{t} in an action of Appeale from the Judgment of the County Court at Salisbury After the Attachment Courts Judgment Reasons of Appeale & euidences in the Case produced were read Comitted to the Jury & are on file wth the Reccords of this Court the Jury brought in their virdict they found for the defendant Confirmation of the former Judgment & Costs of Courts fiuety nine shillings & two pence

Exec Issued out 9th m^{r}ch 76

Ring ag^{t} Buswell

Robe^{r}t Ring plaintiff ag^{t} w^{m} Buswell deffendant in an action of Appeale from the Judgment of the County Court at Salisbury = After the Attachm^{t} Courts Judgment Reasons of Appeale & euidences in the Case produced were read Co$\tilde{m}$itted to the Jury and are remayning on file wth the Reccords of this Court the Jury brought in their virdict they found for the deffend^{t} Confirmation of the forme^{r} Judgment & Costs of Courts fowe^{r} pounds fowe^{r}teen shillings & six penc =

Bennet ag^{t} Gridley

Jno Bennet plaintiff ag^{t} widdow Elisabeth Gri$\tilde{d}$ley deffendant in an action of Appeale from the Judgment of the Comissione^{r}s Court after the Attachment Courts Judgment Reasons of Appeale & Euidences in the Case produced were read co$\tilde{m}$itted to the Jury & are on file wth the Reccords of this Court the Jury brought in their virdict they found for the deffend^{t} Confirmation of the forme^{r} Judgment & Costs of Courts on Jno Bennets motion by his wife the bond was chancerjed to six pounds in all 8^{li} 14^{s}. =

Lowle ag^{t} Gerrish

Benjamin Lowle plaintiff ag^{t} Capt Wm Gerrish deffend^{t} in an action of Appeale from the Judgment of the County Court at Ipswich = this ac$\tilde{c}$on was called & by default it fell =

Woodbridge agt Wms

Thomas woodbridge plaintiff against Nathaniel willjams deffendant in an action of Appeale from the Judgment of the County Court in Boston After the Attachment Courts Judgment Reasons of Appeale & euidences in the Case produced were Read Comitted to y^c^ Jury & are on file wth the Reccords of this Court the Jury brought in their virdict they found a speciall virdict i e In Case that Goods estate & person be vnde^r^ Attachment & remajne so by Attest of the officer who se^r^ved the same wch Consequently must haue Issued eithe^r^ by Judgment of the Court to wch y^e^ ꝑty was Attached or else cease in itself if thus circumstanced it Cann Come vnde^r^ the law title Conveyances sect 3^d^ & be Acompted Imprisonment or dures as also y^t^ in Case a pe^r^secuting * another vpon bond for performance of Award wherein he makes the first breach himself doe Impede his prosecution then wee finde for the plaintiffe the Reuersion of the former Judgment of Court & Costs of Courts = But if othe^r^ wise wee find for the defendant

[59] 1677

Confirmation of the former Judgment & Costs of Courts. The Court on due Consideration finds for the deffend^t^ as aboue = The Court declared also by y^e^ Gouerno^r^ that they lookt not at it as a speciall virdict on Request of y^e^ plaintiff [h]is bond is chanceried to two hundred & forty pounds seuen shillings & three pence mony = & Costs of Courts = fforty one shillings & tenn penc

Bennet agt Symonds

Henry Bennet plaintiff ag^t^ Herlakinden Symonds deffendant in an Acc̄on of Appeale from the Judgment of the County Court at Salem = After the Attachm^t^ Courts Judgment Reasons of Appeale & euidences in the Case produced were Read Comitted to the Jury & are on file wth the Reccords of this Court the Jury brought in their virdict they found for the deffend^t^ tenn pounds mony & Costs of Courts = three pounds sixteen shillings & 4^li^ : †

execution Issued out for 13. 16. 4. march 13. 7 6/7

Ephrajm Turne^r^ plaintiff ag^t^ w^m^ Harris deffendant in an action of Appeale from the Judgment of the County Court in Boston After the Attachm^t^ Courts Judgment Reasons of Appeale & euidences in y^e^ Case produced were read Comitted to the Jury & are on file wth the reccords of this Cour^t^ the Jury brought

execution Issued out & Ret^d^. for 17 : 6 : 3

* Probably an error for "prosecuting." † Error for "4^d^."

in their virdict they found for the deffendant Confirmation of the forme^{r} Judgment & Costs of Courts = thirty shillings.

Daniel Epp^{s} Atturney to Capt Tho: Daniel plaintiff ag^{t} Benj^{a}: marshall deffend^{t} in an Accon of Appeale from the Judgment of :. ^

The partjes Appearing in Court & declaring they were Agred the plaintiff wthdrew his Accon as the other

Idem vsus Idem = ‖ Edmnd marshall ‖ was alike wth draune =

Idem vsus Edmund marshall from sajd Court this also was wth-draune

Hudson ag^{t} messenger

Wm Hudson plaintiff ag^{t} John messenger deffendant in an Accon of Appeale from the Judgment of the Comissione^{r}s Court After y^{e} Attachment Courts Judgment Reasons of Apeale & euidences in the Case produced were Read Comitted to the Jury & Remajne on file wth the Reccords of this Court the Jury brought in their virdict they found for the deffendant Confirmation of the forme^{r} Judgment & Costs of Courts = twenty five shillings

Exec Issued out 13. march 76. for 7 : 13 11 — — — —

6. 8 11
1 5
7. 13. 11.

ma [ior]s * sentenc

Robe^{r}t ma[ior] plaintiffe on Appeale from the sentence of the Comissione^{r}s i e m^{r} stoddard & m^{r} Clarke After the sentenc & Reasons of Appeale wth Euidence in the Case produced were Read Comitted to the ~~Jury~~ ‖ Bench ‖ & are on file wth the Reccords of this Court the ~~Jury~~ Court Confirmed the Judgment of the Comissioners & Costs of Court =

Phillips sentenc

Zachary Phillips plaintiff on Appeale from the Sentence of the Comissione^{r}s i e m^{r} Stoddard & m^{r}. Clarke = After the sentenc & euidences in the Case produced wre Read & are on file the Court Confirmd the Judgm^{t} of the Comission^{rs} & Granted Costs of Courts

nowells sentenc

michael Nowell plaintiff on Appeale from the sentence of the Comissione^{r}s i e m^{r} stoddard & m^{r} Clarke After the sentence & euidences in the Case produced were Read Comitted to the Jury & are on file the Court Confirmd the Judgment of the Comissione^{r}s & Granted Costs.

* Or Maires ?

[60] 1677

Whereas at the County Court held at Boston in octobe[r] last Charles oughtred Atturney to m[r] Sampson Sheaffe obteyned Judgment against John Blackleach as principall debto[r] and Against John Poole as his sue[r]tje for one hundred fivety fowe[r] pounds five shillings & two pence in mony from which Judgment the sajd John Poole appealed but since is sattisfied that the sajd debt is due therefore the sajd Poole Confesse[s] Judgment against himself &c for the foresajd sum̄e together with all charges at the County Court and occasioned by the Appeale and In Regard the lawes frees sue[r]tjes if execution be not extended in a moneth yet he Assents that execution be Granted and may be levyed vpon himselfe and estate at any time after the expiration of three monthes if in the Interim the execution vpon the forme[r] Judgment be not levyed upon the sajd Blackleach or his Estate This Judgment was Acknowledged in open Court as aboue written by John Poole merchant Against himself & his estate ꝑ 12 m[r]ch 1676/7

pooles Judgm[t] ag[t] himself:

Execution Issued out for y[e] [Su]me 29 June 77 & dd to cha: oughtred E R S

as attests Edw Rawson Secrety

Jn[o] ffllynt of Salem being presented by the Grand Jury was Indicted by the name of John flynt for not hauing the feare of God before your eyes & being Instigated by the divill did on or about the month of octob[r] last kill Eljaze[r] Coates Contrary to the peace of ou[r] Soueraigne Lord the King his Crowne & dignity the lawes of God & of this Jurisdiction.

Jn[o] flints Indictm[t]

To w[ch] Indictment he holding vp his hand at the barr pleaded not Guilty putt himself on his tryall by God & the Country the Jury was Impaneld & sworne and after all the euidences in the Case produced were read Comitted to the Jury & are on file wth the Reccords of this Court the Jury brought in their virdict: they found him not Guilty of wilfull murde[r] but Guilty of manslaughter =

found Guilty of manslaughter

Jn[o] flynt the Court Considering of yo[r] offence doe sentence yow to pay a fine to the Country of twenty pounds as also twenty pounds more to the father of the sajd Coates all in mony ‖ w[th] y[e] witnesses costs ‖ & that yow stand Comitted till the sentence be ꝑformed =

fined 20[li] to y[e] Country & 20[li]: to Robe[r]t Coates

In Ans[r] to the peticon of Edmund ffllynt in behalf of his son John ffllynt The Court doth Grant sixe

Ans[r] to his petiĉon

months time for payment of the fine[s] Imposed for w[ch] sufficient bond being Given to the Tresurer & partjes Concerned paying prison fees & chardges he is Released =

Peeter Bent Jun of Sudbury in New England being by the Grand Jury presented was alike Indicted for not hauing the feare of God before his eyes and being Instigated by the divill did about 29 July last kill Joseph Bent late of the same Towne Contrary to the peace of our Soueraigne Lord the king his Crowne & dignity = to which he pleaded not Guilty put himself on God & y[e] Country for his tryall: After y[e] euidences in the Case produced were Read Comitted to the Jury and are on file the Jury brought in their virdict they found him not Guilty of wilfull murde[r] but find him Guilty of killing him by Chanc medley ~~by~~ || or || Casualty = Peter Bent the Court Considering of your offence doe sentence yow to pay as a fine to y[e] Country tenn pounds & as a fine to yo[r] Aunt the widdow of Peeter Bent the sume of twenty pounds both in mony & pay the charges of Court for y[e] witnesses standing Comitted till y[e] sentenc be pformed In Answe[r] to the peticon of Peter Bent the Court [ ]ed him also sixe months time for y[e] payment of y[e] fines as aboue & on like termes is dischardged =

Peter Bent fined 10

[61] 1677

Wm Waldron Indictmt

W[m] Waldron now Residant in Boston being presented by the Grand Jury was Indicted by the name of w[m] waldron of Boston in the County of Suffolke ffor not Hauing the feare of God before his eyes & being Instigated by the divill in Nouembe[r] ^ by himselfe & his partne[r] Henry Lauton as his orde[r] w[th] whom he left his Comission did vnlawfully su[r]prize & steale away seventeen Indian[s] men weomen & children & in y[r] vessell called the endeavour of Boston Carrjed & sent them to ffyall & there made sale of them Contrary to the peace of our Soueraigne Lord the king his Croune & dignity the lawes of God & of this Jurisdiction: entituled man stealing To which Indictment he pleaded not Guilty putt himselfe on God & the Country for his tryall = Afte[r] y[e] euidences & pleas in the Case were Read & heard the Jury brought in their virdict they found him not Guilty =

Jn[o] Haughtons Indictment

Jn[o] Haughton of Boston marriner being presented was Indicted by the name of John Haughton for that yow not hauing the feare of God before your eyes being Instigated by the Divill did take into your vessell the endeavor seventeen Indians men weomen & children & Carrjed them away to ffyall & there were sold Contrary to the peace of our Soueraigne Lord the King his Croune & dignity the lawes of God & of this Jurisdiction title man stealling to wch Indictment he pleaded not Guilty put himselfe on God & the Country for his tryall After the euidences & pleas in the Case were Read & heard the Jury brought in their virdict they found him not Guilty according to the Indictment of man stealling But Guilty he being Shipmaster of the Catch Endevor wherein 17 Indians were receaved on board & carrjed away to ffyall that he did not beare due testimony against the Imployers act therein: — Jno Haughton the Court hath Considered yor offenc & doe sentenc yow to pay a fine of twenty pounds in mony pay the ffees of Court & stand Comitted till the sentenc be performed =

In Ansr to the peticon of John Houghton the Court abates him tenn pounds of his fine he Giving security to ye Tresurer for the payment of the other tenn pounds in mony to the Tresurer of ye County * in six months wch is don & on file

Daniel Deane wm keene Tho: wilder Jno wilder steven mattock & Tho Goble Jun had their bill of Costs Granted them for their Attendance at the Court on the examination & Triall of ye Gobles & Nath wilder wch came to fower pounds tenn shillings in mony to ye Treasurer ——

6 witnesses Costs in ye Gobles Case =

In Ansr to the petition & Request of the Toune of Dedham Capt Daniel ffisher shall be & hereby is Impowred to Joyne such persons together in marriage as either of them be legally be † published in dedham and the other alike published in any other Toune or both there =

Capt ffishers power to marry &c

Jno Lawrence jun of Sudbury in the County of midlesex being presented by ye Grand Jury was Indicted by the name of John Lawrence for that he not having the feare of God before his eyes & being instigated by the divill did Comitt Bestiallity wth a mare in Cambridge bounds vpon the 5th day of September last Contrary to the peace of our Soueraigne Lord the King his Croune & dignity the lawe of God and of this Jurisdiction entituled Bestiality = to wch Indictment he pleaded not Guilty put

Jno Laurenc Indictmt

* Error in the record for "Country."

† This word is evidently superfluous.

himself on Tryall by God & the Country After the Indictm[t] & all the euidences in the Case produced were read Cōmitted to the Jury and are on file wth the Reccords of this Court the Jury brought in their virdict they found him not Guilty.

[62]

Jn[o] Earthy being brought before the Court was ordered to be secured till the Court Called him & his^& Left Gardiner acknowledged themselues bound in forty pounds apeec to John Hull Tresurer of the Country that the sajd John Earthy shall appeare before the Court & Answer w[t] shall be layd ag[t] him at or before the next Court of Assistants

M[r] John Glouer was Called being bound ouer to this Court he was Called proclamation made three times in Court none Appearing Against him his bond was dischardged =

10 Sept 1676 whereas vpon the examination & Tryall of W[m] waldron & othe[r]s for seizing Indians at the Eastward & making sale of them at ffyall as it Appeared to the Court that part of the produce of that voyage was sold to m[r] John Hubbard by m[r] John Glouer who was Concerned in that voyage and the mony yet in the sajd Hubbards hand It was Concluded that the sajd mony should remajne in the sajd Hubbards hands Responsible to the charge of Recouery of sajd Indians or othe[r]wise vpon hearing might Appeare to be Just to* declared in Court to sajd Glouer being not entred as

17 Ap[r] = 77 on Adj[t]. Concluded the Court doeth now orde[r] the entry of the same Accordingly

m[r] Isaack Waldron hauing a chardge draune vp ag[t] him by orde[r] of the Court wch being read desired the libe[r]ty of the law for to haue a Jury wch was Granted he paying for y[e] entry & was donn y[e] charge was against m[r] Isaack waldron of Boston Apothecary

(1st) for his Injurious and reflective speeches & bold Affirmations in his charging the wo[r]p[ffl] Symon Bradstreet Esq[r] one of the Assistants of his maj[tis] Court of Assistants in the open County Court in January last Contrary to trueth saying that the sajd m[r] Bradstreet had not or did not present the originall bond he tooke Against him the sajd waldron binding him ouer to that Court to Answe[r]

---

* Error of the record for "& so." See note on page 91.

for his mischarging seuerall persons as Capt Thomas Marshall Joell Jenkins &c Againe & Againe saying that he presumed
& denjed that to be the originall bond &c In his (2ly)
bold Affirmation at the sajd County Court the same tjme of his tryall that what he had donn was by the Advice & order of sayd mr Bradstreet or else he had not don it & this Reitterated Contrary to truth =
for his bold rejtterated abusive Reflections Againe & (3ly)
Againe in like words in his Reasons of Appeale from the Judgment of the sajd County Court to this Court of Assistants agt the sd worpffl mr Bradstreet before the Country thereby endeavoring to bespatter & Asperse him of whom this Country hath had so long experience of his sincere able & faithfull Administration of Justice = which being Read wth the euidences in the Case produced Comitted to the Jury & are on file wth the Reccords of this Court the Jury brought in their virdict they found him Guilty of the whole charge in the 3 Articles = wm* waldron the Court hath Considered of your offence & doe sentenc yow to pay fjve pounds fine to the Country in money & to make Confession of yor Reflection vpon & Abuse of mr Bra[d]street in the three articles chardged against you

[63] 1677

on Munday next to the satisfaction of the Court or pay twenty pounds mony as a fine to the Country standing Comitted till the sentence be pformed he had liberty to goe home on his parrol till 2d day. when he Came & in open Court presented his Acknowledgment under his hand & was =

To the Right Honorble Jno Leueret Gou̅ & the Rest of ye honord magistrates now Assembled, at the Court of Assistants in Boston. =

The Humble petiĉon of Isaac Waldron. =

Humbly sheweth unto yor Honors that he is troubled & much greived that he hath any way occasioned your Honors Displeasure against him especially by his bold, & passionate speeches wch seemed to your Honors as though he endeavored to Impaire yor Honors Dignity, & Authority But it was neuer in his thoughts so to doe; as by his Actions any time this five or sixe yeares last past may appeare; in wch

* Error in the record for "Isaac."

Isack waldrons Acknowledgm^t

time he hath alwayes obeyed you^r Comands and not only so but willingly, and Contentedly in all things whatsoeuer; and he supposeth hath troubled the Courts as litle as most haue donne; except these two last Courts, which he was Rather Compelled to it, then desired it wherefore he beseecheth you^r Hono^rs, that yow would be pleased, to excuse and pardon him & take of the fine from of him being it is the first time he was convicted of any Crime he Comitted against your Hono^rs, and also by reason his crime was only words spoke in his passion and was no such abominable action, but may be pardoned, if you^r Hono^rs please according to the Holy word of God as in math the 12th 32 wherein it is thus written whosoeuer speaketh against the son of man || which is to be vnderstood the son of God or God man || it shall be forgiven him, so consequently if what is spoken against Jesus Christ Shall be forgiven Then certeinly yor pœnitent petitione^rs words against you^r Hono^rs may be forgiven him. Againe in Luke 17. 3. If thy Brother trespasse against thee Rebuke him and if he repent forgive him; if he trespasse against thee seuen times in a day and seuen times a day turne againe saying I Repent Thou shalt forgive him which if you^r Hono^rs please to forgive you^r Humble petitione^r it shall obliege him neuer to offend yow more and for euer to pray for you^r Hoño^rs that God would endue yo^w wth his holy spirit enrich yow wth his heavenly Grace prosper yow wth all Happiness and bring yow all to his euerlasting Kingdome through Jesus Christ ou^r Lord ou^r Saviou^r & Redeeme^r =

Isaac Waldron

his ffine Remitted to ffive pounds (5li)

The Court Accept^s of this Acknowledgm^t & therevpon orde^rs him to pay only the five pounds mentioned in his sentenc to the Country =

Dep^t Gou & [m^r w^m] Wm Hathorne fined 40^s apeece

Itt is Ordered that the Deputy Goūno^r samuel Symonds Esqr. and majo^r willjam Hauthorne departing hence before the Court was Adjourned are fined forty shillings apeece to be estreated to the Tresure^r to be charged on their Accounts =

[64] 1677

Walter Gendall bound ouer =

Walte^r Gendall was Called & seuerall euidences Read y^t were produced ag^t him othe^rs not being present he was by mittimus sent to the keepe^r of the prison in Boston in orde^r to his trjall nex^t Court of Assistants =

Hugh drury & mary his wifes order

In the Case of Hugh Drury & mary his wife The Court after a due hearing of the Case & euidences therein produced Doe declare that they Doe enjoyne them both to liue togethe[r] according to the ordinance of God as man & wife

This Court was dissolved 13th march 1676. =

Att A Court of Admiralty or Court of Assistants held at Boston y[e] 17[th] of Aprill 1677

present
Jn[o] Leuet Esq[r] Gou
Sam Symonds Esq[r] dep[t] Gou
Symon Bradstree[t]
Tho Danforth
W[m] Hathorne
Edw Tyng
Tho Clarke
Jose: Dudley

Jn[o] Parrick vsus Henry Sandford

In the Case of John Parreck maste[r] of the Catch Brothe[r]s adventure by his Libell & Complaint exhibbited to this Court plaintiffe against Henry Sandiford deffendant for his Injurious and Illegall entring on his sajd ketch on the 4[th] Instant Aprill w[th] three men & by force of Armes tooke & keepes possession of the sajd Catch p[r] according to Attachm[t] Dated in Boston 9[th] of Aprill 1677 refference thereto being had: After the Court had heard & Considered the euidences in the Case produced they Declared Ordered & decreed that the marshall Generall once w[th]in twenty fowe[r] howers goe on board the Catch Brothe[r]s Adventure and deliuer the sajd Catch to John Parricke m[r]. of Sajd Catch w[th] all hir sajles Anco[r]s and appurtenances that belongs to hir & was in hir when he the sajd Sandford tooke hir into his possession And that the sajd Henry Sandford pay vnto the sajd John Parrick for his dammage the summe of eight pounds in money w[th] the Costs of this Court fiue pounds thirteen shillings =

from 10: march 76

whereas in the last Court of Assistants vpon the examination & tryall of W[m] waldron & others ^ seizing Indians at the eastward & making sale of them at Fyall it Appeared to the Court that part of the produce of that voyage was sold to m[r] John Hubbard by m[r] John Glouer who was Concerned in that voyage & the mony yet in the sajd hubbards hands It was then Concluded that the sajd mony should remajne in s[d] Hubbards hands Responsible to the chardge of Recouery of sajd Indians or othe[r]wise vpon hearing might appeare Just & so declared in Court to sajd Glouer which being not entred as Concluded the Court doth now order the entry of the same Accordingly y[e] 17[th] Aprill 1677: = *

* This entered twice on the record. See p. 88.

[65] 1677

present
Jn° Leueret Esqr Gov
Sam Symonds Esqr dep^t Gov
Symon Bradstreet
Wm Hathorn
Jn° Pinchon
Edwd Tyng
Tho: Clarke
Joseph Dudley — —

Wilkins & Loyds libells & Actions wth draune

Att A Court of Admiralty held at Boston 22th of may 1677.

Jn° Wilkins master of the barcque flower in behalfe of himselfe & ouno^rs by his libell & Complaint plaintiffe against Nicholas Page deffendant for his Refusing to pay him for the Hire of the sajd vessell & his & his mates wages amounting in the whole to eighty-one pounds eighteen shillings as in & by the sajd libell doeth & may Appeare Dated 17 may 1677.

The partjes being Called Appeared in Court & declared that they were agreed desiring they might haue their entry mony The Court ordered the secretary to deliuer them halfe their entry mony y^e plaintiff paying the office^rs ffees for seruing entry &c = wch was don

James Loyd sole owno^r of the pinck Hopewell by his libell & Complaint plaintiff against Nicholas skinner late master of the sajd pinck deffendant for his selling & disposing of a parcell of Rigging belonging to the sajd Pinck & refusing to discouer & Giue an account on oath &c as in and by the sajd libell & Attachment refferenc thereto being had doeth & may Appeare = In this Case as aboue the partjes declaring they were agreed like orde^r past =

Courts orde^r as to m^rs Lidget & m^r Pooles Action =

In the Case of m^rs Lydgett & Company plaintiff ag^t Jn° Poole &c deffendt the execution is Respitted till the nex^t Court of Assistants & then to be Issued out vnles the deffendant Reuerse the Judgment or any part of it before that time =

Att a Court of Admiralty held at Boston on Adjournment the 4th of August 1677.

Gideon Baston & Erasmus Bobbat plaintiff by their libell & Complaint exhibbited to this Court in behalfe of themselues & charles Bennet Jn° Addams. w^m kirby & James pettee seamen & marrine^rs belonging to ship Lixborn * merchant whereof Barthol'mew Hopkins is master deffendant for his Refusing to pay them their wages for fiue moneth^s &

* Probably an error of the record for "Lisbon."

one halfe each man at twenty eight shillings ꝑ moneth, After the Court had heard the euidences in the Case produced which are on file The Cour[t] declares that they leaving one month[s] wages for each man due in the sajd maste[r]s hands belonging to each of of * the sajd Seamen from what he brought in & chardged on them particcularly both for brandy Clothes &c according to his Account given in & that he pay them in money i e to Erasmus Bobbat fiuety nine shillings & two pence to w[m] kirby three pounds eight shillings & two pence to Gideon Baston fowe[r]

[66] 1677

pounds seven shillings & nine pence to John Addams three pounds twelue shillings & three pence to James Pettee forty two shillings & tenn pence halfe penny to Charls Bennet five shillings & tenn pence in the whole being seventeen pounds three shillings & eight pence halfe penny † all to be payd in money or in Case the sajd master refuse to give to each of the sajd seamen a sufficient dischardge from the particcular sumes by his Account chardged on them for himself & those of whom they had the same then that he pay vnto each of the sajd seamen sixe pounds sixe shillings in money being fowe[r] months & a half wages due to them & is in the whole thirty seven pounds sixteen shillings and is besides the ‖ month[s] ‖ wages of each of them left in the sajd maste[r]s hands and that he the sajd master pay the Costs & charges of this Court being seven pounds ten shillings

Courts Judgment in Baston Bobbats &c case ag[t] Hopkins

execution Issued out 6 August 77 parties Agreed & so not se[r]ved
[2] R. way =

W[m] Kirby being Complayned on for mutinous Carriage against Bartholmew Hopkins master of the ship Lixbo[r]n merchant here on shoare After the Court had heard the euidences ordered that the sajd kirby make an humble acknowledgment of his miscarriage to his maste[r]s satisfaction or that the master defaulke one halfe mon[th]s pay out of his wages =

Att A Court of Admiralty held at Boston 5[th] of Septembe[r] 1677.

present Jn[o] Leueret Esq[r] Gou̅.
Sam Symonds Esq[r] dep[t] Gou̅

Jabez Hunt marrine[r] & mate of ship Anne by his libell & Complaint exhibbited to the Court

* "of" repeated in the record. † The sum does not agree with the items.

Symon Bradstreet
Daniel Gookin
Daniel Dennison
Tho Danforth
wm Hauthorne
Jno Pynchon
Edwd Tyng
Tho. Clarke
Joseph Dudley
} Esqrs
— — — —

of Admiralty plaintiffe against John Ely master of the sajd ship deffendant for his deteyning his wages & expence & for deteyning eight hundred fforty & five pounds of neuis muscavado[rs] Sugar &c as in the sajd libell & Atttachment Appeares: After the Court had heard & pervsed the euidences in the Case produced they declared they found for the plaintiff and doe orde[r] and decree that as an Issue of this Case the deffendant shall pay unto the plaintiffe twenty pounds five shillings in money on all Accounts to this Court exhibbited & y[t] y[e] master y[e] deffend[t] deliuer the plaintiff his staues w[th] payment for for * freight & Costs & chardges for this Cour[t]:

In Ans[r] to the peticon & motion of m[r] Jn[o] Poole A court of Admiralty was Granted him ag[t] m[r]s Elisabeth Lydget & Company to be held at Boston on the 7[th] Instant at one of y[e] clocke =

[67] 1677

present
Jno Leueret Esq[r] Go[u]
Sam Symonds Esq[r] D[t] Go.
Symon Bradstreet
Daniel Gookin
Daniel Dennison
Tho: Danforth
Wm Hauthorne
Edwd Tyng
Tho. Clarke
Joseph Dudley
} Esqrs
— — — —

Att A Court of Assistants held at Boston 4[th] of Septembe[r] 1677 =

Richard Harris plaintiff against Paul Batt deffend[t] in an Action of appeale from the Judgment of the Commissione[r]s Court in Boston after the Attachment Courts Judgment Reasons of Appeale & euidences in the case produced were read Comitted to the Jury and are on file w[th] the Reccords of this Court the Jury brought in their virdict they found ffor the plaintiff an Abatement of the forme[r] Judgm[t] to fiue pounds eleven shillings seuen penc & costs of Court thirty fowe[r] shillings & eleven penc

[1st Jur]

persons Returnd to Serve on y[e] Grand Jury & sworne are
— — — —
m[r] wm Parkes
Ricd wooddey
Benja Negus
moses Payne
Jno Anderson
Edwd Grant
Antho Pearse
michael Ives
Robt willjams
Jno Phillips
Tho Jenner
Timothy mather
Richd. Leeds
noah wisewall
— — — —

‖ m[r] ‖ Tho Deane ‖ assignee of Jn[o] Glouer ‖ plaintiff against m[r] John Hubbard deffend[t] in an action of Appeale from the Judgment of the County Court In Boston in Aprill last After the Attachment Courts Judgment Reasons of Appeale and euidences in the Case

1st Jur

* "for" repeated in the record.

produced were Read Comitted to the Jury and remayne on file wth the Reccords of this Court the ~~Jury brought in their vi~~ The plaintiff wthdrew his Accon & was ordered to haue his entry mony wch he had =

person[s] Returned to serve on the 1st Jury for tryalls of Appeales life lymb & banishmt

— — — —

mr Nathā: Graues.
Thomas Edwards
Asaph Elljot
Peter Lyon
Tho. Larkin
Samuel Rugles
Nathaniel Brewer
Symon Stone
Samuel Sterne[s]
Humphry Bradshaw
Job Hide
Wm Barret

— — — —

Jonathan Cane execcutor to the last will of Ruth Johnson administratrix to the estate of marmaduke Johnson deceased plaintiff agt Jno Heyward Atturney in behalfe of the Comissioners of the vnited Colonyes deffendt in an action of Appeale from the Judgment of the County Court at charlsTowne in June last After the Attachment & euidences in the case Courts Judgt Reasons of Appeale &c were read Comitted to the Jury & are Remayning on file wth the Reccords of this Court the Jury brought in their virdict they found for the deffendt Confirmation of the former Judgmt & Costs of Courts thirty seven shillings & eight pence. =

[Co 23s]

Jno Scarlet executor to the estate of Capt Samuel Scarlet deceased plaintiff against Wm Prout deffendant in an action of Appeale from the Judgmt of the the * County Court in Boston in Aprill last after ye Attachment Courts Judgmt Reasons of Appeale & euidences in the Case produced were Read Comitteed to the Jury and Remajne on file wth the Reccords of this Court the Jury brought in their virdict they found for the deffendant Confirmation of the former Judgmt & Costs of Courts fforty three † shillings & eight pence =

[dble] ent exec Issued out [28] Sept [77]

Nathaniel Willjams plaintiff against Hanna Calley deffendant in an Accon of Appeale from the Judgmt of the County Court in Boston After the Attachment Courts Judgment Reasons of Appeale & euidences in the Case produced were read Comitted to the Jury and Remajne on file wth the Reccords of this Court the Jury brought in their virdict they found for the plaintiff revertion of the former Judgment & Costs of Courts twenty nine shillings =

* "the" repeated in the record.
† "three" written over "four."

Boston 7 Comission^rs sworne

Capt Tho Bratle majo^r Tho. Sauage Capt Jno Richards m^r John Joyliffe m^r Humphry davy m^r Anthony stoddard Capt Tho clarke were p^resented to this Court as the seuen comission^rs chosen by ye ffreemen for the yeare ensuing wch the Court allowed & Approoved of & tooke their oath all saue maj^r sauage y^t was absent [6 Sept 77]

[68] 1677

ye names of ye 2^d Jury for tryalls of life lymbe & Banishm^t and sworn were
— — — —
m^r Ellis: Barron
Thomas Sauage Junr
Ephraim Sale
samuel Lynde
Thomas Bingley
Tobyas Dauis
Jacob Hewen
Robt Searle dismist 6 Inst
Nath Coolidge
Nath Wilson
Timothy ffoster
w^m Dauis
Benj Thirston in Roome of Robt Searle 6 Inst.
— — — —

Jno Endecott & Jno scottow plaintiffs ag^t Rich^d midlecot Aturney to Joseph Calley hir * husband deffendant in an Action of Appeale from the Judgment of the County Court in Boston July last After the Attachment Courts Judgment Reasons of Appeale & euidences in the Case produced were read Comitted to ye Jury and are remayning on file wth the Reccords of this Court the Jury brought in their virdict they found for the defendant confirmation of the forme^r Judgm^t & Costs of Courts. —

Willjam waldron plaintiffe against James skinner deffend^t in an action of Appeale from the Judgment of the County Court in Boston in Aprill last after the Attachment Courts Judgment Reasons of Appeale & euidences in the Case produced were Read Comitted to the Jury and are on file with the Reccords of this Court the Jury brought in their virdict they found for the deffend^t Confirmation of the forme^r Judgm^t & Costs of Courts thirty five shilling & two penc

Rauson uers Billings

Willjam Rawson plaintiff against Roge^r Billings deffend^t in ^ action of Appeale from the Judgment of the County Court in Boston in July last = After the Attachment Courts Judgment Reasons of Apeale & euidences in the Case produced were read Comitted to the Jury and are Remayning on file wth the Reccords of this Court the Jury brought in their virdict they found for the plaintiff reuersion of the forme^r Judgment & costs of Courts two pounds eleven shillings & eig[h]t penc =

Joy Ag^t Church

Thomas Joy plaintiffe ag^t Joseph Church deffendant in an action of Appeale from the Judgment of the

* Hanna Calley's? See page 95.

County Court in Boston in July last After the Attachment Courts Judgment Reasons of Appeale & euidences in the Case produced were read Comitted to the Jury and are on file w[th] the Reccords of this Court the Jury brought in their virdict they found for the deffend[t] Confirmation of the forme[r] Judgmen[t] & Costs of Courts fiuety three shillings =

Jn[o]. Soames plaintiff ag[t] Darby Bryant deffend[t] in an action of Appeale from the Judgm[t] of the last Comissione[r]s Court After the Attachm[t] the Courts Judgm[t] Reasons of Appeale & euidences in the Case produced were read Comitted to the Jury & are on file w[th] the Reccords of this Court the Jury brought in their virdict they found for the plaintiff reuersion of the former Judgm[t] & Costs of Courts thirty sixe shillings & ten penc.

Soames ag[t] Bryant

36[s]. 10[d]. Costs

Jn[o] Trumble plaintiffe ag[t] Arthur Mason deffend[t] in an acc̄on of Appeale from the Judgm[t] of the County Court at charlsTowne = After y[e] Attachment Courts Judgm[t] Reasons of Appeale & euidences in the case produced were read Comitted to the Jury & are on file wth the Reccords of this Court the Jury brought in their virdict they found for the deffend[t] Confirmation of the former Judgm[t] & Costs of Courts nineteen shillings & ten pence =

Trumble ag[t] mason

Jn[o] Trumble ouned in Court he neu[r] Accounted y[e] debt now sued for to this ounor as payd or any p[t] y[e]rof

— — — — —

[69] 1677

Benjamin Tompson plaintiff against Jn[o] Emery sen̄ deffendant in an Action of Appeale from the Judgm[t] of the last County Court at Ipswich — After the Attachm[t] Courts Judgment reasons of Appeale & euidences in the Case produced were read Comitted to the Jury and are on file w[th] the Reccords of this Court the Jury brought in their virdict they found for the plaintiffe reuersion of the former Judgm[t] & Costs of Court[s] fforty fowe[r] shillings =

Thompson ag[t] Emery

44[s]:

Peter Egge[r]ton sue[r]ty for w[m] maze plaintiff against Daniel mackee deffend[t] in An Action of Appeale from the Judgment of the Comissione[r]s Court in Boston in July last After y[e] Attachment Courts Judgment Reasons of Appeale & euidences in the Case produced were read Comitted to the Jury and are Remayning on file w[th] the Reccords of

makee ag[t] maze or Egge[r]ton =

57[s] : 4[d] mony

this Court the Jury brought in their virdict they found for the deffendant Confirmation of the form[r] Judgment & Costs of Courts seventeen shillings & ffou[r] pence. * =

Sheaffe ag[t]. Palmer := Sampson Sheaffe plaintiff ag[t] Tho. Palmer deffend[t] in an Action of Appeale from the Judgment of the last County Court in Boston After the Attachment Courts Judgment Reasons of Appeale & euidences in the Case produced were Read Comitted to the Jury & are on file wth the Reccords of this Court the Jury brought in their virdict they found for the deffendt Costs of Courts : nine shillings & fowe[r] penc. =

2[d] Jur Barefoot ag[t] Palme[r] Cap[t] walte[r] Barefoot plaintiff against Xtophe[r] Palme[r] deffendant in an action of Appeale from the Judgment of the last County Court at salisbury = After the Attachment Courts Judgment Reasons of Appeale & euidences in the Case produced were Read Comitted to the Jury and are on file wth the Reccords of this Court the Jury brought in their virdict they found for the plaintiff an Abatement of the former Judgment to sixty pounds seven shillings & Costs of Courts sixe pounds fiueteen shillings & sixe penc =

Execution Issued out 9: Sept. 77 for 19[li] : 15 : 6.

1st Golding ag[t] Russell Pete[r] Golding plaintiff ag[t] James Russell execcuto[r] to y[e] Last will & testament of the late Rich[d] Russell Esq[r] deffend[t] in an Acc̄on of Appeale from the Judgm[t] of the County Court in Boston in Aprill last after the Attachment Courts Judgment Reasons of Appeale & euidences in the Case produced were read Com̄itted to the Jury & are on file the Jury brought in their virdict they found for the deffend[t] Confirmation of the form[r] Judgm[t] & Costs of Courts = thirteeen shillings & 2[d]

Bryan ag[t] Soames =non suited= Darby Bryan plaintiff ag[t] Jn[o] Soames deffend[t] in an Acc̄on of Appeale from the Judgment of the last Comissione[r]s Court in Boston the Action & y[e] plaintiff was called three times y[e] plaintiff made default by non Appearance & was non suited =

[70] 1677

^ as to the sadle ^* Jn[o] Griffyn plaintiff against Edw[d] Goue deffend[t] in an Acc̄on of Appeale from the Judgment of the last

* written over "sixteen shillings & ten pence."

* These words with the caret-marks are in the margin of the original record.

County Court at Salisbury After the Attachm[t] Courts Judgment Reasons of Appeale & euidences in the Case produced were Read Comitted^the Jury and are on file w[th] the Records of this Court The Jury brought in their virdict i e a speciall virdict: i e if Left fiske had powe[r] to Impresse a horse & man as a convoy when he was Returning from the country[s] se[r]vice then wee confirme the former Judgm[t] of sallisbury Court & costs of Court if not wee find for the plaintiff the confirmation of m[r] nathaniel Saltonstalls Judgm[t] & Costs of Court The magis[ts] on pe[r]vsall of this Judgment finde for the deffend[t] Costs of Courts: i e three pounds seventeen shilling & sixe pence =

Griffyn ag[t] Goue

memento y[e] Council ordered Edw[d] Gove to deliu[r] to Jn[o] Griffin y[t] bridle sadle &c in his hands insteed of his owne =

= Idem v̄sus Idem on Appeale from s[d] salisbury Court as to Riding his horse After the Attachment Courts Judgment Reasons of Appeale & euidences in the Case produced were read Comitted to the Jury & are on file they brought in their virdict i e a speciall virdict i e if Leiuetenn[t] ffiske had powe[r] to Impress a horse & man as a Convoy when he was Returning home from the Country[s] se[r]vice, then wee Confirme the forme[r] Judgm[t] of Sallisbury Court and Costs of Court if not wee ffinde for the plaintiffe the Confirmation of m[r] Nathaniel Saltonstalls Judgm[t] & Costs of Court [The Magists]* on p̱vsall of this Virdict finde for the deffendant Costs of Courts three pounds sixteen shillings & fowe[r] pence =

Griffin ag[t] Goue

3 16 4

m[r]s Elisabeth || Dauenport aljas Dauis || relict & Administratrix to the estate of y[e] late Cap[t] Nathaniel Dauenport deceased plaintiff ag[t] Edward Shippen deffendant in an Action of Appeale from the Judgment of the last County Court in Boston. After the Attachment Courts Judgm[t] Reasons of Appeale & euidences in the Case produced were read Comitted to the Jury and are remayning file the Jury brought in their virdict they found for the deffendant Confirmation of the forme[r] Judgm[t] & Costs of Courts thirty sixe shillings & tenne penc

m[r]s Dauenport || Aljas Dauis || ag[t] Shippen

Judg[t] v̄ Dauēport 65: 17 10

John Saffyn Atturney to Return wayte plaintiff ag[t] Jn[o] walley defen[t] in an action of Appeale from the Judgment of the last County Court in Boston After the Attachment

Saffin ag[t] Walley.

* This is written over the words "Three po[unds]."

[in fine] Judgt for walley 32. 5. 10

Saffins Abatement 20li & costs of ye Court pap: 13:

Courts Judgment reasons of Appeale & euidences in the Case produced were Read Comitted to the Jury & are on file wth the Reccords of this Court the Jury brought in their virdict they found for the ~~deffendant~~ ‖ plaintiffe ‖ an Abatement of the former Judgment to thirty pounds in mony & Costs of Court

matson agt dispaw

Thomas Matson plaintiff agt Henry Dispaw deffendt in an action of Appeale from the Judgment of the last County Court at Salem After the Attachment Courts Judgment Reasons of Appeale and euidences in the Case produced were Read Comitted to the Jury & are on file wth the Reccords of this Court the Jury brought in their virdict they found for the plaintiff reuersion of the fformer Judgmt & Costs of Courts thirty 2 shillings & 2 penc

[71] 1677

Johnson agt Gardiner =

Mathew Johnson plaintiff as Atturney to Richard Neuars plaintiff agt Richard Gardiner deffendt in an action of Appeale from the Judgmt of the last County Court in Cambridge in aprill last after the Attachments Courts Judgment reasons of Appeale & euidences in the Case produced were Read Comitted to the Jury and are Remayning on file the Jury brought in their virdict they found for the plaintiff a reuersion of the former Judgmt at Cambridg Court & Costs of Courts =

Ballard agt watts

Jervice Ballard plaintiff agt michael watts or his Atturney Benja Dauis Deffendant in an action of Appeale from the Judgment of the County Court in Boston in July last after the Attachment Courts Judgment Reasons of Appeale & euidences in the Case produced were read Comitted to the Jury & are on file wth the Reccords of this Court the Jury brought in their virdict they found for the deffendt Confirmation of the formr Judgmt & Costs of Courts =

Bratle agt Knight & purchis =

Capt Thomas Brattle plaintiff agt Richard Knight ‖ admstrator &c ‖ & olliuer purchis deffendts in an Accon of Appeale from the Judgmt of the County Court in ‖ Boston ‖ ^ April last After the Attachment Courts Judgment Reasons of Appeale & euidences in the Case produced were Read

Comitted to the Jury & are on file wth the Reccords of this Court: ye Court ordering its procedure the Jury brought in their virdict they found for ye plaintiff: the forfeiture of the bond of two hundred & twenty pounds sterling according to bond & Costs of Courts. =

order phibbiting* execution e/r 9 Sept 77 ERS

It is ordered by the Court that no Judgment shall passe nor execution granted in the abouesajd case agt Richard Knight as Admstratr to the estate of mr Jno Payne vntill there be an orderly divission of the sajd estate among the creditors thereto as the law hath provided refferring to non solvent estates. = By ye Court Edwd Rawson Secrety

Hudson agt Rumings =

Capt wm Hudson plaintiffe agt Jno Ruming deffendt in an accōn of Appeale from the Judgment of ye Comissionrs Court in Boston in July last

After ye Attachmt Courts Judgment Reasons of Appeale & euidences in the Case produced were read Comitted to the Jury & are on file wth the Reccords of this Court the Jury brought in their virdict they found for the plaintiff and† abatement of the former Judgment ‖ to three pounds in money ‖ & Costs of Courts twenty sixe shillings.

Sedgwick agt Willis

Robt Sedgwick plaintiff agt Rebeckah willis deffendt in an Accon of Appeale from the Judgmt of the Comissionrs Court in Boston in may last after the Attachment Courts Judgment Reasons of Appeale & euidences in the Case produced were Read Comitted to ye Jury & are on file the Jury brought in their virdict they found for ye plaintiff reuersion of the former Judgment & Costs of Courts twenty eight shillings & 4d

[72] 1677

Mary Drurys Appeale

Mary Drury plaintiffe on Appeale from the sentenc of the County Court last in Boston After the Judgment Reasons of Appeale & ‖ euidences ‖ were Read & pervsed by the Bench to whom she refferd hirself the magists found Confirmation of the former Courts sentence i e. fiue pounds fine[:] and enjoyned hir & sajd Hugh drury to Appeare before the Court on the Adjornmt the 9 of octobr ~~nex~~ next.

---

* The Secretary used the character p here by mistake for p.

† Probably an error in the record for "an."

Phips agt dudson no Attachmt nor Courts Judgmt given in

wm phipps plaintiffe against * Dudson deffendant in an action of Appeale from the Judgmt of the County Court in Boston in Aprill last The plaintiff appeared in Court & Affir[min]g that they had Agreed betweene themselues had liberty to wthdraw his action wch he did =

Mrs Freake † agt Robbinson.

Elisabeth Freake † agt Nathaniel Robbinson deffendt who alike as Aboue wthdrew hir Action =

Walter Gendall his Indictmt

Walter Gendall of or neere blacke point being presented & Indicted by the Grand Jury & left to tryall = was brought to the Barr & was Indicted by the name of walter Gendall for not hauing the feare of God before his eyes & being Instigated by the Divill in the tjme of the warr wth the Indians in a perfidious & treacherous way against the Inhabitants of this Collonyes peace and safety sought to betray them into the ennemyes hands by his Indeavor & Counsell Contrary to the peace of our Soueraigne Lord the King his Croune & dignity ‖ & ‖ the law of this Comonwealth to wch Indictmen[t] he pleaded not Guilty Refferd himself for his tryall to the Bench. The magistrates hauing duely weighed the Indictment & euidences in the Case produced against him found him Guilty of the Indictment & doe therefore sentence yow to Runn the Gantelop thrô the millitary Companyes in Boston on the 10th Instant wth a Roape about his necke that he forfeit all his lands to the Country and be banished out of this Jurisdiction to be gonn by ye 6th of octobe^r nex^t on pœnalty of perpetuall Imp^risonmen^t if he Returne Againe & dischardging the Costs & charges of the prosecution :‸

his Censure

Jno Abbot had [26] Costs

Jno watts Indictment

Jno watts being presented & Indicted by the Grand Jury was brought to the Barr & was Indicted by the name of John watts marriner for not hauing the feare of God before your eyes being Instigated by the Divill in the tjme of the warr wth the Indians did in a perfydious & treacherous way against the Inhabitants of this Colonys peace & safety‸to betray them into the ennemyes hands & hath in or about June last traded powder & shott whereby the ennemy hath binn supplyed Contrary to the peace of our

* This space left blank in the original.

† Or Treake.

Soueraigne Lord the King his Croune & dignity & ye Act of the Council of this Commonwealth.

[73] 1677

~~To which Indictment~~

To wch Indictment he pleaded no^t Guilty put himselfe on his Tryall by God & the bench The Court on consideration of all the euidences in the case produced doe sentence yow to Runn the Gantelop thrô the Company^s that trayne in Boston on second day nex^t being the 10th Instant & Give in his bond of one hundred pounds for his Good behauiour & pay the Costs ‖ & charge ‖ of the prosecution standing comitted till the sentence be performed =

Watts censure

Jno Buttery of marble head was presented & Indicted for Comitting Beastiallity ℞ & left to his tryall

Buttery p^rsented

Whereas Captaine Thomas Bratle contrary to lawe in his reasons of Appeale presented & by him owned in this Court in prosecution of his Appeale against the Administrato^r to the estate of John Payne doth highly reflect vpon the Hono^r of the County Court of Suffolke that barred his plea & granted non suite as donn wholly vpon self Interes^t & for the obteinment of their owne claymes and contrary to law and this after this Courts sence given thereabouts and time Allowed him for a Just resentment thereof which yet by his petition he rather deffends then otherwise The Court doth therefore sentence him to be dischardged from his Comission as Comissione^r in the Towne of Boston & pay one hundred pounds mony & stand comitted vntill his sentenc be ꝑformed

Capt Bratles sentenc

on his peticon his fine Abated to 20^li & ye sent as to ye Comissio^rs place Remitted

Vpon the motion of Abiell Lambe in behalf of his wife late widdow of Joseph Buckminster referring to hir thirds of sajd Joseph^s estate m^r Thomas weld & Thomas Gardiner sen̄ are Appointed a Comittee to Repaire to s^d Lands & set out hir thirds according to lawe

Order abo^t Lambs thirds

Wm Bowdish fined 10^li abated to 5^li

Wm Bowdish of Salem fined tenn pounds for his neglect [or] non Appearanc on his peticon & payment of 5^li to ye marshall y^t was [carrjed]: his fine Abated 5^li

present At A meeting of the Council held at Boston: 1st
Jno Levet Esqr Govr of Novembr 1677
symon Bradstreet
Daniel Gookin
Thomas Clark At ys Council a cirtifficat was presented to the Council undr ^ Charles Gott clarke by ordr of the militia of wenham yt John Bilson & Benja. Kimball were Imprest & marched on the Countrys service vndr the Comand of Capt Hathorn on 25 octobr & Returnd out of the sd service on the 24th of Decembr & Returnd their Armes also = vndrwritt These persons aboue named were left in Garrison at Newitchawannick in Yorkshire & had a ticket from myself wch they alleadge they haue lost: Ri: waldron sar[jt] majr

It is ordered that the Comittee of the Army pass this bill to the Tresurer for payment they taking notice that the bill is sd to be lost &c that it come not Againe.

[74] 1677

In Answer to the peticon of Elisabeth Bowers
Bowers peticon & euidences estreated accordingly = Affir[m]ing therein that hir husband heard not of the Generall Courts Referring his peticon to the next Court in midlesex till it was past It is therefore ordered that the Secretary estreat the peticon & euidences in Benanuel Bowers case to the next County Court at Cambridge to whom It is Refferrd =

Vpon the complaint ‖ & peticon ‖ of mr Isack
1st nouember 1677 foster that there is due to him from kittery the sume of seventy pounds &c The Council Judgeth it meet to Reffer the peticoner to the County Court at Yorke for taking such effectual course & making such ordr therein as may Ansr the peticoners Just expectation therein:

p E R S

mr wm Pope being Complained on for his abusive
wm popes sentanc Carriage in Cursing of the Authority here making an ordr to prevent the spreading of ye smale pox: as also defaming all the weomen in Boston &c. After the euidences pduced
13li, 13. 4d fine or agt him were Read & himself not willing to be trjed by a Jury but reffering himself to the Gouernor & magistrates The Court declared they had Considered of his offences & sentenct him to be whipt wth twenty stripes or to pay twenty markes

fine in money to y^e Country Treasurer standing Comitted till the sentanc be performd

[*Blank space.*]

[75] 1677

Att A Court of Admiralty or Court of Assistants held at Boston the 7^h $7mbe^r$ 1677

present all y^e magists =

John Poole merchant plaintiff against Elisabeth Lydgett execcutrix to Peter Lydget late of Boston merchant $owno^r$ of the catch Content & Company the sajd Poole hauing by his petiĉon & libell complained of breach of charter party in that the Catch Content lett to him & w^m Trott in a voyage to ffyall for three month certeine and nine months vncerteine It Appearing by the euidence that the sajd vessell being disabled by great tempests vpon the sea & the $owno^r$s hauing not prouided materialls for the repaire of the sajd vessell to make hir sufficient for to bring home the merchants Goods she was sould at ffyall for one hundred mill Rees vpon the Consideration of the whole Case The Court finds for the plaintiffe and doe decree that the deffendant pay to the plaintiffe $fowe^r$ hundred pounds damage in money & costs of Courts seven pounds $fowe^r$ shillings =

Poole ag^t Lidged /ent: here should haue binn ent: before =

vide p 45

Att A Court of Admiralty or Court of Assistants held at Boston 27th $Septembe^r$ 1677

Jn° Leueret Esqr Goū
Symon Bradstreet, Daniel Gookin, Tho. Danforth, Edwd Tyng, Thomas Clarke, Joseph Dudley — Esq^{rs}

Jn° Keetch * now Resident in Boston by his libell & Complaint plaintiff against Henry Allin of sajd Boston merchant deffendant for his Refusing to give him an Account of the dispose of a parcell of Ke^rsy^s belonging to m^r w^m $Habe^r$feild of Bristoll & consigned by him the sajd plaintiff to the sajd Allin deffendant as in and by the sajd libell appeareth. After the Court had heard all the pleas and euidences in the Case produced The Court found for the deffendant and did $orde^r$ and decree y^t the said plaintiff shall dischardge the charge of the Court & pay the deffendant his costs sixe shillings =

Jn° Keech Acknowledged in Court that he had received an eleven hogsheads of fish from Henry Alljn as part of the produce of fiueteen

* Or Reetch.

peeces of Kersy of mr Habbe'feilds sent by the sajd Keech to value of about ffforty fowe' pounds = E. R S.

present
Jno Leueret Esqr Gov
Symon Bradstreet
Daniel Gookin
Tho. Danforth
Edwd Tyng
Tho. Clarke
Joseph Dudley
Esqrs
— — — —

At a Court of Admiralty held at Boston 9th of october 1677

Nathaniel Cary master of the Catch Elisabeth & margaret plaintiff in behalfe of himself & Company against the sajd ketch for his & their wages for eleven months at twelve pounds fiue shillings mony In yt Lancellot Talbot his Imployer sent him home from Jamajca wthout any effects & wth a bare noate or bill chardged by him on mr wm Harris of Boston who for want of effects Refused to answer his bill and they being yet without their wages for which they Craue the decree of this Court against sajd Catch as in the sajd Libell appeares After the Court had heard & pervsed the euidences in the Case produced ^ doth decree for the plaintiff one hundred pounds two shillings & tenn penc in mony wth the costs & chardges of this Court three pounds ten shillings & fowe' penc =

[76] 1677

present
Jno Leueret Esqr Gov: *

Att A Court of Assistants or Admiralty held at Boston 15th octobe' 1677

In the Case of Ephraim Angier plaintiff agt Edward winslow master of Catch Johns Adventure The Court vpon all pleas & euidences vpon file Read & Considered finde & decree for the plaintiff the Goods sued for in particcular as mentioned in the libell & owned by the mate or pay fiue hundred pounds money & Costs of Court three pounds twelue shillings =

In the Case of John Noyse plaintiffe against Edward winslow master of Catch Johns Adventure = The Court finds for the plaintiff the Goods sued for in the seuerall particculars mentioned in the libell as owned by the mate vpon pœnalty of three hundred & fiuety pounds money & Costs of Court three pounds fiueteen shillings

present
Jno Leueret Esqr Gov

Att a Court of Admiralty held at Boston 20th decembe' 1677

* No others named as present.

Symon Bradstreet, Thomas Danforth, Wm Hathorn, Edw. Tyng, Tho. Clarke, Joseph Dudley — Esqrs

The ship Speedwell being by warrant & order from the Honble Gouernor directed to the marshall of Suffolk seized & secured wth hir furniture & Ralfe Shelly master & Luke Raster merchant summoned to appeare at this Court to Answer for their breach of the Law for their bringing and Landing of Brandy & breach of the law in that case the warrant & Returne of the marshall therevpon was Read the partjes Allegations & pleas wth the euidences in the Case produced The Court hauing Considered what hath binn prooved & Alleadged in the Case of sajd ship speedwell doe Adjudge the sajd ship speedwell Ralph Shelly master & Luke Raster merchant free from the present seizure hauing entred in England & producing Cocket for their Cargoe But

whereas It Appearth to this Court that Ralph shelly master & Luke Raster merchant of ship speedwell haue broken bulke^ landed in this Harbor of Boston Brandy wthout making entry thereof according to law: This Court Doe Adjudge them to pay twenty shillings p tunn, according to sajd law being sixty pounds money =

In Ansr to the petition of Ralph shelly || mr || & luke Raster merchant of ship speedwell the Court Judgeth it meete on the peticoners payment of thirty pounds money to the Tresurer the other part of their fine is Remitted them. = And It is ordered the Tresurer pay the Costs & charges of the Court =

[77] 1677

present: Jno Leueret Esqr Gou, Samuel Symons Esqr Dt Gou, Symon Bradstreet, Daniel Gookin, Daniel Dennison, Tho Danforth, wm Hauthorne, Edward Tyng, Thomas Clarke, Joseph Dudley — Esqrs

Att A Court of Assistants held at Boston on ye 5th of march 1677

Edward Goue Plaintiffe against Henry Bennet defendant in an action of Appeal from the Judgment of the last County Court at Salem After the Attachment Courts Judgment Reasons of Appeale & euidences in the Case produced were read Comitted to the Jury & are on file wth the Reccords of this Court the Jury brought in their virdict they found for the plaintiffe reuersion of the former Judgment & Costs of Courts fiuety one shillings and two pence =

1st Ju:

The names of ye Grand Jury sworne were =
mr Thomas Hastings
Jno Harrison sen

Joseph How
Thomas Gardiner
John Vyall
Wm Hearsy
Joshua Tydd
Wm Dady
Roge^{r} sumñe^{r} *
Enoch wiswall
Thomas weld
Samuel willjams
John Stone
Wm Bond
— — — —
The names of the first Jury for Appeales life limbe or Banishment sworne were =
— — — —

Capt Dudley Bradstreet Left Jno Osgood &c Selectmen of Andiver plaintiff^{s} against Thomas ffuller deffendant in An action of Appeale from the Judgment of the County Court at Ipswich After the Attachment Courts Judgment Reasons of Appeale & euidences in the Case produced were Read Comitted to to † the Jury & are Remayning on file wth the Reccords of this Court the Jury brought in their virdict they found for the deffendant Costs of Courts [1^{li}] 8^{s} 6^{d}

1st Ju

m^{r} John walley
w^{m} Griggs
w^{m} Coleman
Richd Lowden
Hen: Balcom
John wales
Gamaliel Beamon [sen]
Giles Pason
Nathaniel Holmes
Thomas Prentice [sen]
Richard Ecles
w^{m} Godard —
— — — —
The names ef the second Jury of tryalls as aboue sworn
— — — —
m^{r} samuel seawall
Isaack walker
Jabez Salter
Daniel Smith
James Smith
Tmothy Tyleston
Sam: Paul
stephen willjams
Jno Henneway
Jno ward
Tho Langhorne
John Bisc[o]
— — — —

Jno knight & Tristram Coffin Atturney^{s} for y^{e} Towne of Newbe^{r}y plaintiffs ag^{t} m^{r} Richard Dumme^{r} sen deffend^{t} the Case was Called the Attourney^{s} lette^{r} of Atturney no^{t} being Jointly & seuerally Jno knight being dead the Court declared Actio moritur persona & so it fell. = y^{e} deffend^{t} had his costs thirteen shillings =

Jno Dix[e] plaintiff against Jerremiah morse deffend^{t} in an action of Appeale from the Judgment of the last County Court at Charles Towne After the Attachmen^{t} Cour^{t}s Judgmen^{t} Reasons of Appeale & euidences in the Case produced were read Comitted to the Jury & are on file wth the Reccords of this Court the deffend^{t} pleading it was matter of law & therefore it belonged to the Bench & not to the Jury The magis^{ts} hauing heard the case pleas & euidences therein declard they found for the deffend^{t} Confirmation of the forme^{r} Judgmen^{t} at charls Towne Court ‖ & ‖ Costs of Courts fowe^{r} pounds twelue shillings & ten pence =

Jno Dix plaintiffe against John Hamond deffendant After the Attachment Courts Judgment Reasons of Appeale & euidences in y^{e} Case produced were Read Comitted to the Jury and are on file wth the Reccords of this

first Ju:

* Probably an error in the record for "Sumner."

† "to" repeated in the record.

Court The Jury brought in their virdict they ffound for the deffendant Costs of Courts twenty shillings & eight pence

Robe^{r}t orchard plaintiff against Samuel Pollard deffendant in an action of Appeale from the Judgmen^{t} of the Comissione^{r}s Court in Boston After the Attachment Courts Judgmen^{t} Reasons of Appeale & euidences in the Case produced were read Comitted to the Jury and are Remayning on file wth the Reccords of this Court the Jury brought in their virdict they found for the deffendan^{t} fiuety fiue shillings & tenn pence =

2^{d} Ju

Wm Greene plaintiff ag^{t} John Dauid & Solomon Rainsford deffend^{t} in an Action of Appeale from the Judgment of the County Court in Boston = After the Attachment Courts Judgment Reasons of Appeale & euidences in the Case produced were Read Comitted to the Jury & are on file wth the Reccords of this Court the Jury brought in their virdict they found for the deffendant Costs of Courts forty three shillings & tenn pence = =

exec Issued out

||exec Grted 8 Ap^{r}.||

Edmond Bridges Atturney to phillip English plaintiff ag^{t} James Browne Atturney to Benjamin mazure deffend^{t} in an action of Appeale from the Judgm^{t} of the County Court at Salem After the Attachmen^{t} Courts Judgment Reasons of Appeal & euidences in the Case produced were Read Comitted to the Jury & are on file wth the Reccords of this Court the Jury brought in their virdict & found for the Deffendan^{t} Costs of Courts fiuety nine shillings & sixepenc =

[78] 1677

Philip English plaintiff ag^{t} Benjamin Mazure deffend^{t} in an action of appeale from the Judgment of the County Court at Salem. After the Attachment Courts Judgment Reasons of Appeale & euidences in the Case produced were read Comitted to the Jury & are on file wth the Reccords of this Court the Jury brought in their virdict they found$_{\wedge}$Costs of Courts & tenn shillings dam̃age = the partjes Agreed their Costs in both Cases & damage & Remajned due to James Browne Atturney to mazure thirty sixe shillings & sixpenc

English ag^{t} Mazure

Wm Pitman plaintiff on Appeale from the sentenc of the last County Court at Boston & being Called three times but not Appearing to prosecute his Ap-

Pitmans Bond for ꝓsecution of Appeale forfeited

peale his bond was declared forfeited & Rob[t] Rose had his Costs tenn shillings & sixe penc

Smith ag[t] Bachiler

Robe[r]t smith plaintiffe in an Action of Appeale ag[t] Nathaniel Batchiler deffend[t] After the Attachment Courts Judgment Reason of Appeale & euidences in the Case produced were Read Comitted to y[e] Jury & are on file w[th] the Reccords of this Cour[t] the Jury brought in their virdict they found for the plaintiff Reuersion of the former Judgment the land in Controuersy & Costs of Courts six pounds twelve shillings & eleven penc =

Gardine[r] ag[t] Pudney costs 21 : 4 wch was payd & 20[s] Repd to Gardin[r] in pt of Rent &c. =

Samuell Gardiner plaintiff ag[t] Jn[o] Pudney Deffendant in an acc͠on of Appeale from the Judgm[t] of the County Court at Salem After the Attachment Courts Judgment Reasons of Appeale & euidences in the Case produced were read Com͠itted to y[e] Jury & are on file wth the Reccords of this Court the Jury brought in their virdict they found for the Deffendant Confirmation of the forme[r] Judgment & Costs of Courts twenty one shillings & fowe[r] penc

Gifford ag[t] Lee

Jn[o] Giffords plaintiff ag[t] Jn[o] Lee deffend[t] in an Action of Appeale from the Judgment of the County Court At Ipswich = After y[e] Attachm[t] Courts Judgment Reasons of Appeale & euidences in the Case produced were read Comitted to y[e] Jury & are on file wth the Reccords of this Court the Jury brought in their virdict they found for the plaintiff Reuersion of the former Judgment & Costs of Courts fowe[r] pounds one shillings * & eight penc

ffood ag[t] Legg exec Issued out for 16[li] 9. 5. 1st Ap[ll] 77

James flood plaintiff ag[t] Samuel Legg deffend[t] in an action of Appeale from the Judgm͠[t] of the County Court at Boston in octobe[r] last After the Attachment Courts Judgm[t] Reasons of Appeale & euidences in the Case produced were Read Comitted to the Jury and are on file the Jury brought in their virdict they found for the plantiff Confirmation of the forme[r] Judgm[t] & an Addition of seuen pounds eleven shillings damage & Costs of Courts two pounds fiue shillings & two pence in all sixteen pounds nine shillings & fiue pence

* Error in the record for "shilling."

Blainy ag^{t} ye Kings 3. 2. 4 of wch [fil.]5^{s}

Jno Blainy plaintiffe ag^{t} Elisabeth King exexutrix & Daniel King Ralph King & Guardians to ye children of the sajd Blainy deffendts in an action of Appeale from the Judgm^{t} of the County Court at Salem After the Attachment Courts Judgment Reasons of Appeale & euidences in the Case produced were Read Comitted to ye Jury & are on file the Jury brought in their virdict they found for the plaintiff Reuersion of the former Judg^{t} & Costs of Courts three pounds two shillings & 4^{d}

[79] 1677

2 Jur Dauis ag^{t} winsley

Samuel Dauis plaintiffe against John Winsley deffendant in an Action of Appeale from the Judgment of the County Court at Boston in octobe^{r} last After the Attachment Courts Judgmen^{t} Reasons of Appeale & euidences in the Case produced were read Comitted to the Jury and are on file wth the Reccords of this Court the Jury brought in their virdict they found for the deffend^{nt} Confirmation of the former Judgment & Costs of Courts = The execution is Respitted till the end of the first sessions of the Generall Court and the sue^{r}tjes to Continue a moneth after =

2 Jur

Vshe^{r} ag^{t} Vsher 2 Ju

Hezekiah Vsher plaintiffe against John Vsher deffendant in an accõn of Appeale from the Judgment of the last County Court in Boston After the Attachment Courts Judgment Reasons of Appeale & euidences in the Case produced were read Comitted to the Jury and are on file wth the Reccords of this Court the Jury brought in their virdict they found for the plaintiffe reuersion of the forme^{r} Judgment & costs of Courts thirty two shillings

Olliuer & ag^{t} Tho Laughton & Select men of Lynne

Capt James Olliuer & Thomas Dexter Jun̄ plt ag^{t} the Toune of lynn[e &] the selectmen of lynn Tho. Laughton & deffend^{ts} in an Accõn of Appeale from the Judgment of the County Court at Ipswich as to a nonsuit = the Accon was called & the Court After hearing the Court of Ipswich Judgment Reasons of Appeale & Ans^{r} thereto in the Case Doe Judge meete to conti[nue] this Action to the determination of the Generall Court vpon the Question whither a clarke of the writts in one Toune hath powe^{r} to graunt Sumons or Attachmen^{ts} in another Toune =

Child ag^{t} Longfello^{w} & Dell
37^{li} * 00 10^{d}

Joseph Dell & Wm Longfellow plaintiffs against Allwin Child deffend^{t} in an action of Appeale from the Judgment of the County Court in Boston in octobe^{r} last After the Attachmen^{t} Courts Judgment Reasons of Appeale & euidences in the Case produced were Read Comitted to the Jury and are on file the Jury brought in their virdict they found for the deffend^{t} Confirmation of the forme^{r} Judgmt & Costs of Courts on y^{e} plaintiff^{s} Request the Bond was chanceried to thirty sixe pounds mony & costs of Courts forty shillings & tenn pence =

Oxe ag^{t} Longfello^{w} & Dell
† 137^{li} : 3^{s}. 4^{d}

Wm Longfellow & Joseph Dell plaintiffs ag^{t} Robe^{r}t Oxe deffendant in an action of Appeale from the Judgement of the County Court in octob^{r} last After the Attachment Courts Judgment Reasons of Appeale & euidences in the Case produced were read Comitted to the Jury & are on file wth the Reccords of this Court the Jury found for the deffendant Confirmation of the form^{r} Judgm^{t} & on the plaintiff^{s} Request the Court chanceried the bond to one hundred thirty fiue pounds mony & Costs of Courts : forty three shillings & fowe^{r} penc :

Lydget Ag^{t} Huson

charles Lydget sue^{r}ty for Anthony Roope plt against Thomas Hughson deffend^{t} in an action of Appeale from the Judgment of the County Court at Salem After the Attachment Courts Judgment Reasons of Appeale & euidences in the Case produced were Read Comitted to the Jury and are remayning on file wth the Reccords of this Court the Jury brought in their virdict they found for the deffendant Confirmation of the former Judgment & Costs of Courts

memto : Bridg 3^{s} 10
filing besids ye othe
8 : 08^{d} er 12 6

[79^{2}] 1677

Leuet p Ballard ag^{t} watts p Ben Dauis

Hudson Leueret Atturney to Jarvis Ballard plaintiff ag^{t} mi[ch]aell watts & his Atturney Benjamin dauis deffendant in an action of Appeale from the Judgm^{t} of the County Court in Boston in octobe^{r} last After the Attach-

* Error for "38^{li}."

† Changed from 127^{li}.

ment Courts Judgment Reasons of Appeale & othe[r] euidences in the Case produced were Read Comitted to the Jury & are on file the Jury brought in their virdict they found for the deffendant Confirmation of the former Judgmen[t] & Costs of Courts = fiueteen shillings & sixepenc.

Knight ag[t] Heath

Richard Knight plaintiff ag[t] Thomas Heath deffend[t] in an Action of Appeale from the Judgment of the Comissione[r]s Court After the Attachm[t] Courts Judgm[t] Reasons of Appeale & euidences in the Case produced were Read Comitted to the Jury & are on file the Jury brought in their virdict they found for the deffendan[t] Confirmation of the former Judgmen[t] & Costs of Courts thirty one shillings & fowe[r] pence. =

Smith ag[t] Lidgett.

m[r] John Smith plaintiff against m[r]s Elizabeth Lydget deffend[t] in an Action of Appeale from the Judgment of the last County Court in Boston after the Attachment Courts Judgment Reasons of Appeale & euidences in y[e] case produced were read Comitted to the Jury & are on file w[th] the Reccords of this Court the Jury brought in their virdict they found for the plaintiff Reuersion of the forme[r] Judgment & costs of Courts thirty fiue shillings & eight penc.

Doudens sentenc Re̅u̅st

Leonard Douden plaintiff on Appeale from the sentenc of the last County Court in Boston After the Reasons of Appeale & euidences in the Case produced were read Comitted to the Jury and are on file the Jury found for y[e] plantiffe y[t] he was no[t] guilty of y[e] matter chardged ag[t] him & Re̅u̅st the forme[r] sentenc

Bullis ag[t] Leueret

Phillip Bullis plaintiff ag[t] Hudson Leueret Administrator to y[e] estate of the late Bazaleell Payton deffendant In an action of Appeale from y[e] Judgment of the last County Court at Boston After the Attachm[t] Courts Judgment Reasons of Appeale & euidences in the Case produced were Read Comitted to the Jury and are on file the Jury brought in their virdict they found for the plaintiff Reuersion of the forme[r] Judgmen[t] & Costs of Courts thirty fowe[r] shillings & ten pence =

phipps ag[t] Hamond =

W[m] Phipps plaintiff ag[t] Elisabeth Hamond in an Action of Appeale from the Judgment of the County Court in octobe[r] last in Boston After the Attachment

Courts Judgmen^t Reasons of Appeale & euidences in the Case produced were Read Comitted to the Jury & are on file the Jury found for the deffend^t Confirmation of the former Judgement three pounds in mony or money^s worth & Costs of Courts thirty fiue shillings & tenn penc

Ans^r to Robe^rt Earles peticon & Courts orde^r to Repajre ye prison

In Answer to Rober^t Earle keeper of the prison in boston his peticon It is ordered that the Tresure^r of the Country & the Tresurer of the County of Suffolke shall & are hereby ordered & Impowred to orde^r mee^t Instruments fforthwith effectually & substantially to repaire the prison that escapes of malefacto^rs may be prevented

[80^1] 1677

Samuel Hunting Guilty of manslaugh^tr

he is fined 20^li to the widow of sajd Jno Dexter

Samuel Hunting of charls Toune was presented by ye Grand Jury and Indicted by the name of Samuel Hunting who at or upon the fowe^rth day of Decembe^r last in the woods by shooting of his gunn in the night did kill the person of John Dexter Contrary to the peace of ou^r Soueraigne Lord the king his Croune & Dignitje the lawes of God & of this Jurisdiction being brought to the barr and y^e Question proposed whithe^r Guilty or no^t Guilty he declared he owned the Indictment & Refferrd himself to the Bench as to his triall =

& 5^li to ye Country wch is Respitted

After the Bench had Considered the euidences & pleas declared they found it to be manslaughter And Judged it meet to fine him the sum̄e of twenty pounds to the widdow of the sajd John Dexter towards hir losse & dam̄age and as a fine to the Country five pounds wch is Respitted till the Court take further orde^r

Darby Bryans sentenc

Darby Bryan Resident in Boston being presented by the Grand Jury & was Indicted by the name of Darby Bryan for his not hauing the feare of God before his eyes & being Instigated by the diuil did in or vpon the one & thirtieth day of January last in the night being found in Bed with Abigaile Johnson Comitt the Act of Adultery Contrary to the peace of ou^r Soueraigne Lord the King his Croune & Dignity the lawes of God and of this Jurisdiction being at the Barr & pleading not Guilty on the question whom he would be trjed by sajd by the Bench The Bench hauing heard the euidence & the pleas in the Case did

Adjudge & sentence him to be^by the marshall Gen^ll or his order from the prison to the Gallowes presently after the lecture in Boston & there Cause him to stand wth a Roape about his necke & fastned thereto one howe^r & then taken doune & tyed to a Carts Tayle and at Left ffrary^s doore stripped from the Girdle vpwards on his naked body to be whipped thence to the prison wth thirty nine stripe^s well layd on & there left till he dischardge the chardge of prosecution ‖ to marshall web 6 6 ‖ & ffee^s of Court =

Abigaile Johnson now resident in Boston being presented by the Grand Jury & was Indicted by the name of Abigaile Johnson for that she not having the feare of God before hir eyes & being Instigated by the Divill did in or vpon the one & thirtieth day of January last in the night being found in bed wth Darby Bryan comitt the act of Adultery wth him Contrary to the peace of our Soueraigne Lord the King his Crowne & dignity the lawes of God & of this Jurisdiction to wch Indictmen^t she pleaded not Guilty & put hirself on the triall on the bench who hauing heard the euidences & pleas in y^e Case did Adjudge & senten[ce] hir the sajd Abigaile Johnson to be carrjed by the marshall Generall or his orde^r to y^e Gallowes &c in like manner as aboue in Darby Bryan^s sentence to suffer in all respects =

Abigail Johnsons Indictm^t

no charges but six shillings & 6^d for y^e marshall Gen̄ as to y^e ex-[ec]ution of y^e sentence & fees of Court =

[80^2] 1677

Marea a Spanish Indian servant to stephen ffrench being presented was Indicted by the name of Marea Indian of weymouth for not hauing the feare of God before hir eyes & being Instigated by the diuill did in octobe^r or nouembe^r last murde^r hir child contrary to the peace of ou^r Soueraigne Lord the king his Croune & dignity the lawes of God & of this Jurisdiction = After the Jury had perused the euidences in that Case produced they brought in their virdict they found hir not Guilty. =

Marea Indictm^t

Robe^rt Dendy bound ouer to Ans^r for his Conveying a Gimblett to Cooly &c prisone^rs that Brake the prison & are escaped After the Court had heard the Case they sentenct him to be seuerely whipt wth twenty stripes or pay the fine of twenty

Dendy^s sentenc

pounds money to the Country. In Answe^r to the peticon of Robe^rt Dendy &c the Cour^t Saw Cause to Remitt the fine to forty shillings & fees of Court = y^e 40^s was pajd in Court & by Return wayt sent to y^e Tresu^r.

An^s to Rebeckah Cooly^s petiĉon =

In Answer to the petition of Rebeckah Cooly wife to Richard Cooly that was Cōmitted to prison in orde^r to his triall &c y^t brake y^e prison & is fled &c The Court Respitts y^e Answe^r to hir peticon till the nex^t Court of Assistants =

Ephraim Beamis

Ephraim Beamis of water Towne being Complayned on & bound ouer to this Court for his trapp[ani]ng & Pandoring of mary Willard by his lying & false Information in orde^r to hir being abused by one Jno oynes vnde^r y^e name of one m^r woodman was brought to the barr & charged therew^th desiring his libe^rty to be tryed by a Jury wch was granted him After the pleas & euidences in the case produced were read Cōmitted to the Jury and are on file the Jury brought in their virdict they found him y^e sajd Ephraim Beamis by lying & false Information Guilty of witting & willing trapaning & pandoring of mary willard to the end that John oynes might Cōmitt Adultery with hir = The Court hath Considered of yor offence whereof yow the sajd Ephraim Beamis stands Convicted and doe sentence yow by the order of the marshall Gennerall or his order to be Carrjed to the Gallowes & there Caused to stand wth a Roape about your neck fastned thereto for one howe^r and then taken doune and tyed to ye Carts tayle & at Leiftenn^t Frary^s to be stripped from the Girdle vpwards: & then Cause the executione^r to whip yow thence to the prison wth thirty nine stripes on yor naked body & there leaue yo^w in prison till yow dischardge the || charge of yor || prosecution & pay ffees of Court — which^

Bill of charge for bringing doune Barker & Dickeson =

Thomas Bell & Henry willis of stonington brought & presented their bill of charges for bringing downe John Dickeson & Benja: Barker that had broake Prison wch came to sixe pounds twelue shillings It is ordered that the Tresurer of the Country Dischardge the sajd bill of charges sixe pounds twelue shillings in mony & chardge it^ the keeper of the prisons Account as to his salle^ry. Robe^rt Earle.*

* The keeper of the prison.

[81] 1677

John winsland being bound ouer to Answe^r for his killing of ^ murdering of william Taylor = The grand Jury * on prvsall of the euidences in y^t case brought in their virdict they found him not Guilty of witting or wilfull murder =

[*Large blank space.*]

[82] 1677 †

Att A Court of Assistants or Court of Admiralty held at Boston 24 May 78 & thenc Adjourned to 28th Instant may =

present
Jno Leueret Esqr Gou:
Symon Bradstreet, Daniel Gookin, Tho Danforth, Edw Tyng, Joseph Dudley — Esq^rs
— — — —
On 28: y^e same & Wm Hathorn Esqr

Thomas Bromhall mate Richard peete^rs Laurence Boales & John Ragland marrine^rs of Catch John and Benjamin plaintiffs by their libell & Complaint exhibbited to this Court 24th may 1678 & Adjourned to 28 Instant at one of the clocke against w^m Long m^r of the sajd Catch Jno & Benjamin deffendant = according to Attachment dated 17th may: 1678. who wth the sajd vessell was Attached and bound ouer in one hundred twenty & sixe pounds to respond the decree & Judgment of this Court for that the sajd Deffendant Refused to pay vnto the sajd mate & Company their seuerall wages i e to y^e s^d Bromhall mate twenty fiue pounds ten shillings or thereabout and to the sajd Peeter a thirteene pounds to sajd Boules a tenn pounds ten shillings & to the sajd Ragland a fiuety shillings for their se^rvice donn in sajd Catch as in sajd Attachment & by euidence & sajd maste^rs Acknowledgement appears After the libell Attachment & euidences in the Case produced were read & are on file the Court found for the plaintiff^s and orde^r & decree that the Deffendant m^r & Catch pay vnto Thomas Bromhall twenty fiue pounds fiue shillings to Richard Peete^rs twelue pounds fiueteene shillings to Lawrence Bowles tenn pounds ^ to Jno Ragland fiuety shillings wth Costs & charges of Court three pounds seven shillings & two pence in all fiuety three pounds seventeen shillings & two pence mony. =

execut: Issued out 29^3: 78.

Olliuer Berry Mate Georg Bucknell w^m Lydston John Potts, Phillip Blansheard Jno Kelsey, Tho Cox; Jacob Halgen charles Broune

* Error of the record for Jury of Trials?

† Error in the original for 1678.

& Edward Blancheard marrine^r^s of the Pincke Endeavo^r^ plaintiffs ag^t^ James Lang master of the sajd Pincke endeavo^r^ deffend^t^ according to libell & Complaint exhibitted to this Court & Attachment dated 27th may 1678. The sajd master & pinke being bound ouer to this Court to Respond the plaintiffs for their seuerall wages for se^r^vice donn in sajd Pincke to value of one hundred twenty & fowe^r^ pounds eight shillings & sixe pence or thereabouts expressed in the ~~Attachment~~ || ffoote of the || sajd libell appeares After the libell pleas & euidences in the Case were read & duely Considered of the Court declared they found for the plaintiffs and did orde^r^ and decree that the deffendant pay vnto olliuer Berry nineteen pounds fowe^r^teene shillings to Georg Bucknell eleven pounds seventeen shillings & sixe pence to Phillip Blansheard tenn pounds eleven shillings to w^m^ Lydston eleven pounds sixe shillings to Jno Potts seventeen pounds eight shillings & six pence to John Kelsey nine pounds eight shillings to Thomas Cox tenn pounds twelve shillings to Jacob Halgen tenn pounds eight shillings to charles Broune nine pounds two shillings & to Edward Blansheard seven pounds two shillings in all one hundred & seventeen pounds eight * shillings mony wth Costs & charges of Court three pounds nine shillings & eight pence in all one hundred & twenty pounds seventeen shillings & eight pence each man defalking sixe shillings & eight penc apeece for their proportion of drink mentioned in ye masters Account.

[*The two following paragraphs are on the margin of the page*]:

James Bell marine^r^ of Catch Betty by his libell plaintiff ag^t^ Edwd North master of sajd Catch deffend^t^ for Remainder of his wages as in s^d^ libell on file is exprest After the libell & euidences in the Case produced were Read &c the plaintiff w^th^drew his Accon paying y^e^ deffend^t^ his Costs thirteen shillings =

memento. novembe^r^ 78 y^e^ marshall left wth me nine pounds seuen shillings & fowe^r^ penc to be Reponded † to y^e^ owno^r^s of James Lang.

[83] 1677 ‡

Att A Court of Assistants or Cour^t^ of Admiralty called & sitting in Boston 1st day of July 1678 and Adjourned to y^e^ 9th July 1678.

Jno Culpepper master of the barcq Called the Recouery by his libell & Complaint plaintiff against John woodmansey deffendant as p

* Error in the record for "nine"? † Error in the record for "Responded"?

‡ Error in the record for "1678."

his sajd libel: exhibited to this Court Appeareth for his the sajd woodmansey arresting the Barcq Recouery & Cargoe on pretence of a debt due to him from Zechariah Gillam to whom the sajd Barcq & Cargoe as he pretends doth belong thereby prejudicing the sajd Culpepper & his owno^rs making a stop of the sajd Barcq & Cargoe to his great Damage to value of one hundred pounds as in s^d libell 24 June ‖ 78 ‖ may appeare After the Court had heard the s^d libell & euidences in the Case produced & Considered the same they found for the plaintiff the deliuery of the sajd ship & Goods in such condition as it was seized & fiue pounds damage & Costs of Court three pounds one shilling all in mony. = ~~fiuety three~~

Jno Joanes marriner belonging to the ship treble Croune by his libell & Complaint plaintiff ag^t w^m Sterry master of the sajd ship deffend^t for that he the sajd sterry m^r & Comande^r of sajd ship hath refused to pay vnto the sajd Joanes eight pounds tenn shillings mony due to him for his wages for his se^rvice donn in sajd ship for fiue months twenty six dayes as in sajd libell is expressed as also for deteyning from him the sajd Joanes his chest cloaths & what is in his chest as Instruments &c being also worth tenn pounds more in money in all the sume of eighteene pounds in mony: After the Attachment libell & euidences in the Case produced were read & duely Considered the Court declared they found for y^e deffendant Costs of Court

[*Blank space.*]

[84] 1678

Att A Court of Assistants held at Boston 3^d of Septembe^r 1678. = & Adjourned to the 5th of Septembe^r Inst.

present
Jno Leueret Esqr Gou
Sam. Symon[s] Esqr dept Gou 5th
Symon Bradstreet 3
Daniel Gookin 3
Daniel Dennison 5
Wm Hawthorn 3
Jno Pynchon 3
Edwd Tyng 3
} Esqr

The Grand Jury brought in their bills of present^t & Indictm^t and were discharged = 6 (7)78.

persons Returnd to serve on the Grand Jury sworne

m^r Wm Parkes
Wm English
Wm Bartholmew
Elisha Hutchinson
Dani. Turill

Isaack waldron plantiff against Wm Hende^rson deffend^t in an accon of Appeale from the Judgment of the County Court in Boston in Aprill last After the Attachment Courts Judgmen^t Reasons of Appeale & euidences in the Case produced

execut Issued out 31 m^rch 78 [dd to Mr Norm]

Ralph Haughton
Jno Pelton
Eljas Row
James Cary
Jonas Clarke
Wm maning
Henry Bright
Jno warren
phillip Torrey
— — — —
persons Returnd to serve on ye 1st Jury for trialls of Appeale & for life &c Sworne
— — — —
Left Samuel Rugles
Stephen Burton
Jno V[ya]ll*
Thomas Bill
Dauid Jones
Jno Swett
mathew Solly.
James Prentice
wm Parry
Nathaniel Coolidg
Toby dauis
Tho. moore insted of Jno Swett in ye Capitol Case only:
— — — —

were Read Comitted to the Jury & are on file wth the Reccords of this Court the Jury brought in their virdict they found for the deffendant Confirmation of the forme^r Judgment & Costs of Courts fiuety three shilling & eight pence

mem to 4s fil:

Isaack Waldron plaintiff agt Thomas Tare deffendt in an action of Appeale from the Judgment of the County Court at Portsmouth after the Attachment Courts Judgment Reasons of Appeale & euidences in the Case produced were read Comitted to the Jury & are on file wth the Reccords of this Court the Jury brought in their virdict i e: In Case the Honoured Court doe Judge ye word day† in the top of the Account to be all one wth the word daw in the bottome of the Account then wee finde for the deffendant the Confirmation of the former virdict wth ye Costs of Courts otherwise wee finde for the Apellant Costs of Courts The magists doe finde for the plaintiff Costs of Courts fowe^r pounds sixteen shillings

Francis Nurse plaintiff against Zerrubbabell Endecot defendt in an action of Appeale from the Judgment of the County Court at Salem After the Attachment Courts Judgment Reasons of Appeale & euidences in the Case produced were read Comitted to the Jury and are on file wth the Reccords of this Court the Jury brought in their virdict they found for the deffendant Confirmation of the forme^r Judgmt & Costs of Courts three pounds nineteen shillings & sixe pence. It is ordered by the Goūno^r & magistrates that execution in this Case be suspended till the plaintiffe make his Aplication to the next Generall Court in octobe^r next. =

[85] 1678

Barnes agt Kemball & Wms &c executi Issued out 22(7): 78
The names of ye persons Returnd to serve on the 2d Jury

James Barnes plaintiffe agt Thomas kemble & Richard Willjams deffendt in An action of Appeale from the Judgment of the Comissione^rs Court last in Boston. After the Attachmt Courts Judgment Reasons of Appeale & euidences in the Case produced were

* Written over "White."

† Day, Ship's Captain. As to the words, see the original papers, Suff. Files, Nos. 1734 and 1773.

read Comitted to the Jury & are on file wth the Reccords of this Court the Jury brought in their virdict they found for ye plantiff Reuersion of the former Judgm^t^ & damage fowe^r^ pounds seventeen shillings & three pence & Costs of Courts fiuety one shillings & tenn penc: in all. 7 : 9. 01 :

|| exec Issued out 22 Sep^t^ 78 E R S. ||

of tryalls for Appeals &c sworne — — — — mr Joseph Beaumis Sampson waters Tho: Stanbury James Halsey Jno white Joy[ne^r^] Jno Betts Jno Smith Tho Greenwood Jno Jackson Richard Satle Caleb Lambe Tho : Bird — — — —

Daniel ffairefeild plaintiff ag^t^ Elizabeth fairefeild deffend^t^ in an action of Appeale from the Judgment of the Comissione^r^s Court in Boston. After the Courts Judgment Reasons of Appeale & euidences in the Case produced were read Comitted to the Jury & are on file wth the Reccords of this Court the Jury brought in their virdict they found for the deffendant Confirmation of the forme^r^ Judgment wth seuen shillings more & Costs of Courts twenty & seuen shillings & tenn penc.

Jno Clary plaintiffe against Benja willington deffend^t^ in an action of Appeale from the Judgment of the las^t^ County Court at Cambridge. After the Attachment Courts Judgment Reasons of Appeale & euidences in the case produced were read Comitted to the Jury and are on file wth the Reccords of this Court the Jury brought in their virdict they found for [the] deffendant Confirmation of the forme^r^ Judgment & Costs of Courts = twenty seuen shillings & fowe^r^ penc

Clary Ag^t^ Willington 14 p 1^s^: 4^d^ due executi Issued out Ap^r^ 29, 1679 E R.

Sarah Alcock: widdow relict of the late Sam Alcock plaintiff against Rich^d^ meade deffend^t^ in an Accõn of Appeale from the Judgment of the County Court in Aprill last in Boston = y^e^ partjes being Agreed the plaintiffe had libe^r^ty & did w^th^draw hir Accõn. =

Alcock ag^t^ mead.

Roge^r^ Rose plaintiff ag^t^ Samuel Stowell deffend^t^ in an action of Appeale from the Judgment of the last County Court in Boston after the Attachment Courts Judgment Reasons of Appeale & euidences in the Case produced were read Comitted to the Jury & are on file wth the Reccords of this Court the Jury brought in their virdict they found for the deffnd^t^ Confirmation of the former Judgment & Costs of Courts forty eight shilling^s^ & three pence =

Rose ag^t^ stowell

48. 3^d^: fil 12

Rich. way & Jn° Endecot agt Benj Alford

Richard way & Jn° Endeco[t] plaintiffs as trustees &c to Martha Emery &c ag[t] Benjamin Alford Atturney to Jn° Sweeting of London Adm[inis]trato[r] to y[e] estate of his son Jn° Sweeting deffend[t] in an Accon of Appeale from the Judgment of the County ^ in July last at Boston After the Attachm[t] Courts Judgment Reasons of Appeale & euidences in the Case produced were Read Comitted to the Jury & are on file w[th] the Reccords of this Court the Jury brought in their virdict they found for the deffend[t] Confirmation of the forme[r] Judgmen[t] & Costs of Courts thirty nine shillings & fowe[r] pence =

execution Issu ^

[86] 16[78]

Hull ag[t] Cooke

Cap[t] Jn° Hull plaintiff ag[t] Elisha Cooke Atturney to Cap[t] Jn° wincoll deffendant in an Action of Appeale from the Judgment of the County Court in Boston in Aprill las[t] After the Attachmen[t] Courts Judgm[t] Reasons of Appeale & euidences in the case produced were Read Comitted to the Jury and are on file wth the Reccords of this Court the Jury brought in their virdict i e If according to law a man may sue as an Atturney Irrevocable in another mans name but for his oune vse & behooffe (of him the sajd Atturney) and yet his Attourniship in any respect not Invallid nor thereby made an Assignee then = wee finde for the deffendant a Confirmation of the forme[r] Judgment & Costs of Courts: If othe[r]wise wee finde for the plaintiff & Costs of Courts In this Case the magists finde for the plaintiff Costs of Courts = fiuety nine shillings =

way &c ag[t] Kent

Richard way & Jn° Endeco[t] trustees &c to martha Emery plaintiffs against w[m] Kent & Richard Knight Atturney[s] to Samuel Hauford deffend[ts] in an action of Appeale from the Judgment of the last County Court in Boston After the Attachment Courts Judg[t] Reasons of Appeale & euidences in the Case produced were Read Comitted to the Jury & are on file wth the Reccords of this Cour[t] the Jury brought in their virdict they found for the deffend[t] Confirmation of the forme[r] Judgment & Costs of Courts three pounds fiueteen shillings and tenn pence =

Turner ag[t] Perry

Jn° Turno[r] plaintiff ag[t] Seth perry deffend[t] in an Accon of Appeale from the Judgm[t] of the Comission[r]s Court in Boston the action Called the partjes being Agreed had libe[r]ty to & did w[th]draw his Action.

George Purkis substitute to charles oughtred Atturney to Samuell Sheaffe of London plaintiff in an action of Appeale agt Jno Palmer yt married wth Sarah Relict & Admnstratrix of the estate of John windor as also against the estate of ye late Robe'rt Gibbs in the hands of Jonathan Corwin that married wth Elisabeth the relict &c of sd Gibbs deffendant from the Judgmt of the County Court last in Boston the Accon was called Courts Judgment Reasons of Appeale & Ansr thereto Read on all ^ was heard the Court ordered yt each ^ partjes have their oune pape'rs Againe =

Purkis agt Palmer & Corwin

In the second Accon of Georg Purkis plt agt the same persons in all Respects like order was declard =

Purkis agt Palmr & Corwin

[87] 1678

Theodeʳ Atkinson plaintiffe against Abraham Perkins deffendt in an Accon of Appeale from the Judgment of the County Court last at Salem: After the Attachment Courts Judgment Reasons of Appeale & euidences in the Case produced were Read Comitted to the Jury and are on file the Jury brought in their virdict they found for the plaintiff Reuersion of the formeʳ Judgment & Costs of Courts foweʳ pounds & foweʳ pence

Atkinson agt Perkins

Jno Putman Nathaniel Putman John Dodge &c plaintiff on Appeale from the sentence of the County Court last at Salem. The plaintiff & majoʳ Hawthorn declaring they were agreed had libe'rty to wthdraw their Accon —

Putmans on Appeale &c

Samuel Apleton Junr plaintiff in an action of Appeale agt majoʳ Thomas Sauage deffendant from the Judgment of the last County Court at Salem After the Attachment Courts Judgment Reasons of Appeale & euidences in the Case produced were read Comitted to the Jury & are Remayning on file wth the Reccords of this Court the Jury brought in their virdi[c]t they found for the deffendant Confirmation of the former Judgment & Costs of Courts foweʳ pounds three shillings & seuen pence = Samuel Apleton Junr in open Court he attainted the Jury: = & Samuel Apleton Junr in two thousan[d] pounds & Samuel Apleton & Wm Dounes his sue'rtjes in a thousand pounds apeece acknowledged themselves respectively bound to the Tresurer of the

Apleton agt Sauage

Beammis forman

Country on Condition that Samuel Apleton Jun̄ prosecute his attaint of the sajd Jury at the nex^t Court of Assistants to effect E R S.

Gifford ag^t Lee

Jno Gifford plaintiff in an action of Appeale from the Judgment of the last County Court at Ipswich = || ag^t Jno Lee deffend^t || After the Attachm^t Courts Judgment Reasons of Appeale & euidences in the case produced were read Comitted to the Jury and are on file wth the Reccords of this Court the Jury brought in their virdict they found for the deffendant Confirmation of the former Judgmen^t & Costs of Courts five pounds eight shillings & tenn ^ & though the bond was desired to be chancerjed the partjes were heard ^ Court declared they saw no Cause to Chancerje the bond. =

Lacy ag^t Keene

Thomas Lacy plaintiff in behalf of Robe^rt oxe ag^t Jno Keene deffend^t in an Action of Appeale from the Judgm^t of the County Court in Aprill last after the Attachment Courts Judgment Reasons of Appeale & euidences in the Case produced were Read Comitted to the Jury & are on file wth the Reccords of this Court the Jury brought in their virdict they found for the plaintiff Reuersion of the forme^r Judgment & Costs of Courts fiuety sixe shillings & tenn pence.

[88] 1678

Lacy ag^t ~~oxe~~ || milott || in ye 1st Case abt y^e bond =

Tho Lacy ꝑ Robt oxe plaintiff ag^t Augustin melott deffend^t in An action of Appeale from the Judgment of the County Court at Cambridge Tho Lacy owned himself to his master m^r oxe Atturney & sajd so Appeared in Cambridge Court & doth so at y^s Court m^r James whetcom̄be one of y^e said oxe suertjes for s^d oxe ꝓsecution of the Appeale owned also y^t he was m^r oxe Atturney & stands by him as such to ꝑsecute ye Appeale as he is bound And so it ꝓceeded After the Attachmen^t Courts Judgment Reasons of Appeale and euidences in the Case produced were Read Comitted to the Jury & are on file wth the Reccords of this Cour^t the Jury brought in their virdict they found for the deffendant Confirm̄g the former Judgmen^t & Costs of Courts

Lacy ag^t melot as to Sallery 2 Acti

Tho. Lacy plaintiff ag^t Augustin melot deffendant in an action of Appeale from the Judgm^t of the County Cour^t at Cambridge After the Courts Judgmen^t Reasons of Appeale & euidences in the Case produced were Read

Comitted to the Jury & are on file wth the Reccords of this Court the Jury brought in their virdict they found for the plaintiff Reuersing the forme[r] Judgm[t] & Costs of Courts three pounds eleven shillings & tenn pence =

Boynton ag[t] Crosse

Joshua Boynton pl[t] ag[t] Stephen Cross deffend[t] in an action of Appeale from the Judgm[t] of the County Court at Ipswich partie[s] being Agree[d] y[e] plaintiff had libe[r]ty to & he did w[th]draw his Accon

ffox ag[t] Jn[o] Leueret Esq[r] Gou

Nathaniel ffox plaintiff ag[t] Jn[o] Leueret Esq[r] Gou defend[t] in an action of Appeale from the Judgment of the last County Court in Boston the Partjes being Agreed the plantiff had his libe[r]ty to & he did w[th]draw his action =

Cardin Drabston[s] Indictm[t]

Cardin Drabston of wate[r]Towne spinster being presented by the Grand Jury was brought to the barr & Indicted by the name of Cardin Drabston se[r]vant to Christophe[r] Grant sen for not hauing the feare of God before hir eyes hauing Comitted fornication & brought forth a child on the thirtjeth day of June last pretending the same to be dead borne not Calling any help at hir trauaile being Instigated by the divill murdered it Concealing it fiue days & then buried it in sajd Grants yard Contrary to y[e] peac of ou[r] Soueraigne Lord the king his Crowne & dignity the lawes of God &^this Jurisdiction, to wch Indictment the prisone[r] at the barr pleaded not Guilty put herself on triall on God & the Country after the euidences ag[t] hir were Read & Comitted wth the Indictmen[t] to y[e] Jury & are on file the Jury brought in their virdict they found hir not Guilty of murder according to Indictment

ordered [she] dischardge the wittness & keep[rs] ffees &c:

[89] 1678

xtophe[r] Grants Jn tryall &c

Christophe[r] Grant Jun of WaterTowne being presented by the Grand Jury was Indicted by the name of christophe[r] Grant Jun for not hauing the feare of God before his eyes being instigated by the diuil hauing Comitted fornication wth Cardin Drabston of sajd water Toune spinster whereby she brought forth a child into the world on 30th of June last which was murdered & kept fiue dayes & then buried it Concealled the murde[r] & made no discouery of it Contrary to the peace of our Soueraigne

Lord the King his Croune & dignity the lawes of God and of this Jurisdiction to which Indictment the prisoner at the barr pleaded not Guilty & put himself on his trjall by God & the Country afte[r] the euidences ag[t] him were read & wth y[e] Indictment Comitted to the Jury the Jury brought in their virdict they found him not Guilty according to Indictment

Mary Hare being presented by the Grand Jury was brought to the barr & was Indicted by the name of mary hare wife of Dauid Hare for not hauing the ffeare of God before you[r] eyes & being Instigated by the Divill did Comitt Adultery in the Absenc of your[r] husband who went hence to virginea about the midle of July 1677 & was absent till the midle of may last Contrary to the peace of our Soueraigne Lord the King his Croune & dignity the lawes of God & of this Jurisdiction to wch Indictment she pleaded not Guilty put hirself on triall on God & the Country = After the euidences produced ag[t] hir were Read Comitted to the Jury & are on file wth the Reccords of this Cour[t] the Jury brought in their virdict they found hir not Guilty according to Indictment

mary Hares Indict[t] for Adultery

Also Mary Hare the wife of Dauid Hare was Indicted by the name of mary Hare for not hauing the feare of God before hir eyes being Instigated by the diuill Comitted Adultery in the Absence of your[r] Husband on 13th August last brought a child into the world & for want of timely help murdered it contrary to the peace of ou[r] Soueraigne Lord the King his Croune & dignity the lawes of God & of this Jurisdiction = to which Indictment she pleaded no[t] Guilty & put hirself on triall on God & the Country. After the Indictment & euidences in the Case produced were Read Comitted to the Jury & are on file w[th] the Reccords of this Court the Jury brought in their virdict they found hir not guilty

Mary Hares Indictm[t] for murder

It is ordered y[t] y[e] prisone[r]s discharge all the charges of witnesses & fees of Court

[90] 1678

Tho Kenny negro to francis wyman being bound ouer to this Court from Cambridge made default & his sue[r]tjes being thrice called ffrancis wyman his sue[r]ty Came afterwards while the Cour[t] was sitting w[th] the negro wch was Accepted = & sajd ffrancis wyman Acknowledged himself to stand bound in the same bond he was bound in to the Tresurer of midlesex for the Appearance of his negro Thomas Kenny at the Court of Assistants Sep[t] 1678 that he shall appeare before the nex[t] Court of Assistants in march next as Attests Edw. Rawson secrety

9th of Sep[t] 1678.

Itt is ordered that the Tresurer of the Country m[r] Jn[o] Hull deliuer & pay vnto major Hauthorne (who is Appointed by the Gennerall Court to keepe hampton & salisbury Courts this yeare^the sume of fiuety shillings mony to enable him thereto: = E R S.

Allexande[r] Colman * being Complayned on for his endeavoring to make disturbance of the people in time of publick worship on the last Lords day in the 3[d] meeting house in Boston by Going in wth only a dirty ffrock of Canvice all bloody & no othe[r] cloaths y[e] Constable hauing Carried him to prison he was sent for & being demanded whenc he came he Came from neuis the last place being Askt why he endeavored to make disturbance to the people of God on y[e] Lords day while they were in the publick worship of God &c The Court Considering yo[r] offence sentenc[t] yow † to be whipt w[th] 15 stripes on y[e] naked bod[y] well lajd on & by y[e] constable to be sent out of Toune putting on his frock

In answe[r] to the petition of m[r]s Hope Ambrose Informing that hir husband m[r] Samuel Ambrose hath absented himself from hir vpwards of fowe[r] yeares & left hir not only w[th]out due prouission for the maintenance of hirself & children but as Appeares by the testimony of w[m] Timbe[r]leg & John Hunt in Jamajca hath broake his marriage Couenant & keepes another woman at Jamajca as his whore & hath || had || carnall fellowship w[th] hir seuerall times || & w[th] others || as he hath boasted The Court Judgeth it meete to declare that he hath broake his marriage Couenant w[th] hir and so she is at libe[r]ty to marry w[th] another man = past E R S

Hope Ambrose divorce

Vpon the difference betweene Hugh march & Dorcas his wife It was put to the Question whither Hugh march and the sajd Dorcas might still lawfully live as man & wife The Court Resolued it on the negative =

Courts Resolue as to Hugh march & Dorcas his wife ||

* Or Calman. † Written over the word "him."

[91] 1678

Att A Court of Assistants or Court of Admiralty held at Boston 14th of octobe^r^ 1678

present
Jno Leueret Esqr
Go^u^
Symon Bradstreet
Daniell Dennison
Tho Danforth
Jno Pinchon
Edwd Tyng
Joseph Dudley
— — — —

m^r^ Dominick Bodkin plaintiffe by his libell & Complaint exhibbited to this Court bearing date 10 Instant ag^t^ m^r^ Robe^r^t Brimsden deffend^t^ for that he the sajd Brimsden hath broken the Charter party by Coming away from virginea wth the vessell called the Beginning & one necke master of ye sajd barcq leauing him in a strajng place & forcing him to his great damage to leaue his Concernes & follow him hither where he hath wayted on him for fiue months if possible to receive sattisfaction &c as in the sajd Attachment Refferenc thereto being had appeares After the plea^s^ & euidences in the Case produced by the parties the Court declared they found for the deffendant Costs of Court twenty eight shillings & fowe^r^ pence =

Att A Court of Assistants || or || Admiralty held at Boston the 8th of nouembe^r^ and Adjourned to the 13th Jnstant 1678

present
Jno Leueret Esqr
Go^u^
Symon Bradstreet
Esqr D G.
Daniel Dennison
Tho Danforth
w^m^ Hauthorne Esq^rs^
Edwd Tyng.—
Nathani: Saltonstall
— — — —

In the Case of Paul Creane Boat swajne of the ship James ffrygott in behalfe of himselfe & Jno ffreeman Gunner Othra Christo^r^pher Carpenter Jno Coale Jno wheatly Jno Smalebones Anthony viner & Joseph Good[uin] marriners of s^d^ ship plaintiff^s^ against sajd ship James ffrygot & Robe^r^t Daniel the now master thereof deffendant according to the libell & Complaint wth the Attachment of sajd Creane bearing date &c for that the sajd Robe^r^t Daniel successor of Solomon Blackleach now master hath refused and doth to pay them their wages as Justly Appeares by their Account Giuen in amounting to seventy one pounds twelue shilling^s^ & fiue pence after the Court had heard the Case pleas & euidences therein produced they declar'd they found for the plaintiffs that the deffendant ship &c pay the plaintiffs their wages in mony seventy one pounds twelue shillings & fiue pence damage & Costs & Charges of Court ffowe^r^ pounds seven shillings =

Dominicke Bodkin merchant plaintiffe against John Necke of Boston marriner late master of the barcq called the beginning deffendant according to libell Complaint & Attachment bearing date the 6th Instant as therein & thereby refference thereto being had more Amply Appeareth After the Court had heard all the pleas & euidences produced by the plaintiffe and deffendant The Court doth order & decree that the deffendant pay the plaintiffe the ballance of the Account three pounds sixteen shillings penny halfe penny wth twenty pounds damage in money and Costs of Court three pounds eleven shillings and sixe pence in all twenty seven pounds seven shillings & seven pence halfe penny =

[92] 1678

In the Case betweene mr wm Taylor mr Richard wharton & Capt Peeter Hawto* Atturneys to Captaine Barnard Lemoigne plaintiff & Capt Tho. white mr Samuel Rauenscro[f]t er & their Complices deffendts for disposing & sharing the Goods of a dutch prize or prizes named the Griffin and Nassaw stranded on the Island nantuckett and taken in the bay of metansis in Cuba by virtue of a Commission granted to the sajd Barnard Lamoigne by m[onseer] Le [Seu] Ponsaw Gouno r for the ffrench king at the Turtudoes and the Coasts of Domingo by wch Comission the sajd Capt Le-moigne was obleidged to returne with his pri[z]es by him taken to Petit Guauare† his Commission Port This Court hauing heard the pleas & Allegations of both partjes doe find for the plaintiff and doe Adjudge that the sajd dutch prize Called the Griffyn wth all hir Goods and other moneys or estate taken in the sajd shipps ought to haue binn Carrjed to the said Comission Port, and therefore doe decree that the sajd ships & Goods & money produced by the sale of any of the sajd goods and all other moneys & estate taken in the sajd ships be deliuered to the sajd Capt La-moigne or his Atturneys; he or they giuing bond with sufficient suertjes to value of fower thousand pounds that the sajd ship & goods shall wth all convenient speed (the dainger of the seas excepted ^ be sajled and brought to the sajd Port for the behooffe of the sajd le-moigne & Company taking wth him either all if they be willing or so many of them as shall be sufficient to make their pleas for their shares & Interest as also Henry Jacob the Gunner of the sajd ship who hath petitioned this Court on behalfe of his ownors that he may there make his pleas And In Case the sajd Le-moigne or his Atturneys shall refuse or neglect to give in bond as aforesajd at or before the 15th of the next moneth then the sajd ship & goods shall be seized & remajne in such officers ^ as shall

* "Otto" in the County Court Record. † Or Guanare.

be appointed by the Gou̅nor & Council till furthe^r^ orde^r^ be taken and the deffend^t^ to pay Costs of Court twenty fiue pounds twelue shillings & sixe pence = y^s^ Court is dissolued

Att a Court of Admiralty or Cour^t^ of Assistants held at Boston 2^d^ January 1678

Henry Wheeler late master of the ship Recouery in behalfe of himself & owno^r^s by his libell & complaint exhibbited to this Court bearing date 28th of Decembe^r^ 1678, plaintiffe against m^r^ Anthony Cheeckly and ljdia his wife formerly the wife of the late Benjamin Gibbs & Adminstratrix to his estate deffendant In an Accõn of the Case largely exprest in the aboue mentioned libell and is for not sattisfying him for the hire of sajd ship Recouery for eight months & one third of a moneth at thirty fiue pounds ℘ moneth wch amounts to two hundred ninety one pounds thirteene shillings & fower pence as also for chardges & disbursments and what one Recoured for his wages as in the sajd libell is exprest as by sajd wheelers oath on file &c = After the Attachment and

[93] 1678

euidences in the Case produced were read & duely Considered of the Court declared they Adjudged and did order and decree for the plaintiffe after the deduction of the late Benjamin Gibbs Credit the summe of three hundred sixty two pounds fiueteen shillings and fiue pence in money out of the estate of the late Benjamin Gibbs y^e^ Costs of Court [five ?] pounds [12^s^] shillings ‖ 6^d^ ‖ being included in y^t^ sume aboue =

This Court was dissolued = E R S.

Att A Court of Admiralty or Court of Assistants held at Boston 15th may 1679 and Adjourned to 29th may 1679 *

present
Symon Bradstreet ‖ Esqr ‖ Gou̅
Sam Danforth Esqr Dep^t^ Gou̅
Daniel Gookin
Daniel Dennison
Wm Hawthorne
John Pinchon
Edwd Tyng
Joseph Dudley
Nathan[^ll^] Saltonstall
Humphry Davy
Esq^rs^
— — — —

John ffrancis Boatswayne John Middleton Carpenter John Todd Peter ffletcher & Richard Derry marriners of & lately belonging to the ship Endeavo^r^ plaintiff^s^ Against Samuel Smith Comande^r^ of sajd ship endeavo^r^ deffend^t^ for Refusing to pay them their seuerall wages in mony to the said ffrancis

* This and the three following records of admiralty courts were evidently entered by the Secretary out of their chronological order. They should have been entered after the record of the March term, 1678-9, which ends on page 98 of the original.

after the Rate of forty fiue shillings ℘ month till y[e] s[d] ship arrived at Barbadoes & from that time forty eight shillings ℘ moneth, to John Todd after the Rate of thirty three shillings ℘ moneth & to Peter ffletcher & Richard Derry their wages after the Rate of thirty two shillings ℘ moneth & John midleton his wages after the Rate of three pounds tenn shillings ℘ moneth as by the Portlidge bill may Appeare & m[r]s Acknowledgment in Court After the libell Attachment & euidences in the Case produced were Read & duely Considered The Court orde[r]s & determine for the sajd Boatswajne & seamen fiuety fowe[r] pounds ten shillings money as their full wages to be diuided in proportion amongst them at the Rates vpon which they were shipped as in s[d] libell & Complaint defaulking what they haue Received of the saj[d] m[r] & Costs of Court fower pounds nineteen shillings & two pence. ═

Att A Court of Assistants or Admiralty held at Boston 31 may 1679

present as aboue ═ Goū Dep[t] Goūno[r] &c as

Phillip welch Thomas Smith & Peeter michael marriners of the Catch olliue branch by their libell & Complaint exhibbited to this Court plaintiff ag[t] Edward Barnes master of sajd Catch & sajd Catch deffendant for that the sajd Edward Barnes Refuseth to pay unto Peeter welch his wages for eleven months & a halfe se[r]vice at forty shillings ℘ mo twenty three pounds money and to Thomas Smith for his wages for tenn mon[ths] one half at twenty seuen shillings ℘ month fiueteene * pounds three shillings & sixe penc and to Peete[r] mitchell for his wages fowe[r]teen pounds fowe[r]teen shilling[s] in all fiuety one pounds seventeen shillings & sixpenc mony After the libell & Complaint & euidences were Read & duly considered The Court Judged it meet to declare and decree that the sajd Edward Barnes y[e] master & sajd Catch pay vnto the aboue sajd Plaintiffs the sajd some of ffiuety two pounds seven shillings † & sixe pence mony & Costs of Court three pounds eight shilling[s] deducting what they haue Received ═ ‡ In Ans[r] to the peticon of Elizabeth Lisley The Court on pervsall & consideration of the euidences in the Case doe grant the peticone[r]s request and doe declare hir to be freed from hir Couenant of marrjage made w[th] y[e] aboue named Robert Lisley § : — :

welch &c ag[t] Catch olliue Branch

Elizabeth Lysleys diuorce

* Fourteen ?

† Fifty-one pounds seventeen shillings ?

‡ What follows here was probably inserted at a later date.

§ His name does not appear before in the record.

[94] 1679

present
Symon Bradstreet Esq[r] Gou
Thom: Danforth Esq dep[t] Gou
Daniel Gookin
W[m] Hauthorn
Jn[o] Pynchon
Edw[d] Tyng
Joseph Dudley
Humphry Davy
Esq[rs]

Att A Court of Assistants or Court of Admiralty sitting in Boston the 14[th] of June 1679

Samuel Smith Comander of the ship endeavou[r] plaintiff in behalfe of himself & owno[r]s ag[t] John ffrancis Jn[o] midleton John Todd &c according to his libell ^ Attachm[t] bearing date 12 June 79 After the Courts pervsall of the sajd libell & euidences in the Case produced The Court Adjudged for the plaintiff & doe Orde[r] & decree that the deffendant[s] pay the plaintiffs fowe[r] pounds damage in mony & three pounds fiueteen shilling & fowe[r] pence as Costs ═

The Deposition of Thomas Sexton now master of the ship Elizabeth being in London in the month of february last past did receive A ve[r]ball direction or orde[r] from old m[r] Elkin to keepe a bayle of Goods or deliuer it vnto m[r] John wayte In Case his son Nathaniel Elkin were dead the which Bajle of Goods doth belong vnto m[r] Edward Bass merchant in London & the Cause of old m[r] Elkin his giving such orde[r] vnto me was because he himself as he told me stood bound vnto m[r] Basse that his sonn Nathaniel Elkin should make him the sajd Bass Returnes for the goods the Bayle is marked NE no 7

deposed in Court 14 June 1679. ꝑ Edw. Rawson secre[ty]

Att A Court of Assistants or Admiralty held at Boston 25th octobe[r] 1679

willjam marston mate John Anay Boatswajne nicholas Ginnop Gunner Edward North Hugh may Jacob ketore Henry Gabricke George wood michael Caswell Thomas mande[r] & John Perrin marriners belonging to the ship Apollow ××* & Henry Hollaway m[r] of s[d] ship defend[t] for that he sajd Hollaway m[r] Refuseth to pay the aboue mentioned w[m] marston mate Jn[o] Anay Boat swayne nicholas Gunnop Gunner w[th] y[e] s[d] marrine[r]s their seueral wages for their se[r]vice performed in s[d] ship for seven mon[ths] & eight dayes from Jamajca to the Lagoone of Tr[o[s]] † in y[e] bay of Campeacha & thenc to Boston as ꝑ portlidg Bill &c as ꝑ Attachm[t]

Henry Holloway appeard in Court & owned y[t] y[e] seuall sums mentioned ×× in the libell was & Is Justly due to y[e] seuall seamen to be p[d] y[em] in mony here only had no[t] effects in his hands to dischardg them ××

* These marks are in the original. † Terminos ?

dated in Boston 21th octobe^r^ 1679 may Appeare x x after the Court had heard the pleas of plaintiff & deffend^t^ they did determine order & decree that the sajd ship Apollow & sajd master || thereof || Henry Holloway should pay vnto the plaintiffs. i: e. to w^m^ marston mate for his wages twenty one pounds sixteen shillings being 3^li^ ꝑ mon'h to John Annay twenty one pounds sixteen shillings to Nicholas Gunnop Gunner after 40^s^ ꝑ mo. fowe^r^teen pounds twelue shilling to Hugh may after 39^s^ ꝑ mo. fowe^r^teene pounds fowe^r^ shillings to Jacob Katore fowertene pounds fowe^r^ shillings to Henry Gabrick after thirty fiue shilling ꝑ mo. twelue pounds fiueteene shillings & six pence to Georg wood ye like twelue pounds fiueteen shilling & sixe penc to michael Caswell the like twelue pounds fiueteen shillings & six pence To Thomas mander at 29^s^ ꝑ mo. tenn pounds eleven shillings and six pence & to Georg Perrin after 30^s^ ꝑ mo. tenn pounds nineteen shillings each mans time being 7 mo & 8 dayes in all, one hundred sixty one pounds on[e] shilling * all in money wth costs of Court fowe^r^ pounds fowe^r^ shillings & sixe pence mony.

[95] 1678

Att A Court of Assistants held at Boston 4th march 1678.

present
Jno Leueret Esqr Gou̅n^r^
Symon Bradstreet Esqr dep Go.
Daniel Gookin, Daniel Dennison, Tho: Danforth, Edw Tyng, Joseph Dudley, Natha̅ Saltonstall — Esq^rs^

Grand Jurymen Returnd & Sworn were
m^r^ w^m^ Parkes
Edwd Drincker
Jno Harrison sen̄
ffrancis Hudson
moses Payne
Tho Tollman
Thomas Trott
w^m^ Gary
Randall Nicholls
Aron Ludkin
Samuel Andrewes
Richd Dana
Tho fflegg

Samuel Apleton Jun̄ plaintiff in an Acc̄on of Attaint from the last Court of Assistants ag^t^ the Jury there whereof m^r^ Joseph Beamis was foreman deffendts the plaintiffe and deffendant Appeared pleaded to the Case both lette^r^s of Atturney was produced & owned in Court after all the pleas and euidences in the Case produced were heard Read & Comitted to the Jury the Jury brought in their virdict they found for the plaintiffe Reuersion of the forme^r^ Judgment & Costs of Courts sixe pounds sixteen shillings =

Mary ffigg plaintiffe against Thomas Bake^r^ deffend^t^ In an action of Appeale from the Judgment of the last County Court in Boston After the Attachment Courts Judgment Reasons of Appeale & eui- 20^li^ mony

* This amount indicates that Edward North's share (fourteen pounds twelve shillings ?) was omitted by the Secretary in making up his record.

wm Goddard

— — — —

Jury men Returned for Appeales life limbe &c sworne were ~~1st Jury~~

|| for ye Attaint ||

— — — —

mr Jno Long.
wm whitwell
wm Hobby
Jervas Ballard
Jacob Hewins
Henry Leadbetter
James white
Obadia Hawes
Tho. Edwards
Tho walker
Tho Bligh sen̄
Jno waite
Jno may
Joseph Griggs
Jno Ruggles
Samuel Craft
Nath Rand
Jno Trumball
wm Agur
stephen ffrancis
ffrancis Boman
Jno Benjamin
Jno Trajne
Jno Neuisson

— — — —

dences in the Case produced were read Com̄itted to the Jury and remajne on file wth the Reccords of this Court the Jury brought in their virdict they found for the deffendant Confirmation of the former Judgment & costs of Courts. [32s.]

Jno Pickard & Ezekiel Northend plaintiffs in an action of Appeale agt Wm * Longfellow deffendt from the Judgment of the last County Court in Salem † = After the Attachment Courts Judgment Reasons of Appeale and euidences in the Case produced were Read Comitted to the Jury and are on file wth the Reccords of this Court the Jury brought in their virdict i:e a speciall virdict origine &c ‡ the Court finds for the deffendant Confirmation of the Judgment of the bench at Salem Court & Costs of Courts fiuety nine shillings & eight pence

Tho Leauer sen̄ plaintiff in an action of Appeale agt Phillip Nelson deffendt from the Judgment of the last County Court at Ipswich Atturneys in ys Ac̄on Appearing & shewing their power the plaintiff declaring that the Ac̄on was Agreed wth consent of ye Court wth drew his Ac̄on =

James Smith plaintiff agt michael Bouden deffendant in an action of Appeale from the Judgment of the County Court at Salem After the Attachmt Courts Judgment Reasons of Appeale & euidences in the Case produced were read comitted to the Jury and are on file wth the Reccords of this Court the Jury brought in their virdict they found for the deffendant the Confirmation of the former Judgment at Salem Court i e thirty nine pounds two shillings & Costs of Courts forty fower shillings & fower pence =

James Smith plaintiffe against michael Bouden deffendant in an action of Appeale from the Judgment of the County Court last in Boston After the Attachment Courts Judgment Reasons of Appeale & euidences in the Case produced were Read Comitted to the Jury & are

* Written over "Jno."   † Written over "Boston."

‡ For details of this case see Court Files Suffolk No. 1792, where is the original special verdict at the County Court, and also a copy of the record of the Court of Assistants, attested by the Secretary, more full and differing somewhat from this.

on file wth the Reccords of this Court the Jury brought in their virdict they found for the deffend^{t} Confirmation of the forme^{r} Judgmen^{t} [&] Costs of Courts thirty two shillings & fowe^{r} pence =

Capt James Olliuer & Tho: Dexter plaintiffs against the Towne of lynn deffend^{t} in an action of Appeale from the Judgment of the last County Court at Salem. After the Attachment Courts Judgment reasons of Appeale & euidences in the Case produced were read Comitted to the Jury & are on file wth the Reccords of this Court the Jury brought in their virdict they found for the defendant Confirmation of the former Judgm^{t} & Costs of Courts fiue pounds fowe^{r}teen shillings & two pence =

[96] 1678

Richard Acco^{r}man plaintiffe against Thomas vallentine deffendant in an Accõn of Appeale from the Judgment of the last County Court at Boston After the Attachment Courts Judgment Reasons of Appeale & euidences in the Case produced were read Comitted to the Jury and are on file wth the Reccords of this Court the Jury brought in their virdict & found for the deffendant Confirmation of the forme^{r} Judgment ^ Costs of Courts thirty two shillings

Exec Issued out

pe^{r}sons Returnd to serve on the 1st Jury of trialls for Appeales for life limbe &c sworne were =

— — — —

m^{r} John Neuison
James white
Henry Leadbetter
Tho Langhorne
Jno wayte
Jno Rugles
Samuel Craft
Joseph Ryall
Nathaniel Rand
w^{m} Agur
ffrancis Boman
Jno Trajne

— — — —

Thomas Clarke plaintiffe against John Allin deffendant in an action of Appeale from the Judgmen^{t} of the last County Court at Hampton. After the Attachment Courts Judgment reasons of Appeale & euidences in the Case produced were read Com̃itted to the Jury & are on file wth the Reccords of this Court the Jury brought in their virdict they found for the deffendant Confirmation of the former Judgm^{t} & Costs of Courts = three pounds twelue shillings =

exec Issued out 8 1 78

persons Returnd to se^{r}ve on the 2^{d} Jury of tryall for Appeale life limbe &c sworne =

— — — —

m^{r} Jno Long
Wm Hobby
Jaruis Ballard
Jacob Hewin
Tho Bligh
Jno man
Daniell Turell Junr
obadiah Hawes
Joseph Griggs
stephen ffrancis
Jno Benjamin
Symon Coolidge

— — — —

Joseph knight plaintiff ag^{t} Sam: Peacocke deffend^{t} in an action of Appeale from the Judgm^{t} of the Commissione^{r}s Court in Boston After the Attachment Courts Judgment Reasons of Appeale and euidences in the Case

exec Issued out 7 may 79 for 3 : 12 : 6

produced were read Comitted to the Jury and are remayning on file wth the Reccords of this Court the Jury brought in their virdict they found for the deffendant Confirmation of the former Judgment & Costs of Courts twenty sixe shilling^s^ & sixe pence

y^e^ bill 12^li^

exec Issued out

Theode^r^ Atkinson plaintiffe against Abraham Pe^r^kins deffendant in an action of Appeale from the Judgment of the County Court at Ipswich = After the Attachment Courts Judgment Reasons of Appeale & euidences in the Case produced were read Comitted to the Jury & are Remayning on file wth the Reccords of this Court the Jury brought in their virdict they found for the deffendant Confirmation of the former Judgm^t^ & Costs of Courts =

Atkinson ag^t^ Pe^r^kins

exec Issued out

Theode^r^ Atkinson plaintiff against Abraham Pe^r^kins deffend^t^ in an accon of Appeale from the Judgment of the County Court at Salem last after the Attachment Courts Judgment Reasons of Appeale & euidences in the Case presented were Read Comitted to the Jury & are on file wi^th^ the Reccords of this Court the Jury brought in their virdict they found for the deffend^t^ Confirmation of the forme^r^ Judgment & Costs of Courts three pounds seven shillings & fowe^r^ pence =

Roby & boulte^r^ ag^t^ Evans

executi: Issued out 11 1/mo 78.

Henry Roby & Nathaniel Boulter plaintiff ag^t^ Robe^r^t Evans ‖ deft ‖ in an Action of Appeale from the Judgment of the County Court last at Hampton after the Attachment Courts Judgment Reasons of Appeale & euidences in the Case produced were Read Comitted to the Jury & are on file wth the reccords of this Court the Jury brought in their virdict they found for the plaintiff Reuersion of the forme^r^ Judgm^t^ & Costs of Courts

[97] 1678

Boulter ag^t^ wilson

Nathaniel ~~Moore~~ ‖ Boulter ‖ & w^m^ moore plaintiff ag^t^ Humphry wilson defend^t^ in an Action of Appeale from the Judgment of the last County Court at Hampton After the Attachment Courts Judgm^t^ & Reasons of Appeale wth y^e^ euidences in the Case produced were read Comitted to the Jury and are on file wth the Reccords of this Court the Jury brought in their virdict they found for the deffendant Confirmation of the forme^r^ Judgm^t^ & Costs of Courts ffiuety nine shillings & tenn pence =

m^r^ Jonathan Tyng plaintiff ag^t^ nicholas chadwell deffendant in an action of Appeale from the Judgment of the County Court at Salem After the Attachm^t^ Courts Judgment Reasons of Appeale & euidences in the Case produced were read Comitted to the Jury & are on file wth the Reccords of this Court the Jury brought in their virdict they found for the plaintiff reusion of the forme^r^ Judgment & Costs of Court thirty * fiue shillings

Tyng ag^t^ Chadwell

exec Issued out

Nathaniel Jacob plaintiff ag^t^ Ephrajm & Isack ffellowes deffend^t^ in an action of Appeale from the Judgment of the County Court at Salem After the Attachment Courts Judgment Reasons of Appeale & euidences in the Case produced were read Comitted to the Jury & are on file wth the Reccords of this Court the Jury brought in their virdict they found for the deffendant Confirmation of the forme^r^ Judgment & Costs of Courts = three pounds fiueteen shillings & 4^d^ =

Jacob ag^t^ ffellowes

m^r^ Hezekiah Vshe^r^ plaintiff against John Vshe^r^ deffend^t^ in an Accon of Appeale from the Judgmen^t^ of the County Court in Boston in octobe^r^ last After the Courts Judgmen^t^ Reasons of Appeale & euidences in the Case produced were read Comitted to the Jury & are on file wth the Reccords of this Cour^t^ the Jury brought in their virdict they found for the defend^t^ Confirmation of the forme^r^ Judgm^t^ & Costs of Courts the plaintiff desired his bond might be chanceried the Court on Consideration of the pleas on both sides chanceried the bond sued to fiuety pounds mony & Costs ffiuety two shillings & 6^d^.

Vsher ag^t^ Vsher

Jno man Plaintiffe ag^t^ majo^r^ Thomas Savage deffend^t^ in an action of Appeale ffrom the Judgmen^t^ of the Comissione^r^s Court in Boston The Accon was Called the Reasons not being Given in season i e Daylight The Court declared the Accon ought no^t^ to proceed & ye Court Granted the deffendt his Costs

man Ag^t^ Sauage

Abell Porter plaintiff ag^t^ Edwd Cater deffend^t^ in an Accon of

* Written over the word "twenty."

Porter agt Cater

Appeale ffrom the Judgment of the Court of Associats at Portsmouth: this Accon was also Called no Reasons Returned so the Accon fell & Costs granted to the deffendt & the bond declard to be forfeited =

Gatchells Indictmt er

Bethyah Gatchel was presented & Indicted by the name of Bethiah Gatchell for not hauing the feare of God before hir eyes & being instigated by the diuill Comitted Adultery Contrary ^ the peace of our Soueraigne Lord the King his Croune & dignity the lawes of God & of this Jurisdiction to wch she pleaded not Guilty put hirself on tryall by God & the Country ~~they~~ the Jury finds hir not Guilty according to Indictment the Court enjoyned hir to Appeare before the next County Court at Ipswich to Ansr for hir notorious lying er dischardging fees of Court & Costs of prosecution to be dischardged [Skerry]* Costs 21s allowed

[98] 1678

Ellinor may being Indicted & by the virdict of the Jury of tryalls legally Convicted of whoredome & of hauing a Bastard child in hir husbands absence is sentenced to be tyed to a Carts Tayle & whipt vpon hir naked body from the Prisson to the place of hir aboad not exceeding thirty nine stripes well & seuerely layd on, and also to depart out of the Toune of Boston wth in tenn dayes next Comeing after hir Correction and not to returne againe wthout licence from the Gounor or two magistrates vnder his or their hands in writting and in Case after that time the sajd Elljnor may shall be found in Boston or any of the precincts thereof Contrary to this Order she shall be Apprhended by the Constable on notice given by any of the Inhabitants of the sajd Toune & Comitted to Bridewell there to remajne vntill the Councill or Court of Assistants shall Give further order Concerning her: she dischardging ffees of Court & Costs of wittnesses to be dischardged =

Ellinor mays Sentenc

In Ansr to the peticon of Rebeckah Coolys as to a divorce The Court Judgeth it meet to declare that on pervsal of the euidences agt Richard Cooly that the sajd Rebeckah is free and set at liberty frō hir marriage Couenant wth hir sajd Husband Richard Cooly =

— — — —

Boston 19 mrch 1678/9

vnder a true Copie of the Judgment of this Court in the Case betweene mr Hezekiah vsher plaintiff agt

* Henry Skerry of Salem, marshal ?

mr Jno vsher as on ye other side of this page is word for word stands vnder writt & endorst as followeth Received the sume of fiuety one pounds nineteen shillings & eight pence of mr Hezekiah Vsher Junior in mony by virtue of the wthin written or aboue Judgment of a Court of Assistants as aboue expressed — 50 : 19 8 * wittnes maudit Engis (endorst ℘ John Vsher = march 20 78/9

Maudet Engis of Boston Aged about seventy yeares being deposed before vs doth say that he sawe mr Hezekiah vsher on the 19th day of this Instant pay his brother mr John Vsher of Boston the sume mentioned in the Receipt on the back side vnder the Copy of the Judgment of the Court of Assistants and that he saw mr John Vsher to signe and deliuer the sajd Receipt and did put his hand as a witnes thereof sworne by maudet Engis the day & yeare aboue written before vs

Daniel Gookin
Edward Tyng

Entred & Recorded in perpetuam Rei memoriam At Request of the sajd mr Hezekiah Vsher the 3d day of July 1679

p Edwd Rawson secret

[99] 1678

Att A Court of Assistants held at Boston the 2d of September 1679

present
Symon Bradstreet Esq Gou
Tho Danforth Esqr dept Go.
Daniel Gookin
Daniel Dennison
Wm Hathorn
Edward Tyng
Joseph Dudley
Nathaniel Saltonstall
Humphry Davy
Esqrs

Trystram Coffin Atturney to Richard Lowle & Capt wm Gerrish plaintiffs agt Benjamin Lowle deffendant in an Accon of Appeale from the Judgmt of the County Court at Ipswich After the Attachment Courts Judgment Reasons of Appeale & euidences in the Case produced were read Comitted to the Jury & are on file wth the Reccords of this Court the Jury brought in their virdict they found for the plaintiff reuersion of the former Judgment & Costs of Courts sixe pounds nineteen shillings & eight pence
1st Jry

— — — —
persons Returnd to serve on ye Grand Jury sworne were
— — — —
Capt Daniel Henchman
John Blake
Richrd woody
Jno Conney
John Scarlett

* The amounts given here in the record do not agree with each other or with the amount stated in the record of the judgment. See above p. 137 for the judgment referred to.

Tho Tyleston
Tho Dauenport
Wm Clough
Jno Pentecost
Jonas clarke
Wm maning
Wm Bond.
— — — —
persons Returnd to serve on ye 1st Jury of tryalls for Appeales life lymbe & sworne were
— — — —
mr Anthony checkley
Thomas Edwards
Bozoone Allen
Thomas Jenner
Jacob Green Jun̄
Ezra Clap:
Timothy Tyleston
Samuel Andrewes
noah wisewalle
John Bisco
John Morse
Daniel Brewer
— — — —

Stephen Butler plaintiffe against willjam Hollowell Jun̄ Benja Hollowell & Edward Ashley deffendts in an action of Appeale from the Judgment of the last County Court at Boston After the Attachment Courts Judgment Reasons of Appeale & euidences in the Case produced were read Comitted to the Jury & are on file wth the Reccords of this Court the Jury brought in their virdict they found for the deffendants a Confirmation of the fformer Judgment ~~In part that~~* In part that is to say the moyety of the houses & lands which belonged to the estate of Benjamin Ward according to Inventory or fower hundred pounds in money & Costs of Courts ffiuety sixe shillings & tenn pence =

2d Ju.

Abraham Broune of [Salis]bury plaintiff against Samuel ffellowes deffendant in an Action of Appeale from the Judgment of the last County Court at Salisbury After the Attachment Courts Judgment reasons of Appeale and euidences in the Case produced were read Comitted to the Jury and are on file wth the Reccords of this Court the Jury brought in their virdict they found for the plaintiff Reuersion of the former Judgment & Costs of Courts three pounds fower shillings & fower pence =

2d Ju.

1st Ju

willjam Griggs plaintiff agt peeter chocke deffendt in an Accon of Appeale from the Judgment of the ~~Comissione's~~ ‖ County ‖ Court in Boston: After the Attachment Courts Judgment Reasons of Appeale & euidences in the Case produced were Read Com̄itted to the Jury and are on file wth the Reccords of this Court the Jury brought in their virdict they found for the deffendant Confirmation of the former Judgment & Costs of Courts = twenty shillings & sixe pence

Stephen Bussell plaintiff Against samuel Ballat deffendant in an action of Appeale from the Judgment of the County Court at charlsToune After the Attachment Courts Judgment Reasons of Appeale & euidences in the Case produced were∧Comitted to the Jury & are on file wth the Reccords of this Court the Jury brought in their virdict they found for the plaintiff reuersion of

2d Jur

* Written over the words "& Costs of Courts" and then both cancelled.

the forme^r Judgment & Costs of Courts forty three shillings & two pence :

Peeter chocke plaintiff ag^t Nathaniel Peirce deffendant in an action of Appeale from the Judgment of the Comissione^rs Court in Boston After the Attachment Courts Judgmen^t Reasons of Appeale & euidences in the Case produced were Read Comitted to the Jury & are on file wth the Reccords of this Court the Jury brought in their virdict they found for the deffendant Confirmation of the forme^r Judgm^t & Costs of Courts sixteen shillings & tenn pence

[100] 1679

George Purkis Atturney to Laurence Baske^rvill plaintiff against the Goods or estate lately belonging unto John windor merchant in the hands of John Palmer who marrjed the relict & Admnstratrix of y^t estate & the Goods or estate belonging to the late Robe^rt Gibbs as also the Goods of James whetcomb deffend^ts in an Acc̄on of Appeale from the Judgment of the County Court in Boston After the Attachment Courts Judgment Reasons of Appeale & euidences in the Case produced were read Comitted to the Jury & are on file the Jury brought in their virdict they found for the deffendants Costs of Courts thirty fiue shillings & tenn pence. 1st Ju

persons Returnd to serve on ye 2^d Jury for trialls of Appeales life ljmbe & sworn

mr Edward Willis
Robe^rt Howard
Thomas moore
Eljas Row
Elljce Wood
Richd Norcross
Thomas streight
w^m Gary
John Gore
Thomas Longhorne
w^m Coleman
James Hubbard

Henry Allin & Company plaintiff ag^t w^m Tomljn deffend^t in an Acc̄on of Appeale from the Judgment of the County Court in Boston After the Attachment Courts Judgment Reasons of Appeale & euidences in the Case produced were Read Comitted to the Jury & are on file wth the reccords of this Court the Jury brought in their virdict they found for the deffendant Costs of Courts eighteen shillings & fowe^r pence / 1st Jury

John Veren plaintiffe against John ffros^t deffendant in an action of Appeale from the Judgment of the Comissione^rs Cour^t in Boston After the Attachment Courts Judgment reasons of Appeale & euidences in the Case produced were read Comited to the Jury & are on file wth the Reccords of this Court the Jury brought in their virdict they found for the deffend^t thirty

veren ag^t frost

two yrds of noyl'es Canvas at 18d ℘ yrd or forty eight shilling and sixe penc money & Costs of Courts twenty two shillings & 4d.

2 Jur.

woodbridge agt Hendrick
exec Issued out 26 Apr 83

Thomas Woodbridge Atturney & suerty to Capt Paul white plaintiff agt Jotham* Hendrick deffendt in ^ Accon of Appeale from the Judgment of the County Court at Salisbury. After the Attachment Courts Judgmt Reasons of Appeale & euidences in the Case produced were read Comitted to the Jury and are on file wth the Reccords of this Court the Jury brought in their virdict they found for the deffendt Confirmation of the former Judgment & Costs of Courts thirty shillings =

2 Jury

Idem agt Heath

heath Apprd not er

Thomas woodbridge Atturney & suerty to Capt Paul white plaintiff against Josiah Heath deffendant in an Accon of Appeale from the Judgment of the County Court at Salisbury After the Attachment Courts Judgment Reasons of Appeale & Euidences in the Case produced were Read Comitted to the Jury & are on file wth the Reccords of this Court the Jury brought in their virdict they found for the deffendant Confirmation of the former Judgment & Costs of Courts =

1st Jur

Legg agt flood

Samuel Legg plaintiff against James fflood defendant in an action of Appeale from the Judgment of the last County Court at Boston After the Attachment Courts Judgment Reasons of Appeale & euidences in the Case produced were read Comitted to the Jury and are on file wth the Reccords of this Court the Jury brought in their virdict they found for the plaintiff three pounds nine shillings & nine pence damage in mony & Costs of Courts.

[101] 1679

Rock agt ffranks

Joseph Rock plaintiff agt Sarah ffrancks widdow deffendt in an Accon of Appeale from the Judgment of the County Court in Boston After the Attachment Courts Judgmt Reasons of Appeale & euidences in the Case produced were Read Comitted to the Jury and are Remayning on file wth the Reccords of this Court the ~~Jury brought in their virdict~~ ^ † to whome it only belongd

* Written over "Abraham."

† There is evidently an omission here in the record of the word "magistrates."

hauing on s[d] Rocks Request chanceried his bond declared they Confirmed the Judgment of the County Court wth Costs of Courts = thirty seuen shillings & eight penc

Jn[o] Pickard & Ezekiel northen as they are Lott layers &c plaintiff ag[t] willjam Longfellow deffendant in an Acc̄on of Appeale from the Judgment of the County Court at Salem After the Attachment Courts Judgmen[t] Reason[s] of Appeale & Euidences in the Case produced were read Comitted to the Jury & are on file wth the Reccords of this Court the Jury brought in their virdict they ffound for the plaintiff Reūsion of the former Judgment & Costs of Courts fiue pounds twelue shillings & six pence

Pickard &c ag[t] longfell[w] 1 Action as to divission of lands

2 Jur

Jn[o] Pickard & ezekiel northend plaintiff ag[t] willjam Longfellow deffend[t] in an Action of Appeale from the Judgment of the County Court at Salem: After the Attachment Courts Judgment Reasons of Appeale & euidences in the Case produced were read Comitted to the Jury and are on file w[th] the Reccords of this Court the Jury brought in their virdict they found for the deffendant Confirmation of the forme[r] Judgment & Costs of Courts three pounds four[e]teen shillings & two pence=

Pickard ag[t] Longfellow — — — — 2d Jur

Samuel Pepen plaintiff in an action of Appeale ag[t] Benjamin marshall deffend[t] from the Judgment of the County Court at Salem = After the Attachmt Courts Judgment Reasons of Appeale & euidences in the Case produced were Read Comitted to the Jury and are Remayning on file wth the Reccords of this Court the Jury brought in their virdict they found for the plaintiffe reuersion of the forme[r] Judgm[t] & Costs of Courts three pounds sixteen shillings and sixe pence =

1st Ju:

Pepen ag[t] marshall

M[r]s Elisabeth Dunster & Jonathan Dunster plaintiff ag[t] Ebenezar Prout deffendant in an Action of Appeale from the Judgment of the County Court at Charles Towne: After the Attachment Courts Judgment Reasons of Appeale & euidences in the Case produced were Read Comitted to y[e] 11 of y[e] Jury by consent of both partjes & are on file the Jury brought in their virdict they found for y[e] deffendant Confirmation of y[e] forme[r] Judgm[t] & Costs of Courts thirty two shillings & two pence =

2 Jury

Dunster ag[t] Prout

exec Issued out

wisewall ag^t keene

Jno wisewall plaintiff ag^t Jno Keene deffend^t in an Accon of Appeale ffrom the Judgment of the County Court at Boston After the Attachment Courts Judgment & Reasons of Appeale & euidences in the Case produced were read Comitted to the Jury and are on file wth the Reccords of this Court the Jury brought in their virdict they found for the plaintiff reuersion of the former Judgment & Costs of Court the magist^s sen^t y^e Jury out once & Againe on this virdict but they^no^t Altering = they Refferd y^e Reception till 20th octobe^r

[102] 1679

Jno. Warner ag^t Benja: francklin

Execution of y^s Judgm^t was suspended 20 8ber 1679 vide othe^r side

Jno warner plaintiff ag^t Benja: ffrancklјn deffend^t in an Accon of Appeale from the Judgment of the County Court at Boston After the Attachment Courts Judgment Reasons of Appeale & euidences in the Case produced were read Comitted to the Jury & are on file wth the Reccords of this Court the Jury brought in their virdict they found for the plaintiff twenty pounds nineteene shilling damage in mony & Costs of Court:

mary Bishop^s diuors

In Ans^r to the petition of mary Bishop for a divorce from hir husband Job Bishop he hauing absented himself from hir seventeen yeares and since marrјed to anothe^r woman in the Barbadoes & liues wth hir as his wife as Appeares by testimony the Court Grants hir request a divorce from Job Bishop hir late husband =

Conway^s sentenc

Morris Conway being Comitted to prison for Inticeing others to steale a boate & turn pyrate &c After his examination wth the euidenc was Read to him being at the Barr the Court = sentenc^t him to be whip^t wth fiueteen stripes paying chardges of prosecution & ffees standing Comitted till the sentenc be performed =

Shephardsons sentenc

George shepardson being alike Comitted for Inticing & perswading morrice Conway to steale a boate & Run away wth it after the Court had Considered his Case & euidences Alike sentenc^t him to be whip^t wth fiueteen stripes paying charg of prosecution & ffees standing Comitted till the sentenc be performed

Richard chambe^{r}layne bein[g] in like manner Accused & Comitted the Court Considering his Case presented he was Admonisht & on his paying ffees was dischardged =

Chambe^{r}lain Admō nis^{t} & ffees =

Sara Bradbrooke being Comitted for stealling a peec of silke ffarrendine Coulord found wth hir seuerall yrds of blacke fowe^{r} penny Ribboning fowe^{r} skeynes of silke from m^{r} Hezekiah vsher as also a smale brass ketle & two porringers the Court sentenc^{t} hir to pay vnto m^{r} Hezekiah vsher seven pounds as full payment for treble damag^{es} as also to pay unto m^{r} Samuell Shrimpton twenty shillings in full for treble Damages & y^{t} yow be whipt wth ~~twenty~~ || tenn || stripes paying ffees of Court standing Comitted till this sentenc be performed =

Sarah Bradbrooks sentence

Sarah Bradbrook in Court Accused Thomas Compton then In Court m^{r} Hezekiah vshe^{r}s se^{r}vant for bring[ing] the sajd ffarrendene silke & Ribboning to hir about 3 or 4 nights after the late fier in Boston & deposed the same on hir solemn oath on wch sd Compton was Comitted. he denjed the fact tho some of ye same Ribboning was on hir shirt necke & hands & Joseph Pears Coming in to ye Cour^{t} & declaring he had seene this quantity of silk & Coulor ye same in sd Compton^{s} hand some short time after the fier. Compton was sent for & sajd Pears deposed to ye trueth of his Affirmation The Court declard that he was Convicted of stealing y^{e} sd Farrendene & silke &c & sentenct him to pay half the aboue mentioned treble damages to m^{r} vsher and to be seuerely whipt wth twenty stripes seuerely layd on paying ffees of Cour^{t} & standing Comitted till this sentence be performed =

Tho Comptons sentenc

[103] 1679

Joshua Atwater on suspition of hauing a hand in the late dreadfull fire in Boston his examination & euidence were Comitted to y^{e} Grand Jury who brought in they found him not guilty & so he was dischardged =

Josh Atwaters$_{\wedge}$

Peeter Lorphelin ffrenchman on the 8th of August last being Accused for Rash Insulting speeches in the time of the late Conflargration = thereby Rendring himself Justly suspitious of hauing a hand therein was seized on & Comitted to the Goale in Boston and being examined = Authority Judged it meet to orde^r his chest & writtings to be searcht into by the Constables in presence of some other Gent^n Appointed to see it don, in whose chest was found two or three crucibles a melting pan a strong paire of shee^rs to clip mony & seuerall clippings of the massachusets mony & some other Instruments & on his examination where he had them & what money^s he had clipped, & how long he had vsed that trade to wch after Counsell Given that he would speake the trueth; It was vajne to hide it those being found in his Custody; he solemnly Called God to wittnes that he had not clipt any money^s, that the Instruments ~~er~~ found wth him he had tooke them out of a privatee^rs chest in ou^r Harbou^r vnde^r Lamojgnes powe^r being sent by Authority to search their chests & persisted in that bold & Impudent lye so was Comitted to prison Againe but in a day or two he sent a letter to the secretary in which he declared that what he had so Affirmed before Authority was false & that he had received the sajd Instrum^ts & Clippings of mony from a privateere about fowe^r or fiue yeares since as sent to him from sajd Privatee^r by a woman where sajd Privateere lodged thô he knew not the womans name All which Considered The Court Considring you^r offense so prooved Against yo^w sentenceth yo^w to stand vpon the pillory two howers & then to haue both you^r eares cut off by the executioner and to give bond in fiue hundred pounds wth two suertjes to the sattisfaction of the Gou̅no^r & Council for you^r good Abearance for y^e future & pay chardges of prosecution & ffees of Court standing Comitted till the sentenc be performed = wch sentenc was executed Accordingly — — — —

Peter Lorphlyins sentence — — — —

y^s Court was Adjournd to 20 october 79 E R S

wiswall & warners executions suspended

At the Courts Adjournment held at Boston 20th of octobe^r 1679 It is ordered that the executions in both wisewalls & francklins or warners cases be suspended til the Court take further order =

Warners libe^rty

On the peticon of John Warner the Court Judgeth it meet to orde^r that the sajd John Warner now In prison be releast & set at libe^rty paying his prison chardges =

Jno Sparrey^s libe^rty to sell Jno Kelly =

In Ans^r to the peticon of John Sparrey relating to John Kelly a prisoner & his debtor. The Court Judgeth it meete to take of the forme^r ljmitation of selling the prisone^r onely to those of this Colony & leaue him to the libe^r^ty of the law for the disposing of him = E R S

In A Answer to the peticon of mary white for a divorce from hir husband Joseph white ^

[104] 1679

major Hawthons fine of 40s remitted E R S *

mr Ezekel Knight yt married mr valentine Hills widdow presenting an order of ye Court of Assists 2d Sept 62 Impowring Elder HateEvill nutter Leift Hall & Ensigne Jno Dauis of oyster Riuer as Comissiors to vejw ye seũll lands mills woods lately in possession of sajd valentine Hill &c and either to lay out ye Iust due & thirds of such mills lands houses to ye sajd mary &c or make Iust full & due Composition wth all & euery ye persons for hir Interest therein Appearing & sajd Elder nutter being dead & mr Joseph Hill vncapable & left Hall remote yt nothing as yet hath binn donn on his the sajd Knights request It is ordered yt ensigne Jno Dauis Capt wincoll & Capt ffrost shall & hereby are desired and Impowred forthwith to see the sd former order be duely executed & hir the sajd marys thirds layd out as by that order was Appointed & yeir returne made thereof to ye Court of Assistants vnder their hands in march next = by ye Court E R S †

Att A Court of Assistants or Court of Admiralty held at Boston 24th Septembe 1679

Shapleigh & Nag agt Craty =

Nicholas Shapleigh & Richard Naggs marriners of ship Jno Adventure plt agt Andrew Craty master &c deffendt & ship for ‖ yeir ‖ wages &c as ꝑ libell. The pltffs & deffendants appearing in Court declared they were Agreed & the plaintiff wthdrew his Accon =

ye charges of Court 3li declared

Nicholas shapleigh & Richard nags being sworne saith that to the Information of the french Counterband goods & brandy brought in the ship Jno Adventure on their oathes Affirmed that they knew not of any that wt they mentioned in their libell it was the slip of the pen. = The Court fined the sajd Naggs & shapleigh tenn shillings apeece for their pernitious lye to ye Country. = attests E R S

shapleigh & naggs find 10s apeec for yeir lye wch mrsh webb tooke as he told me =

---

* See p. 90.

† The above record and the memorandum as to Hawthon's fine appear to have been inserted at a later date in the small blank space at the top of the page.

Att A Court of Assistants or Court of Admiralty sitting in Boston 26 January & from thence Adjourned to y^e^ 2^d^ of february 1679

present
Symon Bradstreet Esqr Gov
Tho Danforth Esqr dep^t^ Gov Esqr
Daniel Gookin
Edwd Tyng
w^m^ Staughton
Joseph dudley
Peter Bulkley
Humphry Dauy
& also App^r^d
Daniell Dennison
Nathaniel Saltonstall
4th ffebr. 79
— — — —

In the Case of John Goose late master of Barcq Hope by his libell & Comp^t^ dated 20 January last plaintiff ag^t^ Hugh Campbell merchant & ownor of the sajd barcq deffendant for his the sajd Campbells denying to pay the sajd Goose his wages as mentioned in the sajd libell with other his charges expended and denying to give the plaintiffe security for the seamens wages = After the Court had pervsed and Considered of the pleas and euidences in the Case produced they ordered and decreed that the deffendant pay vnto the plaintiffe tenn pounds damage in mony & is in full of all his wages &c & Costs of Court fiue pounds sixteen shillings

Court charge 3 : 6. 8.
Execution Issued out 20 febr 1679 for 15^li^ 16 : = E R S =

[*Blank space.*]

[105] 1679

Pelton ag^t^ Campbell

In the Case of Robert Pelton late mate of the barcq Hope by his libell & Complaint exhibbited to this Court dated 20th of January 1679 last Against Hugh Campbell merchant & owno^r^ of the sajd barcq deffendant for his the sajd Campbels denying to pay him his wages as he was mate and a short time master of the sajd vessell as also his disbursments in sajd vessell as in the sajd Lybell is exprest refference thereto being had After the Court had heard the Case Considered the plea & euidences in the Case produced the Court ordered and decreed that the deffend^t^ pay vnto the plaintiffe seuen pounds mony in full of all his wages &c & Cost of Court fowe^r^ pounds seventeene shillings and sixe pence: Campbell had pelton^s^ bill of exchaing in open Court returnd to him againe a[nd] not medled w^th^ =

execution Issued out 13 febr 1679 for 11^li^ : 17^s^. 6.

Hugh Campbell vs Jno Goose

In the Case of Hugh Campbell merchant & owno^r^ of the barq Hope by his libell & Complaint exhibbited to this Court dated 28th of January last plaintiff against John Goose late master of the sajd Barcq deffend^t^ for his breach of charte^r^ party and damages exprest at large in the sajd libell refference thereto being had After the Court had heard the pleas & euidences in that Case produced The Court adjudged for the plaintiffe fiueteeen pounds in mony & damage & Costs of Court sixe pounds sixteene shillings —

execution Issued out 19th febr 79 for 21li 16s

— — — —

Att A Court of Assistants on Adjourmt or Court of Admiralty held at Boston first day of June 1680

present
Symon Bradstreet Esqr Gou̅
Tho Danforth Esqr deps Go.
Daniel Gookin
Daniel Dennison
Jno Pynchon
Edwd Tyng
Wm Stoughton
Joseph Dudley
Peeter Bulkley
Nath Saltonstall
Humphry Dauy
wm Broune Sen̅
Jno Hull
Jno Richards
James Russell
Peter Tilton

— — — —

Edward Randolph Esqr In behalfe of our Soueraigne Lord the king &c by his libell or declaration Plaintiffe against the Pyncke expectation mr Tho Gretian master hir tackle & Appurtenances as forfeited & seized to and for his majestyes vse &c as in his declaration on file more fully doth and may Appeare: The Case was Called the sajd mr Randolph Appeared Thomas Gretian Appeared by mr Anthony Cheeckly his Atturney who produced his power wch was Read the warrant & declaration was ‖ also ‖ Read mr cheeckly Atturney aforesajd pleaded much for a non siute seuerall papers produced wch are on file were read as the Acts of Parljament in Book of Rates p 158 &c

mr Edward Randolph in open Court declared that he did heere desire to ꝓsecute his Information Given into this Court as Informer on his majtys behalfe &c mr cheeckly still pressing for a non suite It was put to the Question to the Court by

[106] 1679

the Depty Gou̅nor whither the deffendant on what was pleaded should haue a non suite Granted him or not It was resolued on the Affirmative a non suite is Granted by the Court The Dept Gou̅ declard the non suit & dismist the Jury:

persons Returnd to serve on ye Jury & sworn were

— — — —

mr Tymothy Prout sen̅
John Walley
James whetcombe
Benjn walker
Tho Edwards
Natha Byffeild
Tho sauage Jun̅
wm ffoster
Richard sprague
Andrew Belchar
Phillip Knell
John Blayny

— — — —

At this Court mr Samuel Shrimpton Appeared and declaring that mr Randolph had seized seventeene butts of his brandy distilled he being ready to proove by his servant that he distilled it wch mr Randolph declared was sattisfactory to him & also to the Court the Court declared the sajd Brandy to be free.

The Court Adjourned themselues to the 8th Instant at one of the clocke in order in order * to a hearing of mr Randolphs Case

present
Tho Danforth Esqr dept Gov̄
Daniel Gookin
John Pynchon
Nathaniell Saltonstall
Humphry Davy
Thomas Sauage
Jno Hull
James Russell
Peter Tylton
John Richards
} Esqrs

— — — —
persons Returnd to serve on this Jury were & sworne
— — — —
mr John Saffyn
~~mr~~ christopher clarke
Dauid Edwards
stephen Burton
Anthony Hayward
Tho moore
Edwd willis
Wm clarke
Nathan: Cary
Nathan: Heyman
Henry Sandiford
Thomas Lynes
— — — —

Att an Adjourment of the Court of Assistants ~~or Admiralty~~ held at Boston 8 June 1680

Edward Randolph Esqr Collector surveyor & searcher of his majtys Customs in New England as well for & in behalfe of our Soueraigne Lord ~~the~~ king Charles the seccond &c and the Honnored Symon Bradstreet Esqr as for himselfe &c as in his libell or declaration bearing date the third of June 1680 Amply Appeares plaintiffe against Thomas Gretian mr of ~~ship~~ Pinck expectation & Against the sajd Pinck hir tackle and Appurtenances defendt as forfeited to and for his Majtjes vse &c as in his declaration Refference thereto being had may Appeare &c The Case was Called mr Randolph Appeared so did Thomas Gretian hauing binn sumoned (together wth his Atturney mr Anthony checkly) the libell & declaration wth other his euidences by him produced in Court were Reade together wth the pleas and euidences produced by the deffendant which being duely Con[si]dered of was Comitted to the Jury who brought in their virdict: i e they found for the deffendant Costs of Court ye deffendant brought in his bill of Costs wch afterward he desired to wthdraw by order of the Gov̄nor it was deliuered out to him =

No 4

Tucker &c agt Loyd
present Symō Bradstreet Esqr Gov̄ §
Tho Danforth Esqr dept Gov̄
Daniel Gookin
Edwd Tyng
wm staughton
Joseph Dudley
Peter Bulkley

Att A Court of Assistants or Court of Admiralty held or sitting in Boston 7 August 1680 ‡

Edwd Tucker Jno Tucker Richard Hicks & francis Hicks marriners & seamen belonging to ship michael of Bristol plaintiffe Against Abraham Loyd master & Comander of sajd ship & sajd ship deffendant in an action of the Case for that the sajd master not only

* Two words repeated in the record.

‡ The record of this and the two preceding Courts was evidently entered out of its chronological order.

§ The names of the magistrates were apparently written in at a later date.

refuseth to pay them their wages having altered his designe & voyage ^ doth also refuse to sett them at libe^r^ty as in their libell & Complaint exhibbited to this Court dated the 6th of August Inst refference thereto being had may Appeare the partjes plaintiff & deffendants appeared And after the Court had heard their plea^s^ & maste^r^s Ans^r^ & Considered the Case = ^ determined & ordered that the sajd master Abraham loyd pay the sajd seamen all their wages i e to Edward Tucker seven pounds fowe^r^ shillings to John Tucker his wages seven pounds fowe^r^ shillings to Richard Hicks his wages seven pounds fowe^r^ shillings and to ffrancis Hicks his wages seven pounds fower shillings and also pay them their Costs of Court fowe^r^ pounds tenn shillings = And that the seamen goe their voyage to London wth sajd master =

Humphry Davy
Tho Sauage
Jno Hull
[Jno] Richard[s]
[James] Russell

[107] 1679

Att A Court of Assistants held at Boston 2^d^ day of march 1679.

present
Symon Bradstreet Esqr Gov
Tho Danforth Esqr dep^t^ Gov
Daniel Gookin
Daniel Dennison
w^m^ Stoughton
Joseph dudley
Peeter Bulkley
Nathaniel Saltonstall
Humphry Davy
— — — — } Esq^rs^

Thomas Hill plaintiff against Wm Obbinson deffendant in an action of Appeale from the Judgment of the County Court in Boston Afte^r^ the Attachment Courts Judgment reason^s^ of Appeale & euidences in the Case produced were read Comitted to the Jury & are on file the Jury brought in their virdict they found a speciall virdict: If the lessor not performing his part of the Couenant doth disobleige the lessee from his part of the Couenant then wee finde for the deffendant Confirmation of the forme^r^ Judgement of the forme^r^ Court & Costs of Courts If not wee finde for the plaintiffe tenn pounds in money & Costs of Courts the Court Resolues this question on the negative that the lesso^r^s non-pformance of the Couenant doth not disobleige the lesse * & determins for the ~~deffendant confirmation of the former judgment~~ || plaintiff that the deffendant pay the plaintiff || tenn pounds money & Costs of Courts three pounds fower shillings & eight pence. —

persons Returnd to se^r^ve on the Grand Jury & sworne were =
— — — —
m^r^ John Long.
ffrancis douse
Jerremiah ffitch
Joseph Dauis
Bartholmew cheeue^r^s
John Bateman
Samuel Willjams
John May
Henry Bright
Gregory Cooke
Isack Jones
Tho Jenner
John Stone
Samuel Andrewes
— — — —

persons Returnd to se^r^ve on y^e^ || 1st || Jury of trjalls for Appeales life limbe & Banishm^t^
— — — —

Hannah Negro plaintiff in an Accon of Appeale

* lessee ?

mr John Hubbard
Thomas Newman
John watson
Suball Seaver
John whitney
Benja: Garfeild
Roger Sumner
James ffoster
Thomas Tucke
John Cutler Juñ
Isack willjams
Peeter Towne

from the sentence of the last County Court in Boston as to ye mulk = After the Courts sentenc was read &c the Jury brought in their virdict they found the sajd Hannah Negro Guilty of matter of fact then chardged vpon hir & Costs of Courts

Thomas Holmes plaintiff agt major Thomas Clarke deffendt in an action of Appeale from the Judgment of the last County Court in Boston = After the Attachment Courts Judgment Reasons of Appeale & euidences in the Case produced were read Comitted to the Jury & are on file. the Jury brought in their virdict they found for the deffendant Confirmation of the former Judgment & Costs of Courts the bench hauing heard the plaintiffs Atturney & the deffendant pleas did chancerje the bond to the principall sume according to bond one hundred & Twenty pounds money to be pajd yearely twenty fower pounds the first payment was to beginne the first of July 1675 and so on the first of July yearely successiuely as mentioned in the bond wth sixe ℔ Cent for Interest wch Comes in all to the 9th Inst to one hundred thirty nine pounds three shillings [with fforty *] fiue shilings & two pence costs = 45s 2d || execution Issued out 10 mrch 79 ||

Joshua Scottow plaintiff agt Samuel wheelewright deffendt in an Accon of Appeal from the Judgment of the County Court in Boston After the Attachment Courts Judgement reasons of Appeale & euidences in the Case produced were read Comitted to the Jury & are on file wth the reccords of this Court the Jury brought in their virdict they found for the deffendant Confirmation of the formr Judgment & Costs of Courts fiue pounds fiueteen shillings & ten pence

martyn agt Briggs &c

Richard martjn plaintiffe agt Jno Briggs & Benjamin martyn deffendants in an Action of Appeale from the Judgment of the County Court at charlsTowne After the Attachment Courts Judgment reasons of Appeale & euidences in the Case produced were read Comitted to the Jury & are on file wth the Reccords of this Court the Jury brought in their virdict that if the sd Richard martyn Coming to New-England Contrary to his Contract wth his men though not prooved a deliuering port doe release them from that voyage as in law pag 95 sect 9 then wee find for the

* Written over the cancelled words "and two pence Costs."

deffendants Confirmation of the former Judgment & Costs of Courts if not wee find for the plaintiff Reuertion of the forme[r] Judgment & Costs of Courts The bench declares & determines for y[e] deffendants three pounds fowe[r] shillings & six penc

Ann Dauenport Atturney to francis dauenport he now being p[r]sent plaintiff in an Accon of Appeale from the Judgment or setlement of y[e] estate of w[m] snelling deceasd by y[e] County Court in Boston. This Case was Called & non suited becaus the reasons of Appeale were no[t] signed w[th] hir name.

[108] 1679

persons Returned to serve on y[e] 2[d] Jury for trialls of Appeale & for life limb & banishment = sworne

— — — —

m[r] Jerremiah Dummer
Pen Townsend
John Endecott
Isack Newell
Robe[r]t Herrington
Samuel釋ternes
Samuel Paul
Joseph Leeds
Richard Louden
Samuel Ballard
Jonathan Hydes
Thomas Langhorne

— — — —

Cap[t] Daniel Henchman in behalf of himself & Left Richard woody Guardians to the 5 children of Anne Hitt plaintiff ag[t] the sentence or setlement of the County Court last in Novembe[r] of y[t] estate after y[e] County Courts Judgment &c was Read wth the euidences in the Case produced This Court Confirmes the setlement of the County Court

Isack waldron plaintiff ag[t] George walton deffendant in an action of Appeale from the Judgment of the Court of Associats at portsmouth 30th Sep[t] 79 after the Courts Judgment & Reason[s] of Appeale was Read y[e] partjes i e. ye plaintiff & deffend[t] by his Atturney Hen Roby Appeared ‖ [&c] ‖ y[e] Atturney pleaded It was not now in o[r] Jurisdiction & not to be tryed here wch y[e] plaintiff accepted of & so it fell =

Byfield ag[t] Taylor & messenger

Nathaniel Byfeild execcuto[r] of the last will of the late Cap[t] Thomas Clarke plaintiffe against John Taylor & Symeon messenger deffend[t] in an Action of Appeale from the Comissione[r]s Court in Boston = After the Attachment Courts Judgment Reasons of Appeale & euidences in the Case produced were read Comitted to the Jury & are on file the Jury brought in their virdict they found for the plaintiffe reuersion of the former Judgment & three pounds fiueteene shillings damage ‖ in money ‖ & Costs of Courts thirty seuen shillings & tenn pence =

Cap[t] Nicholas Manning plaintiff ag[t] Resolued whight & Abigaile

Manning agt white

his wife relict of the late wm Lord defendant in An action of Appeale from the Judgmt of the County Court at Salem After the Attachment Courts Judgment Reasons of Appeale & euidences in the Case produced were read Comitted to the Jury and are on file wth the Reccords of this Court the Jury brought in their virdict they found for the deffendant Confirmation of the former Judgment & Costs of Courts twenty eight shillings & sixe pence =

Hooke agt Pike

mr wm Hooke plaintiffe agt major Robert Pike deffendt In an Action of Appeale from the Judgment of the County Court at Sallisbury After the Attachment Courts Judgment Reasons of Appeale & euidences in the Case ‖ produced ‖ were read Comitted to ye Jury before virdict ‖ came in ‖ by Consent of partjes the Case was refferred to the hearing of Capt John Apleton Capt John whiple & maximillian Jewet who are to Goe on the place heare both partjes & determine & conclud the Case the partjes Acknowledging themselues bound in one hundred pounds apeece each to other to stand to & abide the determination of the whole Case & Costs of Courts Capt Apleton to Appoint time & place of meeting between this & Aprill & that it be ended before 1st of may next the whole Case by order of ye Court was dd to Plaintiff & deffendant in open Court =

Apleton agt Porter

Jno Apleton Jun̄ plaintiffe agt Abell porter deffendant in an action of Appeale from the Judgment of the County Court at Boston after the Attachment Courts Judgment reasons of Appeale and euidences in the Case produced were read Comitted to the Jury & are on file wth the reccords of this Court the Jury brought in their virdict they found for the deffendant Confirmation of the former Judgment & Costs of Courts ‖ After ye Court had heard ye partjes pleas [for ?] a chancery of ye bond they Judged it meet i e ‖ ~~on hearing of partjes~~ the bench ‖ to ‖ chancery * the bond to forty fiue pounds mony & Costs of Courts the plaintiff taking the debts & Goods in virginea to himself ye Costs allowed being fower pound sixteene shillings and two pence =

exec Issued out 19 mrch 79 for 49. 16. 2d E R S

* First written "chanceried."

[109] 1679

mr Nicholos Paige & mr Jno Poole plaintiffs in an action of Appeale agt mr Paul Dudley & Capt Edward Tyng deffendt from the Judgment of the County Court at Boston After the Attachment Courts Judgment Reasons of Appeale & euidences in the Case produced were read Comitted to the Jury and are on file wth the Reccords of this Court the Jury brought in their virdict they found for the deffendants Confirmation of the former Judgment & Costs of Courts forty three shillings &c =

Paige &c agt dudley &c

John Willjams plaintiff in an Accon of Appeale agt James Townsend deffendt from the Judgment of the County Court at Boston this Accon was Called no Reasons Appeard signed by a legall Atturney nor vnder ye plaintiffs hand the plaintiff was declard to be non suited & the deffendant to haue his Costs seven shillings =

Wms agt Tounsend

Jno Endecot plaintiffe on Appeale from the sentence of the County Court at Boston in November last this Accon was Refferd by yr plaintiff to ye eleven of the Jury After ye Courts sentenc was read wth ye euidences produced the Jury brought in their virdict they found ye plt not guilty of matter of fact =

Jno Endecot dischrg

John Giffford plaintiffe against Robert Lord marshall of Ipswich deffendt in an action of Appeale from the Judgment of the County Court at Salem after the Attachment Courts Judgment reasons of Appeale & euidences in the Case produced were read Comitted to the Jury & are on file wth the Reccords of this Court the Jury brought in their virdict they found for the deffendt Confirmation of the former Judgment & Costs of Courts forty shillings and two pence

Gifford agt Lord

Execution Issued out 27 mrch 80

Thomas Wells plaintiff agt Edward Allin deffendt in an Action of Appeale from the Judgment of the Comissioners Court in Boston After the Attachmt Courts Judgment Reasons of Appeale & euidences in the Case produced were read Comitted to the Jury & are on file wth the reccords of this Court the Jury brought in their virdict they found for ye deffendant confirmation of the former Judgment & costs of Courts

wells agt Allin

Swann Agt Browne & Ela =

Robe'rt Swann plaintiff agt Left George Browne & Daniel Ela Atturneys for the Towne of Hauerill deffendts in an Action of Appeale from the Judgment of the County Court at Sallisbury after the Attachment Courts Judgment Reasons of Appeal & euidences in the Case produced were read Comitted to the Jury and are on file wth the reccords of this Court the Jury brought in their virdict they found for the defendant Confirmation of the former Judgment & Costs of Courts fiue pounds sixe shillings & eight pence =

Quilter agt Quilter

ffrancis Quilter plaintiffe against Joseph Quilter deffendant in an Action of Appeale from the Judgment of the County Court at Ipsuich this Accon was Called & being testified & owned that the partjes were Agreed ye plaintiff wthdrew hir Action

[110] 1679

Dafforne agt ~~Dauson~~ || Keene || 1st Jur

John Dafforne plaint agt Jno Keene deffendant in an action of Appeale from the Judgment of the County Court in Boston After the Attachment Courts Judgmen[t] Reasons of Appeale & euidences in the Case were read comitted to the Jury and are on file wth the Reccords of this Court the Jury brought in their virdict they found for the deffendant Confirmation of the former Judgment & Costs of Courts thirty ~~thre~~ || nine || shilling & eight* pence =

Elljot agt Dauson 1st Jury —

Henry Elliot plaintiff Contra Georg Dauson deffendant In an action of Appeale from the Judgment of the County Court in January last After the Courts Judgment Reasons of Appeale & euidences in the Case produced were read Comitted to the Jury & are on file wth the Reccords of this Court the Jury brought in their virdict they found for the Appellant reuersion of the former Judgment & costs of Courts = forty six † shillings & two pence — Henry Elljot in open Court engaged that he would deliuer the Indian to George Dauson or his order dead or aliue =

Broune agt Trumble 1st Jur.

James Broune plaintiff against John Trumble deffendant in an action of Appeale from the Judgment of the County Court at charlsTowne after the Attachment Courts Judgment reasons of Appeale & euidences in the Case

* Written over "six." † Written over "fluety one."

produced were read Comitted to the Jury & are on file the Jury brought in their virdict they found for y^e deffend^t that the plaintiff deliuer the goods sued for or in defect thereof seven pounds fiueteene shilling^s & eleven pence in merchantable pay wth in two moneths time & costs of the forme^r Court =

exec issued out 17 may 80 for 8 : 18 : 9 E R S.

Samuel Bellingham Esqr plaintiffe against Capt Lawrence Hamond & margaret his wife execcutrix to y^e last will of the late Francis willowby Esqr deffendant in an action of Appeale from the Judgment of the County Court at Cambridge in octobe^r last After the Attachment Courts Judgment Reasons of Appeale & euidences in the Case produced were read Comitted to the Jury and are on file wth the Reccords of this Court the Jury brought in their virdict they found for y^e ‖ deffend^t ‖ the forfeiture of the bond one hundred pounds starling money of England & Costs of this * ‖ & ‖ forme^r Court[s]: 15^s 10^d This Judgm^t is to stand entred according to law from ye nex^t Court of Assistants in Septembe^r nex^t

Bellingham ag^t Hamond 1st Jur:

w^m west ‖ plt ‖ ag^st Nicholas Paige Atturney to Benjamin Barter deffend^t in an Action of Appeale from the Judgment of the County Court in Novembe^r last at Boston After the Attachment Courts Judgment Reasons of Appeale & euidences in the Case produced were read Comitted to the Jury and are on file wth the Reccords of this Court the Jury brought in their virdict i e If stopping of mony due by bill of exchainge by Attaching of it in the hands of him by whom the bill of exchainge is draune be a sufficient barr for the non payment of the money sued for then wee find for the plaintiff reuersion of the former Judgment & Costs of Courts if no^t wee find for the deffendant Confirmation of the forme^r Judgement & Costs of Courts = The Bench resolues this Question on the negative & so determines this Case for the deffendant Confirmation of the former Judgment & Costs of Courts three pounds eight shillings

West con^t Nicco. Paige

[111] 1679

Peter chocke plaintiffe ag^t w^m morgan deffendant in an Action of Appeale from the Judgm^t of the Comisso^rs Court in Boston After the Attachment Courts Judgmen[t] Reasons of Appeale & euidences in the Case produced

Chocke Contr^a: Morgan 2^d Jur:=

* Written over "the."

were read Comitted to the Jury and are on file w[th] the Reccords of this Court the Jury brought in their virdit they found for ^ reuersion of the former Judgment & twenty eight shillings damage & Costs of Courts forty sixe shillings =

exec Issued out 3: Aug[t] 80 for 3: 14[s]: er

Thomas wate[r]s being Comitted to prison for comitting a Rape on the body of Bethya Johnson The Grand Jury presenting of him & by their bill left to further Tryall was brought to the barr and was Indicted by the name of Thomas wate[r]s late Resident of wooborne for not hauing the feare of God before his eyes & being Instigated by the Diuil did sometime in January last Comitt a rape on the body of Bethya Johnson daughter of John Johnson of s[d] wooborne Contrary to the peace of ou[r] Soueraigne Lord the king his Croune & dignity the lawes of God & of this Jurisdiction to which Indictment he pleaded no[t] guilty ^ put himself on God & the Country for his trjall After the euidences in the Case produced were read Comitted to the Jury & are on file w[th] the Reccords of this Court the Jury brought in their virdict they found him not Guilty according to Indictment The Court Considering the Case orde[r]ed him to pay the charge of his tryall & all the wittnesses y[t] were Against him & that once w[th]in tenn dayes he depart this Jurisdiction & no[t] returne into it Againe w[th]out licence first obteyned from the Court on penalty of being Comitted to prison there to lye till he be dischardged thenc by orde[r] of Authority paying ffee[s] of Court & then be dischardged the prison =

Tho wate[r]s his Indictment er

Att y[e] Adjorm[t] of y[e] Court of Assistants 20 may 1680

Courts act as to Hugh Clarke & Abiel Lambe

In the Case of Hugh Clarke & Abjel Lambe the Court sees no cause to abate of the last Court of Assistants Judgment =

m[r] ‖ Jn[o] ‖ Alden producing his bill of Costs in the Accon betweene him & majo[r] Thomas Clarke Amounting to five pounds fowe[r] shilling & sixe penc being testified by maj[r] sauage then Speake[r] y[t] Costs of Courts was allowed thô the clarke wrote only Court wch y[e] clark likwise ouning the Court of Assistants now on Adjourm[t] Allowed the costs to be fiue pounds mony =

Jno Alden[s] Costs vide Gen̄ Court may 1677

whereas in the Case betweene m^r^ Porter & m^r^ Apleton depending in the Court of Assistants about the Chancering of a bond of Arbitration It appeares (through Inadvertency) that Judgment is entred Contrary to the Intention & order of the Court for a respitt vntill a further hearing It is hereby ordered & declared that the sajd Judgment be null & voyd in lawe and all acts since donne by either partje in prosecution of the sajd Judgment be in like manner null & voyd vntil the sajd Apleton haue opportunity of further plea whereunto he shall be Admitted before the end of the next Court of Assistants in September or the Court take further order therein :

past at Courts Adjourm[t] 4 June 1680

[*The following is written in the small blank space left at the foot of the page, as if inserted by the Secretary at a later date.*]

The Grand Jury presenting Elisabeth morse y[e] wife of w[m] morse ‖ she ‖ was Indicted by the name of Elisabeth morse for that she not hauing the feare of God before hir eyes being Instigated by the diuil & hauing had familiarity wth the diuil contrary to the peace of our Soūaigne Lord the King his croune & dignity y[e] lawes of God & of this Jurisdiction: After the prison[r] had pleaded not Guilty & put hirself on God & y[e] Country for triall y[e] euidences product were read Comitted to the Jury y[e] Jury brought in their virdict they found hir Guilty according to Indictment & had sentenc^

[112] 1680

Att a Court of Assistants or Court of Admiralty sitting in Boston 7[th] of August 1680 =

present
Symon Bradstreet Esq[r] Goū
Tho Danforth Esq[r] dep[t] Goū
Daniel Gookin
Edw[d] Tyng
Joseph Dudley
Peeter Bulkley
Humphry Davy
Tho Sauage
John Hull
James Russell

Jn[o] macklish Carpenter[s] mate James mullen Cooper Jn[o] sauage Jn[o] Thomas & michael Johnson marrine[r]s of ship Herron plaintiff[s] ag[t] Cap[t] Jn[o] Ely master of the sajd ship deffendants in an action of the Case according to their libell exhibbited to sajd Court bearing date the 4[th] of August 1680 the partjes plaintiffe & deffend[t] Appeared And after the Court had heard their pleas & Ans[rs] & Considered their euidences in the Case produced This Court determined & order'd that Cap[t] Jn[o] Ely the master pay the sajd seamen their seuerall wages to this day viz[t] to Jn[o] macklish for his tenn month[s] & 5 odd day[s] service at forty five shillings ꝑ m° is twenty two pounds ten shillings to James mullin for his like time at twenty 8ˢ ꝑ mo. fowe'teene pounds. To Jn° Thomas for his time at twenty fiue shillingˢ ꝑ m°: twelve pounds tenn shillings To Jn° Sauage for his time at twenty fowe' shillingˢ ꝑ mo twelve pounds & to michael Johnson for seuen monᵗʰˢ & odd days at twenty shillings ꝑ m°. seven pounds fower shillings deducting what they already haue had and two monᵗʰˢ wages ꝑ man to be reserved in the maste's hands for security of their service in the Remayning Voyage & the sajd plaintiffs to pay Costs ℓ 15ˢ:

present
Simon Bradstreet Esqʳ Gou
Tho. Danforth Esqʳ depᵗ Gou
Edward Tyng, Joseph Dudley, Peter Bulkley, Humphry Dauy, Tho. Sauage, Wm Browne sen, John Hull — Esqʳˢ

— — — —

persons Returned to serve on the Jury & sworne were

— — — —

mʳ James Whetcombe
Nathaniel Greene
Thomas Thatcher
Edward Bromefeild
Richard Harris
James Loyd
Samuel Chickley
Arthur Tanner
John Balston Juñ
John Cutler
Solomon Phipps
Enoch moore

Att A Court of Assistants held at Boston on Adjournmt 20ᵗʰ of August 1680

Edward Randolph Esqʳ by his Information exhibbited to this Court prosecuting in his Majestyes name* as in sajd Information refference thereto being had may Appeare plaintiffe ℓ Against Jonathan Jackson and Nathaniel Ballard maste's of two sloopes loaden wᵗʰ tobaccoᵉˢ and other Goods deffendants going downe as Informed to ship S't John of Dublin lying out of Coṁand of the Castle, After the Information and evidences in the Case produced were read Coṁitted to the Jury and are on file wᵗʰ the Reccords of this Court the Jury brought in their virdict vizᵗ In the Case depending betweene Edward Randolph Esqʳ plaintiffe & Jonathan Jackson & Nathaniel Ballard Deffendants The Jury finds for the deffendants Costs of Court which was Granted them three shillings =

[*Page 113 is blank with the exception of the date 1680 at the top of the page.*]

[114] 1680

present
Symon Bradstreet Esqʳ Gou

Att A Court of Assistants held at Boston 7ᵗʰ 7ber 1680 =

* Written over "behalfe."

John Bateman plaintiffe against Robe^rt Taft deffendant in an action of Appeale from the Judgment of the County Court in Boston in Aprill last. After the Attachment Courts Judgment Reasons of appeale and evidences in the Case produced were read Comitted to the Jury & are on file wth the Reccords of this Court the Jury brought in their virdict they found for the deffend^t Confirmation of the forme^r Judgment & Costs of Courts the plantiffe desired his bond might be chancerjed the Court hauing heard the plainff^s pleas & the deffendants Ans^r chanceried the bond to fiueteene pounds dam̄age in mony ye Costs Included all but filings : 2. 6

Daniel Gookin
Daniel Dennison
Edward Tyng
Wm Stoughton
Joseph Dudley
Peter Bulkley
2 Humphry Davy
1 Nath. Saltonstall *
Thomas Sauage
John Hull
John Richards
James Russell

— — — —

Grand Jury were sumond Appeard & were Called but no occasion p^rsenting were discharged vide day book

— — — —

Thomas Hill plaintiff ag^t w^m obbinson deffend^t in an action of Appeale from the Judgment of the County Court in Aprill last After the Courts Judgment reasons of Appeale & euidences in the Case produced were read Com̄itted to the Jury & Remajne on file wth the Reccords of this Court the Jury brought in their virdict i e a speciall virdict That if the deffendant giving the plaintiff the key & saying It was the key of his doore if that give^s the plaintiff a Reentry then wee find for the deffendants Costs of Courts & if so Giving & Receiving the key gives no reentry then wee finde for the plaintiff tenn pounds damages in mony & Costs of Courts = The Court on the Consideration of this virdict Resolue^s it for the deffendant Costs of Courts nineteene shillings & tenn pence :

persons Returned to serve on the 1st Jury of trialls & sworne were =

— — — —

m^r Samuel Legg
Jno clarke marriner
w^m Harris
James Taylor
Nathaniel Thayer
Tho Bacon
w^m Dauis
Richard Stowers
nicho: meade
obadiah Swift
Jno Barnard
Sam Leuermore =

— — — —

persons Returnd to serve on the 2^d Jury for trialls of Appeale & sworne were =

— — — —

Thomas Hill plaintiff ag^t w^m Obbinson deffend^t in an action of Appeale from the Judgment of the County Court in Boston in Aprill last After the Attachment Courts Judgment Reasons of Apeale & euidences in the Case produced were read Com̄itted to the Jury and are on file wth the reccords of this Court The Jury brought in their virdict they found for the deffendant fiueteene pounds in money damage & Costs

m^r Elizu^r Holliock
Jonathan Bridgham
Isack walker
Jabez Tatman
James Loudon
Isaack ffowle
Desire Clap
Thomas Strajte
Jno Jackson
nicholas ffessingden
Andrew Boardman
John ffuller

* The numbers against these two names are in the original record and were intended to correct an error of arrangement.

of Court reūsing the former Judgment as to the otheʳ part Costs two pounds foweʳ shillingˢ & two pence —

Resolved white plaintiffe against Nicholas mañing deffendant in An Action of Appeale from the Judgment of the last County Court at Ipswich After the Attachment Courts Judgment Reasons of Apeale & euidences in the Case produced were read Comitted to the Jury & are on file the Jury brought in their virdict they found for the plaintiffe yᵉ Reuersion of the former Judgment & Costs of Courts sixe pounds two shillings & six pence =

executi Issued

Willjam Rauson Atturney to Jame* Greene plantiff agᵗ John Bakeʳ deffedᵗ ‸an action of Appeale from the Judgment of the Comissionʳs Court After the Attachment Courts Judgment Reasons of Appeale & euidences in the Case produced were read Comitted to the Jury and are on file wᵗʰ the Reccords of this Court the Jury brought in their virdict they found for the deffendant Costs of Courts. the magists Comended the Case to the Jury once & Againe & sent the Jury forth to consᵈer of it but they persisted & declard they † they Could not alter their virdict yᵉ Costs Agreed on was twelue shillings

Rauson agᵗ Bakeʳ

[115] 1680

Samuel Pelton plaintiff ag̃ᵗ Sam. Tompson & John Thompson Atturneyˢ to wᵐ Thompson in an Action of Appeale from the Judgment of the County Court at Boston Afteʳ the Attachment Courts Judgment & Reasonˢ of Appeale and euidences in the case produced were Read Comitted to the Jury and are on file wᵗʰ the Reccords of this Court the Jury brought in their virdict they found a speciall virdict If according to law A ‡ sueʳty may sueʳty may § sue the principle for the foretime ⸸ of that bond wherein they are Jointly and seuerally bound Then the Jury finde for deffendant the Confirmation of the former Judgment & Costs of Courts, But if the law be otherwise the Jury finds for the plaintiffe the reuertjon of the former Judgment & Costs of Courts The Court on

Pelton agᵗ Thompson =

* Error in the record for "James." See the letter of Attorney in No. 1889, Court Files, Suffolk.

† Error of the record for "that."

‡ Written over "of."

§ Two words repeated in the record.

⸸ Error in the record for "forfeiture," as appears by the original verdict on file.

Consideration of this virdict Resolues the Question for the deffendant & grants Costs of Courts =

Phillip knight plaintiff ag[t] Thomas Caue deffendant in an action of Appeale from the Judgment of the County Court at Salem After the Attachment the Courts Judgment Reasons of Appeale and euidences in the Case produced were read Comitted to the Jury and are on file wth the Reccords of this Court: The Jury brought in their virdict they found for the deffendant Confirmation of the former Judgment & Costs of Court

Knight ag[t] Caue

Richard Hall & Elizabeth his wife plaintiffe against & Elizabeth his wife plaintiffe Against * Tho weld deffendant ‖ after y[e] Attachm[t] Courts Judgm[t] Reasons of Appeale er Read & Comitted to y[e] Jury y[e] Jury brought in y[e]ir virdict ‖ Confirmation of the former Judgment & Cost of Court[s] twenty seven shilling[s] & sixpence. =

Richd Hall p[lt] ag[t] Tho weld: —

Thomas walter plaintiff against John Gifford deffend[t] = After the Attachm̃[t] Courts Judgment & Reasons of Appeale & euidences in the Case produced were read Comitted to the Jury & are on file wth the Reccords of this Court the Jury brought in their virdict they found for the plaintiff Reusion of the fforme[r] Judgment & Costs of Courts

walter ag̃[t] Gifford

Thomas walter plaintiff ag̃[t] John Gifford deffendant deffend[t] † After the Attachment Courts Judgment Reasons of Appeale & euidences in the Case produced were read Comitted to the Jury and are on file wth the reccords of this Court the Jury brought in their virdict they found ffor the deffendant Confirmation of the former Judgment wth an Addition of twenty pounds more money damage & Costs of Courts three pounds three shillings

walter ag[t] Gifford

Samuel Dutch plaintiffe Against Roger Darby deffendant in An action‸Appeale from the Judgment of the County Court at Ipswich After the Attachment Courts Judgment Reasons of Appeale & euidences in the Case produced were read Comitted to the Jury & are on file w[th] the Reccords of this Court the Jury brought in their virdict they ffound for the plaintiff reuersion of the forme[r] Judgment & Costs of Courts sixe pounds fowe[r]teen shillings & sixe pence

Dutch ag̃[t] Darby

---

* Six words repeated in the record. † Written over "plaintiff."

[116] 1680

Hoare agt Cooke

John Hoare Assignee of marshall Richard wayte plaintiff against mrs Elisabeth Cooke & mr Elisha Cooke execcutorix & execcutor of ye late Left Richard Cook deffendt in an action of Appeale from the Judgment of the County Court at Cambridge in Aprill last After the Attachmt Courts Judgment Reasons of Appeale & euidences in the Case produced were read with the Generall * Courts Judgment 11th octobe 1665 The Court declared they Allowed of the County Courts Judgment for a non suit. =

Everden agt smith

walter euerden plaintiff against Richard Smith deffendt in an Action of Appeale from the Judgment of the Comissioners Court in Boston in August last both partjes Appearing in Court declaring they were Agreed The plaintiff had liberty & did wthdraw his Action =

Sam Bellingham Esqr vsus James Russell Esqr =

Samuel Bellingham Esqr plaintiff against James Russell Esqr deffendant After ^ Attachment Courts Judgment Reasons of Appeale & euidences in the Case produced were read Comitted to the Jury & are on file the Jury brought in their virdict they found for the deffendant Confirmation of the former Courts Judgment twenty one pounds ten shillings & Costs of Courts —

Butler agt Hollowell &c

Execution Issued out 9 novemb. 80 dd mr checkly =

Stephen Butler plaintiff agt wm Holowell Benjamin Holowell & Edwd Ashely deffendt in an action of Appeale from the Judgment of the County Court in Boston After the Courts Judgmt Attachment Reasons of Appeale & euidences in the Case produced were read Comitted to the Jury & are on file wth the Reccords of this Court the Jury brought in their virdict they found for the deffendant Confirmation of the former Judgment & costs of Courts || sixe pounds sixe shillings ||

maning agt Broune & Bartholmew

Nicholas maning plaintiff against John Broune sen & Henry Bartholmew in an action of Appeale from the Judgment of the County Court at Salem After the Attachment Courts Judgment Reasons of Appeale & euidences in the Case produced were Read Comitted to the Jury & are on file wth

* These last three words written over the words "Comitted to the Jury."

the Records of this Court the Jury brought in their virdict they found for the ~~plaintiff~~ ‖ deffendant ‖ Confirmation of the former Judgment & Costs of Courts fiuety six shillings & fower pence =

Lambe agt Clark

Abiell Lambe plaintiff agt John Clarke deffendant in An action of Appeale from the Judgment of the County Court in Boston After the Attachment Courts Judgment & Reasons of Appeale & other euidences in the Case produced were Read comitted to the Jury and are on file wth the Reccords of this Court the Jury brought in their virdict they found for the plaintiff thirteen pounds six shilling & eight pence. Reṽsing the former Judgment three pounds seventeen shillings & two penc

Greely agt woodbridge

Phillip Greely plaintiff agt Thomas woodbridge deffendt in an Action of Appeale from the Judgment of the County Court at Ipswich After the Attachment Courts Judgment Reasons of Appeale & euidences in the Case produced were read Comitted to the Jury and are on file wth the Reccords of this Court the Jury brought in their virdict they found for the deffendant Confirmation of the former Judgment and Costs of Courts

[*The following is entered on the lower edge of the page.*]

Trott agt Gourdon

Barnard Trott plaintiff ‖ on Appeale from the Judgmt of the County Court in Boston ‖ agt Abra Gourdon plaintiff & deffendt Apprd & declard they were Agreed the plaintiff as in other cases had liberty granted & did wthdraw his Accōn

[117] 1680

wayte agt Lewis

Returne wayte plaintiff agt Samuel Leuis deffendt in an action of Appeale from the Judgment of the County Court at Charles Towne after the Attachment Courts Judgment Reasons of Appeale & euidences in the Case produced were read comitted to the Jury and are on file wth the Reccords of this Court the Jury brought in their virdict they found for the plaintiff Reuersion of the former Judgment & Costs of Courts fiuety fiue shillings & six pence

℘ Elish Cook

mrs Elisabeth Cooke execcutrix & mr Elisha Cooke execcutor to the last will of ‖ ye late Left ‖ Richd Cooke pltff. agt James olliuer deffendant in an action of

Appeale from the Judgment of the County Court in Boston After the Attachm[t] Courts Judgm[t] Reasons of Appeale & euidences in the Case produced were read comitted to the Jury and are on file w[th] the Reccords of this Court the Jury Brought in their virdict they found for the Deffendant[s] Confirmation of the forme[r] Judgment & Costs of Courts = The plaintif declard he Attainted the Jury || for erro[r]s or mistakes || & in open Court Elisha Cooke in behalfe of his mother & for himself w[th] Isaack Addington his suerty Acknowledged Jointly & seuerally || themselues ꝑ || bound in tenn pounds to the Tresure[r] of the Country on Condition that the sajd Elisha Cooke should prosecute his Attaint of the Jury as to matter of Erro[r] at the next Court of Assistants to effect = E R S

Cooke ag[t] Olliuer

John Hoare plaintiffe against Elisabeth Cooke execcutrix & Elisha Cooke deffend[t] in an Action of Appeale from the Judgmen[t] of the County Cour[t] at Cambridg after the Attachment Courts Judgment Reasons of Appeale & euidences in the Case produced were read with * the Copie of the Gennerall Courts Judgment in Barr of prosecution the Court declared the plaintiff was non suited =

Hoare ag[t] Cooke

Peter Ege[r]ton plaintiff ag[t] m[r]s smith widdow deffendant in an Action of Appeale from the Judgment of the County Court at Boston the plaintiff being three times Called & making default by his non Appearance he was non suited & his bond declared to be forfeited: & Katherin Smith had hir Costs Granted 6[s] 10[d] =

Eggerton ag[t] Smith

W[m] Pitts plaintiff Against Enock Badcock deffend[t] in an action of Appeale from the Judgment of the County Court at Boston After the Attachment Courts Judgment Reasons of Appeale & euidences in the Case produced were read Comitted to the Jury & are on file wth the Reccords of this Court the Jury brought in their virdict they found for the deffend[t] Confirmation of the forme[r] Judgm[t] 9[li] 18[s] mony damage & costs of Court

Pitts ag[t] Badcock

[118] 1680

ffrancis davenport hauing entred bond to prosecut his Appeale from the sentanc or Judgm[t] of the County Court in Boston & no Action entred & the Deffend[t] † Patch

ffrancis Dauenport

---

* Written over "Comitt."

† This space left blank in the original.

Appearing for his Costs the Court declared he had forfeited his bond =

Daniel mathew on Appeale from the Judgm[t] of the County Court in Boston The Case was Called but no reasons Rendred but that he was vnsattisfied The Court declare[d] the Case was non suited & bond forfeited

Mathews bond forfeited

Ralph Powel plaintiff against m[r] John Cotton deffend[t] In an action of Appeale from the Judgment of the County Court in Boston in July last After the Attachment Courts Judgment Reasons of Appeale and euidences in the Case produced were read Comitted to the Jury and are on file wth the Records of this Court the Jury brought in their virdict they found for the Deffendant Confirmation of the forme[r] Judgment 4[li] mony damage & costs of Courts forty seven shillings & sixe pence

Powell ag[t] Cotton

Henry Ellit plaintiff ag[t] Geoge Dauson deffend[t] in an Action of Appeale from the Judgment of the County Court in Boston After the Attachm[t] Courts Judgment Reasons of Appeale & euidences in the Case produced were read Comitted to the Jury and are on file wth the Reccords of this Court the Jury brought in their virdict they found for the plaintiff reuersion of the forme[r] Judgment & Costs of Courts fiuety seuen shillings & sixe pence

Execution Issued out for 57[s]. 6.

[*The following paragraph with the marginal note appears to have been entered by the secretary at a later date.*]

The Court on Consideration of their late Act in June last Reasuming the Chanceryng of m[r] Apleton[s] bond declare they haue chancerjed the s[d] bond to thirty fiue pounds mony & m[r] Aplton to haue the tobacco[s] himselfe

m[r] Aplton bond chanceried =

Nehemiah Pearse plaintiff on Appeale from the Judgm[t] of the County Court in Boston = After the Attachment Courts Judgment Reasons of Appeale & euidences in the Case produced were Read Comitted to the Jury and are on file w[th] the Reccords of this Court the Jury brought in their virdict i e they find him$_{\wedge}$ of the fact chardged

on his peticon the Court Remitted the one halfe of his fine.

Nehe Pearse 2 10

Paige agt Br[in]sden

Nicholas Paige plaintiff agt Robert Brimsden deffendant In an Action of Appeale from the Judgment of the County Court in Boston the partjes being Agreed the plaintiff had liberty & did wthdraw his Accon

[119] 1680 9 Augt 1680

Randolph agt Hutchinson as to tobacos &c

Edward Randolph Esqr &c by his libell & Information plaintiffe agt fiuety hogsheads || & 4 baggs || of tobacco & other Plantation Comoditjes deffendants as in sajd || Information || Refference thereto being had amply Appeareth The Action was Called the Information was Read mr George Hutchinson Appeared in Court & Affirmed & owned the Tobaccos was his And after all the pleas & euidences produced in Court by the plaintiff as also by sajd Hutchinsons Atturney Thomas Norman were Comitted to the Jury wch are on file The Jury Brought in their virdict they found for the deffendant Costs of Court The Court sent out the Jury once & Againe wth the Case further to Consider of it at their Coming in Againe || they declared by their forman || they saw no cause to Alter their virdict as aboue ~~declared by their foreman for the deffendant~~ || but found || for the deffendant Costs of Court

Ans to Susanah Goodwin peticon & hir diuorce thereupon

In the Case of Susannah Goodwin the wife of Edward Goodwin humbly desiring that hir husband hauing wilfully deserted hir for seuen or eight yeares and left hir destitute of all meanes of support for hirself & children as in hir peticõn The Court Judgeth it meet to declare she is set at liberty & from him to marry wth another man

7 Comissioners chosen

~~this court~~ mr Jno Joyliffe Capt Tho Bratle mr Anthony stoddard Capt Elisha Hutchinson mr Jno Saffyn Capt Jno walley & Capt Jno ffaireweather returned as chosen by ye Toune were Aprooued on by ye Court & tooke their oathes as Comissioners for Boston for ye yeare ensuing

Ansr to Sarah Coopers peti:

In Ansr to ye petiõon of Sarah Cooper for a diuors Respitted till she send to hir husband to informe him &c & his estate secured for a convenient time =

This Court is adjourned to the 16 Instant at 3 of the clocke

The Court mett at the time &c and Adjourned to the 23 of Instant at 3 of y^e clock

vpon the Complaint of Thomas walters the Gov̄no^r & magis^ts doe declare that the sajd walters rendering estate ffor the sattisfaction of the execution the officer ought to levy the execution vpon the same as the law directs and the sajd walters performing the same he shall be released from Prison the officer causeing it to be apprized as mony according to lawe = y^s was thus past 16 october following by all y^e magis^ts except m^r saltonstall m^r Russell & is here entred being a vacant place as Attests E R S

Courts declaration or order as To Tho walter execution

Go: 16th october 1680 DG DD ET WS JD PB HD WB TS JR PT *JH

The Court is Adjourned to the 23 Instant at 3 of the clock in ye afternoone

The Court met at the time The Court Considering that no owno^r Appeared for to lay clajme to the 50 hogsheads of tobacco &c and nine barrells till the last day of the Court The Court Judged it meete to order (seuerall difficulties appearing in the Case) that m^r George Hutchingson who Claymes the sajd tobacco &c entring into bond of two hundred pounds wth sufficient sue^rtjes to respond the Judgment of any of his majtjes Courts in this Jurisdiction in Case of further Complaint & prosecution w^thin one yeare of this date for & Concerning the sajd tobacco^s &c the sajd tobacco^s &c on such bond given to be deliuered to the sajd Huchinson he dischardging the warehouse for the same = =

Courts order about y^e 50 hogds of ^ to be dd to m^r Hutchinson in Case &c

Whereas the Honno^rable George Russell Esqr is Convicted by his owne Confession before the Gouerno^r & seuerall of the magistrates of Comitting fornication with mary Pemberton is fined tenn pounds mony as a fine to y^e County of Suffolke to be presently payd & that he Give ‖ in ‖ security to value of ~~one hundred pounds~~ of † fiuety pounds mony to secure this Toune of Boston & county from damage as to main-

Courts order as to Georg Rusell Esqr his Crime:

* These initials stand for Daniel Gookin, Daniel Dennison, Edward Tyng, William Stoughton, Joseph Dudley, Peter Bulkley, Humphrey Davy, William Browne, Thomas Savage, John Richards, Peter Tilton, and John Hull, as appears from the lists of magistrates in other places in the record.

† "of" repeated in the record.

tenance of the child * or that he Giue security to value of one hundred pounds that he Appeare before the nex[t] County Court to Ans[r] for his sajd Crime & Abide y[e] sentenc of the Court —

[120] 1680

16 & 18 Sep[t] 1680

Cap[t] Laurenc Comitt[t]

Capt Laurence Complain[d] on for Affronting the Gou̅no[r]s war[r]ant & shooting at the boate & men in it the kings Jack being thereon ℘ = The Court sentenct him to be Comitted to prison there to remajne sufficiently secured till he Giue his oune bond in a thousand pounds & two sufficient sue[r]tjes in 500[li] a peece starling mony on Condition y[t] sajd Laurenc personally Appeare & Answer what shall be lajd to his Charge & Abide the sentence of the Court w[th]n two moneths =

Nehemiah pearse ½ his fine Remitted him =

The Court Remitted to him † the halfe of his fine

At An Adjourm[t] 16 Sep[t] 1680

It is ordered that the ship Edward & Ann belonging to m[r] Nicholas Paige now Ready to sajle be Imbargued till munday next to accompany the Honno[r]ble the Lord Culpepper in his ship now also bound to sayle for England =

‖ In Ans[r] to y[e] peticõn of stephen Butler The Court Court ‡ ordered a Respitt of y[e] execution ag[t] him till the end of the nex[t] Generall Court in october nex[t] as is desired Attest E R S. ‖

present.
Symon Bradstreet Esq[r] Gou̅
Tho Danforth Esq[r] dep[t] Gou̅
Richd Saltonstall
Daniel Gookin
Edwd Tyng
w[m] Staughton
~~Joseph Dudley~~ ‖
Peter Bulkley
Humphry Davy
Thomas Sauag
John Hull } Esq[rs]
— — — —

At the Court of Assistants on Adjournment 1st of octobe[r] 1680

‖ The Jury Insisting on Caution for their charges the Court ordered the plaintiff to put in tenn pound. ‖

Jurymen Returnd to serve on this Jury & Sworne were
— — — —

Edward Randolph Esq[r] Collector ℘ by his Information bearing date 30[th] of September 1680 plaintiff as in his ‖ s[d] ‖ Information refferenc thereto being had may § Amply Appeareth plaintiffe against steven Clay m[r] & Comande[r] of the Good ship Called the Batchello[r]s Delight of london seazed on by

* The rest of this paragraph appears to have been written later, when the marginal entry was made.

† Nehemiah Pearse, as appears by the margin.

‡ "Court" repeated in the record.

§ Error in the record for "more."

the sajd m[r] Randolph as forfeited to his majty &c the Case was Called the plaintiff & deffendant both Appeared the Information & other euidences in the Case produced were read Comitted to the Jury & are on file the Jury brought in their virdict they found for the defendant Costs of Court:

m[r] Richard Midlecot
Thomas Bligh sen
Richard Bulkley
John olliuer
|| Rich[d] Crispe ||
Anthony Hayword
John Parmite[r]
John winslow
Samuel Ballard
Thomas Addams
Timo. Cutler
Stephen Cadman
— — — —

The Court Allowed the Jury forty eight shillings for their charge & expenc & the Remainde[r] seven pounds twelue shilling[s] to be deliu[d] to m[r] Randolph Againe wch was donn =

The Secretary is ordered that henceforth where any person shall obteyne an order from the Gounno[r] for the sumoning of the magis[ts] to meete in Court of assistants & of a Jury for the tryall of any Case the secretary before he grant warrant for the sumoning a Jury shall require of the plaintiffe tenn pounds in money as Caution to respond the charges of sajd Court and when the Court is ended and the charges of the Court is payd the remainder shall be returned if any be to the sajd Plaintiffe Provided alwayes It shall be lawfull for any plaintiff in any maritime case or any other that shall prosecute the same in any stated Court of Assistants or County Court that shall prosecute the same paying only tenn shillings for the tryall thereof as hath binn customary =

orde[r] for y[e] secret. to take 10[li] Caution befor he sumon[s] a Jury —
— — — —

Josiah Cobbham Acknowledged himself his heires execcuto[r]s & Admstrato[r]s bound in sixty pounds starling mony to James Russell Esq[r] Tresure[r] of y[e] Country on this Condition that he shall & will Appeare before such Court or Courts as shall take Cognizance of the Case and Answer what shall be layd to his * charge by m[r] Edward Randolph in & about the Sloope[s] Carrying of Goods aboord Cap[t] Laurence his ship Contra[r]y to the Act or Acts of Parljament & abide their Judgment this thus donn by orde[r] of y[e] dep[t] Gounnor in Boston 21 octob 80

as Attests

Edw[d] Rawson Sec.

A warrt was signed to m[r] Randolph or Dani Mathews &c

* Written over "this."

[121] 1680

[*The following paragraph is inserted at the upper edge of the page.*]

2[d] octobe[r] 1680 In Ans[r] to Peter Laurenc peticon It is ordered y[t] his fine be remitted to 20[li] & paying 10[li] in mony & giving security his oune bond for y[e] other tenn pounds to y[e] Tresurer at his returne in like siluer E R S

present
Symon Bradstret Esq[r] Gou
Daniel Gookin
Edw[d] Tyng
W[m] Stoughton
Joseph Dudley
Humphry Davy
Tho Sauage
Jn[o] Richards
John Hull
— — — —

Att a Court of Assistants or Admiralty held at Boston in New England 18th of novemb[r]

(19) = 1680 =

John Bouland mate of * the good ship called the Ann & Hester of London by his libell & complaint exhibbited to this Court bearing date the 16th of Novembe[r] plaintiffe against ffrancis Branson master & Comander of sajd ship together with sajd ship hir tackle & Apparrell deffendant for that the sajd ffrancis Branson master of sajd ship aforesajd refused & still doth refuse to pay vnto the sajd Bowland his just wages to the full some of thirty eight pounds in mony after the rate of three pounds fiue shillings ꝑ moneth for service by him donne & performed in sajd ship &c as in the sajd libell ‖ & ‖ Attachment ~~pleas & evidences~~ refference thereto being had may Appeare After the libell Attachment pleas & euidences made & produced before the Court were heard & read The Court declared & Adjudged that It Appeared this was not the seccond deliuery Port & so wages not due & decreed that the plaintiffe pay the deffendant Costs of Court nineteen shillings and sixe pence

Bowland versus Branson.

Henry Basset Boatswayne Zackeriah Lauter Carpenter Richard Butcher Gunner Jasper Eve Richard Odling George fisher Samuel Rochford Benjamin Whittenhall & symon Thomas marrine[r]s of the ship Ann & Hesther of London by their libell & Complaint exhibbited to this Court bearing date 16[th] of Instant November plaintiffs against ffrancis Branson master & comander of sajd ship together therewith the sajd ship deffend[ts] ffor that he the sajd ffrancis Branson master &

Henry Basset & mariners plts. ag[t] ffrancis Branson deffenndt

* "mate of" written over "by his libell."

Comande^{r} of sajd ship ~~together wth the sajd ship~~ ‖ Refuseth and still doth ‖ refuse to pay vnto them their seuerall wages according as is exprest in their libell on Complaint amounting to the summe of one hundred & sixty sixe pounds or thereabouts for their seuerall wages donn & performed by them in sajd ship as in their sajd libell or Complaint is declared refference thereto being had Amply may Appeare = After the libell with Attachment pleas & euidences made in the Case were heard read and pervsed The Court declared & Adjudged that this was not the seccond Port of deliuery and so their wages was not due and therefore decreed that the plaintiffe pay the deffendant his costs twenty sixe shillings money =

Thomas Tompkins Boat swajne xtian Bowles John Ansley & John Tompkins seamen belonging to the ship called the Resolution of London by their libell & complaint bearing date the 17 of novembe^{r} 1680 plaintiff^{s} ag^{t} Capt Richard Cobb ‖ m^{r} ‖ of the sajd ship together wth sajd ship deffend^{t} for that he the sajd Richard Cobb master & Comander as afores^{d} hath refused to pay them their seuerall wages for their services pe^{r}formed in sajd ship

[122] 1680

as in their sajd libell refference thereto being had more Amply may appeare = After the libell Attachment euidences & pleas made read & heard before the Court the Court declared they Adjudged for the deffendant & decreed the plaintiff should pay the deffendant his Costs of Courts —

Att a Court of Assistants or Admiralty held at Boston in New England 2^{d} decem 1680

present
Symon Bradstreet Esqr Gou
Tho. Danforth Esqr dep^{t} Gou
Daniel Gookin
Edwd Tyng
W^{m} staughton
Joseph Dudley
Humphry Davy
John Richards
John Hull
James Russell

Thomas Stevens Boateswayne Richard milson Gunne^{r} and Thomas Longworth marrine^{r}s belonging to the Good ship Called the George of Bristoll by their libell & Complaint exhibbited to this Court plaintiffe against Samuel Isaac master & comander of sajd ship together with sajd ship deffend^{t} for that he the sajd Samuell Isaac master &c refused & still doeth refuse to pay them their seuerall‸ amounting in the whole to forty nine pounds fowerteene shillings or thereabouts not wthstanding his promise

steuens & marrin'rs plt agt Samuel Isack deff't mr of ship resolution *

to cleare them in New England their seuerall wages as in sajd libell refference thereto being had more Amply doth & may Appeare After the libell Attachment pleas & euidences made & produced were heard er the Court declared they Adjudged that the plaintiffes pay the deffendant his Costs i: e seventeene shillings & sixepence

Capt steephen Clay pl agt. mr Daniel Turell

Capt steeven Clay master & Comander of a ship in the Harbor by his libell & Complaint bearing date 29th of november 1680 plantiff against mr Daniel Turell sen deffendt in an Action of the Case for that the sajd Turell buying a ship of him as she lay at charls Toune at Gree[n]es wharfe for forty pound mony refused and still doth refuse to pay him the sajd clay for the same as in the sajd libell refference thereto being had more at large doeth & may Appeare After the libell Attachments & deffendants Answer pleading for a non suite was read & duely Considered of by the Court the Court Adjudged that the plaintiffe was non suited=

Att A Court of Assistants or Admiralty held at Boston ‖ in N Engld ‖ 9th of December 1680

~~wm kelso chirurgeon~~

[123] 1680 9th december 1680

Kelso agt Branson

wm Kelso chirurgeon of ship Ann & Hesther of London by his libell & Complaint exhibbited to this Court bearing date the 4th of December 1680 plaintiff against francis Branson master & Comander of sajd ship together wth sajd ship deffendant for that he the sajd master hath Gonne beyond his power & authority in tirannically & most cruelly beating and abusing him aboard sajd ship for no other reason but because he would not doe the office of a cooke not being bound thereto & shipt only for his chirugeon Calling a Council of warr vpon him and dischardging him of his place thô he offered to hire one to prforme the Cooks office pretending his Cruell vsage of him was his Jealousy that he should report of his bull bayting & fishing on the Lords Day and refusing to pay him his wages & cleare him he being Justly afrajd of his life as in his libell refference thereto

* Error of the Secretary for "The George of Bristoll."

being had more Amply doth & may Appeare After the libell Attachment and euidences in the Case produced were read & duely Considered of The Court declared they Adjudged for the plaintiffe & decreed that he be freed from the ship and that the deffendant pay the plaintiffe all his wages abating only for sixe weekes wch Comes to in all nineteene pounds fiueteen shillings & sixe pence ‖ starling money of England ‖ as also paying the Costs of the Court fowe[r] pounds fiueteene shillings & sixe pence this Country money

John Bowland mate of the Good ship called the Ann & Hester of London by his libell & Complaint exhibbited to this Court bearing date the 1st of December 1680 plaintiffe against ffrancis Branson master & Comander of the sajd shipp together with the sajd ship deffendant for that he the sajd francis Branson master = refused and still doeth refuse to pay him his Wages not withstanding his performance of his sajd service in sajd ship and his particcular promise besides past in the Isle of may in June last * at his the sajd Boulands arrivall in New England and being Agrieved he would pay him his wages and cleare him of his service from the sajd ship as in sajd libell refference thereto being had Amply doth and may Appeare After the libell Attachment and euidences in the Case produced were read and duely Considered of the Court declared that they Adjudged the plantiffe to pay the deffendant his Costs twelue shillings

Bouland ag[t] ffrancis Branson

30 october 1680

[*The following paragraph is written on the lower edge of the page.*]

The Gou͞no[r] & magists. met in a Court of Assistants & ordered in Ans[r] to the peticon of Georg Hutchinson that any orde[r] formerly notw[th]standing if the sajd Georg Hutchinson shall w[th] his sue[r]tjes enter into bond of one hundred ^ to respond the Judgment of any of his majtes Courts in this Colony once within a yeare of this date in Relation to y[e] sd Tobacco then the sd Bond to be voyd =

Ans[r] to m[r] Georg Hutchinson

[124] 1680

At A Court of Assistants or Admiralty held at Boston ‖ in N Eng ‖ 24th of December 1680

present
Tho. Danforth Esq[r] Dep[t] Gou͞
Richd Saltonstall
Daniel Gookin

Edward Randolph esq[r] Collecto[r] of his Majestjes †

* The word "that" apparently was omitted here by the Secretary.
† Written over "ℯ𝓇 by his."

Wm Staughton
Joseph Dudley
Peter Bulkley
Humphry Davy
Tho Sauage
Jno Richards
John Hull
James Russell
— — — —
persons Returnd to serve on the Jury & Sworne were =
— — — —
mr Thomas Jenner
Wm Gilbert
John ffoy
stephen Burton
Thomas Moore
James Loyd
Thomas Berry
Thomas Jolls
Sam Ballard
Joseph Newell
stephen Cadman
John Knight
— — — —

Customes in New England &c by his Information or lybell plaintiffe against Timothy Armitage master of the Good ship Called the two siste^rs of Boston deffendant as in the said Information or libell refference thereto being had more Amply doth & may Appeare After the euidences in the Case produced were read Comitted to the Jury wch are on file wth the reccords of this Court the Jury brought in their virdict they found for the deffendant costs of Court =

Edward Randolph Esqr Collector &c by his Complaint exhibbited to this Court plaintiff prosecuting T[i]mothy Armitage master of ship two siste^rs vpon breach of the act of the fowe^rteenth of the king for Affronting & disturbing him the sajd Edward Randolph in prosecution of his trust & office After the euidences in the Case produced were read &c the Court Judged it meete to sentence the sajd Timothy Armitage to pay as a fine forty pounds money* & stands Comitted till this sentence be performed

mr Randolphs 6† Cases on ys & the other side =
— — — —

Edward Randolph Esqr Collector &c by his libell & complaint plaintiffe agt John Huling master of the ship Called the maydenhead together with the sajd ship defendant as in sajd libell & Complaint refference thereto being had Amply doth & may Appeare After the euidences in the Case produced were read & Comitted to the Jury the Jury brought in their virdict they found for the deffendant Costs of Court all wch ~~is~~ on file wth the Reccords of this Court =

Edward Randolph Esqr Collector of his maj^tjes Customes in New England by his libell and Complaint plaintiff against the Barcque Called the Gift of God and the master thereof as in sajd libell refference thereto being had doth and may Appeare John Brock master of sajd barque or ship being in Court by Consent this Accon proceeded the euidences in the Case produced were read = The Court declared ‖ yt ‖ their sence is that in and from all distinct places & Goverments entrjes must be made by all strainge^rs but It Appearing that the sajd vessell had entred at the Prouince of majne & cleered as the acts of

* Written over the word "fine."

† Written over "4."

trade require & that shee brought hither neither European nor * Plantation Goods doe order hir now to make entry heere as the law provides & pay the plaintiffe fiue pounds Costs & officers ffees =

[125] 1680 1681

Edward Randolph Esqr Collector &c by his libell & Complaint plaintiff agt two hogsheads of Irish yarne &c in the hands of Joseph Harding deffendant as in sajd Libell refference thereto being had more Amply doth & may Appeare The Euidences in the Case were read & Comitted to the Jury who brought in their virdict they found for the deffendant Costs of Court = eight shillings

Edward Randolph Esqr Collector &c by his libell & Complaint plaintiffe against ship expedition & samuel Lugg master thereof deffendant as in sajd Lybell refference thereto being had more Amply doth and may Appeare After the euidences in the Case produced were read Comitted to the Jury and are on file The Jury brought in their virdict they found for the deffendant Costs of Court =

ffrancis Branson Comander of ship Ann & Hesther by his libell and Complaint plaintiffe against wm kelso Chirurgeon by way of Revejw of an Action trjed at the Court of Assistants or Admiralty on the ninth Instant as in sajd libell & Courts Judgment refference thereto being had Amply doth & may Appeare After the libell & euidences in the Case produced were read ~~Comitted to the Jury~~ & are on file with the Reccords of this Court The Court declared that they Judged It meete to order the plaintiff to pay the deffendant his Costs three pounds sixteene shillings & sixe pence =

at ye same Court wthout a Jury was tried & Issued ye Case betweene ffrancis Branson & wm kelso on Revejw

[*The two following records of Admiralty Courts were evidently entered out of their chronological order.*]

Att a Court of Assistant Called & sumoned to sitt in Boston 17th of June 1681

or Admiralty

present
symon Bradstreet Esqr Go
Tho Danforth Esqr dept Gou
Daniell Gookin mjr Genl
wm Stoughton
Joseph Dudley

Tho Gretian master of the Pincke Expectation by his libell & Complaint exhibbited to this Court [and] by his Attachment Bearing

* Written over the word "Goods."

Humphry Davy
Tho Sauage
Jno Richards
Jno Hull
Samuel Nowell
James Russell } Esqrs
— — — —

date the 10th Instant plaintiff against Josiah Torry deffendant for that the sajd Torrey refuseth to pay vnto the sajd Gretian the sume of twenty seven pounds fiueteene shillings & seuen pence money due for disbursements and wages vpon his eighth part of the sajd Pincke for seuerall voyages as p an Account given the sajd Torrey march 21 (1680) & by the libell dated as aboue & other euidences may Appeare &c After the sajd libell & Attachment dated as aboue wth the other euidences produced were Read ~~Comitted to the Jury~~ and duely Considered of by the the * Court the Court declared they Adjudged for the deffendt & Granted him Costs of Court eight shillings & six penc =

[126] 1681

Thomas Gretion master of the Pinck expectation by his libell & Complaint exhibbited to this Court as also by his Attachment dated the 10th Instant June Refferenc thereto being had plaintiff agt Barnard Shinchinke merchant & particularly agt his ye sajd Shinchinks 3/8 parts of sajd Pinck expectation and all hir Appurtenances Attached to value of two hundred pounds to Respond his sajd Complt for that the sajd Shinchink hath not payd the sajd Gretion one hundred & seuen pounds nine shillings & nine penc in mony due for wages and disbursments vpon the sajd ship or Pincke for seuerall voyages as p the sajd libell bearing date date † as aboue & by the Account of the same date & other euidences may appeare &c ‖ ye defendt was Called but not Appeared sumons left at his last aboad mr Joseph Rock as Returnd ‖ After the libell Attachmt Account & other euidences produced were Read & duly Consid[ered] of by ye Court The Court Adjudged for the plaintiffe the balance in the Account sworne to being one hundred & seuen pounds nine shillings & nine penc mony & the chardg & Costs of Court wch Came to three pounds sixteene shillings & fower pence =

ye deffendt called but not Appearing sumons being left at his last place of Aboad mr Rocks as Returnd =

And It is ordered by this Court that Thomas Gretian giving sufficient security wth two suertys by bond to the Tresurer of the Country in two hundred & fowerteen pounds nineten shilling & sixepenc ‖ to ‖ respond the Revejw or Reuersion of the action aboue by ye sajd Barnard Schinkink his heires Attur[n]ey or Agent recouering any Judgment in any Court of his majestjes in this Jurisdiction wthin on yeare & a day from this time relating to what this day past: =

* "the" repeated in the record. † "date" repeated in the record.

Att a Court of Assistants or Admiralty held at Boston in New England the 4th of August 1681. and then Adjourned to the 11th Instant at three of the clock: when they Sat

Paul sharrot or Starast Leifteñnt & Cloice Pieterson mate of ship Salamander a Prize belonging to the Great Prince the Duke of Brandenburgh by their libell & Complaint exhibitted to This Court Dated the 2d of August 1681 plaintiffs against marcellus Cocke Captaine of sajd ship & sajd ship deffendants for their wages i e Paul sharrot or starrast for a sixty fiue pounds sterling for sixteen months and a halfe service and the sajd Clojce Pieterson for the sume of a sixty pounds for like service as in the sajd libell- refference thereto being had more Amply doeth & may Appeare — After the libell the Attachment & other euidences in the Case produced by the plaintiffs & deffendant (who both Appeared in Court) were read and duely Considered of by the Court they Adjudged for the deffendant Ordering the plaintiffs to pay the officers their ffees out of their Caution ^ & the officer to Returne them the rest =

Paul sharrot or starast &c agt marcellus Cock Cap't of salamander

[127] 1680

Att A Court of Assistants held at Boston the 1st of march 1680

present
Symon Bradstreet Esqr Gou
Tho: Danforth Esqr dept Go
Richard Saltonstall
Daniel Gookin
Daniel Dennison
wm staughton
Joseph Dudley
Nathaniel Saltonstall
Humphry Davy
Tho Sauage
wm Broune
John Richards
Jno Hull
Samuel Nowell
James Russell
Bartholmew Gidney
} Esqrs

mrs Elizabeth Cooke executrix & mr Elisha Cooke execcutor plaintiffes in an Action of Appeale on Attaint of the Jury whereof mr Holliok was foreman = Aagainst * Capt James olliuer deffendant: from the virdict of the Jury at the last Court of Assistants After the Attachment the Courts Judgment & euidences in the Case produced were read Comitted to the Jury & are remayñg on file The Jury brought in their virdict i e in the sajd Case depending between the sd mrs Eliza: Cook & mr Elisha Cooke plaintiff and the Atturneys of Captn James olliuer deffendants the Jury finds for the plaintiff seventy two pounds fiueteene shillings and nine pence money & Costs of Courts

ent. p Elis. Cooke

persons Returned to serve on ye Grand Jury & sworne were

mr John Blake
Thomas Berry
James Pemberton
Tho Gardiner
James strawbridge

* So written in the record.

Nathaniel sparhauke
Tobjas Dauis
Phillip Torrey
Robert Herrington
Tho Tyleston sen
Tho Trott
wm Dady
Jno Heyman
— — — —

seuen pounds fowerteen shillings & 4d Reuersing the former Judgment =

wm waters plaintiffe on Appeale from the Judgment or sentence of the County Court at Boston = This Accon was wthdraune by the plaintiff by leaue & licenc of the Court =

Thomas Hill plaintiffe against wm obbinson deffendant in an Accon of Appeale from the Judgment of the County Court in Boston = After the Attachment Courts Judgment Reasons of Appeale & euidences in the Case produced were read Comitted to the Jury & are remayning on file wth the Reccords of this Court the Jury brought in their virdict they found for the deffendant Confirmation of the former Judgment & Costs of Courts

1st Jn

Benjamin Balch plaintiff in an Action of Appeale from the Judgment of the last County Court at Ipswich against wm Dodge Jun deffendant After Calling of ye Accon ys Case by Consent of partjes was refferrd to ye Bench who hearing the Attachmt Courts Judgment reasons of Appeale & euidences in the Case produced the Bench reuerst the former Judgment & Judged for the plaintiff granting him his Costs forty eight shillings —

Josiah Torrey plaintiff in an Action of Appeale from the Judgment of the County Court at Boston agt Tho Gretian deffendant after the Attachmt Courts Judgment Reasons of Appeale & euidences in the Case produced were read Comitted to the Jury & are on file wth the Reccords of this Court the Jury brought in their virdict i e In this Case the Jury finds for the plaintiff that the deffendant in thirty dayes shall give a Just & true Account of all disbursments vpon & earnings of the Pinck expectation according to Attachmt or pay two hundred pounds money to the plaintiff and Costs of Courts reuersing the former Judgment costs 3li = 02s & 4d.

Exec Issued

persons returnd & sworne to serve on ye Jury for Attaints were =
— — — —
Capt Richd Sprague
Richard Harris
Adam Winthrop
Timo Armitage
Jno Scate
Samuel Bridge
Timo Thornton
Ambrose Dawes
Dauid Copp
Sam[u]el Gookin

Mr Joseph Rocke plaintiff against m's Sarah ffranck deffendant in an action of Appeale from the Judgment of the County Court in Boston After the

Attachment Courts Judgment Reasons of Appeale & Euidences in the Case produced were Read Comitted to the Jury & are on file wth the Reccords of this Court the Jury brought in their virdict they found for the deffend^t^ Confirmation of the former Judgment & Costs of Courts 2^li^ 11. 10

31	4	6
2	11	10
33	16	4

Isaac Hill
Abra: Jackson
Daniel Brewer
Abrah How
Benj. Gamblin
Joseph Rise
Jn^o^than Broune
Samuel stearnes
Joseph sherman

[128] 1680

George Carr Sen̄ plaintiff in an action of Appeale ag^t^ Capt Nicholas Paige deffend^t^ from the Judgment of the County Court at Salem After the Attachment Courts Judgment Reasons of Appeale &c were read the deffendant pleading for a non suite It was Granted

Timothy Tyleston
Henry Leadbetter
John Toleman
Daniel Preston
Tho. Jenner
— — — —
persons Returned & sworne to serve on the 1st Jury of Tryalls for Appeales lyfe lymb &c
— — — —

Walter fairefeild plaintiff against Thomas Knowlton deffendant in an Action of Appeale from the Judgment of the last County Court at Salem after the Attachment Courts Judgment Reasons of Appeale and euidences in the Case produced were read Comitted to the Jury and are on file the Jury brought in their virdict they found for the plaintiff reuersion of the former Judgment & Costs of Courts. ═

2^d^ Jur

1st Jur
Capt Richard Sprague
Jno Conney
Solomon Phipps
Jno Parmiter
Samuel Gookin
Samuel Bridge
Abraham Jackson
Joseph Rise
Samuel Stearnes
John Scates
Abraham How
Ambrose Daues *
— — — —
persons Returnd & sworne for to se^r^ve ye 2^d^ Jury of trialls for Appeales life Limbe &c

Joseph Holmes Atturney & substitute of James mathews of new Yorke plaintiff against John Keene deffendant in an Action of Appeale from the Judgm^t^ of the County Court in January last at Boston ═ After the Attachment the Courts Judgment Reasons of Appeale & euidences in the Case produced were Read Comitted to the Jury and are on file wth the Reccords of this Court the Jury brought in their virdict In the Case depending betweene Joseph Homes substitute of Jno dafforne Atturney to James mathews plt & John Keene deffend^t^ the Jury finds for y^e^ deffendant Confirmation of the forme^r^ Judgment the deffend^t^ paying

1st Jur

Capt Richard Wooddy
John Toleman
Daniel Copp
Isack Hill
Daniel Brewer
Benja Gamblinn
Jonathan Browne
Henry Leadbetter
Daniel Preston
Joseph sherman

* Or Dawes.

Timothy Tyleston Timothy Thornton =

the plaintiff thirty fiue shillings money & Costs of Courts * =

— — — —

George Speere plaintiff against Peeter Bracket deffend[t] in an action of Appeale from the Judgment of the County Court at Boston: the plaintiff w[th]drew his Accon hauing leaue from the Court so to doe =

Tho Gretian plaintiff against Stephen Sweathy deffendant in an Accon of Appeale from the Judgment of the County Court at Boston in January last after the Attachment Courts Judgment Reasons of Appeale & euidences in the Case produced were read Comitted to the Jury and are on file w[th] the Records of this Court the Jury brought in their virdict = the Jury found for y[e] deffendant Confirmation of the former Judgment & Costs of Courts = The plaintiff in open Court sajd he did Attaint the Jury ‖ whereof Cap[t] Rich[d] sprague was foreman ‖ for erro[r]s & mistakes and accordingly Tho. Gretian principle & Anthony Checkly & Nathaniel willjams his sue[r]tjes acknowledged themselues Bound in tenn pounds a peece to the Tresure[r] of the Country on Condition that sajd Thomas Gretian shall prosecute this his Attaint at the nex[t] Court of Assistants to effect as y[e] law Requires from y[e] virdict of the Jury whereof Cap[t] sprague was foreman

Greitian ag[t] sweathy 1st Jury Cloathes

Steve[n] Sweatie † plaintiff ag̃t Thom[s] Greatian ‡ deffend[t] in an Action of Appeale from the Judgment of the County Court at Boston in Janũry last After the Attachment Courts Judgment Reasons of Appeale & euidences in the Case produced were read Comitted to the Jury and are on file the Jury brought in their virdict i e they found for the plaintiff Reuersion of the former Judgment and seuenteene pounds sixteene shillings sixe pence mony & Costs of Courts the ~~plaintiff~~ ‖ deffend[t] ‖ Attainted the Jury ‖ whereof Cap[t] Rich[d] sprague was forman ‖ for errors & mistake[s] & Accordingly Tho Gretian principle & Anthony checkly & nathaniel

steph̃ sweathy pltf 1st Jury for wages Idem uersus Idem

* This verdict is on file and agrees with the record.

The appeal is from the judgment (or verdict) of the County Court in an action of Review Jan. 25, 1680–1, when a verdict was rendered for Keen for "26[li] 5[s] 9[d] in money and costs of Court."

The apparent anomaly in the verdict at the Court of Assistants may perhaps be explained as the result of an adjustment, there being several actions pending between the same parties. See Court Files, Suffolk Nos. 1827 and 2052.

† Written over "Tho Gretian." ‡ Written over "Stephen Sweathy."

willjams his sue^r^tjes aknowledged themselues jointly & seuerally bound in tenn pounds apeec to y^e^ Tresure^r^ of the Country as aboue on this Condition that sajd Gretian shall ꝓsecute this his Attaint at y^e^ next Court of Assistants to effect ag^t^ sajd Jury whereof Capt sprage was foreman =

[129] 1680

Thomas Gretian plaintiff ag^t^ Roger stayno^r^ deffend^t^ in an action of Appeale from the Judgment of the County Court in January las^t^ After the Attachment Courts Judgment Reasons of Appeale & euidences in the Case produced were read Comitted to the Jury & are on file The Jury declard they found for the deffendant Confirmation of the former Judgment & twenty two shillings more money & costs of Courts The plaintif Tho Gretian In open court Attainted the Jury for erro^r^s & palpable mistakes & Accordingly sajd Tho Gretian principle & Anthony cheeckly & Nathaniel willjams his sue^r^tjes acknowledged themselues Jointly & seuerally bound in tenn pounds a peec to the Tresure^r^ of the Country on y^s^ Condition that sd Tho. Gretian prosecut this his Attain^t^ of the Jury to effect

1st Jur

Gretion ag^t^ staintor

Idem ꝟsus Idem on Appeale from the Judgment of the County Court at Boston in January last After the Attachment Courts Judgment reasons of Appeale & euidences in the Case produced were read Comitted to ye Jury & are on file wth the Reccords of this Cour^t^ the Jury brought in their virdict they found for the Deffendant Confirmation of the former Judgment & Costs of Courts the plaintiff Attainted the Jury and sajd Thomas Gretian principle & Anthony cheeckley & Nathaniel willjams his sue^r^tjes acknowledged themselues joyntly & seuerally bound in tenn pounds a peece to the Tresurer of the Country on this Condicion that sajd Gretian shall prosecute this his Attaint of s^d^ Jury at the nex^t^ Court of Assistants to effect =

Gretian ag^t^ staintor

Richard Collecot & nathaniel Greenwood plaintiffs ag^t^ John How deffendant in an Action of Appeale from the Judgm^t^ of Ipswich County Court After the Attachment Courts Judgment Reasons of Appeale & euidences in the Case produced ^ comitted to the Jury & are on file the Jury brought in their virdict they found

Collecot &c ag^t^ How

exec Issued out 4 June 1681

– – – –

for the plaintiffs Reṽsion of the former Judgment & Costs of Courts 3li 3s

Robert knight plaintiff in an action of Appeale from ye Judgment of Ipswich Court agt Sam: Leach & onesephirus Allen deffendts After the Attachment Courts Judgment Reasons of Appeale & euidences in the Case produced were read Comitted to the Jury & are on file wth the Reccords of ys Court the Jury brought in their virdict they found for the plaintiff reuersion of the former Judgment and the land in controuersy & Costs of Courts eight pounds fiueteen shillings & tenn pence =

Knight agt Leach er

Jno Playsted plaintiff against George Norton deffendt in an action of Appeale from the Judgment of the County Court at Boston After ye Attachment Courts Judgment Reasons of Appeale and euidences in the Case produced were read Comitted to the Jury & are on file wth the Reccords of this Court the Jury brought in their virdict they found for the plaintiffe reuersion of the former Judgment & Costs of Courts eight pounds fiueteene shillings & tenn pence — —

Playsted agt Norton.

execution Issued out

|| Sam || & Jno Bennet plaintiffs against Leonard Douden* deffendant in An action of Appeale from from † the Judgment of the County Court at Boston ^ January last After the Attachment Courts Judgment reasons of Appeale & euidences in the Case produced were read Comitted to the Jury & are on file wth the Reccords of this Court the Jury brought in their virdict they found for the plaintiffs reuersion of the former Judgment & Costs of Courts

Sam & Jno Bennet plt agt Leonard Douden & Tho Paddy —

[130] 1680

Timothy Yeales plaintiff agt Roger Rose deffendt in an Action of Appeale from the Judgment of the County Court at Boston After the Attachment Courts Judgment reasons of Appeale & euidences in the Case produced were read Comitted to the Jury & are on file wth the Reccords of this Court the Jury

yeales vs. Rose

* By the papers on file it appears that the defendants in this action of appeal were "Leonard Dowden and Thomas Paddy, Administrs to the estate of William Paddy, decd., as Assignees of Hudson Leverett."

† "from" repeated in the record.

brought in their virdict they found for the deffendant Confirmation of the former Judgment & Costs of Courts

Jn° Gifford plaintiff ag[t] Phillip Read deffend[t] in an action of Appeale frō the Judgment of the County Court at Boston = After the Attachment Courts Judgment Reasons of Appeale & euidences in the Case produced were read Comitted to the Jury & are on file w[th] the reccords of this Court the Jury brought in their virdict they found for the deffend[t] D[r] phillip Read Confirmation of the forme[r] Judgment & Costs of Courts the plaintiff in open Court Attainted the Jury ffor erro[r]s & mistakes & accordingly John Gifford principle & John Joyliffe his sue[r]ty Acknowledged themselues Jointly & seuerally bound in tenn pounds apeece to the Tresure[r] of the Country on this Condition that sajd John Gifford shall prosecute this his Attaint of y[e] Jury at the nex[t] Cour[t] of Assistants according to Law:

Gifford ag[t] Reade 2[d] Jur

Attaint

Daniel Heinshaw* plaintiff ag[t] Thomas voss deffendant in an action of Appeale from the Judgment of the County Court in Boston After the Attachm̄n[t] Courts Judgment Reasons of Appeale & euidences in the Case produced were read Comitted to the Jury and are on file w[th] the Reccords of this Court the Jury brought in their virdict they found a speciall virdict i e That if willjam Pond his originall deed w[th] his Assignment & Conveyance & fowe[r]teen yeares possession be more valid in Law then Joseph Homes his latter deed to Thomas vosse now in Court then wee find for the plaintiffe the land now in Controuersy & Costs of Courts but if othe[r]wise wee finde for the deffendant Confirmation of the former Judgment & Costs of Courts ‖ the Bench found for y[e] pltff Reu̅con of the form[r] Judgm[t] & Costs of Courts three pounds thirteen shilling & eight pence (3: 13. 8. ‖

Heinshaw ag[t] vosse

Joseph Joy ‖ & Nath[l] Beale ‖ plaintiff ag[t] Hudson Leueret deffendant in an Action of Appeale from the Judgment of the County Court at Boston in Janu̅y last after y[e] Attachment courts Judgment Reasons of Appeale & euidences in the Case produced were read Comitted to the Jury & are on file wth the Reccords of this Court the Jury brought in their virdict They

Joy &c ag[t] Leueret

* "Daniell Henshaw" in the original verdict on file.

found for the deffendant Confirmation of the forme^r^ Judgment & Costs of Courts the plaintiff in open Court Attainted the Jury ‖ for erro^r^s & mistakes ‖ & accordingly Joseph Joy & nathaniel Beale principles & Joshua Hubbard Juñ their sue^r^ty did acknowledg themselues Joyntly & seuerally bound in ten pounds apeece to the Tresurer of the Country on Condition that sajd Joy & Beale shall prosecut their Attaint at the nex^t^ Court of Assistant[s] according as the law requires

cheeckly ag^t^ Hutchinson

Anthony cheeckley Atturney to Capt Joshua scottow plaintiff ‖ Against Eliakim Hutchinson deffendt ‖ in an action of Appeale from the Judgment of the County Court in Boston After the Attachment Courts Judgment reasons of Appeale & euidences in the Case produced were read Comitted to ye Jury & are on file, the Jury brought in their virdict they found in y^t^ Case betweene m^r^ Anthony cheeckley plaintiff & m^r^ Eliakim Hutchinson deffendant the Jury finds for the deffendant fiue pounds three shillings nine pence mony ‖ Reūsing ye form^r^ Judgmen^t^ ‖ & costs of Courts

1st Jury

Thayer ag^t^ m^r^ Savage

Attaint

Richd Thajer plaintiff against majo^r^ Thomas Sauage deffendt in an Action of Appeale from the Judgment of the County Court at Boston After ye Attachment Courts Judgment Reasons of Appeale & euidences in the Case produced were read Comitted to ye Jury & are on file. In the Case depending between Richard Thayer plaintiff & majo^r^ Thomas sauage deffendant The Jury finds for the deffend^t^ Confirmation of the forme^r^ Judgm^t^ & Costs of Courts Richd Thayer in open Court Attainted the Jury for erro^r^s & mistakes & accordingly Richd Thajer principle & Nath. Thajer & Jno Pittom his sur^e^tjes acknowledged themselues Jointly & seuerally bound in tenn pounds a peece to ye Tresurer of ye Country on condition y^t^ sajd Richd Thaje^r^ shall prosecute this his Attaint at ye next Court of Assistants as ye law requires

[131] 1680

1st Jur

Thajer ag^t^ Clap

Richard Thajer plaintiff against Capt Roger Clap deffendant in an action of Appeale from the Judgment of the County Court in Boston after the Attachment courts Judgment Reasons of Appeale & euidences in the Case produced were read Comitted to the Jury & are on file wth the Reocords of this Court the Jury brought in their virdict they found for the deffendant Confirmation of the former Judgment & Costs of Courts

John Richards plaintiffe against Josiah witter deffendant in an action of Appeale from the Judgment of the County Court at Ipswich after the Attachm[t] Courts Judgment Reasons of Appeale & euidences in the Case produced were Read Comitted to the Jury and are on file w[th] the Reccords of this Court the Jury brought in their virdict they found for the plaintiff reuersion of the former Judgment & Costs of Courts three pounds tenn shillings

Richards ag[t] witter =

execut : Issued out 19 . Ap[r] . 82 . for 3[li] 10[s]

m[r] Jn[o] Saffyn plaintiff against m[r] Robe[r]t Holt deffendt in an Accon of Appeale from the Judgment of the County Court at Boston After the Attachment Courts Judgment reasons of Appeale & euidences in the Case produced were read Comitted to the Jury and are on file w[th] the Reccords of this Court the Jury brought in their virdict they found for the plaintiff reuersion of the former Judgment & Costs of Courts fiuety fower shilling & two pence =

Saffjn ag[t] Holt 2 Jur

Tho voss : plaintiff ag[t] Daniel Heinshaw deffend[t] ~~after the Atta~~ ‖ In an action ‖ of Appeale from the Judgment of the County Court at Boston After the Attachment Courts Judgment Reasons of Appeale & euidences in the Case produced were read Comitted to the Jury & are on file wth the reccords of this Court the Jury brought in their virdict they found for the plantiffe reuersion of the forme[r] Judgment & Costs of Courts fiue pounds one shilling =

voss ag[t] Heinshaw

Abiel Lamb plt agt Tho Hill deffend[t] in an Action of Appeale from the Judgm̄[t] of the County Court at Boston y[e] plaintiff w[th]drew his Accon by leaue from the Court

Lambe ag[t] Hill

Jn[o] Turne[r] Atturney to Ephrajm Turner pltff ag[t] Thaddews micarter deffend[t] in an Action of Appeale from the Judgment of the County Court at Boston the plaintiff w[th]drew this his Accōn by leaue from the Court

Turne[r] ag[t] micarte[r]

Georg foules Costs agt Hudson Leueret

George ffoule had fiue shillings || & 6d || Granted || him for || his costs agt Hudson Leueret for his non psecution* of his Appeale from charls Towne Court 21 10 mo 80. at this Court

Nath Heymans Costs agt Jno moore

Nathan Heyman had fiue shillings Granted him for his Costs agt John moore for his non prosecution of his Appeale at ys Court from charls Towne County Court.

Jno Dyars Indictmt

Jno Dyar of Braintry was Indicted by the name of John dyar of Braintry in the County of suffolke in New England for not hauing the feare of God before your eyes and being Instigated by the diuill on the 31th of January last did wickedly murder and kill Jno Ahattawants Indian by shooting him wth swan shott con'rary to the peace of our Soueraigne Lord the king his crowne & dignity the lawe of God & of this Jurisdiction being brought to the barr to this Indictment pleaded not guilty put himself on God & the Country for tryall After ye Indictment & euidences in ye Case produced were read Comitted to the Jury and are on file the Jury brought in their virdict they found the prisoner at the barr not guilty according to Indictment but Guilty of manslaughter = In the Case of John Dyar found Guilty of manslaughter It is ordered that the sajd^

[132] 1680

pay vnto the widdow of the sajd Indian slajne sixe pounds i e twenty shilling doune in or as mony and twenty shillings more for fiue yeares successively from this day and also dischardg & pay the charg of the wittnesses & his Imprisonment & prosecution of this Case giving good security for performance of this order standing Comitted till it be don. bond was taken & giuen to ye Tresure [] wth 20^wch he pd to sd Ahattawants widdow =

bond dd to ye Tresurer & 20

1st march 168 0/1 || or || 15th mrch

Mary Hale of Boston widdow was Indicted by the name of mary Hale for that yow not hauing the feare of God before yor eyes and being Instigated by the divill hauing had familiarity wth him by the abhorred sin & art of witchcraft did kill & bewitch

* Error of the record for psecution.

one * Smit to death Contrary to the peace of our Soveraign Lord the king his Croune & dignity the lawes of God and of this Jurisdiction = to wch Indictment the prisoner at the Barr pleaded not Guilty put hirself on tryall by God & the Country After the Indictment & euidences in the Case produced were Read Comitted to the Jury & are on file wth the Reccords of this Court the Jury brought in their virdict they found the prisoner at the Barr mary Hale not Guilty according to Indictment =

mary Hales Indictmt

Tho: Dauis & Jno Eggington ‖ ~~Appearing before the Court & being Convicted of being~~ ‖ two Incorrigible theeves & Robbers standing so Convicted & now allso for many reitterated Oaths & Cursings of themselues & others threatning if loose to burne the Towne were sentenct to be seuerely whipt wth twenty stripes & then Returnd to prison =

Dauis & Egginton's Censure &c

Tho. Dauis & Jno Eggerton Appearing before the Court & Conuicted of being Incorrigible Theeves hauing been formerly sentenced for fellonious taking away goods from sundry persons to value of about fiuety pounds and breaking prison before the sentence was performed & since then of stealing from samuel mason to value of Twenty pounds sixe shillings: are sentenced to restore treble damages to the sajd mason and to pay all charges of prosecution & Imprisonment and in Case of non payment to be sold by the sajd samuel Mason wthin one moneth or else by the Treasurer & sent to any of the English Plantations & they are also further sentenced that after their departure or being sent out of this his Majties Colony that they returne no more wthin the ljmitts thereof on payne of death and stands Comitted till this sentence be performed —

Dauis & Eggertons Sentence =

[133]

[*Blank space.*]

Att a Court of Assistants held at Boston 1st June 1681

present Symon Bradstreete Esqr Gov Tho Danforth Esqr dept Gov Dani: Gookin Esqr majr Genl

In Ansr to the peticon of wm morse in behalf of his wife Elisabeth morse & of hirs also. The Court

* Blank space in the record. From the papers on file it appears the name of the person said to be bewitched was "Michael Smith."

Danl Dennison Esqr
Jno Pynchon
Joseph Dudley
Nath Saltonstall
Tho Sauage
Jno Hull
James Russell
Peter Tilton
— — — —

Judgeth it meet to Repreive the sajd Elisabeth morse the Condemned prisoner to the end of the next session in Octobe^r^ and in the meantime order hir dismission from the prison in Boston to Returne home wth hir husband to Newbery Prouided she goe not aboue sixteen Rods from hir Oune house || & land || at any time except to the meeting house in Newbery nor remoove from the place Appointed hir by the minister & selectmen to sitt in whilst there

past. E R S

[*Blank space.*]

[134] 1681

present
Symon Bradstreet Esqr Gov
Richard Saltonstall
Daniel Gookin
Daniel Dennison
Wm Stoughton
Joseph Dudley
Peter Bulkley
Nathaniell Saltonstall
Humphry Davy
Thomas Sauage
John Richards
John Hull
James Russell
Samuel Nowel
Peter Tilton
Bartholmew Gjdney
Samuel Apleton
} Esqrs
— — — —
persons Returnd to serve on the Grand Jury & Sworne were
— — — —
mr Jonas Clarke
Richrd way
Theoder Atkinson
Thomas Duers
Joseph Dauis
wm Dady
Richrd Louden
Tho Tyleston
Tho Tolman
wm Goddard
Tho: ffegg
Tho weld
Jno Stebbins
wm Maning
— — — —

Att A Court of Assistants held at Boston 6th September 1681

Thomas Gretian plaintiff in an Accon of Appeale on Attaint against stephen sweathy Deffendant from the virdict of the Jury whereof Capt Richard Sprague was foreman After the sajd virdict Courts Judgm^t^ Attachment Reasons of Appeale & euidences in the Case produced were read Comitted to the Jury and are on file wth the Reccords of this Court the Jury brought in their virdict they found for the deffendant the Confirmation of the forme^r^ Judgment & costs of Courts.

for wages

Thomas Gretian plaintiff in an action of Appeale on Attaint against stephen Sweathy deffend^t^ from the virdict of the Jury whereof Capt Rich^d^ sprague was foreman After the sajd virdict Attachment Reasons of Appeale & euidences in the Case produced were read Comitted to the Jury & are on file wth the Reccords of this Court the Jury brought in their virdict they found for the deffendant Confirmation of the former Judgment & Costs of Courts

cloths

Thomas Gretian plaintiff in an Action of Appeale on Attajnt agt ~~Stephen sweathy~~ || Roger stainer || deffendt from the virdict of the Jury whereof Capt Richard sprague was foreman After the virdict Attachment Reasons of Appeale and Euidences in the case produced were read Comitted to the Jury and are remajning on file wth the Reccords of this Court the Jury brought in their virdict they found for the deffendant Confirmation of theformer Judgment & Costs of Courts.

for wages

Thomas Gretian plaintiff in an action of Appeale on Attaint against Roger Staynor deffendant from the virdict of the Jury whereof Capt Richard Sprague was foreman. After the virdict Attachment Reasons of Appeale & euidences in the case produced were read Comitted to the Jury and are on file wth the Reccords of this Court the Jury brought in their virdict they found for the deffendant Confirmation of the former Judgment & Costs of Courts

Joseph Joy & Nathaniel Beales plaintiff in an action of Appeale on Attaint agt Hudson Leueret Atturney to Nathaniel Addams deffendt from the virdict of the Jury whereof Capt Richard Sprague was foreman After the virdict Attachment Reasons of Appeale and euidences in the case produced were read Comitted to the Jury & are on file wth the Reccords of this Court the Jury brought in their virdict they found for the deffendant Confirmation of the former Judgment & costs of Courts ~ the Court chancerjed this bond to tenn pounds mony in full of sd Addams damages = & costs of Courts in all foure pounds & two pence

Richard Thajer senr plaintiff in An action of Attaint agt major Thom: Sauage Esqr deffendt. from the virdict of the Jury whereof Capt Richard sprague was foreman. After the virdict of the Jury Attachment Reasons of Appeale & euidences in the Case produced were Read Comitted to the Jury and are on file wth the Reccords of this Court the Jury brought in their virdict they found for the deffendant Confirmation of the former Judgment & Costs of Courts

Thajer agt Sauage

persons Returnd to serve on the Jury for tryalls of the actions of Attaint & sworn were = — — — —

Caps Jno walley
Robert Brimsden
Samuel Jacklin
John Dauis
Jno Newell
Samuel Ballart
Samuel Ketle
Jacob Hurd

[135] 1681

John Cutler Jun
John Brecke
Tymothy ffoster
Isaack Ryall
Elisha ffoster
Jno withrington
Jno Benjamin
Richd whitney
Thomas wilson
Samuel Rugles
Timothy steevens
Thom: Cheny
Samuel Scarborow
Sam: Goffe
Jnoth. R[i]mington
Jno ffuller

— — — —

persons Returnd to serve on the Jury of Tryalls for Appeales life limb & banishmt & 1st sworne were

— — — —

Capt Jno walley
John ffuller
Samuel Ballart
Jno Newell
Jacob Hurd
Sam Scarborow
Isac Ryall
Robert Brimsden
Tho. wilson
Timo Steevens
John Scarlet
wm Roby
|| instead of Sam Jacklin & Tho Cheny dismist ||

— — — —

persons Returnd to serv[ ] on the 2d Jury for Appeal[ ] & sworn were

— — — —

mr Jonathan Rimington
John Davis
Jno Cutler Jun
Samuel Ketle
Jno Brecke
Samuel Goffe
Timo. ffoster
Jno withrington

mr John Gifford plaintiffe in an action of Attaint on appeale againsᵗ Dr Philljp Read deffendant from the virdict of the Jury whereof Capt Richard Woode* was foreman After the virdict Attachment |Courts Judgmt| Reasons of Appeale & euidences in the Case produced were read Comitted to the Jury and are Remayning on file the Jury brought in their virdict they found for the deffendant confirmation of the former Judgment only abating seven pounds & Costs of Courts ~ here ended ye Attaints =

mr James Alljn plaintiff in an Action of Appeale Contra Nathani Putnam deffendt from the Judgment of the last County Court at Salem = After the Attachment Courts Judgment & Reasons of Appeale wth the euidences in the Case produced were read Comitted to the Jury & are on file wth the Reccords of this Court the Jury brought in their virdict they found for the plaintiff reuersion of the former Judgment the land in Controuersy & Costs of Courts fower pounds eighteen shillings & eight pence:

mr Richard wharton plaintiffe in an Action of Appeale Contra Nathaniell Reynold deffendt from the Judgment of the last County Court in Boston = After the Attachment Courts Judgment reasons of Appeale & euidences in the Case produced were read Comitted to the Jury & are on file wth the Reccords of this Court the Jury brought in their virdict they found A† ~~the deffendant confirmation of the former judgment & Costs of Courts~~ || speciall virdict || that is If sajd Reynolds were a legall officer at the time of seizing the hides then wee find for the deffendant Confirmation of the former judgmt & costs of Courts 1li 11s ten penc but if no legall officer then wee finde for the plaintiffe reuersion of the former Judgment & Costs of Courts The Court determins & Judgeth that

* Written over Sprague. † Written over "for."

Left Reynolds was a legall officer & so finds for y[e] deffend[t] confirmation of y[e] forme[r] Judgm[t] & Costs of Courts: m[r] Richard wharton Attainted the Jury for erro[r]s or mistakes and & Accordingly sajd || m[r] || Richard wharton as principall & m[r] Sampson Sheaff his sue ty acknowledged themselues Jointly & seuerally bound & their heires in tenn pounds apeece to the Tresure[r] of the Country & party concerned that sajd wharton shall prosecute his Attaint at the nex[t] Court of Assistants to effect

Richard whitney
Samuel Ruggles
Thomas Cheny
John Benjamin

Thomas Harris butcher plt agt Hannah Long Atturney to w[m] Long in an Acc̃on of Appeale from the Judgm[t] of the County Court in Boston in Aprill last After the Attachment Courts Judgment reasons of Appeale & euidences in the Case produced were read Com̃itted to the Jury and are on file wth the Reccords of this Court the Jury brought in their virdict they found for the deffendant Confirmation of the former Judgment & Costs of Courts

Josiah Torrey plaintiff against Thomas Gretian defend[t] in an action of Appeale from the Judgment of the last County Court in Boston After y[e] Attachment Courts Judgment reasons of Appeale & euidences in the Case produced were read comitted to the Jury and are on file w[th] the Reccord of this Court the Jury brought in their virdict they found for the deffendant Confirmation of the former Judgm[t] & Costs of Courts =

Michael ffarley plaintiff against Edward Lum[m]as deffendant in an action of appeale from the Judgment of the last County Court at Salem After the Attachment Courts Judgment Reasons of Appeale & euidences in the Case produced were read Com̃itted to the Jury & are on file w[th] the Reccords of this Court the Jury brought in their virdict they found for the plaintiff reuersion of the former Judgm[t] & Costs of Courts = thirty two shillings six pence w[ch] wth Costs allowed him at Salem Court 25[s] 4 make in all fifty seven shillings * =

[136] 1681

Peeter Golding & Sarah his wife plaintiff ag[t] Joseph smith deffend[t] in an action of Appeale from the Judgment of the last County Court in Boston After the Attach-

Golding ag[t] smith

* This sum does not agree with the items, but the items agree with the original bill of costs on file. See Court Files Suffolk No. 2008.

ment Courts Judgment Reasons of Appeale & other euidences in the case produced were read Comitted to the Jury & are on file wth the Reccords of this Court the Jury brought in their virdict they found for the plaintiff as an Addition to the former Judgment* fiue pounds mony or else an Acknowledgment to the sattisfaction of the Court & Costs of Courts fiuety three shillings & tenn penc. = Joseph Smith made his Acknowledgment wch was Read in open Court & is in his Case on file wch the Court Accepted of.

Lee agt Heynes

Lee agt Heynes

Joseph Lee plaintiff agt Robert Heynes deffendt in an action of Appeale from the Judgment of the County Court at Ipswich: after the Court had heard the Attachment Courts Judgment Reasons of Appeale & Ansr they Granted the plaintiff a nonsuit the Accon not being trjable at Ipswich & granted him his Costs thirty eight shillings & sixe pence =

knight agt Leach

Robert knight plaintiff agt Samuel Leach & Onesephirus Allen defendants in an Action of Appeale from the Judgment of the County Court at Salem After the Attachment Courts Judgment reasons of Appeale and euidences in the Case were Read Comitted to the Jury and are on file wth the Reccords of this Court the Jury brought in their virdict they found for the plaintiff Reuersion of the former Judgment & the land in Controuersy & costs of Courts

Sam Leach Attainted ye Jury whereof Capt Jno walley was foreman for errors and mistakes & himself principall and Richard norman & philip ffouler his suertjes Acknowledged themselues to be Joyntly & Seuerally bound in forty pounds a peec their heires executs & Admistrs to the Tresurer of ye Country and party Concerned that sajd Leach shall prosecute his Attaint to ye next Court of Assistants to effect =

Ela Agt Chandler

Daniel Ela plaintiff agt Thomas Chandler defendant in an action of Appeale from the Judgment of the County Court at Ipswich after the Attachment Courts Judgment reasons of Appeale & euidences in the Case produced were read Comitted to the Jury & are on file the Jury brought in their virdict they found for the deffendant Confirmation of the former Judgment & Costs of Courts forty one shillings & two penc

* The verdict at the County Court was for the plaintiff (Golding) for twenty shillings and costs. See Court Files Suffolk No. 2003.

James Dauis plaintiff against mary Dauis widdow & Tho Johnson deffend'ts in an Accon of ^ from the Judgment of the County Court at Ipswich. After the Attachment Courts Judgment Reasons of Appeale and euidences in the Case produced were read Comitted to the Jury and are on file the Jury brought in their virdict they found for the plaintiff reuersion of the forme'r Judgment & Costs of Courts — fforty sixe shillings

Dauis vs. Dauis

m'r Thomas Laughton señ Andrew mansfeild & Tho Newhall plaintiff ag't Tho Broune señ deffend't in an Action of Appeale from the Judgment of the County Court at Salem After the Attachment Courts Judgment Reasons of Appeale & euidences in the Case produced were read Comitted to the Jury & are on file w'th the reccords of this Court the Jury brought in their virdict th[e]y found for the plaintiff's reuersion of the former Judgment & Costs of Courts seven pounds one shilling and fower pence

Laughton ag't Broune

[137] 1681

Thomas migeley plaintiff ag't Joseph Smith deffend't in an action of Appeale from the Judgment of the Comissione'rs Court last in Boston Tho migely Came into the Court and declared he w'thdrw his action

Tho migely Case

w'm Lytherland plaintiffe ag't Abell Porter señ deffend't in an action of Appeale from the Judgm̃'t of the County Court in Aprill last in Boston = After the Attachment Courts Judgm̃'t Reasons of Appeale & euidences in the case produced were Read Comitted to the Jury and are on file w'th the Reccords of y's Court the Jury brought in their virdict they found for the deffendant Confirmation of the former Judgment & costs of Courts

w'm Lythe'rland Cont'a abell Porter

Edward Barton plt ag't Daniel Mathews ~~plaintiff~~ ‖ deffend't ‖ in an action of Appeale from the Judgment of the Comissione'rs in Boston after the Attachment Courts Judgment Reason's of Appeale & euidences in the Case produced were read Comitted to the Jury and are on file w'th the reccords of this Court the Jury brought in their virdict they found for

Barton ag't mathews

execution 2's Rec'd

the plaintiff Reūsion of the former Judgment & Costs of Courts = fforty shillings & 4[d]

Sandford agt orchard.

Robe[r]t Sandford plaintiff ag[t] Robe[r]t orchard deffendt in an action of Appeale from the Judgment of the County Court in Aprill last in Boston. After the Attachment Courts Judgment Reasons of appeale and euidences in the Case produced were read Comitted to the Jury and are on file w[th] the Reccords of this Court the Jury brought in their virdict they found for the deffendant Confirmation of the former Judgm[t] wch was 8 : 9. & 10[d] abating three pounds & Costs of Courts wf y[s] Court fowrteen & six penc wch Joseph Holmes engaged for = thirty seven shillings.

exe:

Exec. Issued 17th* Sept:

Porter Cont[a] fflood

Joseph porter plaintiff against James fflood deffend[t] in an Action of Appeale from the Judgment of the County Court in Boston the plt w[th]drew this Accon =

John Parmiter plaintiff on Appeale from the Judgment of the last County Court in Boston after the Judgment of Cour[t] & Reasons of Appeale were read Comitted to the Jury & Read wch are on file the Jury brought in their virdict they found Confirmation of the former Judgment =

Adam winthrop Atturney to wm̄ Harris plaintiff in an action of Appeale from the Judgment of the County Court ag̃[t] michaell Stoakes deffend[t] After the Attachment Courts Judgment reasons of Appeale & euidences in the Case produced were read Comitted to the Jury & are on file wth the reccords of this Court the Jury brought in their virdict they found for the deffendant Confirmation of the former Judgment & Costs of Courts thirty seven shilling

winthrop [℘] Harris ag[t] Stoakes exec Iss[d] out 15 Sep[t]:

Symeon stoddard plaintiff ag[t] Tho. Johnson deffend[t] in an action of Appeale from the Judgment of the County Court in Boston after the Attachment Courts Judgment reasons of Appeale & euidences in the Case produced were read Comitted to the Jury and are on file wth the Reccords of this Court the Jury brought in their virdict they found for the deffend[t] confirmation of the forme[r] Judgment & Costs of Courts

* 17 written over 15.

[138] 1681

Samuel Lord plaintiffe ag^t Timothy Addams deffend^t in an action of Appeale from the Judgment of the County Court at Cambridge after the Attachment Courts Judgment & Reasons of Appeale & euidences in the Case produced were Read Comitted to the Jury & are on file the Jury brought in their virdict they found for y^e plaintiff reūsion of the former Judgm^t & three pounds eight shilling 4^d mony damage & costs of Courts =

Lord ag^t Addams

The Comissione^rs & Selectmen for the Towne of Boston presenting to this Court m^r Henry Sherlot a frenchman y^t is newly come into this Towne as he saj^th a Dancing master ꝑ a person very Insolent & of ill fame that Raues & scoffes at Religion of a Turbulent spirit no way fitt to be tollerated to live in this place and therefor humbly desir[ing] this Court according to their wisdomes to take such orde^r that the sajd sherlott may be remooved & sent away not only out of this Towne but Colony as a person not wth safety to be Admitted to live amongst vs: The Court on pervsall of what was presented voted that m^r sherlot the frenchman dancer & fencer be remooved out of the Country and that he depart accordingly once w^thin two months on pœnalty of Contempt of Authority =

Comission^rs & select mens Complaint ag^t m^r Henry Sherlott

The Courts sentenc

Ann Perry the Court hauing Considered of yor scandalous offence doe sentence yow to be whipt wth fiueteen stripes or pay fiue pounds mony as a fine to the Country dischardging fees of Court standing Comitted till this sentence be performed

An Perry fined. 5^li ꝑ p^d ye Tre^r.

In Ans^r to the peticõn of Samuel Holton of North Hampton humbly desiring to be divorced from mary his now wife Gon from him & sinc her departure hath had a child ꝑ as in y^e euidences in the Case produced ‖ appeares ‖ The Court hauing pervsed & duely Considered of the euidences in the Case Judge it meet to Grant his request & doe sett him free & at libe^rty from hir. =

at Courts Adjourm^t Samuel Holton^s divorce =

Cheffaleer negro servant to Tho Walker brick maker now in Goale on suspition of Joyning wth marja negro in Burning of Dr Swans' & * Lambs

Cheffalee^r negro^s sentence. =

* This space left blank in the record.

houses in Roxbury in July last The Court on Consideration of the Case Judged it meet to orde^r^ that he be kep^t^ in prison till his master send him out of the Country & then dischardg y^e^ charges of Imp^r^isonment wch if he refuse to doe aboue one moneth the Country Tresurer is to see it donn & when y^e^ chardges be defrajd to returne the ouerplus to y^e^ s^d^ walker.

James Pembertons negro sentenc

The like Judgment & sentenc was declard against Jame^s^ pembe^r^tons negro in all respects as a$\tilde{g}$t cheffaleer negro &c

[139] 1681

Marja Negro servant to Joshua Lambe of Roxbury in the County of Suffolke in New England being presented by the Grand Jury was Indicted by the name of marja Negro for not hauing the feare of God before hir eyes & being Instigated by the divil at or vpon the eleventh day of July last in the night did wittingly willingly & felloniously set on fier the dwelling house of Thomas swann of sd Roxbury by taking a Coale from vnde^r^ a still & carrjed it into another Roome and lajd it on ^ floore neere the doore & presently went & crep^t^ into a hole at a back doore of thy master Lambs house & set it on fier also taking a liue Coale betweene two chips & Carried it into the chambe^r^ by which also it was Consumed as by yor * Confession will appeare contrary to the peace of our Soueraigne Lord the king his Croune & dignity the lawes of this Jurisdiction in that Case made & prouided title firing of houses = The prisoner at the barr pleaded & acknowledged hirselfe to be Guilty of y^e^ fact. And accordingly the nex^t^ day being Again brought to the Barr had sentenc of death pronounct a$\tilde{g}$t hir by the Honnō^ble^ Goūno^r^ y^t^ she should Goe from the barr to the prison whenc she Came & thence to the place of Execution & there be burn^t^. = y^e^ lord be mercifull to thy soule s^d^ y^e^ Goū

Marja negroes Indictment & sentence

~~Cheffallja~~ ‖ Jack ‖ negro servant to m^r^ Samuel woolcot of weathe^r^sfeild thow art Indicted by the name of Jack negro for not hauing the feare of God before thy eyes being Instigated by the divill did at or vpon the fowe^r^teenth day of July last 1681 wittingly & felloniously sett on fier Leifteñnt w^m^ Clarks house in north Hampton by taking a brand of fier from the hearth and swinging it vp & doune for to find victualls as by his

Jack negroes Indictm^t^ & sentenc

* Written over "hir."

Confession may Appeare Contrary to the peace of our Soueraigne Lord the King his Croune & dignity the lawes of God & of this Jurisdiction in that Case made & prouided title firing of houses page (52) to wch Indictment at the barr he pleaded not Guilty & Affirmd he would be trjed by God & the Country and after his Confessions &c were read to him & his owning thereof were Comitted to the Jury who brought him in Guilty and the next day had his sentence pronounct agt him by the Gouernor that he should goe from the barr to the place whence he Came & there be hangd by the neck till he be dead & then taken downe & burnt to Ashes in the fier wth Maria negro = The Lord be mercifull to thy soule sajd the Gouernor =

mr Anthony stoddard Capt Thomas Bratle mr John Joyliffe Capt Elisha Hutchinson mr John Saffyn Capt John walley & mr John faire-weather being presented as chosen by the ffreemen of Boston to be Comissioners for the yeare ensuing were Approoved of by the Court & tooke their Oathes as Comissioners for Boston in open Court

7 Comissioners sworne 13 Sept 1681

[139[2]] 1681

wm Cheny of Dorchester in the County of Suffolke in New England planter thou art Indicted by the name of wm Cheny for not hauing the feare of God before thy eyes & being Instigated by the divill did at or vpon the seccond day of August last 1681 ffelloniously Comitt a Rape on the body of experience Holdbrooke thy servant and had Carnall Copulation wth hir by force against hir will shee crying out & was heard the last time as in hir Confession and by euidence will appeare contrary to the peace of our Soueraigne Lord the king his Croune & dignity the lawes of God & of this Jurisdiction title Rape page 15 = to which Indictment he pleaded not Guilty an[d] put himself for tryall on God & ye Country hauing oppertunity to object agt any of ye Jury if he see cause = wch he saw no cause so to doe. And after the Indictment & other euidences in the Case were read & Comitted to the Jury the Jury brought in their virdict they found the prisoner at the barr Guilty: = And the next day had his sentenc pronounct agt him by the Governor That yow Goe hence to the place from whence yow Came & thence to the place of execution & there be hangd by the necke till yow be dead =

wm Chenys sentenc

The Court ordered that the Secretary Issue out his warrants to the

(14 Sep[t] 81) marshall Gennerall for the three Condemned prisone[r]s execution on the next lecture day presently after the lecture according to their sentenc[s]

Georg fairefax : censure = George fairfax being Comitted to prison for Burglary twice once on the Lords day & stole from his master * Raymond and now from Timothy Dwight of Boston in Rings siluer claspes buttons & money wch sajd Dwight Affirmes to be a twenty fiue pounds eleven shill[ing] Running Away from his master more then once being thus Conuicted the Court sentenceth yow to be branded in the forhead wth the letter B and be seuerely whipt w[th] thirty stripes paying trble damages to the partjes from whome yow stole dischardging fees of Court & y[e] prison standing Comitted till sentence be performed : =

to be Brãded whipt

& to make Restitution In Ans[r] to the peticon of Timothy Dwight It is Ordered that the peticõne[r] hath libe[r]ty any time w[th]in this two months to sell the said George fairfax that he Give an account of his sale to his former master † Raymond who w[th] himself ‖ is ‖ proportionably to haue his share or else the Tresurer of the Country may send the sajd George fairfax away & sell him dischardging the charges of Court & Imprisonment & Responding the Remajnder to the partjes Concerned =

Dorcas Smith[s] libe[r]ty to marry In Ans[r] to the petition of Dorcas Smith humbly Crauing the favo[r] of this Court to sett hir at libe[r]ty to marry w[th] another man hir husband xtophe[r] smith hauing absented himself aboue seven yeares [since] she heard of him & not at all in y[t] time sending to hir for hir or hir childs reliefe the Cour[t] on pervsall of the sajd Dorcas hir oath & othe[r] testimony Judg meet to sett yow at libe[r]ty =

[140] 1681

In Answer to the petition of m[r] Henry Jenkins humbly desiring the favo[r] of this Court that his Appeale from y[e] Comissione[r]s Court for wch he hath entred into security for the next Court of Assistants being a strainger & ready to Goe out of y[e] Country may be heard at this Court This peticon was Granted & fryday nex[t] Appointed for the hearing of the Case he presently

M[r] Jenkins Case

* This space left blank in the record.
† This space left blank in the record.

giving in his reasons of Appeale to ye Comissionr^s or their clarke: ye sajd m^r Henry Jenkins desired a Jury & entring his Appeale after his peticon the Comissione^rs Judgment Reason of Appeale & othe^r euidences in the Case were read Comitted to the Jury & are on file the Jury brought in a speciall virdict vizt In y^e Case of m^r Henry Jenkins wee find him Guilty of saying that he was as Good a man as m^r stoddard & saying to the Constable A pox take your tricks = And · if the Constables affirmation on the oath of a Constable be a legall euidenc to convict a man in such a Case then wee find the sajd m^r Jenkins Guilty of saying that the Barber was wayting vpon a better man then the Comissione^rs & saying to the Constable A pox take yow othe^rwise not guilty = The Court on Consideration of this virdict Judg meet to Confirme the Judgment of the Comissione^rs

Comissione^rs Judg^t Confirmd =

Wm King being brought to the barr was told that he was presented by the Grand Jury & now was Indicted for Blasphemy & bid hold vp his hand he refused & sajd he would be trjed by God & the King &c Refusing to be trjed by God & the Country saying he owned not the Country no^r their lawes using many revyling & threatning speeches &c was sent to the Goale from whence he Came.

And at thi^s Court^s Adjournment 21th of octobe^r 1681:

at 8 in ye morning

Wm King was this day brought to the barr from prison for Blasphemous words testified against him & wch he Again in a presumptuous manner before Authority vttered & declared i: e that he was the [Ae]ternall son of God & y^t he was holy & pure as God himself; was at the last Court of Assistants by the Grand Jury presented & left to tryall and sajd King being brought to the barr & Indicted accordingly for sajd Blasphemy but he behaued himself like a mad man and absolutely refused to hold vp his hand & plead to the sajd Indictment and being now at the barr he owned the words spoken & behaued himselfe outragiously as a madman; the euidences against him were read the Court on pervsall of the euidences &c Judg meet to order him to be severely whipt with Twenty stripes, and then Return'd to prison there to lye till ye Council see meet to dischardge him. This sentence was declard to him in open Court &c 21 8: mo 81

This Court of Assistants is dissolued 22

[141]

present
Symon Bradstreet Esqr Gov
Tho: Danforth Esqr dep^t Gov
Richard Saltonstall
Dani: Gookin sen
Dani. Dennison

w^m stoughton
Joseph dudley
Peter Bulkley
Humphry Davy
Nath Saltonstall
Jno Richards
Jno Hull
Sam Nowell
James Russell

Sam. Apleton
— — — —

persons Returnd to serve on Grand Jury & sworne are
— — — —
m^r w^m Parkes
Rich^d way
francis Johnson
w^m Greenow
Jno white
James Bill
John Smith
Dani. Preston
Ti[m^o] Mather
Joseph Tayntor
Jno Bisco
Jno Peirpoint
Sam. Andrews
Randall Niccolls
Eljas Row.
— — — —

Att A Court of Assistan'ts held at Boston 7th of march 1681 —

The Grand Jury was Impanneld & sworne Gaue In their p^resentment & Indictment as to Jno knight & were dischardged

m^r Richard Wharton plaintiffe against ‖ Lef^t ‖ Nathaniel Reynolds deffend^t in An action of Attaint on Appeale from the virdict of the Jury the last Court of asistants in Septembe^r last after the Attachment Courts Judgment Reasons of Appeale & euidences in the Case produced were read Comitted to the Jury and are on file. The ‖ Jury ‖ brought in their virdict i: e a speciall virdict: If finding the [hydes on] board the ship whereof Willjam Marshall was then Comander though there be no sufficient legall euidence to proove how they came there doe forfeite those Hydes being legally seized, and no testimony to proove the ship^s going away, nor to proove any Intention to transport those hides; then wee find for the deffendant a Confirmation of the former Judgment & Costs of Courts, If not we find a reuersion of forme^r Judgments & Costs of Courts The Bench on pervsall of this virdict doe finde for y^e defendant Confirmation of the former Judgment & Costs of Courts forty seven shillings =

Afterwards the magists voted it that they forgaue m^r wharton the Country^s part of the forfeiture of the hides:

Sam Leach & Onnesephirus Allen plaintiffs against Robe^rt knight defend^t in an Action of Attaint on Appeale from the virdict of the Jury at the Court of Assistants in Septembe^r last The plaintiff & deffendant Appeard in Court & declared they were Agreed & humbly desired the Courts favor to grant them Libe^rty to wth draw wch y^e sajd leach did and Accordingly It was wth draune =

owen Parris of Barbadoes plaintiff against Georg fletcher or his Atturney Hugh Babell deffendant in an Accon of Appeale from the

Judgment of the County Court at Boston in octobe^r last After the Attachment Courts Judgment reasons of Appeale and euidences in the case produced were read Comitted to the Jury and are on file the Jury brought in their virdict they found for the Deffendant Confirmation of the former Judgment & Costs of Courts

Parris ag^t Babell ℘ fletcher

ie 8^li 12 : ye Jury [ownd n^o mo.] * ═

[142] 1681

Joseph Webb plaintiff Against Stephen Burton defend^t in an action of Appeale from the Judgment of the County Court at Boston in octobe^r last After the Attachm^t Courts Judgm^t Reasons of Appeale & euidences in the Case produced were read Comitted to the Jury & are on file the Jury brought in their virdict they found for the plaintiffe Reuertion of the former Judgm^t and that the signe † be Returnd in to the Custody of the sajd plaintiff on forfeiture of paying tenn pounds mony & costs of Courts forty shillings & eight penc

1st Ju

ye names of the 1st Jury for trjalls of Appeales Attaints &c & sworne

— — — —

m^r w^m Bond
Edward Smith
James Loyd
w^m Hoare
Jno moore
Joseph Leeds
Joseph Griggs
Tho Longhorne
Edward Jackson
w^m Hagar
Daniel Smith
Jno ffowle

— — — —

Jno vsher plaintiff ag^t Hezekiah vsher & m^r Samuel Nowell executors to ye last will of ye Late Hezekiah Vshe^r defend^ts In an action of Appeale from the Judgment of the County Court in Boston in octobe^r last After the Attachm^t Courts Reasons ‖ of Appeale ‖ & Judgment of Court ‖ & euidences in the Case produced ‖ were Read Comitted to the Jury and are on file ‖ with the Reccords of this Court ‖ the Jury brought in their virdict they found for the plaintiff Reuersion of the forme^r Judgment and that the legacjes given to Hezekiah Browne by ye will of Hezekiah Vsher deceased being fowe^r hundred pounds the wch the plaintiff obteyned a Judgment for in a County Court held in Boston octobe^r 1678 shall be pajd sajd Plaintiff in Goods at mony prize or in deffects thereof mony & Costs of Courts forty sixe shillings & eight penc. ═

exec Issud out 30 7 mo 82 E R

person[s] sumoned to serve on the seccond Jury of tryalls for Appeales Attain^ts &c sworne were

— — — —

m^r Joseph Lynd
James meares
w^m Gilbert
w^m Broune
Thomas moore:
Room [Cas]
Clement maxfeild
James Bird
Jno Ruggles
Tho Parkes
Nath Coolidg
Hen: spring
Isayah Toy
Jno ffoster in R^et w^ts case

* The verdict at the County Court was for 8^li 12^s, interest not being allowed.

† The action at the County Court was for "taking down" &c. a "signe which was John Keen's."

samuel Holmes plaintiff against francis dudson deffend[t] in an action of Appeale from the Judgment of the Comiss[rs] Court in Boston After the Attachment Courts Judgmen[t] Reasons of appeale & euidences in the Case produced were read Comitted to the Jury & are on file wth the Reccords of this Court The Jury brought in their virdict they found for the plaintiff Reuercon of the forme[r] Judgm[t] & Costs of Courts thirty shillings & two pence

w[m] wright sen̄ Atturney to w[m] wright Jun̄ plaintiff ag[t] Joseph weeden defend[t] in an Action of Appeale from the Judgment of the Comissione[rs] Court in Boston after the Attachment Courts Judgment Reasons of Appeale & other euidences in the Case produced Comitted to the Jury & are on file w[th] the Reccords of this Court the Jury brought in their virdict they found for the plaintiff Reuertion of the former Judgment & Costs of Courts thirty fowe[r] shillings & two pence

Tho voss Atturney to Robe[r]t voss plaintiff ag[t] || m[r] || Anthony checkly Atturney to m[r] Pelatiah Glouer deffend[t] in an Action of Appeale from the Judgment of the County Court in Boston After the Attachment Courts Judgment Reason[s] of Appeale and euidences in the Case produced were Read Com̄itted to the Jury and are on file wth the Reccords of this Court the Jury brought in their virdict they found for the deffendant Confirmation of the former Judgment and Costs of Courts forty fowe[r] shillings & fowe[r] pence

[143] 1681

Goulding ag[t] Smith*

Peter Goulding plaintiff ag[t] Thomas midgley deffend[t] in an Action of Appeale from the Judgment of the Comissione[r]s in Boston After the attachment Courts Judgment Reasons of Appeale and other euidences in the Case produced were read Comitted to Jury and are on file w[th] the Reccords of this Court the Jury brought in their virdict they found for the deffendant Confirmation of the forme[r] Judgment and Costs of Courts fiueteen shillings & fowe[r] pence =

Cap[t] Penn Townsend plaintiff against Thomas Johnson deffend[t] in an action of Appeale from the Judgm̄[t] of the County Court in Boston

* It appears by the papers on file that Joseph Smith acted as attorney for Thomas Midgley; Court Files, Suffolk, No. 2065.

after the Attachment Courts Judgm[t] Reasons of Appeale & euidences in the Case produced were Read Comitted to the Jury are on file wth the Reccords of this Court the Jury brought in their virdict they found for the deffendant Confirmation of the former Judgment & Costs of Courts thirty nine shillings & sixpence.

Townsend ag[t] Johnson

execution Issued out

Sam Chapman pltff ag[t] Jn[o] Barry defend[t] in an Action of Appeale from y[e] Judgmen[t] of Ipswich Court Afte[r] y[e] Attachment Courts Judgment Reasons of Appeale & euidences in y[e] Case produced were read Comitted to y[e] Jury & are on file w[th] the Reccords of this Court the Jury brought in their virdict they found A speciall virdict i : e If a man Gives his daughter a legacy when in the will he Calls hir his daughter y[e] wife of such a man & she dye w[th]out Issue before time of payment if it be hir husbands after hir death by Law Then wee find for y[e] deffendant Confirmation of the Judgment of Ipswich Court & Costs of Courts if othe[r]wise wee find for the plaintiff a reuersion of the forme[r] Judgmen[t] & Costs of Courts forty seuen shillings & fowe[r] pence The Court finds for y[e] plantiff Reuersion of Ipswich Court Judgm[t] & Costs of Courts

Chapman ag[t] Barry

Richard shatswell plaintiff ag[t] nehemiah Jewet deffendant in an action of Appeale from the Judgment of the County Court at Ipswich in September last After the Courts Judgment Attachment & Reasons of Appeale wth othe[r] euidences in the Case produced were Read Comitted to the Jury & are on file the Jury brought in their virdict they found for the defendant Confirmation of the forme[r] Judgment & Costs of Courts three pounds & two pence: y[e] plaintiff Attainted the Jury & sajd Richard shatswel principall in ten pounds & Sam Chapman & Joshua windsor his surtjes in five pounds A peece Respectiuely bound themselues to the Treasure[r] of the Country & partjes Concerned on Condition that sajd Richard shatswell should prosecute this his Attaint at the nex[t] Court of Assistan[ts] to effect =

shatswell ag[t] Jewet

m[r] Bond forman

Attaint =

Steven Butler plaintiff Against Anthony Checkley deffendant in an Action of Appeale from the Judgment of the County Court in Boston. = The plaintiff & deffendant Appeared The Attachment Courts Judgment &c were Read and the plaintiff objecting that this Case hath binn heard & determined by two

Butler ag[t] Checkly

if not three Generall Courts & therefore not trjable by an Inferio^r Court vnless by Revejw wth new Euidence or new plea wch was not made ou^t & the defendan^t no^t making it out so to be The Bench declard this Case ought not to proceed: on furthe^r Consideration the Court ordered the procedure of the Case. the euidences were Cōmitted to the Jury & are on file the Jury brought in their virdict they found for the deffendant the Confirmation of the forme^r Judgment & Costs of Courts

stayno^r ag^t Gretian [or] Holmes ag^t checkley =

Joseph Holmes Atturney to Roger Stayno^r plaintiffe agt Anthony checkley Atturney to Thomas Gretian defendant in an action of Appeale from the Judgment of the County Court in Boston after the Attachment Courts Judgment Reasons of Appeale & euidences in the Case produced were read Comitted to the Jury & are on file wth the Reccords of this Court the Jury brought in their virdict Reve^rsion of the former Judgmen^t & Costs of Courts three pounds

Timothy Thornton Tho stanbury Jno dyar samuell Linds chosen Constable wth others in Boston for y^e yeare ensuing tooke their oathes as Constables in open Court As Attests E R S

[144] 1681

wing ag^t Halsey =

Jno wing plaintiff against James Halsey deffendant in an action of Appeale from the Judgment of the County Court in octobe^r last After the Attachment Courts Judgment Reasons of Appeale & euidences in the Case produced were read Comitted to the Jury & are on file wth the Reccords of this Court the Case being Called the Reason^s for the Appeale no^t being seasonably brought in the plaintiff was nonsuited & defend^t had his Costs granted eleven shillings & six penc

Tare ag^t Hinderson

Thomas Tare plaintiff ag^t w^m Hinderson deffend^t in an Action of Appeale from the Judgm^t of the County Court in Boston January last After the Attachment Courts Judgment Reasons of Appeale & euidences in the Case produced were read Comitted to the Jury & are on file the Jury brought in their virdict they found for the plaintiff reuersion of the forme Judgment & Costs of Courts thirty eight shillings

Robe^rt Taft plaintiff on Appeale from the sentence of the County

Court in Boston after the Courts Judgment or sentenc wth the euidences in the Case produced were read Comitted to the Jury and are on file the Jury brought in their virdict they found Confirmation of Jury[s] virdict & Costs of Courts ℘ 31[s] 6 besides fees =

Robt Taft Appeale

Richard Dole & Henry Jacquis plaintiff ag[t] Rich[d] Kent deffend[t] in an action of Appeale from the Judgment of the County Court at Ipswich: After the Attachment Courts Judgment Reasons of Appeale & euidences in the Case produced were Read Comitted to the Jury & are on file w[th] the Reccords of this Court the Jury brought in their virdict they find for the deffendant Confirmation of the forme[r] Judgment & Costs of Courts fowe[r] pounds twelve shilling[s] & two pence.

Dole ag[t] Kent

Anthony checkley sue[r]ty to Thomas Gretian plaintiff against Joseph webb marshall ‖ deffend[t] * ‖ in an Action of Appeale from the Judgment of the County Court in January last at Boston After the Attachment Courts Judgment Reasons of Appeale & euidences in the Case produced were read Comitted to the Jury & are on file wth the Reccords of this Court the Jury brought in their virdict they found for the deffend[t] marshall webb Confirmation of the forme[r] Judgment the forfeiture of the bond sixty pounds in money & Costs of Courts The plaintiff desird the bond to be chancerjed wch was Granted & the Court having heard the plaintiff & defendt did chancery the bond to thirty pounds money the Costs of Courts Included =

Checkly ℘ Gretian plt ag[t] Joseph webb m[r]shall executi Issued out

Returne wayt marshall plaintiff against Joseph Holmes Atturney to stephen Sweathy deffendt in an Action of Appeale from the Judgment of the County Court in Boston in octobe[r] (81) for wages After the Courts Judgment Reasons of Appeale & euidences in the Case produced were read Comitted to the Jury & are on file the Jury brought in their virdict they found for y[e] deffend[t] Confirmation of the forme[r] Judgment & Costs of Courts = forty two shillings & tenn pence =

1st Jur

wajte ag[t] Hom[es] for wages

Return way[t] marshall plaintiff in an Action of Appeale Against †

* Written over "pltf."

† Written over "from the."

Joseph Homes Atturney to steven sweathy ‖ defend[t] ‖ (for cloaths) After the Attachment Courts Judgment Reasons of Appeale & euidences in the Case produced were read Comitted to the Jury and are on file wth the Reccords of this Court the Jury brought in their virdict they found for the deffendt Confirmation of the forme[r] Judgm[t] & Costs of Courts forty shillings & 2[d] — — —

wayt ag[t] Homes execution Issued ag[t] per for 8 : 14. 10.

[144[2]] 1681

march 18, 1681: then presnt in court[t] Symon Bradstreet Esq[r] Gov Tho. Danforth Esq[r] dep[t] Gov Daniel Gookin, Daniel Dennison, wm Stoughton, Joseph Dudley, John Richards, Sam Nowell, Jame[s] Russell, Jn[o] Hull, Benj. Gedney, Sam Apleton Esq[rs] & Secret[y]

Charles chickatabut son of the late Josiah chickatabut sachem of the massachusets, personally Appearing before the Governo[r] & Court of Assistants desiring and made choyce of willjam stoughton & Joseph dudley Esq[r]s for his Guardians during his minority, referring himself wholly to their mannage and Government praying this Courts allowance and acceptance thereof, Willjam Ahauton being present and Interpreting, which was accordingly granted & Ordered to be Recorded the day Abouesajd and accordingly stands here in their booke of Records thus Recorded: p Edw. Rawson Secret ═

Clenton[s] divorce

In Ans[r] to the petition of Rachel Clenton the wife of Lawrence clenton on pe[rus]all of the euidences in Court, The Court Judgeth it meet to Grant the peticone[r]s Request & doe Judge it meet to divorce hir & free hir from hir sajd husband ═

may 24, 1682

In the Gennerall Court ═ In Ans[r] to the peticon of w[m] Kent tave[r]ner[r] The Gov no[r] & magists Judg meet to grant the peticone[r] licence & libe[r]ty to make sale of his wine beere & prouissions exprest in his peticon till the last tuesday in octobe[r] next Attests Edw Rawson Secret

Edward Rawson and w[m] Rawson his son plaintiff[s] in an action of Appeale from from * the Judgment of the bench & virdict of the Jury in Case per of the County Court last in Boston ‖ ag[t] w[m] stoughton & Joseph dudley Esq[rs] Commissione[r]s for y[e] vnited collonyes for y[e] mas-

* "from" repeated in the record.

sachusetts deffendts ‖ as to a nonsuit &c After the Attachment & Courts Judgment were Read the plaintiffs Insisted on & desired as at ye former Court a non suit =

Edwd Rawson Contra

mr Isaack Addington is ordered by the Court to officiat as clarke of this Court in the Case betweene the Comissioners of the Colonjes & mr Edward Rawson & his son mr Wm Rauson 14. 1 168½ signed Thomas Danforth ℘ order

The Appellants Reasons & pleas for a non suite being read & pleaded and the Question put to voate whither the Appellants ought at the County Court to haue had a non suite granted them It was voted by the whole bench in the negative nemine Contradicente and the Cause proceeded to tryall and both the Attachment Reasons of Appeale & all other euidences in the Case produced were Read Comitted to the Jury and are on file in mr Addingtons hands the Jury brought in their virdict they found for the deffendants Confirmation of the former Judgment & Costs of Courts mr wm Rauson desired to Attaint ye Jury but his father mr Edward Rauson who was present refused to Joyne in ye Attaint where vpon it was put to ye question whithr mr wm Rausons Attaint should be allowed premisses considered & voted in ye negative nemine contradicente

The Bench Chanceried the bond & forfeiture thereof to three hundred and thirty pounds in money & Costs of Courts:

21 mrch 168½

[145]

[*Blank space*]

At a Court of Assistants or Admiralty held at Boston 1st June 1682

Edward Randolph Esqr Collector &c.* of his majties Customes &c pltffe by his libell & Complaint agt seven pakes or fardles two hundred paire of stockins more or less two hundred paire of shooes more or less seuerall Caskes hogshds. trunks bayles chests boxe filled opened or not opened &c as in sajd libell is exprest refference thereto being had may Apeare &c on ye behalfe of our Soueraigne Lord ye King the Gouernor & himself &c Contra George Hutchinson deffendt in whose hands they are or were after ye Case was Called the plaintiff & deffendt appear-

present
symon Bradstreet Esq Go
Tho: Danforth Esqr Dept Go
Dani: Gookin
Dani: Denison
John Pinchon
wm stoughton
Peter Bulkley
Nath Saltonstall
Humphry Davy
Nath: Saltonstall †
Sam: Nowell
James Russell
Peter Tilton
Robt Pike
— — — —

* Written over "of." † Entered twice in the original.

Jury men Returnd to serv[e] at ye Court & were swo[rne]

ing & euidences in ye Case produced were read: Comitted to ye Jury the Jury brought in their virdict they found for the deffendant Costs of Court. =

Capt Pen Townsend
Joseph Pearse [Bo*]
Joseph Homes
Robert Seaver sen
wm Gary
Jno Bird
Nehemiah Clapp
Sam Jennison
Joseph pears [watt†]
Jno Blany
ffrancis Boman
John Goues

Edward Randolph Esqr Collector of his majtjes customes in New England &c plaintiff on behalf of his majty the Gou̅nor Symon Bradstreet Esqr & himself by his libell or Information agt Jno Place master of the ship Hope of Boston deffendt for his vndeliuery of his wine before entry made &c as in sajd libell doth & may appeare refference thereto being had after the plaintiffe & defendts Appearing & euidences in ye case were Considered being Comitted to ye Jury they brought in their virdict they found for the deffendant Costs of Court — —

Edwd Randolph Esqr Collector of his majtys Customs in New Engld by his Information on behalfe of our Soueraigne Lord the king & Symon Bradstreet Esqr Gou̅nr & himself plaintiff agt Jno Boury mr of the ship wm of Bristoll & also agt ye sd ship for his vndeliuery of one pipe of sherry wine at marblehead before entry wth the Gou̅nor &c as in sajd Information refference thereto being had may Appeare & after the Court & Jury &c had heard the pleas &c ye Case Comitted to the Jury the Jury brought in their virdict they found for the deffendt costs of Court

[146] 1682

Butcher agt Randolph &c

Robert Butcher as Atturney to Timothy Armitage plaintiff agt Edward Randolph Esqr ‖ defendt ‖ in an Action of Revejw of a Case tried at a Court of Admiralty or Court of Assistants held at Boston the 25 december 1680 wherein the sajd Randolph was then plaintiff & prosecuted sajd Armitage vpon breach of ye Act of the 14th of ye king & obteyned Judgmt agt sajd Armitage then deffendant the sume of forty pounds mony as by sd Judgmt may Appeare &c After the pleas & euidences in the Case produced were read: Comitted to the Jury &c the Jury brought in their virdict they found for the defendant Costs of Court

Samuel shrimpton principle & nicholas paige ‖ his suerty ‖ both of

* Boston? † Watertown?

Boston me^r chants Joyntly & seuerally Acknowledged themselues bound in two hundred pounds to ou^r Soueraigne Lord King charles the seccond &c on Condition that sajd samuel shrimpton shall respond the Judgment and Apprisall of the ship Hope in reference to an Accon of Revejw of the Case trjed at the Court of Assistants 3^d Instant June betweene between * Edward Randolph Esqr Collecto^r &c & John Place master of ship Hope as shall at sajd Court of Revejw sometimes before the 10th of Septembe^r nex^t be determined & recouered by sajd Edwd Randolph

Attests Edw Rawson secret

Att a Court of Assistants or Court of Admiralty held at Boston 15th June 1682

prsent
ye Gou^r
dep^t Gou
w^m stoughton
Peter Bulkley
Humphry Davy
sam. Nowell
Jno Hull
James Russell

Theophilus Poole one of the Adventure^rs in the ship Resolution plaintiff ag^t w^m Phipps Comande^r of the sajd ship & Erasmus steevens and Nicholas Hayword Quartermaste^rs in an Action of the Case for that they the sajd w^m Phipps Comande^r Erasmus steevens & nicholas Hayward Quartermaste^rs not wth standing the sajd Pole was at æquall Charge & did prouide & pay for his oune Armes & Amunition & prouition after their laying out full shares æqually at martjn^s vinyard hath tooke halfe his share & deteynes the same in their the sajd steeven^s & Hawards hands & Refuseth the deliuery thereof to the sajd poole to his great dammage as in the s^d Attachm^t bearing date 12th June Instant 1682 more at large refferenc thereto being had amply doth & may Appeare After ye Attachm^t & euidences therein produced || were read & || the Court had considered thereof the Court did decree & determine that the sajd Erasmus steevens and nicholas Haward Quartermaste^rs of sajd ship resolution in behalfe of the Company shall pay vnto the sajd plaintiff Theophilus Pole the sume of twenty seuen pounds mony of New England for his halfe share that was taken by them the sajd Quarter masters after the divicon at martyns vineyard & three pounds nine penc like mony Costs in all 30^li

[147] 1682

Jno Aires one of the Adventure^rs in the ship Resolution plantiff^e against w^m Phipps Comander of sajd ship & Erasmus steevens & Nich-

* Repeated in the record.

olas Haward Quartrmrs in an action of the Case for that they the sajd wm Phipps Comander & Erasmus steevens & nicholas Hayward Quartermrs notwthstanding the sd Aires was at æquall charge & did provide & pay for his oune Armes Amunition & prouition after their laying out full shares æqually at martyns vineyard hath took halfe his share & deteynes the same in their the sajd steevens & Haywards hands & refuseth the deliuery thereof to the sajd Aires to his great damage: as in the sd Attachmt bearing date 12 June Instant 1682 more at larg refference thereto being had Amply doth & may appeare After the Attachment & euidences in the Case produced were read & the Court had Considered thereof The Court did decree & determine that the sajd Erasmus steevens & Nicholas Hayword Quartermrs of sd ship Resolution in behalfe of the Company shall pay vnto the plaintiff John Aires the sume of twenty seven pounds mony of New England for his halfe share that was taken by them the sajd Quartermrs after the divicon at martjn's vineyard and three pounds nine penc like mony Costs in all thirty pounds =

Thomas Johnson one of the Adventurers in the ship resolution plaintiff agt wm Phipps Comander of sd ship & Erasmus steevens & Nicholas Hayward Quartermrs ‖ defendts ‖ in an action of the Case for that they the sajd Wm Phipps Comander & Erasmus steevens & Nicholas Hayword Quartermrs notwithstanding the sajd Johnson was at æquall charge & did provide & pay for his oune Armes Amunition & prouission after their laying out full shares æqually at martjns vineyard hath tooke halfe his share & deteynes the same in their the sajd steevens & Haywords hands & refuseth the deliuery thereof to the sajd Johnson to his great damage as in the sajd Attachment bearing date the 12th of June Instant 1682 more at large refference thereto being had amply doth & may Appeare after the Attachment & euidences in the Case produced were read and the Court had Considered thereof The Court did decree & determine that the sajd Erasmus steevens and Nicholas Hayword Quartermrs of sajd ship Resolution in behalfe of the Company shall pay vnto the plaintiff Thomas Johnson the sume of twenty seven pounds mony of New England for his halfe share that was taken by them the sajd Quartermrs after the divition at martjns vinyard & three pounds nine pence like mony Costs in all thirty pounds =

Thomas knaps one of the Adventurers in the ship Resolution plaintiff agt wm Phipps Comander of sd ship & Erasmus steephens & Nicholas

Haywards Qu'te'm's deffendants in an Accon of the Case for that they the sajd wm Phipps Comande' & Erasmus steevens & Nicholas Hayward Quarte'm's no' wthstanding the sajd knapps was at æquall charge & did provide and pay for his owne Armes Ammunition & prouission Afte' there lajing out ffull shares æqually at martjns vineyard hath tooke halfe his share & deteynes the same in their the sajd steevens & Haywards hands & refuseth the deliuery thereof to the said knapps to his great damage as in the sajd Attachmt bearing date the 12th of June Instant 1682 more at large refference thereto being had amply doth & may Appeare After the Attachment & euidences in the Case produced were read & the Court had Considered thereof The Court did decree & determine that the sd Erasmus steevens & nicholas Hayword Quarte'masters of sajd ship Resolution in behalfe of the Company shall pay vnto the plaintiff Thomas knapps the sume of twenty seven pounds mony of New England for his halfe share that was taken by them the sajd Qua'term's after the divission at martjns Vineyard and three pounds nine pence like mony Costs in all thirty pounds

[148]

At A Court of Assitants or Admiralty Called by the Gover' & held at Boston 17 Augst 1682

present
Symon Bradstreet Esqr Gov
Tho. Danforth Esqr dept Gov
Daniel Gookin, wm stoughton, Humphry Dauy, Sam Nowell, Jno Hull, James Russell — Esqrs

In the Case of Jno Daniel Carpenter & Cornelius Anderson Cooke in behalfe of themselues & Robe't Tucker Carpente's mate nicholas Austin qu'tr'mr Robe't Read Jno Curtis Jno day John Goodwin Nathaniel Legg Robe't Browne & Richard strout marrine's belonging to ship merchants adventure of London plaintiffs agst Capt wm stone Comande' of the sajd ship on behale of his owno's deffendt. In an Action of the case according to Attachment bearing date the fowe'teenth Instant refferenc thereto being had amply doth & may Appeare After the Court had heard the libell or Complaint Attachment & euidences in the Case produced were read &c The Court Judged & declared that wages is due to the sajd marriners but not payable at this Port And therefore order the deffendt Costs and doe orde' & require the sajd Seamen to repajre to the sajd ship and Attend their duty

present
Symon Bradstreet Esqr Gov
Tho Danforth Esqr dep^t Gov
Daniel Gookin
Daniel Dennison
W^m stoughton
Peter Bulkley
Nath Saltonstall
Humphry Davy
Sam. Nowell
Jno Hull
James Russell
Bartho: Gidney
sam Apleton
Rob^rt Pike
} Esq^rs.

— — — —

[g]rand [J]ury ~~for tryalls of ye attaint~~ were sworne. —
[m^r] Jonas Clarke
Robe^rt walker
Arthur mason
Gamaliel way^t
James Pemberton
Laurenc Douse
Richd Louden
Edwd [Ca]rringlon
Jno Peirpoint
Phillip Torrey
Tho Toleman sen
Tho Trott sen
Jacob Hewens sen
w^m manning
[N]ath^a Sparhauke
Joseph Beamis
Jno whitney
Joseph child :=

Att A Court of Assistant[s] held at Boston 5th Septemb^r 1682

The Grand Jury brought in their presen^tment leauing Jno Neponet Indian to his further Tryall &c

^1m^r Jno Saffyn ^2m^r John Joyliff ^ ^4Cap^t Elisha Hutchinson ^5m^r John faireweath^r ^6Cap^t Tho Bratle being presented to y^s Court w^th (m^r Antho. Stoddard^3 & Capt Jno walley Absent) tooke their oath^s in open Cour^t as Commissione^rs for the Toune of Boston for one yeare & till new be chosen as Attests E R S

Richard shatswell plaintiff in an Accon of Appeale on Attaint Cont^a Nehe[mi] Jewet deffendt after the virdict of ye Jury & euidences in the Case produced were Read Comitted to the Jury and are on file wth the Reccords of this Court the Jury brought in their virdict they found for the deffendant Confirmation of the form^r Judgment^s & Costs of Courts 1^li 17 1.

Thomas Baker plaintiff &c in an Accon of Appeale ag^t Left Jno Putnam deffend^t in an Action of Appeale from the Judgment of the County Court at Salem After the Attachm^t Courts Judgment Reasons of Appeale & euidences in the Case produced were read Comitted to the Jury & are on file wth the Reccords of this Court the Jury brought in their virdict they found for the deffendant Confirmation of the forme^r Judgment & Costs of Courts fowe^r pounds one shilling & sixepenc.

Joseph ffletcher in behalfe of Jno march & Jemima his wife plaint aga[inst] Hugh march sen deffendant in an Action of Appeale from the Judgment of the County Court at Ipswich after the Attachment Courts Judgment Reasons of Appeale & euidences in the Case produced were read Comitted to the Jury and are on file wth the Reccords of this Court the Jury brought in their virdict they found Confirmation of the forme^r Juryes spetiall virdict vizt If the Acquittance in the deed doth Acquitt Hugh march from his promise vpon marriage to Joseph ffletcher on the behalf of Jno march & Jemima his wife then wee finde for the deffendant Costs of Courts otherwise wee finde for the plaintiffe one hundred thirty & two pounds in or as money & Costs of Courts The magists on pervsall of this virdict finds for the plaintiff & his Costs Granted was sixe pounds eleven shillings =

[149]

Joseph webb plaintiff in an action of Appeale ag[t] m[r] sam shrimpton & Cap[t] Pen Tounesend deffend[t]s from the Judgm[t] of the Comissione[r]s Court in Boston After the Courts Judgm̄[t] Reason of Appeale Attachm[t] & euidences in the Case produced were read Comitted to the Jury & are on file w[th] the Reccords of this Court the Jury brought in their virdict they found for the plaintiff reuersion of the forme[r] Judgm[t] & Costs of Courts twenty nine shillings & nine pence =

The Jury for Tryall of the Acc̄on of Attaint sworn both together

— — — —

m[r] Tho Sandford 1 Jur
Samuel cheeckley
Sam Gary
Jn[o] withrington
Jn[o] Dauis
w[m] marshall
Samuel Douse
Pyam Blower
Tho Prentice
Jn[o] Benja[min]
Isack mixter
Nath Holland
~~Rich[d] Crispe~~
2 Jur
Caleb Sever
James Clarke
Daniel Preston
Dauid Jones
Zack[r]y Long
ma[t]hew Solle
Zakery Johnson
Daniel champney
Tho: olliuer
Tho: ffaning
Tho: fflegg
Cap[t] w[m] G[er]* in m[r] Crisp's Room and m[r] Benjn walker in room of fañing

— — — —

Jn[o] wilkins plaintiff ag[t] Ingerman Helge[r]son deffend[t] in an Action of Appeale from the Judgment of the Comission[r]s Court in Boston after the Attachm[t] Courts Judgm[t] Reasons of Appeale & euidences in the Case produced were read Comitted to the Jury & are on file w[th] the Records of this Court the Jury brought in their virdict they found for the deffendant Confirmation of the forme[r] Judgment & Costs of Courts — twenty three shillings & 3[d]

[1. 6]
[9]
exec

Sarah Hauthorn widdow & Nathaniel Haw[t]horn hir son plaintiff[s] against Josiah Roades deffendant in an Accon of Appeale from the Judgment of the County Court at Salem After the Attachm[t] Courts Judgment Reasons of Appeale & euidences in the Case produced were read Comitted to the Jury and are on file w[th] the Reccords of this court the Jury brought in their virdict they found Confirmation of the former Judgm[t] the horse sued for & Costs of Courts three pounds nineteen shillings & tenn penc. —

Seth perry plaintiff against John Hurd deffend[t] in an Action of Appeale from the Judgment of the County Court in Boston After the

* Gerrish ?

Attachm^t Courts Judgment Reasons of Appeale & euidences in the Case produced were read Comitted to the Jury & are on file wth the Reccords of this Court the Jury brought in their virdict they found for the deffend^t Confirmation of the former Judgm^t & Costs of Courts —

Perry ag^t Hurd

Isaak waldron plaintiff ag^t Theophilus ffrary Jno wing &c deffend^ts in an Accon of Appeale from the Judgmt of the County Court last in Boston After the Attachm^t Courts Judgm^t reasons of Appeale & euidences in the Case produced were read Comitted to the Jury & are on file wth the Reccords of this Court the Jury brought in their virdict they found for the deffendants Confirmation of the former Judgmen^t & Costs of Courts forty sixe shillings =

waldron Cont^a ffrary wing &c

Isaack waldron plaintiff ag^t John wisewall Jun deffend^t in an Accon of Appeale from the Judgm^t of the las^t County Court in Boston After the Attachm^t Courts Judgment Reasons of Appeale & euidences in the Case produced were read Comitted to the Jury & are on file wth the Reccords of this Court the Jury found for the deffend^t Confirmation of the former Judgmen^t & Costs of Courts 28^s 8^d

waldron ag^t wiswall

mannasseth Becke plaintiff ag^t Symon Gale * deffend^t in an Accon of Appeale from the Judgment of the las^t County Court in Boston After the Attachment Courts Judgmen^t Reasons of Appeale & othe^r euidences in the Case produced were read Comitted to the Jury & are on file wth the Reccords of this Court the Jury brought in their virdict they found for the deffendant Confirmation of the former Judgmen^t & Costs of Court^s thirty shillings & tenn penc & wch was p^d him wth ye 4^s damage [by E R S]

Beck ag^t Gates

[150]

m^r HerLakenden Symonds plaintiff against Hudson Leueret deffendant in an Action of Appeale from the Judgmen^t of the County Court in Boston After the Attachment Courts Judgment reasons of Appeale & euidences in the Case were read Comitted to the Jury & are on file wth the Reccords of this Court the Jury brought in their virdict they found for the

Symo[nds] Cont^a Leueret

* The name was probably "Gates" as given in the margin.

deffendant Confirmation of the forme^r^ Judgment & Costs of Court ye plaintiff desired his bond might be chancerjed both partjes Appearing The Court chanceried the Bond to one hundred & thirteen pounds thirteen shillings mony & Costs of Courts: and ordered that before execution Issue out m^r^ Leueret deliver vp to the sajd Herlakenden Symonds all deeds bonds & writtings that he hath had and now hath in his hands of the sajd symonds = The sajd Hudson Leueret Came & in the open Court & deliued vp as he sajd all his deeds bonds & writtings to the sajd m^r^ Symonds wch sajd m^r^ Symonds received and acknowledged in Court y^t^ they were all memo^rd^ y^s^ day m^r^ Epps once And againe sajd he tendered m^r^ Symonds person and desired to know whither he was freed m^r^ Leueret in Court declard m^r^ Epps was free and that he was sattisfied & had nothing to say as to him =

martyn ag^t^ Rost

m^r^ Richard martyn plaint against Thomas Rost deffendant in an action of Appeale from the Judgment of the County Court at Boston After the Attachment Courts Judgment Reasons of Appeale & euidences in the Case produced were read Comitted to the Jury & are on file wth the Records of this Court the Jury brought in their virdict they found for the deffendant Confirmation of the forme^r^ Judgment & Costs of Courts sixteen shillings & sixe pence

W^ms^ ag^t^ Brookin exec Issued out for ye costs

Jno williams plaintiff against Jno Brookings defendant In an Action of Appeale from the Judgment of the County Court at Boston after the Attachment Courts Judgment Reason^s^ of Appeale & euidences in the Case produced were read Comitted to the Jury & are on file the Jury brought in their virdict they found for the plaintiff Confirmation of the forme^r^ Judgment & find Costs of this Court for the deffendant =

Thatche^r^ ag^t^ m^r^ Dauy

execution Issued out 5 dec 82 for 30. 2^s^

Judgm^t^ 28^11^. 19^s^. mo.

m^r^ Thomas Thatcher plaintiff ag^t^ Humphry Davy Esqr After the attachm̄^t^ Courts Judgment Reason of Appeale & euidences in the Case produced were read Comitted to the Jury & are on file wth the Reccords of this Court the Jury brought in their virdict they found for the deffend^t^ Confirmation of the forme^r^ Judgment & Costs of Courts twenty three shillings & sixe pence

Exec. Issud [out paid?]

ffisher agt wayte

Jno ffisher plaintiff agt Returne wayte defendant in an Action of Appeale from the Judgment of the County Court in Boston After the Attachment Courts Judgment Reasons of Appeale & euidences in the Case produced were read Comitted to the Jury & are on file wth the Reccords of this Court the Jury brought in their virdict they found for the deffendt Confirmation of the former Judgment & Costs of Courts thirty two shillings & fower pence

Holman agt Deering [paid]

Abraham Holman || & Tho Andrews per || plaintiffs agt Henry Deering Atturney to * michelson deffendant in an Action of Appeale from the Judgment of the County Court In Cambridge the Reasons not being signed by ye plantiff he was nonsuited but on ye deffendt declaring he was not willing to take any Advantag ye Accon proceeded & After the Attachments Courts Judgment Reasons of Appeale & euidences in the Case produced were read Comitted to the Jury & are on file wth the Reccords of this Court the Jury brought in their virdict they found for the deffendant Confirmation of the former Judgment & Costs of Courts forty two shillings & fower pence

[151]

mr Jno Giffords appeale

Jno Gifford plaintiff agt Thomas walter & Richd midlecot deffendts in an action of Appeale from the Judgment of the County Court in Boston After the Attachmt was Read per ye deffendts pleading for a non suit the Court declared a non suite = It hauing binn tryed at ye Gennerall Court || Granting him his Costs 14s. but || on mr Giffords deliuering a paper Information or peticon In Ansr thereto The Court declares that mr Gifford shall be heard in Case he Cann proove that this is a new Action & different from that which the Gennll Court hath heard & determined that mr walter & mr midlecot haue notice to Attend after dinner mr Gifford was brought mr walter Appeared but on hearing what the Court was about turnd away & went out of Court though Called to Attend. After the Court had heard mr Gifford & vejwed seuerall of his papers wch are on file It was put to the voat those that are of the minde that mr walters had no power by his letter of Atturney let them hold vp their hands, not one held vp & so ye Case Issued =

* This space left blank in the record.

mr Hoar. nonsuted

mr Jno Hoare Atturney & Assignee of Daniel Hoare plantiffe ℘ agt wm Kilcup defendt in an Accon of Appeale from the Judgment of the County Court at Boston the* Case was Called plaintiff & deffendt Appeared the Attachment & Courts Judgment was Read the deffendant pleading for a non suite & the plaintiff for his reasons of Appeale Given in to be read the plaintiff giving in the Gennll Courts order debarring him ℘ his reasons signed by him was read the Court Considering the Genll Courts order declared the Case Could not proceed :

Collicot ℘ Contra Sears

execu: Issued out 9, octob: 82

Richard Collicot & Nathaniel Greenwood plaintiffs agt Jno Seaʳs deffendant in an Action of Appeale from the Judgment of the County Court at charles-Towne After the Attachment Courts Judgment reasons of Appeale & euidences in the Case produced were read Comitted to the Jury & are on file wth the Reccords of this Court the Jury brought in their virdict they found for the plaintiffs Reuersion of the former Judgmt & Costs of Courts fiuety two shillings & six pence =

exec Issued out for 11: 16. 10 13 7mo 82 [Engt]

Jno Trumble plaintiff agt Thomas Peck deffendant in an accon of Appeale from the Judgment of the Comissioners Court in Boston After the Courts Judgment reasons of Appeale & euidences in the Case produced were read Comitted to the Jury & are on file the Jury brought in their virdict they found for the deffendant Confirmation of the former Judgment & Costs of Courts

8th Septemb 1682 Randolph agt wallice

Edward Randolph Esqr Collector ℘ by his libells complaints & Attachment bearing date 7 September 82 plaintiff agt Robert wallis master of the pinck good hope as in the sajd libell Complt ℘ in all respects more at larg Appeareth Refferenc thereto being had deffendt After the libell Infformation ℘ was Read & evidences produced in the Case Comitted to the Jury & are on file wth the Reccords of this Court the Jury brought in their virdict they found for the deffendt Costs of Court

Raldolph agt willet ℘

Edwd Randolph Esqr Collector ℘ plaint In an Action of Appeale agt agt † Jno Pitcher and Andrew willet & sloope swallow deffendt. from the Judgment

* Written over "after."

† Repeated in the original.

of the last County Court in Boston after the Information & othe^r^ euidences in the Case were read Comitted to the Jury & are on file ye Jury brought in their virdict they found for the defend^t^ Confirmation of the forme^r^ Judgment & Costs of Courts.

[152]

mr Randolph ag^t^ Catch Newbery &c

Edward Randolph esq^r^ Collecto^r^ &c plaintiff by his Complaint or Informacon ag^t^ ye ketch Newbery Isaac Eveleigh ma^tr^ or Nathaniel Clarke & Dani Dauison owno^r^s of sajd Catch deffendt vpon breach of the Act of the 15th of the King as is more particcularly expressed in s^d^ Information on Appeale from the Judgment of the last County Cour^t^ in Boston. After the Information Reasons of Appeale & euidences in the Case produced were read Comitted to the Jury & are on file the Jury brought in their virdict they found for the deffendants Confirmation of the forme^r^ Judgment & Costs of Courts.

mr Randolph ag^t^ Andr willet & sloope Swallow

Edward Randolph Esqr plaint ag^t^ Andrew willet owno^r^ of the sloop swallowe defend^t^ In an Action of Appeale from the Judgment of the last County Court in Boston After the Attachment Courts Judgment Reasons of Appeale and euidences in the Case produced were read Comitted to the Jury & are on file the Jury brought in their virdict they found for the deffendant Confirmation of the forme^r^ Judgment & Costs of Courts.

in Boston 14: of Sept 82

The Gou & magists || voted || that the bills of Costs &c ag^t^ m^r^ Randolph should be suspended till the Council take further orde^r^

Atkinson ag^t^ woolcot

Jno Atkinson plaintiff against Jno woolcot deffend^t^ in an Action of Appeale from the Judgment of the County Court at Ipswich After the Attachment Courts Judgment Reasons of Appeale & euidences in the Case produced were Read Comitted to the Jury and are on file wth the Reccords of this Court the Jury brought in their virdict they found for the deffendant Confirmation of the forme^r^ Judgm^t^ & Costs of Courts fowe^r^ pounds tenn shillings & tenn penc

Atkinson ag^t^ woolcot

John Atkinson plaintiff against Jno woolcot deffend^t^ in an Action of Appeale from the Judgm^t^ of Ipswich Court After the Attachm^t^ Courts Judgment

Reasons of Appeale & euidences in the Case produced were read Comitted to the Jury & are on file the Jury brought in their virdict they found Reuersion of the forme[r] Judgm[t] and that the deffendant pay the plaintif tenn shillings mony damage & Costs of Courts fiue pounds fiue shillings & eight penc.

John Atkinson plaintiff ag[t] samuel Buckman deffend[t] in an action of Appeale from the Judgmt of Ipswich Court After the Attachment Courts Judgmen[t] Reasons of Appeale & euidences in the Case produced were read Comitted to the Jury & are on file the Jury brought in their virdict they found for the plaintiff reuersion of the forme[r] Judgment & costs of Courts fowe[r] pounds eighteen shillings =

Atkinson ag[t] Buckman

Jn[o] Cleoments plaintiff ag[t] nathaniel merrill defend[t] in an action of Appeale from the Judgm[t] of Ipswich Court After the Attachment Courts Judgmen[t] Reasons of Appeale & euidences in the Case produced were read Comitted to the Jury and are on file wth the Reccords of this Court the Jury brought in their virdict they found for the plantif Reuersion of the former Judgment & that Jn[o] merrill son of Nathaniel merrill shall serve Jn[o] Cleoment in the trade of a Carpenter the space of five month[s] or pay to y[e] sajd John Cleoments tenn pounds in Indian Corn barly or Barly mault & Costs of Courts fiue pounds thirteen shillings & six pence.

Cleoments ag[t] merrill

[153]

Thomas Mekins plaintiff ag[t] Enos kinsley defend[t] in an Action of Appeale from the Judgment of the County Court at northampton after the Attachment Courts Judgm̃t reasons of Appeale & euidences in the Case produced were read Comitted to y[e] Jury & are on file the Jury brought in their virdict they found for y[e] deffendant Confirmation of the former Judgment & Costs of Courts fowe[r] pounds thirteen shillings & tenn penc =

14th mekins Con[ta] Kinsley

Joseph peasley plaintiff Cont̃[a] Josiah clark deffend[t] in an Accõn of Appeale from the Judgment of the County Court at Ipswich the Case was called Attachment ℘ Read no Reasons Appearing signed vnde[r] the Appellants hand ℘ he was non suited =

Peasley ag[t] Clarke

Barton agt mathews

‖ Edward ‖ Barton plantiff agt Daniel mathew deffendt in an Action of Appeale from the Judgment of the County Court at Boston After the Attachment Courts Judgment Reasons of Appeale & euidences in the Case produced were read Comitted to the Jury & are on file wth the Reccords of this Court the Jury brought in their virdict they found for the deffendt Confirmation of the former Judgmt & Costs of Courts ‖ in all ‖ 3li 13

Barton agt mathews

Edward Barton plaintiff Conta Daniel mathews deffendt in an Action of Appeale from the Judgment of the County Court in Boston after the Attachment Courts Judgment Reasons of Appeale & euidences in the Case produced were read Comitted to the Jury & are on file the Jury brought in their virdict they found for ye defendt Confirmation of the former Judgment & Costs of Courts in all three pounds fower shillings six pence =

20li dam:

Graues agt ffarrington

marke Graues plt Conta mathew ffarrington deffendant in an Accon of Appeale from the Judgment of the County Court at Salem After the Attachmt Courts Judgmt Reasons of Appeale & euidences in the Case produced were read Comitted to the Jury and are on file wth the Reccords of this Court the Jury brought in their virdict they found for the deffendt Confirmation of the former Judgment & Costs of Courts

Barret agt Sprague

Capt Tho Barret Atturney to ffrancis Goffreigh plaint by Edwd shippen his Atturney agt Capt Richard Sprague deffendt in an Accon of Appeale from the Judgment of the last County Court in Boston after ye Attachmt Courts Judgment Reasons of Appeale & euidences in ye Case produced were read Comitted to the Jury & are on file the Jury brought in their virdict they found for the deffendt Confirmation of the former Judgmt & Costs of Courts thirty nine shillings & two pence

Ayres agt ffurnell *

exec. Issued out 12 dec. 1683

Jno Ajres plaintiff agt Jno ffurnell defendt in an action of Appeale from the Judgment of the Comissioners Court after the Attachment Courts Judgment Reasons of Appeale & euidences in the Case produced were read Comitted to the Jury & are on file the Jury brought in their virdict they found for the plaintiff Reuersion of the former Judgment & Costs of Courts forty two shigs 9d —

* Or Farwell ?

Jn° Jacob plaint Con^ta^ John Gale deffend^t^ in an Action of Appeale from the Judgm^t^ of the Comission^r^s Court After the Attachm^t^ Courts Judgm^t^ reasons of Appeale & euidences in the Case produced were read Comitted to the Jury & are on file wth the Reccords of this Court the Jury brought in their virdict they found for the plaintiff seven pounds eleven shillings & fiue penc & Costs of Courts

[154]

Hudson Leueret plaint ag^t^ Edwd Randolph Esqr Collecto^r^ &c in an action of Appeale from the Judgment of the Commission^r^s Court After the Attachm^t^ Courts Judgment Reasons of Appeale & euidences in the Case produced were read Comitted to the Jury & are on file the Jury brought in their virdict they found for the deffend^t^ Confirmation of the former Judgm^t^ & Costs of Courts —

Leū^t^ ag^t^ Randolph

In Ans^r^ to the peticon of Ellino^r^ Redding the Goū & magists Comend the peticone^r^ to the selectmen^s^ Care & due releife & that they put it on the Tresure^r^s Account as in other Case for y^e^ Eastern people =

[*Large blank*]

[155] 1682

Att A Court of Assistants held at Boston the 6th of march 1682

present
Symon Bradstreet Esqr Goū
Tho Danforth Esqr dep^t^ Goū
Daniel Gookin
John Pynchon
w^m^ stoughton
Peter Bulkley
Humphry davy
Samuel Nowell
John Hull
James Russell
Bartholmew Gidney
Sam Apleton

no Cause Appearing for ye Grand Jury they were dismist

person^s^ Returnd to Serve on the Jury of trjalls for Appeales &c 1 Jury

Jn° Atkinson plaintiff against James mirrick defend^t^ in an action of Appeale from the Judgment of the County Court at Salem the actions was Called Plaintiff made default by his non Appearanc was non suited & his bond fforfeited

Hannah Haugh widdow plaintiffe Against Edward willis defend^t^ in an Accon of Appeale from the Judgment of the County Court at Boston in october last after the Attachment Courts Judgment Reasons of Appeale & euidences in the Case produced were read Comitted to the Jury & are on file the Jury brought in their virdict they found for the Defendan^t^ Confirmation of the former Judgment & Costs of Courts

mr Joseph Cooke
Samuel Turill
daniel Quinsey
Peter Towne
wm Clough
Jacob Hurd
Henry Bowen
Jonathan Peake
Richd child
Nath: Basham
Timothy Mather
Tho: Trott.
— — — —
2 Jury for tryalls for Appeales &c
— — — —
mr Tho Jenner
Sam. Bridg:
Timo Clarke
James Townsend
Samuel Ballard
Samuel Gore
Tho Bacon
Joseph Beamis
Jnoth Browne
obadiah Hawes
Tho Toleman
Jno Jackson
XJno ffowle

Nathaniel Byfeild Atturney to Daniel Raymond plaintiff Contra Robert orchard deffendant in an Action of Appeale from the Judgment of of * the County Court held in Boston as to a non suite After the Attachmt was Read & euidence on the plaintiffs pleas for a non suit & deffends Ansr The Court declared they Approoved of ye County Courts Judgment & that there should be no stop of the execution from the County Court g[r]añting ye defendt his costs at this Court

execut.

mr wm Parks in case of Solom̃ Phipps &c

Solomon Phips & Josiah wood plaintiffs agt Benanuel Bowers deffendant in an Action of Appeale from the Judgment of the County Court at Cambridg last in october After ye Attachmt Courts Judgment Reasons of Appeale and euidences in the Case produced were read Comitted to the Jury & are on file the Jury brought in their virdict i: e a speciall virdict If according to law the selectmen of Charls Towne haue power to stint & ljmitt what number of Catle the occupiers of mr † Lidgets farme shall keepe on the Account of such land as lye vnfenced to charls Towne Comon then wee finde for the plaintiff a Reuersion of the former Judgment & Costs of Courts if not for the deffendt a Confirmation of the former Judgment & Costs of Courts = The magists finds for the plaintiff

mr saffyn & mr Vsher Came into ye Court & declared they Attainted the Jury for error & sajd Jno Vsher acknowledged him̃self bound in twenty pounds & mr Richard wharton his suerty in tenn pounds to the Tresurer of the Country on this Condicõ that sajd Jno vsher shall prosecute this his Attaint at the next Court of Assistants to effect = as Attests E R S

Josiah wood & Tho white plaintiff agt Benanuel Bowers deffendt in an Acõn of Appeale from the Judgmt of the County Court at Cambridg in october ‖ last ‖ After the Courts Judgmt Reasons of Appeale & euidences in the Case produced were read comitted to ye Jury & are on file the Jury brought in their virdict a speciall virdict i e If according to law the selectmen of charls Towne haue power to stint & ljmit

* "Of" repeated in the record. † Error in the record for "Mrs"?

what number of Cattel ye occupie^rs of m^rs Lydgetts farme shall keepe on the Account of such lands as lye vnfenced to CharlsTowne Comon then wee find for the plaintiff a reuersion of the former Judgm^t & costs of Courts if no^t for the deffendant a Confirmation of the former Judgm^t & Costs of Courts The magists in this Case finds for the plaintiff^s m^r Jno Vshe^r Attainted ye Jury for erro^r & sajd Jno vshe^r principall || in 20^li || & Richd wharton his suerty in tenn pounds acknowledged themselues alike bound to ye Tresurer of the Country on Condition that sajd vshe^r ꝑsecut this his Attaint to effect at ye nex^t Court of Assistants.

[156] 1682

Daniel Gookin Esqr plaintiff Contra Capt Jn^othan wade deffend^t in an Accon of Appeale from the Judgment of the County Court at charls Towne After the Attachment Courts Judgment Reasons of Appeale & euidences in the Case produced were read Comitted to ye Jury and are on file wth the Reccords of this Court the Jury brought in their virdict they found for the deffendant Costs of Courts thirty one shillings & fowe^r penc

Dani Gookin esq^r contr^a Jno,* wade

m^r Thomas Layton Andrew mansfeild & John Burrel plaintiff ag^t Tho. Browne deffendt in An Action of Appeale from the Judgment of the County Court at Salem After the Attachm^t Courts Judgment Reasons of Appeale and euidences in the Case produced were read Comitted to the Jury and are on file with the Reccords of this Court the Jury brought in their virdict they found for the plaintiff^s reuersion of the former Judgment & the land in Controuersy wth Costs of Courts nine pounds fiue shillings

Laughton mansfeild [&] Burell Atturneys for Toune of ljnn Cont. Tho Browne

Moses Peirse plaintiff Cont^a Benjamin mumford deffend^t in an Action of Appeale from the Judgm^t of the last County Court in Boston After the Attachm^t Courts Judgment reasons of Appeale & euidences in the Case produced were read Comitted to the Jury and are on file wth the reccords of this Court the Jury brought in their virdict they found for the deffendant Confirmation of the former Judgment & Costs of Courts fiuety nine shillings & eigh[t] pence y^e Jury declard y^ey medled no^t wth the title of land =

Peirse Cont^a Mumford exec Issued out

* Jn^othan?

Crosby Conta Addams

Joseph Crosby plaintiff Conta Joseph Addams deffendt in an Action of Appeale from the Judgment of the last County Court in Boston After the Attachment Courts Judgment Reasons of Appeale & euidences in the Case produced were read Comitted to the Jury & are on file wth the Reccords of this Court the Jury brought in their virdict they found for the deffendt Confirmation of the former Judgmt & Costs of Courts two pounds fiueteen shilling & two pence.

× ye pleas of ye deffendt heard for a non suit ye Court declaring ye Case should proceed to tryall

Torry agt Gretian

an Attajnt

mr Jo: Cook foreman=

Josiah Torrey plaintiff Conta Tho: Gretian deffendant in an Action of Appeale from the Judgment of the last County Court in Boston After the Attachmt ‖was Read‖× Courts Judgment Reasons of Appeale & euidences in the Case produced were read Comitted to the Jury and are on file wth the Reccords of this Court the Jury brought in their virdict they found for the plaint a Confirmation of the former Judgment and thirty pounds fiue shillings and seven penc more in mony & costs of Courts ye deffendt Tho Gretian sajd he Attained the Jury for erro'rs & Instanct pticularly because the Jury had given thirty pounds fiue shillings & seven penc more then the proceeds of that voyage wth what other he shall make Appeare: And sajd Thomas Gretian principle & mr Anthony checkley & Left Edward willis suretyes acknowledged themselues & heires bound Tho Gretian in 20li & ye suretjes in tenn pounds apeec to the Tresurer of the Country & partjes Concerned that sajd Gretian shall prosecute his Atteynt at the next Court of Assistants to effect

[157] 1682

wayte Conta Homes exec Issued out

Returne wayt plaintiff agt Joseph Homes Atturney to Stephen Sweathy deffendt in an Acčon of Appeal from the Judgmt of the County Court in Boston After the Attachmt Courts Judgment Reasons of Appeale & euidences in the Case produced were read Comitted to the Jury & are on file the Jury brought in their virdict they found for the plaintiff reuersion of the former judgment & Costs of Courts forty shilljngs & six pence =

Newby conta Hinchman exec Issud

Georg Newby plaintiff agt Jno Hinchman deffendt in an Action of Appeale from the Judgmt of the Comission'rs Court after the Attachmt Courts Judgment

Reasons of Appeale & euidences in the Case produced were read Comitted to y[e] Jury & are on file the Jury brought in their virdict they found for y[e] deffend[t] Confirmation of the former Judgm[t] & Costs of Courts 6. 6[d]

Return wayte plaintiff against Jn[o] Plumbe deffend[t] in an Action of Appeale from the Judgm[t] of the County Court in Boston after the Attachm[t] Courts Judgm[t] Reasons of Appeale & euidences in the Case produced were read Comitted to the Jury and are on file wth the Records of y[s] Court the Jury brought in their virdict they found for the defend[t] Confirmation of the former Judgm[t] & Adds twenty shillings more therevnto w[th] costs of Court: Jn[o] Plumbe in open court declard he was Agred w[th] Return wayt — wayte cont[a] pluffi

In Ans[r] to the petition of Elizabeth street wife to Robe[r]t street Humbly desiring she may be diuorc[t] from hir s[d] Husband she producing seu̇ witnesses of his breach of Coueñt & y[t] he hath anothe[r] wife in Jamajca. The Cour[t] on ꝑvsall of the euidences declares the peticone[r] is at libe[r]ty to marry w[th] another man and that she is divorc[t]. — Eliza: strets diuorce

Roge[r] Gilbe[r]t plaintiff Cont[a]: Isa[ck] waldron deffend[t] in an accon of Appeale from the Judgm[t] of the County Court at Boston After the Attachment Courts Judgment reasons of Appeale & euidences in the Case produced were read Comitted to y[e] Jury & are on file w[th] the Reccords of this Court the Jury brought in their virdict they found for the deffend[t] Confirmation of the forme[r] Judgm[t] & Costs of Courts — Gilbe[r]t ag[t] waldrō

Tho newman Cont[a] Lesly Palmer w[th]drawne ꝑ Agreement — Newman Conta Palmer

Antho checkly plaintff cont[a] Rich[d] Patteshall defend[t] in an Action of Appeale from the Judgm[t] of y[e] County Cour[t] at Boston w[th]draune ꝑ Agreem̄[t] — Cheeckly Conta Patteshall

[158] 1683

Att the Court of Assistants Adjourm[t] 17[th] of Aprill 1683 — present Symon Bradstreet Esq[r] Gou̇

Tho Danforth Esqr dep^t Govr
Daniel Gookin
w^m stoughton
Humphry Davy
Sam: Nowell
John Hull
James Russell
} Esq^rs

— — — —

persons Returnd to serve on the Jury for trjalls & sworne before the prisoner who mad no objections &c were

— — — —

m^r Samuel shrimp=ton
Robe^rt Hayward
Tim^o Tyleston
Samuel Hix
w^m meade
Tobjah Dauis
John knights
Joseph Kitle
Joseph Tainter
Benj^a Garfeild
Zackh. Hicks
Natha: Hancock

— — — —

Elisabeth Payne spinster being presented by the Grand Jury, in march las^t * for murdering of hir child was now brought to the Barr & Indicted by the name of Elizabeth Payne spinster for no^t hauing the feare of God before hir eyes & being led by the Instigation † of the diuil did on or about the 6th day of march last wilfully murde^r hir child Contrary to the Peace of ou^r Soueraigne Lord the king his Crowne & dignity the lawes of God and of this Jurisdiction holding vp hir hand at the Barr pleaded no^t Guilty & put hirself on tryall by God & the Country = Accordingly after the Indictment & euidences produced were read Comitted to the Jury and are on file the Jury brought in their virdict no^t Guilty according to Indictmen^t but greatly negligent in not Calling for help for the preservation of the childs life =

The Court on Consideration of the Case for hir fornication sentenct hir to be whip^t wth twenty stripes paying & dischardging the charge of hir trjall & fees of Court stands Comitted till the sentence be performed. =

James ffulle^r of springfeild being presented by the Grand Jury in ma[rch] last & left to further Tryall at this Court was brought to the Barr & held vp his hand & ‖ there ‖ was Indicted accordingly by the name of James ffuller of Springfeild for that he not hauing the feare of God before his eyes & being lead by the Instigation of the diuill did on or about the latter end of octobe^r last most wickedly Call vpon or pray to the Divil for helpe and hath at seuerall times since had familliarity wth him Contrary to the peace of ou^r Soueraigne Lord the king his Croune & dignity & the lawes of ‖ God & of ‖ this Jurisdiction = After the Indictment & euidenc produced agains^t him was Read he owning the charge as sajd by him but denyed the trueth of it saying he had belyed himselfe ‖ his examination & [confession being] ‖ comitted to the Jury and are on file wth the Records of this Court the Jury brought in their virdict they found the prisoner at the barr not Guilty according to Indictment: The Court Consi[der]ing of his wicked & pernicious willfull lying & Continuanc in it till now putting the Country to so great a charge

---

* Quere. See marginal entry at opening of this Court (p. 223) as to Grand Jury not having any cause before it.

† Written over the word "divill."

sentenct the sajd James ffuller to be seuerely whipt wth thirty stripes seuerely lajd on & that he pay fiue pounds mony to the Tresurer of the Country to dischardg the chardges of his triall paying fees of Court× stands Comitted till the sentence be ꝑformd. ×and that in Case ye sd fiue pounds be not pd by ye sd ffuller wthin a month Its left wth ye Tresurer of ye Country to ship him of & dispose of him as he Cann not ‖ exceeding ‖ fower yeares to Ansr the charges past E R S

24 may (83)

[159] 1683

In Ansr to the peticon of mrs mary Sauage: The Court doth Appoint mr willjam Parkes mr Joseph Lynde & Capt Penn Townsend a Committee to set out vnto mrs mary Sauage relict of the Late Thomas Sauage Esqr hir thirds According to law. and to doe it wth what speed they Cann: And deacon wm Parkes is to Appoint time & place of meeting =

In Ansr to the petition of Ann Perry for a divorce from hir husband &c The Court hauing Considered of the Case sees no Cause to grant hir request =

Att a Court of Assistants Called to sitt & sate in Boston 22th of may 1683

at this Court mary Webster wife to wm webster of Hadly being sent downe vpon suspition of witchcraft & Comitted to prison in order to hir tryall was brought to ye Barr the Grand Jury being Impanneld ~~she not excepting against any of them~~ the * Grand Jury on pervsall &c of the euidences Returnd that as ye Grand Jury for our soueraigne Lord the king they did Indict mary webster wife to wm webster of Hadly for that she not hauing the feare of God before her eyes & being instigated by the divill hath entred into Couenant & had familliarity wth him in the shape of a warraneage † & had hir Imps sucking hir & teats or marks found in hir secret parts as in & by seuerall testimonyes may Appeare Contrary to the peace of our Soueraigne Lord the king his Crowne & dignity the

present
Symon Bradstreet Esqr Gou
Tho Danforth Esqr dept Gou
Daniel Gookin
Jno Pynchon
Wm stoughton
Humphry Dauy
Sam: Nowell
Jno Hull
James Russell
Peter Tylton
Daniel ffisher —
— — — —
persons Returnd to serve on the Grand Jury & sworne were mr James Whetcombe

* Written over "held."

† An Indian name for a *black cat*. — *Judd*. See Drake's "Annals," p. 170.

Thomas moore
Eljakim Hutchinson
Jer ffitch
Joseph How
Eljas Row
Richard Louden
Phillip Torrey
Jn° watson
Isack Jones
wm Pond
Richd Eccles
Wm Bond
Jn° Brett
— — — —

lawes of God & of this Jurisdiction ^ on their serious Consideration of the testimonjes did leaue hir to further Tryalle

Christopher Portingall being Accused for Comitting a Rape on the body of Abigaile Crane as by hir Confession & examination appeares The Court ordered them to stand Comitted till they Give bond for their Appearance at the next County Court at charls Towne to Answer what shall be lajd to their charge —

Peter Addams of milton being Comitted to Goale for his stealling a horse or horses ^ =

This Court Adjourned themselues to the 24 Instant at two of the clocke =

then mett & Adjourned Againe to 31th Instant at ye same time

[*Blank*]

[160]

present
Tho. Danforth Esqr dept Go
Daniel Gookin
wm stoughton
Humphry Davy
Sam Nowell
Jn° Hull
James Russell
Dani ffisher
} Esqrs
— — — —
persons Returnd to serve on the Jury & sworn were
— — — —
mr Edward willis
~~ffrancis foxcroft~~
Adam winthrop
Sam Legg
wm Gard
Roger willington

At A Court of Assistants or Admiralty Called to sitt in Boston & satt in Boston 8th June 1683

mr Barnard Randolph deputy Collector searcher & surveyor of his maj'yes Customes in New England by his Information per dated the first of June 1683. then exhibbited (refference thereto being had amply doth & may Appeare) plaintiff against mr Edward Le-Brunn master and merchant of the Good ship called the martha of Jersey wth hir Cargoe and Appurtenances to hir belonging deffendant After the Information pleas and euidences in the Case Given into the Court were read Comitted to the Jury and are remayning on file with the Records of this Court The Jury brought in their virdict they found for the defendant Costs of Court [five] pounds six shillings =

Henry Spring
wm ffoster
Sam. Andrews
Joseph Cooke
Jno Gore
Joshua [La *]
Jno Brick[e] [vide] day booke

This Court was adjourned to ye 14 June next & thence to the 21th & so from weeke to weeke to ye 5 July 1683. E. R S

[*Blank*]

[161] 1683

Att A Court of Assistants held at Boston on their Adjournmt 5th July 1683.

present
Symon Bradstreet Esqr Gou
Daniel Gookin
wm stoughton
Humphry Davy
Samuel Nowell
‸ James Russell
‸ John Hull †

In Answer to the peticon & Complaint of mr John Gyfford exhibbited to this Court in refferenc to a Judgment obteyned by him the sajd Gyfford against mr Thomas walters, at the Court of Assistants in September 1680 to the value of sixty three pounds odd money, yet vnsattisfied as he Informes and Complaines This Court vpon pervsall and examination of the whole proceeding therein doe finde that through the misinformation of the sajd walter & mistake of the officer &c the sajd Judgment is not yet satisfied according to law, either in money or other reall and propper estate of the sajd walters and therefore doe Judge & declare the officers returne vpon the execution to be nul & voyd to all Intents & purposes whatsoeuer, And doe heereby order and Appoint the Secretary to renue the sajd Execution according to the law Anno 1674 title Judgments frustrated &c & the marshall Gennerall forthwith to execute or serve it accordingly. so past E R S

execution Issued out & dd ye marsall Genll

[*Blank*]

present
Symon Bradstreet Gounor

Att A Court of Assistants held at Boston 4th of September 1683

* Lamb?

† The two carets probably indicate that the name of Hull should come before that of Russell.

Daniel Gookin
wm stoughton
Peter Bulkley
Humphry davy
Samuel Nowell
John Hull 2d:
James Russell
Peter Ty[lton]
Bart[holmew] [Gi]dney
Sam[ll] Apleton
John woodbridge } Esqrs

— — — —

persons Returnd to serve on ye Grand Jury & sworne were =
mr wm Parkes
Tho: Bligh.
James Hill
Abell porter
Tho. Toleman
wm ffoster
Eljas Rowe
Giles Pason
wm Bond
Gregory Cooke
Jno stedman
Richd Dana
— — — —

Anthony Cheeckley on behalfe of Thomas Gretian plaintiff against Josiah Torrey deffendt ‖ on Attaint ‖ the sajd Anthony cheeckly in open Court acknowledged himself to stand bound & to be ljable to execution in Case Torrey recoṁed at this Court in steed of mr Gretian. After the Attachment Courts Judgmeñt reasons of Appeale & euidences in the Case produced were read Comitted to the Jury & are on file wth the Records of this Court the Jury brought in their virdict i: e They found a speciall virdict that is If the twenty seven pounds fiueteene shillings seven pence in the accompt given in by sajd Gretian be legall according to the mariti[m]e law page 93 sect. seccond then wee finde for the plaintiff reve'tion of the last Judgment & Costs of Courts If not legall then wee find ‖ for the defendt ‖ Confirmation of the forme' Judgment & Costs ‖ of Courts. ‖ The magists on pervsall of this virdict find for the defendant Confirmation of the former Judgment & Costs of Courts =

mr Jno Vsher & mr Jno Saffyn on behalfe of Benanuel Bowe's plaintiffs on Attaint Conta solomon Phipps & Josiah wood ℘ driue's of charls-Towne Coñon defendants on Attaint after the Attachment Courts Judgment Reasons of Appeale & euidences in the Case produced were read Coñitted to the Jury & are on file wth the Reccords of this Court the Jury brought in their virdict i e they found for the plaintiffs reuersion of the former Judgment & Costs of Courts =.

[162] 1683

persons Returnd to serve on the Jury for Attaints sworn were =
— — — —
mr James Taylor
Jno Cotter
wm sumner
Jno Parmiter
in ye ch. Cases *
James Bird
Ebenezar withrington

mr John Saffyn & mr Jno vsher on behalfe of Benanuel Bowe's plaintiffs Conta Josiah wood & Tho: white drive's of charls-Towne Coñon ℘ defendant after the Attachment Courts Judgment Reasons of Appeale & euidences in the Case produced were read Comitted to the Jury and are on file wth the Reccords of this Court the Jury finds for the plaintiffs reuersion of the forme' Judgment & Costs of Courts =

* Charlestown cases?

Jn° Atkinson plaintiffe Contra John woolcot sen̄ defendt in an Accon of Appeale from the Judgment of the County Court at Ipswich After the Attachment Courts Judgment Reasons of Appeale & euidences in the Case produced were read Comitted to the Jury and are on file wth the Records of this Court the Jury brought in their virdict: they found for the plaintiff Reūsion of the forme^r Judgmt & Costs of Courts in ye Action of ye bill fiue pounds one shilling & two penc.

1st Jury hith'to

John Atkinson plaintiff Conta Jn° woolcot deffendt in an action of Appeale from the Judgment of the County Court at Salem last After the Attachment Courts Judgment reasons of Appeale & euidences in the Case produced ^ and are on file the Jury brought in their virdict they found for the deffendt Confirmation of the former Judgment & Costs of Courts forty nine shillings =

mary Webster wife to wm webster of Hley † hauing binn presented for suspition of witchraft &c by a Grand Jury in Boston 22th of may last & left to furthe^r Tryall was now Called & brought to the barr and was Indicted by the name of mary webster wife to wm webster &c for that shee not hauing the feare of God before hir eyes & being Instigated by the diuil had entred into couenant & had familliarity wth him in the shape of a warraneage & had hir Imps sucking hir & teats or marks found in hir secret parts as in & by seuerall testimonjes may Appeare Contrary to the peace of ou^r Soueraigne Lord the king his Crowne & dignity the lawes of God & this Jurisdiction to wch Indictment making no exception against any of the Jury leauing hirself to be trjed by God & the Country After ye Indictment & euidences in the Case were read Com̄itted to the Jury and are on file the Jury brought in hir virdict they found hir not guilty =

1 Ju:

James Barbar
Ezra Clap
John Betts
Jn° swett in Gretians *
Richd Chicke
Edward Dor
Jn° weld
Jn° Lyon
sam stone
noah wisewall
Xtophe^r Read
Tho. Langhorne
Jn° Goue:
Caleb church
Josiah Jones
Jn° Hamond
Symon Coolidge
Dani Herrington
Samuell Ruggles
Jn° Livermore

— — — —

persons Returnd to se^rve on ye Jury for Appeales &c sworn

— — — —

Mr James Taylor
Wm sumner
Jn° Betts
Jn° weld
Xtophe^r Read
Jn° Goue
Tho Longhorne
Dani. Herrington
Ebenez^r withrington
Josiah Jones
Wm Gennerson
Richd chicke

— — — —

persons Returnd to serve on ye Jury for life & death & afterw^rds for Appeales &c sworne

— — — —

m^r samuel stone
Jn° Parmiter
Jn° Cotter
Ezra Clapp
James Bird
Sam: Douse
Jn° Swett
Edward Dor
noah wisewall
Symon Coolidge
Jn° Hamond
Jn° Liuermore

— — — —

* Gretian's case?

† Hadley. See above, p. 229.

Joshua Rice being Comitted to prison on suspition of Adultery y[e] Grand Jury on ꝑvsall of the euidences presented & Indicted him & left him to furthe[r] Trjall he was brought to the barr & Indicted by y[e] name of Joshua Rice of Boston in the County of Suffolke in new England Cordwayner for that he not hauing the feare of God before his eyes & being Instigated by the divil did on the 24th of August last repaire to the house of Edward Crockett laborer & didst Comitt the foule sinn of Adultery with Elisabeth Crocket his wife Contrary to the peace of our Soueraigne Lord the king his Croune & dignity the law of God & of this Jurisdiction to wch Indictment he pleaded not Guilty & put himself on trjall on God & y[e] Country after his Indictmen[t] & euidences in the Case produced ag[t] the prisoner at the barr were Read Comitted to y[e] Jury & are on file the Jury brought in their virdict they found him not Guilty according to Indictment but found him guilty of lasivious Gross & foule actions tending to Adultery. =

2 Jur

[163] 1683

Crockets Indictm[t]

Elisabeth Crocket wife to Edward Crocket of Boston in the County of Suffolk Labourer being alike presented & Indicted by the Grand Jury was brought to the Barr & was alike Indicted for the like foule Crime wth Joshua Rice att y[e] same time & place & putting hirself on triall by God & y[e] Country pleading not Guilty after the Jury had pervsed the euidences in y[t] Case brought in their virdict as ag[t] Rice =

2[d] Jur

mason Contra Tight

= Arthur mason plaintiff ag[t] Henry Tight defend[t] in an action of Appeale from the Judgment of the County Court at Boston in Aprill last After the Attachment Courts Judgment Reasons of Appeale & euidences in the Case produced were read Comitted to the Jury & are on file the Jury brought in their virdict they found for the deffend[t] confirmation of the former Judgmt & Costs of Courts [thirty] shillings

Roge[rs] Cont[a] Tyte

Gamaljel Roge[r]s plaintiff ag[t] Henry Tite defend[t] in an action of Appeale from the Judgment of the County Court in Boston in Aprill last After the Attachment Courts Judgment Reasons of Appeale & euidences in the Case produced were Read Comitted to the Jury & are on file w[th] the reccords of this Court the Jury brought in their virdict they found for the defend[t] Confirmation of the former Judgment and Costs of Courts thirty seuen shillings & tenn pence ‖ besides x[s] dam̃age ‖ — —

Brisco ⁊ Contra Sparrey

Joseph Bris[c]o: Atturney to Henry wright & Tim[o] Dwight Atturney to Sam Snow plaintiff Con[a] Jn[o] sparrey defendant in an Action of Appeale from the Judgment of the Comissione[r]s Court in June last after the Attachment Courts Judgm[t] & Reasons of Appeale were Read y[e] defend[t] pleaded for a non suit because the Reasons of Appeale were not signed by y[e] principle or Atturney w[ch] was grted

Idem ṽsus Idem.

Joseph Brisco Atturney to Henry wright plaintiff Conta John sparrey defend[t] in an Action of Appeale from y[e] Judgment of the Comissione[r]s Court the Attachm[t] Courts Judgm[t] & Reasons of Appeale were Read ^ was non suited because y[e] time of y[e] Court was mist in y[e] Reasons =

webb ag[t] manly an Attajnt m[r] stone foremãn

Joseph webb marshall of Suffolke plaintiff ag[t] w[m] manly deffend[t] in an Action of Appeale from the Judgment of the Comissione[r]s Court in Aprill last After the Attachment Courts Judgment reasons of Appeale & euidences in the Case produced were read Comitted to the Jury & are on file with the Reccords of this Court the Jury brought in their virdict they found for the defendant Confirmation of the forme[r] Judgm[t] & costs of Courts. =

Joseph webb marshall sajd he Attainted the Jury for erro[r]s & himself as principall in twelve pounds & Returne wayte & Abraham Bliss his sue[r]tjes Acknowledged themselues respectively bound to the Tresure[r] of the Country & party Concernd on Condition y[t] s[d] webb shall prosecute this his Attaint at the nex[t] Court of Assistants to effect =

Jn[o] child plaintiff on Appeale from the sentenc of the Court ^ After the Courts Judgment Reasons of Appeale & euidences in the Case produced were read Comitted to the Jury & are on file the Jury brought in their virdict they found the Appellant Giulty of playing at Cards for thirty sixe shillings mony =

[164] 1683

Nurse ag[t] Endecot

ffrancis Nurse plaintiff× in an action of Appeale from the Judgment of the County Court at Salem last× against m[r] Zerubbable Endicot deffendant After the Attachment

Courts Judgment Reasons of Appeale & euidences in the Case produced were read Comitted to the Jury & are on file the Jury brought in their virdict they found for the deffendant Confirmation of the forme^r^ Judgment & Costs of Courts ‖ In Ans^r^ to m^r^ Allens peticon * ‖ ‖ execution suspended to y^e^ end of y^e^ nex^t^ Genn^l^ Court ‖

Execution Issued out for 7.18.3 dd to m^r^ Homes Atturney 11 Sep^t^ 1683 =

Clark Con^ta^ Smith

Timothy Clarke plaintiff Cont^a^ katherin Smith in behalf of hir sonn John Smith deffendant in an Action of Appeale from the Judgment of the Comission^r^s Court last in Boston After the Attachment Courts Judgment Reasons of Appeale & euidences in the Case produced were read Comitted to the Jury & are on file wth the Reccords of this Court the Jury brought in their virdict they found for the deffendant Confirmation of the forme^r^ Judgment & Costs of Courts forty two shillings

Dewer ag^t^ Browne

Tho Dewer plaintiff against willjam Broune Esqr defend^t^ in an Accōn of Appeale from the Judgment of the County Court in July last at Boston after the Attachment Courts Judgment Reasons of Appeale & euidences in the Case produced were read Comitted to the Jury & are on file with the Reccords of this Court the Jury brought in their virdict they found for the deffendant Confirmation of the forme^r^ Judgment & Costs of Courts.

Apleton ꝯ Hawkes

an Attaint, m^r^ [James Tayl^r^] foreman =

Samuell Apelton sen̄ Esqr & Samuel Apleton Jun̄ plaintiff^s^ Cont^a^ John Hawkes sen̄ & moses Haukes defend^t^ in An Action of Appeale from the Judgment of the County Court at Salem last After the Attachment Courts Judgment Reasons of Appeale & euidences in the Case produced were read Comitted to the Jury & are on file wth the Reccords of this Court the Jury brought in their virdict they found for the plaintiff thirty pounds mony damages and that the deffendants shall make vp the great damm as Good as before in tweluemonths time next ensuing or pay two hundred & fiuety pounds money & Costs of Courts.

The deffendant Attainted the Jury for erro^r^s & himself sajd Jno Hawkes principall in the sume of two hundrd pounds & Thomas skinner & Edward Richards his sue^r^tjes in 100^li^ a peece acknowledged themselues bound to the Treasurer of the Country in sajd somes

* This part is inserted in the margin, but was evidently intended to be read with the words "execution suspended," etc.

Respectively & to the partjes concerned on Condition that sajd Hawkes shall prosecute this his Attaint at the nex[t] Court of Assistan[t]s to effect =

Samuel Nowel Esq[r] & m[r] Hezekiah Vsher Ex-eccuto[r]s to the last will of the late m[r] Hezekiah vsher plaintiff[s] Cont[a] Nathaniel Harwood as Assignee & Atturney to m[r] John Harwood in an Action of Appeale from the Judgment of the last County Court at charlsTowne on a non suite * after the Court had pvsed the Attachment Courts Judgment Reasons of Appeale and euidences in the Case they declared that there ought to be no non suit & Grants the deffendant his Costs nineteen shillings

Hezekiah Vsher ag[t] Nathani Harwood

[165] 1683

m[r] Hezekiah vsher plaintiff Contra Peter Bulkley Esq[r] as Assignee ‖ &c ‖ of m[r] John Harwood defend[t] in an action of Appeale from the Judgment of the County Court at Cambridge in Aprill last After the Attachment Courts Judgment reasons of Appeale & euidences in the Case produced were read Comitted to the Jury & are on file the Jury brought in their virdict they found for the deffendant Confirmation of the forme[r] Judgment & Costs of Courts ‖ The plaintiff Attainted the Jury for erro[r] & Gaue bond ‖

m[r] vshe[r] ag[t] m[r] Bulkley &c

An Attaint m[r] James Taylor foreñ

Wm Harrison plaintiff Cont[a] Thomas Platts deffendt in an Action of Appeale from the Judgment of the last County Court in Boston After the Attachm[t] Courts Judgment reasons of Appeale & euidences in the Case produced were read Comitted to the Jury & are on file The Jury brought in their virdict they found for the plaintiff reuersion of the former Judgment & that the sajd Platts take his chimneys of the sajd Harrisons Ground wth in sixe moneth[s]

Harrison Cont[a] Platts

Execution Issued out

* "On a non suite" here evidently means "on a plea for a non-suit," as appears by the record of the County Court at Charlestown, June 19, 1683, from whose judgment the appeal was taken. At that Court Nathaniel Harwood, as assignee and attorney of John Harwood, was plaintiff, and Samuel Nowell, who married the relict and executrix of Hezekiah Usher, deceased, and Hezekiah, the other executor, were defendants, the action being for the payment of a legacy of fifty pounds. The defendants, Nowell, etc., "pleaded for a non sute because the plaintiff sued as both attorney & assignee, the law saying or & not and, i.e. the one & not both." "The Magistrates ordered the plaintiff to proceed in his plea," that is, the Court refused to order a non suit. The defendants, Nowell, etc., appealed from this decision. The trial, at the County Court, then proceeded, and Harwood obtained a judgment there in his favor. The Court of Assistants confirmed the decision of the County Court, refusing to order a non suit, and accordingly grants Harwood his costs. See County Court Records, Middlesex, 1681-1686, p. 64.

or pay the sajd Harrison forty pounds in money & Costs of Courts fiue pounds & two pence ==

Harrison Conta Platts

Execution Issued:

Wm Harrison plaint Conta Thomas Platts defendt In an action of Appeale from the Judgment of the County Court last in Boston after the Attachmt Courts Judgmt Reasons of Appeale & euidences in the Case produced were read Comitted to the Jury & are on file wth the reccords of this Court the Jury brought in their virdict they found for the plaintiff reuersion of the former Judgment & Costs of Courts forty shillings & fower pence ==

Homes agt chickley

An Attaint mr stone foreman

Joseph Homes plt Conta Anthony Cheeckley || Atturney to stephen Sweathy || deffendt in an Accon of Appeale from the Judgment of the County Court in Boston After the Attachment Courts Judgment reasons of Appeale & euidences in the Case produced were read Comitted to the Jury & are on file wth the reccords of this Court the Jury brought in their virdict they found for the deffendt Confirmation of the former Judgment & Costs of Courts forty sixe shillings & sixe pence; the plt. Joseph Homes Attainted the Jury || for error er || & Joseph Homes principall in twenty pounds & Joseph webb & Xtopher webb his suertjes in tenn pounds apeece acknowledged themselues bound to the Tresurer of the Country & party Concerned on Condition that Joseph Homes shall prosecute this his Attaint at the next Court of Assistants to effect —

Cowell Conta Thornton

= Joseph Cowell plaintiff Conta Timothy Thornton deffendt in an Action of Appeale from the Judgmt of the Comissioners Court in Boston After the Attachment Courts Judgment Reasons of Appeale & euidences in the Case produced were read Comitted to the Jury & are on file the Jury brought in their virdict they found for ye plaintiff reusion of the former Judgment & Costs of Courts 27s 2d.

Bishop Conta Lumas *

Samuel Bishop plaintiff agt Robert Lord marshall deffendt In an action of Appeale from the Judgment of the County Court at Ipswich After the Attachment Courts Judgment Reasons of Appeale & euidences in the Case produced were read Comitted to the Jury & are on file wth the Records of this Court the Jury brought in their virdict they found for the

* Evidently an error for "Lord."

plaintiff Reue[rsi]on of the forme^r Judgm^t ‖ & ‖ tenn pounds & six penc damage according to Execution & Costs of Courts & execution Respitted till ye nex^t Gen^ll Courts ends

Samuell Lummas * plan^t Cont^a w^m Quarles deffend^t in an Action of Appeale from the Judgment of the County Court at Ipswich After the Attachment Courts Judgm^t Reasons of Appeale & euidences in the Case produced were Read Comitted to the Jury and are on file the Jury brought in their virdict they found for ye deffend^t ffowe^r pounds fowe^rteene shillings & fowe^r pence

[166] 1683

Dauis ag^t Gridley

Robe^rt Dauis plaintiff Cont^a Joseph Gridley deffend^nt In An action of Appeale from the Judgment of the last Comissions^rs Court in Boston after the Attachment Courts Judgment Reasons of Appeale & euidences in the Case produced ^ & are on file the Jury brought in their virdict they found for the deffendan^t Confirmation of the forme^r Judgment & Costs of Courts thirty one shillings & eight pence

Perkins ag^t Smith

Edmond Pe^rkin[s] plt Cont^ra Arthur Smith deffend^t in an Action of Appeale from the Judgment of the last County Court in Boston wth drew his action by the Courts leaue Affirming he had Agred wth y^e defend^t = who did not appear

Worden Con^ta Addams

Samuel worden plt Con^ta Nathaniel Addams deffendan^t in an action of Appeale from the Judgment of the County Cour^t in Boston made his non Appearanc y^e defend^t had his Costs =

Lee ag^t Leueret

John Lee plt Conta : Hudson Leueret deffendant in an Action of Appeale from the Judgment of the Comissione^rs Court in Boston after the Attachm^t Courts Judgment Reasons of Appeale & euidences in the Case produced were read Comitted to the Jury & are on file the Jury brought in their virdict they found for the deffendant Confirmation of the forme^r Judgment & Costs of Courts thirty sixe shillings & three pence

Execution Issued out 15 Sep^t 83

* Written over " w^m Quarles."

Mrs Elisabeth manings divorce from Nicholas maning

at [Ipswich *] court

In Answer to the peticon of Elisabeth maning for a divorce from hir husband, Nicholas Maning = It Appearing to this Court on pervsall of the paper's presented that the sajd Nicholas maning was guilty of Incestuous practises with his sister's of which they were Convicted and punished but himself escaped out of this Jurisdiction thereby Avoyding the punishment, and also that he hath not for seuerall yeares past affoorded the sajd Elisabeth any releife for maintenance and hath lately declared In writting vnder his hand & seale that he doth vtterly renounce the sajd Elisabeth and that he will not owne her for his wife or haue any thing to doe with her = All which being Considered by this Court It is by them declared that the sajd Elisabeth is henceforth freed & released from hir marriage ingagement vnto the sajd Nicholas maning — By ye Court Edw: Rawson secret

Courts sentence agt Joshua Rice & Elisa Crocket for their Adulterous Carriages &c

In the Case of Joshua Rice the Court hath Considered your offence, and doe sentence yow on the next fifth day of ye weeke presently after the lecture to be by ye marshall Gennerall to be taken out of ye prison & ‖ wth a Roape abt your necke ‖ Conveyed thro the Towne to the Gallowes & there to be sett on a ladder & stand on full hower wth yor Roap turnd ouer the Gallowes & then to be taken doune & Conveyed to the begining of the street entring the Towne to be stript & tjed to the Carts Tayle & be seuerely whipt wth thirty stripes thrô the streets to the Goale & be there left till yow discharge the charg of yor trjall prison & Court ffees. wch when donn to be releast from prison the like sentenc was passed & published in Court in all respects against & to Elisabeth Crocket wife to † Crocket partner wth him in ~~their~~ odious vile & lustfull carriages = past ER S =

[167] 1683

Launcellot Smith Complayning to the Gouernor & magists then mett against Nicholas Lynch as By attachment produced bearing date the of 1683 both partjes Appeared plaintiff & defendant & desired their Cases might be heard by a Court of Assistants or Admiralty their occasons not permitting to stay till ye County Court The Court ~~ordered the hearing of their Cases at~~

at one of ye clock present the Gouernor dept Gou major Gookin mr stoughton mr Bulkley mr Browne

* The word "Ipswich" appears to be written here over the word "Salem."

† Left blank in the record.

|| Appointed the twelfth Instant at one of ye clock || [at] the Court of Assistants to sitt in Boston 12 october 1683 || at ye time || The Court mett at the time 12th octobe^r 1683 ye plaintiff Launcelot Smith Appeared & presented his libell ye deffendant Nicholas Lynch Appeared || & put in his Ans^r || and after their * || libell & Answ^r wth y^e || Euidences produced & pleas made by both partjes The Court on a full hearing of the partjes declared they found for the plaintiffe eighty pounds mony of this Country & Costs of Courts two pounds sixteene shillings —

m^r Nowell
m^r Russell
m^r Tilton
m^r Apleton
m^r Gidney
m^r Pyke
— — — —

Nicholas Steeresman also then Appeared as Smith aboue in all respects had the like libe^rty wth like Consent of s^d [Li]nch

The Court ordered the hearing of this Case also on 12 octobe^r 1683

The Court mett at the time the plaintiff & deffendant Appeared the defendant † then put In his libell And after the libell Ans^r therevnto euidences in the Case produced & pleas made by both partjes The Cour^t on a full hearing of the partjes declard they found for the deffendant eighty pounds this Country mony damage & Costs of Court [fiue ‡] pounds seventeen shillings —

[*Blank*]

[168] Boston 1683

[*The remainder of the page is blank.*]

[169] Boston 1683

At A Court of Assistants Called by order of y^e Goūno^r &c and satt in Boston 12 novembe^r 1683 =

present
Symon Bradstreet Esqr Govr
Tho. Danforth Esqr dep^t Goū
Daniel Gookin
w^m Stoughton
Joseph dudley
Peter Bulkley
Natha Saltonstall
Humphry Davy
John Richards
Sam Nowell
James Russell
Barthol: Gidney
Robe^rt Pike
J^no woodbridge
Esq^rs
— — — —

Wm Johnson being presented by the Grand Jury was brought to the barr holding vp his hand at the barr was Indicted by the name of willjam Johnston for that he no^t hauing the feare of God before his eyes but Instigated by the divil Confœderating himselfe wth one John Graham & other Sea Roue^rs his Accomplices did together

* Written over "the." † So in the original. ‡ "Fiue" written over "two."

persons Returnd to serve on ye Grand Jury & Sworn were
— — — —
Capt Jno Capen
Jonathan Bridgham
Theodr Atkinson
Joseph Homes
Jno Coney
Wm Gary
Tho Cheny
Richd Hall
Richd Robbins
Jnothan Rimington
John Stone
Jno strettens
Randall Nicholls
S[am:] Heman
— — — —
persons Returnd to serve on ye Jury of tryalls sworn
— — — —
mrJosephTownsend
ffrancis ffoxcraft
Edwd Broomfeild
Jno Endecott
Benja walker
Giles Dyer
Timo ffoster
sam Gookin
Abraham Holman
Henry Spring
Joseph Child Jun
stephen waters
— — — —

with them sometimes in the month of June in this present yeare 1683 on the high sea & neere the Coast of [Can]ady wth force of Armes pirattically assault, seize & take seuerall vessels & the Companyes belonging to them i e a certeine Catch belonging to the Port of Salem John Lambert master and one other barcq belonging to the Port of Boston James Taylor master & another barcq Called the James & Hannah John Earthy master all three belonging to his Majtjes subjects of this Colony of the Massachusetts And also one barcq Called the St Charles ^ Arsneaw master belonging to the Subjects of the ffrench king now in Amity wth his Majty making the men belonging to the sajd vessells prisoners plundering & sharing among themselues the Goods in the sajd vessells found to the value of seuerall hundred pounds sterling Contrary to the peace of our soueraigne Lord the king his Crowne & dignity & the lawes of this Jurisdiction to wch Indictment the prisoner at ye barr pleaded not Guilty & put himself on tryall on God & ye Country After the euidences produced agt him were read Comitted to the Jury the Jury brought in their virdict they found the prisoner wm Johnson at the barr not guilty according to Indictment — The Court ordered yt he be released from his Imprisonment he putting in security of fiue hundred pounds to Ansr any further Complaint of this nature to be made agnt him wthin sixe months by the ffrench or others & ordered yt he discharg Constable Jno Lamberts Charges wch was 35s for himself wittness: er —— he was after his Conti[nu]ing in prison till * ‖ 5th ‖ January ‖ 83 ‖ nothing Appearing agt him more & not able to finde any s[e]curity was † by order of the Gouꝛnr & magists releast his Imprisonmt 5 January 1683 — /

Leonard Pomery being presented by ye Grand Jury & left to tryall was Indicted by the name of Leonard Pomery for that he not hauing the feare of God before his eyes but Instigated by the divill on the fowerth day of September last in the house of Ruth Harding did maliciously wickedly & ffelloniously quarrelling so with Thomas

* The Secretary apparently began to write "Wednesday" here, but cancelled it.
† "Was" repeated in the record.

Pinnock murther him by throwing him downe on the ffloore from a chajre where he satt giving him a cruell blow on the vpper part of his breast neere his throate & kicking him with his ffoote of which wound & blow he presently sickned vojded much blood in clodds & so continued till he djed of sajd blowes as by seuerall euidences may & will appeare Contrary to the peace of our soueraigne Lord the king his Crowne & dignity ^ the lawes of this

[170] 1683

Jurisdiction to wch Indictment the prisoner at the barr pleaded not guilty and put himself on trjall on God & the Country After the euidences in the Case produced were read Comitted to the Jury & are on file the Jury brought in their virdict they found the Prisoner at the Barr Guilty of man Slaughter the Prisoner was againe brought to the barr and had this sentenc i e: to be burnt in the hand & forfeit his Goods & chattels none to be found ye executioner executed the sentenc in ye face of the Court = 20 Novemb 1683

It was ordered that Edward Crocket be hencforth the executioner and that he haue the sallery that Joseph Gridley had =

Att A Court of Assistants held at Boston 4th march 1683 —

present
Symon Bradstreet Esqr Gou
Tho Danforth Esqr dept Gou
Daniel Gookin
wm stoughton
Joseph dudley
Pet[er] Bulkley
Nathaniel Saltonstall
Humphry davy
John Richards
Samuell Nowell
James Russell
Bartholmew Gidney
Samuel Apleton
Robert Pyke

— — — —

persons Returnd to serve on ye Grand Jury & Sworne

— — — —

Capt Tho Jenner
Richd way
Tho Bligh
Theodr Atkinson
Jno Harrison

John Hawkes &c plaintiff Conta Samuel Apleton sen esqr & samuel Apleton Jun defendant in an Action of Attaint on Apeale from the virdict & Judgmt of ye Jury &c the last Court of Assistants After the Attachment Courts Judgmt Reasons for Attaint &c were read Comitted to the Jury & are on file wth the Records of this Court the Jury brought in their virdict they found for the plaintiff Reuersion of the former Judgment & costs of Courts nine pounds

mr Hezekiah vsher plaint Conta Peter Bulkley Esqr defendt in an action of Attaint on Appeale After the attachment Courts Judgment Reasons of Attaint &c were read Comitted to the Jury & are on file wth the Reccords of this Court the Jury brought in their

moses Payne
Giles Pason
Robe[r]t willjams
Sam: Williams
Enock wiswall
w^{m} Trescott
Jacob Huings
Rich Lowden
Laurenc Douse
Jame[s] Trowbridge
Tho olliuer
francis moor
[Tho ffleg or]
John Whitney

virdict they found for the deffend^{t} Confirmation of the former Judgment & costs of Courts

Joseph Webb plaintiff Con^{ta} w^{m} manly deffendant In An action of Attaynt on Appeale from the Judgment of the last Court of Assistants After the ‖ [Attachmt] ‖ Courts Judgment Reasons of Attaint &c were read Comitted to the Jury & are on file wth the Reccords of this Cour^{t} the Jury brought in their virdict they found for the plaintiff reuersion of the forme^{r} Judgment & Costs of Courts

[171]

1683

persons Returnd to serve on ye Jury of Attaints & sworne

— — — —

m^{r} Jonathan Rimington
Jno white
w^{m} Downes
w^{m} Griggs
Isayah Toy
Tho walker
Isaack Goose
Sam: Peirse
Rouland story
Benjamin Gamblin
Samuel Lyon
Benja. Tucker
Samuel Perry
Samuel Paul
Ebenezar Billing
John Breck
w^{m} Ryall
w^{m} Clutterbuck
Nathaniel Nicholls
Tho white
Peter Towne
Andrew Boardman
Jno Bright
Nath Basham

— — — —

Joseph webb plt Contra w^{m} Manly deffend^{t} in an Action of Attaint on Appeale from the Judgment & virdict of the Jury at the Court ‖ of ‖ Assis^{ts}* in sept^{r} † last after the Attachment Courts Judgm^{t} and reasons of Attaint being Read Com̄itted to the Jury and are on file wth the Reccords of this Court the Jury brought in their virdict they found for the plaintiff Reuersion of the forme^{r} Judgment & Costs of Courts three pounds thirteen shillings & two pence

Joseph Homes pl^{t} Con^{ta} Anthony cheeckley Atturney to stephen sweathy deffend^{t} in an Action of Attaint on Appeale from the Judgment & virdict of the Jury in septembe^{r} last. After the Attachment Courts Judgment Reasons of Attaint were read Comitted to the Jury & are on file wth the Reccords of this Court the Jury brought in their virdict they found for the plaintiff reue^{r}sion of the forme^{r} Judgment & Costs of Courts fowe^{r} pounds fowe^{r}- ‖ teene ‖ shillings & sixe pence

m^{r} Downes in m^{r} Apletons Case stood by
ye Case referrd to 23

— — — —

persons Returnd to serve on ye 1st Jury for tryalls of Appeales &c sworne

— — — —

Edmond Perkins plt Cont[r]a Abraham Merrill dfendant in ^ accon of Appeale from the Comission^{r}s Court in Boston After the Attachment Courts Judgment Reasons of Appeale & euidences in the Case produced were read Comitted to the Jury & are on file wth the Reccords of this Court the Jury brought in

*First written "County Court." †First written "october."

their virdict they found for the plaintiff reue'sion of the former Judĝt & three* pounds money damage & Costs of Courts wch they Agred amongst themselues =

wm Rauson plt Conta wm Gilbert deffendt in an action of Appeale from the Judgment of the County Court in Boston ^ octobe' last After the Attachment Courts Judgment Reasons of Appeale & euidences in the Case ꝓduced were read Comitted to ye Jury & are on file wth the Reccords of this Court the Jury brought in their virdict they found for the deffendt Confirmation of the forme' Judgment & Costs of Courts twenty shilling & sixe pence ‖ ye plaintiff Attainted ye Jury & himself in 10li & Jno woodmansy & mr Harrison his suertjes in 5 li apece Gaue [bond gaue] bond to prosecut ꝑ ‖

Wm Harrison plt Conta Thomas Platts defendt in an action of Appeale from the Judgmt of the County Court in Boston in octobe' last After the Attachment Courts Judgment Reasons of Appeale & euidences in ye Case produced were read Comitted to the Jury & are on file wth the Reccords of this Court the Jury brought in their virdict they found for the deffendant Confirmation of the forme' Judgment & costs of Courts ‖ ye plaintiff Attainted ye Jury & himself in 14li & Josep Home & Jos [Cowell] in 7li ꝑ gaue bond to prosecute ‖

mr Jonathan Rimington
Nathll: Basham
Isayah Toy
Isack Goose
Rouland story
Benj. Tucker
wm Clutterbuck
Samuel Paul
Peter Towne
Tho white
Ebenezar Billing
Sam Peirse
— — — —
person Returnd & sworne for ye 2d Jury of Appeales
— — — —
mr Jno Brecke
wm Dounes
Jno white
wm Griggs
Tho walker
Andrew Boardman
Benja Gamblinn
wm Ryall
Nathanll Nicholls
Sam: Lyon
Sam: [Perry]
[†]

wm Harrison plt conta Thomas Platts defendt in an action of Appeale from the Judgment of the County Court in Boston in January last After the Attachment Courts Judgment Reasons of Appeale & euidences in the Case produced were read Comitted to the Jury & are on file wth the Reccords of this Court the Jury brought in their virdict they found for the defendt Confirmation of the form' Judgment & costs of Courts = ‖ ye plt Attainted ye Jury & himself in 10li & his sue'tjes in 5li gaue security to ꝓsecut ye Attaint to effect = ‖

[172] 1683

Condy conta clarke

Wm Condy Admnstrato' to John wilkys estate plt Contra John clarke marriner defendt in an Action of Appeale from the Judgment of the County Court in Boston in

* Written over "costs." † One name worn off (Jno Bright?).

exec

January last after the Attachment Courts Judgment Reasons of Appeale and euidences in the Case produced were read Comitted to the Jury and are on file wth the Reccords of this Court the Jury brought in their virdict they found for the deffendant Confirmation of the former Judgment & Costs of Courts nineteen shillings & eight pence

Moore Conta Porter

exe:

Thomas Moore plaintiff Conta Abell porter Jun̄ defendt in an action of Appeale from the Judgment of the County Court After the Attachment Courts Judgment reasons of Appeale and euidences in the Case produced were read Com̄itted to the Jury and are^wth the Reccords of this Court the Jury brought in their virdict they found for the plaintiff reuertion of the former Judgment wth fower pounds nine shillings & two pence damage in money & Costs of Courts three pounds nine shilling & 8d.

Peirse Conta mumford

Moses Peirse plaint Conta Benjamin mumford deffendt in an Accon of Appeale from the Judgment of the County Court in Boston ‖ octobe^r last ‖ After the Attachment Courts Judgment Reasons of Appeale & euidences in the case produced were read Com̄itted to the Jury & are on file wth the reccords ‖ of ‖ this Court the Jury brought in their virdict they found for the deffendt Confirmation of the former Judgment & Costs of courts thirty eight shillings & eight pence

Torrey Conta Gretian

Josiah Torrey plaintiff Conta Thomas Gretian deffendt in an Action of Appeale from the Judgm̄ent of the County Court In Boston After the Attachment Courts Judgment Reasons of Appeale And euidences in the Case produced were read Comitted to the Jury and are on file wth the Records of this Court the Jury brought in their virdict they found for the plaintiff reue^rsion of the former Judgment & Costs of Courts three pounds sixteen shilling and six pence

Welsh Conta stowe^rs

exec

Thomas welch plt conta: Richard stowe^rs defendt in An Accon of Appeale from the Judgment of the County Court at charlsTowne After the Attachment Courts Judgment Reasons of Appeale and euidences in the Case produced were read Comitted to the Jury and are on file wth the reccords of this Court the Jury brought in their virdict they found for the plaintiff Reuertion of the former Judgment ~~& Costs~~ [wth the two] acres of land in Controūsy & Costs of Courts

[173] 1683

Ezekiel needham plaintiff Contra Benjamin ffarr deffend^{t} in an Action of Appeale from the Judgment of the County Court last at Ipswich After the Attachment Courts Judgment Reasons of Appeale & euidences in the Case produced were read Comitted to the Jury and are on file wth the Reccords of this Court the Jury brought in their virdict they found for the deffend^{t} Confirmation of the forme^{r} Judgment & Costs of Courts fiuety nine shillings & eight pence

needham Con^{ta} farr exec.

John Arnold plaintiff Con^{ta} Zackery Thayer defend^{t} in an action of Appeale from the Judgment of the County Court in Boston in octobe^{r} last After the Attachment Courts Judgment reasons of Appeale & euidences in the Case produced were read Comitted to the Jury and are on file wth the Reccords of this Court the Jury brought in their virdict they found for the deffend^{t} Confirmation of the forme^{r} Judgment & Costs of Courts sixe pounds one shilling and fowe^{r} penc mony damage & ye costs forty eight shillings & eleven penc

Arnold Con^{ta} Thay^{re}

Samuel Legg Plaintiff Con^{ta} Samuel lilly deffend^{t} in an Action of Appeale from the Judgment of the last County Court in Boston After the Attachment Courts Judgment Reasons of Appeale & euidences in the Case produced were read Comitted to the Jury & are on file wth the Records of this Court the Jury brought in their virdict they found for the deffendant Confirmation of the forme^{r} Judgment & Costs of Courts thirty fowe^{r} shillings & two pence.

Legg Con^{ta} Lilly exec.

John Gifford plaintiff Con^{ta} Thomas walter deffend^{t} in an action of Appeale from the Judgment of the County Court in Boston in october last After the Attachment Courts Judgment Reasons of Appeale & euidences in the Case produced were read Comitted to the Jury and are on file wth the Reccord^{s} of this Court the Jury finds for the deffend^{t} Confirmation of the former Judgment & Costs of Courts [Ren^{d} 13. 6]

Gifford Con^{ta} walter

as to a non Suite Bishop Contª Lord

Samuel Bishop plaintiff in ^ action of Appeale Contª Robeʳt Lord In an Action of Appeale from the Judgment of ~~Ipswich~~ ‖ Salem ‖ Court Conᵗᵃ Robeʳt Lord ‖ marshall ‖ defendant &c The Court doe Judge for the plaintiff that he haue the Costs of this Court ‖ 32: ‖ & doe ordeʳ the plaintiffˢ liberty to proceed on the Attachment at the nexᵗ County Court of that County on his former entry mony =

2 Jury

Bishop Conᵗᵃ Andrews & Hovey. —

Samuel Bishop plaintiff Conᵗᵃ John Andrews & Daniel Hovey Admstʳˢ to the estate of the late mʳ Thomas Andrews defendᵗ After the Courts Judgmᵗ Reasons of Appeale & euidences were read Comitted to the Jury & are on file The Jury brought in their virdict i e they found that mʳ Thomas Andrews died in the house of Samuel Bishop and also that the keys of the sajd Andrews were at that time in possession of sajd Bishop = mʳ Bishop not appearing when Called for to be examined his Costs not Allowed ꝑ Curiā 11 mʳch 83

[174] 1683

Thwing Conᵗᵃ Holljock

Edward Thwing & samuel Phillip plt Conᵗᵃ Elizur Holliock defendᵗ in an Acon of Appeale from the Judgment of the County Court in Boston ^ yᵉ entry of yᵉ action the plaintiffs were Called but noᵗ Appearing the Action fell

Brinsdon Conᵗᵃ wharton

Robeʳt Bromsdon Atturney to John Baker plt Conᵗᵃ mʳ Richard wharton deffendᵗ &c In An action of Appeale from the Judgment of the County Court in ~~octobeʳ~~ ‖ January ‖ last After the Attachment Courts Judgment Reasons of Appeale & euidences in the Case produced were read Comitted to the Jury and are on file wᵗʰ the Reccords of this Court the Jury brought in their virdict they found for the plaintiffe Reuersion * of the former Judgment & Costs of Courts ‖ 3ˡⁱ 6ᵈ ‖ the deffendᵗ † sajd he Attainted the Jury ‖ for errors & mistakes ‖ and the sajd Richard wharton principall in tenn pounds and mʳ Hez. vsher and wᵐ Rawson his suertjes in fiue pounds apeece acknowledged themselues bound to the Treasure[r] of the Country & partje Concerned that the sajd mʳ wharton

Attaint [List] [Mʳ Jnᵒ Breks ‡] foreman

* Written over "deffendant Confirmation." † Written over "plaintiff."
‡ Written over "mʳ Remington."

should prosecute his Attaint at the nex[t] Cour[t] of Assistants to effect = E R S

Mr Wharton Cont[a] John Baker

Richard Wharton in behalf of himself & Company plant Con[ta] John John * Baker marriner deffend[t] in an action of Appeale from the Judgment of the last County Court in October † ‖ last ‖ After the Attachment Courts Judgment Reasons of Appeale & euidences in the Case produced were read Comitted to the Jury & are on file wth the Records of this Court the Jury brought in their virdict they found for the ~~plaintiff~~ ‖ deffend[t] ‖ confirmation ‡ of the forme[r] Judgment & costs of Courts three pounds — 6[d]

Tho Saffyn[s] sent.

Thomas Saffin Con[ta]: County Courts Judgment or sentence — After the Courts Judgment Reasons of Appeale and euidences in the Case produced were Read Comitted to the Jury & are on file wth the Reccords of this Court the Jury brought in their virdict they found Confirmation of the County Courts Judgment wch was i e that he should pay vnto Hannah Hounsell two shillings and sixe pence ꝑ weeke in mony towards the maintenance of the child from the time of its birth till the Cour[t] take further order as in s[d] Judgment may Appeare & Costs of Courts & sd Tho Saffyn on 1[st] Aprill 84 Gaue bond in 40[li] & his sue[r]tjes Isack walker & § Elliston his su[r]tjes in 20[li] apeec to ꝑforme y[e] County Courts Judgm[t] relating to Hannah Hounsell.

[175] 1683

wisewall Conta Paige

John wisewall Juñ plant. cont[a] m[r] Nicolas ¶ & m[r]s Anna Paige deffend[t]s in an Action of Appeale from the Judgment of the last County Court in Boston After the Attachment Courts Judgment Reasons of Appeale & euidences in the Case produced were read Comitted to the Jury and are on file with the Records of this Court the Jury brought in their virdict they ffound for the plaintiff reuersion of the former Judgment & Costs of Courts i. e seuen pounds sixteen shilling ~~& three pence~~

The defend[t] in open Court sajd he Attainted the Jury ‖ for error ‖ and the sajd Nicolas Paige Acknowledged himselfe bound In 20[li] sterljng

---

* "John" repeated in the record.
† Written over "January."
‡ Written over "reuersion."
§ Left blank in the record.
¶ Nicholas Paige?

Attaint of ye Jury mr Rimington forman

to the Treasurer of the Country & party Concerned his heires execcutors &c on this Condition that he will prosecute this Attaint at the next Court of Assistants to effect =

monks Conta Courts Judgmt

George moncke plaint Contra ye Comissnrs Courts Judgment After the Courts Judgment & euidences in the Case produced were Read Comitted to the Jury & are on file wth the Records of this Court the Jury brought in their virdict ~~Reuersion~~ they doe not find by any euidenc or Acknowledgment of sajd moncks vpon Record that he hath broken that law title Inkeepers —

Parris Conta Harris

Samuel Parris plt Contra Richard Harris deffendt: the plt wth drew his Action. —

man Conta Bratle

Jno man plaint Conta Thomas Bratle deffendt &c the plaintiff wth drew his Accon. —

Robert Earl presenting his bill or Account relating to James morrison & Thomas Turrill 2 privatees * ye one djed in Prison the other brak prison amounting to fifty one shilling one penny wch ye Court ordered the Tresurer to pay him in mony 7 ffebr 83 E R S

It is ordered that the refference from Salem Court referring to the late mr Wades estate be heard & considered of on 7 Inst at ye chamber after dinner all the brothers clayming at ye time Appeared & produced seuerall writtings = [ye 1†] 5th march it was declard in Court yt ye secretary might Giue Coppie of any of mr wades papers in his hand & Accordingly gaue Capt wade Coppy of the hon Gov oath & on other and now It was ordered ye secretary giue to each their papers wch he did 11th march 1683 E R S

^ Hezekiah king of weymouth doe hereby bind myself in fiue pounds mony to the Tresurer of the Country to sattisfy & pay him or his successors what shall be allowed to the wittnesses & charges of Court in the Case of samuel Bayly as wittnes my hand 4th mrch. 83. Hezekiah: King

wch was twenty three shillings = E R S

---

* Privateers?

† This rendering is very doubtful. The writing looks also as if it might be shorthand. If so, the rendering should be "but on the," which would make the date 5th instead of 15th, agreeing better with the rest of the record.

[176] 1683

Samuel Bayley of weymouth being brought vp & Comitted to prison in orde^{r} to his trjall being Accused of Buggery wth a mare was brought to the Barr & being presented by ye Grand Jury & left to triall was Indicted by the name of John Bayly for that he not having the feare of God before his eyes being instigated by the divill did on the 21th of Novembe^{r} in the woods malitiously wickedly & felloniously Com̄itt that abominable sinn of Buggery wth a mare as by y^{e} seuerall euidences may Appeare Contrary to the peace of ou^{r} Soveraign Lord the king his crowne and dignity the lawes of God & of this Jurisdiction = After the Indictment & euidences produced against the prisone^{r} at the barr the ‖ Grand ‖ Jury brought in their virdict they ‖ did not ‖ find * the ~~prisoner~~ ‖ bill ‖ =

Constable Torrey presenting a bill of charges of shipping Edward Goue The Court ordered the Tresure^{r} of the Country to pay him twenty shillings in full of the s^{d} bill

Att a speciall Court of Assistants Called by y^{e} Goūno^{r} dep^{t} Goū & magists & held at Boston 22 July 1684

present
Symon Bradstreet Esqr Goū
Tho Danforth Esqr dep^{t} Goū
Daniel Gookin
Humphry Davy
John Richards
Samuel Nowell
James Russell
Elisha Cooke
Wm Johnson
J^{no} Hawthorne
} Esq^{rs}

Vines Ellacot being vnder bonds wth sue^{r}tyes for his Appearance on ye Grand Jury^{s} pervsall of the euidences in his case presented him & Indicted him & left him to further Tryall was Called & Appeared & brought to the barr & holding vp his hand there was Indicted by the name of vines Ellacot of Barbadoes now Resident in Boston in New England merchant for that he not having the feare of God before his eyes & being Instigated by the divill on the 10th of June last Riding violently on a horse did wickedly maliciously & felloniously murther Henry Pease by throwing him downe wth s^{d} horse so as he received his mortall wound in his head whereof he djed Contrary to the peace of ou^{r} Soueraigne Lord the king his crowne & dignity the law of God & of

persons Returnd to serve on the Grand Jury & sworne
— — — —
m^{r} Richard Collicot
Gamalljel Wayte
Henry Phillips
Arthur mason
Xtopher Clarke
J^{no} Capin
Tmo Mather
Giles Pason
Randolph Nicholls

* First written "found."

Richard Austen
Henry Bright
Stephen [Cooke]
Samuel Andrews

this Jurisdiction to wch Indictment he pleaded not Guilty & put himself on tryall by God & ye Country the Jury hauing all y^e^ euidences in the case brought in their virdict they found him not Guilty of the Indictment The Court Considering of this virdict & did Judge that m^r^ vines Ellacot dischardg y^e^ chardg of his tryall & that he pay vnto Gurtrude pease the widdow whose husband was

5 li

sl[a]yne tenn pounds mony = wch was donn & so his bonds dischardgd

[177]

persons Returnd to serve on the Jury of trjalls for life & sworne were

— — — —

m^r^ sampson sheaffe
Georg Pordidge
James meeres
Thomas Smith
James Blake
Tobjas Dauis
John knight
John Jackson
Zeck Hicks
willj^m^ Barret
Wm Bond J^n^
will^m^ shaddock

— — — —

Phillip Darland of Beverly in the County of Essex miller being presented by the Grand Jury for Ou^r^ Soueraigne Lord the king & left to further Tryall was brought to the barr where holding vp his hand was Indicted by the name of Phillip Darland of Bevrly aforesajd for that he not hauing the feare of God before his eyes being Instigated by the Divill did on the 16th day of this Instant July in the orchard of Dauid Perkins of sajd Beuerly Comitt Adultery with mary knights the wife of John knights of Jeoffery^s^ Creeke as by both euidences & Confession of sajd mary will Appeare Contrary to the peace of our Soueraigne Lord the king his Crowne & dignity the lawes of God & of this Jurisdiction to wch Indictment he pleaded not Guilty & put himself for tryall on God & the Country after the euidences in y^e^ Case produced were read Comitted to the Jury & are on file the Jury brought in their virdict they found the Prisone^r^ at the barr not guilty according to Indictment but found him Guilty of vile filthy and abominably libidinous Actions wth mary knights wife of John knights of Jeffery Creeke = The Court Considering his offence sentenct him to be returned to prison & from thenc on y^e^ morrow p^r^sently after the lecture to be taken thence by the marshall General wth a Guard & Conveyed to y^e^ place of execution & ther caused to stand on howe^r^ wth a Rope about his neck Cast ouer the Gallowes & thenc to be taken downe & fastned to the Carts tayle & whipt seuerely on his naked ba[c]ke to the prison againe not exceeding forty stripes & there left till the chardge of his Tryall & wittnesses wth fees of Court be dischardged.

mary knights wife to John knights of Jeoffery^s^ Creeke in the County off Essex for the same offenc being alike presented was brought

to the barr & alike holding vp hir hand was Indicted by the name of mary knights the wife of s[d] John knights as aboue s[d] for that she not hauing the feare of God before hir eyes & being Instigated by the divill did on the 16th of y[s] Instant July in the orchard of Dauid Perkins Comitt Adultery wth Phillip Darland of Beuerly in the sajd County miller Contrary to the peace of our Soueraigne Lord the king his Crowne & dignity the law[s] of God & of y[s] Jurisdiction to which Indictment she pleaded not Guilty & alike put hirself on tryall as aboue After the euedences in the Case produced were Read Comitted to the Jury & are on file the Jury brought in their virdict as aboue in all Respects adding the word whorish to y[e] Actions The Court sentenc[t] hir in all respect as they had Phillip Darland as aboue & ^
wch sentenc was executed & they Returnd to Prison

[178] 1684

seuerall of the magis[ts] being not well in the County of Essex and so not likely ^ at that County Courts Adjourm̃[t] on wednsday next the Council Judged it meet to desire & Appoint Thomas Danforth Esq[r] dep[t] Goṽ & James Russell Esq[r] to goe & keepe the sajd County Court on adjournmt wth y[e] magis[ts] of y[t] County = Boston 24 July 1684
ER.S.

Joseph Gatchell being presented & Indicted by the Grand Jury for our Lord the king for blaspemy ℮r 22 July 84
and by them put on Tryall, the sajd Joseph Gatchell was sent for out of Prison & being at the barr at the last after many Refusalls to hold vp his hand at the barr or to plead to his Indictment did hold vp his hand & pleaded not Guilty to the Indictment which was Read & was that he y[e] sajd Joseph Gatchell being so presented was Indicted by the name of Joseph Gatchell of Marblehead for that he not hauing the feare of God before his eyes being Instigated by the diuill at the house of Jerremiah Gatchell in discourse about Gennerall Salvation, (wch he sajd was his beleife) and that all men should be saued, being Answered that ou[r] Saviou[r] christ sent forth his disciples & Gaue them Com̃ission to preach the Gospell [i e] that whosoeuer Repents & beleives shall be saued; to which Joseph Gatchell Answered if it be so, he was an Imperfect Saviou[r] & a foole, And this was a yeare agoe & somewhat more, as ꝑ the euidences of Elisabeth Gatchell and since in the moneth of march last past & at other times & places hath vttered seuerall hor-

rid blasphemous speeches saying ther was no God, divill or hell, as in and by their euidences may Appeare Contrary to the peace of our Soueraigne Lord the king his Croune & dignity the law of God & of this Jurisdiction to wch as before he pleaded not Guilty & put himself on his tryall by God & the Country = After the Indictmt and euidences in the Case produced were read Comitted to the Jury & are on file the Jury brought in their virdict: wee find the prisoner at the Barr Joseph Gatchell Guilty as followeth that being aboue a yeare Agoe & somewhat more at the house of Jerremiah Gatchell in discourse about Gennerall Salvation which he sajd was his beleife & that all men should be saued being answered that our Sauiour christ did send forth his disciples & Gaue them Comission to preach the Gospell that whosoeuer repents & beleives the Gospell shall be saued that ~~then~~ he did then & there vtter these words that if it were so he was an Imperfect Sauiour & a foole =

The Court Adjournd to ye 7th August at 2 of ye clock & then mett And in Ansr to the petition of mary knights prisoner It is ordered that the keeper discharge hir the prison at present ~~taking~~ on condicon that shee pay forty shillings mony to the Treasurer of ye Country towrds the charge of hir trjall [once] wthin three months or else yt she be sent for & comitted to prison till ye mony be pajd.

This Court Adjourned itself to ye 14 August at 2 of ye clock & mett & Adjournd to the 21 of same at 2 of ye clocke

& proceeded & then mett

The Court sent for ye prisoner Joseph Gatchell & on Consideration of the Crime whereof he stands Convicted by the Jury did sentenc him ye sd Gatchel to be returnd from this place to the pillory to haue his head & hand put in & haue his toung drawne forth out of his mouth & peirct through wth a hott Iron & then to be returnd to the prison there to Remajne vntill he sattisfy & pay all ye charges of his tryall & ffees of Court wch Came ^ seuen pounds shillings The marshall Genrll taking necessary help wth him is to see ye execution of ys sentenc ꝑformed

2[8] Aug 1684 ys Court was dissolued

[179]

Att a Court of Assistants held at Boston 2d September 1684

present
Symon Bradstreet Esqr Gou
Tho Danforth Esqr dept Gou

Willjam Harrison plaintiff Conta Thomas Platts

defend^t in an action of Appeale on Attaint After the Attachment Courts Judgment Reasons for Attaint & other euidences in the Case produced were Read Comitted to the Jury and are on file wth the Records of this Court the Jury brought in their virdict they found for the deffendant Confirmation of the forme^r Judgment & Costs of Courts [two] pounds sixe shillings = exec Issued out

Willjam Harrison plaintiff Contra Thomas Platts defend^t in an Action of Appeale on Attaint after the Attachment Courts Judgment Reasons for Attaint & other euidences in the Case produced were read Comitted to the Jury & are on file with y^e Reccords of this Cour^t the Jury brought in their virdict they found for the deffendant Confirmation of the forme^r Judgment & Costs of Courts two pounds ten shillings & fowe^r pence Execu^t Issued out for 4^li &c

Capt Nicholas Paige & Ann his wife plain^t Contr^a John Wisewall Jun defend^t in an Action of Appeale on Attaint After the Attachment Courts Judgment reasons of Appeale & euidences in the Case produced were read Comitted to ye Jury & are on file wth the Reccords of this Court the Jury brought in their virdict they found for the deffendant Confirmation of the forme^r Judg^t & Costs of Courts.

Willjam Rauson plain^t Cont^r Wm Gilbert defend^t in an action of Appeale on Attaint After the Attachment Courts Judgment reason^s of Attaint and euidences in the case produced were read Comitted to the Jury and are on file wth the Reccords of this Cour^t the Jury brough^t in their virdict they found for the defendant Confirmation of the forme^r Judgment & Costs of Courts —.

Henry Tyte plain^t Con^ta Arthur mason defend^t in an Action of Appeale from the Judgmen^t of the

Daniel Gookin
Nath Saltonstall
Humphry dauy
Jno Richards
Robe^rt Pyke Esq^rs
Jno Woodbridge
Elisha Cooke
Wm Johnson
Jno Hathorne
Elisha Hutchinson
Samuel Seawall
— — — —
persons Returnd to serve on y^r Grand Jury
— — — —
m^r Symon Lynde
Eljakim Hutchinson
Jarvis Ballard
Richard wharton
Samuel Shrimpton
John Pynchon
Lawrenc Douse
Samuel Ketle
Robe^rt willjams
Samuel willjams
Henry Leadbetter
Thomas Tyleston
Tho ffox
Richard Setle
Jno stedman
W^m maning
— — — —
persons Returnd to serve on ye Jury of Attaints & Appeales &c for Attaints & sworne
— — — —
m^r Sam Parris
Jno marrion
Joseph Parsons
Richard Crispe
Bozoone Allen
Sam Phipps
Peter ffoule
Dani: Smith
Zecharyah Long
James Louden
James mellowes
Tho cheny [sen]
stephen willjams
Samuel Pason
Richard Hall
Increase Sumer *
Charles Davenport
Jno minot
Samuel Hix

* Sumner?

Jn° mosse
Jn° Coolidge
Isa Ryall
Jn° Hamond
Jn° spring
— — — —

County Court in April last in Boston After the Attachment Courts Judgmen' reasons of Appeale & euidences in the Case produced were Read Comitted to the Jury and are on file wth the Records of this Cour^t the Jury brought in their virdict they found for the deffendt confirmation of the forme^r Judgment & Costs of Courts thirty nine shillings & six penc & 7^s dam̄ =

Jn° Putnam plaint Con^ta Thomas Baker deffend^t in an acti[on] of Appeale ffrom the Judgment of the County Court at Ipswich: After the Attachm^t Courts Judgment Reasons of Appeale & euidences in the Case produced were read Comitted to the Jury and are on file wth the Records of this Cour^t the Jury brought in their virdict they found for the plaintiff reuersion of the former Judgt & Costs of Courts three pounds eleven shillings & sixepenc =

In the Case of Sarah Cooper ‖ late ‖ wife to Thomas Cooper The Court on pe^rvsall of the euidences in the Case produced she suing for a divorce the Court grants hir Request =

[180] 1684

2^d * Jury for Appeale wer Returnd & sworne
m^r [Edward willy †]
Richard Crispe
Peter foule
James Louden
James mellowes
stephen willjams
Richard Hall
Charles Dauenport
Jn° mosse
John Hamond
Jonathan Bridgam
John Scarlet in behalf of Incr. Su[mn]e^r went sick hom:
— — — —

1st ‡ Jur. persons Returnd to se^rve on Appeale & sworn
m^r Sam Parris
Joseph Parsons
Bozoone Allen
Dani. Smith

m^r Nicholas Paige & Ann^a his wife plaint Con^ta m^r John wisewall sen̄ & m^rs Elisabeth ‖ Cooke ‖ Executrix to ye late Left Richard Cooke defend^t in an Action of Appeale from the Judgment of the last County Court in Boston After the Attachment Courts Judgment Reasons of Appeale & euidences in the Case produced were read Comitted to the Jury & are on file with the Reccords of this Court the Jury brought in their virdict, they found for the deffend^ts Confirmation of the former virdict & Costs of Courts.

m Jn° wisewall sen̄ & m^rs Elizabeth Cooke executrix to y^e late Left Rich Cooke plaintff^s Conta Capt Nicholas Paige & defend^t In An Action of Appeale from the Judgm^t of the last County Cour^t in Boston as to a non Suite = on a full hearing of both plaintiff^s & deffend^t The Bench doe Give Judgmen^t for the plantiffs and doe declare that the pape^rs in ques-

* Written over "1st." † Or Willis. ‡ Written over "2d."

tion ought to have been deliuered to the former Jury: & Grants y^e^ plaintiffs Costs of Courts

Zeckaryah Long
Thomas Cheny
Samuel Pason
Isack Ryall
John Mynot
Samuel Hix
John Coolidge
John Spring

Jeremiah Toy plaintiff Con^ta^ James Loyd defend^t^ in an Action of Appeale from the last County Court in Boston After the Attachment Courts Judgm^t^ Reasons of Appeale & euidences in the Case produced were read Comitted to the Jury and are on file wth the Reccords of this Court the Jury brought in their virdict they found for the deffendant Confirmation of the forme^r^ Judgm^t^ & costs of Courts: two pounds fiueteen^ & fowe^r^ pence Exec. Issued out

Thomas Harwood plaint Con^ta^ Jerremiah Toy defend^t^ In an action of Appeale from the Judgment of the last County Court in Boston after the Attachmen^t^ Courts Judgmen^t^ Reasons of Appeale & euidences in the Case produced were read Co͞mitted to the Jury.& are on file wth the Reccords of this Court the Jury brought in their virdict they found for the deffendant Confirmation of the forme^r^ Judgment & Costs of Courts three pounds one shilling & sixe pence =

Harwood Con^ta^ Burton

John Harwood ‖ [sen] ‖ plan^t^ Contr^a^ Stephen Burton deffend^t^ in an Action of Appeal from the Judgment of the last County Court in Boston After y^e^ Attachment Courts Judgmen^t^ Reasons of Appeale & euidences in the Case produced were read Co͞mitted to the Jury and are on file wth the Reccords of this Court the Jury brought in their virdict they found for the deffendant^ Costs of Courts.

Pe^r^kins Con^ta^ ffenn^o^

Edmond Pe^r^kins plt Cont^a^ John ffenn^o^ defend^t^ in An Action of Appeale from the Judgment of the last County Court in Boston after the Attachm^t^ Courts Judgm^t^ Reasons of Appeale & euidences in the Case produced were read Co͞mitted to the Jury & are on file wth the Records of this Cour^t^ the Jury brought in their virdict they found for ye deffend^t^ Confirmation of the former Judgm^t^ & Costs of Courts three pounds eight shillings & six penc The plaintiff Attainted the Jury for errors ‖ & mistakes ‖ and himselfe in twenty pounds & willjam Payne & Joseph Homes sue^r^tjes in tenn pounds Apeece acknowledged themselues heirs &c in sajd sumes respectively bound to

Attaint
m^r^ Tho Parris *
fore͞man

* Error of the Secretary for "Sam Parris"? See the list of jurymen.

the Treasurer of the Country & party Concerned that the sajd Edmond Perkins shall prosecute his Attaint ag[t] the Jury at the nex[t] Court of Assistants to effect

Sarah Coopers Ans[r]

In the Case of Sarah Cooper late wife to Thomas Cooper The Court on pe[r]vsall of y[e] euidences in y[e] Case produced she suing for a divorce y[e] Court Grants hir Request &c *

[181] 1684

Jn[o]son Cont[a] mills †

Jn[o] mills plaintiff Conta John Johnson sen deffend[t] in an Accon of Appeale from the Judgment of the County Court at charles Toune After y[e] Attachment Courts Judgment reasons of Appeale & euidences in the Case produced were read Comitted to the Jury & are on file the Jury brought in their virdict they found for the defendant Confirmation of the forme[r] Judgment damag nine pounds Costs of Courts thirty nine shillings & eight pence =

Basse Cont[a] Crosby Attaint

Samuel Basse plaint Cont[a] Joseph Crosby defend[t] in an action of Appeale from the Judgment of the County Court in Boston After y[e] Attachment Courts Judgment Reasons of Appeale & euidences in the Case produced were read Comitted to the Jury & are on file w[th] the Recorrds of this Cour[t] the Jury brought in their virdict they found for y[e] deffend[t] Confirmation of the former Judgm[t] & Costs of Courts.— ~~Joseph~~ ‖ xtopher ‖ Webb Atturney to s[d] Basse &c Attainted y[e] Jury for error and himself as & on behalf of y[e] p[r]incipall in fiueteene pounds & Joseph webb his sue[r]ty in 15[li] acknowledged themselues respectively bound & their heires &c in s[d] somes to the Tresurer of the Country & party Concernd that sajd Webb shall prosecute his Attaint at y[e] nex[t] Court of Assis[ts] to effect —

Douning Cont[a] Boober

Richard Douning plaintiff ag[t] Joseph Boober ‖ & Joane his wif ‖ deffend[t] In an Action of Appeale ffrom the Judgm[t] of the County Court in Salem. After the Attachment Courts Judgm[t] Reasons of Appeale & euidences in the Case produced were read Comitted to the Jury and are on file wth the Records of this Cour[t] the Jury brought in their virdict they found for the deffend[t] Confirmation of the former Judgment & Costs of Courts = three pounds nineteen shilling[s] & sixe penc

* This is a repetition of the record on the preceding page of the original.
† So in the original.

Tho: Bake[r] plaint Con[ta] James Pemberton defend[t] in an action of Appeale from the Judgment of the County Court in Boston After the Attachment Courts Judgment Reasons of Appeale & euidences in the Case produced were read Comitted to the Jury & are on file wth the Reccords of this Court the Jury brought in their virdict they found for the deffend[t] Confirmation of the forme[r] Judgm[t] & Costs of Courts two pounds tenn shilling exec ^

Baker Con[ta] Pemberton

Symon Bradstreet Esq[r] Gou̅ plt Con[ta] Peter Coffyn deffend[t] in an action of Appeale from the Judgment of the County Court In Boston the plantiff w[th]drewe his Action ═

Gou̅ Bradstreet Con[ta] Coffyn

Cap[t] daniel Epps pl[t] Conta m[r] Henry Bennet deffend[t] in An action of Appeale from the Judgment of the County Court at Salem. After y[e] Attachmt Courts Judgment Reasons of Appeale & euidences in the Case produced were read Comitted to the Jury and are on file w[th] the Reccords of this Court the Jury brought in their virdict the Jury found for the Appellant Reuersion of the former Judgment & the Indian Boy in Controuersy to be deliuered the Appellant w[th]in tenn days time or twenty pounds money[s] & Costs of Courts fiue pounds sixe shillings & three penc

Epps Cont[a] Bennet

Samuell Bagly * plt Contra James webster deffend[t] in an Action of Appeale from the Judgment of the County Court in Boston in Aprill last After the Attachment Courts Judgment Reasons of Appeale & euidences in the Case produced were Read Comitted to the Jury and are on file wth the Records of this Court the Jury brought in their virdict they found for the deffend[t] Confirmation of the former Judgmen[t] 7[li] mo damage & Costs of Courts forty shillings & 8[d]

Bagly * Conta webster

[182] 1684

James Tounsend pl[t] Con[ta] Tho Edwards defend[t] In an action of Appeale from the Judgment of the County Court In Boston after the Attachment Courts Judgment Reasons of Appeale & euidences in the Case produced were read Comitted to y[e] Jury & are on file w[th]

* Or Bayly.

the Records of this Court the Jury brought in their virdict they found for ye plaintiff ~~confirmation~~ || Reuersion || of the former Judgment & that the defendant Give to the plaintiff a true & Just accompt of the part of the ship sued for & earnings wthin one years time or two hundred pounds money And the house & land Attached to Abide for security & Costs of Courts three pounds one shilling & fower pence =

Townsend Conta Tho Edwrds —

Roger Adams plaint Conta Jno Baker of Roxb[ury] deffendt in an action of Appeale from the Judgmt of the County Court held at Boston in Aprill last After the Attachment Courts Judgment Reasons of Appeale & euidences in the Case produced were read Comitted to the Jury & are on file with the reccords of this Court the Jury brought in their virdict they found for ye Appellant reuersion of the former virdict & that the deffendant deliu in to the Appellant the estate sued for according to Inventory or forty two pounds seuen shillings & nine penc & Costs of Courts [42s] & 10d

Addams Conta Baker [An A]ttant

Jno Baker Attainted the Jury for error & himself principle in twenty pounds & Joseph Homes & Joseph Cowell suertjes in tenn pounds a peec acknowledgd themselves Respectively bound in sd somes to the Treasurer of the Country & party Concernd that sajd Baker shall psecut his Attaint to effect at ye next Court of Assistants

Heman Conta Chapen

Nathaniel Heman Conta John Chapen deffendt in an Action of Appeale from the Judgmt of the Commission's Court in Boston the plantiff wthdrw his Accon

wardell Conta Pittam

Elizabeth wardell plt Conta Jno Pittam in an Action of Appeal from the Judgmt of ye Commision's Court the plant wthdrw ye Accon:

Edward Allen plant Con'a Asaph Elljot defendt in an Action of Appeale from the Judgmt of the Comissioner's Court held in Boston After the Attachment Courts Judgment Reasons of Appeale & euidences in ye Case produced were read Comitted to the Jury & are on file the Jury brought in their virdict they found a speciall virdict i e if the law be that the Appellants appearing & Joyning Issue as Adm[ini]strator to Abraham Spencer deceased & no other testimony to vs Appearing to proove him so be sufficient to make him liable to ye former Judgment as Adm[ini]strator then wee find for

Allin Conta: Elliot

the deffend[t] Confirmation of the form[r] Judgment w[th] costs of Courts If the law be otherwise wee find for y[e] Appellant Reūsing the former Judgm[t] w[th] Costs of Courts = the Benc[h] finds for y[e] defend[t] Confirmation of the forme[r] Judgmen[t] wth Costs of Courts damage sixe pounds eighteen shillings & eight penc mony & Costs 29[s] 10[d]. =

Homes Cont[a] Sheffeild

Joseph Homes plan[t] Conta Ann sheffeild als Perry defend[t] in an Action of Appeale from the Judgmen[t] of the County Court in Boston After the Attachment Courts Judgment Reasons of Appeale & euidences in the Case produced were read Comitted to the Jury & are on file || wth the Records of y[s] Court || the Jury brought in their virdict they found for the defendant Confirmation of the form[r] Judgm[t] wth Costs of Courts y[e] plaintiff Attainted the Jury for error

2[d] Jur Edw. willy * forem[n]

[183] 1684

and the sajd Joseph Homes principle [in] twenty pounds & Joseph Webb and John Bake[r] in tenn pounds apeece acknowledged themselues respectively bound in those sums to the Treasurer of the Country & party Concerned that Joseph homes shall prosecute his Attaint to effect at the nex[t] Court of Assistants to effect =

Apleton Con[ta] Marshall

Samuel Apleton Juñ plan[t] Con[ta] Thomas Marshall defend[t] in an action of Appeale from the Judgmen[t] of the County Court at Salem: After the Attachmen[t] Courts Judgmen[t] Reasons of Appeale & euidences in the Case produced were read & Comitted to the Jury they brought in their virdict they found for the defend[t] Confirmation of the forme[r] Judgm[t] & Costs of Court forty sixe shillings & two penc =

W[m] Dyre Esq[r] Conta Elisha Hutchinson Esq[r]

W[m] Dyre Esq[r] || pln[t] || Con[ta] Elisha Hutchinson Esq[r] deffend[t] in an Action of Appeale from the Judgment of the County Court last in Boston After the Attachment Courts Judgment Reasons of Appeale & euidences in the Case produced were read Comitted to the Jury & are on file w[th] the Records of this Court the Jury brought in their virdict they found for the defendant Confirmation of the forme[r] Judgment & Costs of Courts the plaintiff desired his bond might be chanceried The Court hauing heard the plaintiff & defend[t]s pleas as to the Chancering of the

* Or Willis.

bond did chancery it to sixty-eight pounds fiue shilling^{s} & tenn penc mony & Costs of Courts two pounds sixteen shillings & sixe pence.

Samuel Ingolls plain^{t} Conta Thomas Bishop deffend^{t} in an action of Appeale ‖ from the Judgment of the County Court at Salem ‖ After the Attachment Courts Judgment Reasons of Appeale & euidences in the Case produced were Read Comitted to ye Jury & are on file two of ye Jury being Ill plaintiff & deffend^{t} Consented to stand to ye tens Award ye plaintiff provided it might be no prejudice to his Case as to after proceedings & so the Jury brought in their virdict i: e If the law be y^{t} the Affirmation of the ~~defendant~~ Appellant and the testimony of samuel Bishop to proove the payment of the Appellants rent for seven yeares payable to John Bishop and Thomas Bishop their heires and Assignes vnto them or either of them the sume of twenty one pounds tenn shilling for the first yeare and so Annually vnto the end of seven yeares payable at the house of Samuel Bishop and by the affirmation of Appellant and the testimony of the sajd Samuel Bishop wherein he saith that sixe pounds tenn shillings pajd in mault which was the Remainde^{r} of Rent remayning of all the rents & payments that Concerned Samuell Ingolls lease which was Given him by John & Thomas Bishop for seue[n] years discharge the Appellant = or if the law be that the sajd Samuel Ingolls be ljable to the Suite of Thomas Bishop for the sajd seven yeares Rent wthout John Bishops Joyning with him if not ^ wee finde for the Appellant Reūsing the former Judgment wth Costs of Courts If the law be otherwise wee finde for the defend^{t} coufirmation of the former Judgment wth Costs of Courts * The magis^{ts} on pervsall of this virdict doe Judge & declare for the Appellant Reūsion of the forme^{r} Judgment & Costs of Courts — After the Case was heard & Judgment declared on the

Samuel I[n]golls Conta Tho: Bishop

[184] 1684

the † behalfe of the Appellant Samuel Ingolls reuersing the forme^{r} Judgment & Granting Costs to s^{d} Ingolls, the sajd Ingolls & Thomas Bishop both in open Court to prevent execution Issuing out, and for prevention of future trouble in law did Agree as followeth: The sajd Ingolls for peace sake doth engage to beare his oune Charges which he

* The language of this verdict is not clear, but the record agrees with the original verdict on file. (See Court Files, Suffolk, No. 2243.)

† "the" repeated in the record.

is out in prosecution of the Case from the begining the sajd Thomas Bishop is also to beare whateuer Costs he hath binn at about sajd Case = further the sajd Ingolls is to giue || bill || to sajd Thomas Bishop of tenn pounds in Currant neat Catle Corne or porke to be deliuered at the house where sajd Bishop[s] Brother djed jn Ipswich: vpon the giving of his bill the sajd Thomas Bishop doeth hereby give the sajd Ingolls a Receipt & full discharge of the whole seven yeares Rent sued for, acquitting not only from himself but from the successo[r]s of his Brother John Bishop who is in the originall lease mentioned as one of the lesso[r]s of the sajd farme which ljes in Ipswich And It is mutually Agreed that the bill of tenn pounds as aboue being given by Ingolls to Thomas Bishop then the sajd Ingalls may w[th] leaue of the County Court for Essex take vp the originall lease as is there lodged whereby a future tryall or trouble about y[e] seven yeare[s] Rent sued for may be prevented;

Ingolls & Bishop[s] Agreement=

Tho: Bishop
Samuel Ingolls

Boston 11 Sept 1684 This agreement was signed and the bill was ouned to be giuen accordingly in Court the day & yeare aboue sajd as Attests

Edward Rawson Secre[ty]

Samuel Bishop plaintiff Contr[a]. Josiah Clarke deffendant in an action of Appeale from the Judgment of the County Court at Salem After the Attachment Courts Judgment Reasons of Appeale & euidences in the Case produced were Read Comitted to the Jury and are on file wth the Records of this Court the Jury brought in their virdict they found for y[e] defendant Confirmation of the forme[r] Judgment & Costs of Court

Bishop Cont[a] clarke

This Court was Adjourned to the tenth Instant at 8 of y[e] clock & from thenc diem ꝑ djem till y[e] 19[th] & then to the 20 & thenc to the 25[th] of Septembe[r] 1684 =

W[m] Dyre Esq[r] exhibbited to the Honno[r]ble Goūno[r] A large libell or Articles on 4[th] Instant ag[t] Cap[t] michaell Andreason [Comma]nde[r] of the ship Triumpue[z] & his Com[pan]y ꝑ wch the Gouerno[r] Com[mun]icated After some Consideration to the magists & Court who Considering thereof as the Courts Occasions would ꝑmit the Court being Adjournd from time to tjme as Aboue at y[e] Adjourm[t] on 19[th] Instant

Judged it meete to grant ye Request of sajd Capt michael Andreson ^ orde^rd ye secretary to Grant him a Coppy of sajd large libell to give their Answe^r thereto in the morning at 8 or 9 of y^e clock to wch time the Court was Adjourned wch was don & 20 Instant sajd Michaell Andreson Came & gaue In his Ans^r & seūll depositions &c

& on 25 Instan^t to wch time y^e Cour^t was Adjourd day by day The^r examinations & Cou^rts observations therevpon is on file =

The Cour^t hauing examined the spanish wittnesses who much Contradicting their oune oaths the Courts Judgment was &c

The Court hauing pervsed the spanish euidences ‖ &c ‖ finding the persons thervnto Attesting to be [s]paniards now

[185] 1684

the enemys of the french king and his subjects & Captaine michael Andresons prisone^rs, and that what is contejned therein is almost in euery Artickle very false, as Appeares by Comparing this with what was taken from their oune mouthes in their oune language in open Court by m^r John Champlyn & Dr Hughes their Interprete^rs no[w] on file doe Judge that either their former Interpreter (if they had any) was not ~~faith~~ ‖ skill ‖ full in their language or that the spanyards did sweare very falsly, and that therefore their oathes ought not to haue binn affixed to this paper nor any Credit to be given therevnto as such and doe further orde^r that this be endorsed vpon the originall taken by m^r faireweather — wch is donne = The Judgment of the Court Whereas Wm Dyre Esqr presented to this Cour^t a large Accusation or lybell against Capt michael Andreson & Company who is now in this Port with his ship Called the Trampeuz being Admitted by this Gouernmen^t to Come In heere to fitt his ship he declaring he was a man of warr in the ffrench kings Service whom the sajd Dyre Accused of Pyracy and presented testimonjes now on File which this Court hath examined and Considered as also the Answe^rs testimony^es and Comission presented by sajd Andreson; And upon the whole the Court sees no ground to put sajd Andreson upon trjall for Piracy and doe Allow him libe^rty to proceed on his buisniess; requiring him with all Convenient speed to depart out of this Port according to his Majesties Proclamation; And not to Carry with him any Amunition out of this Colony nor take on board more prouissions then shall be necessary for his transportation to his Commission port = past 25: 7: 84 ꝑ Curiã Edwd: Rawson secret

In Answer to a Complaint exhibited by Cap[t] Jonathan wade to this Court w[th] Refference ‖ y[e] actings of y[e] County Court of Essex in order ‖ to the last will of his ffather m[r] Jn[o]than wade deceased & the setlement of his estate, It is ordered by this Court that s[d] Cap[t] wade ‖ giving ‖ vnder his hand in writing the prticculars wherein 9 Sep[t] 84

[186] 1684

he Judges that the County Court of Essex hath donn him wrong his Appeale made to this Court shall be fully heard and Considered. By y[e] Court Edw[d] Rawson secret

In Answer to the petition of m[r] Jonathan wade It is Ordered that the Secretary write to the clarke of Salem County Court forthwith to remitt and send to him all the originall peticons orde[r]s wills and othe[r] pape[r]s in his hands forme[r]ly deliuered into that Court from any of the sonns of the late m[r] Jonathan wade of Ipswich. This Court hauing heereby ordered a hearing of the Case on Appeale At the Adjornmt of this Court to be held in Boston on the 17[th] day of octobe[r] next at one of the clocke at wch time & place the Aboue sajd m[r] Jonathan wade & his brethe[r]n are ordered to be sent vnto to be present & Attend their Concernes therein. =

past Edw. Rawson Secre[t]

Cap[t] Jonathan wade hauing at a former session of this Court p[r]sented his Complaint against the Acts of the Court of Essex relating to the estate of his father m[r] Jonathan wade deceased and in that desired that an hearing might be allowed him in that matter at this Court the Court for that end was Adjourned to this day to heare him & ordered that the sajd Jonathan & his other Brothe[r]s m[r] Nathaniel & m[r] Thomas wade[s] appearance & the originall pape[r]s ‖ to be ‖ remitted ~~hither and~~ to this Court ‖ By the Clerks of the County courts of Essex w[ch] w[n] it was done and the papers remitted hither & * ‖ Cap[t] wade ordered to proceed; He refused to make any plea and sajd he desired not an Appeale in the Case, But that the first will of his father (which was denyed by the Court to be accepted as his fathe[r]s will) might without any alteration be deliuered to him; which this Court see[s] no Cause to grant without an hearing, and therefore all partjes Concerned are dismissed, At y[e] Court by Adjourm[t] 17 october 1684

* These twenty words, between the upright parallels, are in the margin of the record and in a different hand, apparently that of Isaac Addington, the successor of Secretary Rawson.

And the Secretary is hereby ordered to returne to the seuerall Clarkes of the County Courts of Essex all the Individuall orde^rs, pape^rs & originalls or Coppies that were by the sajd Clarkes transmitted to him

[187]

present
Symon Bradstreet Esqr Go
Tho Danforth Esqr dep^t Go
Daniel Gookin
Humphry Davy
John Richards
Sam. Nowell
James Russell
sam Apleton
Robe^rt Pike
Elisha Cooke
Wm Johnson
Elisha Hutchinson
samuel || Sewall || Esq^rs

— — — —

pe^rsons Returnd to se^rve on ye Grand Jury & sworne
Left sam: Ruggles
Joseph How
Jno scarlet
James Hill
James Pecker
Richard Hall
Isack Jones
Timothy Steevens
Richard Louden
Jno Call
dauid ffi[s]ke
Robe^rt Herrington
Tho ffflegg —

— — — —

pe^rson^s Returnd to serve on the Jury for Attaints & sworne

— — — —

Capt Ephrajm Sauage
Symon Daniel
Isack marrjan
Josiah Torrey
Samuel Bignell
Samuel Greene
Saml symson
James ffoster
sam. Capen
Joseph Leeds
Robe^rt Peirpoint

Att A Court of Assistan^ts held at Boston 3^d march 1684

Edmond Perkins plaintiff on Attaynt Con^ta John ffenno defendant in ^ Action of Appeale from the Judgment of the last court of Assistants from the virdict of the Jury whereof * was foreman After the Courts Judgment Reasons for ye Attaint & euidences of the Case produced were Read Comitted to the Jury and are on file wth the Reccords of this Court the Jury brought in their virdict they found for ye deffendant Confirmation of the former Judgment & Costs of Courts, 3, 13^s & Costs of Courts fowe^r pounds 3 shillings & sixepence † fil. p^d

Joseph Homes pltiff in an action of Attaint from the virdict of the Jury whereof * was foreman Con^ta Ann Sheffeild alj^s: Perry de After the Courts Judgmen^t Reasons for Attaint & other euidences in the Case produced were read Comitted to the Jury & are on file wth the Reccords of this Court the Jury brought in their virdict they found for the deffendant Confirmation of the forme^r Judgment & Costs of Co͞urts

Jno Bake^r plaintiff in an Action of Attaint from the virdict of the Jury whereof * was foreman || con^ta Roger Addams deffend^t || . After the Courts Judgment Reason^s for Attaint ~~& other euidences in the Case produced were read~~ the plaintiff was 3 times Called but not Appea[ri]ng was non suited & his bond declared to be forfeited =

Tho Baker plaintiff Conta Wm Condy defendant in an action of Appeale from the Judgment of the

* Left blank in the record. † So in the original.

County Court in Boston After the Attachment Courts Judgment Reasons of Appeale & euidences in the Case produced were read Comitted to the Jury and are on file w[th] the Reccords of this Court y[e] plaintiff w[th]drew his Action by his not Answering to his Call =

samuel Crafts
Benja Sabjn
Ralph Broadhurst
Jn[o] Grauesner
Tho Jenner
Tho Lord
Sam Gookin
Ebenez[r] wisewall
Nicholas Englesbe
Jn[o] Parkhurst
Tho. wilson
John knight
samuel scarborough

— — — —

John Griffyn plaintiff Con[ta] Joseph knight deffendant in an action of Appeale from the Judgment of the County Court in Boston After the Attachmen[t] Courts Judgment Reasons of Appeale & other euidences in the Case produced were read Comitted to the Jury and ar on file the Jury brought in their virdict they found for the plaintiff Reuersion of the former Judgment & Costs of of Court wch by Consent of Xtophe[r] webb Atturney to s[d] Griffin was brought on chancery of y[e] bond in all to six pounds & filing 2[s]

[188] 1684

Jn[o] Norman plaint Cont[a] Benja: Orne deffend[t] in an action of Appeale from the Judgment of y[e] County Court at Salem after the attachm[t] Courts Judgment Reasons of Appeale & euidences in the Case produced were read Comitted to the Jury & are on file wth the Reccords of this Court the Jury brought in their virdict they found for the deffendant ~~reuersion~~ || confirmation || of the former Judgment & Costs of Courts ~~three~~ || two || pounds ninteen shillings & 8[d]

Norman Con[ta] Orne

ffrancis Wyman || plt || Conta Henry sumers defend[t] in an Action of Appeale from the Judgment of the County Court at Cambridg after the Attachment Courts Judgment Reasons of Appeale & euidences in the Case produced were read Comitted to the Jury & are on file w[th] the Reccords of this Court the Jury brought in their virdict they found for the plaintiff Reuersion of the former Judgm[t] & Costs of Courts ℘ fiue pounds two shillings & ten pence

wyman Against sumers

Thomas Baker plaint Conta Thomas & Joseph Pembe[r]ton defend[t]s in an action of Appeale from the Judgment of the County Court in Boston After the Attachment Courts Judgment Reasons of Appeale & othe[r] euidences in the case produced were read comitted to the Jury &

Bake[r] conta Tho & Jose pembe[r]ton executi: Issued out

are on file wth the Reccords of this Court the Jury brought in their virdict they found for ye plaintiff Confirmation of ye former Judgment on shilling* Addition & costs of Courts; damage & costs in all eight pounds fowe^r^ shillings & Sixe pence

Jackljn Conta Pemberton

Samuel Jackljn plt Conta Thomas Pembe^r^ton deffend^t^ in an Action of Appeale from the Judgm^t^ of the County Court in Boston After the Attachm^t^ Courts Judgment Reasons of Appeale & euidences in the Case produced were read Comitted to ye Jury & are on file wth the Reccords of this Court the Jury brought in their virdict they found for the plaintiff Reuersion of the former Judgment || & || ten pounds fiueteen shilling || mony || damage & costs of Courts fower pounds eighteen shilling^s^ & fowe^r^ penc †

Dawes ag^t^ Petit

Jn^o^than dawes plt Con^ta^ Henry Petit deffend^t^ in an action of Appeale from the Judgm^t^ of the Commission^r^s Court the plaintiff w^th^drew his Accon

m^r^ Edwd will[is ‡] Con^t^ Capt Sauage. =

m^r^ Edward will[is] plt Conta Capt Ephraim Sauage deffend^t^ in an action of Appeale from the Judgment of the County Court in Boston after the Attachment Courts Judgment reasons of Appeale & euidences in the Case produced were read Comitted to the Jury & are on file the Jury brought in their virdict they found for the deffend^t^ Confirmation of the former judgment & costs of Courts thirty nine shilling^s^ & 4^d^ in all

Brookes Conta Muzzey.

Tymothy Brookes plt Conta Benjamin Muzzey deffend^t^ in an action of Appeale from the Judgment of the County Court at Charlestown after the Attachm^t^ courts Judgm^t^ Reasons of Appeale & euidences in the Case produced were read Comitted to the Jury & are on file with the Reccords of this Court the Jury brought in their virdict they found for the defend^t^ Confirmation of the forme^r^ Judgm^t^ w^th^ [tenn] pounds Abatement & Costs of Courts

* At the County Court the verdict was for Baker for 5£. Baker appealed from that verdict.

† At the County Court the verdict was for the defendant, Pemberton, costs of court, the suit being for £10 15s damage.

‡ Or Willy. It is Wyllys in the County Court Record.

[189] 1684

Jn° Endecott Atturney to John Roberts * plt Con^ta^ Jn° Heyward Atturney to John Coleman [plaintiff Conta John Heyward & †] defend^t^ in an action of Appeale from the Judgmen^t^ of the County Court in Boston after the Attachmen^t^ Courts Judgmen^t^ Reasons of Appeale & euidences in the Case produced were read Comitted to the Jury and are on file the Jury brought in their virdict they found for y^e^ defendant Confirmation of the forme^r^ Judgment & Costs of Courts thirty nine shillings = damag. 32. 16.‡ 6: in all 34 16. 6.

Endecot conta Heyward.

Robe^r^t Bronsdon pl^t^ Con^ta^ Jn° Conney ‖ sen ‖ defend^t^ in an Action of Appeale from the Judgmen^t^ of the County Cour^t^ in Boston after the Attachm^t^ Courts Judgment Reasons of Appeale & euidences in the Case produced were read Comitted to the Jury & are on file wth the Reccords of this Court the Jury brought in their virdict they found for y^e^ defendant Confirmation of the former Judgment & Costs of Courts fiueteen shillings & sixe pence =

Bronsdon Con^ta^ Coney

Jn° Marrian Administrato^r^ to y^e^ estate of y^e^ late Tho Batt plan conta m^r^s mary Lake widow executrix ℮ in an Action of Appeale from the Judgm^t^ of the Comission^r^s Court after the Attachment Courts Judgment Reasons of Appeale & euidences in the Case produced were read Comitted to the Jury & are on file the Jury brought in their virdict they found a speciall virdict If a dead man^s^ bookes well kept be legall we find for ye deffend^t^ Confirmation of the forme^r^ Judgment & Costs of Courts if not then wee find for the plaintiff Costs of Courts the magists voted for ye plaintiff.

Marian Con^ta^ Lake

Benja ffarr plt Con^ta^ Josiah witter deffend^t^ in an Accon of Appeale from the Judgment of the County Court at Ipswich the plt desiring & pleading for a non suite because the letter of Atturney was not prooved the Court on hearing of the parties granted the plaintiff a non Suite wth Reūsion of the forme^r^

ffarr Con^ta^ witter

* Joseph Roberts in the County Court Record.

† These five words are superfluous, as appears by the description of the parties in the County Court Record.

‡ 17 in the County Court Record.

Judgment in the Case wth Costs of Courts fiuety one shilling & sixe penc

Peter Coffin Conta Symon Bradstreet Esqr

Tristram Coffyn Atturney to Peter Coffyn plant Conta Symon Bradstret Esqr Gou̅no^r^ deffend^t^ ^ After the Attachment Courts Judgment Reasons of Appeale & other euidences in the Case produced were read Comitted to the Jury & are on file wth the Records of this Court the Jury brought in their virdict they found for the deffendant Confirmation of the former Judgment & Costs of Courts

Symon Bradstreet Esqr plt Conta Peter Coffyn defendant in an action of Appeale from the Judgment of the County Court in Boston after the Attachment Courts Judgment Reasons of Appeale & euidences in the Case produced were Read Comitted to the Jury & are on file wth the Reccords of this Court the Jury brought in their virdict they found for the defendant Confirmation of the former Judgment & Costs of Courts

Richard Dawes plaint Conta Georg newby In an action of Appeale from the Judgment of the County Court in Boston the plantf wthdrew his Accon being Agreed

[190] 1684

Atkinson Conta miller —

John Atkinson plt Conta mathew miller defendant in an Accon of Appeale from the Judgment of the County Court at Salem after the Attachment Courts Judgment Reasons of Appeale & euidences in the Case produced were read Comitted to the Jury & are on file wth the Records of this Court the Jury brought in their virdict they found for the plaintiff reuersion of the former Judgmt & Costs of Courts three pounds fiue shillings & sixe penc

Joseph Holmes Conta James Russell esqr

ten pounds [18s] country pay & 28li 7s. 6d mony

Joseph Homes plant Contra James Russell esqr deffendt In an Action of Appeale from the Judgment of the County Court in Boston After the Attachmt Courts Judgment Reasons of Appeale & euidences in the Case produced were read Comitted to the Jury and are on file wth the Records of this Court the Jury brought in their virdict they found for the defendt Confirmation of the forme^r Judgm^t & Costs of Courts forty [9^s] 4^d in all forty one pounds 14^s 6^d =

Samuel Gibson plt Conta Christophe^r Read deffend^t In an action of Appeale from the Judgm^t of the County Court at Cambridg: After the Attachment Courts Judgment Reasons of Appeale & euidences in the Case produced were read Comitted to the Jury & are on file wth the Records of this Court the Jury brought in their virdict they found for the plaintiff reuersion of the former Judgment & Costs of Courts fiuety shillings &c

Gibson Conta Read

Georg Norton plaintiff Con^ta John Plaisted in an Action of Appeale from the Judgment of the County Court at Boston afte^r the Attachment Courts Judgmen^t Reasons of Appeale & euidences in the Case produced were read Comitted to the Jury & are on file wth the Records of this Court the Jury brought in their virdict they found for the deffendant Confirmation of the forme^r Judgment & Costs of Courts thirty one shillings & nine penc

Norton Conta Plaisted

m^r Richd wharton m^r Hezekiah vshe^r Daniel Turel Jun & Jno white pl^t Conta Joseph Smith defend^t in An Action of Appeale from the Judgment of the County Cour^t in Boston After the Attachment Courts Judgment Reasons of Appeale & euidences in the Case produced were read Comitted to the Jury & are on file they brought in their virdict they found for ye deffend^t Confirmation of the form^r Judgm^t & Costs of Courts this Judgm^t Respited till ye Adjournm^t of y^s Court i e 19th instant &c

Wharton &c Conta Smith

Hannah Armetage Came into this Court ^ made choyce of John ffloyd of Rumley marsh to be hir Guardian The Court orde^rs & Alloues of hir choyce of of Jno ffloyd to be hir Guardian as Attest Edw Rawson Secr

Hannah Armitage Guardian

[191] 1684

Wee the Grand Jury for our Soueraigne Lord the king doe p^rsent and Indict John Dounton son of w^m Dounton of Salem in the County of Essex for that he the sajd John Dounton no^t hauing the feare of God before his eyes & being Instigated by the divill on the 29th octobe^r last did wickedly maliciously & ffelloniously murther Rebeckah Booth by discharging a Gunn in the house of Jn° Hende^{r}son of sajd Salem Contrary to the peace of our Soueraigne Lord the king his Crowne & dignity the lawe of God & of this Jurisdiction title murder. = the Grand Jury found not this bill but ~~found~~ ‖ Indict & prsent ‖ him the sajd John Dounty * of Salem for chance medly by Careless discharging of a Gunn was the death of Rebecka Booth. = The Court considering of this virdict did sentenc the sajd John Dounton to pay vnto the Parents of the sajd Rebecka Booth the sume of fiue pounds in mony & that he pay tenn pounds mony as a fine to the Country or be whip^{t} wth fiueteen stripes publickly at Salem on the nex^{t} lecture day paying also all charges of prosecution & ffees of Court standing Comitted till this sentence be pe^{r}formed = wch his father w^{m} dounton vnde^{r}took & obliged in open Court = This Court was Adjourned to y^{e} 19 Instant & y^{e}n mett.

In Answer to the petition of m^{r} Richard wharton m^{r} Hezekiah Vsher John white and ~~John~~ Daniel Turell Jun̄ humbly desiring in their Complaint that the bond betweene them and Joseph Smith might be chancerjed The Court doe chancery thir bond of eighty pounds to sixty pounds money and in Answer ‖ to their ‖ crauing further remedy against the wrong and Injustice to them susteyned by sajd Smith & Complices with Refferenc to the Dowboy of Gold This Court do order that the sajd ‖ Ri^{d} ‖ wharton and partne^{r}s giving one hundred and twenty pounds bond to prosecute their Complaint against the sajd Smith & Complices at the nex^{t} County Court at Boston & so from Court to Court vntill a legall end be put therevnto ^ In the meane tjme execution vpon the aboue sajd Judgment shall be respitted

per Curiam Edw. Rawson secret

This aboue written orde^{r} was published in open Court as Attests E. R. S.

[192]

And the sajd m^{r} Richard Wharton Hezekiah Vsher Daniel Turell Jun̄^{r} & John white Acknowledged themselues theire heires ꝑr Jointly and seuerally bound in one hundred & twenty pounds to Jame^{s} Russell Esqr Treasure^{r} ꝑr and to the partjes Concerned that they shall & will performe the aboue written orde^{r} in all respects = this donn 19th march 1684 attests

Edward Rawson secret

* Error of the record for "Dounton."

Att A Court of Assistan^ts held at Boston by the Gov̄no^r & Compn^y of the Massachusetts Bay in New England the first day of Septemƀ 1685

present
Symon Bradstreet Esqr Gov̄
Tho Danforth Esqr dep^t Gov̄
Daniel Gookin sen̄ Esqr
w^m Stoughton
Nathaniel Saltonstall
Humphry Davy
John Richards
Samuel Nowell
James Russell
Samuel Apleton
Elisha Cooke
w^m Johnson
Jno Hathorne
Elisha Hutchinson
Samuel Seawall
} Esq^rs

The Grand Jury brought in their Indictments & presentments y^t of Jn^othan Gardiner they found him not Guilty ꝑ the other two of Vrjah Cloemen^ts y^t forme^rly named himsell Ball they left to trjall ꝑ

persons Returnd to serve on the Grand Jury & were sworne were

Capt Jno Holdbrooke
Nathaniel Greene
Abell porter
James whetcombe
Richd Dauy
Tho Leighton
Caleb Hubbard
Daniel Preston
Jno mayho.
w^m Goddard
w^m Bond
Randall Nicholls
Eljah Row
Joshua Beale

mary Peacoke wife & Atturney to sam: Peacock now p^resent plaint contra w^m Pen ‖ def. ‖ in an action of Appeale from the Judgment of the County Court in Boston. After the Attachment Courts Judgment Reasons of Appeale & euidences in the Case produced were read Comitted to ye Jury & are on file wth the Record^s of this Court the Jury brought in their virdict they found for the deffendant Confirmation of the forme^r Judgmen^t i e possession of the House & land sued for & Costs of Courts forty seuen shillings & eight pence

1 Ju

John Norman plt Con^ta Benja: Orne deffend^t in an Accon of Appeale from ye Judgment of the County Court at Ipswich After the Attachment Courts Judgment reasons of Appeale & euidences in the Case produced were read Comitted to the Jury and are on file wth the Reccords of this Court the Jury brought in their virdict they found for the deffendan^t Confirmation of the forme^r Judgmen^t & Costs of Courts forty eight shillings & three penc:

1 Ju.

Benjā Rice pl^t Con^ta m^r Wm Avery deffendant in an Accon of Appeale from the Judgment of the Comissione^rs Court in Boston after the Judgment Attachment Reasons of Appeale & euidences in the Case produced were read Comitted to the Jury & are on file ‖ wth the Records of this Court ‖ the Jury brought in their virdict a speciall virdict y^t if the [y^e] plts not denying his hand in the Comissione^rs Court be in law æqui[u]olent ‖ to ‖ an owning of ~~his hand~~ ‖ it ‖ then wee find for ye defend^t Confirmation of the forme^r Judgmen^t & Costs of Courts if no^t then for

2 Ju

ye plaintiff reuersion of the former Judgment & Costs of Courts the Bench determins for the deffendant & Granted him his Costs of Courts

Wm Gilbert plaint Conta Bartholmew Gidney Esqr Attur[ney] deffendt In || an || Accon of Appeale from the Judgment of the County Court in Salem After ye Attachmt Courts Judgt Reasons of Appeale & euidences in the Case produced were read Comitted to the Jury and are on file the Jury brought in their virdict they found for the plaintiff reuercon of the former Judgment & costs of Courts two pounds thirteen shillings & sixe pence

2d Jur

[193] 1685

persons Returnd to serve on ye 1st Jury for Appeales life limbe &c & sworne were
— — — —
mr stephen ffrench
Henry Bartholmew
Jno ffuller Lynn
Peter Lyon
Jno Dauis
Isack Brookes
Jno Sawin
Phineas sprague
steeven payne
Jnothan Preston
Richd stowers
Nathaniel Thajre
— — — —
persons Returnd to serve on ye 2d Jury for tryalls of Appeales for life limbe &c Sworne
— — — —
mr wm Clarke
Nathaniel willjams
2d for ‡ mr Edwd Broomfeild
Benja Walker
Jno ffuller Cam. §
Antho Sprague
Jno Baxter
James Bird
Isack Newell
Tho ffuller woo ¶
wm Rauson

Joseph Lee plt Conta Jno waingright * deffendt in an Accon of Appeale from the Judgment of the County Court at Ipswich after the Attachment Courts Judgmt reasons of Appeale & euidences in the Case produced were read Comitted to the Jury & are on file wth the Records of this Court the Jury brought in their virdict they found for the plaintiff an abatement of the former Judgment fower pounds three shillings & sixe pence & costs of this Court wch was thirty fower shillings: & on his peticon the Judgmt & execution therevpō was Respitted for 3 months from ys day 8 † of Sept 85

2d Ju:

Benjãin marshall plt Conta Jno Cogswell deffendt in an action of Appeale from the Judgment of the County Court at Salem After the Attachment Courts Judgment Reasons of Appeale & euidences in the Case produced were read Comitted to the Jury & are on file wth the Reccords of this Court the Jury brought in their virdict they found for the deffendt Confirmation of the formr Judgment & Costs of Courts two pounds five shillings.—

1 Ju

Samuel Jackljn plt Conta Thomas Parris defendant in an action of Appeal from the Judgment of the County Court in Boston After ye Attachment Courts Judgment reasons of Appeale & euidences

* Wainwright? † Changed from 3. ‡ Foreman. § Cambridge. ¶ Woburn.

in the Case produced were read Comitted to ye Jury & are on file ‖ w^{th} ‖ the Records of y^s Court the Jury brought in their virdict they found for ye plaintiff reuersion of the former Judgm^t & Costs of Courts forty nine shillings ⌣ exec Issud out 7 7b^r for 2 : 9^s.

2^d Ju :

Jn^othan Phillips
Jn^othan Bridgham
instd of m^r Clark
when [list]

Samuel Gibson plaintiff in an Action of Appeale from Cambridg Courts sentence After the Courts sentenc & euidences in the Case produced were read Comitted to the Jury & are on file wth the Records of this Court the Jury brought in their virdict they found for the plaintiff Reūercon of the Courts sentenc 2^d

Amo^s Marret p^{lt} Con^{ta} Ephrajm Cutter defend^t in an Action of Appeale from the Judgm^t of the County Court at Cambridge After the Attachm^t Courts Judgment Reasons of Appeale & euidences in the Case produced were read Comitted to the Jury & are on file wth the Records of this Court the Jury brought in their virdict i e If a person^s oune euidence & wounds wth other euidences that thinke they heard y^e ꝑson y^t is wounded Cry out be euidenc in law then ye Jury finds A Confirmation of the forme^r Judgm^t or sentenc If not euidenc in law then the Jury finds a reuersion : of ye former sentence. The magis^{ts} determines for ye Courts sentence ═ 1st Ju

Jno Trayne plt Conta Samuel Barnard deffend^t in an action of Appeale from the Judgm^t of the County Court at charlsToune After the Attachm^t Courts Judgment Reasons of Appeale & euidences in the Case produced were read Comitted to the Jury & are on file wth the Reccords of this Court the Jury brought in their virdict they found for the plaintiff Reūsion of the forme^r Judgm^t & Costs of Courts ‖ in all ‖ fowe^r pounds fowe^rteen shillings & fowe^r penc

Trayne ag^t Barnard
25 at Camb. & costs
vide 198 p.

Bethy Arche^r wife & Atturney to hir husband Jno Arche^r ꝑ p^{lt} Conta Benja Pickmand defend^t in an accon of Appeale from the County Court at Salem afte^r the Attachment Courts Judgmen^t Reasons of Appeale & euidences in the Case produced were read ^ objections made ag^t the ꝓcesse the Court declared that there was no legall process & Granted ye plaintiff hir Costs two pounds tenn shillings and fowe^r pence ═

[194] 1685

2d Ju Boober Conta Downing

Joseph Boober Conta Richard Douning deffendant in an Accon of Appeale from the Judgment of ye County Court at Salem after the Attachmt Courts Judgment Reasons of Appeale & euidences in the Case produced were read Comitted to the Jury & are on file wth the reccords of this Court the Jury brought in their virdict they found for the deffendant Confirmation of the former Judgment & Costs of Courts one pound nine shillings & tenn penc

2d Jur Hitchins agt Broune

Daniel Hitchins plt Conta Tho: Browne deffendt in an action of Appeale frō the Judgment of the County Court at Ipswich After the Attachment Courts Judgment Reasons of Appeale & euidences in the Case produced were read Comitted to the Jury & are on file wth the Records of this Court the Jury brought in their virdict they found for ye pltff Reusion of the former Judgmt & Costs of Courts three pounds fiue shillings & six penc The Court ordered that execution Gon forth in ys Case being suruptitiously obteyned shall be respitted & Returnd to ye secretary on 2d day next & deteyned till ye Courts further ordr (ye originall Bond sent for & Returnd =

Courts order to deteyne &c

mr Peter Sarjant & Elisabeth his wife pltff Conta mr Henry Shrimpton ‖ one of ye executors &c ‖ deffendt In an Action of Appeale from the Judgment of the County Court in Boston After the Attachmt Courts Judgment Reasons of Appeale & euidences in ye Case produced were read Comitted to the Jury & are Remayning on file with the Reccords of this Court the Jury brought in their virdict they found for the defendant Confirmation of the former Judgments & Costs of Courts

2d Jur Sarjant Conta Shrimpton.

1st Jur Apleton Conta Roads 1 Acti:

mr Samuel Apleton Jun pltf Conta Henry Roads defendt in an Action of Appeale from the Judgment of the County Court at Salem After the Attachmt Courts Judgment Reasons of Appeale & euidences in the Case produced were read Comitted to the Jury & are on file wth the Records of this Court the Jury brought in their virdict i.e If ye law Gives power to a single magistrate to trye title of land & Giue damage

|| in || an action of trespasse when both partjes clajme title then wee find for the deffendant Confirmation of the forme^r Judgment & Costs of Courts If the law gives no such powe^r then wee find for the plaintiff reuertion of the forme^r Judgm^t & Costs of Courts = the Bench determined for the plaintiff seven pounds nineteen shillings & eight pence costs

m^r Samuel Apleton plt^f Conta Henry Roads deffend^t in an Action of Appeale frō the Judgment of the County Court at Salem after y^e Attachm^t Courts Judgm^t Reasons of Appeale & euidences in the Case produced were read Comitted to the Jury & are on file wth the Records of this Cour^t the Jury brought in their virdict a speciall virdict in ye same words as aboue the bench as aboue determined for the plaintiff & gted him his Cost seuen pounds eighteen shillings & tenn penc

1st Ju: Apleton Con^ta Roads

Samuel Apleton Con^ta Samuel wakefeild deffend^t at a County Court held at Boston from the Comissio^rs in An action of Appeale after the Attachment Courts Judgmen^t Reasons of Appeale & euidences in the Case produced were read Comitted to the Jury & are on file the Jury brought in thei^r virdict they found for the Deffendt Confirmation of the form^r Judgm^t & Costs of Courts

1st Jury

Apleton Con^t wakefeld

Benjamin Chambe^rlajn plain^t Conta Nathaniell Billings deffend^t in an action of Appeale from the Judgment from the County Court at Cambridg after the Attachment Courts Judgmen^t Reason of Appeale & euidences in the Case produced were read Comitted to the Jury and are on file wth the Reccords of this Court the Jury brought in their virdict they found for the deffendan^t Confirmation of the form^r Judgment & Costs of Courts three pounds nine shillings & eight pence

Chambe^rlajn Conta wakefeild *

[195] 1685

Samuel Walke^r plan^t Conta Roger vicke^rs defend^t || in an Action of Appeale from the Judgment of the comissioners court || After ye Attachm^t Courts Judgment reasons of Appeale & euidences in the case produced were read Com̄itted to y^e

1 Jur. & 1. Accō

* Evidently an error of the Secretary for "Billings."

vickers agt walker as to Indent 8li D & 31 : 6d Costs

Jury & are on file wth the Records of this court the Jury brought in their virdict they found for the deffendant Confirmation of the former Judgment & Costs of Courts one pound eleven shillings & six penc

vickers Conta walker for worke —

Joseph vickers plaint Conta Samuel Walker defendt in an Accon of Appeale from the Judgment of the Comissioners Court After the Attachmt Courts Judgment reasons of Appeale & euidences in the Case produced were read Comitted to the Jury & are on file wth the Records of this Court the Jury found for the deffendt Confirmation of the former Judgment & Costs of Courts one pound 9s & dam 30s

Vickers Conta Walker

Joseph vickers plant Con'a Samuel walker defendt in an action of Appeale from the Judgment of the Comissionrs Court after the Attachmt Courts Judgment Reasons of Appeale & euidences in the Case produced were read Comitted to the Jury & are on file wth ye Records of ys Court the Jury brought in their virdict they found for the plaintiff Reuertion* of the former Judgment & Costs of Courts thirty two shillings & fower penc :

2 Jury Hendrick agt Dauis

filings pd. 3 : 4. 6

Jonathant Hendrick plaint Conta James dauis in an Accon of Appeale from the Judgment of the County Court of Salem† After the Attachmt Courts Judgment Reasons of Appeale & euidences in the Case produced were read Comitted to the Jury & are on file wth the Records of this Court ye Jury finds for the plaintiff Reuersion of the former Judgment & Costs of Courts 52 : 10

Baker agt Hundlocke

in all 99, 04. 8. execut: Issued out 9. Sept (.85)

Thomas Baker plaint Conta Edward Hunlocke deffendt in an Accon of Appeale from the Judgment of the County Court in Boston After the Attachment Courts Judgment Reasons of Appeale & euidences in the Case produced were read Comitted to ye Jury & are on file wth the Records of this Court the Jury found for the deffendant Confirmation of the former Judgment & Costs

---

* Written over "deffendant confirmation."

† Written over "Commissioners Court." By the papers on file it appears that the appeal was by Jotham Hendrick from the County Court at Ipswich. See Court Files No. 2338.

of Courts, two pounds fowerteen shillings & two penc the Court chanceried ye bond to ninety six pounds tenn shillings —

Robe'rt Pike esqr plt Conta Nathaniel winsley deffendt in an Accōn of Appeale from the Judgment of the County Court at Salem After ye Attachmt Courts Judgmt Reasons of Appeale & euidences in the Case produced were read Comitted to the Jury & are on file the Jury brought in their virdict they found for the plaintiff Reuision of ye former Judgment & Costs of Courts

Edward Richards Robe'rt Potter seņ samuel Johnson Attu'n'ys for ye Towne of lynn plt conta sam: Apleton Juņ deffendt in an Accōn of Appeale from the Judgmt of the County Court at Salem After the Attachmt Courts Judgment Reasons of Appeale from the Judgmt of the County Court at Salem After the Attachment Courts Judgment Reasons of Appeale * & euidences in ye Case produced were read Comitted to the Jury & are on file the Jury brought in their virdict they found for the defendt Confirmation of the former Judgment & Costs of Courts

[196] 1685

Samuel Pearce plt Contra Jno Haward defend in an Accōn of Appeale from the Judgment of the Comissioners Court In Boston After ye Attachmt Courts Judgment Reasons of Appeale & euidences in the Case produced were read Comitted to the Jury & are on file wth the Records of this Court the Jury brought in their virdict they found^ Pearse Conta Hayward

Gilbe'rt Cole plaint Conta Joseph Homes defendt in an Accon of Appeale from the Judgment of the County Court in Boston. After the Attachment Courts Judgment Reasons of Appeale & euidences in the Case produced were read Comitted to the Jury & are on file wth the Records of this Court the Jury brought in their virdict they found for the defendant Confirmation of the former Judgment & Costs of Courts thirty seven shillings Gilbert Cole Conta Jo. Homes damg. 10li mony Cost 37s

Robe'rt Blood Juņ plt Conta samuel knight defendt in an Accōn of Appeale from the Judgment of the County Court at charlsToune After

* Seventeen words repeated in the record.

Blood agt Knight 9li. 2s. 10 Execution Issued out 17th Septt 85

ye Attachment Courts Judgment Reasons of Appeale & euidences in the Case produced were read Comitted to the Jury & are on file wth the Records of this Court the Jury brought in their virdict they found for the defendt Confirmation of ye former Judgmt & Costs of Courts seventeen shillings & six penc in all damage ꝑ 9li. 02 10

Mulligans sentence to Return to Ireland ꝑ undr pœnalty of 20li

Hugh mulligen plaint on Appeale from the Judgment or sentenc of the Countty Court in Boston After the Courts sentenc & euidences in the Case ꝓduced were read Comitted to the Jury & are on file wth the Records of this Court the Jury brought in their virdict they found a Confirmation of the County Courts sentenc & costs of Courts i e defray ye charg of Tryall:

Lilly Conta payne

Edward Lilly plaint Conta Wm Payne Blacksmith In An action of Appeale from the Judgment of the County Court in Boston After ye Attachmt Courts Judgmet Reasons of Appeale & euidences in the Case produced were read Comitted to the Jury & are on file wth the Records of this Court the Jury brought in their virdict they found for the defendant Confirmation of the former Judgment & Costs of Courts nineteen shillings & 10d wch added to ye damage [mō *] & other Costs in all is twenty seven pounds fiueteen shillings 10d money.

widdow wardell nonsuited

widdow wardell plaintiff Contra mr Symon Lynde deffendt in An Accon of Appeale from the Judgment of the County Court in Boston the plaintiff not Appearing being three times Called was non suited & the bond declared forfeited & defendt had his Costs sixe shillings

Stoddard agt mr Davy

mr Anthony Stoddard plt Conta Humphry Davy esqr deffendt in an action of Appeale from the Judgment of the County Court in Boston After the Attachment Courts Judgment reasons of Appeale & euidences in the Case produced were read Comitted to the Jury & are on file wth the Reccords of this Court the Jury brought in their virdict they found for the deffendant costs of Courts †

* Money? The verdict at the County Court was for 26li in money and Costs of Court, 16s.

† The original verdict on file is "for the deffendant confirmation of ye former Judgment & Cost of Courts." See Suffolk Court Files No. 2338.

Joseph Hiller plaintiff Contra ffrancis Burrowes deffendt in an action of Appeale from the Judgment of the County Court in Boston after the Attachment Courts Judgement Reasons of Appeale and euidences in the case produced were read Comitted to the Jury and are on file with the Reccords of this Court the Jury brought in their virdict they found for the defendant Confirmation of the former Judgment & Costs of Courts

Hiller agt Burrowes

☞ p: 201 [Adj]

ordered ye secretary Issue out warrant for ye discharge of Jnothan Gardiner out of prison he paying the prison fees, ye Grand Jury not finding ye bill

[197] 1685

John Saffyn plaintiff Conta Stephen Burton deffendt in an Action of Appeale from the Judgment of the County Court in Boston after the Attachment Courts Judgment Reasons of Appeale & euidences in the Case produced were read Comitted to the Jury & are on file with the Records of this Court the Jury brought in their virdict they found for the defendant Confirmation of the former Judgment & Costs of Courts two pounds two shillings =

Saffyn agt Burton
Costs 2li 2s 0
memto filing vnpd 2s 6.

Henry Roads plaintiff Conta Samuel Apleton deffendt in an Action of Appeale from the Judgment of the County Court in Ipswich after ye Attachment Courts Judgment Reasons of Appeale & euidences in the Case produced were read Comitted to the Jury & are on file wth the Records of this Court the Jury brought in their virdict they found for the plaintiff reusion of the formr Judgmt twelue shillings damage & Costs of Courts = forty one shillings

Roads agt Apleton

Dr Phillip Read Conta michael Bacon deffendt in an Action of Appeale from the Judgment of the County Court at Cambridge after the Attachment Courts Judgment reasons of Appeale & euidences in the Case produced were read Comitted to the Jury & are on file wth the Records of this Court the Jury brought in their virdict they found for the deffendant Confirmation of the former Judgment & Costs of Courts in all thirty one shillings & fower penc =

Read agt Bacon

Costs 31 . 4
fil. 3 . 8 vnpd

wharton Conta Smith

mr Richd wharton mr Hezekiah Vsher Daniel Turel Jun & John white plt Conta Joseph Smith deffendt in an Accon of Appeale from the Judgment of the County Court in Boston After the Attachment Courts Judgment Reasons of Appeale & euidences in the Case produced were read Comitted to the Jury & are on file wth the Reccords of this Court the Jury brought in their virdict they found for ye plaintiff reuersion of the former Judgment & sixty pounds money damage & Costs of Courts seuen pounds seuen shillings & sixe pence =

on his peticon both executions respitted: 10 Sept 85 =

Saffyn agt Baxter

Tho Saffyn Conta John Baxter In An Action of Appeale from the Judgmt of the County Court In Boston After the Attachmt Courts Judgment Reasons of Appeale & euidences in the Case produced were read Comitted to the Jury & are on file wth the Records of this Court the Jury brought in their virdict they found for ye plaintiff fower pounds abatement of ye former Judgment & Costs of || ys || Court thirty fower shillings & tenn pence —

Execution Issued out agt Saffyn for 7. 5: 4 11 Sept 85 =

Homes agt chickley

Joseph Homes plt Conta Anthony cheeckley In An Action of Appeale from the Judgment of the County Court at Boston || &c || After the Attachment Courts Judgment Reasons of Appeale & euidences in the Case produced were read Comitted to the Jury & are on file with the Records of this Court the Jury brought in their virdict they found for the plaintiff reuersion of the former Judgmt & Costs of Courts || ye defendt Attainted ye Jury 17 Sept 85 for errors & mistakes ^ gaue In his reasons || Antho checkly as principall in sixty pounds & mr Richard Harris of Braintry & Jno. Keech of Boston his suertjes in thirty pounds apeece mony acknowledged themselues respectiuely bound to ye Tresur of ye Country & party Concerned yt sd Anthony cheeckly shall prosecute his Attaint of ye Jury agt ye Jurys virdict at ye next court of Assistants whereof * mr Edwd Bromfeild was foreman

Attest. Edwd Rawson secret

Richard chick plt Conta Edward doe: deffendt in an ac[ti]on of Appeale from the Judgmt of † ye plaintiff Appeared not but sajd yt ye partjes were Agreed

* So in the original.

† This space left blank in the record.

[198] 1685

M^{r}s Hannah Haugh plaint Conta Abraham Hill defend^{t} in an action of Appeale from the Judgment of the [County] Court at [CharlesToune *] as to the non suite granted ag^{t} hir. After the Attachment Courts Judgment Reasons of Appeale & euidences produced$_{\wedge}$ = the Court determined for the plaintiff & Granted hir the Costs of this Court and remitted the Case to the former Court to be heard & determined on the originall writt & former entry =

Haugh Conta Hill fil: 1. 6.

Costs 29^{s}

Samuel Bernard Complayning that he is in prison vpon execution granted by this Court Against ‖ him ‖ to John Trayne for fowe^{r} pounds fowe^{r}teene & fower pence It Appearing that the Judgment amoun^{t}s to no more than three pounds sixe & fowe^{r} pence The Court declares the sajd execution voyd & Be^{r}nard to be released as being falsly Imprisoned / And an execution yet lyes for Trajne for the sajd sume of three pounds six & fow^{r} pence. = And It is ordered that the Secretary Issue out a warrant to the keeper of the prison at Cambridge to discharge the sajd Samuell Bernard his prison as on y^{e} execution granted against him on suit of John Trayne whch was donn Accordingly

Courts Judgm^{t} to Releas Bernard

18 Sep^{t} 1685

Vriah Cleomen^{t}s y^{t} Called himself by the name of John Ball being presented by the Grand Jury & left to further Trjall was brought out of ye prison to ye Barr: was † Indicted by the name of vryah cleoments ‖ or ‖ y^{t} lately Came from England in the Pyncke Adventure John Balston master for that he not hauing the feare of God before his eyes but being Instigated by the devill did vpon the nineteenth day of July last in this present yeare 1685 being the Lords day Comit a Burglary on the dwelling house of Sarah Noyse widow in Boston entring the sajd house stole thence about ninety fiue pounds in money Contrary to the peace of ou^{r} Sou$^{\sim}$aigne Lord the king the Lawes ‡ of God and of this Jurisdiction to wch Indictmen^{t} holding vp his hand at y^{e} Barr he pleaded not giulty put himself on God & the Country for his Tryall & no^{t} excepting against any of the Jury Impanneld After his Accusation by James olliuer whose mony It was y^{t} he stole wth the euidences in the

Cleoments Indictm^{t} & sentenc as to m^{r} James oliuers Acusat

* Written over "Cambridge." † Written over "being."
‡ Written over "his Crowne."

Case produced against him were read Comitted to the Jury & are on file the Jury brought in their virdict the prisoner being at the barr they found him Guilty according to Indictment The Court proceeded to & did sentenc him being so convicted & found Guilty as aboue to be branded wth the letter **B** on ye forhead & haue his Right eare Cutt of dischardging ye charge of ye witnesses tryall & fees & then make treble Restitution to the party Injuried & in deffect thereof to be

[199] 1685

sold to any of the English plantations =

[*Blank space*]

Cleoments Indictmt as to James Pecker & his sentenc

Vryah Cleoments that had falsly Called himself by ye name of John Ball being presented by the Grand Jury & left to further Tryall was brought out of the prison to the Barr & there Indicted by the name of vryah Cleoments &c that lately Came from England in the Pynke Adventure John Balston master for that he not hauing the feare of God before his eyes but being Instigated by the divill did vpon the twelfth of July last in this present yeare 1685 being the Lords day Comitt a Burglary on the dwelling house of James Pecker housewright in Boston entring the sd house stole about tenn pounds in money & some Ribbon Contrary to the peace of our soueraigne Lord the king his Croune and dignity the lawes of God & of this Jurisdiction To wch Indictment holding vp his hand at the Barr he pleaded not Guilty put himself for tryall on God & ye Country (not excepting against any of the Jury Impaneld ^ = After the Indictment his Accusation by James Pecker wth his ye sd Cleoments examinations & euidences in the Case produced against him were read Comitted to the Jury & are on file the Jury brought in their virdict they found him Guilty according to Indictment = The Court proceeded to & did sentenc him to be Againe Branded with the letter **B** on his forehead & haue his left eare Cutt of dischardging the charge of the wittnesses & Tryall & fees of Court & then making treble Restitution to the party Injuried & on defect thereof to be sold to any of the English Plantations =

[*Blank space*]

Wm Clapp ‖ marriner ‖ being Comitted to prison on suspition of being Confœderate wth vriah Cleoments aliast Jno Ball was brought to y^e^ Barr & there m^r^ James olliuer exhibbited his Complaint ag^t^ him for being confœderate wth vriah cleoments in stealing concealing & helping to spend the mony stolne by him out of m^r^s Noyes her house as ꝑ euidence & his oune Confession will Appeare: Jno Channell is also complajned against on the same effect signed

By James Oliver

wch Complaint being read in Court ag^t^ sajd w^m^ Clapp: he ans^r^d he was no way Guilty & desired to be trjed by ye Jury wch was granted him & After the Complaint & all the euidences & examinations & Confessions taken before ye Comissione^r^s &c were read Comitted to the Jury & are on file wth the Records of this Court the Jury brought in their virdict they found him the sajd w^m^ clapp Guilty according to ye Complaint John * french foreman &c The like Complain^t^ was Read ag^t^ Jno channell & on like tryall by

Courts sentence ag^t^ w^m^ Clap & Jno chan^ll^ on Complt of m^r^ James oliuer &c

[200] 1685

like Jury as in Clap^s^ in all respects

The Court proceeded to sentenc them the sajd John channon & w^m^ Clap for their offences being Convicted & stand Guilty of being Confœderate wth vriah Cleomen^t^s in stealing Concealing & helping to spend the money stolne from the sajd oliuer out of m^r^s Noyes hir house as ꝑ euidence & their oune Confession to pay tenn pounds a peece mony as a fine to the Countrey & be Returned to y^e^ prison there to remajne for one month & discharging the wittnesses & tryall & fees of Court then to be dischardged = In Ans^r^ to the petiĉon of w^m^ Clapp Its ordered that on his paying his fine & charges of Tryalls &c he shall be releast his Imprisonm^t^ The like favou^r^ was granted to Jno channell

from 17th Septemb. 85

Joseph Homes Sen̄ & Jun̄ principalls being bound ouer wi^th^ sue^r^tjes that they Appeare at ye nex^t^ Court of Assistants to Answer what they shall be charged with for being present at the expending receiving & privy to the Concealing of any of the mony stolne out of the house of m^r^s Noyce in Boston & abide the orde^r^ of the Court Joseph Homes sen̄ & Jun̄ were Called & appeared & it being put to them whither they would be trjed by the Bench or by ~~the~~ Jury, they each after othe^r^ refferd themselues to the Bench =

Joseph Homes sen^r^ was heard & was Admonished for his vncomely speech abt m^r^ williams =

* The original verdict on file is signed by "Steph. ffrench fforeman."

Jose[p]h Homes Jun̄ being Accused to be accessory to the Burglary & Theft Comitted at the house of m^r^s Noyce by vryah cleoments by his after being at the expence of some of the money & receiving vntold & Concealing a part thereof vntill pursued & challenged by the owno^r^s and ~~taking a part thereof~~ ‖ hauing referred ‖ himself to the Court without a Jury the Cause being heard He is Adjudged to pay tenn markes as a fine to the Country, to suffer fowe^r^teen day^s^ Imprisonment & pay fees of Court prosecution & prison & then be dischardged

18. Sep^t^ 1685: In Ans^r^ to y^e^ petition of Joseph Homes Junr It is ordered that the said Joseph Homes Junr on payment of his fine &c be released & dischardged = y^e^ same fauo^r^ was Granted to w^m^ clap & Jno channon

Courts Adjo^rmt^ 18 Sep^t^ 85 The Court Respitted as before the execution in smith ag^t^ m^r^ wharton &c & in m^r^ whartons ag^t^ m^r^ Smith till this Courts Adjour[nment] to 2^d^ wednesday in octobe^r^ nex^t^ at one of the clock to wch time this Court was Adjourned =

This Court was Adjourned to y^e^ 14th of octobe^r^ 85 at one of y^e^ clock to wch time y^e^ Genl Court had binn Adjourned

[201]

The Court mett at y^e^ time of Its Adjourm^t^ 14 of octobe^r^ 1685 & so day by day to y^e^ ending of the session.

m^r^ Jno Bisco Appeared & Complayned agains^t^ his servant James farrell with John macolly servant to m^r^ Joseph sherman that Gott into the cellar of * Neue^r^son as in their Confession

[*Blank space*]

Itt is Ordered that James Pecker shall haue forthwith deliuered to him out of the mony that vrijah cleoments stole from m^r^ James oliuer twenty fiue shillings money (the sajd cleoments not only owning that he did steale Peckers mony but also had about fiuety shillings of sajd Pecke^r^s mony in his hands and put it into m^r^ olive^r^s mony) and also that ‖ i. e. Robt Butcher † ‖ the Constable that seized cleoments

* Left blank in the record. † Written in the margin.

two suites of cloathes hatt stockings shooes silve[r] Buckles Button shirt & necke clothes & handthecherfs || w[th] y[e] seven shillings y[t] Clap borowed, & two shillings Channon borowed of s[d] cleoments ꝑ before m[r]s Noy[s] hovse was broken up || deliuer them to sajd Pecker the sajd Pecker to pay what is Justly due to Sam Lincolne y[e] Taylor

In answer to the motion of Joseph Helljer* The Court chanceried his bond to one hundred & eight pounds mony & Costs of Courts

It is ordered that John Channons fine of tenn pounds be Abated to sixe pounds

[*The rest of the page is blank*]

[202] 1685

Att A Court of Assistants held at Boston 2[d] of march 1685

present
Symon Bradstreet Esq[r] Gou[r]
Thomas Danforth Esq[r] dep Go.
Daniel Gookin
w[m] stoughton
Joseph dudley
Humphry davy
John Richards
Sam Nowell
James Russell
Sam: Apleton
Robe[r]t Pyke
Elisha Cooke
w[m] Johnson
Jn[o] Hathorn
Elisha Hutchinson
Samuel seawall
} Esq[rs]

The Grand Jury brought in their presentments & Indictments & were discharged.

m[r] Anthony Checkley plaintiff in an Action of Appeale on Attaint Contra [the] y[e] virdict of y[e] Jury whereof m[r] Edward Bromefeild was foreman & ag[t] Joseph Homes Defendant After the Attachm[t] the || Courts Judgm[t] & || Jury[s] virdict & euidences in the case were read Comitted to the Jury and are on file the Jury brought in their virdict therevpon & is on file viz[t] they found for the defendant Confirmation of the former Judgment & Costs of Courts fower pounds eleven shillings & sixpence to sajd Homes

— — —

persons Returnd to serve on y[e] Grand Jury & sworne were

— — — —

m[r] symon Lynde
Rich[d] way
Jabez Totman
Henry Leadbetter
Stephen Lincolne
w[m] Torrey Jun[r]
Andrew Belchar
Joseph ketle
Allexande[r] marsh
Samuel Andrewes
Jn[o] Bright

Anna Haugh plain[t] Con[ta] Abraham Hill defendan[t] || In an Action of Appeale from the Judgmt of y[e] County Court at ~~Boston~~ || Cambridge || After the Attachment Courts Judgment Reasons of Appeale & euidences in the Case producd were read Comitted to Jury & remajne on file wth the Records of this Court the Jury brought in their virdict therevpon they found

* See page [196]

Nath Coolidge
James flood
Nath. Sternes
— — — —

for the plaintiffe reuersion of the former virdict & twenty pounds mony damage & Costs of Courts three pounds eight shillings & 4[d]

George Kirbee plaintiff In An Action of Appeale from the Judg[t] of the County Court in Boston in octobe[r] last after the Attachmen[t] Courts Judgmen[t] Reasons of Appeale and euidences in the Case produced were read Comitted to the Jury & are on file the Jury brought in their virdict therevpon they found for the defendant the Revertion * of the form[e]r virdict & Judgment & Costs of Courts one pound ten shillings & eight pence =

Sarah Barret Plaintiff on Appeale from the sentence of the County Court in Boston After the Courts sentence & euidence in the Case produced were read Comitted to the Jury & are on file the Jury brought in their virdict they found Confirmation of the forme[r] sentence 5[li] fine er †

Sarah ‡ Barret plaintiff on Appeale from the sentence of the County Court in Boston After the Courts sentenc & euidences in the Case produced were read Comitted to the Jury & are on file wth the Records of this Court the Jury brought in their virdict therevpon they found Confirmati[on] of y[e] sentenc 5[li] mony er

persons Returnd to serve on the Jury of Attaints & Appeales & for life limbe & banishmen[t] & sworne were
— — — —
m[r] Samuel phipps
w[m] Gilbert
Isayah Toy
Bozoune Allen
Richard Banks
obadiah Gill
Cleomen Coldham
Henry Bowen
Sam Gore
Jn[o] Tolman
Ebeneza[r] Billing
w[m] Greene
on the othe[r] side

m[r] Jonathan Corwin Administrato[r] to the estate of y[e] late Cap[t] Georg Corwin plt ‖ In an action of Appeale from y[e] Judgment of Salem Court ‖ Conta w[m] Dounton & John La[under] defendants After the Attachments Courts Judgment Reasons of Appeale & euidences in the Case produced were read Comitted to the Jury & are on file with the Records of this Court the Jury brought in their virdict therevpon & found for the deffendants Confirmation of the former Judgmen[t] & Costs of Courts three pounds 3[d] damage was 12 ^

[203] 1685

Symon Gross
Sam: Holbrooke

George Dauson plt Conta Cap[t] Jn[o] wing defendant In an action of Appeale from the Judgment of the

---

* Written over "Confirmation." † er written over "& Costs."

‡ Written over "Jn[o]than." There were two Appeals from the County Court by Sarah Barret.

County Court at Charls Toune after the Attachment Courts Judgment Reasons of Appeale & euidences in the Case produced were read Comitted to the Jury & are on file wth the Reccords of this Court the Jury brought in their virdict therevpon they found for the deffendant || confirmation of the former Judgment & || Costs of Courts =

Sam. ketle
Joseph Cro[s]by
Tho. Olliuer
noah wisewall
Joseph Mason
w^m^ shaddock
Ebenezer flegg
natha: Bullard
James foule
ffrancis Burrell

— — — —

persons Returnd to serve on y^e^ 1st Jury for Appeales life & sworne—
m^r^ Sam Phipps
I[s]ayah Toy
Richd Banks
francis Burrell
Henry Bowen
Jno Tolman
w^m^ Greene
Sam Holbrooke
Joseph Crosby
noah wisewall
w^m^ Shaddock
natha Bullard
w^m^ Gibson insteed of Toy in 3 or 4 Act[ions]

— — — —

George Dauson plt Cont^a^ George Pite & defendant in an Action of Appeale from the Judgment of the County Court at charls Toune After the Attachment Courts Judgment reasons of Appeale & euidences in the Case produced were read Comitted to the Jury & are on file wth the Reccords of this Court the Jury brought in their virdict they found for the deffendant Costs of Courts.

Abraham Holman & Plaintiff Cont^a^ nathaniel Hanckock & Jno Goue defend^ts^ in an Action of Appeale from the Judgment of the County Court at charls-Toune After the Attachmen^t^ Courts Judgment reasons of Appeale & euidences in the Case produced were read Comitted to the Jury & are on file wth the Reccords of this Court the Jury brought in their virdict they found for the plaintiff reuertion of the forme^r^ Judgment & Costs of Courts.

Whereas In the Case betweene Cambridge Selectmen plt & ye drum̃e^r^s of the Toune defendants a testimony hath binn read in this Court signed & sworne by Jerremiah Holman & Abraham Holman wch doth appeare to this Court to be very rash & presumptuous & to the Drume^r^s prejudice in their Case, if false, This Court doeth refer * the examination thereof vnto the County Court of middlesex & to give Judgment therein as they shall see Cause

w^m^ Marshall plt Cont^a^ W^m^ marbell deffendant In an action of Appeale from the Judgment of the County Court at charls Toune After the Attachment Courts Judgment reasons of Appeale & euidences in the case produced were read Com̃itted to the Jury & are on file wth the reccords of this Court the Jury brought in their virdict they found for the ~~plaintiff~~ || defendant || Confirmation of the

w^m^ marshall Conta w^m^ marble ℘ defend: 16, 10 dam & costs 2.9 mem^t^ 5 ent 2.4 ff

* Written over "doe therefore."

former Judgm[t] i e sixteen pounds ten shillings damag mony & Costs of Courts forty nine shilling[s]

marshall Cont[a] Soley ℘ Soley 33[li]. da. mony & 57[s] costs fil. 2:4 post ent 10.

w[m] marshall plt Contra Sarah Soley widdow defend[t] In an acti[on] of Appeale from the Judgment of the County Court at charlsToune After the Attachment Courts Judgment reasons of Appeale & euidences in the Case produced were read Comitted to the Jury & are on file the Jury brought in their virdict they found for the defendant Confirmation of the forme[r] Judgment i e thirty three pounds ‖ mony ‖ & fifty seuen shillings Costs

marshall cont[a] moor ℘ moore 55[li] mony & Costs of Courts 2=13.6 Add entry [&] filing 2 57. 15.6

w[m] marshall plaint Con[ta] Enoch moore defend[t] in an Action of Appeale from the Judgment of the County Court at charlsToune After the Attachmen[t] Courts Judgment reasons of Appeale & euidences in the Case produced were read Co͞mitted to the Jury and are on file wth the Reccords of this Court the Jury brought in their virdict they found for the deffendant Confirmation of the former Judgment i e fiuety fiue pounds mony & Costs of Courts fiuety three shillings & sixpenc.

[204] 1685

Gates Conta Jn[o] ffoskett

Symon Gates Gates* Plaintiff In An Acc͞on of Appeale from the Judgment of the County Court at Cambridge ‖ contra Jn[o] ffoskett ‖ After the Attachment Courts Judgment Reasons of Appeal & euidences in the Case produced were read Co͞mitted to the Jury & are on file with the records of this Court the Jury brought in their virdict they found for the plaintiff reu͞sion of the forme[r] Judgmen[t]s & Costs of Courts fiuety one shilling[s] & sixe pence =

Homes Con[ta] Olliuer

Joseph Homes Jun͞ plaintiff Conta Nathaniel Olliuer defend[t] In Action of Appeale from the Judgment of the County Court in Boston octobe[r] last After the Attachment Courts Judgment Reasons of Appeale & euidences in the Case produced were read Comitted the Jury & are on file with the Records of this Court the Jury brought in their virdict they found for

* Repeated in the record.

the plaintiff * Confirmation of the former Judgment & Costs of Courts w[ch] was ten shillings & sixe penc ℘ & acknowldgd p[d] =

Turell conta Jn[o] Cowell

Daniel Turell Turell † Juñ Atturney to Nicho: Inglesby plt Con[ta] Joseph ‡ Cowell Atturney to w[m] Shaddock § deffendt In An Action of Appeale from the Judgment of the Commissione[r]s Court in Boston After the Attachment Courts Judgment Reasons of Appeale & euidences in the Case produced were read Comitted to the Jury & are on file w[th] the Reccords of this Court the Jury brought in their virdict they found for the deffendant Confirmation of the forme[r] Judgm[t] & Costs of Cour[ts] nineteen shillings —

Bullard Conta Richards

Nathaniel Bullard & John Herse plt. Con[ta] County Courts sentenc or determination as to y[e] probat of y[e] will of ¶ Richards After the Courts Judgment & setlement & othe[r] euidences in the Case produced were Read The Bench declared they Confirmed the forme[r] Judgment of the County Court in Boston & gaue the defendants Costs three pounds one shilling & tenn penc :

Bacon Conta mack-[quinis] filings to pay

michael Bacon plt Con[ta] Daniel [Maguinis] deffendant In an Action of Appeale from the Judgment of the County Court at Cambridge in octobe[r] last After the Attachment Courts Judgment Reasons of Appeale & euidences in the Case produced were read Comitted to the Jury & are on file wth the Records of this Court the Jury brought in their virdict they found for the plaintiff Reuersion of the former Judgment & Costs of Courts thirty sixe shillings & 8[d]

Cox Conta : Hiskett

Rowland Coxe plaintiff Cont[a] Daniel Hiskett defend[t] in an action of Appeale from the Judgment of the County Court in octobe[r] last after the Attachment Courts Judgment reasons of Appeale & euidences in the Case produced were Read Comitted to y[e] Jury & are on file wth the Records of this Court y[e] Jury brought in their virdict they found

filing to pay

* Error of the record for "defendant"? † Repeated in the record. ‡ Written over "Jn[o]."

§ In the papers in the case on file this name is "William Haddock." See Court Files Suffolk, No. 2386.

¶ This space left blank in the record. By the papers on file it appears the name was Edward Richards. See Court Files Suffolk No. 2370.

for the defend^{t} Confirmation of the former Judgm^{t} & Costs of Courts nineteen shilling & 6^{d}

Norden Con^{ta} Scottow

Samuel Norden plaintiff Conta Capt Joshua Scottow defend^{t} in an Action of Appeale from the Judg^{mt} of the Comissione^{r}s Court in Boston After the Attachment Courts Judgment Reasons of Appeale & euidences in the Case produced were Read Comitted to the Jury & are on file wth the Records of this Court the Jury brought in their virdict they found for the defend^{t} Confirmation of ye form^{r} Judgm^{t} tenn pounds mony damage & Costs of Court[s] twenty seuen shillings & 8^{d}

[205] 1685

Patteshall ag^{t} Hiskett

Richard patteshall plaintiff Con^{ta} Steven Heskett defend^{t} in an action of Appeale from the Judgment of the County Court in Boston &c After the Attachment Courts Judgment Reasons of Appeale & euidences in the Case produced were read Comitted to the Jury & are on file wth the Records of this Court the Jury brought in their virdict they found for y^{e} defendant Costs of Courts ninten* || shill || & nine penc

Harrison =

Wm Harrison plaintiff Contra the Courts sentenc wch being read & the euidences in the Case produced were read Comitted to the Jury & are on file wth the Records of this Court the Jury brought in their virdict they found the sajd Harrison Guilty of breach of y^{e} peace —

Hundlocke Contra Blayne & Hubbard

Edward Hunlorck || p his lawfull Atturney || p^{lt} Conta m^{r} Jno Hubbard merchant & John Blajne of ye Island of Je^{r}sy marriner or eithe^{r} of them defend^{t}s after the || Attachm^{t} Courts Judgment & euidences in the Case produced wth y^{e} Reasons were read Comitted to the Jury & are on file with the reccords of this Court the Bench declard they Confirmed the fforme^{r} Courts Judgm^{t} & Costs of Courts = †

Greene Con^{ta} Courts sent

Joseph Greene plaint Con^{ta} ye County Court of Boston^{s} sentence in octob last After the Courts sentenc Reasons of Appeale & euidences in the Case produced

---

* Written over "eleven."

† See p. [206] where this record is more fully entered.

were Read the plaintiff haueing his case to be trjed in open Court put it on this Issue y[t] he denyes y[t] he was not in the Toune at the time all wch put to the Jury they brought in their virdict they found Joseph Greene no[t] Guilty =

m[r] Richd wharton m[r] Hezekiah Vsher Daniel Turell Juñ Blacksmith & John white Joyne[r] plaintiffs ag[t] Joseph Smith deffend[t] in an Action of Appeale from the Judgment of the County Court in Boston defend[t] After the Attachm[t] Courts Judgment Reasons of Appeale & euidences in the Case produced were read Comitted to the Jury & are on file w[th] the Reccords of this Court the Jury brought in their virdict they found for the deffendant Confirmation of the form[r] Judgment & Costs of Courts

m[r] wharton & pl[t]ffs Conta Joseph Smith

The plaintiff[s] in open Court sajd they Atteinted the Jury whereof Bozoone Allen was foreman & gaue in their reasons w[ch] are on file And sajd m[r] Richard wharton m[r] Hezekiah vsher Daniel Turell Juñ & John white Joyner came & Joyntly & seuerally acknowledged themselues respectively bound in one hundred & seventy pounds money to the Treasure[r] of the Country for the time being and party[s] concerned that hauing Attainted the Jury whereof m[r] Bozoune Allen was foreman for error only in the Case betweene them & Joseph Smith on the Condition that they will prosecute their Attaint at the nex[t] Court of Assistants to effect as Attests

bond for ꝑsecution

Edw[d] Rawson secre[t]

[206] 1685

Samuel Nowell Esq[r] plaint Conta Gyles Goddard deffendant in an Action of Appeale from the Judgment of the County Court in Boston octobe[r] last. || Giles Godard being 3 times Called no[t] Appearing his bond was dec[lrd] forfeited* || After the Attachment Courts Judgment Reasons of Appeale & euidences in the Case produced were read Comitted to the Jury & are on file wth the Records of this Court the Jury brought in their virdict they found the defendant Guilty of defrauding sajd Nowell and betraying his trust in not deliuering vp three truncks which were Comitted to his trust and Care in wch were sundry Rich & choyce Goods of diuers sorts and also Gold & Siluer for all wch doe finde for the plaintiff one hundred & twenty pounds damag in mony & Costs of Courts

m[r] Nowell ag[t] Gyles Goddard

* Written in the margin.

ffrancis Stepneys sent

ffrancis Stepney plaintiff In an action of Appeale from the sentenc & Judgment of the County Court* in Boston January last After the Courts sentenc Reasons of Appeale & euidences in the Case were read (the plaintiff being sick & not Appearing at ye Court when Called & also ye like Called at ye Courts Adjournmt 26 of march 86 Cirtifficat being Given of his Illnes & his surtys for ꝓsecution pr[ess]ing that they may be dischardged refusing to stand further bound nor willing to proceed ^ the Court declared the suertjes were dischardged & that the Judgment of the County Court agt sd stepney to stand good against him

Ansr to mr Antho checkleys mo[ti]on er

In Ansr to ye motion or peticōn of mr Anthony checkley It was voted that his fine of tenn pounds to the Country in the Case of Attaint shall be respitted till the end of the next sessions of ye Genell Court past E R S

mrs Margaret Hundlock Conta: mr Jno Hubbard & Jno bolajne. =

mrs margaret Hundlock wife & Atturney to mr Edward Hundlock plaint Conta mr Jno Hubbard & John Belajne deffendts in an Action of Appeale from the Judgment of the County Court as to a nonsuit after the Attachment Courts Judgment Reasons of Appeale & euidences in the Case produced were read ~~Comitted to~~ ‖ er ‖ The magists Confirmed the former Judgmt of the County Court at Boston & Costs of Courts = †

Morgans Indictmt

James morgan being Indicted by the name of James Morgan of Boston for not hauing the feare of God before his eyes being Instigated by the diuill ffor that he not hauing the feare of God before his eyes ‡ on the tenth day of december last in the house of constante worcester widdow in Boston did about ten of the clocke that night wickedly maliciously & felloniously wound kill & murder

[207] 1685

Joseph Johnson Butcher of sajd Boston Butcher § by running a spitt into his belly a litle aboue the navell of which wound about three dayes after the sajd Johnson djed as in & by the euidences more fully

* Written over "Court of Assistants."

† See above p. [205]. There was only one case at the County Court.

‡ Repeated in the record. § Repeated in the record.

may Appeare Contrary to the peace of ou^r Soueraigne Lord the king his Croune and Dignity the lawe of God & of this Jurisdiction being at the Barr & holding vp his hand whiles Indicted pleaded not Guilty Referd himself for trjall to God & ye Country hauiḡ his optunity to object against any of the Jury wch he saw no Cause to doe only ag^t one Isayah Toy y^t had binn of ye Jury of Inquest Ebenezar Billing was sett in his roome after the Jury had pervsed the euidences^ brought in their virdict they found the prisoner at the barr guilty according to Indictment he was Remanded unto prison & being thenc brought to the barr y^e Goūno^r Askt him what he had to say why sentenc of Death should not be pronounct ag^t yow = The Goūno^r proceeded saying yow James morgan for the murther yow haue Comitted are to Goe henc to y^e place whence yow Came & from thence to the Gallowes & there be hangd by y^e neck till yow be dead & y^e Lord haue mercy on you^r soule

The secretary was ordered to Issue out his warrant to the marshall Generall to take a sufficient guard wth him on the 11th Instant presently after ye lecture & see execution of this sentence ꝑ wch was donn Accordingly

Mary fflood the wife of Henry ffloodl of Boston in the County of Suffolke in New England Cordwayner was Indicted by the name of mary fflood for that shee no^t hauing the feare of God before hir eyes & being Instigated by the diuill on the 28th day of february last early in the morning did wickedly maliciously & fœloniously kill and murder thy youngest daughter of about thirteene weekes old by giving it seuerall stroakes of thy ffist Contrary to the peace of our Soueraigne Lord the king his Croune & Dignitje the lawes of God and of this Jurisdiction holding vp hir hand at the Barr & pleaded not guilty saying she would be trjed by God & the Country hauing optunity to object ag^t any of the Jury wch she sajd shee had none. = the Case & euidences given in ag^t the prisoner at the barr was read Comitted to the Jury who after Consideration thereof they brought in their virdict they found the prisone^r at the barr no^t Guilty according to Indictment

[208] 1685

Joseph Indian of martjns vineyard ^ by the name of Joseph Indean for that he not hauing the feare of God before their* eyes and being instigated by the divill on the 12th or 13th of february last did wickedly maliciously & felloniously kill & murder his squaw or wife (she being

* So in the record.

at the watchhouse on the necke in Boston at nine of the clocke at night well and that he after that time drew her the sajd squaw on the ground to the ljme house a considerable distance and left hir there with seuerall mortall wounds on hir head whereof on the 15th of sajd february early in the morning ^ was found dead contrary to the peace of our Soueraigne Lord the king his Croune and Dignity the laues of God & of this Jurisdiction the sajd Indian holding vp his hand at the barr pleaded to this Indictment not guilty saying he would be trjed by God and the Country: there being a Jury of one halfe English & the other halfe Indians had his libe'ty to object any ^ them being Called one by one but making no objection the euidences being Read yt were produced agt him & Comitted to v they brought in their virdict thereupon they found him not Guilty according to Indictment but found him Guilty of vnnaturalenes and barbarous Cruelty towards his wife. = So was Remanded to prison Againe & thenc brought to the barr where & when the honnorbl Gou̅nor sajd howeuer Joseph Indean yow are cleered by the Jury, yet they found yow Guilty of cruelty to your wife The Court sentents yow to be seuerely whipt with thirty stripes and also pay forty shillings mony for ye ꝓsecution and that within a weeke or be sold by the Treasurer out of this Country to any of his majtjes plantations dischardging your prison ffees =

4 mrch 85. E R S Andrew Pittymee Indian Interpreter was sworne In Court truely to Interpret what the Court declares to him and also what the prisoner at the Barr Answe'rs are to the Court =

This Court Adjourned by the Gou̅nor &c to the 26th of Instant march the Court mett at the time 26 march 1686

[209] 1686

Att An Adjourment of the Court of Assistants ‖ & Co[uncil] ‖ held at Boston the 26th of march 1686.

present
Symon Bradstreet Esqr Gou̅
Tho Danforth Esqr dept Gou
Daniel Gookin
wm Stoughton
Joseph dudley
Humphry Dauy
Jno Richards
James Russell
wm Johnson
Jno Hathorne
Samuel Seawall
— — — —

Jno Lugger clarke of his majtjes Customes by his bill of Information Given into this Court declares that the ship Elisabeth of Boston whereof Thomas Bossinger was master lately Imported certeine forreigne Com̄oddtje vizt wine Brandy &c without due entrys & cleering from England Contrary to the act of ye fiueteenth of Charles the second &c for which sajd ship ljes vnder seizure humbly desiring that the ‖sd ‖ ship

& Appurtenances in all respects may receive tryall & Condemnation according to that law This Case by Consent of sajd partjes Came to tryall And after the Cour[t] had duely pervsed & heard the wittnesses did Judge the sajd ship Elisabeth with hir tackle & Appurtenances to hir belonging to be forfeited to his Maj[ty] and according to the aboue recited law did passe sentence of Condemnation on hir accordingly

m[r] Richard wharton & m[r] Daniel Allen of Boston merchants by their libell exhibbited to the Court & Attachment therevpon dated 12[th] march $\frac{85}{6}$ plaint[ffs] Conta w[m] marshall Enock more Sarah Soley widdow &c = After the libell & Attachment & sumons were read‸

[*Blank space.*]

Att this Court Information was Given in as followeth the Hon-no[r]ble Gove[r]no[r] and magis[ts] lately Assembled in the County Court at Boston doe Informe the Council now Assembled that m[r] Samuell shrimpton being sumoned to Attend sajd Court in a Civill Case in a Proud & contemptuous manner declared himself that there was no Gou̅no[r] & Company of which the Gou̅ had a Certifficat or Citation & therefore he would make no Answer to the sumons Giuen him for his Appearance & Added therevnto seuerall reviling words = The Cour[t] ordered the marshall to goe & tell m[r] shrimpton that the Cour[t] would speake wth him, w[ch] he did & returnd he was not at home Gonn to Nodles Island & sajd he had left Information & that they sajd they would send to him but he not Com̅ing the Court Adjourned to the nex[t] fifth day at three of the clocke & ordered the Secretary to lett m[r] shrimpton know y[t] at the time he should attend the Court p[r]sently after the lecture = & warrant Issued out to y[e] marshall Gen̅ll for y[t] end 27 of sd march & is on file

1[st] of aprill 1686 y[e] Court mett at the time

present the Gou̅no[r]
dep[t] Gou̅no[r]
w[m] stoughton
Joseph dudley
Jn[o] Richards
James Russell
Elisha Cooke
w[m] Johnson
Elisha Hutchinson
Samuel Seawall =
— — — —

y[e] marshall Generall Returnd his warrant as to m[r] shrimpton who Appeared & gaue in his ‖ paper & ‖ Answer and was = I did say there is no Gouerno[r] and Company of this place in being that the Gou̅no[r] had a signiffication of the dissolution of the charter of this Colony And that I was not willing to submitt to lawes made since that day, And wha[t] I sajd to the Gou̅n[r] as to wrong donn I then explained to be only in refference to an Arbitration wherein his Honnor was one & wthout any reflection wth respect to any Judiciall Act and if any heat then expressed it was occasioned by my being called after two or three theives And as I apprhended at mr sargeants chojce the Gou̅no r Asking him if he would then haue his Cause called saying there was but a thin Court not wth standing the fiue senior magists of the Court were present*

[210] 1686

The Court of Assistants & Council Adjourned to the 15 of sajd Aprill at three of the clock in the Afternoone †

present
Symon Bradstreet Esqr Gou̅
Tho Danforth Esqr dept Gou̅
Daniel Gookin
Willjam stoughton
×Joseph dudley ‡
Humphry Davy
Jno Richards
James Russell
×Sam Apleton ‡ Esqrs
Robert Pyke
Elisha Cooke
Wm Johnson
Elisha Hutchinson
Samuell Seawall
— — — —
persons Returnd to serve on ye Grand jury 17 Aprill 86 & sworn were =
Capt Pen Tounsend
2 James Hill
3 Tho Jenner
4 wm ffoster
5 Jno watson
[6] Sam Champney
7 Sam Wms sen̅
8 Richd Hall
9 Clemt maxfeild
[10] Jno Richards
11 [James §] Tounsend
Joseph Child. =
— — — —
persons Returnd to serve on the Jury of Trjalls: were —
mr Edwd willey
Jno Atwood
Jno moore

Att A Court of Assistants or Admiralty held at Boston on the 15th of April 1686

The Court mett at the time and at the request of mr willjam woodrope of the Island of St Christophers now Resident in Boston A Court of Admiralty is granted him against mr John Keech of Boston in the County of Suffolk merchant And also Against mr Timothy Thorneto[n] of the sajd Boston in New England & County ^ merchant defendants &c to be held at sajd Boston on the 22th of Instant Aprill at three of the clock in the Afternoone = he the sajd woodrope giving in his libell & Caution seasonably to the secretary which he sajd woodrope did the next day being the 16th Instant as certified at the bottome of sajd libell may Appeare

At this Adjournmt mr Samuel Shrimpton Appeared in Court ^ an Information wch is on file & was Read which when he had heard sajd he denjed all that was therein and sajd he had the last time Given in his Answer in writting the seuen seu̅ll euidences sumoned appeard all but ¶ & Gaue in their euidences wch were read & sworne to bef[o]re him & are on file: he sajd he would be trjed by a Jury = which the Court Granted him & ordered the secretary to Issue out his warrants to the seuerall Tounes for a Grand Jury & Jury of tryalls wch was donn in vsuall

* This record appears to have been crowded into a blank space left at the bottom of the page.
† This paragraph is written at the upper left-hand corner of the page.
‡ See below, record of April 17, 1686. § Written over "Joseph." ¶ Blank space in the record.

form & are on file = And ordered mr Shrimpton to Giue fiue hundred pounds bond then on the 17th Instant to Appeare & Answer what shall be then lajd to his charge & both Court & Council Adjourned to 17th Instant at 8 of the clocke in the morning.

Ephraim Sarl
Nathani Cary
Edwd wilson
francis moore
Dani Champney
Samuel Clap
wm Ryall
Ebenezar white
Sam: Jennison

17th of Aprill 1686 The Court mett at yt time, the Gou̅no^r & magistrates the same as Aboue except 2 wth ys × :* warrant Issued out on ys date to ye mrshall Gen[erall]

The Grand Jury brought in their Indictment. =

Wee the Grand Jury for our soueraigne Lord the king in the Massachusets Colony doe present & Indict mr Samuell Shrimpton of Boston merchant for yt he at the County Court sitting in Boston on the 22th of march last in a contemptuous violent & seditious manner & wth a loud voyce did in open Court say that he was brought there by mr Sargants order & not by ye Courts & that he denyed any such thing in being as Gouernor & Company of this Colony and that he stood there to Justify it & denyed their power, and they might send him to prison if they pleased wch words in the same manner he repeated ~~againe~~ ‖ ouer ‖ & ouer againe wth diuers other seditious words & expressions as by the euidences will & may Appeare thereby defaiming the Generall Court & sajd County Court & caused such a tumult in the Court as euidently tended to the high breach of his Maj'jes Gouernment heere & all this Contrary to the peace of our Soueraigne Lord the king his Croune & Dignitje & the laues of God & of this Jurisdiction & particcularly the law title Courts Sect 6: wee find this bill & leaue it to further Tryall

Penn Tounsend foreman In the name of the rest of the Jury

It is ordered the secretary Issue out his warrant to the marshall Generall Jno Green to Attach the person of mr Samuel Shrimpton & that he Giue his bond wth suertjes in a thousand pounds to Appeare

[211] 1686

before the Court on 5th day next at two of the clock to which time the Court is Adjourned & on his refusall to give bond accordingly to Co̅mitt him to prison till the time of the Adjournment = mr shrimpton Appeared not = †

* See above in the margin of record of April 15, 1686.

† See note on next page.

The Court of Assistants is Adjournd till ye 22 Instant at two of ye clock *

Att an Adjournment of the Court of Assistants ‖ or Admiralty ‖ held at Boston 22th of Aprill 1686

present ye Gov̄nor
Tho Danforth Esqr dept Gov̄

Dani: Gookin
wm stoughton
‖ Joseph dudley ‖
Humphry Davy
James Richards
‖ Samuel Nowell ‖
James Russell
Robert Pike
Elisha Cooke
wm Johnson
Elisha Hutchinson
Samuel Seawall
} Esqrs

— — — —

Jurymen Returnd to serve at this Court of Assistants or Admiralty & sworne were

— — — —

mr Edward willey
Jno Atwood
Jno moore
Ephraim Serll
Nathanl Cary
Edward Wilson
ffrancis moore
Daniel Champney
Samuel Clap
wm Ryall
Ebenezer white
Samuel Jennison

— — — —

The libell presented to this Court by mr willijam woodrope of the Island of St Xtophers now Resident in Boston & ounor of the sloope the Brothers Adventure together wth the Attachment bearing date the 16th Instant thereby Complayning against Jno keech of sajd Boston in the County of Suffolke in New England merchant for that he the sajd keech by his Attachment bearing date the first day of october last 1685 did Attach his sajd sloope Brothers Adventure to the County Court held at Cambridge the 6th day of sajd octobe' vnder pretence of a debt due to him from the estate of Sa[nct]illo Heynes of sajd Island of St Xtophe'rs & there recouered a Judgment & execution therevpon & thereby deteyning the same vessell as in his sajd libell more fully & largely is expressed to his the sajd woodropes great dam̄age The Court on pervsall & on due Consideration of the euidences & pleas in the Case made & produced by both partjes wth the virdict of the Jury there vpon doe Adjudge declare & decree that the sajd sloope brothers Adventure with all hir tackling Apparrell & furniture to hir belonging as deliuered by sajd Execution to sajd keech be in all respects deliv̄ed vp to the sajd wm woodrope, as also that the sajd Keech pay vnto him the sajd woodrope the sume of twelue pounds ten shillings mony dam̄age & fiueteen pounds money as Costs of Court in all twenty seuen pounds tenn shillings money. =

The lybell of mr wm woodrope of the Island of St Xtophe'rs now Resident in Boston in the County of Suffolke in New England & ounor of the sloope brothers Adventure together with the Attachment bearing date the 16th day of this Instant Aprill thereby Complayning against mr Tymothy Thornton of sajd Boston in the County aforesajd merchant

* The last two paragraphs appear to be crowded into the blank spaces at the bottom of p. [210] and at the top of p. [211].

ffor that he the sajd Thornton by his Attachment bearing date the first day of octobe[r] last 1685 did Attach his sajd sloop Brothe[r]s Adventure to the County Court held at Cambridge the 6[th] of sajd october vnder pretence of a debt due to him from the estate of sa[nct]illo * Heynes of sajd Island of St Xtophe[r]s & there recouered a Judgment & execution therevpon and thereby deteyning the sajd vessell as in his sajd Lybell more ffully & largely is expressed to his the sajd woodropes great damage The Court on pervsall & due Consideration of the euidences & pleas in the Case made & produced by both partjes with the virdict of the Jury therevpon doe Adjudge declare & decree that the sajd sloope brothe[r]s Adventure with all hir tackling Apparrell & furniture to hir belonging as deliu[r]ed by execution to sajd Thornton be in all respects deliuered vp to the sajd w[m] woodrope, as also that he the sajd Thornton pay vnto him the sajd woodrope the sume of twelue pounds tenn shillings money dam̃age & fiueteene pounds money as Costs of Court in all twenty seven pounds tenn shillings mony:
both the aboue & this decree past by the Court of Assistants or Admiralty As aforesajd

Attests

Edward Rawson Secret

[212] 1686

The marshall Generall made returne of his warrant relating to m[r] Samuel shrimpton w[ch] is on file the Indictment was Read

m[r] Samuel shrimpton Appeared at this Courts Adjournm[t] as on the other side & exprest himself that he had many objections against the legality of the Indictment

[The rest of this page and pages [213], [214], and [215] are blank in the original.]

[From here to page [238] inclusive the record is in the handwriting of Isaac Addington.]

[216]

Grand jury Sworn. Bernard Trott ffforeman Moses Paine

At a Court of Assistants for the Colony of the Massachusetts Bay, held at Boston the 24th. of Decemb[r]. 1689. continued upon Adjournm[t]. from the 3[d].

* Or Samvillo.

Thomas Harwood
Arthur Mason
John Marion Senr.
John Capen
Isaac Jones
Robert Pierpont
William Garey
Sam^{ll}. Stone sen^{r}.
Richd Danie
Richard Lowden
Henry Spring
— — — —
Jury of Tryals sworn.
Elizur Holyoke Foreman/.
Edward Thomas
Jacob Melyne
Isaia Tay
Joseph Griggs
Sam^{ll}. Craft
James Bird
Joseph Weekes
Sam^{ll}. Hasting
Edwd. Winchip
W^{m}. Welsteed sen^{r}.
Benj^{a}. Garfield.
— — — —

of September 1689./. Anno R:R:^{s} et Reginae Gulielmi et Mariæ nunc Angliæ &c^{a}. p^{m}m^{o}.

Present.

Thomas Danforth Esqr. Deputy Govern^{r}.

John Richards Samuel Appelton William Johnson Samuel Sewall John Phillips Jeremiah Swayne	Esq^{rs}.	Nathan^{l}. Saltonstal James Russell Elisha Cooke Elisha Hutchinson John Smith —	Esq^{rs}.

Gibson Fawer P^{lt}. vers^{s}. George Cable Def^{t}. — on Appeale from the Judgem^{t}. of the County Court for Suffolke holden at Boston 30th. July. 1689./ where he brought his suite against the said George Cable for ‖ deteining in his possession & refusing to give the ‖ Pl^{t}. Possession of a House Shop Warehouse and Garden in Boston on the North side of the drawbridge, And Judgement was given against him for costs of Court. Both party^{s} appeared by their Attourney^{s}. and joyned issue The Jury brought in their Verdict and found for the Appellant, ye Revertion of the former Judgement & the Possession of the House, Shop, warehouse and Garden sued for and costs of Courts; allowed Forty two shillings and two pence./ Execution issued 31°. Decemb^{r}. 1689./

1 Jury

Jury of Tryals sworn./
L^{t}. Jonath^{n}. Remington Foreman./
Nath^{ll}. Thayer
Samuel Lillie
Thomas Downe
W^{m}. Griggs
John Ruggels sen^{r}.

[217]

John Watson
Joseph Leeds
Hopestill Humphry
John Simpson
Daniel Warren
John Bond

John Usher Esqr. P^{lt}. Vers^{s}. John Frizell Def^{t}. — on Appeale from the Judgement of the County Court for Suffolke holden at Boston 30th. July 1689. Both party's by their Attourny^{s}. joyned issue. The Jury brought in their Verdict. They found for the Defend^{t}. Confirmation of the former Judgement being Twenty pounds five shillings & eight pence money and cost of Courts allowed ^

1. Jury

There being shown forth an Order from his Majesty in Councill of the 26th. of September ult. Comanding the Magistrates at Boston in New-England & others whome it may concern to take notice of his Royal will and pleasure that the Appell^t. John Usher Esqr. be not molested in his person or Estate upon the acco^t. of his being Treasurer & Receiver General of his Maties. Revenue in New-England until his Maties. pleasure be be further known ^

Jotham Grover of Boston Brasier Pl.
vers^us.
Thomas Bulkley of Boston Merch^t. Def^t.
} on appeale
from the Judgement of the County Court for Suffolke holden at Boston the 30th. of July. 1689. The partys joyned issue The Jury brought in their Verdict, They found for the Def^t. Confimation of the former Judgement being seven pounds thirteen Shillings nine pence in money and cost of Courts 2 Jury

Samuel Massey late Prison keeper of Boston Pl^t
vers^us.
William Robie of Boston Merch^t Def^t
} on appeale from the Judgement of the County Court for Suffolke holden at Boston the 30th. July. 1689. The party^s. appeared and joyned issue, The Jury brought in the Verdict. They found for the Defend^t. Confirmation of the former Judgement being Ten pounds in money || damage || and costs of Courts 2 Jury.

Hugh Stone of Andover Husbandman being Indicted by the Juro^rs. for our Sovereign Lord and Lady the King and Queen, upon their oath's, for that the said Hugh Stone upon the twentyeth day of April. 1689. at Andover afores^d. &c. did feloniously kill and murder Hannah his wife, contrary to the peace of o^r. Sovereign Lord and Lady the King and Queen their Crown and dignity, the Law's of God and this Colony. —

Upon which Indictment the aforesaid Hugh Stone being arraigned, Pleaded Guilty, and was remanded back to Prison./ 25th. Decemb^r.

26° Decemb^r / the afores^d. Hugh Stone being brought to the Barr, The Court did Award that for the felony and murder aforesaid by him the said Hugh Stone committed as aforesaid, of which he hath confest himselfe guilty sentance of death be pronounced against him = which

[218]

was accordingly done by Thomas Danforth Esqr. Deputy Governo^r. That is to say, That he the afores^d. Hugh Stone be carried back to the place from whence he came and from thence to the place of Execution there to be hanged untill he be dead. — And Ordered that John Green Marshall Generall take care and see that this Sentance be duely executed upon the said Hugh Stone on Thursday ye. second of January next; And that the Secretary (being thereto appointed by Law) signe a warrant for the same. /.

25th. 10br/. Hannah Hutchinson wife of Samuel Hutchinson of Andover being Indicted by the Jurors. for our Sovereign Lord and Lady the King and Queen upon their Oath's, For that the said Hannah Hutchinson at Andover aforesd. before the felony and murder comitted by Hugh Stone of Andover aforesd. upon Hannah his late wife, That is to say, upon the nineteenth daye of April. 1689. the same Hutchinson at Andover aforesd. unto the ffelony and murder aforesd. comitted by the said Hugh Stone as aforesd. him the said Hugh Stone did feloniously and maliciously excite abett and procure &ca. prout in the Indictment [&] Upon which Indictment the said Hannah Hutchinson being arraigned, pleaded not guilty and put her selfe upon Tryal by God and the Country. The first Jury of Tryals were called whereof mr Elizur Holioke is Foreman, and the Prisoner makeing no challenge against any of them, They were Sworn for her Tryal, and past upon her. The Jury brought in their Verdict, That is to say, That they do not find Hannah Hutchinson Guilty of the crime whereof she hath been Indicted. — The Court Ordered that the said Hannah Hutchinson be discharged upon her paying of ffees & charges.

26th. 10br. / Robin Negro Servant of Andrew Gardner of Muddy River being Indicted by the Jurors. for our Sovereign Lord and Lady the King and Queen, upon their Oaths, For that the said Robin Negro at Muddy River aforesd. upon the second day of August. 1689. did slay and kill John Cheeny of Cambridge, giveing him a mortall wound on the head with a stick, of which wound the said John Cheeny languished and on the sixth day of the said month of August dyed & prout in the Indictment. Upon which Indictment the said Robin negro being arraigned pleaded not guilty and put himselfe upon Tryal

[219]

by God and the Country. The first Jury of Tryalls whereof mr Elizur Holyoke is ffforeman were called, and all appeared and answered save Edward Thomas, in whose roome Nathanl. Thayer was put on, and the prisoner makeing no challenge against any of them, they were sworn for his Tryal, and past upon him; The Jury brought in their Verdict That is to say, They find Robin Negro guilty of manslaughter.

mr Edward Thomas One of the Jurors sumoned for the Tryals at this Court, makeing default in appearance when called (at the Impaneling of a Jury to pass upon Robin the Negro) was fined five shillings./.

The Court Adjourned unto Tuesday the seventh day of January next at nine in the morning./

Anno R: Rs. et Reginæ Gulielmi et Mariae pmo. Tuesday the seventh of January. 1689.

The Court met by Adjournmt. and sat de die in diem (Except the Sabbath) untill the seventeenth of ye same month.

Holden by Thomas Danforth Esqr Deputy Governor.

James Russell		John Richards—		
Samuel Appelton		William Johnson—		
John Hathorne	Esqrs	Elisha Hutchinson	Esqrs	
Samuel Sewall		John Phillips —		
John Smith		Jeremiah Swayne.		

Grand jury Sworn.
mr. Bernard Trott Foreman
Moses Paine
Tho: Harwood
Arthur Mason
John Marion Senr:
John Capen
Isaac Jones
Robt. Pierpont
William Garey
Richd Lowden
Henry Spring
John Alden Senr.
Richd. Buckley
Samuel Lynde
Ephraim [S]ale

8o. Janry.

Severall Bills of Indictment against divers prisonrs. for piracy and murder were comitted to the Grand jury./.

9th. the Grand jury brought in their bills of Indictment & were dismist untill munday the 13th instant at one oclock./.

9o. Thomas Hawkins of Boston marrinr being presented & Indicted by the Jurors for our Sovereign Lord and Lady the King and Queen upon their Oath's, vizt that the sd Thomas Hawkins upon ffriday the ninth day of August, 1689. upon the high seas that is to say, about three Leagues from halfe way Rock in ye. massachusetts Bay upon the Katch Mary of Salem Hellen Chard master and upon the said Master and men being = in

[220]

Jury of Tryals sworn.
Elizur Holyoke Foreman
Jacob Melyne
Isaia Tay
Joseph Griggs
Samuel Craft
James Bird
Samll. Hasting
Joseph Weekes
Edwd: Winchip
Wm. Welsteed Senr.
Benja. Garfield.
Tho: Downe
— — — —

in number about five of their Majties. Liege people, then and there in the King and Queens peace and about their lawfull Imployments being, with force and Armes an assault did make and as a Felon and Pirate with guns and Swords did Enter and the said Katch with all her appurces. and Lading of ffish being the value of sixty pounds of the goods and chattels of their Maties. Liege people from the said Master feloniously and piratically tooke and carryed away contrary to the peace of our Sovereign Lord and Lady the King and Queen their Crown and dignity and the Laws and Statutes in that behalfe made and provided. The aforesaid Thomas Hawkins being arraigned at the Barr upon the said Indictment pleaded not guilty and put himselfe upon Tryal by God and the Country. A Jury was ca'ld and Sworn to pass upon him (Elizur Holyoke being foreman of said Jury^ the Evidences, were sworn and the case comitted. The Jury gave in their Verdict, Vzt. They find Thomas Hawkins Guilty of the Piracy whereof he hath been Indicted. The Court Adjudged the said Thomas Hawkins to have the Sentance of death passed upon him (which was

17o Janry

accordingly pronounced against him by the Deputy Governor.) That is to say, That he said Thomas Hawkins be returned to the place from whence he came and from thence be carryed to the place of Execution and there be hanged by the neck

23d.

untill he be dead. The Court likewise Ordered that John Green Marshall Generall cause this Sentance to be Executed upon the said Thomas Hawkins on Munday the Twenty Seventh of this Instant January, And that the Secretary (being thereto by Law appointed) signe warrant for the same./

John Newhall tertius of Lynn yeoman and Thomas Witt of the same place yeoman being presented and Indicted by the Jurors for our sovereign Lord and Lady the King and Queen upon their Oath's That is to say, That the said John Newhall tertius and Thomas Witt upon the fifteenth day of Novembe^{r}. 1688. in the s^{d}. Town of Lynn at the House of Theophilus Baily, not haveing the fear of God before their Eyes, but being led by the instigation of the devil of their malice forethought upon the body of Ralph King jun^{r}. of Lynn afores^{d}. with force and Arms a violent assault did make and with their hands Feet and Knees did strike kick, stamp and crush the said Ralph King jun^r. thereby giveing him many grievous and mortall wounds and bruises of which wounds and bruises he did grievously Languish untill the 22th day of the said November and then of the afores^d. mortall wounds and bruises dyed. And so the said John Newhall tertius and

[221]

Thomas Witt of their malice forethought the said Ralph King junio^r. in manner and forme afores^d. did feloniously kill and murther contrary to the peace of our Sovereign Lord and Lady the King and Queen their Crown and dignity the Laws of God and this Colony. The afores^d John Newhall tertius and Thomas Witt being brought to the Barr and severally arraigned upon the afores^d. Indictment, thereto severally pleaded not guilty and put themslves upon Tryal by God and the Country The Jury was ca'ld, (m^r. Elizur Holyoke ffforeman) and sworn to pass upon their Tryal, the Evidences were sworn and the case comitted. The Jury gave in their Verdict upon Each of them severally. V^zt. The Jury find John Newhall tertius guilty of manslaughter. The Jury find Thomas Witt Guilty as an accessory of manslaughter. Ordered that the said John Newhall Tertius pay two third parts of the charges of prosecution amounting to the sume of Thirty six pounds nineteen shillings and ffour pence; That the said Thomas Witt pay one third part of the charges of prosecution amounting to the sume of Eighteen pounds nine shillings and Eight pence, the whole being ffifty ffive pounds nine shillings. And that they pay their Prison charges and fees of Court and remain in custody untill this order be performed.

Thomas Pound of Boston marriner being Indicted by the Jurors for our Sovereign Lord and Lady the King and Queen upon their Oath's by three severall bills of Indictment, as follow^th. That is to say. 1st. That he s^d Thomas Pound upon ‖ friday ‖ the ninth day of August 1689 on the high sea's ‖ vz^t ‖ about three Leagues from halfe way Rock in the Massachusetts Bay, upon the Katch Mary of Salem Hellen Chard master and upon the s^d. master and men with force and Armes an Assault did make And as a Felon and pirate wth. swords and Guns did enter, and the s^d. Katch wth her appur^ces. and Lading of Fish being the value of sixty pounds of the goods and Chattels of their Majesties Liege people from the said Master feloniously tooke and carryed away &c^a. 2^d. Also that he said Thomas Pound upon the twenty seventh day of August. 1689. on the high sea's Vz^t. in martyns vineyard Sound, upon the Briganteen merrimack of Newbury John Kent master an Assault did make and with force and Armes the said Briganteen did Enter and out of the said Briganteen of the goods and Chattels of their Majesties Liege People to the value of fforty pounds feloniously & piratically from

[222]

from the s^{d}. John Kent did take and carry away. ℘^{a}. prout in ye Indictm^{t}. 3^{d}. Indict^{mt}. That the said Thomas Pound on the fourth day of October 1689. upon the high sea's That is to say, in Martyns Vineyard Sound upon the sloop Mary of Boston then sayling under their Maties. Colours and upon the Comander namely Samuel Pease and Company, then and there upon their Maties. Service, said Pound being under a Red fflagg which he in defiance of their ma^{ties}. Authority purposely put up at the head of the mast, with force and Armes an Assault did make and with Bulletts which he out of small Gun's feloniously shott the body of the said Samuel Pease in severall places did strike and mortally wound, of which mortall wounds the said Samuel Pease did grievously languish untill the twelfth day of the said October and then of the said mortall wounds dyed. And so the said Thomas Pound of his malice forethought on the day aforesaid the said Samuel Pease in manner and forme afores^{d}. did feloniously kill and murther contrary to the peace of our sovereign Lord and Lady the King and Queen, their Crown and dignity, the laws of God and this Colony, —. The said Thomas Pound, being arraigned at the Barr upon Each of said Indictments severally, confes't himselfe guilty of the charge laid in his Second Indictment as afores^{d}. relating to the Briganteen Merrimack John Kent Master, unto the other two Indictments pleaded not guilty and put himselfe on Tryal by God and the Country. The Jury were called and Sworn, who upon a full hearing of the Evidences sworn on behalfe of their ma^{ties}. and what was said by the prison^{r}. in his defence, brought in their Verdicts and found the s^{d}. Thomas Pound guilty of the Felony and piracy whereof he hath been Indicted; And also guilty of the felony and murder whereof he hath been Indicted. The Court adjudged the said Thomas Pound to have the sentance of death pronounced against him (which was accordingly declar^{d}. by the Deputy Govern^{r}.) That is to say, That he said Thomas Pound be returned to the place from whence he came and from thence

Jury of Tryals Sworn.
Elizur Holyoke Foreman.
Isaia Tay
Joseph Griggs
Samuel Craft
James Bird
Joseph Weekes
Samuel Hasting
Edward Winchip
W^{m}. Welsteed Senr.
Benj^{a}. Garfield
Thomas Downe
Nath^{ll}. Thayer.
— — — —

17th. Jan^{ry}.

be carryed to the place of Execution and there be hanged by the neck untill he be dead. /

23^{d}. The Court likewise ordered that John Green marshall Generall cause this sentance to be executed upon the s^{d}. Thomas pound — on Munday the twenty seventh of this instant January and that the secretary (being thereto by Law appointed $_{\wedge}$ signe warrant for the same.

[223]

13° Thomas Johnston of Boston Marrin^{r} Indicted by the Jurors for o^{r}. Sovereign Lord and Lady the King and Queen upon their Oath's by three severall Indictments.

1st Indictm^{t}. That the said Thomas Johnston upon the ninth day of August 1689 on the high Sea's that is to say, about three Leagues from halfe way Rock in the Massachusetts Bay upon the Katch Mary of Salem Hellen Chard master and upon the said master and men with force and Armes an Assault did make and as a Felon and Pirate with swords and Gun's did Enter and the said Katch with her appur^{ces}. and Lading of Fish being the value of Sixty pounds of the goods & Chattels of their ma^{ties}. Liege people from the said master feloniously did take and carry away &c^{a}. prout in the Indictm^{t}. 2^{d} Indictm^{t}. That the said Thomas Johnston on the twenty seventh day of August 1689, upon the high seas That is to say, in martyns Vineyard Sound upon the Briganteen merrimack of Newbury John Kent master an Assault did make and with ffforce and Armes did Enter and as a Felon and Pirate of the goods and Chattels of their ma^{ties}. Leige People of the value of Forty pounds from the said master did feloniously take and carry away &c^{a}. prout in the Indictm^{t}. 3^{d}. Indictm^{t}. That the said Thomas Johnston on the fourth day of October. 1689. on the high sea's, That is to say in martyns vineyard Sound upon the Sloop Mary of Boston then sayleing under their ma^{ties}. Colours and upon the Commander namely Samuel Pease and Company then and there upon their ma^{ties}. Service, said Johnston being under a Red fflagg which in defiance of their ma^{ties}. Authority was purposly put up at the head of the mast with force and Armes an assault did make and with bullets out of small Gun's which he feloniously shot, the body of the said Samuel Pease in severall places did strike and mortally wound, of which mortall wounds the said Samuel Pease did greivously Languish untill the twelfth day of the said October and then of the said Mortal wounds dyed and so the said Thomas Johns[t]on of his malice forethought on the day aforesaid in manner and forme afores[d]. did feloniously kill & murther, contrary to the peace of our Sovereign Lord and Lady the King and Queen their Crown and dignity, the Laws of God and of this Colony. The said Thomas Johnston was arraigned upon Each of said Indictments Severally and thereto pleaded not guilty and put himselfe upon Tryal by God and the Country. The Jury were called and Sworn who upon a full hearing of the evidences sworn on behalfe of their ma[ties]. and the defence made by the Prisoner, brought in their Verdicts and found the said Thomas Johnston guilty of the severall piracys whereof he stood Indict[d]. As also guilty of the Felony and Murder whereof he stood Indicted as afores[d]. The Court adjudged the said Thomas Johnston

y[e] former Jury. Eliz[r]. Holyoke Foreman &c[a]. onely Nath[a]. Thayer taken off and Jacob Melyne put on in his Roome.

17th day

[224]

to have the Sentance of death pronounced against ‖ him ‖ (which was accordingly pronounced by the Deputy Govern[r].) That is to say, That he said Thomas Johnston be returned to the place from whence he came & from thence be carryed to the place of Execution and there be hanged by the neck untill he be dead. The Court likewise ordered that John Green marshall Generall cause the afores[d]. sentance to be executed upon the afores[d]. Thomas Johnston on Munday the twenty seventh of January instant, And that the secretary (being thereto appointed by Law) signe warrant for the same. /

13[o]

Eleazer Buck marrin[r]. Indicted by the Jurors for our Sovereign Lord and Lady the King and Queen upon their Oath's by three severall Indictm[ts] viz[t]. That the said Eleazer Buck upon ffriday the ninth of August 1689 on the high sea's That is to say, about three Leagues from halfe way Rock in the Massachusetts Bay upon the Katch Mary of Salem Hellen Chard master and upon the s[d]. master and men their Majesties Liege People with force and Armes an Assault did make and as a Felon and Pirate with Guns and Swords did enter and the s[d]. Katch with all her appur[ces]. and Ladeing of Fish being the value of sixty pounds of the goods and chattels of their Ma[ties]. Liege people tooke & carryed away &c[a]. And that the said Eleazer Buck upon the twenty seventh day of August. 1689. on the high Sea's That is to say in Martin's Vineyard Sound upon the Briganteen merrimack of Newbury John Kent master an assault did make and with force and Armes did Enter and out of the said Briganteen of the goods and Chattels of their Majesties Liege People of the value of ffforty pounds from the said John Kent feloniously and piratically did take and carry away &c^{a}.

And that the said Eleazer Buck upon the fourth day of Octob^{r}. 1689 on the high sea's that is to say, in Martins Vineyard Sound, being under a Red Flagg in defiance of their ma^{ties}. Authority purposly put up at the head of the mast, upon the sloop Mary of Boston then sayleing under their ma^{ties}. Colours and upon the Comãnder namely Samuel Pease and Company then & there upon their ma^{ties}. service being, with force & armes an Assault did make &c. and of his malice forethought the said Samuel Pease did feloniously kill and murther, contrary to the peace of our Sovereign Lord and Lady the King and Queen their Crowne & dignity the Laws of God and of this Colony. The said Eleazer Buck was arraigned upon Each of said Indictments severally and to the first relating to the Katch Mary of Salem, pleaded guilty, unto the other two Indictments pleaded not guilty and

Jury of Tryals Sworn.
m^{r} Jon^{a}. Remington Foreman
Nath^{a}. Thayer
Sam^{ll}. Lillie.
w^{m} Griggs.
John Ruggles Senr.
John Watson
Joseph Leeds
Hopestill Humfrey
John Simpson
Daniel Warren
Richard Way.
John White./

[225]

put himselfe on Tryal by God and the Country. A Jury was cal'd and Sworn, Who upon a full hearing of the Evidences sworn on behalfe of their ma^{ties}. and the defence made by the prisoner, brought in their verdicts and found the said Eleazer Buck Guilty of the Felony and piracy whereof he stands indicted. As also Guilty of the Felony and murder whereof he stands Indicted. The Court adjudged the said Eleazer Buck to have the sentance of death pronounced against him (which was accordingly pronounced by the Deputy Governo^{r}.) That is to say, That the said Eleazer Buck be returned to the place from whence he came and from thence be carried to the place of Execution, and there be hanged by the neck untill he be dead. The Court likewise Ordered that John Green marshall Generall cause the afores^{d}. sentance to be Executed upon the said Eleazer Buck, on munday the twenty seventh of this instant January. And that the secretary (being thereto appointed by Law) Signe warrant for the same.

17th day

23th. day

John Sickterdam, being Indicted by the Jurors for our Sovereign Lord and Lady the King and Queen upon their Oath's, for feloniously and piratically takeing and carrying away the Katch Mary of Salem Hellen Chard ma^{r}. with appur^{ces}. and Ladeing of Fish being the value of sixty pounds of the goods and Chattels of their ma[ties]. Leige People, upon the ninth day of August. 1689. on the high sea's viz[t]. about three League's from halfeway Rock in the Massachusetts Bay. &c[a]. And that the said John Sickterdam upon the twenty seventy day of August. 1689. on the high sea's viz[t]. in Martyns Vineyard Sound, upon the Briganteen Merrimack of Newbury John Kent Master an assault did make and with force and Armes did Enter and out of the said Briganteen of the goods and Chattels of their Ma[ties]. Liege people of the value of Forty pounds from the said John Kent feloniously and piratically did take and carry away &c[a].

Also that the said John Sickterdam upon the fourth day of Octob[r]. 1689. on the high Sea's, that is to Say, in martyns vineyard Sound being under a Red ffagg in defiance of their ma[ties]. Authority purposly put up at the head of the mast, upon the sloop Mary of Boston then Sayling under their M[aties]. Colours, and upon the Comand[r]. namely Samuel Pease then and there upon their ma[ties]. Service being, with force and Armes an assault did make &c[a]. and of his malice forethought the said Samuel Pease did feloniously kill and murther, contrary to the peace of our Sovereign Lord and Lady the King and Queen their Crown and dignity, the Law's of God and of this Colony. Upon which aforesaid three Indictments the s[d]. John Sickterdam being arraigned severally, thereto pleaded not guilty and put himselfe upon Tryal by God and the Country. The Jury was

The Jury of w[ch]. Elizur Holyoke is Foreman

[226]

was called and sworn, who upon a full hearing of the Evidences sworn on behalfe of their ma[ties] and the defence made by the Prisoner ^ The Jury brought in their Verdicts. That is to say, To the first Indictm[t]. about the Katch Mary, The Jury found the said John Sickterdam guilty of the Felony and piracy whereof he stood Indicted. To the second Indictm[t]. relating to the Briganteen Merrimack The Jury found the said John Sickterdam guilty of the Felony and piracy whereof he stood Indicted. To the third Indictm[t]. relating to the killing and murdering of Cap[ne]. Sam[ll]. Pease, The Jury found said John Sickterdam guilty of the Felony and murder whereof he stands Indicted. The Court Adjudged the said John Sickterdam to have the sentance of death pronounced against him (which was accordingly pronounced by the Deputy Govern[r].) That is to say, that he said John Sickterdam be returned to the place from whence he

17th. day

came and from thence be carried to the place of Execution and there be hanged by the neck untill he be dead.

William Dun being Indicted by the Juro^{rs}. for our Sovereign Lord and Lady the King and Queen 14^{d}. upon their Oath's, That is to say, That the said William Dun upon the 27th. day of August. 1689. on the high sea's that is to say in martyn's vineyard Sound, upon the Briganteen Merrimack of newbury John Kent master and his Company an assault did make and with force and Armes the said Briganteen did Enter and out of the said Briganteen of the goods and Chattels of their ma^{ties}. Liege people to the value of Forty pounds feloniously and piratically did take and carry away, contrary to the peace of our Sovereign Lord and Lady the King & Queen their Crown and dignity ℘^{a}. Upon which Indictment he was arraigned put himselfe upon Tryal and was acquitt^{d}. by the Jury.

William Dun being Indicted and arraigned upon two severall Bills found against him by the Grand jury, That is to say, That the said William Dun upon Friday the ninth of August. 1689. upon the high Seas (that is to say) about three Leagues from halfeway Rock in the Massachusetts Bay, then & there upon the Katch Mary of Salem Hellen Chard master and upon the said master and men ℘^{a}. with fforce and Armes an Assault did make and as a Felon and Pirate ~~did~~ with Guns and Swords did enter ℘^{a}. and the s^{d}. Katch with all her appur^{ces}. and Lading of Fish being of the value of sixty pounds of the goods and Chattels of their Maties. Liege people

[227]

did feloniously take and carry away contrary to the peace of our Sovereign Lord and Lady the King and Queen their Crown and dignity and the Law ℘^{a}./. The other Bill or Indictm^{t}. That the said William Dun on the fourth day of October. 1689. upon the high sea's That is to say in martins Vineyard Sound near Tarpolin Cove upon the Sloop Mary of Boston then Sayling under their Maties. Colours & upon the Com̄ander namely Samuel Pease and Company being in number about twenty of their Maties. Liege People then & there upon their Maties. service being ℘^{a}. with force and Armes an Assault did make, and with bullets which he out of small Guns feloniously shot, the body of the said Samuel Pease in severall places did strike and mortally wound of which mortall wounds he did grievously Languish untill the twelfth day of the said Octob^{r}. and then of the s^{d}. mortal wounds dyed. And so the Juro[rs]. upon their oath's do say that the said William Dun upon the high seas afores[d]. the day & year afores[d]. of his malice forethought the said Samuel Pease in manner and forme afores[d]. did feloniously kill and murther contrary to the peace of our Sovereign Lord & Lady the King and Queen their Crown and dignity and the Laws of God and this Colony. Upon which afores[d]. two severall Indictments the said William Dun was severally arraigned and to Each of them pleaded Guilty. The Court Adjudged the said William Dun to have the sentance of death pronounced against him (w[ch]. was accordingly pronounced by the Deputy Governo[r].) That is to say That he said William Dun be returned to the place from whence he came and from thence be carryed to the place of Execution and there be hanged by the neck untill he be dead./.

17th day

14d.

Richard Griffin of Boston Gun Smith being arraigned upon a Bill found against him by the Grand jury, That is to say, that the said Richard Griffin upon the fourth day of October 1689. upon the high seas, that is to say, in Martyns Vineyard Sound near Tarpolin Cove upon the Sloop Mary of Boston then Sayling under their Ma[ties]. Colours and upon the Comander namely Samuel Pease & Company being in number about twenty of their Ma[ties]. Liege people then and their upon their Ma[ties]. Service being p[ra]. with force and armes an Assault did make and with Bullets which he out of small Guns feloniously Shot, the body of s[d]. Samuel Pease did strike in severall places and mortally wound, of which mortal wounds the said Samuel Pease did grievously Languish untill the twelfth day of the said October and then of the said mortal wounds dyed, And so the Jurors upon their Oath's do say that the said [228] Richard Griffin upon the high Seas aforesaid the day and year aforesaid of his malice forethought the said Samuel Pease did feloniously kill and murther contrary to the Peace of our Sovereign Lord and Lady the King and Queen their Crown and dignity and the Laws of God and this Colony. The said Richard Griffin pleaded not Guilty and put himselfe upon Tryal by God and the Country. The Jury found said Richard Griffin guilty of the Felony and Murder whereof he stands Indicted./.

The Jury whereof Elizur Holyoke is Foreman....

14d.

Richard Griffin being arraigned upon a Bill found against him by the Grand jury, That is to say, that the said Richard Griffin upon Friday the ninth day of August. 1689. upon the high Sea's that is to say, about three Leagues from halfe way Rock in the Massachusetts Bay, then and there upon ye Katch Mary of Salem Hellen Chard Master and upon the said Mastr. and men &ca. with force and Arme's an Assault did make and as a Felon and Pirate with Guns and Swords did Enter and the said Katch with all her appurces. and Lading of Fish being the value of sixty pounds of the goods and Chattels of their Maties. Leige People from the said master feloniously and piratically did take and carry away &ca.

The said Richard Griffin pleaded not Guilty and put himselfe upon Tryal by God and the Country, And upon what himselfe confest on his Tryal without farther Evidence The Jury found said Richard Griffin Guilty of the Felony and piracy whereof he stands 17th day
Indicted. The Court Adjudgd. said Richard Griffin to have the sentance of death pronouncd. against him (which was accordingly pronounced by the Deputy Governor.) That is to say, That he said Richard Griffin be returned to the place from whence he came and from thence be carried to the place of Execution and there be hanged by the neck untill he be dead./.

Edward Browne being Indicted arraigned and 14d
tryed for feloniously killing and murthering of Capne. Samuel Pease, as is laid in said Indictment, said Edward Browne pleading not guilty, And William Warren and Samuel Watts witnessing for him that he was deteined on board the vessell as a Prisoner and a force put upon him; The Jury brought in their verdict That Edward Browne is not guilty: whereupon he was Acquitted ^ of his Imprisonment./.

The Jury whereof Jona. Remington is Foreman —

Benjamin Gallop, Abraham Adams junr. and Colburn Turell
[229]
making default in attending the Court to give Evidence for their Maties. against Richard Griffin and others then to come to their Tryal were Fined Ten shillings apeice. Afterwards upon hearing their Excuse the Court remitted the Fine./.

Daniel Lander being arraigned upon a Bill found 15d.
against him by the Grand-jury That is to say, That the said Daniel Lander upon Friday the ninth day of Augst. 1689. upon the high Sea's, That is to say about three Leagues from halfeway Rock

in the Massachusetts Bay, then and there upon the Katch Mary of Salem Hellen Chard Master and upon the said Master and men &c^a. with force and Armes an Assault did make and as a Felon and Pirate with Swords & Guns did Enter &c^a. And the s^d. Katch with all her appur^ces. and Ladeing of Fish being of the value of sixty pounds of the goods and Chattels of their Maties. Liege People from the said master feloniously and piratically tooke and carryed away, contrary to the peace of our Sovereign Lord and Lady the King and Queen their Crown and dignity and the Laws &c^a. The said Daniel Lander to this Indictment pleaded not guilty and put himselfe upon Tryal by God and the Country. The Jury found said Daniel Lander guilty of the Felony and piracy whereof he stands Indicted./.

Daniel Lander being arraigned upon a Bill found against him by the Grandjury, That is to say, That the said Daniel Daniel * Lander upon the fourth day of October. 1689. upon the high Sea's That is to say, in martins vineyard Sound near Tarpolin Cove, upon the Sloop Mary of Boston then Sayleing under their Maties. Colours, and upon the Comander namely Samuel Pease and Company being in number about twenty of their Maties. Liege People then and there upon their Maties. Service &c^a. with force & Armes an Assault did make and with Bullets which he out of small Guns feloniously shot the body of the said Samuel Pease in several places did strike and mortally wound, of which mortal wounds the s^d. Samuel Pease did grievously Languish untill the twelfth day of the said October and then of the said mortal wounds dyed. And so the Juro^rs. upon their Oath's do say that the said Daniel Lander upon the high seas afores^d. on the day and year afores^d. of his malice forethought the said Samuel Pease in manner and forme afores^d. did feloniously kill and murther contrary to the Peace of our Sovereign Lord and Lady the King and Queen their Crown and dignity the Law's of God and this Colony. To this Indictment he pleaded not guilty and put himselfe upon Tryal by God and the Country: The Jury found s^d. Daniel Lander guilty of the Felony and murder whereof he stands Indicted. The Court Adjudged the said Daniel Lander to have the sentance of death pronounced against him, (which was pronounced accordingly by the Deputy Governo^r.) That is to say, That he said Daniel Lander be returned to the

The Jury whereof m^r Elizur Holyoke is Foreman

17th. day

* Repeated in the record.

place from whence he came and from thence be carryed to the place of Execution and there be hanged by the neck untill he be dead.

[230]

William Warren being arraigned upon a Bill found against him by the Grand Jury That is to say, That the said William Warren upon Friday the ninth day of August. 1689. upon the high seas about three Leagues from halfeway Rock in the Massachusetts Bay, then and there upon the Katch Mary of Salem Hellen Chard Master and upon the said Master and men ℘r^{a}. with force and Armes an Assault did make and as a Felon and Pirate with Guns and swords did Enter ℘r^{a}. and the said Katch, with all her appur^{ces}. and Ladeing of Fish being the value of sixty pounds of the goods and 15^{d}.
Chattels of their Maties. Liege People from the said Master did feloniously and piratically take and carry away, contrary to the Peace of our Sovereign Lord and Lady the King and Queen their Crown and dignity and the Laws ℘r^{a}. To this Indictment he pleaded not guilty and put himselfe upon Tryal by God and the Country, The Jury found said William Warren Guilty of the Felony and Piracy whereof he stands Indicted. The Jury whereof m^{r} Jon^{a}. Remington is Foreman —

William Warren being arraigned upon a Bill found against him by the Grand jury, That is to say, That the said William Warren upon the fourth day of October. 1689. upon the high Seas, that is to say in Martyns Vineyard Sound near Tarpolin Cove upon the sloop Mary of Boston then Sayling under their Maties. Colours and upon the Comānder namely Samuel Pease and Company being in number about twenty of their Maties. Liege People then and there upon their Maties. service being, said William Warren under a Red Flagg which in defiance of their Maties. Authority was purposly put up at the head of the mast with force and Armes an Assault did make, and with Bulletts which he out of small Guns feloniously shot, the body of the said Samuel Pease in Severall places did strike and mortally wound, of which mortall wounds the said Samuel Pease did grievously Languish untill the twelfth day of the said October and then of the said Mortall wounds dyed; And so the Juro^{rs}. upon their Oath's do say That the said William Warren upon the high seas afores^{d}. on the day and year afores^{d}. of his malice forethought the said Samuel Pease in manner and forme aforesaid did feloniously kill and murther contrary to the peace of our Sovereign Lord and Lady the King and Queen their Crown and dignity & the Laws of God and this Colony. To this same Jury

Indictment he pleaded not guilty and put himselfe upon Tryal by God and the Country. The Jury found him guilty of the Felony and Murder whereof he stands Indicted. The Court Adjudged said William Warren to have the sentance of death pronounced against him (which was accordingly pronounced by the Deputy Governo[r].) that is to say, That he said William Warren be returned to the place from whence he came and from thence be carried to the place of Execution and there be hanged by the neck untill he be dead.

17th. day

[231]

Samuel Watts being arraigned upon a Bill found against him by the Grand jury for Felony and piracy in takeing and carrying away the Katch Mary of Salem Hellen Chard Master with her appur[ces]. and Ladeing of Fish &c[a].
pleaded not guilty and put himselfe upon Tryal by God and the Country, And was acquitted by the Jury of the charge laid against him./.

Samuel Watts being arraigned upon a Bill found against him by the Grand jury That is to say, That the said Samuel Watts upon the fourth day of October 1689, upon the high Seas, that is to say in martins vineyard Sound near Tarpolin Cove upon the sloop Mary of Boston then sayling under their Ma[ties]. Colours & upon the Coḿander namely Samuel Pease and Company being in number about twenty of their Ma[ties]. Liege people then and there upon their Ma[ties]. Service s[d]. Watts being under a Red Flagg, which in defiance of their Ma[ties]. Authority was purposly put up at the head of the mast, with force and Arḿes an Assault did make and with Bullets which he out of small Guns feloniously shot; the body of the said Samuel Pease in severall places did strike and mortally wound, of which mortall wounds the said Samuel Pease did grievously Languish untill the twelfth day of the said October and then of the said mortall wounds dyed. And so the Juro[rs]. upon their Oath's do say that the said Samuel Watts upon the high Seas afores[d]. on the day and year afores[d]. of his malice forethought the said Samuel Pease in manner and forme aforesaid did feloniously kill and murther contrary to the peace of our Sovereign Lord and Lady the King and Queen their Crown and dignity and the Laws of God and this Colony.
To this Indictment he pleaded not guilty and put himselfe upon

Tryal by God and the Country. The Jury found said Samuel Watts guilty of the Felony and Murder whereof he stands Indicted. The Court Adjudged said Samuel Watts to have the sentance of death pronounced against him (which was accordingly pronounced by the Deputy Governo^r.) That is to say, That he said Samuel Watts be returned to the place from whence he came and from thence be carryed to the place of Execution and there be hanged by the neck untill he be dead./.

The Jury whereof mr. Elizur Holyoke is Foreman — — — —

17th day

William Coward, Peleg Heath, Thomas Storey and Christopher Knight marrin^rs. being Indicted and a Bill found against them by the Grand jury. That is to say That the said William Coward, Peleg Heath, Thomas Storey and Christopher Knight upon the one and twentyeth day of Novemb^r. 1689. in the first year of their Maties. Reign in the Evening of that day in nantasket Road in the Massachusetts Bay then and there upon the Katch Elinor of Boston Wm Shortriggs master then at an Anchor in the said Road Lying & being, and upon part of the s^d. Katches seamen or Company and passengers to the number of seven of their Maties. Liege people then on board the said Katch in the King and Queens peace being a violent Assault did make and with force and Armes that is to say, with Swords and Guns as Pirates and Felons did Enter. And the said Seamen or Company and passengers in great fear of Body put, and the said Katch [232] with all her appur^ces. together with severall Cloth's of the Masters and Seamen And severall goods and money belonging to his Maties. Liege people to the value of Two hundred pounds did from the said Seamen and passengers feloniously and piratically take and carry away, contrary to the peace of our sovereign Lord and Lady the King and Queen their Crown and dignity, the Laws & Statutes in that behalfe made and provided. Upon which Indictment the within named Peleg Heath, Thomas Storey and Christopher Knight were Severally arraigned tryed and by the Jury found guilty of the Felony & Piracy whereof they stand Indicted — The within named William Coward refusing to hold up his hand or plead to the Indictment was remanded back to Prison. The next day said William Coward was

15th & 16th days. of Jan^ry. present also mr. Jon^a. Corwin

Jury of Tryals sworn
Jonath^n. Remington Foreman
Nath^ll. Thayer
William Griggs
John Ruggles Senr.
John Watson
Joseph Leeds
Hopestill Humfrey
John Simpson
Daniel Warren
Richard Way
John White
John Waite
— — — —

16^d./

again sent for and set to the Barr who still refusing to hold up his hand or plead to the Indictm^{t}. the Jury were called and he makeing no challenge, were sworn, The Indictment was read and the Evidences for their Maties. called and Sworn, and the prisoner allowed to speake for himselfe. The Jury found the said William Coward guilty of the Felony and Piracy whereof he stands Indicted./. The Court Adjudged the said Peleg Heath, Thomas Storey, Christopher Knight and William Coward to have the sentance of death pronounced against them. That is to say, That the said William Coward be returned to the place from whence he came and from thence be carried to the place of Execution and there be hanged by the neck untill he be dead./. That the said Peleg Heath be returned to the place from whence he came and from thence be carried to the place of Execution and there be hanged by the neck untill he be dead. That the said Thomas Storey be returned to the place from whence he came and from thence be carried to the place of Execution and there be hanged by the neck untill he be dead./. That the said Christopher Knight be returned to the place from whence he came and from thence be carried to the place of Execution and there be hanged by the neck untill he be dead./. The Court likewise ordered that John Green Marshall Generall cause this sentance to be Executed upon the said William Coward on Munday the twenty seventh of January instant And that the Secretary (being thereto appointed by Law) signe warrant for the same.

The sentence declared unto Each of the s^{d}. persons severally by the Deputy Govern^{r}.

23d. day Jan^{ry}.

17th January 1689
Present
Tho. Danforth Esqr. Dep^{t}. Govr.
John Richards
James Russell
Sam^{ll}. Appelton
W^{m}. Johnson
John Hathorne
Elisha Hutchinson
John Smith
Jonath^{n} Corwin
John Phillips
Jeremiah Sweyne

The Court Adjudged and ordered that the severall persons hereafter named tryed at this Court for their lives, That is to say Thomas Hawkins found guilty of Piracy, Thomas Pound, Thomas Johnston, Eleazer Buck John Sickterdam William Dun Richard Griffin, Daniel Lander and William Warren severally found guilty of ffelony Piracy and Murder, Samuel Watts found guilty of murder. William Coward, Peleg Heath, Thomas Storey and Christopher Knight severally found guilty of Felony and Piracy ha[ve]

[233]

the Sentance of death pronounced against Each and every of them (That is to say) to be returned to the place from whence they came and from thence be carried to the place of Execution and there be hanged by the neck untill they be dead. — which Sentance was pronounced against Each of the said persons severally by the Depty. Governo[r]. They being brought and Set to the Barr.

Post Meridiem

John Newhall Tertius of Lyn found guilty of Man Slaughter, is Ordered to pay two third parts of charges of prosecution, prison charges and Fees, amounting to Thirty six pounds nineteen Shillings and four pence (the whole being ffifty ffive pounds Ten shillings) and to remain in custody untill he performe it.

Thomas Witt of Lynn found guilty as accessory of Man Slaughter is ordered to pay one third part of the charges of prosecution prison charges and Fees. amounting to Eighteen pounds nine Shillings & Eight pence (the whole being ffifty ffive pounds Ten shillings) and to remain in custody untill he performe it./.

Robin Negro found guilty of Man Slaughter, is Ordered to pay the charges of prosecution prison charges and Fees and to remain in custody untill he performe it./.

Adjourned to Munday the 20[th] of January instant 1689 at one a clock and then met.

Present Thomas Danforth Esq[r]. Dep[t]. Gov[r].

Wait Winthrop		John Richards	
James Russell		William Johnson	
Elisha Cooke	Esq[r]s	Samuel Shrimpton	Es'q[r]s
Elisha Hutchinson		Samuel Sewall.	
John Phillips.			

William Neffe being imprisoned upon an accusation for deserting their Ma[ties]. Garrison at Falmouth where he was posted a private Centinel and confederating with Thomas Pound Thomas Hawkins &c[a]. in their piracy, said Neffe appearing in Court and it being certified that he was enticed and deluded away from the Garrison by his Corporal And that he tooke the first Opportunity to leave the pirates, Escaping from them and applyed himselfe to the next Magistrate. The Court discharged him He paying for a Gun which he had of the Country[s]. store and saith he disposed of for his Support./.

Adjourned to Thursday 23th. of January instant at nine in the morning and then met./.

Present. Thomas Danforth Esqr. Dep^ty. Govern^r.

Wait Winthrop		John Richards	
Sam^ll. Shrimpton		William Johnson	Esq^s.
Sam^ll. Sewall	Esq^s	Elisha Hutchinson	
John Smith		John Phillips	
Jon^a. Corwin			

Ordered that Thomas Pound, Thomas Hawkins, Thomas Johnston William Coward and Eleazer Buck ffive of the condemned prison^rs. sentanced to be hanged, be Executed on Munday next the twenty

[234]
seventh of January instant, notice thereof to be forthwith given them by the Marshall; And that John Green Marshall Generall cause the Sentance of this Court pronounced against them to be Executed upon them and every of them on Munday the said 27th. instant. And the Secretary (being thereto appointed by Law) to signe warrant for the same./.

The Court dismist.

[*The rest of this page is blank.*]

[235]
Anno R : R^s. et Reginæ Gulielmi et Mariæ Secundo./
Massachusetts s^s./.

At a Court of Assistants held at Boston, April. 8th. 1690. being adjourned from the fourth day of March last past. —

Present./. Thomas Danforth Esqr. Dep^t. Govr.

John Richards James Russell Elisha Hutchinson John Phillips	Assis^ts.	Wait Winthrop William Johnson Samuel Sewall	Assist./^s

Jury of Trials or Petit Jury = Sworn Cap^ne. W^m. Greenoug[h] Sam^ll. Marshall John Dyer Abrah^m. Blish	Sarah Fowler of Boston Wine Retailer. P^lt . . . vers Thomas Clarke of Boston Pewterer Def^t.	On appeale from the Judgment of the County Court Sitting in Boston 19°. No-

vemb^r. 1689. The Reasons of Appeale Answers and Evidences in the case were read and com̃itted to the Jury; The Jury found for the Defend^t. Confirmation of former Judgement, That is to say, Twenty ffour pounds in money damage and costs of Courts. Allowed Two pounds thirteen Shillings and four pence./. Execution issued 5°. May. 1690./. 2^d. Jury.

Is^a: Newell Senr.
Moses Draper
Tho: Lord Senr.
Isaac Fowle
Sam^ll. Buck
John Capen
Joseph Russe[ll]
Noah Bema[n]

Edmund Perkins of Boston Shipwright P^lt. Vers. John Winslow of Boston Merch^t. Def^t. On appeale from the Judgement of the County Court sitting in Boston ffebruary 25°. 1689. where the P^lt. Sued the said Winslow for unloseing and takeing away a certain Boat of the pl^ts. with the Oares, and not returning and delivering said Boat to the pl^t. to the damage of ffifteen pounds &c^a. according to attachm^t. And was cast to pay costs of Court. The Reasons of Appeale Answers and Evidences in the case produced were read and com̃itted to the Jury, The Jury found for the P^lt. Revertion of the former Judgement, and that John Winslow deliver to Edmund Perkins the Boat in controversy in as good repair as she was when he tooke her away, with twenty Shillings damage and costs of Courts, allowed Thirty Eight shillings and two pence./. 1^d. Jury

Petit Jury = Sworn
M^r. David Jeffr[y]
Timothy Clar[k]
W^m. Phillips
Jacob Mel[yn]
Tho: Carter
Sam^ll. Marshall
Zech^a. Johnson
John Skeat[s]
John Grosven[or]
John Holbroo[k]
Stephen Wat[ ]
Sam^ll. Hix

John Keech was put on y^e Jury in roome of Tim^o. Clarke [who is]

[236]

Willaim Arbucklė Merch^t. P^lt. (on appeale from the Judgement of the County Court sitting in Boston. 25.° February ult.) vers. Robert Bronsdon Adm^r. to the Estate of Edward Bricknall late of Boston marrin^r. dece^d. Defend^t. where the said Bronsdon recovered Judgem^t. against said Arbuckle for Five hundred pound's Sterling money of England Penalty of the Charter party and costs of Court.

Arbuckle vers. Bronsdon.

The Jury finde for the P^lt. Reversion of the former Judgement and costs of Courts./. 2^d Jury./.

Balck vers. Bronsdon &c.

William Black marrin^r. master of the Pinke Mary P^lt. (on Appeale from the Judgement of the County Court sitting in Boston 25°. February ult.) vers. Robert Bronsdon Merch^t. and Isaac Greenwood marrin^r. Def^ts. which Judgement was for the Deft^s. costs of Court.

2^d Jury. The Jury find for the Def^ts. costs of Courts.

Black vers. Bronsdon &c.

William Black P^lt. (on appeale from the Judgement of the County Court sitting in Boston 25°. ffebruary ult). vers. Pinke Mary, Robert Bronsdon and Isaac Greenwood Owners Def^ts. which Judgem^t. was for the P^lt. vizt. Twenty eight pounds one shilling in money and costs of Court. The Jury finde for the Def^ts.*

2^d Jury. Reversion of the former Judgem^t and costs of Courts.

Black vers. Bronsdon./.

William Black P^lt. vers. Robert Bronsdon Def^t. on appeale from the Judgem^t. of the County Court sitting in Boston 25°. February ult. which is for the Def^t. costs of Court.

2^d Jury. The Jury find for the Def^t. costs of Courts.

Foxcroft vers. Eyres./.

1^d. Jury

Charles Lidgett and Francis Foxcroft Execto^rs. to Anthony Heywood. P^lts. vers. Thomas Eyres Def^t. on Appeale from the Judgement of the County Court in Boston. 25° Feb^ry. ult. where the said Eyres recovered costs of Court. The Jury finde for the Def^t. costs of Courts.

Robineau vers. Assailley.

Stephen Robineau Marrin^r. Master of the Katch Amitie P^lt. vers. Peter Assailly jun^r. Merch^t. Def^t. on appeale from the Judgement of the County Court sitting in Boston 25° ffeb^ry. ult. vizt. Thirty pounds and costs of Courts recovered by the

[237]

1^d Jury

said Assailly ag^t. him said Robineau. The Jury find for the P^lt. Reversion of the former Judgement and costs of Courts.

* In this case and some others the original title of the case in the County Court is retained.

Elisha Hutchinson and Penn Townsend Plts. vers. Gyles Fyfield and Timothy Clarke Defts. on appeale from the Judgemt. of the County Court Sitting in Boston 19°. Novembr. 1689. for costs of Court recovered by the said Fifield and Clarke.

Hutchinson &c vers. Fyfield &c 2d Jury. Exon issued March 25.91

The Jury find for the Defts. costs of Courts, allowd. Thirty Six shillings.

Susanna Walker Plt. vers. Hezekiah Usher Deft. on appeale from the Judgement of the County Court sitting in Boston. 25°. February ult. where said Hezekiah Usher recovered of the sd. Susanna Walker Judgement for Forty five pounds six shillings and four pence in money and costs of Court. The Jury find for the Deft. Confirmation of the former Judgement and costs of Courts.

Walker vers. Usher 1d Jury

David Waterhouse of Boston Mercht. Plt. vers. Seth Perry Deft on appeale from the Judgement of the County Court Sitting in Boston 19°. Novembr. 1689. where said Perry recovered Ten pounds in money damage and costs of Court against the said Waterhouse. The Jury finde for the Plt. Reversion of the former Judgement and costs of Courts

Waterhouse vers. Perry. 1d Jury.

George Mountjoy of Boston Marrinr. Plt. vers. Samuel Hemlock of Boston Marrinr. Deft. on appeale from the Judgemt. of the County Court sitting in Boston 25° ffebruary ult. which Judgement was for the said Hemlock agt. said Mountjoy for Forty pounds in money damage and costs of Court.

Mountjoy vers. Hemlock 1d Jury

The Jury ^ for the Deft. confirmation of the former Judgemt. That is to say Forty pounds in money damage and costs of Courts. allowed Three pounds six shillings and sixpence.

Execution issued 8°. May 1690

Samuel Banks of Yorke Plt. vers. John Child of Boston Taylor Deft. on Appeale from the Judgement of the County Court Sitting in Boston. 19°. Novembr. 1689. where said Child recovered Judgemt. for Ten pounds four Shillings in money & costs of Court. The Jury find for the Deft. Confirmation of the former Judgement, That is

Banks vers. Child. Execution issued 25°. April. 1690.

to Say, Ten pounds four shillings in money and costs of Courts, allow^{d}. Twenty Eight Shillings. 6^{d}.

[238]

Brentnal vers. Hamlin 2^{d} Jury.

Execution issued 28^{d} April. 1690./

Thomas Brentnal formerly of Rumney Marish now of Wadeing River P^{lt}. vers. Thomas Hamlin and Esther his wife late widow and Adm^{x}. to the Estate of Thomas Platts late of Boston dece^{d}. Def^{t}. on Appeale from the Judgem^{t}. of the County Court sitting in Boston. 19°. Novemb^{r}. 1689. where the said Hamlin recovered Judgement for One hundred twenty ffive pounds in money according to Agreement and Costs of Court. The Jury find for the Def^{t}. Confirmation of former Judgemt, That is to say, one hundred Twenty ffive pounds in money according to Agreement and costs of Courts allowed Thirty ffour Shillings Sixpence.

English vers. Stebbins 2^{d} Jury.

Phillip English of Salem P^{lt}. vers. Rebecca Stebbins of Boston widow Def^{t}. on Appeale from the Judgem^{t}. of the County Court sitting in Boston 19°. Novemb^{r}. 1689. where the said Rebecca Stebbins recovered Judgem^{t}. against the said Phillip English vizt. for the delivery of the Boat and appurtenances sued for, at Salem within Ten dayes next, and three pounds in money damage and costs of Court; Or in default thereof Twenty pounds in money and costs of Court. The Jury find for the Def^{t}. Confirmation of former Judgement and costs of Courts, allowed.

April 10th. 1690.

present, also Robt. Pike John Hathorne Jonath^{n}. Corwin

Upon reading the Petition of Phillip Goss marrin^{r}. Setting forth that Hannah his wife is married to one at Jamaica with whome she now lives and by him hath had a Child. And produceing a Certificate from the Clerke of the Parish of the said Hannah^{s}. being married to one John Morrey, besides severall Evidences thereof, Praying for a divorce. Ordered that the said Phillip Goss be and hereby is divorced from the said Hannah and discharged from all conjugal duty and Obligation unto her for maintenance or Dowry.

The Court dismist./

[From here the record appears to be in the handwriting of Joseph Webb, who was Clerk of the Suffolk County Court, and seems to have acted as Secretary for the Court of Assistants, Addington having become an Assistant as appears by the record.]

[239]

Anno R R^{s} et Reginæ Gulielmi et Mariæ Angliæ &c. Tertio
Massachusetts ss /

At a Court of Assistants holden at Boston Septem^{r}. 2, 1690.
Present

The Hon^{rble}. Simon Bradstreet Esqr Govern^{r}.

Thomas Danforth Esqr. deputy Govern^{r}.

Maj^{r}. Gen^{ll}. Wayt Winthrop	Assist^{ts}	James Russell	Assist^{ts}.
William Johnson		Samuel Sewall	
Elisha Hutchinson		Isaac Addington	
John Phillips			

PETER DE VAULX of Boston Merch^{t}. Pl^{t}.
vers.
ROBERT SHELSTON of Boston Labourer def^{t}.
on Appeale from the Judgem^{t}. of ye County Court held in Boston Aug^{o}. 12th. on Adjournm^{t}. from 29 July 1690, for assaulting & beating ye s^{d} De Vaulx, where s^{d} De Vaulx was cast, costs of Court. The Attachm^{t}. Courts Judgem^{t}. & Reasons & Evidences in the case being read were cōmitted to the Jury, who returned with their Verdict vizt. They found for the Appel^{t}. Reversion of the former Judgem^{t}. and five shillings in money dam̄age and five shillings costs.

ROBERT SWAN sen^{r}. of Haverhil Pl^{t}.
vers.
SIMON WAINWRIGHT Atturney of Fr. Wainwright def^{t}.
On appeale from the County Court of Salem the last tuesday in June 1690 where the s^{d}. Wainwright recovered Judgem^{t}. for eighty five pounds nineteen shillings & eleven pence in wheat, Rye, corne porke or merchantable fatt beefe hides tallow at 2^{d} ℘ li according to accomp^{t}. & costs of Court. The Parties joyned issue.

The Attachm^{t}. Courts Judgem^{t}. Reasons of Appeale & Evidences in ye Case being read were committed to the Jury and are on file The

Jury returned their verdict they found for the defend[t]. confirmation of former Judgem[t]. and costs of Courts. /

[*Blank.*]

John Crode of Salem Ex[r]. of the last will and testam[t] of m[r]s Elizabeth Price, [Pl[t]] vers. Capt Jn[o]. Price Surviving Ex[r]. of Cap[t]. Walter Price defendt. On Appeale from Salem Court the last tuesday in June 1690 according to Attachm[t]. dated 5[th]. June 1690 where s[d] Croad recovered Judgem[t]. viz[t]. the Estate in controversy according to the will of m[r]s Eliz[a]: Price &c and costs of Court The Attachm[t]. Courts Judgem[t]. Reasons of Appeale & evidences being read were comitted to y[e] Jury, The Jury returned their verdict viz[t]. They found for the defend[t]. Revertion of the former Verdict & costs of Courts.

[240]

John Pynchon of Boston merch[t] Pl[t].
vers.
John Forster & David Waterhouse merch[ts]. def[ts]. } On Appeale from the Judgem[t] of the County Court holden in Boston Aug[o]. 12th. on Adjournm[t]. from 29. July 1690, where the s[d] John Foster & David Waterhouse recovered Judgem[t]. Possession of the Messuage or Tenem[t] ‖ &c ‖ sued for in the Attachm[t]. & costs of Court. The Reasons of Appeale, answers and Evidences in the Case being read were comitted to y[e] Jury. The Jury returned wth. their Verdict viz[t]. They find for the Pl[t]. Revertion of the former Judgem[t]. and costs of Courts./

Thomas Fosket of Charlestowne Pl[t].
vers.
Hannah Foskett widow defend[t]. } The Pl[t]. was non-suited not giving in his Reasons in time according to Law

Vincent Stilson of Marblehead Pl[t]. . .
vers.
Cap[t]. Nath[ll]. Norden &c Selectmen of Marblehead def[ts]. } On Appeale from the Judgm[t]. of Salem Court 24th. of June 1690, where s[d] Cap[t]. Norden &c recovered

Judgem^{t}. fifty five shillings in money according to Bill and costs of Court. The Parties join'd issue. The Reasons of Appeale & Evidences in the Case being read & comitted to the Jury and remain on file The Jury returned their Verdict vizt. They find for the defend^{ts}. Confirmation of the former Judgem^{t}. & costs of Co^{rts}.

NATHANIEL GOOKIN & * his wife Pl^{ts} vers. EPHRAIM SAVAGE &c. . . . . defend^{ts}. — The Pl^{ts} nonsuited not giving in the Reasons in time according to Law.

MARY SAVAGE Spinster Pl^{t}. vers. EPHRAIM SAVAGE &c^{a}. defend^{t} — The Pl^{t} was nonsuited not giving in her Reasons in time according to Law./

JOSEPH LAMPSON Constable of Maldon pl^{t}. vers. CAP^{t}. WILLIAM GREEN defend^{t}. — On appeale from the Judgem^{t}. of Charlestowne Court July 1°. 1690 on adjournm^{t}. where s^{d}. Capt. Green recovered Judgem^{t}. for a staff or paire of Colo^{r}.s to be returned to him as when taken away or six pounds in money & Costs of Court. The Reasons of Appeale & Evidences in the case being read and comitted to the Jury, The Jury returned their verdict vizt They find for the defend^{t}. the Colours in Controversy or three pounds ten shillings in money & costs of Courts.

Lampson vers. Green 1 Jury

DANIEL REA of Salem. Pl^{t}. vers. CAP^{T}. JOHN PUTNAM of Salem def^{t}. — On Appeale from the Judgem^{t}. of Salem Court June 24th. 1690 where said Putnam recovered Judgem^{t}. the land in Controversey & costs of Court: The Reasons of Appeale answers & Evidences in the Case being read & comitted to the Jury, The Jury returned their Verdict, vizt. They find for the defend^{t}. Confirmation of the former Judgem^{t}. & Costs of Courts./

Rea vers. Putnam 2 Jury.

* Left blank in the record.

Stanbridge vers. Goffe

JOHN STANBRIDGE pl^t. vers. Samuel Goffe defend^t. on an Appeale from the Judgem^t. of Cambridge Court April 15°. 1690 on a Replevin for a Negroeman named Jn°. Cream, where s^d Goffe recovered six pence damage & costs of Court. The Reasons of Appeale and answers & evidences in ye Case being read were comitted to ye Jury, the Jury returned their verdict vizt. confirmation of the former Judgem^t. & costs of Courts./

2 Jury.

[241]

Adams vers Mountfort

ESTHER ADAMS Adm^rx. to the Estate of Capt. Sam^ll: Adams Executor of the last will & Testam^t. of Thomas Adams Pl^t. vers. HENRY MOUNTFORT of Boston Merchant . . defend^t. } On Appeale from the Judgem^t of the County Court holden at Cambridge, in April, 1690, where s^d Mountfort recovered Judgem^t. ag^t. the Appellant One hundred & ffifty pounds currant money of New England and costs of Court. The Courts Judgem^t. Reasons of Appeale & evidences in the Case produced being read & pleas made the Case was comitted to the Jury. The Jury returned their verdict, vizt. They found for the Appell^t. The Revertion of the former Judgem^t. & costs of Courts.

Execution issued Sept. 19. 1690

GILES FIFIELD of Boston Marrin^r Pl^t. vers. GEORGE BRADLEY Merchant def^t. } On Appeale from the Judgem^t. of the County Court holden in Boston Aug°. 12. on Adjournm^t. from the 29th. July 1690. where the s^d. Bradley recovered Judgem^t. ag^t. the s^d Fifield One hundred twenty one pounds seven shillings money by Bill of Exchange & Twenty One pounds more money damages & costs of Court. The Courts Judgem^t. Reasons of Appeale defend^ts. Answer & evidences in the Case produced & pleas by both parties made, the Case was comitted to the Jury, The Jury returned their Verdict thereon vizt. They find for the defend^t. Confirmation of the former Judgem^t. & costs of Courts.

Fifield vers Bradley

1. Jury

ALICE FRANCIS &c^a. of Cambridge Pl^ts. vers. THOMAS DANFORTH Esqr. defend^t. } the Appell^ts. was nonsuited not giving in their Reasons in time . . . . . .

THOMAS EDWARDS Marriner Pl^t^.
vers.
ZECHARIAH JARVIS . . . . def^t^ } On Appeal from the Judgm^t^. of the County Court holden in Boston on 12°. Aug°. by adjournm^t^. from the 29 of July 1690. where s^d^. Jarvis recovered Judgem^t^. ag^t^. the Appell^t^. The goods sued for according to Invoice in Twenty dayes or pay One hundred & ninety pounds Eighteen shillings & one penny in money dam̄age & costs. The Courts Judgem^t^. Reasons of Appeale & evidences in the Case being read were comitted to the Jury who returned their Verdict thereon, vizt. They find for the Plaint. The Revertion of the former Judgement & Costs of Courts.

Edwards vers. Jarvis. 1 Jury.

JOHN NEWMARSH of Ipswich Pl^t^.
vers.
PETER BERRY of Ipswich defend^t^. } On Appeale from the ‖ Judgem^t^ of y^e^ ‖ County Court holden at Salem June 24th. 1690 where s^d^ Berry recovered Judgem^t^. ag^t^. the Appell^t^. Forfeiture of ye bond two hundred pounds money & costs. The Courts Judgem^t^. Reasons of Appeale and Evidences in the Case being read & com̄itted to the Jury. The Jury returned their Verdict thereon vizt. They find for the Appell^t^. The Revertion of the former Judgem^t^. & costs of Courts.

Newmarsh vers. Berry.

PETER BERRY of Ipswich Pl^t^.
vers.
JOHN NEWMARCH of Ipswich def^t^ } On Appeale from the Judgem^t^. of Ipswich Court March 25. 1690. where s^d^. Newmarch recovered Judgem^t^. ag^t^. the Appell^t^. for twenty foure pounds according to Bill & three pounds six shillings more dam̄age & costs ^

Berry vers. Newmarch

[*Blank.*]

[242]

PETER BERRY of Ipswich Pl^t^.
vers.
JOHN NEWMARCH of Ipswich def^t^. } On Appeale from the Judgem^t^. of the Court held at Ipswich March 25°. 1690: where s^d^. Newmarch obteined Judgem^t^. ag^t^. the Appellant fifty nine pounds according to bill & ten pounds more dam̄age and costs of Court. The Courts Judgem^t^. Reasons of Appeale,

Berry vers. Newmarch

answers & Evidences in the Case being read were comitted to the Jury. ^

[*Blank.*]

Capt. Cyprian Southack Comander of the ship Porcupine by his libel & Information Exhibited unto this Court, Giving the Court to understand & be informed that in pursuance of a Comission given him by the Lords Comissioners for Executing the office of Lord High Admiral of Engld. bearing date the 16th. day of July Anno. 1689. In the First yeare of ye Reign of Our Soveraign Lord & Lady William & Mary now King & Queen over England &ca. and Instructions thereto annexed for the takeing or seizing any merchant ship or ships belonging to France or ship or ships of any dominion under the French Power, or any ship or ships trading to or from ffrance or any ffrench Dominion, and to bring such ship or ships into any Port or Ports within their sd. Maties William & Mary's Soveraignty or of their ffriends or Allies to be proceeded agt. as suspected Prize He the sd Capt. Cyprian Southack cruising upon the Banks of Newfoundland in the sd. ship Porcupine on the 20th day of July in the second year of their sd Majties ^ over England &c did take & seize the ship called the Gift of God belonging to France of ye Burthen of Eighty Tonns or thereabouts whereof one Romain L'Cordier a ffrenchman Subject to ye ffrench King was master laded with ffrench wine brandy, fish & salt navigated with Frenchmen Enemies to their sd. Majties. William & Mary, and is become a lawfull Prize to the sd. Cyprian Southack who hath brought the same into this Port for the Condemnation thereof as the Law in that case directs. Praying the advice of this Court, for the Condemnation & Confiscation of ye aforesd. Ship the Gift of God together with all her rigging, tackle ffurniture amunicōn and apparel to ye sd Cyprian Southack as a free & lawful Prize according to the Comission & Instructions given to him as aforesd., and ye several Proclamations Laws & Statutes in that case made & provided.

Upon reading & due Consideration of ye afore recited Comission & Instructions, and hearing the Confession of the sd. Romain L'cordier late Master and Tout saints Le sont late mate of the within named ship Gift of God (both of them personally Appearing in Court. ^ The Court do adjudge declare & decree the sd. Ship Gift of God, with all her rigging tackle ffurniture apparel and lading to be lawfull Prize & confiscate unto the sd Capt. Cyprian Southack as belonging to ye Subjectes of the ffrench King King,* Enemies to their Maties. William & Mary King & Queen of Engl^d &c at the time of the takeing & seizing thereof.

[243]

Cap^tn. Cyprian Southack Commander of the ship Porcupine by his libell and Information exhibited unto this Court, Giveing the Court to understand & be informed, That in pursuance of a Comission given him by the Lords Com^rs. for executing the office of Lord High Admirall of England &c bearing date the 16th day of July Anno 1689 in the first yeare of the Reign of o^r. Soveraign Lord & Lady William & Mary now King & Queen over England &c^a. and Instructions thereunto annexed for the takeing or seizing any Merchant ship or ships belonging to ffrance, or ship or ships of any dominion under the ffrench Power, or any ship or ships tradeing to or from ffrance, or any ffrench dominion not haveing their Maj^ties. Pass or by their Maties. Power, and to bring such ship or ships into any Port or Ports within theire s^d. Maties. William and Mary's Soveraignty or of their friends or Allies to be proceeded against as suspected Prize, And whereas farther the s^d. Cyprian Southack by his s^d. libell gives the Court to understand, That the ship William of Waymouth of the burthen of seventy Tons or thereabouts whereof one Jacob Chubb of s^d Waymouth in the Kingdome of England was Comander was in ye month of October last past taken from s^d. Jacob chubb then master thereof with the seamen thereunto belonging by the Portugal Frigott of the Harbour of S^t. Mallo in ffrance, Privateers, Enemies of their Maties. William & Mary, and was by them carryed in || to || the s^d. Harbour of S^t. Mallo in France, and there made Prize, and adjuged publickly to one W^m. Vincent s^r. of Bas sa blous Burgess and Merch^t. dwelling in s^d. Town of s^t. Malo, & subject of the French King And farther that the s^d Jacob Chubb haveing confederacy & combination with one Jacob Seale of the Island of Jersey merch^t. and correspondency &c with the afores^d William Vincent & others Subjects of the ffrench King did there contract & agree at s^t. Malo afores^d. wth. s^d w^m. Vincent for the s^d Ship William of Waymouth wth. her Rigging ffurniture & Apparel, and afterwards sailes wth. s^d ship loaded with ffrench wines, brandy, bread, salt & linnen for Newfoundland haveing lettpasses & certificates from the s^d ffrench King, and his subordinate Officers wth. special charge to observe the Orders of the s^d. ffrench King &c against the form & effect of their

* Repeated in the record.

Maties. William & Mary's Proclamation of warr and divers other Proclamations lawes statutes & ordinances in such cases made & provided.. And whereas the sd. Capt. Cyprian Southack further informes that by vertue of his aforemencōned Coñission & Instructions to him given, cruising upon the Coast of New-foundland in the ship Porcupine, on the twenty seventh day of June in the second yeare of their Majties. Reign over England &c at Scilly Cove in Newfoundland he took & seized the sd William of Weymouth loaded as aforesd whereof the sd Jacob Chubb was master, with all her Cargo, sailes Cables &c trading to & from France under the Protection of the ffrench King, contrary to the Coñission & Instructions thereunto annexed, Proclamations laws statutes & ordinances aforesd, and the sd. Capt. Cyprian Southack hath brought sd. Ship into this Port [244] for Condemnation thereof as the Law directs and desires the advice of this Court in the premisses and due process in the Law, and the Judgemt. sentence & decree of this Court for Condemnac̄on and Confiscation of sd. Cargoe & the ship William with all her guñs, rigging tackle &c to the sd. Cyprian Southack & company as a free & lawfull Prize according to the aforesd. Coñission & Instructions, statutes & Ordinances in that case made & provided.

The Court upon several Considerations & difficulties in this Case refer the same to be tryed & determined by the High Court of Admiralty of England.

Capne. Cyprian Southack Coñander of the ship Porcupine by his libell and Information exhibited unto this Court, Giveing the Court to understand & be informed, that in pursuance of a Coñission given by the Lords Coñrs. for Executing the office of Lord High Admirall of England &c bearing date the 16th day of July Anno 1689 in the first year of the Reign of our Soveraigne Lord & Lady William & Mary now King & Queen over England &c And Instructions thereunto annexed for the takeing & seizing any Merchant ship or ships belonging to ffrance or ship or ships of any dominion under the ffrench Power or any ship or ships trading to or from France, or any ffrench Dominion, not haveing their Maties. Pass, or by their Maties. Power, and to bring such ship or ships into any Port or Ports within their Maties. William & Mary's soveraignty or of their ffriends or Allies to be proceeded agt. as suspected Prizes, And whereas further Capt. Cyprian Southack in sd. Libell gives this Court to understand & be informed, That the ship Richard of Boston

afores^d. Burthen One Hundred & Forty Tunns whereof William Harris was late master belonging to the Subjects of King William & Queen Mary bound from New England to London was by the ffrench King's Subjects taken from s^d. William Harris about the month of June or July in the yeare 1689, and carryed into S^t. Malo in ffrance, and there made a Prize, and ffarther, That Frederick Clutterbuck of the City of London Merchant in S^t. Mallo afores^d. bought s^d. ship Richard, and all her appurtenances of the s^d ffrench Kings Subjects or Allies, and in & upon s^d. ship Richard in s^d Port of S^t. Mallo afores^d. a Considerable Cargoe of Goods of the Growth, Production & manufacture of the Kingdom of ffrance s^d. Clutterbuck did lade & ship, vizt. ffrench Brandy, French wine, ffrench Canvas & lines and French Provisions which he there bought of the ffrench Kings Subjects And with the s^d. ship Richard now called the ffrederick & his cargoe of French Goods & Provisions, under the ffrench Kings Protection & Pass (one Caleb Barnes being master) did saile directly from the Port of S^t. Malo in France to Bonavis * Road in Newfoundland one of their Maties. King William & Queen Mary's Plantations in Newfoundland did there sell & dispose of their cargoe of ffrench Goods not having landed the same in England Wales or Berwick, nor haveing any cleering Pass or Protection from their Maj^ties. or any of their Officers in England Wales or Berwick, which is contrary to the Express Coñand of their Maties. in the Proclamation of warr which expressly forbids all their Maties. Subjects to hold any correspondence or Combination with the ffrench King or his subjects and
[245]
contrary to severall other laws & orders in that behalfe made & Provided And the s^d Capt Cyprian Southack by vertue of his Comission, and according to the Instructions thereunto annexed hath legally seized the s^d ship Richard otherwise called the ffrederick, with all her Guns, Am̃unition, Tackle Fur[n]iture and apparel, and her loading, and brought them into this their Maties. Port of Boston to be proceeded with according to law, Praying the Advice of this Court &c. as in the s^d libell is set forth. Issue is joyned, for Breach of their Maties. Proclamac̃on of Warr

Upon hearing the several Pleas and Allegations of both Parties, Nothing appearing That the ship had any ffrench Goods on board at the time of seizing her, but being laden with ffish./

The Court adjudge declare & decree for the defend^t. (That is to say) That the s^d ship Richard al̃s Frederick with all her

* Bonavista?

guñs Am̃unicõn Tackle, Apparel, Furniture, and lading of Fish be released from the s^d seizure and delivered unto the s^d Frederick Clutterbuck.

Henry Toltwood of Newberry Indicted by the Jurors for our Soveraign Lord and Lady the King & Queen, upon their Oaths, ffor that the s^d. Henry Toltwood on the thirteenth day of the month of August in the yeare 1690 in the second year of their Maties. Reigne at a certain Place called Rowley woods in the Massachusets ^ wth. fforce & armes in & upon Elizabeth Horsely of Rowley afores^d in the Colony afores^d a Maid of the Age of Eighteen yeares then & there in the Peace of God & the King & Queen being did make an Assault, and ag^t. the will of the s^d. Elizabeth Horsly ffelloniously did Ravish & carnally know, Against the Peace of o^r. soveraigne Lord & Lady the King & Queen, and contrary to the laws of England & of this Colony in that Case made & provided. On s^d Indictment was arraigned, pleaded not guilty, put himselfe upon Tryall, by God & the Country. The Jurors upon their Oathes say, That s^d Henry Toltwood is not guilty according to Indictment.

[246]

Grand Jury

m^r. John Dossett
Arthur Mason
Thomas Bligh
Jeremiah Fitch
Isaac Jones
John Bird
Samuel Gookin
Samuel Gore
Benjn. Tucker
Solomon Phipps
John Call
John Warren sen^r.
Thomas Flegg jun^r.

At a Court of Assistants holden at Boston March 3^d. 1690/1

Present.

The Honble. Simon Bradstreet Esqr. Govr.
Thomas Danforth Esqr. Deputy Govr.

Wait Winthrop William Johnson Elisha Hutchinson Isaac Addington Jonath^n. Corwin	Esq^rs Assist^ts.	James Russell Samuel Appleton Samuel Sewall John Smith	Esq^rs. Assist^ts.

Jury of Tryalls

m^r John Gardner
John Cotta
John Blake
David Jones
Sam^ll. Oldham
John Squire
James Draper
John Davis
John George

WILLIAM BOLDERSON of Boston Adm^r of the estate of THOMAS THURTON late of Boston dec^d. Pl^t.
1. Jury vers.
WILLIAM COLMAN of s^d Boston def^t.

On Appeale from the County Court held in Boston Octob^r. 28, 1690, where the defend^t. sued the Appell^t. in an Action of the case for non paym^t. of three pounds fifteen shillings & five pence money due for severals deliv^rd. s^d

Thurtons wife in the month of November 1688 &c and recovered Judgem^t^. Twenty two shillings 6^d^ money & costs. The Reasons of Appeal & Evidences in the Case being read & pleas made, The Case was comitted to the Jury, The Jury find for the defend^t^. Confirmation of the former Judgem^t^. twenty two shillings six pence & two pound twelve shillings & eleven pence more in money & costs of Courts.

Samuel Lord
Samuel Blunt
Isaac How

2 Jury

Elizur Holioke
William Downe
Nathll. Glover
Desire Clapp
John Sharp
Isaac Morris
Isaac Newell
Samuel Douse
Samuel Kettle
Philip Shattock
Richard Child
Samll. Gaskill

ELIZABETH LOFT, Ex^rx^. of Richd Loft dec^d^ Pl^t^.
1. Jury vers.
NATHANAEL OLIVER of Boston Merch^t^. def^t^.
} On Appeale from the County Court held at Boston Jan^r^y 27. $169^0/_1$

where the Appell^t^. sued y^e^ def^t^. in an action of debt of six pounds two shillings money due for Malt & was cast costs of Court. The parties Joyned issue The Courts Judgem^t^. Reasons of Appeal & Evidences were read & comitted to the Jury The Jury find for the Appel^t^. Revertion of the former Judgem^t^. and six pounds two shillings in money damages and Costs of Courts

S^R^. WILLIAM PHIPPS late Comander of the ffrigott the Golden Rose Appel^t^.
vers.
ROBERT BRONSDON of Boston merch^t^. def^t^.
} On Appeal from the County Court held at Boston

Jan^r^y 27. $169^0/_1$ where the s^d^ Robt. Bronsdon sued the Appell^t^. for deteining severall sums mentioned in three severall Bills vizt Tho: Cloft, Henry Gabrick, John Bloar, George Wright & Edwd. Nayler & the Appell^t^. cast twenty five pounds seventeen shillings six pence money & costs. The Reasons of Appeal & evidences of the Case being read and pleas made the Case was comitted to the Jury. The Jury returned their Verdict. They find for y^e^ Appell^t^. Revertion of the former Judgem^t^. and Costs of Courts.

S^R^. WILLIAM PHIPPS KN^T^. als W^m^. Phipps late comander of y^e^ ffrigot Golden Rose Appel^t^.
vers.
ROBERT BRONSDEN of Boston Merch^t^. def^t^.
} On Appeal from the County Court holden at Boston Jan^r^y 27 $169^0/_1$

[247]

Where the Appell^{t} was sued in an Action of Debt of One hundred ^ in mony due by one Obligation under the Appel^{ts}. hand & seale dated 15th. decemb^{r}. 1683. and was cast to pay one hundred pounds penalty of the bond & costs from wch he appealed. The Courts Judgem^{t}. Reasons of Appeal & Evidences in ye case being read were comitted to ye Jury. The Jury find for the Appel^{t}. Revertion of the former Judgem^{t}. & costs of Courts.

S^{R}. WILLIAM PHIPPS, otherwise Capt. W^{m}. Phipps late comander of y^{e} ffrigot Golden Rose Appell^{t}.
vers.
ROBERT BRONSDON of Boston merch^{t}. defend^{t}.

On Appeal from the County Court holden at Boston 27th of January 169^{0}/$_{1}$ where the Appell^{t}. was sued by the s^{d} Robt. Bronsdon in an action of Debt for non paym^{t}. of two hundred pounds due by vertue of an obligation bearing date 11th. Jan^{r}y 1683, and was cast two hundred pounds penalty of the bond & Costs, from wch. Judgem^{t}. he appealed. The Courts Judgem^{t}. Reasons of Appeale & Evidences in the Case being read were committed to the Jury, The Jury returned their Verdict, They find for the Appell^{t}. Revertion of the former Judgem^{t}. & costs of Courts.

THOMAS BULKLEY of Boston Merch^{t}. Appel^{t}.
vers.
NATHANIEL THAYRE & JOSEPH PARSON ^ both of Boston Merch^{ts} defend^{ts}.

On Appeal from the County Court held in Boston October 1690, where the s^{d} Thayre & Parsons sued the Appel^{t}. for a true Acco^{tt}. of goods & Merchandize with ye effects as sold at Providence s^{d} Goods being loaden on board Ship Concord Gregory Sugars Comander &c and the Appell^{t}. was cast to give a just & true Acco^{tt}. of s^{d} Goods & merchandize within thirty dayes or pay One hundred & six pounds seven shillings & foure pence money &c The Reasons of Appeal & Evidences in the Case were read & comitted to ye Jury. The Jury find for ye defend^{ts} Confirmation of the former Judgem^{t}. & costs of Courts.

PETER TOPPAM of Newbery appel^{t}.
vers
JACOB TOPPAM of s^{d} Newbery defend^{t}.

The Appell^{t}. & defend^{t}. made an Agreem^{t}. under hand & seal as a finall issue between them and desired liberty of the Court to withdraw their Action wch. was granted

[248]

Stephen Small of Salem Appel^t^. vers John Bullock . . . defend^t^. On appeale from the County Court of Salem 25th. 9^ber^. 1690 which Judgem^t^. was for s^d^ Bullock the land in controversy & costs The reasons of Appeal & evidences in ye case were read & comitted to the Jury, The Jury find for the def^t^. Confirmation of ye former Judgem^t^. & costs of Courts.

Thomas Smith of Boston blacksmith Pl^t^. vers. George Hiskett of Boston Marr^r^. defend^t^. On Appeal from the County Court held in Boston October 28. 1690, at wch. Court Judgem^t^. was for the s^d^. Hisket Eight pounds twelve shillings six pence & to secure him from Tho: Roberts & to give him a deed of sale for one quarter part of the ship built by s^d^. Roberts &c within ten dayes or to pay to ye s^d^ Hisket one hundred & forty pounds money & costs

The Courts Judgem^t^. Reasons of Appeal & evidences in the case being read were comitted to ye Jury. The Jury find for ye Pl^t^. Revertion of the former Judgem^t^. & costs of Courts. Execution issued May 27, 1691.

Palty Dorrell widow & Martha Bent, Pl^t^. vers John Foster & Abigail his wife &c def^ts^. On Appeal from the County Court held at Boston 27 Janry 1690/1 where Judgem^t^. was for the s^d^ ffoster &c Possession of the house & land sued for & costs. The Courts Judgem^t^. Reasons of Appeal & evidences in the case being read, The Case was comitted to the Jury. The Jury find for the Appel^t^. Revertion of the former Judgem^t^. and Costs of Courts.

John Bigg of Boston merch^t^. Pl^t^. vers. Thomas Harwood & Rachell his wife def^t^. On Appeal from the County Co^rt^. holden in Boston October 28th. 1690 where s^d^. Harwood & Rachell his wife sued the Appell^t^. for refuseing to give possession of a certain Messuage or Tenem^t. in Boston belonging to s^d Tho: Harwood and Rachel his wife in right of s^d Rachel &c where Judgem^t was for Possession of ye Messuage or Tenem^t. sued for & costs. The Reasons of Appeal, answers & evidences in the case being read were comitted to the Jury. The Jury find for the Appel^t. Revertion of the former Judgem^t. & Costs of Courts.

NICOLAS TIPPET of Boston merch^t. Appel^t.
vers.
S^r. TIMOTHY THORNHILL of Barbados Barr^t. def^t } On Appeal from ye County Court holden in Boston 27th Jan^ry. 169^0/1 where Judgem^t. was for s^d Thornhill fourteen hh^ds & sixteen Tearces of Muscovado sugar & costs. The Courts Judgem^t. Reasons of Appeal & evidences in the Case were read & comitted to the Jury. The Jury find for the def^t. confirmation of ye former Judgem^t. & costs of Court.

[249]

JOHN BLANEY sen^r of Salem Pl^t.
vers.
WILLIAM DUNTON of Salem Goalkeep^r def^t } On Appeal from the County Court held at Salem 25th. 9^br: 1690 where Judgem^t. was ^ s^d W^m. Dunton the pl^t. sixteen pounds, two shillings in money & ^ costs. The Reasons of Appeal & evidences in the Case being read, were comitted to ye Jury The Jury find for the defend^t. Confirmation of the former Judgem^t. and costs of Courts./ upon the motion of m^r Christopher Webb ye Appel^ts. Attorney the Execution is respited.

JAMES ADLINGTON of Boston Marrin^r. Pl^t.
vers.
ANN FERNES widow & Adm^rx. of Peter fferns def^t. } On Appeal from the Judgm^t. of the County Court holden at Boston October 28. 1690. where Judgem^t. was for s^d ffernes Ninety three pounds money & costs. The Reasons of Appeal & Evidences in the Case being read & comitted to ye Jury. The Jury find for the Defend^t. Confirmation of the former Judgem^t. & costs of Court.

PHILIP ENGLISH of Salem Merch^t^. Pl^t^.
vers.
PHILIP CROMWELL of s^d^ Salem defend^t^. } On Appeal from the County Court at Ipswich Sepr. 30th. 1690, where Judgem^t^. was for the def^t^. cromwell costs of Court.

The Reasons of Appeal Answers and Evidences in the case being read were committed to the Jury. The Jury returned their Verdict vizt. They find for ye def^t^. Confirmation of the former Judgem^t^. and costs of Courts.

SAMUEL HEMLOCK of Boston Mar^r^. Pl^t^.
vers.
GEORGE MOUNTJOY of s^d^ Boston Mar^r^. def^t^. } On Appeal from ye County Court holden at Boston 28th October 1690 where Judgem^t^. was for the Pl^t^. Mountjoy, Forty Pounds money & costs. The Courts Judgem^t^. Reasons of Appeal & Evidences in the case were read & coñitted to the Jury. The Jury find for the def^t^. Confirmation of the former Judgem^t^. & costs of Court.

JONAS CLAY of Boston mar^r^. Pl^t^.
vers.
NATHAN^LL^. JEWELL of Boston mar^r^ def^t^. } On Appeal from the Judgem^t^. of the County Court held at Boston October 28th. 1690 where Judgem^t^. was for s^d^ Jewell Three Pounds twelve shillings & nine pence money & costs. The Reasons of Appeal & Evidences in the case being read were coñitted to ye Jury. The Jury find for the appellant, Revertion of the former Judgem^t^. & costs of Courts.

[250]

THOMAS CLARKE of Boston Pl^t^.
vers.
SETH WYMAN of Woobourn def^t^. } On Appeal from ye County Court held at Boston Octob^r^. 28. 1690 where Judgem^t^. was for the Pl^t^. Thomas Clark Ten hundred weight of good merchantable hopps according to Bill or twenty pounds in money in ten dayes & costs. The Reasons of Appeal and Evidences were read & coñitted to ye Jury. The Jury find for the def^t^ Revertion of the former Judgem^t^. & costs of Court.

THOMAS EYRE of Boston Marrin^r Pl^t. vers JOHN EYRE of Boston Merch^t. def^t.	The Appell^t. withdrew.

The Court being informed that Samuel Newton of Marlborough did sometime since marry with Rebekah his late Unkle Isaac Newton's widow (by whom she hath issue one Daughter), and hath lived wth her as his wife by whom he hath had two children. The s^d Parties both appearing and confessing the truth of what is above written. Upon consideration thereof, The Court do Judge the s^d. Persons at the time of s^d Marriage to have stood within the line of Affinity forbidden Marriage by the word of God, as also by the Law of England and their living together incestious, And therefore forbid the s^d Persons any Cohabitation or fellowship together as man & wife for the future, under the severest penalty.

Mary Stebbins, wife of Samuel Stebbins of North hampton complaining to this Court, That her s^d husband Sam^ll. Stebbins dureing the time of their marriage hath committed Fornication with divers other women by whom he hath had several Bastard children, and now for some yeares past hath withdrawn himselfe from the fellowship & cohabitation with her s^d. Mary; Praying that she may obtein a Bill of Divorce; It's Ordered that a Notification of the s^d. compl^t. & Petition be sent unto the s^d. Samuel Stebbins, with the time appointed for hearing the same at the adjournm^t. of this Court April 16, 1691. That so he may have oppertunity then to appear, and shew cause (if any he have) why the s^d. Mary should not have her Peticõn in y^t. behalfe granted.

m^r. Samuel Gookin was by the Court of Assistants appointed Marshall General for the time & untill further order by the Gen^ll Court and tooke his Oath in open Court.

The Court adjourned to 17th. March 169^0/1

[*Large Blank.*]

[251]
Jahleel Brenton Genl̃ collector surveyor & searcher of their Maties. Customs in New England who as well for their Maties. as for Simon

Bradstreet Esqr. Govern^r. of their Majesties Colony in New England as for himself coming into the Court of our s^d. Soveraigne Lord & Lady the King & Queen afores^d.

Giveing s^d. Court to know & be informed. That whereas there is one Act of Parliament made in the ffifteenth yeare of the Reign of King Charls the second over England &c^a. Entituled An Act for the Encouragem^t. of Trade; in which Act among other things it is Enacted. That from & after the five & Twentieth day of March, one thousand six hundred sixty foure No Comodities of the Growth, Production or Manufacture of Europe shall be imported into any Land, Island, Plantacon, Colony Territory or Place to his Matie. belonging, or which shall hereafter belong unto or be in the Posession of his Maj^ty. his heires or Successo^rs in Asia, Africa or America (Tangier only Excepted) but what shall be bonâ fide & without Fraud laden & shipped in England Wales or Towne of Berwick upon Tweed, and in English built Shipping, or which were bonâ fide bought before the first day of October, one thousand six hundred sixty two, and had such certificate thereof as is directed in one Act of this present Parliament entituled an Act for preventing ffraud & regulateing abuses in their Maties. Customes, & whereof the master & three fourths of the Marrin^rs at least are English

[252]

And which shall be carryed directly thence to the s^d. Lands Islands Plantations Colonies Territories or Places, and from no other Place whatsoever by land or water, ^ And if by water of the ship or vessell in which they were imported with all her guns, tackle furniture amunition & apparel, One third to his Ma^ty. his heires & successo^rs. One third part to the Govern^r. of such land Island Plantation Colony, Territory or Place into which such goods were imported, If ye s^d. ship Vessell or goods be there seized or Informed ag^t. & sued for, otherwise that third also to his Ma^ty. his heires & successo^r.s and the other third part to him or them who shall seize inform or sue for the same, in any of his Maties. Courts, in such of the s^d lands, Islands Colonies, Plantations, Territories or Places where the offence was comitted, or in any Court of Record in England by Bill Information, plaint or other Action, wherein no Essoyn, Protection or wager in law shall be admitted.

And ffarther the s^d. Jahleel Brenton Giving s^d. Court to know & be informed that Nicolas Lawrence master of the Katch Salisbury, the Paines & penalties of the fore recited Act not regarding, did on or about the ninth day of February in the year of our Lord One Thousand six hundred & ninety in the second year of their Maties. Reign import in the Katch Salisbury into Boston aforesaid a Colony or Place belonging to their s^d. Maj^ties. in New England several Goods & Merchandizes of the Growth, Production or manufacture of Europe, which was not bonâ fide & without fraud laden & shipped in England Wales or Towne of Berwick upon ^, The goods imported are as followeth, One chest conteining Twelve peices of Kersey, sixteen peices of worsted stuffs, foure peices of silk crape, twenty peices of Scottish cloth seventeen Papers of Buttons, two peices of Friez, one peice of white & one peice of Red Bayes, one peice of course striped stuff, Two Bailes conteining sundry peices of Fustians or demitys. One Baile conteining twelve peices peices* of white & foure peices of browne linnen, one small Baile conteining twelve peices of Hamborough linnen q^t. 449½ Ells — In a Rugg is conteined seven broad peices & foure peices & an halfe of Ticking, One bag of Haberdashery — Forty Barrels of powder, ffive hh^ds. of Nailes — one smal bundle conteining four peices of silk crape, six peices of worsted stuffs, Three papers of Buttons, which goods & merchandize are justly become forfeited, as also the Katch Salisbury with all her Guns, Ammunition, furniture & apparel, one third part to their Maties. one third part to Simon Bradstreet Govr. and the other third part to Jahleel Brenton as afores^d who sues for the same praying the advice of the Court & Judgement accordingly.

Nicolas Lawrence master of ye s^d Katch Salisbury comes into Court the day & year above-written, and to the matter of ye Information pleads, Not guilty; Issue is thereupon joyned, And after a full hearing of ye Pleas & Evidences offered by Each party. The Jurors upon their oaths say. They find for the Pl^t. The Forfeiture of the Goods & Katch Salisbury according to Information, The Court receiv[e] and record their Verdict, and enter up Judgem^t. accordingly./

Nicolas Lawrence afores^d appealed from this Judgem^t. unto the Lords Comissio^rs. of the High Court of Admiralty of Engl^d. wch. was granted, and himselfe as Principal and Col^l. Nicolas Paige as surety bind themselves their heires Ex^rs & Adm^rs jointly & severally in ye sum̃ of ffive hundred pounds curr^t. money of New-Engl^d to their Maties. King William & Queen Mary & to the parties concerned, on Condition s^d Nicolas Lawrence shall prosecute his Appeal before ye Lords Comiss^rs with Effect and shall pay all such costs & dam̃ages as shall by s^d comiss^rs ^ awarded ag^t them

* Repeated in the record.

[253]

At a Court of Assistants holden in Boston September 22th. 1691 by Adjournment from the first day of sd. September./

Grand Jury sworn

Present.

Simon Bradstreet Esqr. Governr.

James Russell, William Johnson, John Hathorn, Elisha Hutchinson, John Phillips — Esqrs. Assistts.

William Stoughton, Samuel Appleton, Samuel Sewall, Isaac Addington — Esqrs. Assistts.

Capt. Edwd Wylly foreman
James Green
Thomas Downe
Robert Bronsdon
Seth Perry
Edward Dorr
John Capen
Thomas Tilestone
Samuel Ballard
John Knight
Samuel Stone
John Tidd
John Whitney

Edward Neeland senr Husbandman Plt. vers Isaac Foster senr. . . . defendt. } On Appeal from the County Court held at Salem June 30th. 1691, where the sd Foster recovered Judgemt. the land in controversy & costs The Courts Judgemt. Reasons of Appeal & evidences in the case being read & committed to the Jury. The Jury find for the defendt. Confirmation of the former Judgemt. & costs of Courts.

Jury of Tryalls sworn

Capt. Richd Crisp foreman.
Edward Crick
Thomas Davis
Thomas Stanbury
John Scott
Joseph Leeds
John Capen junr.
John Watkins
Nathanll. Adams
Abraham Hill
William Russell
Thomas Hammond

John Paul of Lynn . . Plt. vers Tieg A Barrow of Boston deft. } On Appeal from the County Court held at Salem June 30th. 1691. where Judgement was for ye Plt. Tieg A Barrow the land in controversy & costs. The Courts Judgmt. Reasons of Appeal & Evidences in the ^ were read & committed to ye Jury The Jury find for the defendt. Confirmation of ye former Judgemt. & costs of Courts.

John Clark . . Plt vers Abiel Lamb deft. } The plt. ^

John Burnam junr of Chebacco of Ipswich Appelt. vers. Robert Cross senr. of Chebacco of Ipswich defendt. } On Appeal from ye Judgmt. of the County Court holden at Salem

2 Jury of Tryals sworn

mr Caleb Church foreman.
George Ellistone

Josiah Holland
William Chaplin
Ephraim Pason
William Pratt
Nicolas Lobdell
Joseph Simons
Samuel Gibson
Bartholomew Green
Saml^l. Herrington
John Hastings.

30th June 1691 In an Action of the Case, for that sd. John Burnam as a Trespasser for several late yeares improved a certain parcel of salt marsh of sd. Crosses conteining by Estimation neer Thirty Acres lying at Chebacco aforesd & still keeps the plt. out of posession to his dam̄age one hundred pounds money according to attachmt. dated 12o. June 1691. at wch. Court the Jury found for ye plt. the land in controversy &c from wch. the defendt. appealed The Attachmt. Courts Judgemt. Reasons of Appeal & Evidences in ye Case being read com̄itted to ye Jury & are on file wth. the Records of this Court, The Jury returned their verdict thereon vizt. [254]
They find for the Appellant, Revertion of the former Judgemt & costs of Courts.

Joseph Mason of Watertown Appelt.
vers.
John Stone &ca. selectmen of Watertown defts.

On Appeal from the Judgemt. of the County Court held at Cambridge April 7th. 1691, where sd selectmen sued the Appellt. in an Action of the Case for neglecting Gathering the Rates made for the use of the Towne & com̄itted to sd Mason to collect & levy as ℘ Attachmt on file bearing date March 21. 169$\frac{0}{1}$ where the Jury found for ye Jury found for* ye plts. Fifty five pounds Eight shillings eleven pence mony & costs from wch. Judgemt. the deft. appealed. The Courts Judgemt. Reasons of Appeal, Answer & evidences in the Case being read & pleas by both parties made, the case was com̄itted to ye Jury. The Jury returned their Verdict thereon vizt. They find for ye Appelt. Revertion of the former Judgemt. & costs of Courts.

Rebekah Stebbins of Boston widow Plt.
vers.
Philip English of Salem defendt.

On a scire facias on a Judgmt. of the County Court holden at Boston November 19th. 1689 & confirmed by the Court of Assistts. April 8th. 1690 where sd Stebbins recovered Judgemt. for the delivery of a boat & appurtenances in ten dayes and three pound in money dam̄age or in default thereof to pay Twenty pounds in money & costs. The defendt.

* Repeated in the record.

pleaded he had ^ a legall tender of s[d] Boat according to Judgem[t]. which issue was cōmitted wth. the evidences to the Jury. The Jury returned their verdict. They do not find a legall tender. The Court determine and give Judgem[t]. for seventeene pounds being the remaining part of the Judgement & costs.

BENJAMIN WALKER of Boston Merch[t] Pl[t].
vers
JAMES HAWKINS of s[d]. Boston Bricklayer def[t]. } On Appeal from the County Court held in Boston July 18th. 1691, where the Appell[t]. sued s[d]. Hawkins for not paying y[e] pl[t]. five pounds ten shillings money due by Agreem[t]. & promise &c w[ch]. Judgem[t]. was for the defend[t]. costs of Court. The Reasons of Appeal and evidences in the Case were read & cōmitted to y[e] Jury. The Jury find for the Appell[t]. Revertion of the former Judgem[t]. and five pounds & ten shillings in money dāmages & costs of Courts Execution issued Oct 6. 1691

WILLIAM WARREN of Boston Appel[t].
vers
ELLIS CALLENDER of Boston def[t]. } On Appeal from the Cōmission[rs] Court holden at Boston July. 14th. 1691 where s[d] Calender had Judgem[t]. Ten bushells of salt & costs. The Courts Judgem[t]. Reasons of Appeal and Evidences in the case were read & cōmitted to the Jury. The Jury find for the Appellant Revertion of the former Judgm[t]. & costs of Courts.

AMOS MARRETT Pl[t].
vers.
JAMES HOLLAND defend[t]. } On Appeal from the County Court held at Charlstowne June. 19th. 1691 by adjournm[t]. where s[d] Holland obteined Judgem[t]. ffifty shillings money or the Mare in controversy. The Reasons of Appeal & evidences in the case were read & cōmitted to y[e] Jury The Jury find for y[e] defend[t]. confirmation of y[e] former Judgem[t]. ffifty shillings mony dāmage & costs of Courts Execution issued october 5, 1691.

[255]
THOMAS DENNIS of Ipswich Pl[t].
vers.
JOHN WAINWRIGHT of s[d]. Ipswich def[t]. } On Appeal from the County Court holden at Ipswich March 31. 1691. where Judgem[t]. was for the s[d]. Wainwright Fifty shillings money dāmage &

costs &c The Courts Judgm^t^. Reasons of Appeal & Evidences in the case were read comitted to ye Jury The Jury find for the Defend^t^. Confirmation of the former Judgem^t^. & costs of Courts.

Capt. STEPHEN CROSS of Ipswich Plantff.
vers.
JOHN LOW Terti. Atto^rny^. to SAM^LL^. YOUNGLOVE, def^t^

On Appeal from the County Court held at Ipswich March 31st. 1691. where the Judgem^t^. of Maj^r^ Sam^ll^. Appleton was confirmed. The Reasons of Appeal & Evidences in the case were read & comitted to the Jury, The Jury find for the Pl^t^. Revertion of the former Judgem^t^. & costs of Court.

WILLIAM FAIRFIELD of Wenham Pl^t^.
vers
JOHN FAIRFIELD of Ipswich def^t^.

On Appeal from the County Court held at Ipswich March. 31. 1691. in an action of Trespass where Judgem^t^. was for the defend^t^. costs of Court. The Courts Judgem^t^. Reasons of Appeal & Evidences in the Case being read & comitted to the Jury. The Jury find for the Appell^t^. Revertion of the former Judgem^t^. and Two shillings & nine pence money damage & costs of Courts.

PHILIP WHITE of Beaverly Pl^t^.
vers.
GEORGE STANLEY of s^d^. Beaverley def^t^.

On Appeal from the County Court holden in Ipswich 31st. March 1691. where the Jury found for ye defend^t^. costs. The Courts Judgem^t^. Reasons of Appeal & evidences in the Case were read & comitted to ye Jury. The Jury find for the Appell^t^. Revertion of the former Judgem^t^. and Twelve Pounds ten shillings damage the one Third money, the other two Thirds in Country pay & costs of Courts.

COL^L^. NICOLAS PAIGE Attorney of Capt. Andrew Dolbery appel^t^.
vers.
JACOB MORRELL of Salisbury shipwright, def^t^.

in an action of Appeal from the County Court holden in Ipswich, March 31, 1691. where the Appell^t^. was cast, the Jury finding for the pl^t^. the Hull or body of the ship in Controversey or seven hundred pounds money dam̃age & Costs of Court. The Courts Judgem^{t}. Reasons of Appeal and Evidences in the case produced being read were committed to the Jury & are on file, The Jury returned their Verdict thereon, vizt. They find for the defend^{t}. Confirmation of the former Judgem^{t}. six hundred & ninety pounds money & Costs of Court.

[256]

Capt. Ebenezer Prout Pl^{t}.
vers.
Caleb Brooks, Isaac Fox & John Whitmore defend^{ts}.

On Appeal from the County Court held in Charlstowne June 19th. 1691. where the Appel^{t}. sued ye defend^{ts}. for withholding from ye pl^{t}. ye Possession of one Messuage or Tenem^{t}. within ye bounds of Medford &c. And Judgem^{t}. was for the defend^{ts}. Costs of Court. The Courts Judgem^{t}. Reasons of Appeal & Evidences in the case being read were com̃itted to the Jury. The Jury find for ye defend^{ts}. Confirmation of the former Judgem^{t}. & costs of Courts.

George Lason Com̃ander of ye Pink or Buss Two Brothers - - Pl^{t}.
vers.
Jahleel Brenton Gent Collect^{r}. survey^{r}. &c of their Maties Customs in New Engl^{d} def^{t}.

On Appeal from ye County Court holden in Boston on 25th. Aug^{o}. 1691 continued by Adjournm^{t}. from 28th July foregoing, where the Appel^{t}. was cast by the Jury upon the Act of ye 12°. Caroli secundi Regis entituled an Act for the encourageing & increasing of shipping * Confiscation of the Pink or Buss Two Brothers & the Goods on board her. The County Courts Judgem^{t}. Reasons of Appeal Information & Evidences in the Case produced ~~being produced~~ being read & Pleas made in the Case by both ye Appel^{t}. & defend^{t}. The Case was com̃itted to ye Jury, who returned their Verdict thereon. vizt. They find for ye Appell^{t}. The Revertion of ye former Judgm^{t}. ag^{t}. the Pink or Buss, Two Brothers. Jahleel Brenton Gent̃ collect^{r} &c appealed from this Judgem^{t}. to their Maj^{ties}. in Council wch. was granted.

* This space left blank in the record.

William Hall who marryed Sarah ffowler of Boston wine retailer Plt. vers. Benjamin Backway of Boston Marriner defendt. } On Appeal from ye Judgmt. of the County Court held in Boston April 28th. 1691. where the Appellt. was cast to pay Twenty six pounds in money & costs of Court upon sale of Nathanael Force a Negro man who was sold to sd. Backway by sd Sarah Fowler &c The Courts Judgemt, Reasons of Appeale and Evidences in the Case produced were read & comitted to ye Jury. The Jury find for the Appellt. Revertion of the former Judgemt. & costs of Court.

John Tyler of Charlstown Plt. vers Henry Wright of Boston Carpenter Deft } On Appeal from ye Comissionrs Court holden in Boston July 14. 1691. where the Appelt. was cast to pay Twenty foure shillings seven pence money & costs. The Courts Judgemt. Reasons of Appeal & Evidences in the case were read & comitted to ye Jury. The Jury find for ye deft. Confirmation of the former ^ twenty foure shillings seven pence money damage & costs of Courts.

[257]

David Waterhouse of Boston mercht. Plt. vers Robert Luist Marriner mr. of the ship Providence defendt. } On Appeal from ye County Court holden in Boston ~ April 28th. 1691. where Judgemt. was for the defendt. costs of Court. The Courts Judgemt. Reasons of Appeale & Evidences in the case were read & comitted to ye Jury, The Jury find for the defendt. Confirmation of the former Judgemt. and costs of Courts.

Nathanael Oliver of Boston Mercht. Plt. vers Elizabeth Loft Exrx. of Richd. Loft decd deft. } On Appeal from ye County Court holden in Boston April 28th. 1691. where Judgemt was for the defendt. Costs of Court. The Courts Judgement Reasons of Appeal & Evidences in the case were read & comitted to ye Jury The Jury find for the defendt. Confirmation of the former Judgement & Costs of Courts.

GEORGE BALL of Boston Marrin^{r}. Pl^{t}. vers WINSOR SANDEY of s^{d} Boston Marrin^{r}. Def^{t}. } On Appeal from the County Court holden in Boston July 28th. 1691. where Judgem^{t}. was for the Pl^{t}. Sandey Twenty one pounds seventeen shillings & three pence money & costs. The Courts Judgem^{t}. Reasons of Appeal & Evidences in the case were read & coñitted to ye Jury The Jury find for the defend^{t}. Confirmation of the former Judgem^{t}. Twenty one pound seventeen shillings three pence mony & costs of Courts.

[*Blank.*]

GEORGE READ of Wobourn pl^{t}. vers WILLIAM PEARSE of s^{d} Woobourn def^{t}. } On Appeal from the County Court held at Cambridge April 7th 1691. In an Action of trespass where the Appel^{t}. was cast costs of Court The Courts Judgem^{t}. Reasons of Appeal & Evidences in the Case produced were read & committed to the Jury. The Jury find for the defend^{t}. confirmation of the former Judgement & Cost of Courts. Execution issued october 3, 1691.

[258]

JOHN TYLER of Charlstowne Pl^{t}. vers HENRY WRIGHT of Boston defend^{t}. } The pl^{t}. withdrew.

George Monck Taverner on Appeal from the Judgem^{t}. of the Coñiss^{rs} Court held in Boston May 12. 1691 where he was fined ffforty shillings in money as a fine to the County &c The Courts Judgem^{t}. Reasons of Appeal & Evidences being read and coñitted to ye Jury. The Jury find for the Appell^{t}. Revertion of the former Judgment.

WILLIAM MUMFORD of Boston Slater Pl^{t}. vers. EDWARD WYLLYS of Boston Merch^{t}. def^{t}. } On Appeal from the Judgm^{t} of the Coñission^{rs} Court held in Boston April 7th. 1691 in an Action of Review, where the Appell^{t}. was cast to pay two pounds fourteen shillings & eleven pence money & costs. The Courts

Judgem^{t}. Reasons of Appeal & Evidences in ye Case were read & comitted to the Jury. The Jury find for the Appell^{t}. Revertion of the former Judgem^{t}. & costs of Courts.

JOHN HAYWARD of Roxbury Merch^{t}. Pl^{t}. vers THOMAS BULKLEY of Boston Merch^{t}. defend^{t}. } On Appeal from the County Court holden in Boston July 28. 1691. where the Judgem^{t}. was for ye Pl^{t}. Bulkley. Thirty eight pounds in money & costs. The Courts Judgem^{t}. Reasons of Appeale & evidences in the Case were read & comitted to the Jury. The Jury find for the defend^{t}. Confirmation of the former Judgem^{t}. & costs of Courts.

SETH PERRY of Boston Pl^{t}. vers BENJ^{N}. ALFORD of Boston Merch^{t}. def^{t}. } On Appeal from the County Court holden in Boston 28th. July. 1691. where the Appell^{t}. was cast to pay Fourteen pounds three shillings money & costs, The Courts Judgem^{t}. Reasons of Appeal & Evidences in ye Case were read & comitted to the Jury. The Jury find for the defend^{t} Confirmation of the former Judgement & costs of Courts. Ex^{con}. issued Dec^{r}: 1. 1691

Capt^{ne}. John Alden Comander of the sloop Mary of Boston by his Libell or Information Exhibited unto this Court giveing the Court to understand & be Informed, That by vertue of a Comission given him by the Honrd. Govern^{r} & Council of the Massachusets Bay in New-England & Instructions thereunto or orders in which is one clause comanding him in case he met wth. any ship or vessell belonging to the ffrench King or his subjects in his going or returning from Port Royall to seize them wth. their lading if within his power & bring them to Boston in order to their Tryal, He the s^{d} Alden on the first day of April in the year 1691, at Port Royal afores^{d} did take or seize a Vessel or Barque called the Speedwell burthen about Twenty three Tuns wch. did belong to one of the French Kings Subjects whose name is s^{t}. Tobin, wch Barque was sometime Giles S[eres] [259]
of Ipswich in New-Engl^{d}. and in an hostile maner taken from him by the French Kings Subjects & kept in their possession above Eighteen months until the time he s^{d} Alden tooke her &c praying the Advice of

this Court in the premisses & due process in the law & ye Judgemt. sentance & decre of the Court for the condemnation of sd Barque Speedwell & her appurtenances accordingly

Upon Reading & Due consideration of Comission & Evidences presented, The Court decre the sd Barque Speedwell a lawfull Prize to the Captor.

Captne. Cyprian Southack Comander of the Ship Porcupine by his libel and Information exhibited unto this Court, giveing the Court to understand and be Informed that in pursuance of a Comission given him by ye Lords Comissionrs for executing the office of Lord High Admiral of England &c bearing date the sixteenth day of July 1689, in the first yeare of the Reign of Our soveraigne Lord & Lady William & Mary King & Queen over England &c and Instructions thereto annexed for the taking or seizing any Merchant ship or ships belonging to France, or ship or ships of any Dominion under the French Power, or any ship or ships trading to or from France or any French Dominion & to bring such ship or ships into any Port or Ports within their sd. Maties. William & Mary's Soveraignty or of their ffriends or Allies to be proceeded agt. as suspected Prize. He the sd. Capt. Cyprian Southack cruising in sd. Ship Porcupine neer the Isle of Persy in Northern France on the eighth day of June in the Third yeare of their Maties. Reigne over England &c. did take & seize a small Ship or Barque called the st. John Frigott of Quebeck whereof one master Millevashe (or Thousand Cow) was Comander being burthen about fforty Tuns or thereabouts belonging to the French Kings subjects haveing on board severall sorts of French Goods suitable for an Indian trade, and is become a lawfull Prize to the ‖ sd ‖ Cyprian Southack who hath brought the same into this Port for the Condemnation thereof as the Law directs, praying the Advice of this Court in the premisses and due process in the law, & that Judgement might pass agt. sd. Ship or Barque called st. John ffrigott together wth. all her rigging, tackle, furniture apparell & cargoe to ye sd Cyprian Southack as a free & lawfull Prize according to the Comission & Instructions given to him as aforesd & ‖ ye ‖ Proclamatio~ and Statutes in that case made & provided

Upon the Reading & Consideration of the Evidences produced both English & ffrench, that the ship or Barque st. John ffrigott of Quebeck did at the time of her takeing belong to the Inhabitants of Quebeck subjects of the French King & Enemies to their Ma[ties]. William & Mary King & Queen of England &c. The Court do adjudge declare & decree the s[d] ship s[t]. John Frigot of Quebeck with all her rigging tackle apparell & loading to be a lawful prize to the s[d] captor.

[260]

Capt[ne]. Samuel Adams Comander of the Briganteen Boneta by his Libel and Information exhibited unto this Court, giveing the Court to understand & be informed, That in pursuance of a Comission given him by y[e] Honor[ble]. Simon Bradstreet Esq[r]. Govern[r]. of this their Ma[ties]. Colony of the Massachusets Bay, with y[e] consent of y[e] Council bearing date y[e] 23[d]. day of ffebruary Anno Dm. 169$^0/_1$ in the third year of the Reign of o[r]. soveraign Lord & Lady William & Mary by the Grace of God of England Scotland France & Ireland King & Queen defend[r]s of the ffaith &c and Instructions thereto annexed did permit and allow him s[d]. Samuel Adams to take the Comand of Cap[t]. of the s[d] Briganteen Boneta of Boston belonging to their Majesties good & loyall Subjects in the Colony afores[d]. by them at their owne proper costs & charges fitted & set forth for the securing these coasts & the seas adjacent from the attacks and spoiles of the ffrench King subjects upon & ag[t]. their Ma[ties]. good subjects, and for weakning the power of their Ma[ties]. enemies the French by vertue of which Comissions & Instructions thereto annexed especially in obedience unto the pursuance of the ffifth Article of the s[d] Instructions viz[t]. you are to bring in all ships or Vessels or goods of the enemies which you shall seize or take from the ffrench the declared & professed Enemies to the Crown of England into this Port to be proceeded ag[t]. as suspected‸ And the s[d]. Cap[t]. Adams in the in the * s[d]. Briganteen Boneta, cruising upon the Banks of Newfoundland upon the second day of June 1691 in the Third year of their Ma[ties]. Reign, the Ship called y[e] Marquess Royan, ‸ whereof was master or Comander Peter Richard one of the French Kings Subjects) of burthen about one hundred & ffifty Tuns, manned with ffrench men, and belonging to the ffrench Kings Subjects, haveing on board her a quantity of ffrench salt & core ffish & some Earthen ware did attack & seize & into this their Ma[ties]. Port have brought in order to an adjudication & condemnation as a lawfull Prize, Praying the Advice of this Hon[rd]. Court and due Process in the law & that a Sentance of Condemnation may pass ag[t]. s[d]. Ship her Guns Amunition Tackle Apparel furniture and loading as afores[d]. as a lawfull Prize to be divided,

* Repeated in the record.

(the Guñs & Am̃unition in her taken to be to the sole use of their Maties. King William & Queen Mary, and the ship her Tackle Apparel ffurniture & goods among the s^d Samuel Adams, the owners & setters forth of the s^d Briganteen & her Company according to Instructions afores^d. and Articles between the owners of s^d. Briganteen & himselfe & Company, And Proclamacõn & statutes in that case made & provided^

Upon Reading & Consideration of the Evidences produced and ye Confession of Jaques Jamet, Charls de Champs and ffrancis Boreau three ffrenchmen of the Company belonging to s^d. Ship Marquess of Royan at ye time of her being taken, that ye s^d ship did wholely belong unto Monsr. Abraham Michard Merch^t. in Rochell a subject of the French King.

The Court do adjudge & decree the s^d. Ship Marquis of Royan with all her rigging Tacklin Apparell & lading to be a lawfull Prize ‖ un ‖ to the ‖ s^d. ‖ Captor./

[261]

John Cutler jun^r. on Appeal from the sentance of the County Court held at Charlstowne June 19th. 1691. where s^d. Cutler was sentenced to pay twenty pounds money as a fine &c. For Reproachfull words by him uttered ag^t. the present authority &c. The Courts Judgem^t. Reasons of Appeal & Evidences in the Case were read & com̃itted to ye Jury. The Jury return their Verdict. They find the Appell^t. not guilty.

JAHLEEL BRENTON Gent Collect^r. surv^r &c of their Maj^ties. Customs in New-Engl^d Pl^t. vers. Pink. THREE BROTHERS, Thomas Wilkinson Commander def - - - } Upon his libell or Informacõn for Breach of the Act of the 12° of King Charles ye second Intituled an Act for the Encourageing & increasing of shipping &c and also for Breach of one other Act of the 15°. of s^d. King Charles Intituled an Act for the incouragem^t of trade &c as is at large recited in the Information. The Pl^t. setting forth that the s^d. Pink imported Sundry Goods wares & merchandize of ye Growth Production & Manufacture of Europe vizt. Fifty tons salt, two hundred Cask of Raysins, five hh^ds. of Brimstone, one Butt & two smaller cask of Oile Sundry cask of wine &c The defend^t. Thomas Wilkinson pleaded not Guilty and both parties Joyn Issue. The Information, defend^ts. Answer and Evidences in the case being read and Pleas by both parties made The Case was comitted to the Jury. The ‖ Jury ‖ return their Verdict on their Oaths viz[t]. They find the Pink Three Brothers, whereof Thomas Wilkinson is Comander, not Guilty according to Information. The Court Record this Verdict. Jahleel Brenton Gent. Pl[t]. Appealed from this Judgem[t]. to their Ma[ties]. in Council & gave bond to prosecute his s[d] Appeal wth effect.

m[r]. John Croad appeared in Court of Assistants Septemb[r]. 22. 1691. & presented his Petition shewing forth, that he recovering a Judgem[t]. at the last County Court held in Salem ag[t]. Cap[t]. John Price surviving Executo[r]. of the last will & Testam[t]. of Cap[t]. Walter Price sometime of Salem dec[d]. From w[ch]. Judgement s[d]. Cap[t]. John Price appealed & since that time y[e] s[d]. Cap[t]. John Price is dead, and neither Ex[rs]. nor Adm[rs]. appearing to prosecute s[d] Appeal, and none Appeal being entred, The Petition[r]. desired that his appearance to defend s[d]. Case might be entred & recorded, w[ch] was granted & is accordingly done./

m[r]. ffrancis Burroughs, m[r]. James LLoyd & m[r]. Benj[a]. Alford are comissioned & appointed a comittee to apprize the Katch Salisbury Nicolas Lawrence late Comander with her Tackle & Apparel &c and the Goods imported in s[d] Katch now under the seizure of Jahleel Brenton Gent collect[r]. survey[r]. &c of their Ma[ties] Customes in New-England and to make report of their doings herein under their hands to this Court with what Convenient Speed they can. — — —

m[r]. Hezekiah Usher Petitioning the Court, that he might have an hearing of two actions he comenced ag[t]. the Adm[rs]. of m[r]. Richard Wharton late of Boston merch[t]. dec[d]. at July Court, 1691. The Court grant he shall have an hearing of y[e] s[d] cases at Octob[r]. Court upon y[e] same Process & Entry.

[262]

Josiah Littlefield bound over to this Court by the County Court of Salem to answer for his uttering such words as that he would sweare point blank that he knew some men that had sold the Indians Powder & shot & being Examined denyed the same. The Court order him to pay ten shillings money fine to their Ma[ties]. & fees of Court, standing comitted &c[a].

Joseph Downer of Newberry bound over to this Court by the County Court of Salem to answer for reporting that the Indians killed a man at ye eastward and so they might well enough for that ye Indians had powder & shot sold them under a pretence of cut Tobacco &c s^d Downer acknowledged in Court that he spake unadvisedly, and humbly begg'd the Courts Pardon, upon wch. the Court dismissed him paying ffees of Court.

26th Sep^t. Elizabeth Emmerson single woman Daughter of Michael Emmerson of Haverhill in the County of Essex being indicted by the Jurors for o^r Soveraigne Lord & Lady King William & Queen Mary upon their Oathes. For that the s^d. Elizabeth Emmerson being with child with two living Children or Infants on Thursday night the 7th. of May 1691 before day of Fryday morning at Haverhill afores^d in the house of Michael Emmerson afores^d by the Providence of God two Bastard Children alive did bring forth, and the s^d. Elizabeth Emmerson not haveing the feare of God before her Eyes but being instigated by ye Devil of her malice forethought, the s^d two Infants did feloniously kill & murther, and them in a small Bagg or cloath sewed up, and concealed or hid them in s^d Emmersons house untill afterwards, that is to say, on sabbath day May the tenth 1691, the s^d two Infants in the yard of s^d Emmerson in Haverhill afores^d. did secretly bury contrary to the peace of Our Soveraign Lord & Lady the King & Queen, their Crown & dignity, the Laws of God, and the Lawes & Statutes in that case made & provided

Upon which Indictment the s^d. Elizabeth Emmerson was arraigned and to the Indictment pleaded not guilty & put herselfe upon Tryal by God & the Country, * a Jury was impannelled being the first Jury, whereof m^r. Richard Crisp was foreman, and were accordingly sworne (the prisoner making no challeng) The Indictment Examination & evidences were read, & the prisoner made her defence, The Jury return their Verdict, The Jury say, That she s^d. Elizabeth Emmerson is guilty according to Indictment. The Court order, That sentance of Death be pronounced ag^t. her.

[263]

Comissionrs of Boston M^r. John Joyliffe, Capt. Penn Townsend, Capt. Theophilus ffrary, m^r. Edwd. Bromfield m^r Jeremiah Dumer & m^r. John Eyre chosen Comission^rs for the Towne of Boston

* Left blank in the record.

were sworne before the Court September 29. 1691. & m^r^. Tim^o^. Thornton was sworn about a week after.

Fanning discharg'd

Elizabeth ffanning, after Proclamation by an Oyes. three times made in Court October pr^o^. 1691. That if any Person or Persons could give in Evidence ag^t^. s^d^ Elizabeth of Treason, ffelony or High Misdemeanor, they should come in & be heard, for y^t^. shee stood on her deliverance, and none appearing s^d^. Elizabeth was discharged.

Denmarke indicted

Bridget Denmarke servant maid of Duncan Cambell of Boston Stationer Indicted by the Jurors for o^r^. Soveraigne Lord & Lady the King & the Queen upon their Oathes, for that the s^d^ Bridget Denmarke on the tenth day of April 1691. about seven or eight of the clock in the evening of that day with force & armes upon Rice Griffin of Boston labourer upon the wharf neer the dock in Boston in the Peace of God & the King being an Assault did make & with force & violence with her hands into the dock the s^d^ Rice Griffin did wilfully & maliciously thrust & thereby him by drowning in the water & mudd in the s^d^ dock being, felloniously kill & murther, contrary to the Peace of o^r^ s^d^ Lord & lady the King & Queen their Crown & dignity, the Laws of God, & the laws & statutes in y^t^ case made and provided. Upon which Indictment s^d^ Bridget denmark was arraigned, pleaded not guilty, & put her^ upon Tryall by God & ye Country. The Jury is impanelled whereof m^r^ Richd Crisp is forem̃, & sworne (the s^d^ Bridget makeing no challenge) upon the Tryall & past upon her. And brought in their Verdict, that is to say. The Jury say they find s^d^ Bridget Denmark Guilty of M̃anslaughter by accident ꝑ chance

oct^r^ pr^o^.

Ordered, that s^d^ Bridget denmark pay twenty pounds fine to their ma^ties^. and to pay charges of prosecution & fees of Court, and to remain in Prison till this order be ꝑformed.

Richard Lillie son of Edward Lillie ‖ late ‖ of Boston Cooper Indicted by the Jurors for our Soveraign Lord & Lady William & Mary King & Queen of England &c upon their Oaths, ffor that the s^d^ Richard Lillie upon the 25 day of July last past about five a clock in the afternoon in the Harbor of Boston afores^d^ on board the Briganteen Samuel, John Robinson master, upon Charles Hopkins of Boston, an Assault did make giving him a mortall

2d

wound in the groin by discharging a Buckaneer Gun at him of wch. wound he died. Upon which Indicted the s^d^ Richard Lillie being arraigned pleaded not Guilty, and put himselfe upon Tryall by God & the Country. The first Jury of Tryalls were called whereof m^r^. Rich^d^. Crisp was foreman, and the prisoner makeing no challenge were sworn for his Tryal & past upon him. And the Jury brought in their Verdict, that is to say, They find s^d^. Rich^d^. Lillie guilty of Manslaughter by Misadventure. The Court order s^d^. Richd Lillie to pay ffive pounds money a fine to their Maties. & twenty pounds money to Margaret the widow of s^d^ Charles Hopkins, & charges of Prosecution & fees of Court & to remain in Prison till he pform this sentance.

[264]

In answer to the Petition of John Cutler jun^r^. praying that he may have an hearing of his case, on an appeal from the County Court holden in Charlstowne in December 1689. The Court granted the Petitioner his request. vizt. That his Case shall be heard at the next Court of Assistants to be holden in Boston in March next, and in the mean time that Execution be respited

Attest Joseph Webb cler

The Court was adjourned to the sixteenth of October at nine a clock in the Morning & then sate.

Present The Honble. Simon Bradstreet Esqr. Govr.

Samuel Appleton	Esq^rs^. Assist^ts^	James Russell	Esq^rs^. Assist^ts^.
John Hathorn		Samuel Sewall	
Elisha Hutchinson		Isaac Addington	
John Phillips		John Smith	

Martin Williams a stranger late Resident in Salem Bricklayer being presented & indicted by the Jurors for our Soveraigne Lord & Lady the King and Queen upon their Oaths, That is to say, That s^d^. Martin Williams intending falsly craftily & deceitfully to defraud the Good People of this their Maties. Colony of New-England, at Salem afores^d^ on the sixth day of April 1691. in the Third yeare of their Maties. reigne, Five peices of false counterfeit money of false & mixt mettals to the likeness of Spanish money called peices of Eight, not being the proper Coine of the Kingdome of England, but the same being curr^t^. in this

Williams Indicted

their Ma[ties]. Colony of the Massachusets in New-Engl[d]. and others their Ma[ties]. Colonies & Plantations in America, falsly did counterfeit, make & coine. And upon the s[d] sixt day of April 1691 about nine a clock in the Evening, one of the s[d] false counterfeit peices of Eight for y[e] value of six shillings curr[t]. money of this Colony did utter & put away contrary to the laws & statutes in that case made & provided. The s[d] Martin Williams being brought to the Barr & arraigned upon s[d] Indictment pleaded not guilty, and put himselfe upon Tryall by God & the Country. The Jury was called (Cap[t]. Richard Crisp foreman) & sworn to pass upon his Tryall, the Evidences in y[e] Case were read (the witnesses appeared) and owned by s[d] Williams. The Case was comitted to y[e] Jury, The Jury gave in their Verdict, viz[t]. They find the s[d] Martin Williams guilty of falsly & ffraudulently uttering of false Counterfeit money according as is expressed in the Indictment. The Court order that the s[d]. Martin Williams shall stand three ‖ severall ‖ Lecture dayes in Boston, in the Pillory, one houre each time after the lecture wth. a Paper signifying his Crime, and that he pay charges of Prosecution, and ffees of Court & Prison & remain in Custody till this Order be performed. /

Jury Sworne

Cap[t]. Richard Crisp
Edward Creeck
Thomas Stanbury
John Scott
Joseph Leeds
John Capen jun[r].
Nathanael Adams
Abraham Hill
William Russell
Thomas Hamond
Nath[ll]. Norden
James Barnes

Ordered that John Newhall Tertius of Lynn & John Blaney be sent for to appeare at the Court of Assist[ts]. on their Adjournm[t].

The Court adjourned to the second Tuesday in Decemb[r]. next at one of the clock in y[e] Afternoon.

[265]

The Court mett, and adjourned to Wednesday 9th of December at nine a clocke morning, thence to the Eleventh at One a clock in the afternoon

Order about Nic: Lawrence's Appeale

Whereas Nicolas Lawrence late master or Comander of the Katch Salisbury had given bond to prosecute his Appeale before the Comissioners of the High Court of Admiralty, from a Judgem[t]. Jahleel Brenton Gent. Collect[r]. &c of their Ma[ties]. Customs in New-Engl[d]. recovered on an Informacon vers s[d] Katch Salisbury &c, which ^ never intended when they granted his appeal but to their Ma[ties]. in Council,

Ordered, that the entry be rectifyed & amended according to the true Intent & as the s[d] Appeale was granted

Court adjourned to Thursday the 24th decemb[r]. thence to 25th. at one a clock

Hannah Owen's sentance.

Hannah Owen of Braintree comitted to the Prison in Boston for that by indirect meanes Josiah Owen & s[d] Hannah Owen procured a marriage ~~notw~~ they being within the line of kindred or affinity forbidden Marriage by the Word of God & Statutes of England, Appeared, and owned she was s[d]. Josiah owen's Brothers Relict. The Court do order, That the s[d] Hannah do for the future no more cohabit wth. s[d] Josiah Owen, or have fellowship with him as with an husband, and that she make a publick acknowledgement of her sin & evil before the Congregation at Braintree on their Lecture day, or on the Lords day.

[*Blank.*]

[266]

At a Court of Assistants holden in Boston March pri°. 169½

Present

Simon Bradstreet Esq[r]. Gov[r].

Thomas Danforth Esq[r]. Dep[ty]. Gov[r].

James Russell, Wait Winthrop, John Phillips — Esq[rs]. Assist[ts].

William Stoughton, Samuel Sewall, Isaac Addington — Esq[rs]. Assist[ts].

Grand Jury sworne

L[t]. Richard Way
Jarvis Ballard
Thomas Harwood
Thomas Bannister
John Cotta
Henry Bowen
John Watson
Henry Garnsey
Thomas Trott sen[r].
Rich[d]. Lowden
Thomas Bligh
Thomas Cheeney
James Hubbard
Richard Norcras
Theophilus Roads

Cap[t] Edward Wylly of Boston shopkeeper Pl[t]. vers Edward Thomas of s[d] Boston Merch[t]. def[t]. — On Appeal from the Comission[rs] Court held in Boston december 24. 1691. where Judgem[t]. was for the Pl[t]. Thomas Three pounds sixteen shillings money & costs. The Courts Judgem[t]. Reasons of Appeal & Evidences in the Case being read & comitted to y[e] Jury. The Jury find for the defend[t]. Confirmation of the former Judgem[t]. & costs of Courts.

Jury of Tryalls sworn

mr. Jacob Melyne forem̃
Roger Kilcupp
Jabez Salter
John Henneway
Isaac Newell
Thomas Morey
James ffoster
Increase Sumner
James Blake
Joseph Kettle
John Simson
Reuben Luxford

NATHANAEL THAIRE of Boston Plt. vers. ELIZABETH TOWNSEND Relict of James Townesend - - - deft. } On Appeal from the Judgmt. of the County Court held in Boston October 27. 1691. where Judgemt. was ^ the Plt. That the defendt. do forthwith deliver to ye Plt. Possession of the pt of the house sued for as it was layd out by Order of Court & costs. The Courts Judgemt. Reasons of Appeal & Evidences in the Case were read, and com̃itted to the Jury. The Jury find for the defendt. Confirmation of the former Judgemt. & costs of Courts. Execution issued March 28. 1692

2 Jury of Tryals sworn

mr. Jonathn. Remington
Robert Cumbey
William Hobbey
Jacob Newell
Robert Spurr
Samuel Kettle
Joseph Ryall
Nicolas ffessondon
Jason Russell
Amos Merrit
Thomas Straite
Jonathan Smith

ARTHUR MASON Guardian to Tho: Gatliff son of Jonathn. Gatliff of Boston Marrinr. decd. Plt. vers. SAMUEL LEGG of Boston Marrinr. deft. } On Appeal from ye Judgmt. of the County Court hat * at Boston October 27. 1691. where the Plt. recovered Judgemt. agt. ye Appelt. Ten Pounds in money & costs. The Courts Judgemt Reasons of Appeal & evidences were read & com̃itted to ye Jury. The Jury find for the Appellt. Revertion of the former Judgemt. & costs of Courts.

ANDREW BELCHAR Mercht. Plt. vers JAMES LLOYD Mercht. defendt. } On Appeal from the County Court holden in Boston January 26th. 1691½ where Judgemt. was for the defendt. costs of Court, the Appellt. sueing ye deft. in an action of Debt for non paymt. of two hundred & fifty pounds justly due by one Obligation or charter party under ye hand & seale of sd James LLoyd indented & made 22th July 1691 for going into ye parts of Nova Scotia not in Amity wth. the King of Engld. &c as is more at large specifyed in ye Attachmt. & Courts Judgemt. The Appellt. desired a special Jury of Merchts &c and he would be at ye charge wch. was accordingly granted

* Error in the record for "held"?

[267]

Special Jury sworn

Capt. Edward Wyllys
Robert Howard
David Jefferyes
Nathanael Carey
John Balston
William Welsted
Richard Way
James Barnes
John Hayward
William Griggs
Samll. Phipps
Joshua Gee

and a Jury sumoned whose names are in the Margent. The Courts Judgemt. Reasons of Appeale & evidences in the case were read & Pleas made. The case was comitted to the Jury. The Jury returned their Verdict thereon vizt. They find for the Appellt. Revertion of the former Judgemt. & forfeiture of the charter Party, two hundred & ffifty pounds money & costs of Courts

James Lowden Appellant from the County Court at Cambridge October 6th. 1691. where the Court sentenced sd. Lowden to pay five pounds in money fine to ye County & fees of Court &c being found Guilty of slaundering mr. James Russell in the discharge of his Magistraticall office. The Courts Judgemt. Reasons of Appeal & evidences being read were comitted to ye Jury. The Jury find Confirmation of the former Judgemt. and costs of Courts.

Hovey vers. Perkins

Daniel Hovey senr. of Ipswich Plt. vers Abraham Perkins defendt. } On Appeal from the Judgmt of the County Court held at Ipswich Septembr. 29. 1691. where Judgemt ^ for the Plaintiff the land in controversy & costs. The Courts Judgemt. Reasons of Appeal & Evidences in the case were read & comitted to the Jury. The Jury find for the Appellt. Revertion of the former Judgemt. & costs of Courts.

Perry vers. Alford.

Seth Perry of Boston Plt. vers. Benjn. Alford of sd Boston defendt. } On Appeal from the County Court holden in Boston 26th January 169½ in an action of Review, where the Appellt. was cast Costs of Court. The Courts Judgmt. Reasons of Appeal & Evidences in the case were read & given to ye Jury. The Jury find for the defendt. Confirmation of former Judgemt & costs of Courts.

Waite vers Newhall

John Waite Plt. vers. Thomas Newhall defendt. } On Appeal from the Judgemt. of ye County Court held at Charlstowne decembr. 29. 1691. where the Jury found for sd Newhall ye Plt.

foure pounds money according to Bill & costs. The Courts Judgem^t. Reasons of Appeal & Evidences in the case being read & committed to ye Jury, The Jury find for Thomas Newhall Confirmation of ye former Judgem^t. & costs of Courts.

Somes vers Lake

JOHN SOMES of Boston Appel^t. vers. LANCELOTT LAKE of s^d Boston defend^t. } On Appeal from the County Court of Suffolke Jan^{ry}. 26. 169½ where the defend^t. recovered Judgem^t. ag^t. the Appell^t. That he give the defend^t. an Acco^{tt}. of the Goods sued for & costs of Court. the s^d Lancelot Lake sueing for an acco^{tt} with the Produce of Sundry Goods & merchandize as ℘ Attachm^t. The Courts Judgement, Reasons of Appeal & evidences in the case being read & committed to the Jury. The Jury returned their Verdict, They find for the defend^t. Confirmation of the former Judgement and do adde that the Appell^t. shall within one month give acco^{tt}. to ye defend^t. of his disposall of the Goods he rec^d. as Attourney of ye def^t. & now sued for, or pay to ye def^t. in curr^t. money, two Hundred twenty foure pounds & costs of Courts.

[268]

Arnold vers. Belcher

JOHN ARNOLD Prison keeper in Boston - - - - Pl^t. vers. JOSEPH BELCHAR of Braintree defend^t. } On Appeal from the Judgem^t. of the County Court holden in Boston October 27th. 1691. where Judgem^t. was for the Pl^t. Belchar ffourteen pounds nineteen shillings & ten pence mony & costs. The Courts Judgem^t. Reasons of Appeal & evidences in ye case being read and comitted to the Jury The Jury find for the Appell^t. Revertion of the former Judgem^t. & costs of Courts.

Davison ver Potter

DANIEL DAVISON ‖ jun^r ‖ of Ipswich Pl^t. vers. EDMOND POTTER of Ipswich defend^t } On Appeal from the County Court held at Ipswich Sep^t. 29. 1691. Where the Judgem^t. was Confirmation of ye former

Judgem^t^. & costs of Courts. The Courts Judgem^t^. Reasons of Appeal & Evidences in the case being read & comitted to ye Jury. The Jury find for ye defend^t^. Confirmation of the former Judgement & costs of Courts.

Smith vers Nash

THOMAS SMITH of Boston Smith Pl^t^.
vers.
JOSEPH NASH of Boston Marrin^r^. def^t^.
} On Appeal from the Judgem^t^. of the Comission^r^s Court held at Boston decemb^r^. the 29th: 1691. Where Judgem^t^. was for the pl^t^. Nash ffort y shillings in money and costs. The Courts Judgem^t^. Reasons of Appeal & Evidences in the case were read & comitted to ye Jury. The Jury find for the defend^t^. Confirmation of the former Judgem^t^. & costs of Courts.

Dunclin vers Witherett

NATHAN DUNCLIN of Charlstown Mar^r^ Pl^t^.
vers.
WILLIAM WITHERETT of Boston Merch^t^. defend^t^.
} On Appeal from the Judgem^t^. of the County Court holden at Boston October 27. 1691. where Judgem^t^. was for the defend^t^. Costs of Courts The Courts Judgem^t^. Reasons of Appeal & Evidences in the case were read & comitted to the Jury. The Jury find for the defend^t^ Confirmation of the former Judgem^t^. & costs of Courts.

Peggey vers Crisp

EDWARD PEGGY of Boston Pl^t^.
vers
RICHARD CRISP of Boston defend^t^.
} On Appeal from the Judgem^t^. of the County Court held at Boston January 27. 169$\frac{1}{2}$ where Judgem^t^. was for the pl^t^. Thirteen pounds in p^s^. of Eight at five shillings a peice & costs. The Courts Judgem^t^. Reasons of Appeale & Evidences in the case were read & comitted to y^e^ Jury. The Jury find for the Appell^t^. Revertion of the former Judgem^t^. & costs of Courts.

Shrimpton vers Brenton

SAMUEL SHRIMPTON Esq[r]. Owner of the Briganteen Mary . . . Appel[t] vers JAHLEEL BRENTON Gent Collector survey[r] & searcher of their Ma[ties]. Customs in New Engld def[t]. } On Appeal from the Judgem[t]. of the County Court holden in Boston ffebruary 17th continued by Adjournm[t]. from 26th January 169½ upon an [269]
Information or libell against the Briganteen Mary, for the breach of the Act of the 12° of King Charles the second Entituled an Act for y[e] Incourageing & increasing of shipping & Navigation &c[a]. as also upon y[e] Act of ‖ y[e] ‖ 25th of the s[d] King Charles as is more at large Expressed in the County Courts Judgem[t]. said Briganteen being forfeited for haveing her full ladeing of hides & Tobacco not giving bond nor paid duties for the same according as ꝑ s[d] Act is required. Issue is thereupon Joyned. The Courts Judgem[t]. Reasons of Appeal, the defend[ts]. answer & Evidences in the case being read, and Pleas by both parties made, The case was comitted to y[e] Jury. The Jury upon their Oathes return their verdict for the Appellant. Revertion of the former Judgement.

Lambe &c vers Clarke attorny.

ABIEL LAMBE & SOLOMON RAYNSFORD Pl[t]. vers M[R] ADAM WINTHROP Treasurer of the County of Suffolk by John Clark his Atto[rny]. defend[t]. } On Appeal from the County Court holden in Boston on the 27th day of October 1691. where the Appell[t]. was cast forfeiture of the Bond one hundred & fifty pounds money & costs of Court. The Courts Judgem[t]. Reasons of Appeal & Evidences in y[e] Case being read committed to the Jury & are on file, The Jury returned their verdict thereon viz[t]. They find for y[e] defend[t]. Confirmation of the former Judgement & costs of Courts.

GEORGE DANSON Pl[t]. vers CAP[T]. JOHN WING def[t]. } This action fell, no reasons of Appeal being returned.

Milner vers. Wing

NATHANIEL MILNER Marrin^{r}. Pl^{t}. vers CAP^{T}. JOHN WING of Boston defend^{t}. } On Appeal from the Judgem^{t}. of the County Court holden in Boston Octob^{r}. 27th. 1691. where Judgem^{t}. was for the pl^{t}. Jno Wing seven pounds twelve shillings & eight pence & costs. The Courts Judgem^{t}. Reasons of Appeale and Evidences in the case were read & comitted to ye Jury. The Jury find for the defend^{t}. Confirmation of the former Judgem^{t}. & Costs of Courts.

CAP^{T}. JOHN MARCH of Newbery Pl^{t}. vers. RICHARD CARR of Salisbury def^{t}. } The Appell^{t}. was nonsuited on non appearance, & ye def^{t}. Rich^{d}. Carr moved ye Court for his Costs, wch. was granted for his Attendance &c at this Court wch. amounts to twenty eight shillings wth. certificate. The costs at Ipswich Court & before Maj^{r}. Saltonstall not being brought into this Bill of costs but left to Ipswich Court bill that is allow^{d} there.

attest J. Webb cler

Stanbury vers Harris

THOMAS STANBURY of Boston Pl^{t}. vers. RICHARD HARRIS of s^{d} Boston Defend^{t}. } On Appeal from the Judgem^{t}. of the County Court January 26th. 169½ where the Judgem^{t}. was for the defend^{t}. costs of Court The Courts Judgem^{t}. Reasons of Appeal

[270]

and Evidences in the Case were read & comitted to the Jury. The ^ find a special Verdict to this effect. That George ^ * shipmaster lands from on board his ship, a parcell of salt in the warehouse of ye defend^{t}. which s^{d}. salt was shipped on board by William Ball as appeares by receipt under George Ball's hand, we find proved that this salt was sold by s^{d}. W^{m}. Ball unto the pl^{t}. as appeares by the Testimonyes of Richard Arnold that saw it measured unto ye pl^{t}. as also owned by the defend^{t}. as appeares by the testimony of Thomas Edwards, also that he agreed with the pl^{t}. about the warehouse room for s^{d} salt as appeares by the testimony of s^{d} Edwards & m^{r}. Epaphras Shrimpton If therefore the

* Ball?

defend^{t}. is by law obliged to deliver s^{d} salt to ye pl^{t}. on his demand without the special order of George Ball who first delivered the same to him, we find for the pl^{t}. the salt in Controversy wth. Revertion of the former Judgem^{t}. & costs of Courts. If otherwise for the defend^{t}. Confirmation of ye former Judgem^{t}. & costs of Courts.

The Magistrates on consideration of the * declare for ye Appell^{t}. the salt in controversy, Two hundred sixty seven bushells & costs of Courts.

Foy vers Robie

CAP^{T}. JOHN FOY of Boston Marrin^{r}. Pl^{t}. vers WILLIAM ROBIE of Boston Merch^{t}. ffeofee in trust for Mary Loder late wife of John Loder def^{t} } On Appeal from the Judgem^{t}. of y^{e}. County Court holden in Boston Octob^{r}. 27 1691. where Judgem^{t}. was for ye Pl^{t}. Robie, Two hundred pounds mony and costs. The Courts Judgem^{t}. Reasons of Appeale & evidences in ye Case produced were read & comitted to ye Jury The Jury return a speciall verdict That if the Execution levyed on the ship Dolphin, and possession given to m^{r}. Robie of the same do invest the right & power in m^{r}. Robie as ffeoffee in trust then we find for the defend^{t}. confirmation of the former Judgem^{t}. & costs of Courts, if otherwise we find for the Appell^{t}. Revertion of the former Judgem^{t}. & costs of Courts

The Magistrates declare for the Appellant Revertion of the former Judgement & costs of Courts.

Green ver Fox.

SAMUEL GREEN in behalfe of himselfe and as Attorney to his Brethren Pl^{t}. vers THOMAS FOX defend^{t}. } On Appeal from the County Court held at Charlestowne decemb^{r}. 29. 1691. where Judgem^{t}. was for the defend^{t}. Title to ye land in controversy & costs of Court. The Courts Judgement Reasons of Appeale and evidences in the case produced being read & comitted to ye Jury The Jury find for the defend^{t}. Confirmation of the former Judgement & costs of Courts.

* Left blank in the record.

[271]

Stratton vers. Gidley.

RICHARD STRATTON Appell^t. vers. HEZEKIAH GIDLEY defend^t. } On Appeal from the Judgem^t. of the County Court at Charlstowne in december 1691. where s^d Hezekiah Gidley sued s^d. Stratton for illegally possessing himselfe of an house & land in Chelmsford &c which of right belonged to s^d Gidley's father & wch. he dyed seized of as his owne proper real Estate &c and recovered Judgem^t. ag^t. the Appell^t. Title to ye land in controversy & costs of Court. The Courts Judgem^t. Reasons of Appeale & Evidences in the Case were read & comitted to ye Jury The Jury find for the defend^t. Confirmation of ye former Judgem^t. & costs of Courts allowed two pounds eight shillings ten pence. Execution issued for Costs March. 25. 1692

Tay vers Harwood

JEREMIAH TAY of Boston Marrin^r. Pl^t. vers. THOMAS HARWOOD & Rachel his wife def^t. } On Appeal from the Judgem^t. of the County Court holden in Boston Jan^ry 26. 169½ where Judgem^t. was for ye Pl^t. Possession of the house & land sued for & costs of Court. The Courts Judgem^t. Reasons of Appeal & Evidences in the Case were read & comitted to the Jury. The Jury find for the Appellant Revertion of the former Judgem^t. & costs of Courts.

Thatcher vers Thatcher

MARY THATCHER of Boston widow. Pl^t. vers. M^R. PETER THATCHER of Milton def^t. } On Appeal from the Judgem^t. of the County Court holden in Boston January 26. 169½ where Judgement was for the Pl^t. The Possession of the house & land sued for & costs of Court. The Courts Judgem^t. Reasons of Appeal & evidences in the Case were read & comitted to ye Jury The Jury find for the Defend^t. Confirmation of the former Judgem^t. and costs of Courts.

Checkley vers. Grigs

CAP^T. ANTHONY CHECKLEY Pl^t. vers. WILLIAM GRIGGS defend^t. } On Appeal from the Commission^rs. Court held in Boston ffebruary 9th. 169½ where the Judgmt. was for the Plt. six pounds money & costs of Court. The Courts Judgemt. Reasons of Appeal & Evidences in the case were read & comitted to the Jury. The Jury return their Verdict vizt. They find for the defendt. Confirmation of the former Judgemt. & costs of Courts. Execution issued March 23. 169½

[*Here ends the record of the Sessions of the Court of Assistants.*]

[Record of Executions.]

[The following record of executions is at the end of the volume, the paging beginning with the third leaf from the end, the preceding two leaves being blank. The beginning of each page of this part of the original record is indicated here by [1a] [2a] &c. The whole of this record is in the handwriting of Edward Rawson, the Secretary.]

[1a]

Att this end of the Court of Assistants booke of Records stands Recorded such executions as haue binn Returnd & by y[e] partjes Concerned so desired to be so entred at words in length &c

Att A Court of Assistants held at Boston y[e] 2[d] Septembe[r] 1673.

ffatherGon Dinely Administrato[r] to the estate of John Dinely deceasd plantiff ag[t] the estate of Cornelius stenwicke in the hands of Cap[t] w[m] Dauis In an action of Appeale from the Judgment of the County Court at Boston in July last = After the Attachment Courts Judgment Reasons of Appeale & euidences in the Case produced were read Comitted to the Jury and are on file wth the Reccords of this Court the Jury brought in their virdict they found for the Appellant Reuersion of the forme[r] Judgment wth the land in Controuersy & Costs of Courts fowe[r] pounds ten shillings & two pence = This Judgment stands entred as the law directs from march nex[t] 167$\frac{3}{4}$ That this is A true Copy taken out of the Courts book of Reccords

Attests Edw[rd] Rawson Secr[ty]

To Edward Mitchelson marshall Generall or his deputy These require yow in his Majtys name by way of execution to levy & execute the Judgmen[t] aboue written in all respects and deliuer the same wth two shillings for this execution to Fathe[r]Gon Dinely administrato[r] administrato[r] * aforesajd and is in sattisfaction of the aboue sajd Judgment granted him by the Court of Assistants sitting in Boston as aboue sajd making yo[r] returne as the law directs & not faile dated in Boston 9[th] of march 167$\frac{4}{5}$ By y[e] Cour[t] Edward Rawson secrety vnd[r]writt

* Repeated in the record.

This Execution was se^r ved according to the aboue written order and the land deliuered to the Appellan^t only wee did not gett any Costs Capt Dauis being but an Atturney deny ^ to pay any Costs this 22 of (1) mo 167 4/5 Edward michelson marshall Geñ^ll

This execution & Return is entred & Recorded word for word & Compared wth the originall on file this 8th Aprill 1675 at Reques^t of fathe^r gon Dineley ℘ Edw: Rawson secre^t

[*Blank*]

[5^a] *

Att A Court of Admiralty or Court of Assistants held at Boston in New England the 16th of Decembe^r 1675

In the Case brought to this Court by the libell & complaint of Nicholas skinner master of the ship Doue in behalfe of himself & Company plaintiff (against the sajd ship Doue nicholas moulder p^t ouno^r of the sajd ship and James Loyd his Assignee defendan^ts) for wages for himself sajd skinner & Company and expenses lajd out on the sajd ship. This Court finds for the plaintiffe ‖ & orders and decrees that the defendant ^ unto the plaintiffe ‖ the sume of two hundred and sixteen pounds nine shillings & fower pence damage in money & costs of this Court three pounds sixteen shillings That this is a true Copie taken out of the Courts Reccords Attests Edward Rawson Secre^ty

To Edward mitchelson marshall Generall or his deputy.

These Require yow in his Maj^tys name to levy by way of execution on sajd ship Doue Nicholas moulder & James Loyd his Assignee in mony the sume of two hundred and twenty pounds fiue shillings and fowe^r pence and deliuer the same to Nicholas skinner master of the sajd ship Doue in behalfe of himself & Company for wages & expenses &c as aboue in all respects hereof not to faile. Dated in Boston this 21th decembe^r 1675

By ye Court Edward Rawson Secre^ty

underwritt

That this is A true Copie of ye execution Attests Edw Rawson secret

Boston 28 decembe^r 1675

Wee whose names are vnde^r written being chosen by m^r Nicholas

* (*Pages [2^a], [3^a], and [4^a] are blank except that in the upper left-hand corner of page [3^a] is entered " This Executiõ entred 21 of xbr 78." This page [5^a] is numbered in Rawson's hand 5, and is the only page at this end of the book which has an original numbering.*)

moulder mr Nicholas skinner & the marshall Generall for the Country to Aprise the Pincke * Doue whereof is mr † mr Nicholas skinner wth hir Appurtenances belonging unto sajd Pincke Doue an Inventory of sajd Pincke & Appurtenances being produced to us and the particculars shewed unto us and vpon our vejwing and ouerhaling of them ꝑticcularly wee doe Apprize the sajd Pincke and Its Appurtenances at the sume of fower hundred forty & fower pounds mony as witt[n]es our hands the day & yeare abouesajd christopher Clarke Joseph Cocke nathaniel Greenwood.

vndr writt & Anext this execution was served on the pinck Doue that was Apprised money as will Appeare by the Aprisement also so much of the vessell was prized and deliuered vnto mr skinner the wch' execution amounted to two hundred twenty pounds fiue shillings and fiuety shillings for the serving of this execution wch' I Received of mr skinner as wittnes my hand the sume is two hundred twenty two pounds fiueteen shillings wch' is the whole of the execution as ‖is‖ abouesajd and deliuered the same vnto mr skinner for the sattisfying of the aboue written judgment = 27 $\frac{10}{mo}$ 1675 Edward mitchelson marshall Generall

The Judgment execution Aprisement & deliuery by the marshall Generall as aboue written stands here Recorded word for word wth the originall on file as Attests Edward Rawson Secrety

[*Page 6a is blank.*]

[7a]

Att A Court of Assistants or Admiralty held at Boston 24th of may & Adjourned to 28th sajd may 1678

prsentt
Jno Leueret Esqr Gou
Symon Bradstreet
Daniel Gookin
Tho Danforth
Wm Hathorne
Edwd Tyng
Joseph Dudley Esqr

Tho Bromehall mate Richard Peeters Lawrence Bowles & Jno Ragland marriners of Catch Jno & Benjamin plaintiffs by their libell & complt exhibbitted to this Court 24th may Instant & Adjourned to twenty eighth Instant at one of the clocke against wm Long master of the sajd Catch deffendt according to Attachment who wth the sajd vessell was bound ouer in one hundred twenty sixe pounds mony to respond the decree & Judgment of this Court for that the sajd deffendant refused to pay vnto the sajd mate & company their seuerall wages i e to the sajd Thomas Bromhall mate twenty fiue pounds ten shillings or thereabouts & to the sajd

* Written over "ship." † Master.

Richard Peete^{r}s a thirteen pounds to sajd Bowles ten pounds tenn shillings and to ye sajd Ragland fiuety shillings for their se^{r}vices donn in the sajd Catch as in sajd Attachm^{t} & euidences & sajd maste^{r}s Acknowledgm^{t} that the sajd marrine^{r}s had binn wth him a tenn or eleven mon^{ths} After the libell Attachmen^{t} & euidences in the Case produced were Read and are on file The Court found for the plaintiff^{s} and orde^{r}s & decrees that the deffend^{t} master & Catch pay vnto Tho Bromhall twenty fiue pounds fiue shillings to Richard Peete^{r}s twelue pounds fiueteen shillings To Lawrenc Bowles ten pounds $_{\wedge}$ to John Ragland fiuety shillings wth Costs & chardges of Court three pounds seven shillings & two pence in all fiuety three pounds seventeen shillings & two pence = execution Issued out for y^{e} same 29th may 78 = & was

To Edward Mitchelson marshall Gennerall or his deputy

In his Majtjes name yo^{w} are Required by way of Execution to levy on the person of w^{m} Long master of the Catch John & Benjamin wth hir Apparrell & furniture in mony the sume of fiuety pounds tenn shillings and deliuer the same wth two shillings for this execution together with three pounds seuen shillings & two pence for Court charges & Costs in mony to Thomas Bromhall twenty-fiue pounds fiue shillings to Richard Peete^{r}s twelue pounds fiveteen shillings to Lawrenc Bowles tenn pounds $_{\wedge}$ to Jno Ragland fiuety shillings in all wth costs & charges three pounds seuen shillings & two penc and is in sattisfaction of a Judgment & decree of the Court of Admiralty granted to them for so much making you^{r} Returne as the law directs Dated in Boston the 29th of may 1678 =

By the Court Edward Rawson Secre^{ty}

vnde^{r}writt

I haue seised the master & Catch John & Benjamin and haue Apprised the same as will Appear vnde^{r} their hands hereto Annex^{t} the 31th $\frac{3d}{mo}$ 1678. Edward Mitchelson Generall marshall

Annex^{t} = An Apprisement of the Catch John & Benjamin w^{m} Long Comand^{r} may 31th 1678

	li	s	d
majnsajle one hundred & sixteene yards fifty eight shillings Jebsajle 13. 4^{d} sprit sajle thirteene shillings & fowe^{r} pence — — — — — —	04.	04.	04
majne top sajle ten shillings missen six shillings three pence one hundred weight Junke sixe shillings	01.	02.	03
nine barrells sixe shillings Cable forty shillings Runing Rigging in hold & blocks 20^{s} —	01.	06.	00

	li	s	d
Iron potts & a frying pan ten shillings pewter dish & wooden platte^rs 2^s Can hooks 1^s	00.	10	00
spikes & chajne plates for store ten shillings on Anchor 35^s grindston 1^s — — — — — —	02	06	00
standing & Runing Rigging fiuety shillings boate mas^t & sajle & oares fiuety shillings — — — —	05	00	00
The Hull masts & yards seventy & fiue pounds —	75	00	00
willjam Condy John ffoy Nathaniel Greenwood	92:	19.	11*

vnde^rwritt

know all men by these presents that on the one & thirtieth day of may 1678 w^m Condy John ffoy & nathaniel Greenewood Came before me vnde^r writt and deposed that they being chosen by willjam Long master

[8^a]

and the seamen of the sajd Catch & the marshall Gennerall Edward mitchelson on behalfe of the Country to make an Aprajsement of the sajd Catch & Appurtenances aboue written Came before me and tooke their oathes that they would make a due Aprisement of the same which ‖ also ‖ they haue signed vnde^r their hands as Attests Tho Brattle Comissione^r. /

stands endorst on the originall execution Returned

This is to Certify that this execution is sattisfied and the men is pajd their wages and the vessell was sold according to the Apprisemen^t as will Appeare vnde^r their hands and what remajnes I shall rese^rve till further orde^r

Edwd mitchelson m^rsh^ll Genll

And at the ffoote of all is writt:

This is to Certify whom it may Concerne that I vnde^rwritt hauing seized the aboue mentioned Catch & had hir & hir Appurtenances duely Apprized on oath as is aboue written and sold the same one halfe to John keech for forty fowe^r pounds & to John Turell & John ffoster the othe^r halfe for the like sume wch was in full of the execution

Edward mitchelson marshall Gen^ll

That the Courts Judgment execution therevpon Granted & Returnd wth the endorsm^t of the Catch^s Apprisement on oath the marshalls returne of Sattisfaction made to ye seamen of their wages as also

* The figures in this account are given as in the record, although they do not agree with each other. It is not possible to explain the discrepancies.

of his sale of the sajd Catch to the sajd John keech John Turell & John ffoster ffor eighty eight pounds & his deteyning the Remainde^r in his hands till further orde^r one after the othe^r stands entred & Recorded word for word in the sajd Cour^t of Admiralty booke of Records for such transactions is Attested by Edward Rawson Secre^ty

13th June 1678 =

[9^a] 1681

Att A County Court held at Salem the 29th 4/mo 1680:

John Broune sen̄ Ruling Elde^r of the church of Salem & Henry Bartholmew merchant ouersee^rs & feoffees in trust for the children of Robe^rt Grey late deceased plaintiff^s against Nicholas manning defendant in an action of the Case ꝑ according to Attachment dated the 14th of June 1680 the Attachment wth what other euidences in the Case produced were read Cōmitted to the Jury and are on file The Jury brought in their virdict they found for the plaintiff the forfeiture of the mortgage vizt the house & land mortgaged & Costs of Court — Nicholas Maning the defendant Appeales from this virdict to the nex^t Court of Assistants & Gaue bond to prosecute ꝑ = This is a true Coppie — Hilljard veren Cleric = Copia vera. Attes^ts Edward Rawson Secre^t

Att A Court of Assistants held at Boston 7th Septembe^r 1680

Jno Broune & Hen Bartholm̄ execution recorded

Nicholas Mañing plaintiffe on Appeale against John Broune sen̄ and Henry Bartholmew deffendants as ouersee^rs & feoffees in trust as is aboue from the Judgment of the County Court at Salem last After the Attachmen^t Courts Judgmen^t reasons of Appeale & euidences in the Case produced were read Comitted to the Jury and are on file with the Reccords of this Court the Jury brought in their virdict they found for the deffendant Confirmation of the former Judgment & Costs of Courts two pounds sixteene shillings & fower pence = That this is A true Copie of the Courts Judgment taken out of their Reccords Attests Edward Rawson Secret

To Edward Mitchelson marshall Gennerall or his deputy In his Mājjes name yo^w are Required to extend this execution on the house & land now in possession of Nicholas maning as aboue mentioned in the County Cou^rts Judgment as forfeited by his mortgage bearing date 14th of march 1664 which Judgment is Confirmed by the Court of Assistants as in their Judgment aboue also written being true Copies of sajd Judgments as Appeares and deliuer vnto the sajd John Broune

& Henry Bartholmew ouersee^rs & trustees as is aboue declared quiet peaceable & full possession thereof together therewith yo^w are alike required to levy by way of Execution on the Good^s estate or person of nicholas maning in money fiuety sixe shillings & fowe^r pence & deliuer the same wth two shillings for this execution to the sajd Jno Broune & Henry Bartholmew as abouesajd and is in sattisfaction of sajd Judgment so Confirmed making you^r returne as the law directs hereof yo^w are no^t to fajle dated in Boston 22th day of Septembe^r 1680 By ye Court Edward Rawson Secre^t

By virtue hereof I depute Henry skerry my lawfull deputy for the execution of this warrant Edwd mitchelson marshall Gen^ll endo^rs^t stands

I went to the house that Nicholas maning had in possession and made demand of the houses and land morgaged by Nicholas Maning and levyed this execution vpon the houses and land and deliuered them to John Broune sen̄ and as Henry Bartholmew and gaue him quite* peaceable and full possession of all the houses and land according to the Tenno^r of this execution dated this 2^d day 8 mo 1680 in full sattisfaction of this execution ꝑ me Henry skerry marshall Genne^rlls deputy. unde^r writt

I also levyed After demand of the money for Costs and none Could be had on the shoop of nicholas maning^s for the mony and then wee chose fiue† men

[10^a]

men Carpende^rs & were then sworne by m^r Broune assistant of Salem vizt Nathaniel Pickman sen̄ and John Norton who Aprized it then at sixe pounds fiueteene shillings mony and I deliuered it to John Broune sen̄ and as Henry Bartholmew & gaue to him quite & peaceable possession and the marshalls due is in this shoop according to the tenno^r of this execution in full sattisfaction of this execution this 2^d 8 mo 1680

ye executiō & Returne was Returnd to me 5th Aug^st 1681 E R S —

wee whose names ^ vnde^rwritten being chosen & sworne to Aprise a shop of Nicholas maning Gunsmith wee doe Aprize the shop to be valyed at sixe pounds fiueteen shillings [in] money in the Ground as the shop stands on now

annext.

2 octo^be^r 80

Nath Pickman John Norton

Taken vpon oath that this Apprizement is true according to our best Judgment before willjam Broune Assistant:

---

* quiet ?

† So in the record.

the execution Returne of the marshall Genlls deputy vpon it w[th] the Aprizement on oath || & annex[t] || as they stand vnde[r] writ the Courts Judgm[ts] one after the other stands here thus entred & Recorded word for word Agreeing w[th] their Originall from y[e] day of its Returne to me vnde[r]writt i e 5[th] August 1681 in perpetuam rei memoriam at Request of m[r] Henry Bartholmew p Edward Rawson secre[t]

To Jn[o] Greene marshall Gennerall or his deputy Joseph Webb marshall of Suffolke =

In his Maj[t]jes name you are heereby required to levy on the Goods or estate of Barnard Schinking merchant where ev[e]r they may be found or in defect thereof on his sajd three eight parts of the pinck expectation w[th] the Appurtenances thereto belonging to the value of one hundred & eleven pounds thirteen shillings & one penny money and deliuer the same w[th] two shillings for this execution vnto Thomas Gretian marriner & master of sajd Pinke Expectation and is in sattisfaction of a Judgment Granted him for so much by the Court of Assistants sitting in Boston 17th Instant as the Ballance of his Account Given into the sajd Court & sworne vnto wth his Costs &c granted him making you[r] returne hereof to the Court as the law directs dated in Boston 25 of June 1681

By the Court Edward Rawson Secre[t]

on y[e] originall Annex[t] June 27. 1681.

I extended this execution on the three eights of the ship or Pincke Expectation shewed me to be the estate of m[r] Bernard schinking merchant the whole ship being Apprized by m[r] Jonathan Balston m[r] Timothy Prout sen[r] [&] m[r] Thomas Moore as p an Inventory of particculars to wch they subscribed their names will Appeare at two hundred & seven pounds two shillings & fower pence three eighths of which amounts to seventy seven pounds thirteen shillings & fowe[r] pence halfe penny and likewise fower pounds fiueteene shillings more being the propper estate of sajd schinking distinct from the ship in all amounting to eighty two pounds eight shillings & fower pence halfe penny, and || out of which || deducting forty fower shillings for ffees & charges at the Apprizement there remajns eighty pounds fower shillings & fower pence halfe penny, which estate so Apprized I deliuered vnto thomas Gretian in part sattisfaction of this execution there remayning to compleate the same the sume of thirty one pounds one shilling & eight pence halfe penny.

Joseph webb marshall of Suffolk m[r]shall Genrll deputy

New England 27th of August 1681:

This execution marshalls Returne of its extension & ye Aprizement vnder ye three Apprizers hands from ye day aboue written when it was Returnd stands thus recorded in the Court of Assistants booke of Reccords as Attests

Edward Rawson Secrety

[11a] 1681

Annext

wee whose names are herevnto subscribed being chosen & desired by mr Thomas Gretian & Joseph webb marshall of suffolke marshall Gennералls deputy in Behalfe of mr Barnard schenking merchant & in behalfe of the Country to Apprize some of the estate of sajd mr schinking here in New England in order to the sattisfaction of an execution bearing date 25th. June 1681 to value of one hundred & eleven pounds & fiueteen shillings & one penny mony as ℘ sajd execution may appeare refference thereto being had, hauing vejwed the Pincke or ship expectation three eights of which Pincke or ship is Affirmed to be sajd mr schinkings wee doe value the whole ship as followes wth all her Appurtenances —

	li	s	d
Impr'imis The Hull Boat masts yards & standing Rigging as now she ljes	100 =	00 —	00
3 Anchors about thirteen hundred weight — —	020	00	00
1 sheet Cable 14c 2 smaller Cables & an Hauser about 22c — — — — — — — — —	035	00	00
4 smale Guns wth Carriages 12 hundred weight —	014 —	00	00
2 majn sailes 2 foresajles 2 foretop sajles one majntop sajle 1 mizen about 7 hundred & seventeen yards 717 about halfe worne — — — — —	027 —	02 —	04
8 C. weight of smale Rigging & blockes more propperly his oune particcular estate distinct from the ship	006	00	00
	202 =	02 —	4
2 pr of Hand screwes being Rusty & old — —	001 —	10 —	00
1 Copper Keetle weighing twenty seven pounds 27	001 —	10 —	00
1 pr stilyards rusty & wanting some fitting —	000 —	10 —	00
12 pounds of pewter at 12d ℘ li — — — —	000 —	19 —	00
27th June 81	206 —	11 =	4

Jonathan Balston
Timothy Prout sen
Tho moore

Jonathan Balston Timothy Prout and Thomas Moore gaue in this

Apprizement of the Pincke expectation vpon oath before me Symon Bradstreet Gou̅no^r. =

More since taken notice of belonging to the ship

6 muskets & 1 smale fowling peece 3 sword blades 2 Crowes of Iron 1 deep sea lead 1 sounding lead 5 compasses halfe doz^n Glasses a Cross cutt saw valued by the above named Gentlemen at — —	05 = 00 — 00
belonging to m^r schinking 1 Iron pot & on old stewpan at	6^s

recorded as on y^e oth^r side

[12^a]

Att A County Court held at Boston 27th July 1680.

Wm Hollowell Jun̄ Benjamin Hollowell & Edward Ashley who marrjed mary Hollowell or their lawfull Atturney plaintiffs Cont^ra Stephen Butler sen̄ deffend^tt in an Accon of Revejw of an action Comenced & prosecuted by the now plaintiff^s ag^t the sajd Stephen Butler at a County Court in Boston in July last for wth holding (und^r pretence of right by execcutorship to Mary ward late wife to Benjamin ward & othe^r false p^rtences ^ an estate to the value of fower hundred pounds or thereabouts which did belong vnto Benjamin ward aforesajd and now is the propper right of the plan^ts who are the right & vndoubted heires of sajd Benjamin ward &c^a according to Attachm^t the Attachment & euidences in the Case produced being read & Com̄itted to the Jury wch are on file the Jury brought in their virdict they found for the plaintiffs the houses & lands & appurtenances therevnto belonging sued for & Costs of Court The Deffend^t Appealed from this Judgmen^t vnto the nex^t Court of Assistants & Gaue bond for prosecution to effect This is A true Copie as Attests Is^a Addington Cler. Copia vera Attests Edwd Rawson Secre^t

Att A Court of Assistants sitting in Boston 7th 7ber 1680

Stephen Butler plaintiff ag^t w^m Hollowell Jun̄ Benj. Hollowell & Edward Ashley deffend^ts in an Action of Appeale from the Judgment of the County Court in Boston After the Attachment Courts Judgment Reasons of Appeale & euidences in the Case produced were read Comitted to the Jury & are on file wth the Reccords of this Court the Jury brought in their virdict they found for the deffendants Confirmation of the forme^r Judgment & Costs of Courts sixe pounds sixe shillings =

Copia vera Attests Edwd Rawson Secret

To Edward Mitchelson marshall Gennerall

In his Maj'jes name yo^{w} are required to levy by way of Execution on the houses lands and Appurtenances thereto belonging ‖ as ‖ in the Judgment of the County Court aboue written and is there exprest and also in Costs in mony from stephen Butler the sume of sixe pounds sixe shillings and deliuer the same wth two shillings for this Execution to w^{m} Hollowell Benjamin Hollowell & Edward Ashley or their Atturney and is in sattisfaction of the Judgment of the Court of Assistants sitting in Boston the 7th of September last Confirming the same making you^{r} returne as the law directs dated in Boston this 9th of Novembe^{r} 1680.

By the Court Edward Rawson Secre^{t}

To Jno Greene marshall Genll, or his deputy

In his Maj'jes name yo^{w} are Required to levy by way of Execution on the houses & lands yet remayning & not Compleated wth the Costs according to the Judgment of the County Court & Court of Assistants as aboue exprest lately belonging to Benjamin ward deceased &c and deliuer the same wth two shillings for this execution to the Aboue mentioned Hollowells &c or their Atturney m^{r} Anthony cheekley as sattisfaction to the ‖ sd ‖ Judgments making your returne as the law directs & not fajle Dated in Boston 1st of August 1681

By the Court Edward Rawson Secret

I hereby depute marshall Returne wayte
to extend this execution August 2, 1681

Jno Greene marshall Genn^{ll}

[13^{a}]

Nouembe^{r} 12th 1680.

I extended this execution on the house & Ground where Roger Browne now liueth wth all the appurtenances thereto belonging or Apperteyning as also vpon the house & Ground where willjam Robbins now liueth with all Appurtenances ‖ & priueledges ‖ thereto belonging as also vpon the halfe of an orchard Adjoyning to m^{r} Nathaniel Olliuers ground also vpon a slip of Ground Runing doune from the orchard to the Corner of stephen Butlers dwelling house which ljeth wthin the fence also vpon the halfe of a smith^{s} shop in the occupation of w^{m} Robbins also vpon a part of a wharfe lying on the north west side of willjam Hollowells ware house also vpon the Ground that Thomas Smith^{s} shop stands vpon & deliuered possession of all the before mentioned premisses vnto m^{r} Anthony checkley Atturney to w^{m} Hollowell Jun̄ Benja^{n}: Hollowell & Edward Ashley that Is to say I extended this execution vpon all the houses & lands Intended in the same except a house wch was Benja[n] wards dwelling house, which stephen Butler Jun̄ his wife Inhabitts and kept possession of being big wth Child I was desired not to eject hir in that Condition also I haue not extended for the Costs

Return Way[t] marshall Gen[l] deputy

This Returne was made by Return wayt 25 July 1681

August 14th 1681.

I extended this execution on the house and land formerly belonging to Benja[n] ward dece[d] which Jacob wilkinson lately liued in according to the Judgment of the County Court & Court of Assistants as aboue exprest & deliũ[d] the same to m[r] Anthony checkley Atturnje to w[m] Hollowell Benja[n] Hollowell & Edward Ashley & for Costs of Courts I extended this execution on the person of Stephen Butler sen̄ and for want of money to sattisfy haue Comitted him to prison marshalls fees two pounds ten shillings in all nine pounds. Returne wayt marshall Genneralls deputy

This Execution & marshalls Returnes stands thus entred & Recorded in the Courts Booke of Reccords for executions word for word Agreeing w[th] the originall on file this 17[th] of octobe[r] 1681 as Attests Edw[d] Rawson Secrety

Att A Court of Assistants or Admiralty held at Boston 2[d] January 1678 Henry wheeler late master of the ship recouery in behalfe of himself & owno[r]s by his libell & complaint exhibbited to this Court bearing date 28[th] of Decembe[r] 1678 & then given in plaintiff against m[r] Anthony checkly and Lyddea his wife formerly the wife of the late Benjamin Gibbs & Administratrix to his estate defendant In an action of the Case largely e[x]prest in the aboue mentioned libell and is for not sattisfying him for the tjme of the sajd shipp Recouery for eight monet[hs] and one third of a moneth at thirty fiue pounds ℘ moneth which amounts to two hundred ninety one pounds thirteene

[14[a]]

shillings and fowe[r] pence, as also for charges and disbursments and what one recouered for his wages as in the sajd ljbell is exprest as by sajd wheele[r]s oath on file After the Attachment and euidences in the Case produced were read and duely Considered of The Court declared they Adjudged and did order and decree for the plaintiffe after the deduction of the late Benjamin Gibbs his creddit the sume of three hundred fiuety sixe pounds fiueteene shilling[s] & ‖ eleven penc ‖ in

money and Costs of Court fiue pounds ninteen shillings & sixe pence ||
In the whole three hundred sixty two pounds 15 05[d] ||
estate
mōy * out of the estate of the late Benjamin Gibbs =
That this is a true Copie taken out of the Courts Records Attests Edward Rawson secret

To Edward mitchelson marshall Gennerall or in
vnd'writt
his absence to the marshall of the County of Suffolke

In his majtjes name yo[w] are Required to levy by way of Execution on the Goods or estate of the late Benjamin Gibbs in the hands of Lyddia his relict or Administratrix to the sajd Benjamin Gibbs his estate as in the Coppie of the Court of Assistants or Admiralty[s] Judgment or decree aboue exprest in all exprests † the sume of three ^ sixty two pounds fiueteene shillings and fiue pence in mony and deliuer the same with two shillings for this execution to Henry wheeler late master of the ship Recouery in behalfe of himself and ouno[r]s as aboue is exprest and is in sattisfaction of the aboue mentioned Courts Judgment & decree hereof yow are not to fajle making you[r] Returne as the law directs dated in Boston this 4[th] day of January 1678

By the Court Edward Rawson Secre[t]

endorst

January 4 & 24: 167$\frac{8}{9}$

This execution was extended on the estate of m[r] Benjamin Gibbs in the hands of m[r] Anthony checkley who married Lydea relict & Adminstratrix to the estate of the late Benjamin Gibbs to value of two hundred & nine || pounds || as may Appeare by the seuerall Invoyces of said Goods wch Goods were shewed me and ouned by m[r] checkley & his wife

[15[a]]

to belong to sajd Gibbs estate and the same was deliuered to m[r] James Barton ꝑ order & and as Atturney of Henry wheeler ^ onely since the Invojces & deliuery a pewter still valued at 1[li] 5[s] was returned and thirty shillings for a Porringer and twelue shillings for a great chaire not yet payd) by virtue of this execution ꝑ Joseph Webb marshall of suffolke

I Received of m[r] Barton 35[s] in ꝑ[te] of fees

I leveyed vpon m[r] Gibbs out wharfes valued at one hundred & nine pounds twelue shillings as ꝑ Invoyce and deliuered them to m[r] James Barton as aboue

Joseph webb marshall

---

* Money? † respects ?

Wee whose names are vnderwritten being chosen by m^{r} James Barton as Atturney to Henry wheeler & m^{r} Anthony checkley as he marrjed Lyddia administratrix to the estate of m^{r} Benjamin Gibbs deceased & Joseph webb marshall of Suffolke as Apprise^{r}s of Certeine Goods in order to the sattisfaction of an Execution obteyned on sajd Judgment bearing date January 4th 1678 the Goods presented to us Janua^{r}y 14th 1678 wee Apprized as follows

It 1 scriptore somewhat broken 7^{li} 13 Turkey wrought chaires at 7^{s} 6^{d} ꝑ peece 4. 17. 6	11 — 17 — 06
It 6 Red chaires at 6^{s} 6 apeece 1^{li} 19 : [10]* And-Irons at 5^{li} 10 — — — — — — — —	07 — 09 — 00
It 4 Tables at 4^{li} = 1 round Table at 1^{li} = 1 looking Glass wth the brasses 2^{li} — — — — — —	07 — 00 00
It 1 map or Globe of y^{e} world 1^{li} = 10 pewte^{r} platters & 11 plates & smale dishes ‖ [at 63^{d} p^{li} 17^{li}] ‖ 4^{li} = 3^{s}	05 — 03 — 05
It 3 Candlesticks & sockets: 15^{s} = 1 Cubbord 15^{s} 1 Iron ba[lke ?] at 15^{s}. — — — — — — —	02 — 05 — 00
1 Turky wrought Carpet at 2^{li} = 10^{s} 6 searge chaires at 6^{s} 6^{d} apeece 2 stooles at 4^{s} 6^{d}	04 — 18 — 00
It 1 bed boulster bedstead greene silke quilt Curtains & valliants bed tester & [gu]ilt head [peec]	15 — 00 — 00
It 4 searg chaires at 7^{s}. 6^{d} & 2 stooles 5^{s} apeece 2^{li} { 1 [Gu]ilt couch 3^{li} — — — — — — — —	05 — 00 — 00
It 1 dutch table 18^{s} 1 looking Glasse 15 1 scripto^{r} & a little table vnd^{r} it at 6^{li} — — — — —	07 — 13 — 00
It 6 turky wrought chajres [C]R at 14^{s} a peece 04^{li}. 4^{s} = 2 p^{r} AndIrons at 1^{li}. 15^{s}	05 — 19 — 00
It 6 [peñd†] Turky wrought chajres at 10^{s} apeece — — — — — — — — — — —	03 — 00 — 00
1 square bed 1 suite of white Curtejnes 1 suite of searg Curtains wth Goulden & sad Coulored freings whiting & blankets & bed steed — — —	16 — 00 — 00
It 1 Ciprus chest at — — — — — — —	02 — 00 00
It 1 negro man named Hecto^{r} — — — — —	35
	131 — 04 — 00‡

John woodmansey
Ephraim Sauage
Robe^{r}t Sedgwicke

* Or "to." † Or "prud." ‡ The total does not agree with the items.

m^r^ Jno Woodmansey mr Ephraim Sauage & m^r^ Robe^rt^ Sedgwicke being chosen Apprize^r^s of the estate aboue mentioned did make oath that setting aside all sinister respects they haue Apprised as aboue to the value & is mony to the best of their vnde^r^standings sworne vnto Janu̅. 14 1678 before me Edward Tyng Ass^t^.

Janu^r^y 14 167$\frac{8}{9}$

Annex^t^ Boston 22^d^ January 167$\frac{8}{9}$

wee whose names are vnde^r^ written being chosen and sworne before Capt Thomas Brattle on the day and yeare aboue written to Apprize the draw bridge in Boston and [16^a^]
shop Joyning to it which shop is in the occupation of Henry messenger wth any other shop or priuiledge belonging to sajd Bridge which priueledg may Appeare further refference being had to a deed vnde^r^ the hand & seale of Joshua Scotto to Benja: Gibbs which deed beares date the twenty sixth day of february one thousand sixe hundred seventy & fower doe Apprise the sajd Bridge shop^s^ and priuiledges &c at thirty pounds mony as wittnes our hands =

Edward Lilly
Nathaniel Greenwood —

Drawbridge at 30^li^

Invoyce of Goods at Benjamin Gibbs house taken on Execution and Apprized January 23, 1678 p m^r^ woodmansey and m^r^ Ephrajm Sauage and m^r^ Robert Sedgwicke sworne before the wo^r^p^ll^ Edward Tyng Esqr Asistant

	li	s	d
Imprimis 1 great ketle at 18^d^ p^li^ 46^li^ — —	03 —	09 —	00
seuerall peices of pewter at 13^d^ p^li^. 64^li^ — —	03 —	09 —	04
10 Caster Hatts for weomen & men at 6^s^ p peece	03 —	00 —	00
29 felts hatts old fashion at 2^s^ — 6^d^ p peice —	03 —	12 —	06
1 pewter still bottom & Iron — — — —	01 —	05 —	00
1 pewter server at — — — — — —	00 —	15 —	00
6 netts — — — — — — — — —	06 —	00 —	00
1 handchech'erfe box wth frame — — — —	00 —	08 —	00
1 bedsteed old fashion — — — — — —	01 —	10 —	00
1 wainscot chest — — — — — — —	01 —	05 —	00
48 y^rds^ of thread sattjn at 3^s^ p y^rd^ — — —	07 —	04 —	00
A parcell of lace Galloone & hatt ljnings &c —	06 —	00 —	00
1 siluer porringer at 30^s^ — — — — —	01 —	10 —	00
14 y^r^ds of dyaper at 3^s^ p y^rd^ — — — —	02	03	06

[17a]

1 great Red chajre at	00	12	00
some sajles that mr Barton shewed me to belonged to sajd estate valued in the Inventory at 6li or thereabouts which sajles were after Replevied by mr Anthony checkley	Li42.	03.	04
Attested ꝑ Joseph webb marshall Boston 10th of January 1678	131.	04.	11
	42.	03.	9
wee whose names are vnderwritten being chosen by mr James Barton & marshall Joseph webb to Apprize an estate shewed vs to be belonging formerly	30.	00.	0
	203.	08	[8]

to mr Bejami Gibbs now deceased there being a parcell of wharfing prsented to us vizt fiuty fower foote of an outward wharfe wch wharfe wee doe apprize at thirty two shillings ꝑ foote & eighteen foot of wharfe joyning to a parcell of wharfe of mr Edward shippens wch sd eighteen foote of wharfe being in that Capacitje that now Its wanting neere three foote of its hight the which eighteen foot wee doe Apprize at twenty six shillings ꝑ ffoote as wittnes our hand —

Edward Lillje
Nathaniel Greenwood

That the Copie of the Court of Assistants & Admiraltys Judgment in the Case then trjed in Boston 2d January 1678 betweene Henry wheeler plaintiffe against mr Anthony Checkley & Lydja his wife (late wife to Capt Benjamin Gibbs deceased and Administratrix to his estate) wth the Copie of the execution on that Judgment marshalls Returne therevpon wth the Apprisers Apprisement of the seuerall parcells of Goods on their oathes wth ye seuerall Invoyces thereof annexed therevnto at the request of mr James Barton Atturney to sajd Henry wheeler so signed stands thus entred & recorded in the Court of Assistants booke of Records for executions word for word Agreeing with the originalls on file this 27th of Decembr * [1684] as Attests Edward Rawson Secrety

Att A County Court held at Boston 29° July 1684

Ann sheffeild aljs Perry ‖ plt ‖ Conta Joseph Homes of Boston defendant in an Action of the Case for that the sajd Homes hath possessed himselfe in, & doth refuse to give hir possession of a parcell of land and building thereon lying at the South end of Boston neere the windmill point which of right doth belong to the plaintiff it being lately

* Written over January.

hir husband sheffeilds deceased letters of Adminstration being Granted to the plaintiffe with all due damages. The Attachment and euidences in the case produced being read and Committed to the Jury

[18[a]] 1684

which are on file the Jury brought in their virdict they found for the plaintiff possession of the house and land sued for & costs of Court= Copia vera Attes[ts] Is[a] Addington cler. —

Copia vera Attes[ts] Edward Rawson Secre[t]

The deffendant Appealled from this Judgment to the nex[t] Court of Assistants in Septembe[r] ffollowing where that Case was trjed and Judgment passed i: e Confirmation of the County Courts Judgm̃t from which sajd Judgment Joseph Homes the deffendant by Attaint carrjed the Case to the Court of Assistants to be held in Boston the third of march Instan[t], where the case was trjed and alike — Confirmation of the sajd County Courts Judgment as aboue as is Attested ꝑ Edward Rawson Secrety

Copia vera Attes[ts] Edw[d] Rawson Secre[ty]

To John Greene marshall Generall or his lawfull deputy

Yow are heereby Required in his Maj[tys] name to Giue possession of the house and land mentioned in the County Courts Judgment a true Copie whereof is aboue written ^ which hath been Confirmed by both Courts of Assistants aboue also Certified and declared) to the aboue mentioned Ann sheffeild Aljas Perry as she is Administratrix of hir late husband sheffeilds estate as also to levy on his estate or person in mony the sume of two pounds thirteen shillings for Costs of Courts and deliuer the same with two shillings more for this execution or in want of mony for sajd Costs to sattisfy the sajd Ann Perry alja[s] sheffeild yow are alike required to seize the person of the sajd Homes [sen[r].] and him Com̃itt vnto the safe keeping of the prison keeper in Boston vntill he make payment acccording to this execution or othe[r] wise be released by the sajd Perry aljas sheffeild or by order of lawe hereof fajle not as yow will answer the Contrary at you[r] Perrill

[19[a]] 1684

and make returne of your doings herein vnde[r] your hand as the law directs for which this shall be you[r] sufficyent warrant dated in Boston 7th march 1684 ꝑ Curiam Edward Rawson secre[t]

Copia vera Attes[ts] Edward Rawson secre[ty]

[i]ndorst 7th march 1684

I haue Giuen possession of the house and lands vnto Ann Perry in all respects according to the execution and Judgment of the Courts wth-in here exprssed: I also levyed this execution vpon the mony of Joseph Homes the sume of two pounds fiueteene shillings mony wth two shillings for my ffees and deliuer the sajd mony vnto Ann Perry =

John Greene marshall Genll

That what is here entred & stands Recorded from the true Copies & originall Attachment Courts Judgments execution therevpon & marshall Generalls Returne therevpon in this & the other two fore-going paiges is thus Recorded in the Court of Assistants booke of Records word for word Agreeing therewth on Request of sajd Ann Perry ꝑ ‖ 16 may 1685 ‖ is Attested by Edward Rawson Secrety

To the marshall Gennerall John Greene or his deputy

In his Majtjes name yow are required to levy by way of execution the Goods estate or person of Richard Downing (in Case) in mony three pounds nineteene shillings & sixe pence and deliuer the same [with two shillings] for this execution to Joseph Boober as Costs as also the house & land in controuersy according to Attachment ꝑ and is in sattisfaction of the Judgment of the Court of Assistants sitting in Boston 2d Septemb^r 1684 making yor Returne hereof to the Court as the law directs dated in Boston the ninth day of september 1684 By the Court Edward Rawson secret

vnder writt I doe Assigne & Impower marshall skerry of Salem to be my lawfull deputy to levy this execution as wittnes my hand this tenth day of September 1684: John Greene marshall Generall

I Recd: as part of ye ffees of Jone Boober three shillings then doe yow demand the whole endorst this 27th of September 1684 =

I levyed this execution before vpon the house & land all of it that was John Bennets which I deliuered the house & land to Joseph Booby by turfe & twigg & gaue to them quiet possession wthall the priuiledges & Appurtenances belonging to it the house & land that Richard Downing liued then ~~levyed~~ in according to the Attachment also I levjed in mony of Richard Dounings fower pounds one shilling & deliuered it to Joseph Booby & his wife to the full sattisfaction of this execution as for them ꝑ me Henry skerry marshall

this execution & returne stands thus here entred & Recorded 4th Septembr 1685 at Request of Joan Booby wife to Joseph Booby As Attests

Edw: Rawson secret

[20^{a}] 1685

To John Greene marshall Gennerall or his Deputy

You are Required in his Maj^{t}jes name by virtue hereof to levy in Execution of the money of Thomas ‖ Baker ‖ & John Baker or either of them the some of ninety Nine pounds fower shillings and eight pence with two shillings more for this execution, and deliuer the same to Edward Hundlocke or his order which is to sattisfy a Judgment‸ ~~granted & confirmed to him ye sd Edward Hundlocke or his order which is to sattisfy a Judgment~~ granted & Confirmed to him the sajd Edward Hundlocke‸ ~~or his order which is to sattisfy a Judgm^{t}.~~ ‖ recouered at the Court of Assistants Sitting ‖ in Boston the first of this Instant September in money and for want of money or other estate of the sajd Thomas and John Baker or either of them you are alike required to seize the person or persons of the sajd Thomas and John Baker or either of them, and him or them to Comitt to the safe keeping of the prison keeper in Boston vntil the sajd Thomas and John Baker or either of them, make paymen^{t} according to this execution, or otherwise be released by the sajd Hundlocke, or by order of law‸* hereof fayle not as yow will Answer the Contrary at your perrill and make returne of your doings herein vnde^{r} your hand as the law directs for which this shall be you^{r} sufficient warrant dated in Boston this sixteenth day of September 1685

Hundlocks executiō ag^{t} Tho. & Jno Bake^{r} &c

By the Court Edward Rawson Secret

This is A true copie of the originall execution Attests Edwd Rawson secre^{ty}

endorst

September the 21th 1685

I have levyed this execution on the house and land of Thomas Baker sittuate lying and being in Boston in the lane Commonly Called Hudson^{s} lane or wing lane and

[21^{a}] 1685

is bounded easterly by the land of ‖ m^{r} ‖ Symon Lynde by the lane on the front southerly by the house and land now in the tenure and occupation of w^{m} Parsons westerly; by the new End of sajd Bake^{r}s house northerly to say the old end of sajd house to the midle of the chimney^{s} with the land whereon it stands measuring from the midle of the chimney^{s} to the southerly Corner of the house about twenty three foote more or less, thence to the street twenty three foote foure Inches and fifteen foote front to the lane besides the Gate way,

* This caret mark is in the original record.

And I also levyed on a kitchin on the easterly side of sajd house being about sixteene foote fowe[r] Inches long and twelue foote and three Inches broad with the land on which it standeth and also the land rainging from the N. west Corner of sajd kitchin to the reare of sajd Bakers land measuring about two foote there from the corner next m[r] Lynes land and so from the south west Corner of the || s[d] || kitchin all the land on a streight ljne to the Gate way reserving a passage way for the vse and bennefit of both houses vizt the house now levyed vpon and the new end of sajd Bake[r]s house which house and land so butted and bounded and measuring as aboue was apprized by m[r] Joseph Townsend and m[r] Joseph Homes : =

[then] chosen * by m[r] Edward Hundlocke Thomas Baker & myself at one hundred and two pounds || money || being the house & land John Cotta Constable of Boston attached by sajd Bake[r]s order to respond the Judgment and I deliuered possession of the premisses to m[r] Edward Hundlock he paying me my fees forty shillings with other charges John Greene marshall Generall

This is a true Copie of y[e] marshall Genlls Returne Attests Edw[d] Rawson secret

vnde[r] writ as endorst

[22[a]] 1685

Wee the subscribe[r]s willjam Parson[s] Joseph Tounesend and Joseph Homes being chosen by m[r] Edward Hunlock m[r] Thomas Bake[r] and the marshall Generall to Apprise an house and land of Thomas Bakers to sattisfy an Execution of m[r] Hunlocks against Thomas Baker and John Baker or either of them for ninety nine pounds sixe shillings and eight pence whith † marshalls fees and other charges to value of one hundred and two pounds wee hauing vejwed the sajd house and land sittuate lying and being in the lane Comonly Called Hudsons lane, or wings lane, shewed us to be the estate of Thomas Baker and was Attached by the Constable of Boston; in our presents Affirming that to be the estate he Attached to Answer the Complaint of sajd Hunlock wee doe Apprize the front par[t] of the house viz[t] the Old part to the middle of the Chimney[s] with the land whereon it stands measuring about two and twenty ffoote to the Corne[r] of the house and also the land betweene sajd house and the lane also a smale kitchin about sixteen foote long and about twelue ffoote and fower Inches wide being and lying on the easterly side of y[e] sajd house with the land whereon it stands and a slip of land from the northwest

Apprisement [er]

* Written over "that were." † with?

Corner of sajd kitchin on a streight ljne to the reare of sajd Bakers land it measuring there about two foote, it being about thirty nine foote from the reare to the kitchin also a slip of land runing from the sout west corner of sajd kitchin on a streight ljne to the Gate reserving the passage way for the vse of both parts of sajd houses the part so prized and that remajnes sajd Bake[r]s wee Aprize the premisses at one hundred and two pounds money wittness our hands this one and twentjeth day of Septembe[r] 1685

Joseph Tounsend
Josep Homes

Boston 24° october 1685
vnde[r] writ &
annex[t] as endorst

[23[a]] 1685

Aprizers oath

Joseph Tounsend and Joseph Homes two of the Apprize[r]s appearing made oath that the aboue written is a Just and true and æquall Apprizement of the estate therein specified according to their best Judgment and Conscience without any partiality or sinister respects Jurat Corã Isa. Addington Comission[r].

This is A true Coppy of the Aprisement so signed & y[e]re oath[s] therevpon Attests Edward Rawson Secre[t]

29 octobe[r] 1685

That the Execution marshall Generalls extention and deliuery thereof are truely word for word Compared w[th] the originalls & Aprisement as aboue one after the other || & || stands thus recorded in the Court of Assistants booke of Records for executions so signed at the request of m[r] Edward Hunlocke; being therew[th] Compared & is on file Attests this 29[th] day of octobe[r] 1685 Edw[d] Rawson secret

To John Greene marshall Generall

yow are Required in his Maj[t]jes name by virtue hereof to levy on the ketch freindship of Boston hir tackle Apparrell & furniture with all hir appurtenances to value in mony the sum̃e of eighty sixe pounds seven shillings in these seuerall sum̃es with two shillings more for this execution and deliuer the same in these seuerall sum̃es i: e to Andrew Elljot late master of the sajd Catch in behalfe of himselfe & charles Driuer mate, Abraham Avis & Joseph mosse marrine[r]s and John Avant Boy for their seuerall wages granted to them for their seuerall seruices in sajd ketch for eight moneths & twenty fower dayes each of them and is to sajd Andrew Elljot thirty fiue pounds fower shillings for his tjme after fower pounds ꝑ moneth To charles driuer eighteen pounds eighteene shillings for his seruice To Abraham Avis for his wages for like time twelve pounds sixteene shillings and to Joseph mosse for his wages for like time twelue pounds seventeene shillings and to John Avant Cabbin boy for his wages for like time sixe pounds twelue shillings as

[24a] 1686

as per portlidge bill given in and sworne to In Court (three pounds one shilling excepted) to be deducted out of the wages of charles Driver & Abraham Avis wages in the whole eighty sixe pounds sixteene shillings the costs of Court Included making your returne of your doings heerein vnder your hand as the law directs for which this shall be your sufficient warrant Dated in Boston the 14th of may 1686

By the Court Edward Rawson secret

Stands Indorst

wee whose names are vnderwritten being chosen to prize the Ketch ffreindship Burdened about thirty tunns desired by the marshall Gennerall & mr Jarvis Ballard mr Bolens Atturney & the master of the sajd Catch Andrew Elliott shewed by the marshall Gennerall which he levelled * vpon by virtue of an execution dated the 14th of may 1686, which sajd ketch with her boate tackling furniture & Apparrell & all other Appurtinances at seuenty eight pounds Current money of new England as wittness our hands this 19th day of may 1686

willjam ffoster
micaell Shuite
Samuell Greenow

vnderwrit 19th may 1686

I Levjed this within execution vpon the ketch ffreindship & Andrew Elliot was Comander as with hir tacklings Apparrell furniture and Boat Anchors Cables with sajd ketch and all hir Appurtenances was Aprised by persons legally chosen and sajd ketch with all hir Appurtenances I deliuered vnto Andrew Elljot at seventy eight pounds mony to pay the men according to theire proportion and sajd master and mate

John Green marshall Generall

That this execution on the other side and the Appraisement with the marshall Generalls extention & deliuery of the ketch freindship wth hir boate Anchors tacklings apparrell And Appurtenances vnto the sajd Andrew elljot late master of the said vessell for the ends & vses therein

* Error in the record for "levied"?

exprest & so signed stands here thus recorded word for word Compared wth the originall left on file from y[e] sajd 14th of may & 19th of sajd may at request of sajd Elliot Attests

Edward Rawson secret

[Between this page [24[a]] of the record of executions and the last page [271] of the other part, the record of the Court there are nine blank pages, except that on one of them is written in an ancient hand "Boston Jan[y] 2 1650."]

INDEX.

INDEX.

PAGE

AASANEMESET, JAMES, (Jury) 22
ABBOT, JOHN, ment^{d}. in margin 102
ABUSIVE SPEECHES. (*See* CRIMES.)
ACCORMAN, RICHARD, ag^{t}. Vallentine 135
ACOMPANUT (alias JAMES), Indian, case of, (murder) 53
ACT. (*See* ACTS.)
ACTION
  dies with the person (Newbury ag^{t}. Dummer) 108
  new, declaration of Court as to, (Gifford ag^{t}. Walter &c.) 218
ACTS or ACT
  of council of Commonwealth (case of John Watts) 103
  of parliament, in book of rates p. 158, (libel &c. ag^{t}. pink Expectation) 149
    (case of Josiah Cobbham) 171
    as to fraud &c., (information ag^{t}. Lawrence) 343
    as to trade " " " 343
  of 12th Charles II, as to shipping (Lason ag^{t}. Brenton, Coll^{r}.) . . 349
    (libel ag^{t}. pink Three Brothers) 355
    (Shrimpton ag^{t}. Brenton, Coll^{r}.) 366
  of 14th Charles II., breach of, (information ag^{t}. Armitage) 176
    (Armitage ag^{t}. Randolph) 210
  of 15th Charles II., (complaint ag^{t}. ketch Newbery &c.) 220
    (information ag^{t}. ship Elizabeth) 296
    as to trade (libel ag^{t}. pink Three Brothers) 355
  of 25th Charles II., (Shrimpton ag^{t}. Brenton, Coll^{r}.) 366
ADAMS or ADDAMS
  Abraham, Junr. &c., case of, (default) 315
  Esther, adm^{x}., ag^{t}. Mountfort 330
  John, &c., seamen &c. of ship Lixborn Merchant, (libel &c.) . . 92–3
  Joseph, Crosby ag^{t}., ... 226
  Nathaniel, Joy &c. ag^{t}., ... 191
    Worden ag^{t}., ... 239
    (Jury of trials) 345
    (Jury) 360
  Peter, of Milton, case of, (stealing) 230
  Roger, ag^{t}. Baker 260
    Baker ag^{t}., ... 266
  Samuel, Capt., &c., sureties, (case of Jon^{a}. Crispe &c.) . . . 57
    Bennett ag^{t}., ... 69

PAGE

ADAMS or ADDAMS, *continued.*
Samuel, Capt., execr., his admx. agt. Mountfort 330
commander of brigantine Boneta (libel &c.) . . . 354–5
Thomas, (Jury) 171
admx. of his execr. agt. Mountfort 330
Timothy, Lord agt., ... 197
ADDAMS. (*See* ADAMS.)
ADDINGTON
Isaac, Mr., appointed to implead Shapleigh 12
surety on bond of attaint (Execx. &c. of Cooke agt. Olliver) . 166
Mr., to officiate as clerk (Rawson &c. agt. Stoughton &c. commrs.) 209
Esqr., assistt., present at Court 2 Sept. 1690 327
3 Mar. 1690–1 336
22 Sept. 1691 345
16 Oct. 1691 359
1 Mar. 1691–2 361
clerk, copy attested by, ... 387
commr., oath before, (Hundlocke agt. Baker &c.) (execn.) . 391
ADLINGTON, JAMES, of Boston, mariner, agt. admx. of Ferns 340
ADMINISTRATOR, liability of, (Allen agt. Elliot) 260
ADMIRALTY, COURT OF. (*See* ASSISTANTS, COURT OF.)
ADMIRALTY, HIGH COURT OF
in England, case referred to, ... 334
appeal to, (information agt. Lawrence) 344
Commrs. of, (order on appeal of Lawrence) 360
ADULTEROUS CARRIAGE } (*See* CRIMES.)
ADULTERY }
ADVENTURE (pink), (case of Uriah Cleoments) 283, 284
AFRICA mentd. (information agt. Lawrence) 343
AGLIN, WM., Teudor agt., ... 7
AGUR
Wm., (Jury for attaint) 134
(1st Jury of trials &c.) 135
AHATTAWANTS, JNO., (Indian), murder of, (case of Jno. Dyar) . . . 188
AHAUTON
———, (Jury) 22
William, interpreter, (choice of guardians by Chickatabut) . . 208
AIRES. (*See* AYRES.)
ALCOCK
Sam., his relict, agt. Meade 121
Sarah, relict of Sam. Alcock agt. Meade 121
ALDEN
John, agt. Clark 66, 158
Capt., commander of sloop Mary of Boston (libel &c.) . . . 352
Senr., (Grand Jury) 305
ALFORD
Benjamin, atty., execrs. of Shepheard agt., ... 79

PAGE

ALFORD, *continued.*
Benjamin, atty., trustees &c. of Emery &c. agt., ... 122
of Boston, mercht., Perry agt., ... 352
Mr., &c., appointed to apprize ketch Salisbury . . . 356
of Boston, Perry agt., ... 363
ALLEN or ALLIN
——, Mr., pet. of, mentd. (Nurse agt. Endicot) 236
Bozoone, agt. Whiple 26
answer to pet. of, ... 29
case of, (reflections on Magistrates &c.) 29
(1st. Jury of trials &c.) 140
(Jury for attaints) 255
(1st. Jury for appeal) 256
(Jury of attaints &c.) 288
foreman of jury, (Wharton &c. agt. Smith) 293
Daniel, Mr., &c., of Boston, merchants, (libel &c.) 297
Edward, Wells agt., ... 155
agt. Elliot 260
Henry, (Grand Jury) 32
of Boston, merchant, (libel &c.) 105
& Co. agt. Tomlin 141
James, &c., trustees &c., Rice agt., ... 24
Mr., agt. Putnam 192
John, Capt., (Grand Jury) 1
Clarke agt., ... 135
Onesephirus, &c., Knight agt., ... 184, 194
agt. Knight 202
ALLIN. (*See* ALLEN.)
AMBROSE
Hope, Mrs., wife of Mr. Sam. Ambrose, pet. for divorce 127
Samuel, Mr., pet. for divorce by his wife Hope 127
AMERICA
mentd. (information agt. Lawrence) 343
(case of Martin Williams) 360
AMESBURY (Town of), John Ash of, ... 50
AMITIE (ketch), master of, agt. Assailly 324
AMY, MARTHA, (case of Cole &c.) 12
ANAY (or ANNAY), JOHN, boatswain of ship Apollow, &c. agt. Hollaway &c. . 132–3
ANDERSON or ANDREASON, ANDRESON
Cornelius, &c., (libel &c.) 34
Dutchman, case of, (piratically seizing &c.) . . 35
found guilty of theft &c. . . 36
cook of ship Merchants Adventure, &c., agt. Stone . . 213
David, Mr., (libel &c.) 75
John, (Grand Jury) 94
Michaell, Capt., commander of ship Triumpuez, &c. (libel &c.) . . 263–4
ANDOVER (Town of)
Selectmen of, agt. Fuller 108

PAGE

ANDOVER (Town of), *continued.*
Hugh Stone of, husbandman 303–4
Sam[l]. Hutchinson of, ... 304
ANDREASON / ANDRESON } (*See* ANDERSON.)
ANDREWES or / ANDREWS }
John, &c., adm[rs]., Bishop ag[t]., ... 248
Samuel, (Grand Jury) 24, 32, 133, 151, 202, 252, 287
(1st. Jury of trials &c.) 140
(Jury) 231
Thomas, &c., ag[t]. Michelson 218
Mr., his adm[rs]., Bishop ag[t]., ... 248
ANGIER, EPHRAIM, ag[t]. Winslow 106
ANN & HESTER / ANN & HESTHER } (ship)
of London, mate &c. of, (libel &c.) 172, 174, 175, 177
ANNA NEGRO
&c., presentments &c. ag[t]., ment[d]. in margin 25
servant to Mrs. Lynde, case of, (infanticide) 29
order for execution of her sentence 33
ANNAY. (*See* ANAY.)
ANNE (ship), mariners &c. of, (libel &c.) 94
ANSLEY, JOHN, &c. seamen of ship Resolution of London, (libel &c.) . 173
ANTONIO (ship)
ment[d]. (answer to pet. of Alvin Child) 12
of Lisbon (case of Shapleigh) 13
ANUSQUENUT (alias JOHN), Indian, case of, (murder) 54
APELTON / APLETON / APLTON. } (*See* APPLETON.)
APOLLOW (ship), mariners of, ag[t]. Hollaway &c. 132–3
APPEAL, jury for trials of. (*See* JURY for trials.)
APPELTON / APPLETON } or APELTON, APLETON, APLTON
——, Mr., and Mr. Porter, case between, ... 159
bond chanceried 167
present at Court 12 Oct. 1683 241
case of, ment[d]. in margin 244
John, Capt[t]., &c., case referred to, (Hooke ag[t]. Pike) 154
Jun[r]., ag[t]. Abell Porter 154, 159, 167
Samuel, &c. sureties on bond of attaint, (Apleton ag[t]. Savage) . . 123
Jun[r]., ag[t]. Savage 123–4
plaintiff, attaint of jury, (Beamis, foreman) . . . 133
Esq[r]., present at Court 6 Sept. 1681 190
present at Court, 7 Mar. 1681 202
Esq[r]., present at Court, 18 Mar. 1681 208
5 Sept. 1682 214

PAGE

APPLETON, &c., *continued.*
Samuel, present at Court, 6 Mar. 1682 223
Esqr., present at Court, 4 Sept. 1683 232
Senr., Esqr., &c. ag^t^. Hawkes, &c. 236
Junr., &c. ag^t^. Hawkes, &c. 236
Hawkes &c. ag^t^., ... 243
Sen., Esqr., &c., Hawkes, &c. ag^t^., ... 243
present at Court 4 Mar. 1683 243
Junr., ag^t^. Marshall 261
Esqr., present at Court 3 Mar. 1684 266
1 Sept. 1685 273
Mr., Junr., ag^t^. Roads 276–7
ag^t^. Wakefeild 277
Junr., Town of Lynn ag^t^., ... 279
Roads ag^t^., ... 281
Esqr., present at Court 2 Mar. 1685 287
15 Apr. 1686 298
24 Dec. 1689 302
7 Jan. 1689 305
present at Court 17 Jan. 1689 320
Esqr., Assist^t^., present at Court 3 Mar. 1690–1 336
22 Sept. 1691 345
Maj^r^., judgment of, (Cross ag^t^. Younglove) 348
Esqr., Assist^t^., present at Court 16 Oct. 1691 359
ARBUCKLE, WILLIAM, merch^t^., ag^t^. adm^r^. of Bricknall 323
ARCHER
Bethy, wife & atty. to Jno. Archer, &c. ag^t^. Pickmand 275
John, his wife & atty. &c. ag^t^. Pickmand 275
ARMETAGE or ARMITAGE
Hannah, choice of guardian 271
Timothy, master of ship Two Sisters of Boston, (information &c.) . 176
(Jury for attaints) 180
by atty. ag^t^. Randolph 210
ARMY, comm^tee^. of, order as to, (certificate &c. for payment for service under Hathorn) 104
ARNOLD
John, ag^t^. Thayer 247
prison keeper in Boston, ag^t^. Belchar 364
Richard, testimony by, ment^d^. (Stanbury ag^t^. Harris) 367
ARROWSMITH, EDWARD, appointed constable of Pemaquid 12
ARSNEAW, ——, master of bark St. Charles, (case of Wm. Johnson) . 242
ARSON. (*See* CRIMES.)
ASH
John, of Amesbury, (case of Sam. Guile) 50
Mary, wife of Jno. Ash, (case of Sam. Guile) 50
(allowance for Treasurer &c.) 50

PAGE

ASHELY or ASHLEY
Edward, &c., Butler agt., ... 140, 164
(who married Mary Hollowell), &c. agt. Butler (execn.), 380–382
&c., Butler agt., (execution) 380–382
ASHTON
Henry, Gibbs agt., ... 2
complaint of, mentd. (case of Benja. Gibbs) 2
Bonner agt., ... 3
ASIA mentd. (information agt. Lawrence) 343
ASSAILLEY or ASSAILLY
Peter, Junr., merchant, Robineau agt., ... 324
ASSAULT. (*See* CRIMES.)
ASSISTANTS, COURT OF, or COURT OF ADMIRALTY
Assistants, Court of, second book of records 1
book of records for executions, 371, 379, 382, 386, 388, 391
Admiralty, Court of, book of records for, mentd. 376
Assistants, or Admiralty, Court of, "day book" mentd. in margin, 16, 231
Assistants, Court of, 2 Sept. 1662 mentd. (order for Mrs. Hill's dower), 147
Sept. [1673] mentd. (Clarke agt. Bartlet) . . 2
2 Sept. 1673 mentd. (Dinely agt. Stenwick) (execn.) 371
3 Mar. " 1
7 " " 11
11 " " 10
11 " [1673] 12
13 " 1673 . . . . 11, 13
adjourned to 14 Mar. 1673 14
14 Mar. 1673 14
adjourned to 23 Mar. 1673 14
Admiralty, Court of, 9 Apr. 1674 mentd. (order for Treasr. to pay Kent &c.) 36
Assistants, or Admiralty, Court of, 10 Apr. 1674 . . . . . 13, 14, 15
Assistants, Court of, 28 May 1674 15
29 May 1674 16
6 June " 15, 16
1 Sept. " 16
adjournment of, to 9 Oct. 1674 23
9 Oct. 1674 23
Admiralty, Court of, 21 Oct. 1674 23
Assistants, Court of, 2 Mar. " 24
5 Mar. 1674 25
special Court of, 11 Mar. 1674 32
Court of, adjourned to 13 May [1675] 31
13 May 1675 33
Assistants or Admiralty, Court of, 17 May 1675 34
Assistants, Court of, 24 May 1675 34

PAGE

Assistants, Court of, &c., *continued.*
Assistants, Court of, 17 June 1675 36
Assistants or Admiralty, Court of, 17 June 1675 39
6 Aug. 1675 41
30 " " 43
Assistants, Court of, 7 Sept. 1675 43
Assistants or Admiralty, Court of, 13 Sept. 1675 52
Assistants, Court of, 18 Sept. 1675 52
[Assistants], Court of, adjourned to 21 Sept. 1675 51-2
Assistants or Admiralty, Court of, 1 Oct. 1675 55
Assistants or Admiralty, Court of, 4 Oct. 1675 55
19 Nov. 1675 . . . . . 55, 58
Assistants, Court of, adjourned to 30 [Nov. 1675] . . . 57
4 Dec. 1675 58
Assistants or Admiralty, Court of, 16 Dec. 1675 . . . . . 58, 372
Assistants Court of, 7 Mar. 1675-6 . . . . 56, 58
14 Mar. 1675-6 61
Assistants or Admiralty, Court of, 29 Mar. 1676 61
21 July 1676 62
Admiralty, Court of, 26 July 1676 62
31 July 1676 63
22 Aug. [1676] 63
28 " 1676 63
Assistants, Court of, 5 Sept. 1676 64
[Assistants], Court of, 10 Sept. 1676 88
adjourned to 13 [Sept. 1676] 70
13 Sept. 1676 70
Assistants or Admiralty, Court of, 9 Oct. 1676 75
adjourned to 12 Oct. 1676 . . 75
23 Oct. 1676 76
26 " " 76
5 Mar. " 77
Assistants, Court of, 6 Mar. 1676 77
(case of Isaac Waldron for abusive speeches) . 88
10 Mar. 1676 91
12 " " 80
[Assistants], Court of, dissolved 13 Mar. 1676 91
Assistants Court of, 17 Apr. 1677 88
Assistants or Admiralty, Court of, 17 Apr. 1677 91
Admiralty, Court of, 22 May 1677 92
4 Aug. 1677 92
Assistants, Court of, 4 Sept. 1677 94
Admiralty, " " 5 " " 93
[Assistants], " " 6 " " allowance &c. of Bratle &c. comm^rs^. 96
Assistants or Admiralty, Court of, 7 Sept. 1677 105
27 Sept. 1677 105
Admiralty, Court of, 9 Oct. 1677 106

PAGE

ASSISTANTS, COURT OF, &c., *continued.*

Assistants or Admiralty, Court of, 15 Oct. 1677 106
Admiralty, Court of, 20 Dec. 1677 106
Assistants, " " 5 March " 107
Assistants or Admiralty, Court of, 24 & 28 May 1678 . . 117, 373, 374
1 & 9 July 1678 118
Assistants, Court of, Sept. 1678 ment[d]. (case of Tho[s]. Kenny, Negro) 127
3 & 5 Sept. 1678 119
Assistants or Admiralty, Court of, 14 Oct. 1678 128
8 & 13 Nov. 1678 128
2 Jan. 1678 . . 130, 382, 383, 386
Assistants, Court of, Mar. [1678–9] ment[d]. (case of Tho[s]. Kenny, negro) 127
4 Mar. 1678 133
19 Mar. 1678–9 138
Assistants or Admiralty, Court of, 15 & 29 May 1679 130
31 May 1679 131
14 June " 132
Assistants, Court of, 2 Sept. 1679 139
Assistants or Admiralty, Court of, 24 Sept. 1679 147
Assistants, Court of, 20 Oct. 1679 146
Assistants or Admiralty, Court of, 25 Oct. 1679 132
26 Jan. 1679 148
2 Feb. " 148
[Assistants], Court of, 4 Feb. 1679 148
Assistants, " " 2 Mar. " 151
20 May 1680 158
Assistants or Admiralty, Court of, 1 June 1680 149
Assistants, Court of, 4 June 1680 159
8 June 1680 150
Assistants or Admiralty, Court of, 7 Aug. 1680 . . . . . 150, 159
[Assistants], Court of, 9 Aug. 1680 168
adjourned to 16 Aug. 1680 168
Assistants, Court of, 20 Aug. 1680 160
[Assistants], " " adjourned to 23 Aug. 1680 169
Assistants, " " Sept. 1680 ment[d]. (order on pet. of Gyfford) . 231
7 Sept. 1680 . . . . . 160, 376, 380–382
[Assistants], Court of, 16 & 18 Sept. 1680 170
Assistants, " " 1 Oct. 1680 170
order as to caution money 171
[Assistants], Court of, 2 Oct. 1680 172
16 Oct. 1680 169
30 " " 175
Assistants or Admiralty, Court of, 18 Nov. [1680] 172
2 Dec. 1680 173
9 " " 174, 177
24 " " 175
Assistants or Admiralty, Court of, 25 Dec. 1680 ment[d]. (Armitage ag[t]. Randolph) 210

PAGE

ASSISTANTS, COURT OF, &c., *continued.*

Assistants, Court of, 1 Mar. 1680 179
1 June 1681 189
Assistants or Admiralty, Court of, 17 June 1681 177
4 Aug. 1681 and adjourned to 11 Aug. 1681 179
Assistants, Court of, Sept. [1681] (appeal from, on attaint)
(Wharton ag[t]. Reynolds) 202
(Leach &c. ag[t]. Knight) 202
Assistants, Court of, 6 Sept. 1681 190
[Assistants], Court of, 13 Sept. 1681 Boston comm[rs]. sworn . . 199
14 Sept. 1681 200
21 Oct. 1681 201
Assistants, Court of, dissolved 22 Oct. 1681 201
7 Mar. 1681 202
[Assistants], Court of, 18 Mar. 1681 208
Assistants, Court of, 21 Mar. 1681–2 209
Assistants or Admiralty, Court of, 1 June 1682 209
Assistants, Court of, 3 June [1682] (bond by Shrimpton &c.) . . 211
Assistants or Admiralty, Court of, 15 June 1682 211
17 Aug. 1682 213
Assistants, Court of, 5 Sept. 1682 214
[Assistants], Court of, 8 Sept. 1682 ment[d]. (Randolph ag[t]. Wallis) . 219
14 Sept. 1682 220
Assistants, Court of, 6 Mar. 1682 223
17 Apr. 1683 227
22 May 1683 229
[Assistants], Court of, adjourned to 24 [May 1683] 230
31 [May 1683] 230
Assistants or Admiralty, Court of, 8 June 1683 230
[Assistants], Court of, adjourned to 14 June [1683] 231
21 June [1683] 231
5 July 1683 231
Assistants, Court of, 5 July 1683 231
[Sept. 1683] (appeal from, on attaint)
(Hawkes &c. ag[t]. Apleton &c.) 243
(Webb ag[t]. Manly) . . 244
Assistants, Court of, 4 Sept. 1683 231
12 Oct. " 240–1
12 Nov. " 241
4 Mar. " 243
[Assistants], Court of, [5] Mar. 1683 ment[d]. (order on est. of Wade), 250
Assistants, special Court of, 22 July 1684 251
[Assistants], Court of, 22 & 24 July 1684 253
adjourned to 7 Aug. 1684 254
14 Aug. 1684 254
21 " " 254
dissolved 28 Aug. 1684 254

PAGE

ASSISTANTS, COURT OF, &c., *continued.*
Assistants, Court of, 2 Sept. 1684 254
mentd. (Boober &c. agt. Downing) 388
[Assistants], Court of, 9 Sept. 1684 265
adjourned to 10 Sept. 1684 263
19 Sept. 1684 263
20 " " 263
25 " " 263
17 Oct. 1684 265
Assistants, Court of, 3 Mar. 1684 . . . . 266, 387
[Assistants], Court of, adjourned to 19 Mar. 1684 272
19 Mar. 1684 272
Assistants, Court of, 1 Sept. 1685 273
mentd. (Hundlocke agt. Baker &c.) 389
[Assistants], Court of, 18 Sept. 1685 286
adjourned to 14 Oct. 1685 286
14 Oct. 1685 286
Assistants, Court of, 2 Mar. 1685 287
[Assistants], Court of, 4 Mar. 1685 296
Assistants, Court of, adjourned to 26 Mar. 1686 296
and Council 26 Mar. 1686 . . . . . 294, 296
[Assistants], Court of, 1 Apr. 1686 297
Assistants, Court of, & Council adjourned to 15 Apr. [1686] . . 298
Assistants or Admiralty, Court of, 15 Apr. 1686 298
[Assistants], Court of, and Council adjourned to 17 Apr. 1686 . . 299
[Assistants], Court of, 17 Apr. 1686 299
Assistants, Court of, adjourned to 22 Apr. 1686 300
Assistants or Admiralty, Court of, " " " 300, 301
Assistants, Court of, 3 Sept. 1689 . . . . 301, 302
24 Dec. 1689 301
[Assistants], Court of, adjourned to 7 Jan. 1689 305
7 Jan. 1689 305
15 & 16 Jan. 1689 319
17 Jan. 1689 320
adjourned to 20 Jan. 1689 321
23 Jan. 1689 321
Assistants, Court of, 4 Mar. 1689 322
Assistants, Court of, 8 Apr. 1690 . . . . 322, 346
[Assistants], Court of, 10 Apr. 1690 326
Assistants, Court of, 2 Sept. 1690 327
3 Mar. 1690-1 336
[Assistants], Court of, adjourned to 17 Mar. 1690-1 342
16 Apr. 1691 mentd. (complaint by Stebbins) . 342
Assistants, Court of, 1 Sept. 1691 345
22 Sept. 1691 354
(pet. by Croad) 356
[Assistants], Court of, 29 Sept. 1691 Boston Commrs. sworn . . 358
1 Oct. 1691 (case of Fanning) 358

PAGE

ASSISTANTS, COURT OF, &c., *continued.*
[Assistants] Court of, adjourned to 16 Oct. 1691 359
9 Dec. 1691 360
11 " " 360
24 " " 361
25 " " 361
Assistants, Court of, 1 Mar. 1691–2 361
(*See also* BENCH and MAGISTRATES.)

ASSOCIATES, COURT OF
at Portsmouth (Porter agt. Cater) 138
30 Sept. 1679 (Waldron agt. Walton) 153

ATKINS, THO., agt. Joy 21

ATKINSON
Abigail, by her father Theodore, agt. Williams 4
John, agt. Woolcot 220
Buckman 221
Mirrick 223
Woolcot, Senr., ... 233
Woolcot 233
Miller 270
Theodore, Senr., by atty. agt. Williams 4
(Jury of trials &c.) 33
Theodore (Grand Jury) 59, 190, 242, 243
agt. Perkins 123, 136

ATTACHMENT
whether to be accounted imprisonment &c. (Woodbridge agt. Williams) 83
question as to power of clerk of writs to grant, (Olliver &c. agt. Lynn &c.) 112
of bill of exchange (West agt. Barter) 157

ATTAINT
Jury of. (*See* JURY of attaint, list of.)
Bonner agt. Heyman [Bonner & Lawton] 1
Woodmansey agt. Joy 45, 59
Apleton agt. Savage 123, 124, 133
Execx. &c. of Cooke agt. Olliver 166, 179
Gretian agt. Sweathy 182, 190
Sweatie agt. Greatian 182, 183
Greatian agt. Staynor 183, 191
Gifford agt. Read 185, 192
Joy &c. agt. Leveret 186
Thaier agt. Savage 186, 191
Joy &c. agt. Addams 191
Wharton agt. Reynolds 193, 202
Knight agt. Leach &c. 194
Leach &c. agt. Knight 202
Shatswell agt. Jewet 205, 214
Rawson &c. agt. Stoughton &c., commrs. 209
Phips &c. agt. Bowers 224, 225

PAGE

ATTAINT, *continued.*
Torrey ag^{t}. Gretian 226
Bowers ag^{t}. Phipps &c. 232
Gretian ag^{t}. Torrey 232
Webb, marshal, ag^{t}. Manly 235, 244
Apelton &c. ag^{t}. Hawkes &c. 236, 237
Usher ag^{t}. assignee &c. of Harwood 237
Homes ag^{t}. Sweathy 238, 244
Hawkes &c. ag^{t}. Apleton &c. 243
Usher ag^{t}. Bulkley 243
Harrison ag^{t}. Platts 245, 255
Rauson ag^{t}. Gilbert 245, 255
Baker ag^{t}. Wharton 248, 249
Wisewall ag^{t}. Paige &c. 249, 250
Paige &c. ag^{t}. Wisewall 255
Perkins ag^{t}. Fenno 257, 258, 266
Basse ag^{t}. Crosby 258
Addams ag^{t}. Baker 260
Homes ag^{t}. Sheffeild 261, 266
Baker ag^{t}. Adams 266
Homes ag^{t}. Cheeckley 282
Checkley ag^{t}. Homes 287
Wharton &c. ag^{t}. Smith 293
Votes on pet. of Checkley in "the case of attaint" 294
Sheffeild ag^{t}. Homes (exec^{n}) 387

ATTORNEY
action by, for his own use (Hull ag^{t}. Wincoll) 122
power of, vote as to, (Gifford ag^{t}. Walter &c.) 218

ATWATER
Joshua, ag^{t}. Balston 44
case of, (incendiarism) 145

ATWOOD
John, (Jury of trials) 298
(Jury) 300

AUSTEN or AUSTIN
Nicholas, quartermaster of ship Merchants Adventure, &c. ag^{t}. Stone 213
Richard, (Grand Jury) 252

AUTHORITY, reproachful words ag^{t}., (*See* CRIMES.)

AVANT, JOHN, cabin boy, &c. ag^{t}. ketch Freindship, (exec^{n}.) . . . 391–2

AVERY, WM., Mr., Rice ag^{t}., ... 273

AVIS, ABRAHAM, &c. mariners, ag^{t}. ketch Freindship, (exec^{n}.) . . . 391–2

AYRES or AIRES, EYRE, EYRES
John, adventurer in ship Resolution, ag^{t}. Phipps &c. 211, 212
ag^{t}. Furnell 222
of Boston, merchant, Eyre ag^{t}., ... 342
Mr., &c., chosen comm^{rs}. for Boston & sworn 357
Martha, Mrs., widow, by atty. ag^{t}. Chenery 26

PAGE

AYRES, &c., *continued.*
Thomas, exec^rs. of Heywood ag^t., ... 324
of Boston, mariner, ag^t. Eyre 342

BABELL, HUGH, atty., Parris ag^t., ... 202–3
BACHELLORS DELIGHT. (*See* BATCHELLORS DELIGHT.)
BACHILER. (*See* BATCHILER.)
BACKWAY, BENJAMIN, of Boston, mariner, Hall ag^t., ... 350
BACON
John, &c., mariners, (libel &c.) 40
Michael, Read ag^t., ... 281
ag^t. [Maguinis] 291
Thomas, (1st Jury of trials &c.) 161
(2nd Jury of trials &c.) 224
Wm., &c. by atty. agt. Town of Hampton 19
BADCOCK, ENOCK, Pitts ag^t., ... 166
BADGE, WEARING OF. (*See* PUNISHMENT, Miscellaneous.)
BAGLY (or BAYLY), SAMUEL, ag^t. Webster 259
BAILY or BAYLY
———, Mr., (libel &c. of Toton) 43
John, of Rochelle, merchant, his agent &c. (libel &c.) 55
Samuel, case of, ment^d. (bond by King) 250
of Weymouth, case of, (buggery) 251
(or Bagly) ag^t. Webster 259
Theophilus, house in Lynn ment^d. (case of Newhall &c.) 306
BAKER
John, Greene ag^t., ... 162
by atty. ag^t. Wharton 248
mariner, Wharton & Co. ag^t., ... 249
principal on bond of attaint (Adams ag^t. Baker) 260
of Roxb[ury], Adams ag^t., ... 260
&c., bond of attaint (Homes ag^t. Sheffeild) 261
ag^t. Addams 266
&c., Hundlocke ag^t., (execution) 389, 390
Richard, (Grand Jury) 35
Thomas, &c. ag^t. Putnam 27
Figg ag^t., ... 133
ag^t. Putnam 214
Putnam ag^t., ... 256
ag^t. Pemberton 259
Condy 266
Pemberton &c. 267
Hunlocke 278
&c., Hundlocke ag^t., (execution) 389, 390
house &c. on Hudsons (or Wing) lane, Boston, ment^d. (Hundlocke ag^t. Baker &c.) (exec^n.) . . 389–391
BALCH, BENJAMIN, ag^t. Dodge 180
BALCOM, HEN., (1st. Jury for appeals &c.) 108

PAGE

BALE, BENJAMIN, (Jury of trials &c.) . . . 85–6

BALL
George, of Boston, mariner, agt. Sandey . . . 351
receipt by, mentd. (Stanbury agt. Harris) . . . 367–8
John, (alias Uriah Cleoments) (Grand Jury indictments) . . . 273
case of (burglary) . . . 283–4
(case of Wm. Clapp) . . . 284
William, salt shipped by, (Stanbury agt. Harris) . . . 367

BALLARD
Jarvis, agt. Watts . . . 100
by atty. agt. Watts &c. . . . 112
(Jury for attaint) . . . 134
(2d. Jury of trials &c.) . . . 135
(Grand Jury) . . . 255, 361
Mr., atty., (Elliot &c., agt. ketch Freindship) (execn.) . . . 392
Nathaniel, &c., Randolph agt., . . . 160
Samuel, (2d Jury of trials &c.) . . . 153, 224
(Jury) . . . 171, 176
(Grand Jury) . . . 345

BALLART OR BALLAT
Samuel, Bussell agt., . . . 140
(Jury for attaint) . . . 191
(1st. Jury of trials &c.) . . . 192

BALLAT. (*See* BALLART.)

BALSTON OR BOLSTON
John, (1st. Jury of trials &c.) . . . 78
Junr., (Jury) . . . 160
master of pink Adventure (case of Cleoments) . . . 283–4
(Special Jury) . . . 363
Jonathan, (Grand Jury) . . . 35
Atwater agt., . . . 44
Mr., (1st. Jury of trials &c.) . . . 70
&c. appraisers, (libel &c. agt. Schinking) (execn.) . . . 378–9

BANISHMENT. (*See* PUNISHMENT.)

BANKS
Richard, (Jury of attaints &c.) . . . 288
(1st. Jury for appeals &c.) . . . 289
Samuel, of York, agt. Child . . . 325

BANNISTER, THOMAS, (Grand Jury) . . . 361

BARBADOES
mentd. (libel &c. of Measure) . . . 39
(Francis &c. agt. Smith) . . . 131
(case of Mary Bishop) . . . 144
Owen Parris of, . . . 202
Vines Ellacot of, merchant, . . . 251
Sr. Timothy Thornhill of, Barrt., . . . 340

BARBAR, JAMES, (Jury for attaints) . . . 233

PAGE

Barefoot or }
Barefoote }
Walter, ag^t. Shackford 67
Capt., ag^t. Palmer 98
Barker, Benja., &c., bill of charges for, ... 116
Barnard or Bernard
James, (1st. Jury for trials &c.) 17, 78
John, " 25, 161
(Jury of trials &c.) 32
Samuel, Trayne ag^t., ... 275
order on complaint of, ... 283
Barnes
Caleb, master, (libel &c. of Southack) 335
Edward, master of ketch Ollive Branch, &c. (libel &c.) 131
James, ag^t. Kemble &c. 120
(Jury) 360
(Special Jury) 363
Baron. (*See* Barron.)
Barrat. (*See* Barret.)
Barret or Barrat
John, &c. bond by, ... 57
order as to rendezvous & marching "with the forces" . . 58
Sarah, plaintiff, (appeal) 288
Tho., Capt., atty., ag^t. Sprague 222
Wm., (2d. Jury for trials) 18
(1st " " ") 95
(Jury of trials &c.) 252
Barron or Baron
Ellis, (or Elliz) (Grand Jury) 17, 44, 59
Mr., (2d. Jury for trials &c.) 96
Barrow, Tieg A., of Boston, Paul ag^t., ... 345
Barry, Jno., Chapman ag^t., ... 205
Barter, Benjamin, West ag^t., ... 157
Bartholmew
Abraham, Mr., &c. (libel) 76
Henry, &c., Manning ag^t., ... 164
(1st. Jury for appeals) 274
merchant, &c. overseers &c., ag^t. Manning (execn.) . 376–378
Manning ag^t., (execn.) . 376–378
Wm., Mr., (Jury of trials &c.) 32
(Grand Jury) 78
(Grand Jury) 119
Bartlet
Joseph, Clarke ag^t., ... 1–2
Robert, ag^t. James &c. (Marblehead Commons) 20
Barton
Edward, ag^t. Mathews 195, 222
James, Mr., atty., (libel &c. of Wheeler &c.) (execn.) . 383, 384, 386

PAGE

BA[R]TY, JARVICE, part owner of ship George, &c. (complaint &c.) . . 41
BARUCH, ——, &c., Gibbs agt., ... 49
BASHAM
Nathl., (1st. Jury for trials &c.) 224, 245
(Jury of attaints) 244
BASKERVILL, LAURENCE, by atty. agt. est. of Windor &c. 141
BASS or BASSE
Edward, Mr., merchant in London (depn. by Sexton) 132
Samuel, agt. Crosby 258
BAS SA BLOUS, Wm. Vincent of, burgess &c. 333
BASSE. (*See* BASS.)
BASSET
Henry, boatswain of ship Ann & Hesther (libel &c.) 172
Wm., agt. Waldron 78
BASTARD, security for, (case of Geo. Russell) 170
BASTO, negro slave to Cox, case of, (rape) 74
BASTON, GIDEON, &c. seamen &c. of ship Lixborn Merchant (libel &c.) . 92–3
BAT. (*See* BATT.)
BATCHELLORS DELIGHT (ship) of London, master &c. of, information agt., . 170
BATCHILER (or BACHILER), NATHANIEL, Smith agt., ... 110
BATEMAN
John, (Grand Jury) 35, 151
agt. Taft 161
BATT or BAT
Paul, agt. Harris 20, 28
case of, (reflections declared in reasons of appeal) . . . 31
Harris agt., ... 94
Tho., his admr. agt. Lake 269
Timothy, agt. Seaverns 9
&c. sureties on bond of attaint (Woodmansey agt. Joy) . 45
Wells agt., ... 48
BATTEN or BATTYN, BUTTYN
Benjamin, (1st. Jury of trials &c.) 17
William, (case of Amy Wellen) 15
BATTYN. (*See* BATTEN.)
BAXTER
John, (2d. Jury for trials &c.) 274
Saffyn agt., ... 282
BAYLY. (*See* BAILY.)
BEALE or BEALES
Joshua, (Grand Jury) 273
Nathaniel, &c. agt. Leveret 185, 186
principals on bond of attaint (Joy &c. agt. Leveret) . 186
agt. Adams 191
BEAMIS, BEAMMIS or BEAUMIS
——, foreman, mentd. in margin 123

PAGE

BEAMMIS, &c., *continued.*
Ephraim, of Watertown, case of, (lying &c.) 116
Joseph, (1st. Jury of trials &c.) 25
(Grand Jury) 65, 214
Mr. (2d. Jury for trials &c.) 121
foreman, (Apleton's attaint of jury) 133
(2d. Jury for trials &c.) 224
BEAMON, GAMALIEL, [Senr.,] (1st. Jury for appeals &c.) 108
BEAUMIS. (*See* BEAMIS.)
BECK or BECKE
Mannasseth, agt. Gale (or Gates) 216
BECKFORD. (*See* BICKFORD.)
BEERS
Richard, (Grand Jury) 25
Left., (Grand Jury) 32
BEGINNING (bark), (libel &c. agt. Brimsden) 128
BELAINE. (*See* BLAINE.)
BELCHAR or BELCHER
Andrew, (Jury) 149
(Grand Jury) 287
merchant, agt. Lloyd 362
Joseph, of Braintree, Arnold agt., ... 364
BELKNAP, JOSEPH, Mr., &c., attys., agt. trustees &c. of Bellingham . . 24
BELL
James, mariner of ketch Betty (Libel) 118
John, " " ship George, &c. (Complaint &c.) 41
Thomas, &c., of Stonington, order on bill of charges 116
BELLINGHAM
Richard, Esqr., his trustees &c., Rice agt., ... 24
Samuel, Esqr., agt. Hamond &c. 157
agt. Russell 164
BEMA[N], NOAH (Jury of trials) 323
BENCH
case referred to, (case of Benanuel Bowers) 3
point of law belonging to, (Admr. of Coggan & wife agt. Clarke) . 4
declaration by, (Hutchinson agt. Payne) 28
case referred to, (case of Robert Ma[ior]) 84
(case of Walter Gendall) 102
law belonging to, (Dix[e] agt. Morse) 108
sentence by, (case of Darby Bryan) 114
case referred to, (case of Saml. Hunting) 114
sentence by, (case of Abigail Johnson) 115
bond chanceried by, (Holmes agt. Clarke) 152
determination by, (Martin agt. Briggs &c.) 153
to chancery bond (Apleton agt. Porter) 154
former judgment made null (Apleton agt. Porter) 159

PAGE

BENCH, *continued.*
case referred to, (Balch ag^{t}. Dodge) 180
finding by, (Heinshaw ag^{t}. Voss) 185
(Wharton ag^{t}. Reynolds) 202
declaration by, (Butler ag^{t}. Checkley) 206
vote by, as to attaint whether to be allowed when one party refuses to join (Rawson &c. ag^{t}. Stoughton &c., comm^{rs}.) 209
vote by, as to non-suit (Rawson &c. ag^{t}. Stoughton &c., comm^{rs}.) . 209
order and vote by, (Gifford ag^{t}. Walter &c.) 218
judgment by, (Wisewall &c. ag^{t}. Paige &c.) 256
finding by, (Allen ag^{t}. Elliot) 261
determination by, (Rice ag^{t}. Avery) 274
(Apleton ag^{t}. Roads) 277
(Haugh ag^{t}. Hill) 283
case referred to, (case of Joseph Homes, Sen., &c.) 285
declaration by, (Bullard &c. ag^{t}. County Court sentence) . . . 291
(Hunlorck ag^{t}. Hubbard &c.) 291
(*See also* MAGISTRATES and SPECIAL VERDICT.)
BENDISH, THOMAS, M^{r}., &c., Elson ag^{t}., ... 59
BENJAMIN
Edw., mariner, wages of, (libel &c. ag^{t}. ship Nevis factor) . . . 76
John, (Jury for trial of attaint) 134, 192
(2^{d}. Jury for trials &c.) 135, 193
(1st. Jury for trials &c.) 215
BENNET
Charles, &c., seamen &c. of ship Lixborn Merchant (libel &c.) . . 92, 93
Henry, ag^{t}. Symonds 83
Gove ag^{t}., ... 107
Mr., Epps ag^{t}., ... 259
John, &c., case of, (neglect of Wilson, &c.) 11
ag^{t}. Addams 69
ag^{t}. Gridley 69, 82
&c., ag^{t}. Douden 184
house &c. of, ment^{d}. (Boober & wife ag^{t}. Downing) (exec^{n}.) . 388
Richard, (Grand Jury) 24
Samuel, &c., case of, (neglect of Wilson, &c.) 11
& wife, complaint by, (case of Anna Edmunds) 11
&c., ag^{t}. Douden 184
Sarah, (case of John Bennet &c.) 11
BENT
Joseph, of Sudbury (case of Peter Bent, Junr.) 86
Martha, &c., ag^{t}. Foster & wife 339
Peeter, Junr. of Sudbury, case of, (murder) 86
BERNARD. (*See* BARNARD.)
BERRY
Olliver, mate of pink Endeavor, &c. (libel &c.) 117, 118
Peter, of Ipswich, ag^{t}. Newmarch 331
Newmarsh ag^{t}., ... 331

PAGE

BERRY, *continued.*
Thomas, (Jury of trials) 56
(Jury) 176
(Grand Jury) 179
BERWICK ment[d]. (libel &c. ag[t]. ship Richard) 335
BERWICK UPON TWEED ment[d]. (information ag[t]. Lawrence) 343–4
BESTIALITY. (*See* CRIMES.)
BETTS
John, (2[d] Jury for trials &c.) 121
(Jury for attaints) 233
(Jury for appeals) 233
BETTY (ketch), mariner of, (libel) 118
BEVERLY (Town of)
David Perkins of, ... 252
Phillip Darland of, miller 252–3
Phillip White &c. of, ... 348
BICKFORD (or Beckford), CHRISTOPHER, (inquisition) 33
BIGG, JOHN, of Boston, merchant, ag[t]. Harwood & wife 339
BIGNELL, SAMUEL, (Jury for attaints) 266
BILBOA, payment at, ment[d]. (libel ag[t]. Bartholmew &c.) 76
BILL of exchange, attachment of, (West ag[t]. Barter) 157
BILL
James, (Grand Jury) 202
Thomas, (1st Jury for trials, &c.) 120
BILLING or BILLINGS
Ebenezer, (Jury for attaints) 244, 288
(1st Jury for trials &c.) 245
(case of James Morgan) 295
Nathaniel, Chamberlain ag[t]., ... 277
Roger, Rawson ag[t]., ... 26, 96
(1st Jury of trials) 66
Mr. (2nd Jury of trials) 71
BILSON, JOHN, (certificate & order for pay[mt]. &c. under Hathorn) 104
BINGLEY or BINGLY
Thomas, (Jury of inquest) (inquisition on Bickford) 34
(2[d] Jury for trials &c.) 96
BIRD
James, (2[d] Jury of trials &c.) 25, 71, 203, 274
(1st " " " ") 66
(Jury for attaints) 232
(Jury for trials &c.) 233, 302, 306, 308
John, (Jury of trials &c.) 35–6
(Jury) 210
(Grand Jury) 336
Thomas, &c., surety of Smith ag[t]., ... 69
(2[d] Jury for trials &c.) 121

PAGE

BISCO or BISCOE
John, (Grand Jury) 78, 202
(2d Jury for trials &c.) 108
(1st " " " ") 140
Mr., complaint agt. Farrell &c. 286

BISHOP
Job, pet. for divorce by his wife Mary 144
John, mentd. (Ingolls agt. Bishop) 262
Margaret, execx., &c., agt. Wainewright 60
Mary, wife of Job Bishop, pet. for divorce 144
Samuel, agt. White 20
agt. Gold 47
execr., &c., agt. Wainewright 60
agt. Lord, marshal 238, 248
agt. admrs. of Andrews 248
agt. Clarke 263
Thomas, mentd. (Bishop agt. White) 20
Gold agt., ... 21
agt. Gold 47
atty., mentd. (Bishop agt. Gold) 47
his execr., &c., agt. Wainewright 60
Ingolls agt., ... 262–3

BLACK
William, agt. pink Mary, &c. 324
agt. Bronsdon 324
mariner &c., of pink Mary, agt. Bronsdon &c. 324

BLACKLEACH
John, Mr., &c., Court of Admiralty granted on motion of, ... 63
&c., merchants, (libel &c.) 63
Sheaffe agt., ... 85
Solomon, master of ship James Frygot (libel &c. of Creane &c.) . 128

BLACK POINT
Jno. Glandfeild of, ... 15
Wm. Battyn of, ... 15
Walter Gendall of, ... 102

BLAGE, NATH., (1st Jury of trials &c.) 59

BLAINE (or BLAYNE, BELAINE, BOLAINE) JOHN, of Island of Jersey, marr., Hunlorck agt. 292, 294

BLAINY. (*See* Blaney.)

BLAKE
James (2d Jury of trials &c.) 45
(Jury of trials &c.) 252, 362
John, (Mr.) (Grand Jury) 17, 65, 78, 139, 179
(Jury of trials &c.) 336

BLANCHARD or BLANCHEARD, BLANDCHARD, BLANSHEARD
Edward, &c., mariners of pink Endeavor (libel &c.) 118
George, his son, &c., case of, (coining base money) 22

PAGE

BLANCHARD, &c., *continued.*
Joseph, &c., case of, (coining base money) 22
bond by, ... 22
Phillip, &c., mariners of pink Endeavor (libel &c.) 117-18
BLANCHEARD }
BLANDCHARD } (*See* BLANCHARD.)
BLANEY or BLAINY, BLANY, BLAYNY
John, ag^{t}. King, exec^{x}., &c. 111
(Jury) 149, 210
Senr., of Salem ag^{t}. Dunton 340
&c., order as to, ... 360
BLANSHEARD. (*See* BLANCHARD.)
BLANY. (*See* BLANEY.)
BLASPHEMY. (*See* CRIMES.)
BLAYNE. (*See* BLAINE.)
BLYANY. (*See* BLANEY.)
BLESSING (ship), master of, &c. (libel &c.) 58, 59
BLIGH
Thomas, Sen., (Jury for trial of attaint) 134
(2^{d} Jury of trials &c.) 135
Sen., (Jury) 171
(Grand Jury) 232, 243, 336, 361
BLISH, ABRAHAM, (Jury of trials) 322
BLISS, ABRAHAM, &c., sureties on bond of attaint (Webb ag^{t}. Manly) . . 235
BLOAR. (*See* BLOWER.)
BLOOD, ROBERT, Junr., ag^{t}. Knight 279-80
BLOWER }
BLOWERS } or BLOAR
John, ment^{d}. (Phipps ag^{t}. Bronsdon) 337
Pyam, (1st Jury of trials &c.) 17, 215
(Grand Jury) 53
BLUNT, SAMUEL (Jury of trials) 337
BOALES. (*See* BOWLES.)
BOARDMAN
Andrew, (2^{d}. Jury of trials &c.) 60, 161, 245
(Jury of attaints,) 244
Wm., Senr., (2^{d}. Jury of trials &c.) 25
BOBBAT, ERASMUS, &c., seamen &c., of ship Lixborn Merchant (libel &c.) . 92-3
BODKIN
Dominick, merchant, ag^{t}. Necke 128
Mr., libel, &c., ag^{t}. Brimsden 128
BOLAINE. (*See* BLAINE.)
BOLDERSON, WILLIAM, of Boston, adm^{r}., ag^{t}. Colman 336
BOLEN, ——, Mr., ment^{d}. (Elliot, &c., ag^{t}. ketch Friendship) (exec^{n}.) . 392
BOLSTON. (*See* BALSTON.)
BOLTON
Nicholas, (1st. Jury of trials) 66
(2^{d}. Jury of trials) 71

PAGE

Boman
Francis, (Jury for attaint) 134
(1st. Jury of trials &c.) 153
(Jury) 210
Bonavista Road in Newfoundland, sale at, ... 335
Bond
declared forfeited by County Court (Clarke agt. Bartlet) 2
chancery of, (Bennet agt. Gridley) 82
prosecution upon, as to, (Woodbridge agt. Williams) 83
chancery of, (Woodbridge agt. Williams) 83
verdict for forfeiture of, (Brattle agt. Knight, admr., &c.) 101
declared forfeited (Wm. Pitman, plaintiff, appeal) 110
chanceried (Dell &c. agt. Child) 112
(Longfellow &c. agt. Oxe) 112
(Usher agt. Usher) 137
declared forfeited (Porter agt. Cater) 138
chancery of, (Rock agt. Francks) 143
(Holmes agt. Clarke) 152
(Apleton agt. Porter) 154
forfeiture of, (Bellingham agt. Hamond &c.) 157
of arbitration, as to chancery of, (Porter agt. Apleton) 159
chancery of, (Bateman agt. Taft) 161
declared forfeited (Egerton agt. Smith) 166
forfeiture of, (Davenport agt. Patch) 166
chancery of, (case of Mr. Apleton) 167
forfeiture of, (case of Daniel Mathew) 167
chancery of, (Joy &c., agt. Addams) 191
(surety of Gretian agt. Webb, marshl.) 207
chancery &c. of, (Rawson &c., agt. Stoughton &c., commrs.) . . . 209
chancery of, (Symonds agt. Leverett) 217
forfeiture of, (Atkinson agt. Mirrick) 223
chancery of, (Dyre agt. Hutchinson) 261–2
declared forfeited (Baker agt. Addams) 266
chancery of, (Griffyn agt. Knight) 267
chancery of, (order on pet. of Wharton &c.) 272
(Baker agt. Hunlocke) 279
forfeiture of, (Wardell agt. Lynde) 280
chancery of, (answer to motion of Hellier) 287
declared forfeited (Nowell agt. Goddard) 293
forfeiture of, (Lambe &c., agt. Winthrop, Treasr. &c.) 366
Bond
——, Mr., foreman, mentd. (Shatswell agt. Jewet) 205
John, (Jury of trials) 302
William, (2d. Jury of trials &c.) 18
(Grand Jury) 108, 140, 230, 232, 273
Mr. (1st Jury of trials &c.) 203
Ju., (Jury of trials &c.) 252
Boneta, (brigantine) commander of, (libel &c.) 354

PAGE

BONNER
John, agt. Heyman &c. [Bonner & Lawton] 1
agt. Ashton 3
&c., Gibbs agt., ... 18
BOOBER or BOOBY
Joan[e], & husband Joseph, Douning agt., ... 258
" " " " agt. Douning (execn.) 388
Joseph, & wife Joane, Douning agt., ... 258
agt. Douning 276
and wife Joan, agt. Douning (execn) 388
BOOBY. (*See* BOOBER.)
BOOK of Rates, p. 158, acts of parliament in, (libel of Randolph) . . 149
BOOTH, REBECKAH, murder of, (case of John Dounton) 272
BOREAU, FRANCIS, &c., confession by, mentd. (libel of Adams) . . . 355
BOSSINGER, THOMAS, master &c. (information of Lugger) 296
BOSTON (Courts at,)
County Court at 2–5, 7–9, 15, 17, 18, 21, 24–29, 31, 44–50, 59, 60, 65, 66, 68, 69, 77–81, 83, 85, 88, 89, 94–103, 109–113, 119, 121–125, 133–135, 137, 140–142, 144, 151–157, 161, 162, 164–168, 180–187, 192, 193, 195, 196, 203–209, 215–220, 222, 223–227, 234, 236–239, 245–249, 256, 257–261, 267–274, 276–282, 288, 290, 291–294, 297, 302, 303, 322–328, 330, 331, 336–341, 346, 347, 349–352, 362, 363–369, 371, 380–382, 386
(*See also* County Court Suffolk)
Commissioners Court in, ... 6, 7, 20, 46, 67, 81, 94, 97, 98, 101, 109, 120–122, 135, 137, 141, 153, 155, 157, 164, 195, 204, 215, 219, 236, 238, 239, 244, 260, 273, 279, 291, 292, 347, 350, 351, 361, 365, 369, 370
(*See also* Commissioners Court)
Court of Assistants at, . . . 1, 15, 16, 24, 34, 36, 39, 41, 43, 52, 55–58, 61, 64, 75–77, 89, 91, 94, 96, 106, 107, 117–119, 128, 130–132, 133, 138, 139, 146, 147–151, 159, 160, 172–179, 189, 190, 202, 209–211, 213, 214, 223, 229–231, 241, 243, 251, 253, 254, 265, 266, 273, 287, 296, 298, 300, 301, 322, 327, 336, 345, 359, 361, 371–373, 376, 378, 380–382, 386, 387–389
(*See also* Assistants)
Meeting of Governor & Council at, ... 23, 104, 296, 297
Court of Admiralty at, . . . 34, 39, 41, 43, 52, 55, 58, 61–63, 75, 76, 77, 91–94, 106, 117, 118, 128, 130, 131, 132, 147–149, 159, 172–179, 209, 210, 211, 213, 230, 298, 300, 372, 373, 382, 386
(*See also* Assistants)

PAGE

Boston (Town of,)
constable of, return of warrant by, (case of Geo. Cole etc.) . . . 12
Ship Expectation fitted in, ... 16
Ordinances of Christ in, ... 21
prison in, commitment to, (case of Mary Parsons) 31
Governor and Magistrates in, ... 32
constable of, (inquisition on body of Bickford) 33
Mr. Humphry Warren of, merchant 34
Mr. John Freake of, ... 35–39
Robert Houghton of, ... 39, 42
ment^d^. (libel, etc. ag^t^. Bull) 40
Thomas Patten of, ... 43
ment^d^. (case of Maurice Bret) 51
(case of Zechariah Crispe) 51
Maurice Brett of, ... 56
Mary Gibbs of, ... 57
Anthony Stoddard, commissioner in, ... 66
freemen in, choice of [commissioners] allowed, etc. 67
Thos. Davis late resident in, ... 70
John Bucknam of, ... 73
Robert Cox, etc. of, ... 74
constables chosen in, and oath 80
Wm. Waldron, &c., of, ... 86
Mr. Isack Waldron of, ... 88
prison in, (case of Walter Gendall) 90
attachment dated in, 9 Apr. 1677 (libel &c. ag^t^. Sandiford) . . 91
commissioners in, sworn 96
military companies in, ... 102–3
Capt. Tho. Brattle discharged as comm^r^. of, sentence remitted, . . 103
defaming women in, (case of Wm. Pope) 104
Henry Allin of, ... 105
John Keetch of, ... 105
Peter Lydget of, merchant 105
Mr. Wm. Harris of, ... 106
harbor of, ment^d^. (case of ship Speedwell &c.) 107
Darby Bryan of, ... 114
keeper of prison in, order on pet. of, ... 114
Abigaile Johnson of, ... 115
lecture in, (case of Darby Bryan) 115
Third Meeting House in, ... 127
John Necke of, ... 128
ment^d^. (Marston &c., ag^t^. Hollaway &c.) 132–3
banishment from, (case of Ellinor May) 138
Mr. John Usher of, ... 139
Maudet Engis of, ... 139
fire in, ment^d^. (case of Joshua Atwater &c.) 145
gaol in, commitment to, (case of Peeter Lorphelin) 145–6
comm^rs^. chosen for, & oath 168

PAGE

BOSTON (Town of,) *continued.*
security for, (case of Geo. Russell) 169
order of Dep^{ty}. Gov. in, 21 Oct. 1680 (case of Cobbham) 171
harbor in, ship in, ment^{d}. (libel &c. ag^{t}. Turell) 174
ship Two Sisters of, ... 176
Mary Hale of, ... 188
prison in, ment^{d}. (answer to pet. of Morse) 190
comm^{rs}. &c. for, complaint ag^{t}. Sherlot, dancing master &c. . . . 197
freemen of, comm^{rs}. chosen by, & oath 199
Timothy Dwight of, ... 200
constables chosen in, & oath 206
Ship Hope of, ... 210
Saml. Shrimpton &c. of, merchants 211
comm^{rs}. of, oath by, ... 214
Edward Crocket of, ... 234
Joshua Rice of, ... 234
port of, bark belonging to, (case of Wm. Johnson) 242
Vines Ellacot now resident in, merchant 251
John Keech of, ... 282
Sarah Noyes of, ... 283
James Pecker of, ... 284
house of Mrs. Noyes in, ... 285
Constante Worcester of, widow 294
James Morgan of, ... 294
Joseph Johnson of, butcher 294
Henry Flood of, ... 295
ship Elisabeth of, ... 296
watch house on the neck in, ... 296
Mr. Richard Wharton &c., of, merchants 297
Mr. Wm. Woodrope &c., of, ... 298, 300
Mr. Saml. Shrimpton of, merchant 299
house &c. in, ... 302
Jotham Grover, &c., of, ... 303
Wm. Robie, &c., of, ... 303
Thomas Hawkins of, mariner 305
Thomas Pound of, mariner 307
sloop Mary of, ... 308, 309, 311–314, 316–318
Thomas Johnston of, mariner 309
Richard Griffin of, gunsmith 314
ketch Elinor of, ... 319
Sarah Fowler, &c., of, ... 322
Edmund Perkins, &c., of, ... 323
Edward Bricknall of, ... 323
David Waterhouse of, merchant 325
George Mountjoy &c., of, ... 325
John Child of, tailor 325
Rebecca Stebbins of, widow 326
Thomas Platts of, ... 326

PAGE

BOSTON (Town of,) *continued.*
Peter De Vaulx &c., of, ... 327
John Pynchon of, merchant 328
Giles Fifield of, mariner 330
Henry Mountfort of, merchant 330
ship Richard of 334
Wm. Bolderson &c., of, ... 336
Nath[l]. Oliver of, ... 337
Rob[t]. Bronsdon of, merchant 337–8
Thomas Bulkley &c., of, merchants 338
George Hiskett of, mariner 339
John Bigg of, merchant 339
Thomas Smith of, blacksmith 339
land &c. in, ... 340
James Adlington of, mariner 340
Nicholas Tippet of, merchant 340
George Mountjoy of, mariner 341
Jonas Clay &c., of, mariners 341
Samuel Hemlock of, mariner 341
Thomas Clarke of, ... 341
Thomas Eyre &c., of, ... 342
ment[d]. (information ag[t]. Lawrence) 344
Tieg A. Barrow of, ... 345
Rebekah Stebbins of, widow 346
Benjamin Walker &c., of, ... 347
Wm. Warren &c., of, ... 347
David Waterhouse of, merchant 350
Henry Wright of, carpenter 350
Nath[l]. Oliver of, merchant 350
Sarah Fowler &c., of, ... 350
George Ball of, mariner 351
Henry Wright of, ... 351
Winsor Sandey of, mariner 351
Wm. Mumford &c., of, ... 351
sloop Mary of, ... 352
ment[d]. (libel ag[t]. bark Speedwell) 352
Benj. Alford of, merchant 352
Seth Perry of, ... 352
Thomas Bulkley of, merchant 352
brigantine Boneta of, ... 354
Mr. Richard Wharton of, ... 356
comm[rs]. for, sworn 29 Sept. 1691 357–8
Duncan Cambell of, stationer 358
Edward Lillie of, cooper 358
Rice Griffin of, laborer 358
lecture day in, ... 360
Capt. Edw[d]. Wylly of, shopkeeper 361
prison in, ... 361

PAGE

Boston (Town of,) *continued.*
Nathl. Thaire of, ... 362
Samuel Legg &c., of, mariners 362
Benjamin Alford of, ... 363
Seth Perry of, ... 363
John Arnold, prison keeper in, ... 364
John Somes of, ... 364
Wm. Witherett of, ... 365
Edward Peggy &c., of, ... 365
Thomas Smith &c., of, ... 365
Capt. John Wing of, ... 367
Thomas Stanbury &c., of, ... 367
Capt. John Foy &c., of, ... 368
Jeremiah Tay of, mariner 369
Mary Thatcher of, widow 369
execution dated at, 21 Dec. 1675 372
29 May 1678 374
22 Sept. 1680 377
4 Jan. 1678 383
appraisement dated at, 22 Jan. 1678–9 385
appraisement at, ... 385
Drawbridge in, mentd. 385
Joseph Homes of, ... 386
prison keeper in, (Sheffeild agt. Homes) 387
Hudsons (or Wing) lane in 389
prison keeper in, mentd. (Hundlocke agt. Baker &c.) 389
John Cotta, constable of, ... 390
appraisers oath dated at, 24 Oct. 1685 391
ketch Freindship of, ... 391
execution dated at, 14 May 1686 392
Bouden, Michael, Smith agt., ... 134
Bouland (or Bowland), John, mate of ship Ann & Hester (libel &c.) . 172, 175
Boules. (*See* Bowles.)
Boulter
——, (Colcord?) Roby &c. agt., ... 7
Nathaniel, &c., agt. Evins 6, 136
atty., Hampton agt., ... 43
&c., agt. Wilson 136
Boury, Jno., master of ship Wm. of Bristol, &c., information agt., . . . 210
Bowdish, Wm., of Salem, case of, (neglect or non appearance) 103
Bowen
Henry, (1st Jury for trials &c.) 224
(Jury of attaints &c.) 288
(1st Jury of appeals &c.) 289
(Grand Jury) 361
Bowers
Benanuel, case of, ... 3
referred to County Court, Cambridge 104

PAGE

BOWERS, *continued.*
Benanuel, Wood &c. agt., ... 224
Phips &c. agt., ... 224
by attys. agt. Phipps &c. 232
Elisabeth, order on pet. of, ... 104
BOWLAND. (*See* BOULAND.)
BOWLES or BOALES, BOULES.
Christian, &c., seamen of ship Resolution (libel &c.) 173
John, (Grand Jury) 32, 35
Laurence, &c., mariners of ketch John & Benjamin (libel &c.) . . 117
" " " " " " " " " (execn.) 373-4
BOYNTON, JOSHUA, agt. Cross 125
BRACKET
Peter, (Grand Jury) 32
Speere agt., ... 182
BRADBROOK or BRADBROOKE
Sarah, case of, (stealing) 145
BRADLEY, GEORGE, merchant, Fifield agt., ... 330
BRADSHAW
Humphry, (2d Jury of trials &c.) 71
(1st Jury of trials &c.) 95
BRADSTREET or BRADSTREETE, BRADSTRET
Dudley, Capt., &c., Selectmen of Andover, agt. Fuller 108
Simon or Symon, Esqr., Honble. Govr. Esqr., Depty. Govr.,
present at Court, 1, 15, 16, 23, 24, 32-36, 41, 43, 52, 55, 58, 61, 65, 70, 76, 77, 91, 92, 94, 105-107, 117, 119, 128, 130-133, 139, 148, 149, 150, 151, 159, 160, 170, 172, 173, 177, 179, 189, 190, 202, 208, 209, 213, 214, 223, 227, 229, 231, 241, 243, 251, 254, 266, 273, 287, 296, 298, 327, 336, 345, 359, 361, 373.
injurious speeches agt., (case of Isaac Waldron) 88
present at meeting of Council in Boston 1 Nov. 1677 . . . 104
mentd. (libel agt. Gretian &c.) 150
&c., information agt. Boury &c. 210
libel agt. Place 210
agt. Coffyn 259, 270
Coffyn agt., ... 270
mentd. (information agt. Lawrence) 342-344
commission by, ... 354
oath before, (libel agt. Schinking) (execn.) 380
BRADSTREETE BRADSTRET (*See* BRADSTREET.)
BRAINTREE (Town of)
Jno. Dyar of, ... 188
Mr. Richard Harris of, ... 282
Hannah Owen of, ... 361
Joseph Belchar of, ... 364

PAGE

BRANDENBURGH, Duke of, ment^{d}. (libel ag^{t}. Cocke &c.) 179
BRANDFORD in England ment^{d}. (case of Ruth Read) 10
BRANDING. (*See* PUNISHMENT, miscellaneous.)
BRANSON
Francis, master &c. of ship Ann & Hester, &c., libel &c.
of Bouland ag^{t}., . 172, 175
of Basset, &c., ag^{t}., . 172
of Kelso ag^{t}., . . 174
ag^{t}. Kelso . 177
BRATLE or BRATTLE
Thomas, atty., Knight ag^{t}., ... 8
Mr., (Grand Jury) 56
Capt^{t}., &c., comm^{rs}., [Boston], allowed &c. by the Court . 67, 96
ag^{t}. Knight, adm^{r}., &c. 100–1
case of, (reflections on Suffolk County Court) . . 103
&c. chosen comm^{rs}. for Boston & oath 168, 199
&c. oath as " " " 214
Man ag^{t}., ... 250
comm^{r}., oath before, (libel &c. ag^{t}. Long) 375
Capt^{t}., appraisers sworn before, (libel &c. ag^{t}. Checkly &c.) (exec^{n}.) 385
BRAYDEN, James, (Jury of trials) 56
BREACH OF THE PEACE. (*See* CRIMES.)
BRECK, or BRECKE, BREKS, BRICKE, BROCK
John, master of bark Gift of God, &c., libel ag^{t}., ... 176
(Jury for attaint) 192, 244
(Mr.) (2^{d}. Jury for trials &c.) 192, 245
(Jury) 231
[John], [Mr.], foreman, ment^{d}. in margin 248
BRECKE, BREKS (*See* BRECK.)
BRENTNAL, THO^{S}., formerly of Rumney Marsh, now of Wadeing River ag^{t}. Hamlin & wife . . . 326
BRENTON
Jahleel, Gent., Coll^{r}., &c., information ag^{t}. Lawrence . . . 342–344
Lason ag^{t}., ... 349
libel ag^{t}. pink Three Brothers &c. . . . 355–6
(appraisement of ketch Salisbury) 356
(order on appeal of Lawrence) 360
Shrimpton ag^{t}., ... 366
BRET or BRETT
John, (Grand Jury) 230
Maurice, of Boston, case of, (murder) 51
(adultery) 56
(contemptuous carriage) 57

PAGE

BREWER
Daniel, (Jury for trials) . . . 35, 37
(1st Jury for trials) . . . 140
(Jury for attaints) . . . 181
(2d. Jury for trials &c.) . . . 181
Nathaniel, (1st. Jury for trials &c.) . . . 17, 95
BRICKE. (*See* BRECK.)
BRICKNALL, EDWARD, of Boston, mariner, his admr., Arbuckle agt., . . . 323
BRIDEWELL, commitment to, (case of Ellinor May) . . . 138
BRIDG. (*See* BRIDGE.)
BRIDGAM. (*See* BRIDGHAM.)
BRIDGE or BRIDG.
——, mentd. in margin . . . 112
Edwd., (Jury of trials) . . . 35, 37
Samuel, (Jury for attaints) . . . 180
(1st. Jury for trials &c.) . . . 181
(2d. Jury for trials &c.) . . . 224
BRIDGES, EDMOND, atty., agt. Mazure . . . 109
BRIDGHAM or BRIDGAM
Jonathan, (1st. Jury for trials &c.) . . . 70
(2d. Jury for trials &c.) . . . 161
(Grand Jury) . . . 242
(2d. Jury for appeals) . . . 256
instead of Mr. Clark (2d. Jury of trials &c.) . . . 275
BRIGGS
Abraham, assignee, Leveret agt., . . . 50
Rauson agt., . . . 65
Gifford agt., . . . 65
Jno, &c., Martin agt., . . . 152
BRIGHT
Henry, (Grand Jury) . . . 1, 25, 32, 59, 120, 151, 252
Jno., (Jury of attaints) . . . 244
(2d. Jury of trials &c.) . . . 245
(Grand Jury) . . . 287
BRIMSDEN } (*See* BRONSDON.)
BRINSDON }
BRISCO, JOSEPH, atty., &c., agt. Sparrey (2 actions) . . . 235
BRISTOL (Town of)
Wm. Haberfeild of, . . . 105
ship George of, . . . 173
ship Michael of, . . . 150
ship William of, . . . 210
BROADHURST, RALPH, (Jury for attaints) . . . 267
BROCK. (*See* BRECK.)
BROMEFEILD. (*See* BROMFIELD.)
BROMEHALL. (*See* BROMHALL.)

PAGE

BROMFEILD } or BROMEFEILD, BROOMFEILD
BROMFIELD }
Edward, (Jury) 160
(Jury for trials) 242
Mr., (2d. Jury for trials, &c.) 274
foreman, mentd. (Homes agt. Cheeckley) 282
(Checkley agt. verdict of jury, &c.) . 287
&c., chosen commrs. for Boston & sworn 357

BROMHALL or BROMEHALL
Thomas, mate of ketch John & Benjamin, &c. (libel &c.) . . 117, 373–4

BROMSDON } or BRIMSDEN, BRINSDON.
BRONSDON }
Robert, libel &c. of Bodkin agt., ... 128
Paige agt., ... 168
(Jury for attaint) 191
(1st. Jury for trials &c.) 192
atty., agt. Wharton 248
agt. Conney 269
admr., Arbuckle agt., ... 323
&c., owners, Black, agt., ... 324
Black agt., ... 324
merchant, &c., Black agt., ... 324
of Boston, merchant, Phipps agt., (3 actions) 337–8
(Grand Jury) 345

BROOKES. (*See* BROOKS.)

BROOKIN or }
BROOKINGS }
John, Williams agt., ... 217

BROOKS or BROOKES
Caleb, &c., Prout agt., ... 349
Isack, (1st. Jury of appeals &c.) 274
Tymothy, agt. Mussey 268

BROOMFEILD. (*See* BROMFIELD.)

BROTHERS ADVENTURE (sloop and ketch)
mentd. (libel, etc. agt. Sandiford) 91
(libel, agt. Keech) 300
(libel, agt. Thornton) 300–1

BROUGHTON
Thomas, (1st. Jury of trials &c.) 59
foreman, mentd. (Woodmansey agt. Frost) 59

BROUNE. (*See* BROWNE.)

BROUNSFORD, ROBT., &c., mariners, (libel, &c.), ... 40

BROWNE or BROUNE
———, Mr., present at Court 12 Oct. 1683 240
Abraham, of Salisbury, agt. Fellowes 140
Charles, &c., mariners of pink Endeavor (libel, &c.) 117–18
Edward, case of, (murder) 315
Elizabeth, (case of Thomas Davis) 70

PAGE

BROWNE or BROUNE, *continued.*
Elizabeth, wife of Wm. Browne, case of, (adultery) 70
George, Left., &c., attys., Swann agt., ... 156
Hezekiah, legacies to, mentd. (Usher agt. execrs. of Usher) 203
James, atty., English agt., ... 109
agt. Trumble 156
John, Senr., &c., Maning, agt., ... 164
&c. overseers, &c., Maning agt., (execn.) 376–7
(Ruling Elder of church of Salem), &c. overseers, &c.,
agt. Maning (execn.) . 376–7
Jonathan, (2d. Jury for trials &c.) 79, 181, 224
(Jury of attaints) 181
Robert, mariner of ship Merchants Adventure, &c. agt. Stone, . . . 213
Roger, house &c. of, (Butler agt. Hollowell &c.) (execn.) 381
Thomas, (2d. Jury of trials &c.) 18
Senr., Laughton, &c. agt., ... 195
Town of Lynn agt., ... 225
Hitchins agt., ... 276
William, Senr., merchant, agt. Letherland 25
of Charlestown, case of his wife Elizabeth, ... 70
Senr., present at Court 1 June 1680 149
20 Aug. 1680 160
16 Oct. 1680 169
Esqr., " " " 1 Mar. 1680 179
(2d Jury of trials &c.) 203
Esqr., Dewer agt., ... 236
Assist., oath before, (Manning agt. overseers &c.) . . . 377
BRUSCO, JNO., (Jury of trials) 57
BRYAN or BRYANT
Darby, Soames agt., ... 97
agt. Soames 98
of Boston, case of, (adultery) 114
mentd. (case of Abigaile Johnson) 115
BRYANT. (*See* BRYAN.)
BUCK
Eleazer, mariner, case of, (piracy &c.) 310, 311, 320, 322
Saml., (Jury of trials) 323
BUCKLEY, RICHD., (Grand Jury) 305
BUCKMAN, SAMUEL, Atkinson agt., ... 221
BUCKMINSTER, JOSEPH, late widow of, order on estate of, ... 103
BUCKNAM
John, of Boston, his wife Sarah mentd. (case of Peter Cole) . . . 73
Sarah, wife of John Bucknam, " " . . . 73
case of, (adultery) 74
BUCKNELL, GEORG, &c. mariners of pink Endeavor (libel &c.) . . . 117, 118
BUFFAM, JOSHUA, mentd. (case of George Cole &c.) 12
BUGGERY. (*See* CRIMES.)

PAGE

BULKLEY
——, Mr., present at Court 12 Oct. 1683 240
Peter or Peeter, Esq[r]., present at Court, 148–151, 159–161, 169, 170, 176, 190, 202, 209, 211, 214, 223, 232, 241, 243
Peter, Esq[r]., assignee &c., Usher ag[t]., ... 237
Usher ag[t]., ... 243
Richard, (1st Jury of trials &c.) 65, 70
(Jury) 171
Thomas, of Boston, merchant, Grover ag[t]., ... 303
ag[t]. Thayre, &c. 338
Hayward ag[t]., ... 352
BULL, JOHN, master of ship Providence (libel &c.) 40
BULLARD
Natha., (1st Jury of appeals &c.) 289
(Jury of attaints &c.) 289
Nathaniel, &c., ag[t]. County Courts judgment as to will of Richards . 291
BULLIS, PHILLIP, ag[t]. adm[r]. of Payton 113
BULLOCK, JOHN, Small ag[t]., ... 339
BURELL. (*See* BURRELL.)
BURGLARY. (*See* CRIMES.)
BURNAM, JOHN, Jun[r]., of Chebacco of Ipswich, ag[t]. Cross 345–6
BURNING to death (case of Maria, negro) 198
BURREL } or BURELL
BURRELL }
Francis, (Jury of attaints &c.) 289
(1st Jury for appeals &c.) 289
John, &c., atty[s]., ag[t]. Browne 225
BURROUGHS or BURROWES
Francis, Mr., &c., appointed to apprize ketch Salisbury 356
Hiller ag[t]., ... 281
BURROWES. (*See* BURROUGHS.)
BURTON
Stephen, (2[d]. Jury for trials &c.) 60
(1st. Jury for trials &c.) 120
(Jury) 150, 176
Webb ag[t]., ... 203
Harwood ag[t]., ... 257
Saffyn ag[t]., ... 281
BUSSELL, STEPHEN, ag[t]. Ballat 140
BUSWELL, WM., Ring ag[t]., ... 82
BUTCHER
Richard, gunner of ship Ann & Hesther, &c. (libel &c.) 172
Robert, atty., ag[t]. Randolph, Esq[r]. 210
constable, (case of Wm. Clapp &c.) 286
BUTLER
Stephen, ag[t]. Hollowell &c. 140
ag[t]. Hollowell &c. 164

PAGE

BUTLER, *continued.*
Stephen, order on pet. of, ... 170
ag^t. Checkley 205
Senr. Hollowell, &c., ag^t., (execution) 380–382
ag^t. Hollowell &c. 380–382
Junr., wife of, ment^d. (Butler ag^t. Hallowell &c.) (exec^n.) . 382
BUTTERFIELD, HENRY, gunner of ship John & Mary, &c. (libel &c.) . . 40
BUTTERY, JN^o., of Marblehead, case of, (bestiality) 103
BUTTOLPH, JN^o., jury of inquest (inquisition on body of Bickford) . . 34
BUTTYN. (*See* BATTEN.)
BYFEILD
BYFFEILD
BYFIELD
Nathaniel, (1st Jury for trials &c.) 59
(Jury) 149
exec^r., ag^t. Taylor &c. 153
atty., ag^t. Orchard 224

CABLE, GEORGE, Fawer ag^t., ... 302
CADMAN, STEPHEN, (Jury) 171, 176
CALEB (Indian), &c., case of, (being open & murderous enemies) . . 76
CALL, JOHN, (Grand Jury) 266, 336
CALLENDER, ELLIS, of Boston, Warren ag^t., ... 347
CALLEY
Hanna, Williams, ag^t., ... 95
Joseph, Endecott &c. ag^t., ... 96
CALMAN. (*See* COLMAN.)
CALUMBINE (Indian), &c., case of, (being open & murderous enemies) . 76
CAMBELL. (*See* CAMPBELL.)
CAMBRIDGE (Town of)
County Court at, ... 2, 22, 27, 57, 100, 104, 121, 124,
(*See also* County Court Middlesex) 157, 164, 166, 197, 218, 224, 237, 267, 271, 275, 277, 281, 287, 290, 291, 300, 301, 330, 346, 351, 363
prison at, commitment to, (case of Benanuel Bowers) 3
ment^d. (case of old Jethro, Indian) 54
ment^d. (case of Jno. Lawrence) 87
(" " Tho. Kenny, negro) 126
Jno. Fuller of, ... 274
prison at, (order on complaint by Bernard) 283
drummers of, Cambridge Selectmen ag^t., ... 289
John Cheeny of, ... 304
Alice Francis &c. of, ... 330
CAMPBELL or CAMBELL
Duncan, of Boston, stationer, case of his servant maid 358
Hugh, merchant & owner of bark Hope, libel &c. of Goose ag^t., . . 148
of Pelton ag^t., . 148
ag^t. Goose . . 184
CAMPEACHY, BAY OF, ment^d. (Marston &c. ag^t. Hollaway &c.) 132

PAGE

CANADA, coast of, (case of Wm. Johnson) 242
CANE, JONATHAN, exec^{r}., ag^{t}. comm^{rs}. of the United Colonies 95
CANNIDA, THOMAS, &c., by atty. ag^{t}. Town of Hampton 19
CANNON, ROBERT, Johnson &c., for owners of ship Dove, ag^{t}., ... 52
CAPEN or CAPIN
Barnard, freeman, oath by, ... 78
(1st Jury for trials &c.) 78
John, Capt., (Grand Jury) 242
(Grand Jury) 251, 302, 305, 345
(Jury of trials) 323
Junr., (Jury of trials) 345
(Jury) 360
Sam., (Jury for attaints) 266
CAPENAWAGEN, &c., appointment of Constable at, ... 12
CAPIN. (*See* CAPEN.)
CAPITAL PUNISHMENT. (*See* PUNISHMENT.)
CARDS, playing at, for money, (case of John Child) 235
CAREY. (*See* CARY.)
CARR
George, Senr., ag^{t}. Paige 181
Richard, of Salisbury, March ag^{t}., ... 367
CARRINGTON, EDW., (Grand Jury) 56, 214
CARTER, THO., (Petit Jury) 323
CARY or CAREY
James (Grand Jury) 120
Nathaniel, master of ketch Elizabeth & Margaret, &c., ag^{t}. ketch Elizabeth & Margaret 106
(Jury) 150, 30
(Jury of trials) 299
(Special Jury) 363
CASTLE, ship St. John of Dublin lying out of command of, (Randolph ag^{t}. Jackson &c.). 160
CASWELL, MICHAEL, &c., mariners of ship Apollow ag^{t}. Hollaway &c. . . 132–3
CATER, EDW^{D}., Porter ag^{t}., ... 137–8
CAVE, THOMAS, Knight ag^{t}., ... 163
CHADWELL
Nicholas, Tyng ag^{t}., ... 137
Tho., (2^{d}. Jury of trials &c.) 60
CHAMBERLAIN or CHAMBERLAYNE
Benjamin, ag^{t}. Billings 277
Richard, case of, (inciting to theft) 145
CHAMBERLAYNE. (*See* CHAMBERLAIN.)
CHAMPLYN, JOHN, Mr., &c., interpreters, (libel ag^{t}. Andreason &c.) . . 264
CHAMPNEY
Daniel, (2^{d}. Jury for trials &c.) 215
(Jury of trials) 299
(Jury) 300
Sam., (Grand Jury) 298

PAGE

CHAMPS. (*See* DE CHAMPS.)

CHANCE MEDLEY
ment^{d}. in verdict (case of Peter Bent, Junr.) 86
in verdict ag^{t}. Dounton 272

CHANCERY. (*See* BOND.)

CHANDLER
Jno., (2^{d}. Jury for trials &c.) 60
Thomas, Ela ag^{t}., ... 194

CHANNELL, (or CHANNON) John, case of, (accomplice in theft) . . 285–287

CHANNON. (*See* CHANNELL.)

CHAPEN, JOHN, Heman ag^{t}., ... 260

CHAPLIN, WILLIAM, (2^{d}. Jury of trials) 346

CHAPMAN
Sam., ag^{t}. Barry 205
&c., sureties, bond by, (Shatswell ag^{t}. Jewet) 205

CHARD, HELLEN, master of ketch Mary of Salem, (case of Thos. Hawkins &c.) 305, 307, 309–311, 313, 315, 316–318

CHARLES II. (*See* under Acts, Brenton, Coll^{r}., Randolph, Coll^{r}., and Majesty.)

CHARLESTOWN (Town of)
County Court at, ... 3, 73, 95, 97, 108, 140, 143, 152,
(*See also* County Court Middlesex) 156, 165, 188, 219, 225, 230, 237, 246, 258, 268, 275, 279, 283, 289, 290, 329, 347, 349, 355, 359, 363, 368, 369
ment^{d}. (case of Anna Negro) 29
Thomas Russell, &c. of, ... 55
Daniel Davisson of, ... 62
lecture day at, (case of Thomas Davis) 70
Wm. Broune of, ... 70
Peter Cole of, ... 73
Samuel Hunting of, ... 114
Greenes wharf at, ... 174
Selectmen of, (Phips &c., agt., Bowers) 224
common ment^{d}., " " " " 224–5
common, drivers of, Bowers ag^{t}., ... 232
Thomas Fosket of, ... 328
John Tyler of, ... 350–1
Nathan Dunclin of, mariner 365

CHARTER of the Colony, dissolution of, ment^{d}. (case of Shrimpton) . . 297

CHARTER PARTY
ment^{d}. (libel ag^{t}. Starr &c.) 23
breach of, (libel ag^{t}. Measure) 42
ment^{d}. (libel ag^{t}. Davisson) 62
breach of, (libel ag^{t}. Wharton & Co.) 63
ment^{d}. (libel ag^{t}. Poole &c.) 64
(libel ag^{t}. Wheeler) 75
(libel ag^{t}. Gibbs) 77

PAGE

CHARTER PARTY, *continued.*
breach of, (Poole ag^{t}. exec^{x}. of Lydgett) 105
ment^{d}. (libel ag^{t}. Brimsden) 128
breach of, (libel ag^{t}. Goose) 148
penalty of, (Arbuckle ag^{t}. adm^{r}. of Bricknall) 323
ment^{d}. (Belchar ag^{t}. Lloyd) 362
forfeiture of, (Belchar ag^{t}. Lloyd) 363
CHASE, JAMES, ag^{t}. trustee of wife &c. of Nanny 17
CHEBACCO
land lying at, (Burnam ag^{t}. Cross) 346
of Ipswich, John Burnam, &c. of, ... 345
CHECKLEY } or CHEECKLEY, CHEECKLY, CHEEKLEY, CHICKLEY
CHECKLY }
———, Mr., exec^{n}. delivered to, (Butler ag^{t}. Holowell &c.) . . 164
Anthony, atty., ag^{t}. Williams 4
Mr., (1st Jury for trials &c.) 17
ag^{t}. Salter 47
atty., (libel ag^{t}. Shice) 58
&c., sureties, bond by, (case of Rich^{d}. Scott) 61
Mr., and wife Lidia, (libel &c.) 130
(1st Jury of trials &c.) 140
atty., (libel ag^{t}. pink Expectation) 149
(libel ag^{t}. Gretian &c.) 150
&c., sureties on bonds of attaint (Gretian ag^{t}. Sweathy) . 182–3
atty., ag^{t}. Hutchinson 186
Mr., atty., Voss ag^{t}., ... 204
atty., Staynor ag^{t}., ... 206
Butler ag^{t}., ... 205
surety, ag^{t}. Webb 207
Mr., &c., sureties on bond of attaint (Torrey ag^{t}. Gretian) . 226
ag^{t}. Patteshall 227
on behalf of Gretian ag^{t}. Torrey 232
atty., Homes ag^{t}., ... 238, 244
principal on bond of attaint (Homes ag^{t}. Cheeckley) . . 282
Homes ag^{t}., ... 282
Mr., ag^{t}. Homes 287
votes on pet. of, ... 294
Capt., ag^{t}. Griggs 369
Mr., atty., ment^{d}. (Buttler ag^{t}. Hollowell &c.) . . . 381–2
& wife Lydia (libel &c.) (exec^{n}.) . . . 382–384, 386
John, Mr., (Jury of trials) 35
foreman, ment^{d}. (case of John Roads &c.) 36
Lidia (or Lyddea), (formerly wife of Benj^{a}. Gibbs) & husband Anthony, (libel &c.) 130, 382–384, 386
Samuel, (jury) 160
(1st Jury for trials &c.) 215
CHEECKLEY }
CHEECKLY } (*See* CHECKLY.)
CHEEKLEY }

PAGE

CHEENEY } (*See* CHENY.)
CHEENY }
CHEEVERS or CHEIVERS
Bartholmew, (Jury for attaint) 2
(2d. Jury for trials &c.) 3
(Grand Jury) 151
CHEFFALEER (Negro)
servant to Thos. Walker, case of, (arson) 197
mentd. (case of James Pemberton's negro) 198
CHEIVERS. (*See* CHEEVERS.)
CHELMSFORD, house &c. in, (Stratton agt. Gidley) 369
CHENERY or }
CHENREE }
John, Ayres agt., ... 26
CHENY or CHEENEY, CHEENY
John, of Cambridge, murder of, (case of Robin, negro) 304
Thomas, (Jury for attaint) 192
dismissed (1st. Jury of trials &c.) 192
(2d. Jury of trials &c.) 193
(Grand Jury) 242, 361
[Senr.] (Jury for attaints) 255
(1st. Jury for appeal) 257
Wm., of Dorchester, planter, case of, (rape) 199
CHICK or CHICKE
Richard, atty., Harris agt., ... 46
(Jury for appeals) 233
(Jury for attaints) 233
agt. Doe 282
CHICKATABUT
Charles, son of Josiah, choice of guardians 208
Josiah, late sachem of Massachusetts, choice of guardians by his son Charles 208
CHICKE. (*See* CHICK.)
CHICKLEY. (*See* CHECKLY.)
CHILD.
Alvin, answer to pet. of, ... 12
Allwin, Dell &c., agt., ... 112
John, case of, (gambling) 235
of Boston, tailor, Banks agt., ... 325
Joseph, (1st. Jury for trials &c.) 70
(Grand Jury) 214
Junr., (Jury of trials) 242
(Grand Jury) 298
Richard, (1st. Jury for trials &c.) 224
(2d. Jury for trials &c.) 337
CHOCKE
Peter, Griggs agt., ... 140
agt. Peirce 141
agt. Morgan 157

PAGE
CHRIST, ordinances of, in Boston, (answer to motion of Wm. Leatherland) . 21
CHRIST THE SAVIOR ment[d]. (case of Joseph Gatchell) 253
CHRISTOPHER, OTHRA, carpenter of ship James Frygot, &c. (libel, &c.) . 128
CHUBB, JACOB, of Waymouth, commander, ment[d]. (libel, &c. ag[t]. ship William) 333-4
CHURCH
Caleb, (Jury for attaints) 233
Mr., foreman, (2[d]. Jury of trials) 345
Joseph, Joy ag[t]., ... 96
CLAP OR CLAPP
Desire, (2[d]. Jury of trials &c.) 161, 337
Ezra, (1st. Jury of trials &c.) 140
(Jury for trials &c.) 233
(Jury for attaints) 233
Nath., (2[d]. Jury for trials &c.) 60
Nehemiah, (Jury) 210
Nicholas, (1st. Jury for trials &c.) 44
Roger, Cap[t]., Thaier ag[t]., ... 186
Samuel, (Grand Jury) 32
(Jury of trials) 299
(Jury) 300
Wm., mariner, case of, (accomplice in theft) 284-287
CLARK OR CLARKE
——, Mr., & Mr. Stoddard, comm[rs]., sentence of, appealed from, (case of Maior, &c.) 84
——, Mr., Jn[o]. Bridgham instead of, (2[d]. Jury for trials &c.) . . 275
Andrew, ag[t]. Nicholls 47
Christopher, Mr., (Grand Jury) 24
(Jury) 150
(Grand Jury) 251
&c., appraisers, (libel &c. ag[t]. ship Dove &c.) (exec[n].) . 373
Edward, Marshal Gen[l]. Dep[ty]., Godfrey ag[t]., ... 8
Hugh, ag[t]. Bartlet 2
bond of, declared forfeited by County Court 2
(Grand Jury) 56
&c., case of, as to, ... 158
James, (2[d]. Jury for trials &c.) 215
John, ag[t]. Bartlet 1, 2
bond of, declared forfeited by County Court 2
&c., surety of Smith ag[t]., ... 69
mariner, (1st. Jury of trials &c.,) 161
Lambe ag[t]., ... 165
mariner, adm[r]. of Wilky ag[t]., ... 245
ag[t]. Lamb 345
atty., Lambe &c. ag[t]., ... 366
Jonah, (Grand Jury) 56
Jonas, (Grand Jury) 1, 24, 32, 35, 44, 53, 120, 140

PAGE

CLARKE, *continued.*
Jonas, Junr., master of ketch Hopewell (libel &c.) 23
Mr., (Grand Jury) 190, 214
Josiah, Peasley ag^t^., ... 221
Bishop ag^t^., ... 263
Mathew, & Co., Herbert ag^t^., ... 80
Nathaniel, &c., owners of ketch Newbery (complaint &c.) 220
Thomas, Esqr., or Major or Mr., present at Court, 1, 12, 15, 16, 23, 24, 32, 33, 34, 36, 41, 43, 52, 53, 55, 58, 61, 62, 63, 65, 70, 76, 77, 91, 92, 94, 105, 106, 107
Thomas, adm^r^. of Coggan & wife ag^t^., ... 3, 4
Major, &c., appointed to allow bills of cost 31
(Courts order as to witnesses) 31
Alden ag^t^., ... 66
Capt., &c., chosen by freemen of Boston allowed &c. by the Court, 67, 96
&c., present at meeting of the Council, Boston, 1 Nov. 1677, 104
ag^t^. Allin 135
Major, Holmes ag^t^., ... 152
Capt. his exec^r^., ag^t^. Taylor &c. 153
Major, Alden ag^t^., as to bill of costs 158
of Boston, pewterer, Fowler ag^t^., ... 322
ag^t^. Wyman 341
Timothy, (2^d^ Jury of trials, &c.) 224
ag^t^. Smith &c. 236
(Petit Jury) 323
&c., Hutchinson &c. ag^t^., ... 325
William, (Jury) 150
Lieut., house of, in North Hampton, ment^d^. (case of Jack, negro), 198
Mr., (2^d^. Jury for appeals &c.) 274
CLARY, JN^o^., ag^t^. Willington 121
CLAY
Jonas, of Boston, mariner, ag^t^. Jewell 341
Steven, master, &c. of ship Batchellors Delight (information, &c.) . 170
Capt., master, &c., (libel, &c.) 174
CLENTON
Lawrence, pet. for divorce by his wife Rachel 208
Rachel, wife of Lawrence, pet. for divorce 208
CLEOMENTS
John, ag^t^. Merrill 221
Uriah (alias John Ball), case of, (burglary) 273, 283–4
ment^d^. (case of Wm. Clapp) 284–287
CLERK of writs, question as to power of, in another town (Oliver &c. ag^t^. Town of Lynn &c.) 111–12
CLIPPINGS of Massachusetts money (case of Peter Lorphelin) 146

PAGE

CLOFT, THO., ment^{d}. (Phipps ag^{t}. Bronsdon) 337

CLOUGH

Wm., (Grand Jury) 140

(1st. Jury for trials &c.) 224

CLUTTERBUCK

Frederick, of London, merchant in St. Mallo, ment^{d}. (libel &c. ag^{t}. ship Richard, 335

Wm., (Jury of attaints) 244

(1st Jury for trials &c.) 245

COALE. (*See* COLE.)

COATES

Eliazer, ment^{d}. (case of Jno. Flynt) 85

Robert, father of Eliazer Coates, ment^{d}. (case of Jno. Flynt) . . 85

COBB, RICHARD, Capt., master of ship Resolution, &c. (libel &c.) . . . 173

COBBHAM, JOSIAH, recognizance by, to answer to Randolph 171

COCK or COCKE

Joseph, &c., appraisers, (libel &c. ag^{t}. ship Dove &c.) (exec^{n}.) . 373

Marcellus, Capt. of ship Salamander, &c. (libel &c.) 179

COFFIN or COFFYN

Peter, Bradstreet ag^{t}. 259, 270

by atty. ag^{t}. Bradstreet 270

Tristram, &c., atty^{s}., ag^{t}. Dummer 108

atty., ag^{t}. Lowle 139

ag^{t}. Bradstreet 270

COGGAN

John, and wife Martha, their adm^{r}. ag^{t}. Clarke 3, 4

Mr., & wife Martha, their adm^{r}. ag^{t}. guardian of Robbinson . 17

Martha, & husband John, their adm^{r}., ag^{t}. Clarke 3, 4

Mrs., & husband John, their adm^{r}. ag^{t}. guardian of Robbinson, 17

COGSWELL

John, Cogswell ag^{t}., ... 59, 66

Marshall ag^{t}., ... 274

Wm., ag^{t}. Cogswell 59, 66

COLCORD

Edward, Roby &c. ag^{t}., ... 7

&c., atty^{s}., ag^{t}. Tilton 7

ag^{t}. Redman 18

ag^{t}. Palmer 19

answer to pet. of, ... 24

ag^{t}. Drake 81–2

COLDHAM, CLEOMEN, (Jury of attaints &c.) 288

COLE or COALE

———, wounding of, (case of John Weaver) 57

Georg (Quaker), &c., case of, ... 12

Gilbert, ag^{t}. Homes 279

Jno., &c., mariners of ship James Frygot (libel &c.) 128

PAGE

COLE, &c., *continued.*
Peter, of Charlestown, case of, (adultery) 73
(case of Sarah Bucknam) 74
COLEMAN. (*See* COLMAN.)
COLLECOT or
COLLECOTT
COLLICOT
Richard, agt. Pinchon, assignee 8
assignee, Sheaffe agt., ... 45
Mr., (Grand Jury) 65, 251
&c., agt. How 183
agt. Sears 219
COLMAN or CALMAN, COLEMAN
Allexander, case of, (disturbance at public worship) 127
John, Roberts agt., ... 269
William, (1st Jury for appeals &c.) 108
(2d Jury of trials &c.) 141
of Boston, admr. of Thurton agt., ... 336
COLONIES, inhabitants of, betrayal of, (case of Walter Gendall &c.) . . 102
(*See also* United Colonies.)
COLONY
seal of, (case of John Weaver) 23
mentd. (order on pet. of John Sparrey) 147
his Majesties Court in, ... 175
banishment from, (case of Thos. Davis &c.) 189
(complaint agt. Sherlot) 197
mentd. (libel agt. Andreason &c.) 264
charter of, dissolution of, mentd. (case of Saml. Shrimpton) . . 297
(*See also* Massachusetts.)
COLONY SOLDIERS mentd. (case of John Indian) 53
COMMISSIONERS
of the United Colonies, estate of Johnson agt., ... 95
for Boston, sworn in Boston 67, 96
oath by, ... 168
&c. for Boston, complaint agt. Sherlot 197
chosen by freemen of Boston, approved by the Court & oath . . 199
for the United Colonies, Rawson &c., agt., ... 208-9
for Boston, oath by, ... 214
mentd. (Apleton agt. Wakefeild) 277
&c., complaint before, (case of Wm. Clapp &c.) . . 285
sworn 29 Sept. 1691 357-8
of the High Court of Admiralty (order on appeal of Lawrence) . . 360
COMMISSIONERS COURT at Boston
Dec. [1673] (Miles agt. Heyden) 6
Jan. 1673 (Teudor agt. Aglin) 7
(Batt agt. Harris) 20
(Harris agt. Greeneoway) 46
(Ruggles agt. Hudson) 65

PAGE

COMMISSIONERS COURT at Boston, *continued.*
(Tyng ag^{t}. Davis) . . . 67
(Wooddey ag^{t}. Speere) . . . 81
(Bennet ag^{t}. Gridley) . . . 82
(Hudson ag^{t}. Messenger) . . . 84
(case of Robt. Maior &c.) . . . 84
(Harris ag^{t}. Batt) . . . 94
July [1677] (Surety of Maze ag^{t}. Mackee) . . . 97
(Soames ag^{t}. Bryant) . . . 97
(Bryan ag^{t}. Soames) . . . 98
May [1677] (Sedgwick ag^{t}. Willis) . . . 101
July [1677] (Hudson ag^{t}. Ruming) . . . 101
(Orchard ag^{t}. Pollard) . . . 109
(Knight ag^{t}. Heath) . . . 113
(Barnes ag^{t}. Kemble &c.) . . . 120
(Fairefeild ag^{t}. Fairefeild) . . . 121
(Turnor ag^{t}. Perry) . . . 122
(Knight ag^{t}. Peacocke) . . . 135
(Man ag^{t}. Savage) . . . 137
(Chocke ag^{t}. Peirce) . . . 141
(Veren ag^{t}. Frost) . . . 141
(Exec^{r}. of Clarke ag^{t}. Taylor &c.) . . . 153
(Wells ag^{t}. Allin) . . . 155
(Chocke ag^{t}. Morgan) . . . 157
(Greene ag^{t}. Baker) . . . 162
Aug. [1680] (Everden ag^{t}. Smith) . . . 164
(Migeley ag^{t}. Smith) . . . 195
(Barton ag^{t}. Mathews) . . . 195
(Answer to pet. of Henry Jenkins) . . . 200–1
(Goulding ag^{t}. Midgley) . . . 204
(Holmes ag^{t}. Dudson) . . . 204
(Wright ag^{t}. Weeden) . . . 204
(Webb ag^{t}. Shrimpton &c.) . . . 215
(Wilkins ag^{t}. Helgerson) . . . 215
(Trumble ag^{t}. Peck) . . . 219
(Aires ag^{t}. Furnell) . . . 222
(Jacob ag^{t}. Gale) . . . 223
(Leveret ag^{t}. Randolph, Collector) . . . 223
(Newby ag^{t}. Hinchman) . . . 226
(Wright ag^{t}. Sparrey) . . . 235
Apr. [1683] (Webb (marshal) ag^{t}. Manly) . . . 235
June " (Wright &c., ag^{t}. Sparrey) . . . 235
(Clarke ag^{t}. Smith) . . . 236
(Cowell ag^{t}. Thornton) . . . 238
(Davis ag^{t}. Gridley) . . . 239
(Lee ag^{t}. Leveret) . . . 239
(Perkins ag^{t}. Merrill) . . . 244
(case of George Moncke) . . . 250

PAGE

COMMISSIONERS COURT at Boston, *continued.*
(Allen ag^{t}. Elliot) 260
(Wardell ag^{t}. Pittam) 260
(Heman ag^{t}. Chapen) 260
(Dawes ag^{t}. Petit) 268
(Adm^{r}. of Batt ag^{t}. Lake) 269
(Rice ag^{t}. Avery) 273
(Walker ag^{t}. Vickers) 277
(Vickers ag^{t}. Walker) 278
(Pearce ag^{t}. Haward) 279
(Inglesby ag^{t}. Shaddock) 291
(Norden ag^{t}. Scottow) 292
14 July 1691 (Warren ag^{t}. Callender) 347
(Tyler ag^{t}. Wright) 350
7 April 1691 (Mumford ag^{t}. Wyllys) 351
12 May 1691 (case of George Monck) 351
24 Dec. 1691 (Wylly ag^{t}. Thomas) 361
29 " " (Smith ag^{t}. Nash) 365
9 Feb. 1691–2 (Checkley ag^{t}. Griggs) 369–70

COMMITTEE OF THE ARMY, order to pass a bill (Certificate &c. for payment for service under Capt Hathorn) 104

COMMONWEALTH
law of, ment^{d}. (Dudson & Co., ship Expectation) 16
(case of Walter Gendall) 102
act of council of, ment^{d}. (case of Jno. Watts) 103

COMPTON, THOMAS, servant to Usher, case of, (stealing) 145

CONCORD (Town of) Stephen Goble, &c., of, ... 71–73

CONCORD (ship) ment^{d}. (Bulkley ag^{t}. Thayre &c.) 338

CONDY
William, adm^{r}., ag^{t}. Clarke 245
Baker ag^{t}., ... 266
&c., appraisers, ment^{d}. (libel &c. ag^{t}. Long) (exec^{n}.) . . 375

CONEY or CONNEY
John, (Grand Jury) 17, 43, 139, 242
&c., ag^{t}. judgment &c. of Stoddard, comm^{r}. 66
(1st. Jury for trials &c.) 181
Sen., Bronsdon ag^{t}., ... 269

CONSTABLE or CONSTABLES
bill of, ment^{d}. (case of John Bennet &c.) 11
appointment of, at Eastward Kennebec, &c. 11, 12
of Boston, return of warrant by, (case of Geo. Cole &c.) 12
warning by, (inquisition on Bickford) 33
chosen at Boston 80
as to his affirmation being a legal evidence (answer to pet. of Mr. Henry Jenkins) 201
chosen in Boston & oath 206

PAGE

CONTEMPTUOUS CARRIAGE. (*See* CRIMES.)
CONTENT (ketch)
owners of, libel ag[t]. Poole &c. 64
ment[d]. (Poole ag[t]. exec[x]. of Lydget) 105
CONTRACT, avoidance of, by a subsequent contract (Hutchinson ag[t]. Payne) . 28
CONVERS, JAMES, &c., sureties, (case of Jn[o]. Parker) 57
CONWAY
Morris, ment[d]. (case of George Shepardson) 144
case of, (inciting to theft) 144
COOK or
COOKE
Elisha, atty., Hull ag[t]., ... 122
Mr., exec[r]., &c., assignee of Wayte ag[t]., ... 164
ag[t]. Olliver 165, 166, 179
&c., Hoare ag[t]., ... 166
Esq[r]., present at Court, 251, 255, 266, 273, 287, 297, 298, 300, 302, 321
Elizabeth, Mrs., exec[x]., &c., assignee of Wayte ag[t]., ... 164
ag[t]. Olliver 165, 166, 179
Elizabeth, exec[x]., &c., Hoare ag[t]., ... 166
Mrs., exec[x]., &c., ag[t]. Paige &c. 256
Paige &c., ag[t]., ... 256
Gregory, (2[d] Jury of trials &c.) 45
(Grand Jury) 151, 232
Jo——, Mr., foreman ment[d]. in margin 226
Joseph, Mr., (Jury of trials &c.) 33
(Grand Jury) 56
Mr., (1st Jury for trials &c.) 224
(Jury) 231
Richard, Left., his assignee, Sheaffe ag[t]., ... 45
his exec[x]., &c., assignee of Wayte ag[t]., ... 164
ag[t]. Olliver 165
agt. Paige &c. 256
Paige &c., ag[t]., ... 256
Stephen, (Grand Jury) 252
COOLIDG
COOLIDGE } or COULIDG
John, (Grand Jury) 17, 44
(Jury for attaints) 256
(1st Jury for appeal) 257
Nathaniel, (1st Jury for trials &c.) 25, 120
(Jury of trials &c.) 32, 57
(2[d] Jury for trials &c.) 96, 203
(Grand Jury) 288
Symon, (1st Jury for trials &c.) 70
(2[d] Jury for trials &c.) 135
(Jury for attaints) 233
(Jury for trials &c.) 233

PAGE

COOLY
——, &c., prisoners, ment[d]. (case of Robert Dendy) . . . 115
Rebeckah, wife of Rich[d]. Cooly, answer to pet. of, ... 116
pet. for divorce 138
Richard, answer to pet. of his wife Rebeckah 116
pet. for divorce by his wife Rebeckah 138

COOPER
Sarah, answer to pet. of, ... 168
late wife to Tho[s]. Cooper, pet. for divorce 256, 258
Thomas, pet. for divorce by his wife Sarah 256, 258

COPP
Daniel, (2[d]. Jury for trials &c.) 181
David, (2[d]. Jury for trials &c.) 25
(Jury for attaints) 180

CORWIN
Elizabeth, wife of Jon[a]. Corwin, (Sheaffe ag[t]. Palmer &c.) 123
George, Capt., his admr. ag[t]. Dounton &c. 288
Jonathan, est. of Gibbs in hands of, &c., Sheaffe ag[t]., ... 123
Mr., adm[r]., ag[t]. Dounton &c. 288
or Esq., Assistant, present at Court 319, 320, 322, 326, 336

COTTA
John, (Jury of trials) 336
(Grand Jury) 361
constable of Boston (Hundlocke ag[t]. Baker &c.) (exec[n].) . 390

COTTER
John, (Jury for attaints) 232
(Jury for trials &c.) 233

COTTON, JOHN, Mr., Powel ag[t]., ... 167

COULIDG. (*See* COOLIDGE.)

COUNCIL
Governor &, meeting of, in Boston 4 Sept. 1674 23
act 15th. Feb. 1674 ment[d]. (libel ag[t]. Rodriego &c.) 34
Governor &, Court of Assistants or Admiralty called by, ... 55
order by, (Griffyn ag[t]. Gove) 99
meeting of, at Boston 1 Nov. 1677 104
Governor &, (Lemoigne ag[t]. White &c.) 130
(case of Peter Lorphelin) 146
Court of Assistants and, adjournment of, at Boston 26 Mar. 1686 . 296
adjourned to 15 Apr. 1686 298
adjourned to 17 Apr. 1686 299
appeal to, (Lason ag[t]. Brenton, Collector) 349
Governor &, commission by, (libel ag[t]. bark Speedwell) 352
ment[d]. (libel &c. ag[t]. ship Marquis of Royan) 354
their Majesties in, appeal to, (libel &c. ag[t]. pink Three Brothers &c.). 356
(order on appeal of Lawrence) 360

COUNCIL OF WAR ment[d]. (libel &c. ag[t]. Branson &c.) 174

COUNTERFEITING. (*See* CRIMES.)

PAGE

COUNTRIES SERVICE
as to impressments on return from, (Griffyn ag^{t}. Gove) 99
certificate and payment for, ... 104

COUNTY
of Essex. (*See* Essex, County of.)
Hampshire. (*See* Hampshire, County of.)
Middlesex. (*See* Middlesex, County of.)
Norfolk. (*See* Norfolk, County of.)
Suffolk. (*See* Suffolk, County of.)
York. (*See* York, County of.)

COUNTY COURT
at Boston. (*See* County Court — Suffolk.)
Cambridge, Charlestown (*See* County Court — Middlesex.)
Dover, Hampton (*See* County Court — Norfolk.)
Ipswich. (*See* County Court — Essex.)
Northampton. (*See* County Court — Hampshire.)
Portsmouth. (*See* County Court — Norfolk.)
Salem. (*See* County Court — Essex.)
Salisbury. (*See* County Court — Norfolk.)
York. (*See* County Court — York.)

COUNTY COURT — Suffolk (or County Court at Boston)
[Jan. 1673-4] (Gibbs ag^{t}. Acton) 2
[Jan. 1673] (case of Benj^{a}. Gibbs) 2
[Jan. 1673-4] (Bonner ag^{t}. Ashton) 3
(Lowle ag^{t}. Skinner) 3
(adm^{r}. of Coggan & wife ag^{t}. Clarke) 4
(Atkinson ag^{t}. Williams) 4
(Pattyn ag^{t}. Dyer) 4
(Pattyn ag^{t}. Winsley) 4
Oct. 1673 (Thayer ag^{t}. Rose) 5
[Jan. 1673-4] (Dudson &c. ag^{t}. Darvall) 5
(case of Joseph Ludden &c.) 5
Jan. 1673 (Ryder ag^{t}. Sharp) 7
Oct. 1673 (Pecke ag^{t}. Lauton) 8
[Jan. 1673-4] (Collecot ag^{t}. assignee of Pinchon) 8
(Knight ag^{t}. Cutt) 8
Oct. 1673 (Shoare ag^{t}. Yale) 9
[Jan. 1673-4] (Joseph Smith, plaintiff) 9
April 1674 (case of John Lowell) 15
[July 1674] (adm^{r}. of Coggan & wife ag^{t}. guardian of Robinson) . 17
(Sands ag^{t}. Hutchinson) 17
(Gibbs ag^{t}. Bonner &c.) 17, 18
(Crispe ag^{t}. Joanes) 18
(Atkins ag^{t}. Joy) 21
Jan. [1674] (Rice ag^{t}. trustees &c. of Bellingham) 24
Oct. [1674] (Broune ag^{t}. Letherland) 25

PAGE

County Court — Suffolk, *continued.*
Oct. [1674] (Newman agt. Smith) 25
(Tounsend agt. Parkeman) 25
(Rawson agt. Glover) 26
Jan. [1674] (Rawson agt. Billing) 26
Oct. 1674 (Legg agt. Davis) 27
Jan. [1674] (Batt agt. Harris) 28
(Hutchinson agt. Payne) 28
Sept. [1674] (Mighill & wife agt. Toppan) 29
Oct. [1674] (Shakeley &c. agt. Winslow) 29
(case of Mary Haukins) 31
April [1675] (Smith agt. Hudson) 44
[July 1675] (Atwater agt. Balston) 44
(Woodmansey agt. Joy) 45
April [1675] (Sheaffe agt. Hunkin) 45
(Smith agt. Rand & Co.) 46
April [1675] (Clark agt. Nicholls) 47
(Checkley agt. Salter) 47
(Greenleafe agt. Gilbert) 48
[July 1675] (Hudson agt. Leveret) 48
(Wells agt. Batt) 48
(Wharton agt. assignee of Joy) 48
(Gibbs agt. Gideon &c.) 49
(Gibbs agt. assignee of Watters) 50
(Leveret agt. assignee of Gifford) 50
[Jan. 1675-6] (Elson agt. Wharton &c.) 59
(Wooddy agt. Harrison) 60
April [1676] (case of Andrew Newcomb) 65
[July 1676] (Rauson agt. Briggs) 65
(Rauson agt. Glover &c.) 65
(Gifford agt. Briggs) 65-6
July [1676] (Alden agt. Clarke) 66
April [1676] (Shoare agt. Gibbs) 68
(Sureties of Fog agt. Williams) 68
[July 1676] (Bennet agt. Addams) 69
(Cowell agt. Elkin) 69
(Surety of Smith agt. Swift &c.) 69
Oct. [1676] (Gibbs agt. Sweete &c.) 77
Jan. " (Isack Waldron, plaintiff) 77
(Basset agt. Waldron) 78
(Jenkins agt. Waldron) 78
[Jan. 1676] (Marshall agt. Waldron) 78
Oct. [1676] (Execrs. of Shepheard agt. Sweeting) 79
(Obbinson agt. Gilbert) 79
Jan. [1676-77] (Edmonds agt. Waldron) 79
(Muzey agt. Waldron) 79
[Jan. 1676-7] (Herbert agt. Clarke & Co.) 80
(Pease agt. Freake) 80

PAGE

COUNTY COURT — Suffolk, *continued.*

[Jan. 1676–7] (Perry ag^{t}. Deane) 80
(Poole ag^{t}. Oughtred) 81
(Turner ag^{t}. Harris) 83
(Woodbridge ag^{t}. Williams) 83
Oct. [1677] (Sheaffe ag^{t}. Blackleach &c.) 85
Jan. [1676–7] (case of Isaac Waldron) 88–9
April [1677] (assignee of Glover ag^{t}. Hubbard) 94
(Exec^{r}. of Scarlet ag^{t}. Prout) 95
[July [1677] (Williams ag^{t}. Calley) 95
April [1677] (Waldron ag^{t}. Skinner) 96
July [1677] (Endecot &c. ag^{t}. Calley) 96
(Rawson ag^{t}. Billings) 96
(Joy ag^{t}. Church) 97
April [1677] (Golding ag^{t}. exec^{r}. of Russell) 98
[July 1677] (Sheaffe ag^{t}. Palmer) 98
(Relict & adm^{x}. of Davenport ag^{t}. Shippen) 99
(Wayte ag^{t}. Walley) 99
July [1677] (Ballard ag^{t}. Watts) 100
April [1677] (Brattle ag^{t}. Knight, adm^{r}., &c.) 100–1
[July 1677] (case of Mary Drury) 101
April [1677] (Phipps ag^{t}. Dudson) 102
(case of Capt. Tho. Brattle) 103
(Greene ag^{t}. David &c.) 109
(Wm. Pitman, plaintiff) 109
Oct. [1677] (Flood ag^{t}. Legg) 110
(Davis ag^{t}. Winsley) 111
[Jan. 1677] (Usher ag^{t}. Usher) 111
Oct. [1677] (Ballard ag^{t}. Watts &c.) 112
(Dell &c., ag^{t}. Child) 112
(Longfellow &c. ag^{t}. Oxe) 112
(Phipps ag^{t}. Hamond) 113
[Jan. 1677] (Bullis ag^{t}. adm^{r}. of Payton) 113
(Smith ag^{t}. Lydget) 113
(case of Leonard Douden) 113
April [1678] (Waldron ag^{t}. Henderson) 119
(Alcock ag^{t}. Meade) 121
[July 1678] (Rose ag^{t} Stowell) 121
April [1678] (Hull ag^{t}. Wincoll) 122
[July 1678] (Trustees &c. of Emery ag^{t}. Hauford) 122
July [1678] (Trustees &c. of Emery, &c. ag^{t}. Sweeting, adm^{r}.) . . 122
[July 1678] (Sheaffe ag^{t}. Palmer &c.) 123
April [1678] (Oxe ag^{t}. Keene) 124
[July 1678] (Fox ag^{t}. Leveret, Govr.) 125
[Jan. 1678] (Figg ag^{t}. Baker) 133
(Smith ag^{t}. Bouden) 134
[Jan. 1678] (Accorman ag^{t}. Vallentine) 135
Oct. [1678] (Usher ag^{t}. Usher) 137

PAGE

COUNTY COURT — Suffolk, *continued.*

(Griggs agt. Chocke) 140
[July 1679] (Butler agt. Hollowell &c.) 140
(Allin & Co. agt. Tomlin) 141
(Baskervill agt. est. of Windor &c.) 141
(Rock agt. Francks) 142
[July 1679] (Legg agt. Flood) 142
(Warner agt. Francklin) 144
(Wisewall agt. Keene) 144
(Hill agt. Obbinson) 151
(Scottow agt. Wheelewright) 152
[Jan. 1679] (Holmes agt. Clarke) 152
(case of Hannah Negro) 152
Nov. [1679] (Est. of children of Anne Hitt) 153
(Estate of Wm. Snelling) 153
(Apleton agt. Porter) 154
(Page &c., agt. Dudley &c.) 155
(Williams agt. Townsend) 155
Nov. [1679] (case of Jno. Endecot) 155
(Dafforne agt. Keene) 156
Jan. [1679] (Elliot agt. Dauson) 156
Nov. [1679] (West agt. Barter) 157
April [1680] (Bateman agt. Taft) 161
(Hill agt. Obbinson) 161
(Pelton agt. Thompson) 162
(Butler agt. Holowell &c.) 164
(Lambe agt. Clarke) 165
(Trott agt. Gourdon) 165
(Egerton agt. Smith) 166
(Execx. &c. of Cooke agt. Olliver) 166
(Davenport agt. Patch) 166
(Pitts agt. Badcock) 166
(Ellit agt. Dauson) 167
(Case of Daniel Mathew) 167
(Nehemiah Pearse, plaintiff) 167
July [1680] (Powel agt. Cotton) 167
(Paige agt. Brimsden) 168
(Hill agt. Obbinson) 180
(Rocke agt. Franck) 180
(Torrey agt. Gretian) 180
(case of Wm. Waters) 180
Jan. [1680] (Mathews agt. Keene) 181
(Speere agt. Bracket) 182
Jan. [1680] (Gretian agt. Sweathy) 182
(Sweatie agt. Greatian) 182
(Gretian agt. Staynor) 183
(Playsted agt. Norton) 184
(Yeales agt. Rose) 184

PAGE

COUNTY COURT — Suffolk, *continued.*
Jan. [1680] (Bennet &c. ag[t]. Douden) 184
(Gifford ag[t]. Read) 185
(Heinshaw ag[t]. Voss) 185
Jan. [1680] (Joy &c. ag[t]. Leveret) 185
(Scottow ag[t]. Hutchinson) 186
(Thaier ag[t]. Clap) 186
(Thaier ag[t]. Savage) 186
(Lamb ag[t]. Hill) 187
(Saffyn ag[t]. Holt) 187
(Turner ag[t]. Micarter) 187
(Vose ag[t]. Heinshaw) 187
[July 1681] (Wharton ag[t]. Reynolds) 192
April [1681] (Harris ag[t]. Long) 193
[July 1681] (Golding & wife ag[t]. Smith) 193
(Torrey ag[t]. Gretian) 193
April [1681] (Lytherland ag[t]. Porter) 195
(Porter ag[t]. Flood) 196
(Stoddard ag[t]. Johnson) 196
April [1681] (Sandford ag[t]. Orchard) 196
[July 1681] (John Parmiter, plaintiff) 196
Oct. 1678 (Usher ag[t]. execrs. of Usher) 203
[1681] (Parris ag[t]. Fletcher) 203
(Usher ag[t]. execrs. of Usher) 203
(Webb ag[t]. Burton) 203
(Townsend ag[t]. Johnson) 204
(Vose ag[t]. Glover) 204
(Butler ag[t]. Checkley) 205
(Staynor ag[t]. Gretian) 206
Jan. [1681] (Tare ag[t]. Hinderson) 206
Oct. [1681] (Wing ag[t]. Halsey) 206
(Rob[t]. Taft, plaintiff) 206–7
Oct. 1681 (Wayt (marshal) ag[t]. Sweathy) 207
Jan. [1681] (Surety of Gretian ag[t]. Webb (marshal)) 207
[Jan. 1681] (Rawson &c. ag[t]. Stoughton &c. comm[rs].) . . . 208–9
(Perry ag[t]. Hurd) 215
(Symonds ag[t]. Leveret) 216
[July 1682] (Becke ag[t]. Gale) 216
(Waldron ag[t]. Frary &c.) 216
(Waldron ag[t]. Wisewall) 216
(Martyn ag[t]. Rost) 217
(Williams ag[t]. Brookings) 217
(Fisher ag[t]. Wayte) 218
(Gifford ag[t]. Walter &c.) 218
(Assignee of Hoare ag[t]. Kilcup) 219
[July 1682] (Complaint ag[t]. ketch Newbery &c.) 220
(Randolph, Coll[r]. &c. Ag[t]. Pitcher &c.) 220
(Randolph ag[t]. Willet) 220

PAGE

COUNTY COURT — Suffolk, *continued.*

(Barton ag^{t}. Mathew) . . . 222
(Barton ag^{t}. Mathews) . . . 222
[July 1682] (Goffreigh ag^{t}. Sprague) . . . 222
Oct. [1682] (Haugh ag^{t}. Willis) . . . 223
(Raymond ag^{t}. Orchard) . . . 224
[Jan. 1682] (Pierse ag^{t}. Mumford) . . . 225
(Wayt ag^{t}. Sweathy) . . . 226
[Jan. 1682] (Crosby ag^{t}. Addams) . . . 226
(Torrey ag^{t}. Gretian) . . . 226
(Checkly ag^{t}. Patteshall) . . . 227
(Gilbert ag^{t}. Waldron) . . . 227
(Wayte, ag^{t}. Plumbe) . . . 227
April [1683] (Mason ag^{t}. Tight) . . . 234
(Rogers ag^{t}. Tite) . . . 234
July [1683] (Dewer ag^{t}. Broune) . . . 236
[July 1683] (Harrison ag^{t}. Platts) . . . 237–8
(Homes ag^{t}. Sweathy) . . . 238
(Perkins ag^{t}. Smith) . . . 239
(Worden ag^{t}. Addams) . . . 239
Oct. [1683] (Harrison ag^{t}. Platts) . . . 245
(Rauson ag^{t}. Gilbert) . . . 245
Jan. [1683] (Admr. of Wilky ag^{t}. Clarke) . . . 245–6
(Harrison ag^{t}. Platts) . . . 245
(Torrey ag^{t}. Gretian) . . . 246
Oct. [1683] (Peirse ag^{t}. Mumford) . . . 246
(Arnold ag^{t}. Thayer) . . . 247
(Gifford ag^{t}. Walter) . . . 247
[Jan. 1683] (Legg ag^{t}. Lilly) . . . 247
[Jan. 1683–4] (Thwing &c. ag^{t}. Holliock) . . . 248
[Jan. 1683–4] (Baker ag^{t}. Wharton) . . . 248
[Jan. 1683] (Wisewall ag^{t}. Paige &c.) . . . 249
[Jan. 1683–4] (case of Thos. Saffin) . . . 249
Oct. [1683] (Wharton & Co. ag^{t}. Baker) . . . 249
April [1684] (Tyte ag^{t}. Mason) . . . 256
[July 1684] (Paige &c. ag^{t}. Wisewall &c.) . . . 256
(Wisewall &c. ag^{t}. Paige &c.) . . . 256
(Harwood ag^{t}. Burton) . . . 257
(Harwood ag^{t}. Toy) . . . 257
(Perkins ag^{t}. Fenno) . . . 257
(Toy ag^{t}. Loyd) . . . 257
(Basse ag^{t}. Crosby) . . . 258
(Baker ag^{t}. Pemberton) . . . 259
(Bradstreet, Gov., ag^{t}. Coffyn) . . . 259
(Tounsend ag^{t}. Edwards) . . . 259
April [1684] (Bagly ag^{t}. Webster) . . . 259
(Adams ag^{t}. Baker). . . . 260
(Homes ag^{t}. Sheffeild) . . . 261

PAGE

County Court — Suffolk, *continued.*
[July 1684] (Dyre ag[t]. Hutchinson) 261
(Baker ag[t]. Condy) 267
(Baker agt. Pemberton) 267
(Griffyn ag[t]. Knight) 267
(Jacklin ag[t]. Pemberton) 268
(Willis ag[t]. Savage) 268
(Bronsdon ag[t]. Conney) 269
(Roberts ag[t]. Coleman) 269
(Bradstreet ag[t]. Coffyn) 270
(Dawes ag[t]. Newby) 270
(Homes ag[t]. Russell) 270
(Norton ag[t]. Plaisted) 271
(Wharton &c. ag[t]. Smith) 271
(Order on pet. of Mr. Rich[d]. Wharton &c.) 272
(Peacock ag[t]. Pen) 273
(Jacklin ag[t]. Parris) 274
(Sarjant &c. ag[t]. Shrimpton, exec[r]. &c.) 276
(Apleton ag[t]. Wakefeild) 277
(Baker ag[t]. Hunlocke) 278
(Cole ag[t]. Homes) 279
(Lilly ag[t]. Payne) 280
(Stoddard ag[t]. Davy) 280
(Wardell ag[t]. Lynde) 280
(case of Hugh Mulligan) 280
(Hiller ag[t]. Burrowes) 281
(Saffyn ag[t]. Burton) 281
(Homes ag[t]. Cheeckley) 282
(Saffyn ag[t]. Baxter) 282
(Wharton &c. ag[t]. Smith) 282
(Sarah Barret, plaintiff) 288
Oct. [1685] (George Kirbee, plaintiff) 288
(Homes ag[t]. Olliver) 290
(Coxe ag[t]. Hiskett) 291
judgment of, Bullard &c. ag[t]., ... 291
(Patteshall ag[t]. Heskett) 292
Oct. [1685] (case of Joseph Greene) 292
(Wharton &c. ag[t]. Smith) 293
Oct. [1685] (Nowell ag[t]. Goddard) 293
Jan. [1685] (Francis Stepney, plaintiff) 294
Gov. &c. assembled in, (case of Sam[l]. Shrimpton) 297, 299
30 July 1689 (Usher ag[t]. Frizell) 302
(Fawer ag[t]. Cable) 302
(Grover ag[t]. Bulkley) 303
(Massey ag[t]. Robie) 303
19 Nov. 1689 (Fowler ag[t]. Clarke) 322–3
25 Feb. 1689 (Arbuckle ag[t]. adm[r]. of Bricknall) 323
(Perkins ag[t]. Winslow) 323

PAGE

COUNTY COURT — Suffolk, *continued.*
25 Feb. 1689 (Black ag^{t}. Bronsdon &c.) 324
(Black ag^{t}. pink Mary &c.) 324
(Exec^{rs}. of Heywood ag^{t}. Eyres) 324
(Robineau ag^{t}. Assailly) 324
19 Nov. 1689 (Banks ag^{t}. Child) 325
(Hutchinson &c. ag^{t}. Fyfield &c.) 325
(Waterhouse ag^{t}. Perry) 325
25 Feb. 1689 (Mountjoy ag^{t}. Hemlock) 325
(Walker ag^{t}. Usher) 325
19 Nov. 1689 (Brentnal ag^{t}. Hamlin &c.) 326
(English ag^{t}. Stebbins) 326
12 Aug. 1690 on adjournment from 29 July 1690
(De Vaulx ag^{t}. Shelston) . 327
(Pynchon ag^{t}. Forster &c.) 328
(Fifield ag^{t}. Bradley) . . 330
(Edwards ag^{t}. Jarvis) . 331
28 Oct. 1690 (Adm^{r}. of Thurton ag^{t}. Colman) 336
27 Jan. 1690–1 (Exec^{x}. of Loft ag^{t}. Oliver) 337
(Phipps ag^{t}. Bronsdon) 337
Oct. 1690 (Bulkley ag^{t}. Thayre &c.) 338
28 Oct. 1690 (Bigg ag^{t}. Harwood &c.) 339
(Smith ag^{t}. Hiskett) 339
27 Jan. 1690–1 (Dorrell, &c. ag^{t}. Foster &c.) 339
(Tippet ag^{t}. Thornhill) 340
28 Oct. 1690 (Adlington ag^{t}. adm^{x}. of Fernes) 340
(Clarke ag^{t}. Wyman) 341
(Clay ag^{t}. Jewell) 341
(Hemlock ag^{t}. Mountjoy) 341
19 Nov. 1689 (Stebbins ag^{t}. English) 346
18 July 1691 (Walker ag^{t}. Hawkins) 347
25 Aug. 1691 by adjournment from 28 July 1691 (Lason ag^{t}. Brenton, Coll^{r}.) 349
28 Apr. 1691 (Hall ag^{t}. Backway) 350
(Oliver ag^{t}. exec^{x}. of Loft) 350
(Waterhouse ag^{t}. Luist) 350
July 1691 (Ball ag^{t}. Sandey) 351
(Hayward ag^{t}. Bulkley) 352
(Perry ag^{t}. Alford) 352
27 Oct. 1691 (Guardian of Gatliff ag^{t}. Legg) 362
(Thaire ag^{t}. Townsend) 362
26 Jan. 1691–2 (Belchar ag^{t}. Lloyd) 362
(Perry ag^{t}. Alford) 363
(Somes ag^{t}. Lake) 364
27 Oct. 1691 (Arnold ag^{t}. Belchar) 364
(Dunclin ag^{t}. Witherett) 365
27 Jan. 1691–2 (Peggy ag^{t}. Crisp) 365
27 Oct. 1691 (Lambe &c. ag^{t}. Winthrop) 366

PAGE

COUNTY COURT — Suffolk, *continued.*
17 Feb. 1691-2 by adjournment from 26 Jan. 1691-2 (Shrimpton agt. Brenton) 366
27 Oct. 1691 (Milner agt. Wing) 367
26 Jan. 1691-2 (Stanbury agt. Harris) 367
27 Oct. 1691 (Foy agt. trustee of Loder) 368
26 Jan. 1691-2 (Tay agt. Harwood and Wife) 369
(Thatcher agt. Thatcher) 369
July [1673] (Admr. of Dinely agt. est. of Stenwicke) (execn.) . . 371
27 July 1680 (Hollowell &c. agt. Butler) (execn.) 380-382
29 July 1684 (Sheffeild agt. Homes) (execn.) 386
COUNTY COURT — Middlesex (or County Court at Cambridge or Charlestown)
Oct. 1673 (Clarke agt. Bartlet) 1, 2
Dec. 1673 (case of Benanuel Bowers) 3
(case of Joseph Blandchard &c.) 22
(Ayres agt. Chenery) 27
Apr. [1676] (case of Geo. Robbins &c.) 57
(Case of Benjamin Symons) 73
June [1677] (est. of Johnson agt. Commrs. of the United Colonies) . 95
(Trumble agt. Mason) 97
Apr. [1677] (Nevars agt. Gardiner) 100
(Order on pet. of Elisabeth Bowers) 104
(Dixe agt. Morse) 108
(Clary agt. Willington) 121
(Lacy agt. Melot) 124
(Oxe agt. Melot) 124
(Bussell agt. Ballat) 140
(Dunster &c. agt. Prout) 143
(Martin agt. Briggs &c.) 152
(Broune agt. Trumble) 156
Oct. [1679] (Bellingham agt. Hamond &c.) 157
Apr. [1680] (Assignee of Wayte agt. execx. &c. of Cook) . . . 164
(Wayt agt. Leuis) 165
(Hoare agt. Cooke, execx., &c.) 166
(Heyman's costs agt. Moore) 188
21 Dec. 1680 (Foule's costs agt. Leveret) 188
(Lord agt. Addams) 197
(Holman &c. agt. Michelson) 218
(Collicot &c. agt. Sears) 219
Oct. [1682] (Phips &c. agt. Bowers) 224
(Wood &c. agt. Bowers) 224
(Gookin agt. Wade) 225
(Case of Christopher Portingall) 230
Apr. [1683] (Usher agt. assignee &c. of Harwood) 237
(Execrs. of Usher agt. assignee &c. of Harwood) 237
(Welch agt. Stowers) 246
(Mills agt. Johnson) 258
(Wyman agt. Sumers) 267

PAGE

County Court — Middlesex, *continued.*
(Brookes agt. Mussey) . . . 268
(Gibson agt. Read) . . . 271
(Marret agt. Cutter) . . . 275
(Trayne agt. Barnard) . . . 275
(Samuel Gibson, plaintiff) . . . 275
(Chamberlain agt. Billings) . . . 277
(Blood agt. Knight) . . . 279
(Read agt. Bacon) . . . 281
(Haugh agt Hill) . . . 283, 287
(Cambridge Selectmen agt. the drummers of Cambridge) . . . 289
(Dauson agt. Pite &c.) . . . 289
(Dauson agt. Wing) . . . 289
(Holman &c. agt. Hanckock &c.) . . . 289
(Marshall agt. Marbell) . . . 289
(Moore) . . . 290
(Soley) . . . 290
(Gates agt. Foskett) . . . 290
Oct. [1685] (Bacon agt. Maguinis) . . . 291
6 Oct. [1685] (libel agt. Keech &c.) . . . 300–1
1 July 1690 (Lampson agt. Green) . . . 329
April 1690 (Adams, admx. agt. Mountfort) . . . 330
15 Apr. 1690 (Stanbridge agt. Goffe) . . . 330
7 Apr. 1691 (Mason agt. Stone &c.) . . . 346
19 June 1691 (Marrett agt. Holland) . . . 347
(Prout agt. Brooks &c.) . . . 349
7 April 1691 (Read agt. Pearse) . . . 351
19 June 1691 (case of John Cutler, Junr.) . . . 355
Dec. 1689 (answer to pet. of John Cutler, Junr.) . . . 359
29 Dec. 1691 (Waite agt. Newhall) . . . 363
6 Oct. 1691 (case of James Lowden) . . . 363
29 Dec. 1691 (Green agt. Fox) . . . 368
Dec. 1691 (Stratton agt. Gidley) . . . 369
County Court — Essex (or County Court at Salem or Ipswich)
(Godfrey agt. Clarke) . . . 8
(Keine agt. Piper) . . . 9
(Sandford agt. Putman) . . . 19
(Bartlet agt. James &c. (Marblehead Commons)) . . . 20
(Bishop agt. White) . . . 20
(Lattimore agt. James &c. (Marblehead Commons)) . . . 20
(Gold agt. Bishop) . . . 21
(Allen agt. Whiple) . . . 26
(Wayte &c. agt. execx. of Dickinson) . . . 26
Sept. [1674] (Gold &c. agt. Putman &c.) . . . 27
(Rouland agt. Hobbs) . . . 27
Sept. [1674] (Gifford agt. Hathorne) . . . 28
(case of Bozoone Allen) . . . 29
(Dumer agt. Gerrish &c.) . . . 44

PAGE

COUNTY COURT — Essex, *continued.*
(Richards ag^t. Putman) 44
(Sandford ag^t. Putman) 44
(Gold ag^t. Putman) 45
(Bishop ag^t. Gold) 47
(Gifford ag^t. Hathorne) 48–9
(Cogswell ag^t. Cogswell) 59, 66
(Exec^{rs}. of Bishop ag^t. Wainewright) 60
(Heynes ag^t. Toppan) 66
(Woodbridge ag^t. Gerrish) 67
(Thompson ag^t. Emmery) 80, 97
(Lowle ag^t. Gerrish) 82
(Bennet ag^t. Symonds) 83
(Matson ag^t. Dispaw) 100
(Gove ag^t. Bennet) 107
(Bradstreet &c. ag^t. Fuller) 108
(English ag^t. Mazure) 109
(Giffords ag^t. Lee) 110
(Gardiner ag^t. Pudney) 110
(Olliver &c. ag^t. Town of Lynn &c.) 111
(Blainy ag^t. King &c.) 111
(surety of Roope ag^t. Hughson) 112
(Nurse ag^t. Endecot) 120
(Apleton ag^t. Savage) 123
(Atkinson ag^t. Perkins) 123
(John Putman &c. plaintiffs) 123
(Gifford ag^t. Lee) 124
(Boynton ag^t. Cross) 125
(Leaver ag^t. Nelson) 134
(Pickard &c. ag^t. Longfellow) 134
(Smith ag^t. Bouden) 134
(Olliver &c ag^t. Town of Lynn) 135
(Atkinson ag^t. Perkins) 136
(Jacob ag^t. Fellowes &c.) 137
(Tyng ag^t. Chadwell) 137
(case of Bethyah Gatchel) 138
(Lowle &c. ag^t. Lowle) 139
(Pepen ag^t. Marshall) 143
(Pickard &c. ag^t. Longfellow) 143
(order on est. of Wade) 150
(Manning ag^t. Whight) 154
(Gifford ag^t. Lord) 155
(Quilter ag^t. Quilter) 156
(White ag^t. Maning) 162
(Dutch ag^t. Darby) 163
(Knight ag^t. Cave) 163
(Manning ag^t. Broune &c.) 164
(Greely ag^t. Woodbridge) 165

PAGE

County Court — Essex, *continued.*
(Balch ag^{t}. Dodge) 180
(Carr ag^{t}. Paige) 181
(Fairefeild ag^{t}. Knowlton) 181
(Collecot &c. ag^{t}. How) 183
(Knight ag^{t}. Leach &c.) 184
(Richards ag^{t}. Witter) 187
(Allin ag^{t}. Putnam) 192
(Farley ag^{t}. Lummas) 193
(Ela ag^{t}. Chandler) 194
(Knight ag^{t}. Leach &c.) 194
(Lee ag^{t}. Heynes) 194
(Davis ag^{t}. Davis &c.) 195
(Laughton &c. ag^{t}. Broune) 195
(Chapman ag^{t}. Barry) 205
Sept. [1681] (Shatswell ag^{t}. Jewet) 205
(Dole &c. ag^{t}. Kent) 207
(Fletcher for March & wife ag^{t}. March) 214
(Baker ag^{t}. Putnam) 214
(Hauthorn &c. ag^{t}. Roades) 215
(Atkinson ag^{t}. Woolcot) 220
(Atkinson ag^{t}. Buckman) 221
(Cleoments ag^{t}. Merrill) 221
(Peasley ag^{t}. Clark) 221
(Graves ag^{t}. Farrington) 222
(Atkinson ag^{t}. Mirrick) 223
(Layton &c. ag^{t}. Browne) 225
(Atkinson ag^{t}. Woolcot) 233
(Nurse ag^{t}. Endicot) 235
(Apelton &c. ag^{t}. Hawkes &c.) 236
(Bishop ag^{t}. Lord, marshal) 238
(Lummas ag^{t}. Quarles) 239
(pet. of Elizth. Manning) 240
(Needham ag^{t}. Farr) 247
(Bishop ag^{t}. Lord) 248
Thomas Danforth &c. to keep, ... 253
(Putnam ag^{t}. Baker) 256
(Douning ag^{t}. Boober & wife) 258
(Epps ag^{t}. Bennet) 259
(Apleton ag^{t}. Marshall) 261
(Ingolls ag^{t}. Bishop) 262–3
(Bishop ag^{t}. Clarke) 263
(Answer to complaint of Wade) 265–6
(Norman ag^{t}. Orne) 267, 273
(Farr ag^{t}. Witter) 269
(Atkinson ag^{t}. Miller) 270
(Gilbert ag^{t}. Gidney) 274
(Marshall ag^{t}. Cogswell) 274

PAGE

COUNTY COURT — Essex, *continued.*

(Lee ag^t. Waingright) . . . 274
(Archer &c. ag^t. Pickmand) . . . 275
(Hitchins ag^t. Browne) . . . 276
(Boober ag^t. Douning) . . . 276
(Apleton ag^t. Roads) . . . 276–7
(Hendrick ag^t. Davis) . . . 278
(Pike ag^t. Winsley) . . . 279
(Town of Lynn ag^t. Apleton) . . . 279
(Roads ag^t. Apleton) . . . 281
(Adm^r. of Corwin ag^t. Dounton &c.) . . . 288
June 1690 (Swan ag^t. Wainwright) . . . 327
($Exec^r$. of Price ag^t. $exec^r$. of Price) . . . 328
24 June 1690 (Stilson &c. ag^t. Selectmen of Marblehead) . . . 328
(Rea ag^t. Putnam) . . . 329
(Newmarsh ag^t. Berry) . . . 331
25 March 1690 (Berry ag^t. Newmarch) . . . 331
25 Nov. 1690 (Small ag^t. Bullock) . . . 339
(Blaney ag^t. Dunton) . . . 340
30 Sept. 1690 (English ag^t. Cromwell) . . . 341
30 June 1691 (Neeland ag^t. Foster) . . . 345
(Paul ag^t. Barrow) . . . 345
(Burnam ag^t. Cross) . . . 345–6
31 March 1691 (Dennis ag^t. Wainwright) . . . 347
(Cross ag^t. Younglove) . . . 348
(Dolbery (ag^t. Morrell) . . . 348
(Fairfield ag^t. Fairfield) . . . 348
(White ag^t. Stanley) . . . 348
(case of Josiah Littlefield) . . . 356
(pet. of Mr. John Croad & decree) . . . 356
(case of Joseph Downer) . . . 357
29 Sept. 1691 (Hovey ag^t. Perkins) . . . 363
(Davison ag^t. Potter) . . . 364
29 June 1680 (Overseers &c. of children of Gray ag^t. Manning) . . . 376

COUNTY COURT — NORFOLK (or COUNTY COURT at SALISBURY, HAMPTON, DOVER OR PORTSMOUTH)

(Martyn & wife ag^t. Winsly & wife) . . . 5
estate of North left to disposal of, (Martin &c. ag^t. Winsly &c.) . 6
(Pike ag^t. Gove) . . . 6
(Roby &c. ag^t. Evins) . . . 6
(Winsly ag^t. Martyn) . . . 6
(Roby &c. ag^t. Colcord) . . . 7
(Town of Hampton ag^t. Tilton) . . . 7
(Gove, assignee, ag^t. Fouler) . . . 8
(Batt ag^t. Severans) . . . 9
(Gove ag^t. Pike) . . . 16
(Chase ag^t. trustee of wife &c. of Nanny) . . . 17
(Colcord ag^t. Redman) . . . 18

PAGE

COUNTY COURT — Norfolk, etc., *continued.*
(Sevy ag[t]. Deering) 18
(Bacon &c. ag[t]. Town of Hampton) 19
(Colcord ag[t]. Palmer) 19
(Jn[o]. Garland & wife, plaintiffs) 46
(Patridge ag[t]. Waynwright) 46
(Waynwright ag[t]. Pickering) 46
(Barefoote ag[t]. Shackford) 67
(Gilman ag[t]. Foulsham) 68
(Sexton ag[t]. Winslow) 68
(Pickering ag[t]. Frost) 69
(Daniel &c. ag[t]. Thornhull) 75
(Greely ag[t]. Young) 81
(Colcord ag[t]. Drake) 82
(Ring ag[t]. Buswell) 82
(Ring ag[t]. Worcester) 82
(Barefoot ag[t]. Palmer) 98
(Griffyn ag[t]. Gove) 99
(Waldron ag[t]. Tare) 120
appointment of Major Hauthorne to keep, ... 127
Clarke ag[t]. Allen 135
(Boulter &c. ag[t]. Wilson) 136
(Roby &c. ag[t]. Evans) 136
(Broune ag[t]. Fellowes) 140
(White ag[t]. Heath) 142
(White ag[t]. Hendrick) 142
(Hooke ag[t]. Pike) 154
(Swan ag[t]. Town of Haverhill) 156

COUNTY COURT — HAMPSHIRE (or COUNTY COURT at NORTHAMPTON)
ment[d]. (case of Mary Parsons) 31
(Mekins ag[t]. Kinsley) 221

COUNTY COURT — YORK (or COUNTY COURT at YORK)
complaint &c. of Foster referred to, ... 104

COURT OF ASSISTANTS. (*See* ASSISTANTS.)

COURT OF ASSOCIATES. (*See* ASSOCIATES.)

COURT, COMMISSIONERS. (*See* COMMISSIONERS COURT at BOSTON.)

COURT, COUNTY. (*See* COUNTY COURT.)

COURT, GENERAL. (*See* GENERAL COURT.)

COUZENS, ANDREW, &c. mariners (libel &c.) 40

COWARD, WILLIAM, &c., mariners, case of, (piracy) 319, 320, 322

COWELL
Edward, ag[t]. Elkin 69
Joseph, ag[t]. Thornton 238
&c., bond by, (Harrison ag[t]. Platts) 245
sureties on bond of attaint (Adams ag[t]. Baker) . . . 260
atty., Inglesby ag[t]., ... 291

PAGE

Cox or Coxe
- Martha, daughter of Rob[t]. Cox (case of Basto, negro) 74
- Robert, of Boston, case of his negro slave, Basto 74
- Rowland, ag[t]. Hiskett 291
- Thomas, &c., sureties, ag[t]. Williams 68
  - mariners of pink Endeavor (libel &c.) 117, 118

Craft or Crafts
- Griffin, (Grand Jury) 1
- Jn[o]., (2[d]. Jury for trials &c.) 79
- Samuel, (Jury for trial of attaint) 134, 267
  - (1st. Jury of trials &c.) 135
  - (Jury of trials) 302, 306, 308

Crane or Creane
- Abigaile (case of Christopher Portingall) 230
- Paul, boatswain of ship James Frygott, &c. (libel &c.) 128

Craty, Andrew, master of ship Jn[o]. Adventure, &c., Shapleigh &c. ag[t]. . 147

Cream, Jn[o]., (negro) replevin for, (Stanbridge ag[t]. Goffe) 330

Creane. (*See* Crane.)

Creeck or Crick
- Edward, (Jury of trials) 345
  - (Jury) 360

Crimes, Misdemeanours, &c.
- adultery, rape, lascivious actions, &c.
  - case of Ruth Read . . . . . (adulterous carriage) 10
    - Benj[a]. Goad . . . . (bestiality) 10
    - Amy Wellen . . . . (adultery) 14
    - Jn[o]. Glandfeild . . . . " 15
    - Tom Indian . . . . (rape) 21
    - Edw[d]. Naylor . . . . (intruding on his late wife) 32
    - Samuel Guile . . . . (rape) 50
    - Maurice Brett . . . . (adultery) 56
    - Mary Gibbs . . . . " 57
    - Elisabeth Broune . . . . " 70–1
    - Tho[s]. Davis . . . . " 70
    - Peter Cole . . . . " 73
    - Benj[a]. Symons . . . . (rape) 73
    - Sarah Bucknam . . . . (adultery) 74
    - Jack (Negro) . . . . (bestiality) 74
    - Basto " . . . . (rape) 74
    - Jn[o]. Lawrence . . . . (bestiality) 87
    - Jn[o]. Buttery . . . . " 103
    - Darby Bryan . . . . (adultery) 114
    - Abigaile Johnson . . . . " 115
    - Christopher Grant, Jun[r]. . . . . (fornication) 125
    - Mary Hare . . . . (adultery) 126

PAGE

CRIMES, MISDEMEANOURS, &c., *continued.*

adultery, &c., *continued.*

case of Bethyah Gatchel . . . . . . (adultery) 138
Ellinor May . . . . (whoredom) 138
Thomas Waters . . . . (rape) 158
George Russell . . . . . . (fornication) 169
Wm. Cheny . . . . (rape) 199
Elisabeth Payne . . . . . . (fornication) 228
Christopher Portingall . . . . . . (rape) 230
Joshua Rice &c. . . (lascivious actions &c.) 234, 240
Samuel Bayly . . . . (buggery) 251
Phillip Darland &c. . . . . (adultery) 252
Samuel Newton & wife . (incestuous cohabitation) 342
Hannah Owen . . . (forbidden cohabitation) 361

murder, manslaughter, infanticide, &c.

case of John Bennet &c. . . . (neglect causing death) 11
Anna Negro . . . . (infanticide) 29
Robert Driver . . . . (murder) 30
Nicholas Faevor . . . . " 32
Maurice Bret . . . . " 51
Zechariah Crispe . . . . " 51
Dorothy Jones . . . . " 51
John Indian . . . . " 53
Little John Indian . . . . " 53
Revp, Indian . . . . " 53
James, alias Acompanut, Indian . . . . " 53
Mampausnackosut, Indian . . . . . " 53
Joseph Spoonhaut, Indian . . . . . " 53
James Nanapatu, Indian . . . . . " 54
John, alias Anusquenut, Indian . . . . " 54
Jn°., alias Mucksumquenut, Indian . . " 54
Muckscumpey, Indian . . . . " 54
Peter, alias Paguskmenut, Indian . . . . " 54
Thomas, alias Mumucksuncasusucquater, Indian " 54
George Robbins &c. . . . . " 57
James Foord (driving over, causing death) 60
Daniel Goble . . . . (murder) 71
Stephen Goble . . . . " 71
Daniel Hoare &c. . . . . " 72
John Flynt . . . . " 85
Peter Bent, Junr. . . . . " 86
Samuel Hunting . . . . . (manslaughter) 114
Marea, Spanish Indian servant . . . (infanticide) 115
John Winsland . . . . (murder) 117
Cardin Drabston . . . . (infanticide) 125
Mary Hare . . . . " 126
John Dyar . . . . . . (manslaughter) 188
Elisabeth Payne . . . . (infanticide) 228
Leonard Pomery . . . . . . (manslaughter) 243

PAGE

CRIMES, MISDEMEANOURS, &c., *continued.*
murder, &c., *continued.*
case of Vines Ellacot . . . . (murder) 251
John Dounton . . . . " 271–2
James Morgan . . . . " 294
Mary Flood . . . . " 295
Joseph Indian . . . . " 295
Hugh Stone . . . . " 303
Hannah Hutchinson . . . . . . " 304
Robin, negro servant . . (manslaughter) 304, 305, 321
John Newhall, tertius, &c. . " 306, 307, 321
Thomas Witt . . . . . " . 307, 321
Thomas Pound . . . . . (murder) 307, 308, 320
Thomas Johnston . . . . . " 309, 310, 320
Eleazer Buck . . . . . " 310, 311, 320
John Sickterdam . . . . . " 311, 312, 320
Wm. Dun . . . . . . " 313, 314, 320
Richard Griffin . . . . . " 314, 315, 320
Edward Browne . . . . . " . . 315
Daniel Lander . . . . . " 315, 316, 320
Wm. Warren . . . . . . " 317, 318, 320
Samuel Watts . . . . . . " 318, 319, 320
Elizabeth Emmerson . . . . . (infanticide) 357
Bridget Denmarke . . . . (manslaughter) 358
Richard Lillie . . . . . " 358–9
witchcraft &c.
case of Anna Edmunds . . . . . . (witchcraft) 11
Mary Parsons . . . . . . " 31, 33
Elisabeth Morse . . (familiarity with the devil) 159
Mary Hale . . . . (witchcraft) 188
James Fuller . . . (familiarity with the devil) 228
Mary Webster . . . . . . (witchcraft) 229, 233
burglary, theft, stealing and selling Indians, &c.
case of Nicholas Shapleigh . . . (concealing goods) 12, 13
Cornelius Andreson . . . . . (robbery) 36
Wm. Waldron . . . . (stealing Indians) 86, 88, 91
Jn°. Haughton . . . . " 87
Morris Conway &c. . . . . (inciting to theft) 144
Richard Chamberlayne . . . . " 145
Sara Bradbrooke &c. . . . . . (stealing) 145
Tho. Davis &c. . . . . . . " 189
George Fairfax . . . . . . (burglary) 200
Peter Addams . . . . . . (stealing) 230
Uriah Cleoments . . . . . . (burglary) 283–4
Wm. Clapp &c. . . . . (accomplice in theft) 284–286
lying, slander, cursing, counterfeiting, gambling, contempt, &c.
case of Joseph Blandchard . . (coining of base money) 22
John Weaver . . . . (lying) 23
Edward Thomas . . . . . . (false oath) 24

PAGE

CRIMES, MISDEMEANOURS, &c., *continued.*
lying, &c., *continued.*
case of Paul Batt . . . . . . (refections) 13
old Jethro, Indian . . . . . (abusive speeches) 54
Jacob Jesson . . . . (obstructing the jury) 55
Maurice Brett . . . (contemptuous carriage) 57
Richard Scott . . . . . (writing untruths) 60
Ezekiel Fogg . . . . . " 61
Mr. Isack Waldron . . (injurious speeches) 88, 89
Wm. Kirby . . . . (mutinous carriage) 93
Capt. Tho. Bratle . . (reflections on County Court) 103
Wm. Bowdish . . . . (non appearance) 103
Wm. Pope . . . . . . (cursing &c.) 104
Robert Dendy . . . . (aiding escape) 115
Ephraim Beamis . . . . . . (lying &c.) 116
Allexander Colman . (disturbance of worship) 127
Nicholas Shapleigh &c. . . . . . (lying) 147
Capt. Laurence . (affronting the Gov[rs]. warrant) 170
Ann Perry . . . . . (scandalous offense) 197
complaint of Boston Com[rs]. ag[t]. Sherlot . . (scoffing) 197
case of Wm. King . . . . (blasphemy) 201
James Fuller . . . . (lying) 228
Jn[o]. Child . . . . (gambling) 235
Joseph Gatchell . . . . . . (blasphemy) 253
Wm. Harrison . . . (breach of the peace) 292
Samuel Shrimpton . . . . . . (contempt) 297, 299
Mr. Edward Thomas . . . (non appearance) 305
Benj[a]. Gallop &c. . . . . . " 315
Wm. Neffe . . . . (deserting) 321
John Cutler, Jun[r]. . . . (reproaching authority) 355
Josiah Littlefield . . . . (false statements) 356
Joseph Downer . . . . . " 357
Martin Williams . . . . (counterfeiting) 359, 360
James Lowden . . . . . . (slander) 363
piracy, &c.
case of Peter Rodriego . . . . (piracy) 35
Jn[o]. Roads, &c. . . . . " 36
Cornelius Andreson . . . . . . " 36
Richard Fouler . . . . " 37
Peter Grant . . . . " 37
Randolph Judson . . . . " 38
John Williams . . . . " 38
John Thomas . . . . " 39
Thomas Mitchell &c. . (concurrence with piracy) 42
Wm. Johnson . . . . (piracy) 242
libel ag[t]. Andreason, &c. . . . . " 264
case of Thomas Hawkins . . . . " 306, 320
Thomas Pound . . . . (piracy) 307, 308, 320
Thomas Johnston . . . . " 309, 310, 320

PAGE

CRIMES, MISDEMEANOURS, &c., *continued.*
piracy, &c., *continued.*
case of Eleazer Buck . . . . . (piracy) 310, 311, 320
John Sickterdam . . . . " 311, 312, 320
Wm. Dun . . . . . . " 313, 314, 320
Richard Griffin . . . . " 314, 315, 320
Daniel Lander . . . . " 315, 316, 320
Wm. Warren . . . . . " 317, 318, 320
Samuel Watts . . . . " 318, 319, 320
William Coward &c. . . . " 319, 320
William Neffe . . . . " 321
assault, personal injury, &c.
case of Jn°. Foster . . . . (accidental shooting) 54
John Weaver . . . . . . (wounding) 57
James Foord . . . (driving over Abigail King) 60
Joseph Indian . . . . . . (cruelty) 296
Henry Toltwood . . . . (felonious assault) 336
treason, sedition, &c.
case of John Lowell 15
Caleb, Indian &c. 76
Walter Gendall &c. 102
John Watts 102
Samuel Shrimpton 297, 299
Elizabeth Fanning 358
arson, incendiarism, &c.
case of Joshua Atwater 145
Peter Lorphelin 145
Cheffaleer, negro 197
Jack, negro 198
Maria, negro 198

CRISP or CRISPE
——— Mr., Capt. Wm. Gerrish in room of, (2d. jury of trials &c.) . 215
Jonathan, &c., bond by, ... 57
order as to rendezvous and marching "with the forces" . 58
Richard, (jury) 171
(cancelled) (1st. jury for trials &c.) 215
(jury for attaints) 255
(2d. jury for appeal) 256
Captain, foreman, (jury of trials) 345
Richard, Mr., foreman, (case of Elizabeth Emmerson) 357
(case of Bridget Denmarke) 358
(case of Richard Lillie) 359
Richard, Capt., (Jury) 360
foreman, (case of Martin Williams) 360
Richard, of Boston, Peggy agt., ... 365
Zackariah, agt. Joanes 18
of Groton, case of, (murder) 51

PAGE

CROAD OR CRODE
John, of Salem, exec^{r}. ag^{t}. exec^{r}. of Price 328
Mr., ag^{t}. Price, exec^{r}., case of ment^{d}. (pet. of Crode & decree) 356
pet. to Court of Assistants 22 Sept. 1691 and decree . 356

CROCKET OR CROCKETT
Edward, laborer, house of, (case of Joshua Rice) 234
of Boston, laborer, case of his wife Elisabeth . . 234, 240
order as to being executioner 243
Elisabeth, ment^{d}. (case of Joshua Rice) 234
wife of Edwd. Crocket, case of, (adultery) . . . 234, 240

CRODE. (*See* CROAD.)

CROMWELL, PHILIP, of Salem, English ag^{t}., ... 341

CROSBY
Joseph, ag^{t}. Addams 226
Basse ag^{t}., ... 258
(Jury of attaints &c.) 289
(1st Jury of appeals &c.) 289

CROSS OR CROSSE
Robert, Senr., of Chebacco of Ipswich, Burnam ag^{t}., ... 345
Stephen, Boynton ag^{t}., ... 125
Capt., of Ipswich, ag^{t}. Younglove 348

CRUELTY. (*See* CRIMES.)

CUBA, Bay of Matanzas in, ment^{d}. 129

CULPEPPER
———, Honble. Lord, ment^{d}. (order as to ship Edward & Ann) . . 170
Jno., master of bark Recovery (libel &c.) 118, 119

CUMBEY, ROBERT, (2^{d}. Jury of trials) 362

CURSING. (*See* CRIMES.)

CURTES OR CURTIS
Jno., mariner of ship Merchants Adventure, &c., ag^{t}. Stone . . . 213
Phillip, (Jury of trials &c.) 32

CUTLER
John, Junr., (1st. Jury for trials &c.) 152
John, (Jury) 160
John, Junr., (2^{d}. Jury for trials &c.) 192
(Jury for trials of attaint) 192
case of, (uttering reproachful words against the Authority) 355
answer to pet. of, ... 359
Tim^{o}., (Jury) 171

CUTT, JN^{O}., Knight, ag^{t}., ... 8

CUTTER, EPHRAIM, Marret ag^{t}., ... 275

DADY, WM., (Grand Jury) 59, 108, 180, 190

DAFFORNE
John, ag^{t}. Keene 156
atty., Joseph Homes substitute of, (Mathews ag^{t}. Keene) . . 181

PAGE

DAMERILLS COVE, &c., appointment of constables at, ... 12
DANA (or DANIE), RICHARD, (Grand Jury) 133, 232, 302
DANFORTH
——, Mr. (Courts order as to witnesses &c.) 31
Samuel, Esq[r]., Dep[ty]. Gov[r]., present at Court 130, 131
Thomas, Mr., Esq[r]., or Dep[ty]. Gov[r].
present at Court, 1, 12, 15, 16, 23, 24, 32–36, 41, 43, 52, 55, 58, 61–63, 65, 70, 76, 77, 91, 94, 105, 106, 107, 117, 128, 132, 133, 139, 148–151, 159, 160, 170, 173, 175, 177, 179, 189, 202, 208, 209, 213, 214, 223, 228–230, 241, 243, 251, 254, 266, 273, 287, 296, 298, 300, 302, 305, 320–322, 327, 336, 361, 373
&c., appointed to keep County Court at Essex 253
sentence by, (case of Hugh Stone) 303
order signed by, ... 209
Esq[r]., Francis, &c. ag[t]., ... 330
DANIE. (*See* DANA.)
DANIEL
Jn[o]., carpenter of ship Merchants Adventure, &c. ag[t]. Stone . . . 213
Robert, master of ship James Frygot, &c. (libel &c.) 128
Symon, (Jury for attaints) 266
Thomas, Capt., &c. (libel &c.) 75
by atty. ag[t]. Benj[a]. Marshall 84
Edmund Marshall 84
DANSON (or DAUSON)
George, Elliot ag[t]., ... 156
Ellit ag[t]., ... 167
ag[t]. Wing 288, 366
ag[t]. Pite &c. 289
DARBY, ROGER, Dutch, ag[t]., ... 163
DARLAND, PHILLIP, of Beverly, miller, case of, (adultery) 252–3
DARVALL
——, Mr. &c., ag[t]. Dudson &c. 15
William, Dudson &c. ag[t]., ... 5
Mr., &c., answer to pet. of, ... 13, 14
DAUES. (*See* DAWES.)
DAUSON. (*See* DANSON.)
DAVENPORT
Ann, atty., appeal (estate of Snelling) 156
Charles, (Jury for attaints) 255
(2[d] Jury for appeals) 256
Elisabeth (alias Davis), Mrs., relict and adm[x]., ag[t]. Shippen . . 99
Francis, by atty., appeal, (estate of Snelling) 153
ag[t]. Patch 166
John (Jury) 37
mariner &c. of bark Endeavor (libel &c.) 77
Nathaniel, (Jury of trials) 56
Capt., his relict & adm[x]. ag[t]. Shippen 99
Tho., (Grand Jury) 140

PAGE

DAVID
(Indian) &c., order as to, ... 54
John, &c., Greene, agt., ... 109

DAVIS
Benjamin, atty., Ballard agt., ... 100
&c., Ballard agt., ... 112
Elizabeth (alias Davenport), Mrs., relict & admx., agt. Shippen . . 99
James, agt. Davis &c. 195
Hendrick agt., ... 278
John, Ensigne, of Oyster River, &c., commrs., (order for dower to widow of Hill) 147
(Jury for attaint) 191
(2d. Jury for trials &c.) 192
(1st. Jury for trials &c.) 215
(1st. Jury for appeals &c.) 274
(Jury of trials) 336
Joseph, Tyng, Esqr., agt., ... 67
(Grand Jury) 151, 190
Mary, widow, &c., Davis agt., ... 195
Robert, mariner of ship John & Mary, &c. (libel &c.) 40
agt. Gridley 239
Samuel, master of ship Nevis factor, &c., libel of Hodsdall, agt., . 63–4
libel of Hooper agt., ... 64
Keith agt., ... 64
libel &c. agt. ship Nevis factor . 76
agt. Winsley 111
Thomas, Legg agt., ... 27
late resident in Boston, case of, (adultery) 70
(case of Elisabeth Broune) 70
&c., case of, (stealing &c.) 189
(Jury of trials) 345
Tobiah, (Jury for trials &c.) 228
Tobias, (1st. Jury of trials) 65
(2d. Jury of trials) 96
(Grand Jury) 180
(Jury of trials &c.) 252
Toby, (1st. Jury for trials &c.) 120
William, (1st. Jury of trials &c.) 25, 161
(2d. Jury of trials &c.) 96
Capt., est. of Stenwicke in hands of, admr. of Dinely agt., (execn.) 371–2

DAVISON OR DAVISSON
Daniel, (Jury for attaint) 3
(1st. Jury for trials &c.) 3
(2d. Jury for trials &c.) 25
of Charlestown, merchant (libel) 62
&c., owners of ketch Newbery (complaint &c.) 220

PAGE

DAVISSON, *continued.*
Daniel, Junr., of Ipswich, agt. Potter 364
DAVY
Humphrey, &c., trustees &c., Rice agt., ... 24
Mr., &c., chosen by freemen of Boston allowed &c. . . 67, 96
Esqr., present at Court, 130–132, 139, 148–151, 159–161, 169, 170, 172, 173, 176, 178, 179, 190, 202, 209, 211, 213, 214, 223, 228–232, 241, 243, 251, 255, 266, 273, 287, 296, 298, 300
Thatcher agt., ... 217
Stoddard agt., ... 280
Richd., (Grand Jury) 273
DAWES or DAUES
Ambrose, (Jury for attaints) 180
(1st. Jury for trials &c.) 181
Jonathan, agt. Petit 268
Richard, agt. Newby 270
Wm., (Grand Jury) 1
DAY, JNO., mariner of ship Merchants Adventure, &c., agt. Stone 213
DAY BOOK mentd. in margin 16, 231
DEANE
Daniel, &c., costs granted to, ... 87
Thomas, Perry agt., ... 80
Mr., assignee, agt. Hubbard 94
DEBTOR, sale of, (order on pet. of Sparrey) 146
DE CHAMPS, CHARLS, &c., confession by, mentd. (libel &c. agt. ship Marquis of Royan) 355
DEDHAM (Town of)
rendezvous at, order as to appearance at, ... 58
pet. for Capt. Daniel Fisher to join persons in marriage 87
DEED of gift, as to being authentic (Atkinson agt. Williams) 5
DEERING
Henry, Sevy agt., ... 18
atty., Holman &c., agt., ... 218
DELL
Joseph, his assignee, agt. Aglin 7
&c., agt. Oxe 112
agt. Child 112
DEMEIRE
Nicholas, father of Wm. Demeire (libel agt. Shice) 58
William, (libel &c. agt. Shice) 56, 58
DENDY, ROBERT, case of, (conveying a gimlet to prisoners) 115, 116
DENISON. (*See* DENNISON.)
DENMARKE, BRIDGET, servant of Duncan Cambell, case of, (manslaughter) . 358
DENNIS
James, &c., (Marblehead Commons) Bartlet agt., ... 20
Thomas, of Ipswich, agt. Wainwright 347

PAGE

DENNISON or DENISON
Daniel, Mr. Esqr., or Major present at Court 1, 15, 16, 23, 24, 33, 34, 36, 41, 43, 52, 58, 65, 70, 77, 94, 107, 119, 128, 130, 131, 133, 139, 148, 149, 151, 161, 169, 179, 190, 202, 208, 209, 214
Major Genl., oath by, ... 22
oath before, (inquisition on body of Bickford) 34
DEPUTY GOVERNOR
present at Court . . . 12, 43, 62–64, 70, 76, 77, 169, 211, 240, 297
&c., fined 52
declaration by, (libel agt. pinck Expectation) 149
order of, in Boston 21 Oct. 1680 (case of Josiah Cobbham) . . 171
sentence by, (case of Thomas Hawkins) 306
(case of Thomas Pound, &c.) 308, 310, 311, 312, 314, 315, 316, 318, 319, 320, 321
DERRY, RICHARD, &c., mariners of ship Endeavor, agt. Smith 130–1
DESERTING. (*See* CRIMES.)
DE VAULX, PETER, of Boston, merchant, agt. Shelston 327
DEW, HESTER, (case of George Cole &c.) 12
DEWER
Thomas, (2d. Jury for trials &c.) 18
Senr., (Grand Jury) 65
agt. Broune 236
DEXTER
John, (case of Saml. Hunting) 114
Thomas, Junr., &c., agt. Town of Lynn &c. 111, 135
DICKESON, JOHN, &c., bill of charges for 116
DICKINSON, THOMAS, his execx., Wayte &c. agt., ... 26
DILLON, JOHN, appointed constable of Monhegin 12
DINELY
Father Gon, admr., agt. est. of Stenwicke in hands of Davis (execn.) . 371–2
John, his admr., agt. est. of Stenwicke in hands of Davis (execn.) . 371
DISPAW, HENRY, Matson agt., ... 100
DISTURBANCE OF WORSHIP. (*See* CRIMES.)
DIVORCE
case of Hugh Drury and his wife Mary 91
pet. by Mary Sanders 30
Mrs. Hope Ambrose 127
Elizabeth Lisley 131
Rebeckah Cooly 138
Mary Bishop 144
Mary White 147
Susannah Goodwin 168
Samuel Holton 197
Dorcas Smith 200
Rachel Clenton 208
Elizabeth Street 227

PAGE

DIVORCE, *continued.*
pet. by Ann Perry 229
Elisabeth Maning 240
Sarah Cooper 256, 258
Phillip Goss 326
Mary Stebbins 342
DIX or DIXE
John, agt. Hamond 108
agt. Morse 108
DIXON, WM., (1st. Jury of trials &c.) 44
DODGE
John, &c., plaintiffs, (appeal) 123
Wm., Junr., Balch agt., ... 180
DOE, EDWARD, Chick agt., ... 282
DOLBERY, ANDREW, Capt., by atty. agt. Morrell 348
DOLE, RICHARD, &c., agt. Kent 207
DOLPHIN (ship), execution levied on, mentd. (Foy agt. Trustee of Loder) . 368
DOMINGO, coasts of, &c. mentd. (Lemoigne agt. White &c.) 129
DOR. (*See* DORR.)
DORCHESTER, (Town of) Wm. Cheny of, ... 199
DORR or DOR
Edward, (Jury for attaints) 233
(Jury for trials &c.) 233
(Grand Jury) 345
DORRELL, PATTY, widow, &c., agt. Foster &c. 339
DOSSETT, JOHN, Mr., (Grand Jury) 336
DOUDEN. (*See* DOWDEN.)
DOUNES. (*See* DOWNES.)
DOUNING. (*See* DOWNING.)
DOUNTON or DUNTON, DOUNTY.
John, son of Wm. Dounton, case of, (murder) 271–2
Wm., of Salem, case of his son John, ... 271–2
&c., admr. of Corwin agt., ... 288
William, of Salem, gaol keeper, Blaney agt., ... 340
DOUNTY. (*See* DOUNTON.)
DOUSE
Francis, (Grand Jury) 44, 151
Laurence, (Grand Jury) 65, 214, 244, 255
Samuel, (1st. Jury for trials &c.) 59, 215
(Jury for trials &c.) 233
(2d. Jury of trials) 337
DOVE (ship)
owners of, agt. Cannon 52
master of, &c., libel &c. agt. ship Dove &c. 58
&c., libel &c. of Skinner &c. agt., ... 58
master of, &c., libel &c. agt. ship Dove &c. (execn.) 372–3
&c., libel &c. of Skinner &c. agt., (execn.) 372–3

PAGE

DOVER (Town of)
County Court at, (Patridge agt. Waynwright) 46
(Waynwright agt. Pickering) 46
Portsmouth &, Courts at, June [1676] (libel &c. agt. Thornhull) . 75
DOW, HENRY, atty., agt. Huggens 43
DOWBOY of gold (order on pet. of Wharton &c.) 272
DOWDEN or DOUDEN
Leonard, case of, ... 113
Bennet &c. agt., ... 184
DOWNE
Thomas, (Jury of trials) 302, 306, 308
(Grand Jury) 345
William, (2d. Jury of trials) 337
DOWNER, JOSEPH, of New England, case of, (uttering false statements) . 357
DOWNES or DOUNES
William, &c., sureties on bond of attaint (Apleton agt. Savage) . . 123
(Jury of attaints) 244
(2d. Jury of trials &c.) 245
DOWNING or DOUNING
Richard, agt. Boober & wife 258
Boober agt, ... 276
Boober & wife agt., (execn.) 388
DRABSTON
Cardin, of Watertown, spinster, servant to Christopher Grant, Senr., case of, (infanticide) 125
mentd. (case of Christopher Grant, Junr.) . 125
DRAKE, ABRAHAM, Colcord agt., ... 81–2
DRAPER
James, (Jury of trials) 336
Moses, (Jury of trials) 323
DRAWBRIDGE in Boston, appraisal of, (libel &c. agt. Checkley & wife) (execn.) 385
DRINCKER, EDWD., (Grand Jury) 133
DRIVER
Charles, mate, &c., agt. ketch Friendship (execn.) 391–2
Robert, &c., presentment &c. agt., mentd. in margin 25
Scotchman, apprentice &c. to Williams, case of, (murder) . 30
(case of Nicholas Faevor) 32
&c., order for execution of, ... 33
DRURY
Hugh, (Grand Jury) 1
(Jury of trials &c.) 33
Left., (2d. Jury for trials &c.) 71
& wife Mary, order of Court enjoining them to live together . 91
(case of Mary Drury) 101
Mary, & husband Hugh, order of Court enjoyning them to live together 91
case of, ... 101
DUBLIN, ship St. John of, ... 160

PAGE

DUDLEY
Joseph, Mr., Esqr., present at Court, 62, 63, 65, 70, 76, 77, 91, 92, 94, 105–107, 117, 128, 130–133, 139, 148–151, 159–161, 169, 170, 172, 173, 176, 177, 179, 190, 202, 208, 241, 243, 287, 296–298, 300, 373
Joseph, Esqr., &c., commrs., Rawson &c. agt., ... 208
chosen as guardians by Chickatabut 208
Paul, Mr., &c., Paige &c., agt., ... 155

DUDSON or DUDSSON
———, Mr., &c., Melynes &c. agt., ... 15
———, Phipps agt., ... 102
Francis, Holmes agt., ... 204
Joseph, &c. agt. Darvall 5
& Co., request of, for judication of ship Expectation, . . 15, 16

DUERS, THOMAS, (Grand Jury) 190
DUKE of Brandenburgh (libel &c. agt. Cocke &c.) 179

DUMER or DUMMER
Jeremiah, Mr., (2d. Jury for trials &c.) 153
&c., chosen commrs. for Boston and sworn 357
Richard, agt. Gerrish &c. 44
Mr., Senr., Town of Newbury agt., ... 108

DUN, WILLIAM, case of, (piracy &c.) 313, 314, 320
DUNCLIN, NATHAN, of Charlestown, mariner, agt. Witherett 365

DUNSTER
Elisabeth, Mrs., &c., agt. Prout 143
Jonathan, &c., agt. Prout 143

DUNTON. (*See* DOUNTON.)
DURE, THO., (Jury of trials &c.) 33
DUTCH, holding a correspondency with, (case of John Lowell) 15
DUTCH, SAMUEL, agt. Darby 163

DWIGHT
Timothy, order on pet. of, ... 200
of Boston (case of George Fairfax) 200
atty., &c. agt. Sparrey 235

DYAR or DYER or DYRE
Giles, Pattyn agt., ... 4
(Jury of trials) 242
John, of Braintree, case of, (murder) 188
&c., chosen constables in Boston & oath 206
(Jury of trials) 322
William, Esqr., agt. Hutchinson, Esqr. 261
libel agt. Andreason &c. 263–4

DYRE. (*See* DYER.)

PAGE

EARL or EARLE
Robert, keeper of prison in Boston, order on pet. of, ... 114
prison keeper, (order on bill of charges of Bell &c.) . . 116
account of, order as to, ... 250
EARTHY
John, case of, ... 88
master of bark James & Hannah (case of Wm. Johnson) . . 242
EASTWARD, constables chosen at, ... 11
seizing Indians at, (case of Wm. Waldron &c.) 88, 91
EASTWICK, PHESANT, (2d. Jury for trials &c.) 60
ECCLES or ECLES
Richard, (2d. Jury for trials &c.) 60
(1st. Jury for appeals &c.) 108
(Grand Jury) 230
EDMONDS or EDMUNDS
Anna, case of, (witchcraft) 11
(case of John Bennet &c.) 11
William (case of John Bennet &c.) 11
agt. Waldron 79
EDWARD & ANN, (ship) belonging to Mr. Nicholas Paige, order as to, . . 170
EDWARDS
David, (Jury) 150
Thomas, (1st Jury of trials &c.) 25, 95, 140
(Jury for attaint) 134
(Jury) 149
Tounsend agt., ... 259, 260
mariner, agt. Jarvis 331
testimony by, mentd. (Stanbury agt. Harris) 367
EDY, JNO., (Grand Jury) 56
EGERTON or EGGERTON or EGGINGTON
Jno., &c., case of, (stealing &c.) 891
Peter, surety, agt. Mackee 97
agt. Smith 166
EGGINGTON. (*See* EGGERTON.)
ELA
Daniel, &c., attys., Swann agt., ... 156
agt. Chandler 194
ELINOR (ketch) of Boston (case of Wm. Coward &c.) 319
ELISABETH. (*See* ELIZABETH.)
ELIZABETH (ship)
master of, dep. by, ... 132
of Boston, Thomas Bossinger, master, (information &c.) . . . 296-7
ELIZABETH & MARGARET (ketch)
Nathaniel Cary, &c., agt., ... 106
master of, &c. agt. ketch Elisabeth & Margaret 106

PAGE

ELKIN
——, Mr., old, ment^d. (dep. by Thomas Sexton) 132
Nathaniel, Cowell ag^t., ... 69
ment^d. (dep. by Thomas Sexton) 132
ELLACOT, VINES, of Barbadoes, now resident in Boston, merchant, case of, (murder) 251–2
ELLES. (*See* ELLIS.)
ELLIOT or ELLIT
Andrew, master, &c. ag^t. ketch Friendship (exec^n.) 391–393
Asaph, (1st Jury for trials &c.) 95
Allen ag^t., ... 260
Henry, ag^t. Dauson 156, 167
Jacob (Grand Jury) 32
ELLIS or ELLES
Edward, (Jury of Inquest) (inquisition on body of Bickford) . . 34
Rich., (2^d. Jury of trials &c.) 71
ELLISTON or ELLISTONE
——, &c., sureties, (case of Thomas Saffin) 249
George, (2^d Jury of trials) 345
ELLIT. (*See* ELLIOT.)
ELSON, JAMES, master of ship Blessing, &c. (libel &c.) 58–9
ELY
John, master of ship Anne (libel &c.) 94
Capt., master of ship Herron (libel &c.) 159
EMBARGO of ship Edward & Ann, order for 170
EMERY or EMMERY
John, Thompson, ag^t., ... 80
Senr. Tompson ag^t., ... 97
Martha, her trustees &c. ag^t. Hauford 122
her trustees &c. ag^t. adm^r. of Sweeting 122
EMMERSON
Elizabeth, single woman & daughter of Michael Emmerson, case of, (infanticide) 357
Michael, of Haverhill, case of his daughter Elizabeth 357
EMMERY. (*See* EMERY.)
ENDEAVOR (bark or pink &c.)
master of, libel &c. ag^t. Paige 77
of Boston, (case of Wm. Waldron) 86
(case of John Haughton) 87
mariners of, libel &c. ag^t. Lang 118
master of, libel &c. of Berry &c. ag^t., ... 118
commander of, Francis &c. ag^t., ... 130
mariners of, ag^t. Smith 130
commander of, &c., libel ag^t. Francis &c. 132
ENDECOT / ENDECOTT or ENDICOT
John, &c. exe^rs., ag^t., Sweeting 79

PAGE

ENDECOT, &c., *continued.*
John, agt. Calley 96
trustees &c. agt. admr. of Sweeting 122
agt. Hauford 122
(2d Jury for trials &c.) 153
case of, ... 155
(jury of trials) 242
atty., agt. Coleman 269
Zerubbabel, Nurse agt., ... 120
Mr., Nurse agt., ... 235
ENDICOT. (*See* ENDECOTT.)
ENGIS
Maudet, of Boston, (70 years) dep. by, ... 139
witness, (Usher agt. Usher) 139
ENGLAND
Brandford in, ... 10
mentd. (libel &c. agt. Bull) 40
(case of ship Speedwell &c.) 107
money of, ... 157, 175, 323
ship Edward & Ann, &c. bound for, ... 170
mentd. (case of Uriah Cleoments) 283–4
(information agt. ship Elisabeth) 296
Lord High Admiral of, ... 332–4, 353
High Court of Admiralty in 334, 344
law of, mentd. (case of Saml. Newton & wife) 342
mentd. (information agt. Lawrence) 343–4
(libel &c. agt. ship Marquis of Royan) 354
statutes of, (case of Hannah Owen) 361
king of, mentd. (Belchar agt. Lloyd) 362
ENGLESBE. (*See* INGLESBY.)
ENGLISH, murder of, (case of Little Jno., Indian) 53
ENGLISH
Phillip, &c., evidence by, mentd. (answer to pet. of Sanders) . . . 31
agt. Mazure 109
by atty., agt. Mazure 109
of Salem, agt. Stebbins 326
merchant, agt. Cromwell 341
Stebbins agt., ... 346
Wm., (grand jury) 119
ENGLISH PLANTATIONS
mentd. (case of Thos. Davis &c.) 189
sale to, (case of Uriah Cleoments) 284
EPPS
———, Mr., (Symonds agt. Leveret) 217
Daniel, atty., agt. Marshall 84
Capt., agt. Bennet 259
ESCAPE, aiding. (*See* CRIMES.)

PAGE

ESSEX (County of)
Beverly in, ... 252
Thomas Danforth, &c. to keep the Court at, ... 253
Salem in, ... 271
Haverhill in, ... 357
ESSEX COUNTY COURT. (*See* COUNTY COURT — ESSEX.)
EUROPE, commodities &c. of, ... 343, 344, 355
EVANS (or EVINS), ROBERT, Roby &c. agt., ... 6, 136
EVE, JASPER, &c. mariners of ship Ann & Hesther (libel &c.) 172
EVELEIGH, ISAAC, master of ketch Newbery, &c. (complaint &c.) . . 220
EVELY, SILVESTER, (Grand Jury) 24
EVERDEN, WALTER, agt. Smith 164
EVERELL, JAMES, &c., Gibbs agt., ... 17, 18
EVIDENCE
sufficient to a legal conviction (case of Goad) 10
special verdict as to, (Ingolls agt. Bishop) 262–3
(Rice agt. Avery) 273–4
(Marret agt. Cutter) 275
EVINS. (*See* EVANS.)
EXECUTION
on person & estate & releasing person, as to, (Colcord agt. Drake) . 81
levying of, on estate rendered, judgment as to, (order on complaint of Walters) 169
EXECUTIONS
book of records for, (Court of Assistants), mentd., 371, 379, 382, 386, 388, 391
EXPECTATION (ship, pink, &c.)
mentd. (request of Dudson & Co.) 16
libel of Randolph, Collr., agt., ... 149, 150
master of, libel &c. agt. Torry 177
agt. Shinchinke 178
mentd. (Torrey agt. Gretian) 180
mariners &c. of, libel agt. Schinking (execn.) 378–380
EXPEDITION (ship), &c., libel &c. of Randolph, Collr., agt. 177
EYRE, EYRES (*See* AYRES.)

FAEVOR or FAVOR
Nicholas, (case of Robert Driver) 30
case of, (murder) 32–3
FAGG, WM., Colony soldier, mentd. (case of John Indian) 53
FAIREFAX. (*See* FAIRFAX.)
FAIREFEILD. (*See* FAIRFIELD.)
FAIREWEATHER
——, Mr., &c., Melynes &c. agt., ... 15
——, Mr., (libel agt. Andreason &c.) 264
John, &c. agt. Darvall 5
Mr., of Boston, case of his negro servant Jack 74
Capt., &c. chosen commrs. for Boston & oath &c. 168
Mr., &c. chosen commrs. for Boston & oath &c. . . 199, 214

PAGE

Fairfax or Fairefax
George, case of, (burglary &c.) 200
mentd. (order on pet. of Timo. Dwight) 200
Fairfield or Fairefeild
Daniel, agt. Elizth. Fairefeild 121
Elizabeth, Daniel Fairefeild agt., ... 121
John, of Ipswich, Wm. Fairfield agt., ... 348
Walter, agt. Knowlton 181
William, of Wenham, agt. John Fairfield 348
Falmouth, his Majesties garrison at, ... 321
False Oath. (*See* Crimes.)
Familiarity with the Devil. (*See* Crimes.)
Faning or Fanning
Elizabeth, case of, (treason) 358
Thomas, (Jury of trials) 35
(2d. Jury of trials) 215
Farley, Michael, agt. Lummas 193
Farr
Benjamin, Needham agt., ... 247
agt. Witter 269
Farrell, James, &c., complaint of Bisco agt., ... 286
Farrington, Mathew, Graves agt., ... 222
Farwell (or Furnell), Jno., Aires agt., ... 222
Favor. (*See* Faevor.)
Fawer, Gibson, agt. Cable 302
Fellowes
Ephraim, &c., Jacob agt., ... 137
Isack, &c., Jacob agt., ... 137
Samuel, Broune agt., ... 140
Felonious Assault, Felony (*See* Crimes.)
Fenno, John, Perkins agt., ... 257, 266
Fernes or Ferns
Ann, widow & admx., Adlington agt., ... 340
Peter, his widow & admx., Adlington agt., ... 340
Fessingden or Fessondon
Nicholas, (2d Jury of trials &c.) 161, 362
Fifeild, Fifield or Fyfield
Giles, (2d Jury for trials &c.) 45
&c., Hutchinson &c. agt., ... 325
of Boston, mariner, agt. Bradley 330
Fifty hogsheads of tobacco &c. (libel &c.) 168–9
Figg, Mary, agt. Baker 133
Fines. (*See* Punishment.)

PAGE

FISHER
——, Capt., &c., atty[s]. (case of James Nanapatú, Indian) . . . 54
Daniel, Capt., impowered to join persons in marriage on pet. of Town of Dedham 87
present at Court 22 May 1683 229
Esq[r]., present at Court 8 June 1683 230
George, &c., mariners of ship Ann & Hesther (libel &c.) 172
Jn[o]., ag[t]. Wayte 218
FISKE
——, Left., ment[d]. (Griffyn ag[t]. Gove) 99
David, (Grand Jury) 266
Nath., Sen[r]., (Jury of trials &c.) 33
FITCH, JEREMIAH, (Grand Jury) 59, 151, 230, 336
FLACK, SAMUEL, son of, ment[d]. (case of Jn[o]. Foster) 54
FLAGG or FLEG, FLEGG
Ebenezer, (Jury of attaints &c.) 289
Thomas, (1st Jury of trials &c.) 59, 65, 70
(Grand Jury) 133, 190, 244, 266
Jun[r]. (Grand Jury) 336
(2[d] Jury for trials &c.) 215
Wm., Colony soldier, (case of John Indian) 53
FLEG / FLEGG } (*See* FLAGG.)
FLETCHER
Georg, Parris ag[t]., ... 202–3
Joseph, for John March & wife ag[t]. Hugh March, Sen[r]., ... 214
Peter, &c., mariners of ship Endeavor, ag[t]. Smith 130–1
FLINT or FLYNT
Edmund, answer to pet. of, ... 85
John, (answer to pet. of Edmund Flynt) 85
of Salem, case of, (murder) 85
found guilty of manslaughter 85
FLOOD
Henry, of Boston, cordwainer, case of his wife Mary, (murder) . . 295
James, ag[t]. Legg 110
Legg ag[t]., ... 142
Porter ag[t]., ... 196
(Grand Jury) 288
Mary, wife of Henry Flood, case of, (murder) 295
FLOWER, (bark) master of, &c. (libel &c.) 92
FLOYD
——, Mr., exec[n]. delivered to, (case of John Bennet &c.) . . . 11
John, constable, ment[d]. (Isaac Waldron, pltf., appeal) 77
of Rumley Marsh, chosen guardian by Armetage 271
FLYNT. (*See* FLINT.)
FOG or / FOGG }
David, (case of George Cole &c.) 12

PAGE

FOG, &c., *continued.*
Ezekiel, answer to pet. of, ... 31
(case of Richard Scott) 60
case of, (writing untruths &c.) 61
his sureties ag^t. Williams 68
FOORD, JAMES, case of, (driving a cart over Abigail King) 60
FORCE, NATHANAEL, (negro) sale of, (Hall ag^t. Backway) 350
FORNICATION. (*See* CRIMES.)
FORREST, WM., seaman, (case of Nicho^s. Shapleigh) 12, 13
FORSTER. (*See* FOSTER.)
FOSKET or FOSKETT
Hannah, widow, Thos. Fosket ag^t., ... 328
John, Gates ag^t., ... 290
Thomas, of Charlestown, ag^t. Foskett 328
FOSTER or FORSTER
Abigail, & husband John, Dorrell &c. ag^t., ... 339
Elisha, (Jury for attaint) 192
Isack, Mr., order on complaint &c. of, ... 104
Isaac, Senr., Neeland ag^t., ... 345
James, (1st. Jury of trials &c.) 59, 152
(Jury for attaints) 266
(Jury for trials) 362
John, case of, (wounding Saml. Flack's son) 54
(2^d. Jury for trials &c.) 203
&c., merchants, Pynchon ag^t., ... 328
& wife Abigail, Dorrell &c. ag^t., ... 339
&c., sale to, (libel &c. ag^t. Long) (exec^n.) 375–6
Tho., (2^d. Jury for trials &c.) 71
Timothy, (Jury for attaint) 2, 192
(2^d. Jury for trials &c.) 3, 96, 192
(Jury of trials) 242
William, (Grand Jury) 65, 232, 298
(Jury) 149, 231
&c., appraisers, (Elliot, &c. ag^t. ketch Freindship) (exec^n.) . 392
FOULE. (*See* FOWLE.)
FOULER. (*See* FOWLER.)
FOULESHAM or FOULSHAM
John, Sen., Gilman ag^t., ... 68
FOWLE or FOULE
George, costs granted him ag^t. Leveret 188
Isaac, (2^d. Jury of trials &c.) 161
(Jury of trials) 323
James, (Jury of attaints &c.) 289
John, (1st. Jury for trials &c.) 203
(2^d. Jury for trials &c.) 224
Peter, (2^d. Jury for appeal) 256
(Jury for attaints) 255

PAGE

Fowler or Fouler
Philip, &c., sureties on bond of attaint (Knight ag^{t}. Leach &c.) . . 194
Richard, (libel ag^{t}. Rodriego &c.) 34
Englishman, case of, (piratically seizing small vessels &c.) . 37
&c., order for execution of, ... 39
Samuel, Gove, assignee, ag^{t}., ... 8
Sarah, of Boston, wine retailer, ag^{t}. Clarke 322
wine retailer (whom Wm. Hall married) (Hall & Backway) . 350

Fox
Isaac, &c., Prout ag^{t}., ... 349
Nathaniel, ag^{t}. Leveret, Esqr., Govr., ... 125
Thomas, (Grand Jury) 1, 44, 255
Green ag^{t}., ... 368

Foxcraft or Foxcroft
Francis, (cancelled) (Jury) 230
(Jury of trials) 242
&c., exec^{rs}., ag^{t}. Eyres 324

Foy
John, (Jury) 176
Capt., of Boston, mariner, ag^{t}. trustee of Loder 368
&c., appraisers, (libel &c. ag^{t}. Long) (exec^{n}.) 375

France
Rochelle in 55
king of, ment^{d}. (Lemoigne ag^{t}. White &c.) 129
subjects of, (case of Wm. Johnson) 242
(libel ag^{t}. Andreason &c.) 264
ships belonging to, &c. 332–334, 353
St. Mallo in, ... 333, 335
king of, vessels &c. belonging to, ... 352
Northern, Isle of Persy in, ... 353
king of, ment^{d}. (libel &c. ag^{t}. ship Marquis of Royan) 354

Francis
Alice, &c. of Cambridge ag^{t}. Danforth 330
John, boatswain of ship Endeavor, &c. ag^{t}. Smith 130
&c., (libel &c.) 132
Stephen, (Jury for attaint) 134
(2^{d}. Jury of trials &c.) 135

Franck. (*See* Francks.)

Francklin
Benjamin, Warner ag^{t}., ... 144
&c., case of, execution in, suspended 146

Francks or Franck, Franks
Sarah, widow, Rock ag^{t}., ... 142
Mrs., Rock ag^{t}., ... 180

Franks. (*See* Francks.)

Frary
———, Lieut., ment^{d}. (case of Darby Bryan) 115

PAGE

FRARY, *continued.*
——, Lieut., ment^d^. (case of Ephraim Beamis) 116
Theophilus, (Grand Jury) 56
&c., Waldron ag^t^., ... 216
Capt., &c., chosen comm^rs^. for Boston and sworn . . 357
FRATHINGHAM. (*See* FROTHINGHAM.)
FRAUD &c., prevention of, Act of Parliament for, ment^d^. (information ag^t^. Lawrence) 344
FREAKE
——, Mrs., Pease ag^t^., ... 80
Elisabeth, Mrs., relict of John Freake, &c. (libel &c.) 34
ag^t^. Robbinson 102
John, (Jury for attaint) 2
Mr., merchant, his relict &c. ag^t^. Rodriego &c. 34
of Boston, (case of Peter Rodriego &c.) 35–39
FREDERICK, ship Richard now called the, (libel &c. ag^t^. ship Richard) . . 335
FREEMAN, JN^o^., gunner of ship James Frygot, &c. (libel &c.) 128
FREEMEN OF BOSTON, comm^rs^. chosen by, ... 67, 96, 199
FREINDSHIP (ketch) of Boston, Elliot &c. ag^t^., (exec^n^.) 391–2
FRENCH
John, (or Stephen) foreman, (case of Wm. Clapp &c.) 285
Stephen, case of his Spanish Indian servant 115
Mr., (1st. Jury for appeals &c.) 274
FRENCH KING. (*See* FRANCE.)
FRIZELL, JOHN, Usher ag^t^., ... 302
FROST
——, Capt., (order for dower to widow of Hill) 147
Charles, mariner of ship George, &c. (complaint &c.) 41
Pickering ag^t^., ... 69
John, Mr., (2^d^. Jury for trials &c.) 45
(Jury for trials &c.) 53
foreman in behalf of jury of appeals, Woodmansey, ag^t^., . 59
Veren ag^t^., ... 141
FROTHINGHAM or FRATHINGHAM
Nath., (2^d^. Jury for trials &c.) 71
Peter, (1st. Jury for trials &c.) 78
FULLER
James, of Springfield, case of, (familiarity with the devil) . . . 228–9
John, (Grand Jury) 17
(1st. Jury for trials &c.) 78, 192
(2^d^. Jury for trials &c.) 161
(Jury for attaint) 192
(Cambridge) (2^d^. Jury of trials &c.) 274
(Lynn) (1st. Jury for appeals &c.) 274
Thomas, Bradstreet &c. ag^t^., ... 108
(Woburn) (2^d^. Jury for trials &c.) 274
FURNELL (or FARWELL), JN^o^., Aires ag^t^., ... 222

PAGE

FYALL
Indians sent to, (case of Wm. Waldron &c.) 86–88, 91
voyage to, (Poole ag[t]. exec[x]. of Lydgett) 105
FYFIELD. (*See* FIFIELD.)

GABRICK or GABRICKE
Henry, &c., mariners of ship Apollow, ag[t]. Hollaway &c. 132–3
ment[d]. (Phipps ag[t]. Bronsdon) 337
GALE
John, Jacob ag[t]., ... 223
Symon, (or Gates), Becke ag[t]., ... 216
GALLOP, BENJAMIN, &c. case of, (default) 315
GAMBLIN or GAMBLINN, GAMLIN
Benjamin (Jury of trials &c.) 83
(Jury for attaints) 181, 244
(2[d] Jury for trials &c.) 181, 245
GAMBLING. (*See* CRIMES.)
GAMBLINN or GAMLIN (*See* GAMBLIN.)
GAMON, ROBERT, appointed constable of Capenawagen &c. 12
GANTLET, running of, (case of Walter Gendall &c.) 102–3
GARD, WM., (Jury) 230
GARDINER or GARDNER
——, Left., &c., bond by, (case of Jn[o]. Earthy) 88
Andrew, of Muddy River, case of his negro servant Robin 304
John, Mr., (Jury of trials) 336
Jonathan, ment[d]. (Grand jury indictments &c.) 273
order as to 281
Richard, Nevars ag[t]., ... 100
Samuell, ag[t]. Pudney 110
Thomas, Sen[r]., &c., committee (order on est. of Lambe) 103
(Grand Jury) 108, 179
GAREY or GARY
Samuel, (Jury for attaint) 2
(1st. Jury for trials &c.) 3, 215
William, (Grand Jury) 78, 133, 242, 302, 305
(2[d] Jury of trials &c.) 141
(Jury) 210
GARFEILD or GARFIELD
Benjamin, (1st Jury for trials &c.) 152
(Jury of trials &c.) 228, 302, 306, 308
GARLAND
Elisabeth & husband John, plaintiffs, (appeal) 46
Jn[o]., & wife Elisabeth, plaintiffs, (appeal) 46
GARNSEY, HENRY, (Grand Jury) 361

PAGE

GARRISON
at Falmouth, deserting of, &c. (case of Wm. Neffe) 321
at Newitchawannick in Yorkshire (certificate & order for payment for service under Capt. Hathorn) . 104
GARY. (*See* GAREY.)
GASKILL, SAM[ll]., (2[d] Jury of trials) 337
GATCHEL or GATCHELL
Bethyah, case of, (adultery) 138
Elisabeth, evidence of, ment[d]. (case of Joseph Gatchell) 253
Jerremiah, house of, ment[d]. (case of Joseph Gatchell) . . . 253–4
Joseph, of Marblehead, case of, (blasphemy) 253–4
GATES
Symon, (or Gale) Becke ag[t]., ... 216
Symon, ag[t]. Foskett 290
GATLIFF
Jonath[n]., of Boston, mariner, guardian of his son Tho[s]., ag[t]. Legg, . 362
Th[o]., (son of Jon[a]. Gatliff), his guardian ag[t]. Legg 362
GEDNEY. (*See* GIDNEY.)
GEE, JOSHUA, (Special Jury) 363
GENDALL, WALTER, of Black Point, case of, (treachery) 90, 102
GENERAL COURT
order of, Oct. 1673 (appointment of constables at Kennebec) . . 11
ment[d]. (Bartlett ag[t]. James &c. (Marblehead Commons)) . . . 20
(Lattimore ag[t]. James &c. (Marblehead Commons)) . . 20
(libel ag[t]. Starr &c.) 23
(case of Peter Rodriego) 35
(order on pet. of Elizabeth Bowers) 104
first sessions of, (Davis ag[t]. Winsley) 111
action continued to determination of, (Olliver &c. ag[t]. Lynn &c.) . 111
ment[d]. (Nurse ag[t]. Endecot) 120, 236
(Courts order to pay Hauthorne) 127
May 1677 ment[d]. in margin 158
judgment 11 Oct. 1665 ment[d]. (assignee of Wayte ag[t]. exec[x]. &c. of Cooke) 164
judgment (Hoare ag[t]. Cooke, exec[x]., &c.) 166
Oct. [1680] (order on pet. of Stephen Butler) 170
ment[d]. (Butler ag[t]. Checkley) 206
24 May 1682, ment[d]. in margin 208
ment[d]. (Gifford ag[t]. Walter &c.) 218
order ment[d]. (assignee of Hoare ag[t]. Kilcup) 219
ment[d]. (Bishop ag[t]. Lord, marshal) 239
adjourned to 14 Oct. 1685 286
ment[d]. (votes on pet. of Checkley) 294
&c., defamation of, (case of Samuel Shrimpton) 299
ment[d]. (appointment of Sam[l]. Gookin as mar[l]. gen[l].) 342
GENERAL SALVATION, disturbance about, (case of Jos. Gatchell) . . 253–4
GENNERSON, WM., (Jury for appeals) 233

PAGE

GEORGE (ship)
of Bristol, mariners of, (libel &c.) 173
of London Derry (complaint &c. agt. Newton &c.) 41
GEORGE, JOHN, (Jury of trials) 336
GERRISH
William, Capt., &c., Dummer agt., ... 44
Senr., Woodbridge agt.,. 67
Capt., Lowle agt., ... 82
&c., by atty., agt. Lowle 139
in Mr. Crisp's room (2d. Jury for trials &c.) . . 215
GIBBS
——, of Boston, case of his wife Mary, ... 57
Benjamin, case of, ... 2
agt. Ashton 2
agt. Bonner &c. 17
case of, mentd. in margin 45
agt. Gideon &c. 49
agt. assignee of Watters 50
Shoare agt., ... 68
libel agt. Wheeler 75
Capt., libel &c. of Wheeler &c. agt., ... 76
agt. Sweete &c. 77
his admx. mentd. (libel &c. agt. Checkly & wife) . . 130
wife &c. of, " " 382–386
deed to, " " 385
Elisabeth, (relict &c. of Robt. Gibbs), wife of Jona. Corwin, mentd. (Sheaffe agt. Palmer &c.) 123
Lidia, (admx. of Benja. Gibbs), wife of Anthony Cheeckly, &c. (libel &c.) 130
Mary, (case of Maurice Brett) 56
of Boston, case of, (adultery) 57
Robert, estate of, in hands of Corwin &c., Sheaffe agt., ... 123
&c., Baskerville agt., ... 141
GIBSON
Samuel, agt. Read 271
plaintiff, (appeal) 275
(2d. Jury for trials &c.) 346
William, (1st. Jury for trials &c.) 59
instead of Toy (1st Jury for appeals &c.) 289
GIDEON, ROULAND, &c., Gibbs agt., ... 49
GIDLEY, HEZEKIAH, Stratton agt., ... 369
GIDNEY OF GEDNEY
Bartholomew, Esqr. present at Court 1 Mar. 1680 179
6 Sept. 1681 190
18 Mar. " 208
5 Sept. 1682 214
6 Mar. " 223
4 Sept. 1683 232

PAGE

GIDNEY or GEDNEY, *continued.*
Bartholomew, Esqr. present at Court 12 Oct. 1683 241
" Nov. " 241
4 Mar. " 243
atty., Gilbert agt., ... 274
Benj., [Bartholomew?] Esqr. present at Court 18 Mar. 1681 . . 208
GIFFORD or GIFFORDS, GYFFORD
John, agt. Hathorne 28, 48, 49
his assignee, Leveret agt., ... 50
agt. Briggs 65
agt. Lee 110, 124
agt. Lord 155
Walter agt., ... 163
(Mr.) agt. Read 185, 192
principal on bond of attaint, (Gifford agt. Read) 185
agt. Walter &c. 218, 247
Mr., allowed hearing (Gifford agt. Walter &c.) 218
order on petn. of, ... 231
GIFFORDS. (*See* GIFFORD.)
GIFT OF GOD (bark or ship)
&c. libel &c. of Randolph, Collr., agt., ... 176
of France, libel &c. of Southack agt., ... 332
GILBERT
John, Greenleafe agt., ... 48
Obbinson agt., ... 79
Roger, agt. Waldron 227
William (Jury) 176
(2d Jury for trials &c.) 203
Rawson agt., ... 245, 255
agt. Gidney, atty. 274
(Jury of attaints &c.) 288
GILL, OBADIAH (Jury of attaints &c.) 288
GILLAM
Ann, (case of Geo. Cole &c.) 12
Benjamin, (Jury of trials) 35
Capt., (Jury) 36
foreman, (case of John Roads &c.) 36
Zechariah, (libel &c. agt. Woodmansey) 119
GILMAN, MOSES, agt. Foulsham 68
GINNOP (or GUNNOP), NICHOLAS, gunner of ship Appollow, &c.
agt. Hollaway &c. 132–3
GLANDFEILD
John, case of, (adultery) 15
of Black Point (case of Amy Wellen) 15
GLOVER
Habbacuck, (1st. Jury of trials &c.) 25
&c., Rawson agt., ... 26, 65
(Grand Jury) 35

PAGE

GLOVER, *continued.*
John, &c., Rawson agt., ... 65
Mr., case of, ... 88
(case of Wm. Waldron &c.) 88, 91
his assignee agt. Hubbard 94
Nathll., (2d. Jury of trials) 337
Pelatiah, &c., Rawson agt., ... 65
Mr., Voss agt., ... 204
GOAD
Benjamin, case of, (bestiality) 10
answer to petn. of, ... 14
as to execution of, ... 14
GOBL or }
GOBLE }
Daniel, of Concord, case of, (murder of Indians) 71
Stephen, " " " " " 71
&c., examination &c. of, mentd. (costs granted to Keene &c.) 87
Tho., Junr., &c., costs granted to, ... 87
GODARD or }
GODDARD }
Gyles, Nowell agt., ... 293
William, (1st. Jury of trials, &c.) 17
(1st. Jury of appeals &c.) 108
(Grand Jury) 134, 190, 273
GODFREY or }
GODFRY }
John, agt. Clarke, marl. genls depty., ... 8
estate of, mentd. in margin 80
GOFFE
Samuel, (Jury of trials) 35
(Jury) 37
(2d. Jury for trials &c.) 192
(Jury for attaint) 192
Stanbridge agt., ... 330
GOFFREIGH, FRANCIS, by atty., agt. Sprague 222
GOLD
John, agt. Bishop 21
Ensign, &c. agt. Putman &c. 27
agt. Putman 45
Bishop agt., ... 47
GOLDEN ROSE (frigate), late commander of, agt. Bronsdon 337–8
GOLDING. (*See* GOULDING.)
GOOD HOPE (pink), master of, (libel &c.) 219
GOODWIN
Edward, pet. for divorce by his wife Susannah, ... 168
John, mariner of ship Merchants Adventure, &c. agt. Stone . . . 213
Joseph, &c., mariners of ship James Frygot, (libel &c.) 128
Susannah, wife of Edwd. Goodwin, pet. for divorce 168

PAGE

GOOKIN
——, Major, (case of Richard Scott) 61
Daniel, Esq[r]., Capt., Major or Major Gen[l].,
present at Court, 1, 15, 16, 23, 24, 32–34, 36, 41, 43, 52, 55, 58, 61, 94, 105–107, 117, 119, 130–133, 139, 148–151, 159, 161, 169, 170, 172, 173, 175, 177, 179, 189, 190, 202, 208, 209, 213, 214, 223, 228, 229–232, 240, 241, 243, 251, 255, 266, 273, 287, 296, 298, 300, 373.
&c., present at meeting of the Council in Boston 1 Nov. 1677 . 104
dep[n]. sworn before, ... 139
Esq[r]., ag[t]. Wade 225
Nathaniel, & wife ag[t]. Savage &c. 329
Samuel, (Jury for attaints) 180, 267
(1st. Jury for trials &c.) 181
(Jury of trials) 242
(Grand Jury) 336
Mr., appointed marshal general 342

GOOSE
Isaac (Jury of attaints) 244
(1st. Jury for trials &c.) 245
John, late master of bark Hope, libel &c. ag[t]. Campbell . . . 148
of Campbell ag[t]., . . 148

GORDON or GOURDON
Abra., Trott ag[t]., ... 165
James, agent &c., (complaint &c. ag[t]. Newton &c.) 41

GORE
John, (2[d]. Jury of trials &c.) 141
(Jury) 231
Samuel, (1st. Jury of trials &c.) 25
(2[d]. " " " ") 224
(Jury of attaints &c.) 288
(Grand Jury) 336

GOSPEL ment[d]. (case of Joseph Gatchell) 253

GOSS
Hannah, wife of Phillip, her marriage at Jamaica to John Morrey. ment[d]. (order on pet. of Goss) 326
Phillip, mariner, pet. for divorce 326

GOTT, CHARLES, clerk, certificate presented by order of the militia of Wenham . 104

GOULDING or GOLDING
Peter, ag[t]. exec[r]. of Russell 98
& wife Sarah ag[t]. Smith 193
ag[t]. Midgley 204
Sarah, & husband Peter ag[t]. Smith 193

GOURDON. (*See* GORDON.)

GOVE or GOVES
Edward, Pike ag[t]., ... 6
assignee, ag[t]. Fouler 8

PAGE

GOVE or GOVES, *continued*.
Edward, ag[t]. Pike . . . 16
Griffyn ag[t]., . . . 98, 99
ag[t]. Bennet . . . 107
(order on bill of charges of Torrey) . . . 251
John, (1st Jury for trials &c.) . . . 17
(Jury) . . . 210
(Jury for appeals) . . . 233
(Jury for attaints) . . . 233
&c., Holman &c. ag[t]., . . . 289
GOVERNOR
present at Court, 11, 41, 43, 58, 62, 63, 64, 70, 76, 77, 169, 211, 240, 297, 299, 300
sentence by, (case of Benj[a]. Goad) . . . 11
admonishment by, (case of George Cole &c.) . . . 12
&c., order as to constables of Kennebec &c. . . . 12
declaration by, (case of Benj. Goad) . . . 14
&c., declaration &c. by, ment[d]. in margin . . . 16
approval of, (complaint of Isaac Griffyn) . . . 19
declaration by, (case of Tom Indian) . . . 22
& Council, meeting of, in Boston 4 Sept. 1674 . . . 23
sentence by, (case of Robert Driver) . . . 30
& Magistrates in Boston, special Court of Assistants called by, . . . 32
sentence by, (case of Nicholas Faevor) . . . 32
Court of Assistants &c. called by, . . . 34
sentence by, (case of Peter Rodriego) . . . 35
& Council, Court of Assistants &c. called by, . . . 55
to be the umpire (Woodbridge ag[t]. Gerrish) . . . 67
sentence by, (case of Daniel Goble) . . . 72
ment[d]. (Woodbridge ag[t]. Williams) . . . 83
& Magistrates, case referred to, (case of Wm. Pope) . . . 104
warrant &c. from, (case of ship Speedwell &c.) . . . 107
& Magistrates, order by, (Nurse ag[t]. Endecot) . . . 120
& Council ment[d]. (Lemoigne ag[t]. White &c.) . . . 130
&c. ment[d]. (case of Ellinor May) . . . 138
& Council ment[d]. (case of Peeter Lorphelin) . . . 146
order of, ment[d]. (libel ag[t]. Gretian &c.) . . . 150
&c., declaration by, on complaint of Walters . . . 169
&c., confession before, (case of Geo. Russell) . . . 169
order from, for summoning the Court &c., (order for ten pounds caution money &c.) 171
& Magistrates in a Court of Assistants ment[d]. (order on pet. of Geo. Hutchinson) 175
sentence by, (case of Maria, negro) . . . 198
(case of Jack, negro) . . . 199
(case of Wm. Cheny) . . . 199
&c., license granted by, to Wm. Kent . . . 208
&c. ment[d]. (choice of guardians by Chickatabut) . . . 208

PAGE

GOVERNOR, *continued*.
&c., Randolph, Coll^r^., in behalf of, (libel &c.) 209
Court of Assistants &c. called by, ... 213
& Magistrates, votes by, ... 220
ment^d^. (answer to pet. of Redding) 223
&c. ment^d^. (complaint ag^t^. Lynch) 240
Court of Assistants called by, ... 241
&c., order by, (case of Wm. Johnson) 242
ment^d^. (order on est. of Mr. Wade) 250
&c., special Court of Assistants called by, ... 251
ment^d^. (libel ag^t^. Andreason &c.) 263
&c., Court of Assistants held by, 1 Sept. 1685 273
sentence by, (case of James Morgan) 295
Court of Assistants adjourned by, ... 296
sentence by, (case of Joseph Indian) 296
&c. assembled in County Court at Boston (case of Shrimpton) . . 297
& Company &c. ment^d^. (case of Shrimpton) 297, 299
&c. of Mass. Bay, commission by, (libel ag^t^. bark Speedwell) . . 352
GOVES. (*See* GOVE.)
GRAFTON
John, libel &c. ag^t^. Shice 55
appearance of, (libel &c. ag^t^. Shice) 58
GRAHAM, JOHN, (case of Wm. Johnson) 242
GRAND JURY
List of, 1, 16, 24, 25, 32, 35, 43, 44, 53, 56, 59, 65, 78, 94, 107, 108, 119, 120, 133, 134, 139, 140, 151, 179, 180, 190, 202, 214, 229, 230, 232, 242–244, 251, 252, 255, 266, 273, 287, 288, 298, 301, 302, 305, 336, 345, 361
Mentioned, impanelled, &c., 10, 14, 15, 29–32, 35, 36, 50–52, 85–87, 102, 114, 115, 125, 126, 158, 161, 198, 201, 202, 223, 228, 229, 233, 234, 242, 251–253, 271, 272, 281, 283, 284, 313, 315–319
Presentments &c., 21, 33, 43, 117, 119, 145, 214, 273, 287, 299, 305–307, 309–311, 313, 314, 336, 357–359
GRANT
Christopher, Senr., case of his servant Cardin Drabston, . . . 125
Junr., of Watertown, case of, (fornication) . . . 125
Edward, (Grand Jury) 59, 94
Peter, (libel ag^t^. Rodriego &c.) 34
&c., case of, (piracy) 36
Scotchman, case of, (piratically seizing vessels &c.) . . 37
&c., order for execution of, ... 39
GRAVES
Marke, ag^t^. Farrington 222
Natha., Mr., (1st. Jury of trials &c.) 95
GRAVESNER. (*See* GROSVENOR.)
GREATIAN. (*See* GRETIAN.)

PAGE

GREELY
Phillip, his assignee agt. Fouler 8
agt. Young 81
agt. Woodbridge 165

GREEN or GREENE
——, wharf of, at Charlestown (libel agt. Turell) 174
Bartholomew, (2d. Jury of trials) 346
Jacob, Junr., (1st. Jury of trials) 140
James, (2d. Jury for trials &c.) 79
by atty., agt. Baker 162
(Grand Jury) 345
John, (Jury of trials &c.) 32, 56
(Grand Jury) 59
marshal general, mentd. 299, 304, 306, 309–311, 320, 322, 378, 381, 387–392
Joseph, case of, ... 292–3
Nathaniel, (Jury) 160
(Grand Jury) 273
Samuel, (Jury for attaints) 266
atty., agt. Fox 368
William, agt. David &c. 109
(Jury of attaints &c.) 288
(1st. Jury of trials &c.) 289
Capt., Lampson agt., ... 329
GREENEOWAY, GEORGE, Harris agt., ... 46
GREENLEAFE, ENOCK, agt. Gilbert 48

GREENOUGH or GREENOW
Samuell, &c., appraisers, (Elliot &c. agt. ketch Friendship) (execn.) . 392
William, (Grand Jury) 202
Capt., (Jury of trials) 322

GREENWOOD
Isaac, &c., owners &c., Black agt., ... 324
Nathaniel, &c. agt. How 183
agt. Sears 219
appraisers, (libel &c. agt. Ship Dove &c.) (execn.) . 373
(libel &c. agt. Long) (execn.) 375
(libel &c. agt. Checkly & wife) (execn.) . 385–6
Tho., (2d. Jury for trials &c.) 121

GREITIAN GRETIAN or GREATIAN.
—— case of, mentd. in margin 233
Thomas, Mr., master of pink Expectation, &c., (libel &c.) 149, 150, 177–8
Torrey agt., ... 180, 193, 226, 246
Sweatie agt., ... 182
agt. Sweathy 182, 190

PAGE

GRETIAN, etc., *continued.*

Thomas, principal on bond of attaint (Sweatie ag[t]. Gretian) . . 182
(Gretian ag[t]. Sweathy &c) . 182–3
ag[t]. Staynor 183, 191
Staynor ag[t]., ... 206
his surety ag[t]. Webb, marshal, ... 207
principal on bond of attaint (Torrey ag[t]. Gretian) . . 226
by atty., ag[t]. Torrey 232
mariner &c. of pink Expectation (libel &c.) (exec[n].) . . 378–9

GREY

Robert, overseers &c. of his children ag[t]. Manning (exec[n].) . . 376
Manning ag[t]., " 376

GRIDLEY

——, widow, Bennet ag[t]., ... 69
Elisabeth, widow, " " 82
Joseph, Davis ag[t]., ... 239
(order as to Edw[d]. Crocket) 243

GRIFFIN (Dutch prize) ment[d]. (Lemoigne ag[t]. White &c.) 129

GRIFFIN or GRIFFYN

John, ag[t]. Gove 98–9
ag[t]. Knight 267
Rice, of Boston, laborer, (case of Bridget Denmarke) 358
Richard, of Boston, gun smith, case of, (murder &c.) . 314, 315, 320

GRIGGS or GRIGS

Joseph, (Jury for trial of attaint) 134
(2[d]. Jury of trials &c.) 135
(1st. " " " ") 203
(Jury of trials) 302, 306, 308
William, (1st. Jury for appeals &c.) 108
ag[t]. Chocke 140
(Jury of attaints) 244
(2[d]. Jury of trials &c.) 245
(Jury of trials) 302, 311, 319
(Special Jury) 363
Checkley ag[t]., ... 369, 370

GRIMES

George, &c., case of, (coining of base money) 22
bond by, ... 22

GROSS, SYMON, (Jury of attaints &c.) 288

GROSVENOR or GRAVESNER

John, (Jury for attaints) 267
(Petit Jury) 323

GROTON (Town of)

Zeckariah Crispe of, ... 51
ment[d]. (case of Old Jethro, Indian,) 54

GROVER, JOTHAM, of Boston, brasier, ag[t]. Bulkley 303

PAGE

GUILE, SAMUEL, of Haverhill, case of, (rape) 50
GUNNOP. (*See* GINNOP.)
GYFFORD. (*See* GIFFORD.)

HABERFEILD, WM., of Bristol, (libel &c. ag[t]. Allin) 105–6
HADDOCK (or SHADDOCK), WM., Inglesby ag[t]., ... 291
HADLY (Town of), Wm. Webster of, ... 229, 233
HAGAR, WM., (1st Jury for trials &c.) 203
HALE, MARY, of Boston, widow, case of, (witchcraft) 188–9
HALF WAY ROCK in Mass. Bay ment[d]. . . 305, 307, 309, 310, 312, 313, 315, 317
HALGEN, JACOB, &c., mariners of pink Endeavor (libel &c.) 117, 118
HALL
——, Leift., &c., comm[rs]., (order for dower to widow of Hill) . 147
Elizabeth, & husband Richard ag[t]. Weld 163
Richard (Jury of trials &c.) 33
(Grand Jury) 53, 65, 242, 266, 298
(libel &c. ag[t]. ship Nevis factor) 76
& wife Elizabeth ag[t]. Weld 163
(Jury of attaints) 255
(2[d] Jury for appeals) 256
William, who married Sarah Fowler of Boston, wine retailer, ag[t]. Backway 350
HALSEY
James, Wing ag[t]., ... 206
(2[d] Jury for trials &c.) 121
HAMLIN
Esther (widow &c. of Tho[s]. Platts) and husband Thomas, Brentnal ag[t]., 326
Thomas, and wife Esther, Brentnal ag[t]., ... 326
HAMOND
——, Capt., &c., answer to pet. of, ... 62
Elisabeth, Phipps ag[t]., ... 113
John, Dix ag[t]., ... 108
(Jury for attaints) 233, 256
(Jury for trials &c.) 233
(2[d]. Jury for appeals) 256
Lawrence, Capt., & wife Margaret, Bellingham ag[t]., ... 157
Margaret, execx., & husband Lawrence, " " 157
Thomas, (Jury of trials) 345
(Jury) 360
HAMPSHIRE, COUNTY OF, Northampton in 33
HAMPSHIRE COUNTY COURT. (*See* COUNTY COURT HAMPSHIRE.)
HAMPTON (Town of)
County Court at, (Martyn &c. ag[t]. Winsly &c.) 5
(Pike ag[t]. Gove) 6
(Roby &c. ag[t]. Evins) 6
(Winsly ag[t]. Martyn) 6
(Roby &c. ag[t]. Colcord) 7
(Hampton ag[t]. Tilton) 7

PAGE

HAMPTON (Town of), *continued.*
by atty^{s}. ag^{t}. Tilton 7
County Court at, (Gove, assignee, ag^{t}. Fouler) 8
(Batt ag^{t}. Severans) 9
Wm. Bacon &c. ag^{t}., ... 19
by atty., ag^{t}. Huggens 43
County Court at, (Gilman ag^{t}. Foulsham) 68
(Sexton ag^{t}. Winslow) 68
& Salisbury Courts, appointment of Hauthorn to keep, ... 127
County Court at, (Clarke ag^{t}. Allin) 135
(Boulter &c. ag^{t}. Wilson) 136
(Roby &c. ag^{t}. Evans) 136

HANCKOCK or HANCOCK
Nathaniel, (Jury for trials &c.) 228
&c., Holman &c. ag^{t}., ... 289

HANNAH (Negro) case of, ... 151–2

HARBOR
of Boston ment^{d}. (case of ship Speedwell &c.) 107
privateer in, (case of Lorphelin) 146
brigantine Samuel in, ... 358
of St. Mallo ment^{d}. (libel &c. ag^{t}. ship William) 333

HARDING
Joseph, two hogsheads of Irish yarn in hands of, (libel &c.) . . 177
Ruth, house of, (case of Pomery) 242

HARE
David, case of his wife Mary, ... 126
Josiah, commander of ship John & Mary, (libel &c. ag^{t}. Smith) . . 41
Mary, wife of David Hare, case of, (adultery & infanticide) . . 126

HARRIS
John, Batt ag^{t}., ... 20, 28
(1st. Jury for trials &c.) 70
Richard, ag^{t}. Batt 94
(Jury) 160
(Jury for attaints) 180
Parris ag^{t}., ... 250
Mr., of Braintree, &c., sureties on bond of attaint, (Homes ag^{t}. Cheeckley) 282
of Boston, Stanbury ag^{t}., ... 367
Thomas, ag^{t}. Greeneoway 46
butcher, ag^{t}. Long 193
William, (2^{d}. Jury for trials &c.) 45
(Jury for trials &c.) 53
Turner ag^{t}., ... 83
Mr., of Boston, (Cary &c. ag^{t}. ketch Elizth. & Margaret) . 106
(1st. Jury of trial &c.) 161
by atty., ag^{t}. Stoakes 196
master, (libel &c. ag^{t}. ship Richard) 335

PAGE

HARRISON
——, Mr., &c., sureties on bond of attaint, (Rauson ag^t. Gilbert) . 245
John, Senr., Wooddy ag^t., ... 60
(Grand Jury) 108, 133
(Grand Jury) 243
William, ag^t. Platts 237, 238, 245, 254–5
found guilty of breach of the peace 292
HARWOOD
John, Mr., his assignee &c., Usher ag^t., ... 237
exec^rs. of Usher ag^t., ... 237
Senr., ag^t. Burton 257
Nathaniel, assignee &c., exec^rs. of Usher ag^t., ... 237
Rachel, & husband Thomas, Bigg ag^t., ... 339, 340
Tay ag^t., ... 369
Thomas, ag^t. Toy 257
(Grand Jury) 302, 305, 361
& wife Rachel, Bigg ag^t., ... 339, 340
Tay ag^t., ... 369
HASTING or HASTINGS
John, (2^d. Jury of trials) 346
Samuel, (Jury of trials) 302, 306, 308
Thomas, (Jury of trials) 35
(Grand Jury) 35, 56, 65
Mr., (Grand Jury) 108
Walter, (Grand Jury) 65
HATHORN HATHORNE or HAUTHORN, HAUTHORNE, HAWTHON, HAWTHORN, HAWTHORNE
——, Major, (Lattimore ag^t. James &c.) 20
——, " &c. fined 52
——, Mr., present at Court 13 Sept. 1676 70
——, Capt., certificate & payment for service under, ... 104
——, Major, &c., declaration by, (Putman, &c. pltf^s.) 123
——, " appointed to keep Hampton & Salisbury Courts &c. . 127
——, " fine remitted ment^d. in margin 147
John, Gifford ag^t., ... 28, 48, 49
Esqr., present at Court, ... 251, 255, 273, 287, 296, 305, 320, 326, 345, 359
Nathaniel, & his mother Sarah ag^t. Roades 215
Sarah, widow, & son Nathaniel " " 215
William, Esqr. or Major,
present at Court, 1, 16, 23, 24, 33–35, 43, 52, 65, 76, 77, 91, 92, 94, 107, 117, 119, 128, 130–132, 139, 373
&c., fined 90
HAUFORD, SAMUEL, trustees &c. of Emery ag^t., ... 122
HAUGH
Anna, ag^t. Hill 287
Hannah, widow, ag^t. Willis 223
Mrs., ag^t. Hill 283

PAGE

HAUGHTON. (*See* HOUGHTON.)
HAUKES. (*See* HAWKES.)
HAUKINS. (*See* HAWKINS.)
HAUTHORN / HAUTHORNE } (*See* HATHORN.)
HAVERHILL (Town of)
Samuel Guile of, ... 50
Robert Swann agt., ... 156
Senr. of, ... 327
Michael Emmerson of, ... 357
HAWARD. (*See* HAYWARD.)
HAWES
Obadiah, (2d. Jury for trials &c.) 18, 135, 224
(Jury of trials) 57
(Jury for trial of attaint) 184
HAWKES or HAUKES
John, principal on bond of attaint (Apelton &c. agt. Hawkes &c.) . 236
Senr., &c., Apelton &c. agt., ... 236–7
&c. agt. Apleton &c. 243
Moses, &c., Apelton &c. agt., ... 236–7
HAWKINS or HAUKINS
James, mariner, (libel &c. agt. ship Nevis factor) 76
of Boston, bricklayer, Walker agt., ... 347
Mary, case of, second punishment remitted 31
Thomas, Sheaffe agt., ... 68
of Boston, mariner, case of, (piracy) . . 305, 306, 320, 322
mentd. (case of Wm. Neffe) 321
HAWTHON / HAWTHORN / HAWTHORNE } (*See* HATHORN.)
HAWTO (or OTTO), PEETER, Capt., &c., attys., agt. White &c. 129
HAYWARD / HAYWORD } or HAWARD, HOWARD, HEYWARD, HEYWOOD
Anthony, (1st. Jury for trials &c.) 59
Mr., &c. chosen constables for Boston & oath 80
(Jury) 150, 171
his execrs. agt. Eyres 324
John, (Jury for trial of attaint) 2
(2d. Jury for trials &c.) 3
of Concord, &c. sureties, bond by, (case of Benj. Symons) . 73
atty., estate of Johnson agt., ... 95
Roberts agt., ... 269
Pearce agt., ... 279
of Roxbury, mercht., agt. Bulkley 352
(Special Jury) 363
Nicholas, quartermaster of ship Resolution, &c., Poole agt., . . 211
Aires agt., . 211, 212
Johnson agt., . . 212
Knaps agt., . 212, 213

PAGE

HAYWORD, etc., *continued.*
Robert, (2d. Jury of trials &c.) . . . 141
(Jury of trials &c.) . . . 228
(Special Jury) . . . 363
HEARSY or HERSE
John, &c., agt. County Court judgment as to will of Richards . . 291
Wm., (Grand Jury) . . . 108
HEATH
Josiah, White agt., . . . 142
Peleg, &c., mariners, case of, (piracy) . . . 319, 320
Thomas, Knight agt., . . . 113
HECTOR (Negro) mentd. (libel &c. agt. Checkly & wife) (execn.) . . . 384
HEINSHAW. (*See* HENSHAW.)
HELGERSON, INGERMAN, Wilkins agt., . . . 215
HELLIER. (*See* HILLER.)
HEMAN
Nathaniel, agt. Chapen . . . 260
Sam., (Grand Jury) . . . 242
HEMLOCK
Samuel, of Boston, mariner, Mountjoy agt., . . . 325
agt. Mountjoy . . . 341
HENCHMAN or HINCHMAN
Daniel, Capt., (Grand Jury) . . . 139
&c., guardians, plaintiffs, (est. of children of Hitt) . 153
Jno., Newby agt., . . . 226
HENDERSON or HINDERSON
Jno., house of, in Salem (case of John Dounton) . . . 272
Wm., Waldron agt., . . . 119
Tare agt., . . . 206
HENDRICK
Abraham, (cancelled), White agt., . . . 142
Jonathan, (Jotham?), agt. Davis . . . 278
Jotham, White agt., . . . 142
agt. Davis . . . 278
HENNEWAY or HENNOWAY
John, (1st. Jury for trials &c.) . . . 44
(2d. Jury for appeals &c.) . . . 108
(Jury of trials) . . . 362
HENSHAW or HEINSHAW
Daniel, agt. Voss . . . 185
Voss agt., . . . 187
HERBERT, JOHN, agt. Clarke & Co. . . . 80
HERRINGTON
Daniel, (Jury for appeals) . . . 233
(Jury for attaints) . . . 233
Robert, (2d. Jury for trials &c.) . . . 3, 153
(1st. " " " ") . . . 44, 78

PAGE

HERRINGTON, *continued*.
Robert, (Grand Jury) 180, 266
Samuel, (2d. Jury of trials &c.) 346
HERRON (ship), mariners of, (libel &c.) 159
HERSE. (*See* HEARSY.)
HESKETT. (*See* HISKETT.)
HEWEN, HEWENS, HEWIN, HEWINS } or HUINGS
Jacob, (Jury for trial of attaint) 3, 134
(1st Jury for trials &c.) 3
(2d. Jury for trials &c.) 96, 135
Senr., (Grand Jury) 214
(Grand Jury) 244
HEYDEN, EBENEZAR, Miles agt., ... 6
HEYMAN
John, &c., Bonner agt., ... 1
(Jury of trials &c.) 33
(Grand Jury) 44, 78, 180
Nathan, (Jury) 150
costs granted him agt. Moore 188
HEYNES
Jonathan, agt. Toppan 66
Robert, Lee agt., ... 194
Sanctillo (or Samvillo), of Island of St. Christophers, est. of, mentd. (libel agt. Keech &c.) 300–1
HEYWARD, HEYWOOD } (*See* HAYWARD.)
HICKS. (*See* HIX.)
HIDE, JOB, (1st Jury for trials &c.) 95
HILL
Abraham, Haugh agt., ... 283, 287
(Jury of trials) 345
(Jury) 360
Isaac, (Jury for attaint) 181
(2d. Jury for trials &c.) 181
James, (Grand Jury) 232, 266, 298
Joseph, Mr., mentd. (order for dower to widow of Hill) 147
Thomas, agt. Obbinson 151, 161, 180
Lamb agt., ... 187
Valentine, Mr., widow of, order for dower 147
HILLER or HELLIER
Joseph, agt. Burrowes 281
bond of, chanceried 287
HILLS, JOSEPH, &c., Dumer agt., ... 44
HILTON, WM., Mr., (1st. Jury of trials &c.) 25
HINCHMAN. (*See* HENCHMAN.)

PAGE

HINDERSON. (*See* HENDERSON.)

HISKETT or HESKETT
- Daniel, Coxe agt., ... 291
- George, of Boston, mariner, Smith agt., ... 339
- Steven, Patteshall agt., ... 292

HITCHINS, DANIEL, agt. Browne 276

HITT, ANNE, children of, as to est. of, ... 153

HIX or HICKS
- Francis, &c., mariners &c. of ship Michael, agt. Loyd &c. . . . 150–1
- Richard, " " " " " " " " " . . . 150–1
- Samuel, (Jury for trials &c.) 228
  - (Jury for attaints) 255
  - (1st. Jury for appeal) 257
  - (Petit Jury) 323
- Zachariah (Jury of trials &c.) 32, 228, 252

HOAR or HOARE
- Daniel, &c., objections agt. Remington as juryman 71
  - of Concord, case of, (murder of Indians) 72
  - his atty. &c. agt. Kilcup 219
- John, assignee, agt. execx. &c. of Cook 164
  - agt. Cooke, execx., &c. 166
  - Mr., atty. &c., agt. Kilcup 219
- Wm., (1st. Jury for trials &c.) 203

HOBBEY. (*See* HOBBY.)

HOBBS, JNO., Rouland agt., ... 27

HOBBY or HOBBEY
- William, (Jury for trial of attaint) 134
  - (2d. Jury for trials &c.) 135, 362

HODGES, HUMPHRY, (Jury of trials &c.) 32

HODSDAL or HODSDALE HODSDALL
- Charles, pilot of ship Nevis factor, (libel &c.) 63–4

HOFFE, SAM., (1st Jury for trials &c.) 78

HOLBROOK or HOLBROOKE HOLDBROOKE
- Experience, servant, (case of Wm. Cheny) 199
- John, (Jury) 37
  - (2d. Jury for trials &c.) 45
  - Capt., (Grand Jury) 273
  - (Petit Jury) 323
- Sam., (Jury of attaints &c.) 288
  - (1st. Jury for appeals &c.) 289

HOLDING, JUSTINIAN, (Grand Jury) 17

HOLIOKE. (*See* HOLYOKE.)

PAGE

HOLLAND
James, Marrett ag[t]., ... 347
Josiah, (2[d]. Jury of trials) 346
Nath., (1st. " " ") 215
HOLLAWAY. (*See* HOLLOWAY.)
HOLLIOCK / HOLLIOK (*See* HOLYOKE.)
HOLLOWAY (or HOLLAWAY), Henry, master of ship Apollow, &c., Marston &c. ag[t]., 132–3
HOLLOWELL or HOLOWELL
Benjamin, &c., Butler ag[t]., ... 140, 164
(exec[n].) 380–382
ag[t]. Butler (exec[n].) 380–382
Mary, (whom Edw[d]. Ashley married) ment[d]. (Hollowell &c. ag[t]. Butler) (exec[n].) 380
William, Jun[r]., &c., Butler ag[t]., ... 140
&c., Butler ag[t]., ... 164
Jun[r]., &c., Butler ag[t]., (exec[n].) 380–382
ag[t]. Butler (exec[n].) 380–382
HOLMAN
Abraham, &c. ag[t]. Michelson 218
(Jury of trials) 242
&c. ag[t]. Hanckock &c. 289
testimony by, ment[d]. (Cambridge Selectmen ag[t]. drummers of Cambridge) 289
Jerremiah, &c., testimony by, ment[d]. (Cambridge Selectmen ag[t]. drummers of Cambridge) 289
HOLMES or HOMES
———, Mr., atty., (Clarke ag[t]. Smith) 236
Joseph, (Jury for trial of attaint) 2
(2[d]. Jury for trials &c.) 3
atty. &c., ag[t]. Keene 181
deed of, ment[d]. (Heinshaw ag[t]. Voss) 185
ment[d]. (Sandford ag[t]. Orchard) 196
atty., ag[t]. Gretian 206
Wayt, marshal, ag[t]., ... 207, 208, 226
(Jury) 210
ag[t]. Sweathy 238, 244
principal on bond of attaint (Homes ag[t]. Sweathy) . . 238
(Grand Jury) 242
&c., sureties on bond of attaint, (Perkins ag[t]. Fenno) . . 257
(Adams ag[t]. Baker) . . 260
ag[t]. Sheffeild 261, 266
principal on bond of attaint (Homes ag[t]. Sheffeild) . . 261
ag[t]. Russell 270
Cole ag[t]., ... 279
ag[t]. Cheeckley 282
Sen[r]. & Jun[r]., case of, (accessory to theft) 285–6

PAGE

HOLMES or HOMES, *continued.*
Joseph, &c., Checkley ag^t., ... 287
Junr., ag^t. Olliver 290
of Boston, Sheffeild ag^t., (exec^n.) 386–388
Mr., &c., appraisers, (Hundlocke ag^t. Baker &c.) (exec^n.) . 390–1
Nathaniel (2^d Jury for trials &c.) 45
(1st Jury for appeals &c.) 108
Samuel, ag^t. Dudson 204
Thomas, ag^t. Clarke 152
HOLOWELL. (*See* HOLLOWELL.)
HOLT, ROBERT, Mr., Saffyn ag^t., ... 187
HOLTON
Mary, pet. for divorce by her husband Samuel 197
Samuel, of North Hampton, pet. for divorce 197
HOLYOKE or HOLIOKE, HOLLIOCK, HOLLIOK
———, Mr., foreman, (Cooke exec^x., &c. ag^t. Olliver) 179
Elizur, Mr., (2^d Jury of trials &c.) 161
Thwing &c. ag^t., ... 248
foreman, (Jury of trials) . 302, 306, 308, 310, 312, 314, 316, 319
Mr., foreman, (case of Hannah Hutchinson &c.) 304
foreman, (case of Thomas Hawkins &c.) 306–7
(2^d Jury of trials) 337
HOME, JOSEP, &c., bond by, (Harrison ag^t. Platts) 245
HOMES. (*See* HOLMES.)
HOOKE, WM., Mr., ag^t. Pike 154
HOOPER, BARTHOLMEW, carpenter of ship Nevis factor, (libel &c.) . . 63–4
HOPE (bark or ship)
owner of, libel &c. ag^t. Goose 148
master &c. of, libel &c. ag^t. Campbell 148
of Boston, master of, libel of Randolph, Coll^r., ag^t., ... 210
ment^d. (bond by Shrimpton &c.) 211
HOPEWELL (ketch or pink)
master of, libel ag^t. Starr &c. 23
ment^d. (libel ag^t. Haughton) 39
(libel ag^t. Measure) 42
formerly the Nightingall (libel &c. ag^t. Shice) 56
owner of, libel &c. ag^t. Skinner 92
HOPKINS
Bartholmew, master of ship Lixborn Merchant, (libel &c.) . . . 92–3
(case of Kirby) . 93
Charles, of Boston, assault &c. (case of Richd Lillie) 358–9
Margaret, widow of Charles Hopkins, (case of Richd Lillie) . . 359
HORSELY, ELIZABETH, of Rowley, (case of Henry Toltwood) 336
HOUGHTON or HAUGHTON
John, of Boston, mariner, case of, (stealing Indians) 86–7
answer to pet. of, ... 87
Ralph, (Grand Jury) 65, 120
Robert, of Boston, mariner &c. of ketch Hopewell, (libel &c.) . . 39, 42

PAGE

HOUNSELL, HANNAH, judgment as to maintenance of her child (case of Thomas Saffin) 249

HOVEY
Daniel, &c., admrs., Bishop agt., ... 248
Senr., of Ipswich, agt. Perkins 363
HOW
Abraham, (Jury of trials &c.) 32
(Jury for attaints) 181
(1st Jury for trials &c.) 181
Isaac, (Jury of trials) 337
Israell, (1st Jury for trials &c.) 17
John, Collecot, &c. agt., ... 183
Joseph, (Grand Jury) 59, 108, 230, 266
HOWARD. (*See* HAYWARD.)
HUBBARD
Caleb, (Grand Jury) 273
James, (2d. Jury of trials &c.) 141
(Grand Jury) 361
John, Mr., (1st. Jury of trials) 65, 152
(case of Wm. Waldron &c). 88, 91
assignee of Glover agt., ... 94
merchant, &c., Hunlorck agt., ... 292, 294
Joshua, Junr., surety on bond of attaint, (Joy &c. agt. Leveret) . . 186
HUDSON
Francis, (Grand Jury) 133
James, Ruggles agt., ... 65
William, Smith agt., ... 44
Capt., agt. Leveret 48
agt. Messenger 84
Capt., agt. Ruming 101
HUDSONS LANE (or Wing Lane) in Boston 389, 390
HUGGENS, JNO., Town of Hampton agt., ... 43
HUGHES, ——, Dr. &c., interpreters, (libel agt. Andreason &c.) . . 264
HUGHSON. (*See* HUSON.)
HUINGS. (*See* HEWINS.)
HULING, JOHN, master of ship Maydenhead, &c. (libel &c.) 176
HULL
John, Treasurer &c., (case of Jno. Earthy) 88
Capt., agt. Wincoll 122
Mr., Treasurer &c., order to pay Hauthorne 127
Esqr., present at Court, 149, 150, 151, 159–161, 169, 170, 172, 173, 176, 178, 179, 190, 202, 208, 211, 213, 214, 223, 228–230, 231, 232

HUMFREY or / HUMPHRY / HUMPHRYS
Hopestill, (Jury of trials) 302, 311, 319
Thomas, appointed constable at Kennebec 12

PAGE

HUNDLOCK / HUNDLOCKE } or HUNLOCKE, HUNLORCK
Edward, Baker ag[t]., ... 278
by atty., ag[t]. Hubbard &c. 292
Mr., his wife & atty. ag[t]. Hubbard &c. 294
ag[t]. Baker &c. (exec[n].) 389–391
Margaret, Mrs., atty., ag[t]. Hubbard &c. 294
HUNKIN, REBECKAH, assignee of Cooke for, Sheaffe ag[t]., ... 45
HUNLOCKE / HUNLORCK } (*See* HUNDLOCK.)
HUNT
Jabez, mariner &c. of ship Anne (libel &c.) 93–4
John, &c., testimony of, ment[d]. (case of Mrs. Hope Ambrose) . . 127
HUNTING, SAMUEL, of Charlestown, case of, (manslaughter) 114
HURD
Jacob, (Jury for trials of attaint) 191
(1st Jury for trials &c.) 192, 224
John, Perry ag[t]., ... 215, 216
HURTLEBERRY HILL, Indians murdered at, (case of Wilder) 71–2
HUSBAND & WIFE
special verdict as to legacy (Chapman ag[t]. Barry) 205
(case of Dorcas & Hugh March) 127
HUSON (or HUGHSON), THOMAS, surety for Roope ag[t]., ... 112
HUSSEY, STEVEN, (case of George Cole &c.) 12
HUTCHINSON
———, Capt., answer to pet. of, ... 32
Edward, Capt., Sands ag[t]., ... 17
Eliakim, ag[t]. Payne 28
Scottow ag[t]., ... 186
(Grand Jury) 230, 255
Elisha, Lef[t]. (1st. Jury for trials &c.) 44
&c., owners of ship Salamander, Woodman ag[t]., ... 61
(Grand Jury) 119
Capt, &c., chosen comm[rs]. for Boston, approved by the Court, and oath, 168, 199, 214
Esq[r].; present at Court, 255, 266, 273, 287, 297, 298, 300, 302, 305, 320–322, 327, 336, 345, 359
Dyre ag[t]., ... 261
&c. ag[t]. Fyfield &c. 325
George, Mr., by atty., (libel of Randolph) 168–9
order on pet. of, ... 175
libel &c. of Randolph, Coll[r]., ag[t]., ... 209
Hannah, wife of Sam[l]. Hutchinson, case of, (abetting &c. the murder of Hannah Stone) 304
Samuel, of Andover, case of his wife Hannah 304
HYDES, JONATHAN, (2[d]. Jury for trials &c.) 153
HYLLIARD, EDWARD, &c., seizing vessels &c. of, (case of Andreson) . . 36

PAGE

IMPRESSING (certificate & order for payment for service under Capt. Hathorn) 104
IMPRESSMENT, special verdict as to, (Griffyn agt. Gove) 99
IMPRISONMENT. (*See* PUNISHMENT.)
INCENDIARISM. } (*See* CRIMES.)
INCESTUOUS PRACTICES. } (*See* CRIMES.)
INDIAN }
INDIANS }
Tom, case of, (rape) 21
from Marlborough, &c., Grand Jury summoned for trial of, . . . 52
James (alias Acompanut), case of, (murder) 53
John, of Marlborough, case of, (murder) 53
Joseph Spoonhaut, case of, (murder) 53
Little Jno., case of, (murder) 53
Mampaus nackosut, case of, (murder) 53
Reup, of Marlborough, case of, " 53
at Lancaster (case of John Indian) 53
David &c., order as to, ... 54
James Nanapatu, case of, (murder) 54
old Jethro, case of, (abusive speeches) 54
John (alias Anusquenut), case of, (murder) 54
(alias Mucksumquenut), case of, (murder) 54
Muckscumpey, case of, (murder) 54
Peter (alias Paguskmenut), case of, (murder) 54
Thomas (alias Mumucksuncasusucquater), case of, (murder) . . 54
killing of, (case of Geo. Robbins &c.) 57
persons ordered to march with the forces [agt. the Indians] . . 58
murder of, (case of Stephen Goble &c.) 71–2
Caleb &c., case of, (being open & murderous enemies) 76
Calumbine &c., case of, " 76
stealing and selling of, (case of Wm. Waldron &c.) 86–88, 91
war with, mentd. (case of Walter Gendall &c.) 102
mentd. (Elliot agt. Dauson) 156
Jno. Ahattawants, murder of, (case of Jno. Dyar) 188
Jno. Neponet, trial of, mentd. 214
Indian boy in controversy (Epps agt. Bennet) 259
Joseph, of Martins Vineyard, case of, (murder) 295–6
found guilty of cruelty to his wife 296
jury one half English and one half Indian (case of Jos. Indian). . 296
Joseph Pittymee sworn as interpreter 296
Indian trade mentd. (libel &c. agt. ship St. John frigott) 353
powder &c. sold to, (case of Josiah Littlefield &c.) 356–7
INFANTICIDE. (*See* CRIMES.)
INFERIOR COURT mentd. (Butler agt. Checkley) 206
INGLESBY OR ENGLESBE
Nicholas, (Jury for attaints) 267
by atty., agt. Shaddock 291
INGOLLS, SAMUEL, agt. Bishop 262–3

PAGE

INGRAM
William, (Jury of trials &c.) 32
(Grand Jury) 53
INTERPRETER (Indian), Joseph Pittymee sworn as, ... 296
IPSWICH (Town of)
County Court at, 8, 9, 20, 21, 26–29, 45, 48, 49, 59, 60, 66, 80, 82, 97, 108, 110, 111, 124, 125, 134, 136, 138, 139, 156, 162, 163, 165, 180, 183, 184, 187, 194, 195, 205, 207, 214, 220, 221, 233, 238, 239, 240, 247, 256, 269, 273, 274, 276, 278, 281, 331, 341, 347, 348, 363, 364, 367. (*See* also County Court Essex.)
Court ment^d. (Knight ag^t. Leach &c.) 184
(case of Elis^th. Maning) 240
costs at, (March ag^t. Carr) 367
Robert Lord, marshal of, ... 155
ment^d. (Ingolls ag^t. Bishop) 263
Mr. Jon^a. Wade of, ... 265
John Newmarsh of, ... 331
Peter Berry, &c., of, ... 331
Chebacco of, John Burnam &c. of, ... 345
Thomas Dennis &c. of, ... 347
Capt. Stephen Cross of, ... 348
John Fairfield of, ... 348
Giles Seres of, ... 352
Daniel Hovey of, ... 363
Daniel Davison, Junr., of, ... 364
Edmond Potter of, ... 364
IRELAND
Londonderry in, ... 41
sentence to return to, (case of Hugh Mulligan) 280
IRON WORKS, owners of, Gold &c. ag^t., ... 27
ISAAC or
ISACK
Samuell, master &c. of ship George, &c. (libel &c.) 173–4
ISLAND OF JERSEY. (*See* JERSEY, ISLAND OF.)
ISLAND OF NANTUCKET. (*See* NANTUCKET.)
ISLAND OF ST. CHRISTOPHERS. (*See* ST. CHRISTOPHERS, ISLAND OF.)
ISLE OF MAY ment^d. (libel &c. ag^t. Branson) 175
ISLE OF PERSY ment^d. (libel &c. ag^t. ship St. John Frigott) 353
IVES, MICHAEL, (Grand Jury) 94

JACK (Negro)
servant to Faireweather, case of, (bestiality) 74
servant to Woolcot, case of, (arson) 198
JACKLIN
Samuel, Mr., &c. chosen constables at Boston & oath 80
(Jury for Trials of attaint) 191
Wm. Roby instead of, (1st. Jury of trials &c.) 192

PAGE

JACKLIN, *continued.*
Samuel, ag^{t}. Pemberton 268
ag^{t}. Parris 274

JACKSON
Abraham, (Jury for attaints) 181
(1st. Jury of trials &c) 181
Edmund, [S], (Grand Jury) 1
Edward, (1st. Jury for trials &c.) 203
John, (2^{d}. Jury for trials &c.) 121, 161, 224
(Jury of trials &c.) 252
Jonathan, &c., Randolph ag^{t}., ... 160

JACOB
Henry, gunner, pet. of, ment^{d}. (Lemoigne ag^{t}. White &c.) . . . 129
John, ag^{t}. Gale 223
Nathaniel, ag^{t}. Fellowes &c. 137

JACOBSON, PETER, &c., by atty., ag^{t}. Winslow 29
JACQUIS, HENRY, &c. ag^{t}. Kent 207

JAMAICA
ment^{d}. (Cary &c. ag^{t}. ketch Elisabeth & Margaret) 106
(case of Mrs. Hope Ambrose) 127
(Marston &c. ag^{t}. Hollaway &c.) 132
(case of Elizabeth Street) 227
(order on pet^{n}. of Phillip Goss) 326

JAMES (Indian)
(alias Acompanut), case of, (murder) 53
(Aasanemeset), (Jury) 22
(Nanapatu), case of, (murder) 54

JAMES
Erasmus, &c., (Marblehead Commons), Bartlet ag^{t}., ... 20
Lattimore ag^{t}., ... 20

JAMES FRYGOT (ship), mariners &c. of, (libel &c.) 128
JAMES & HANNAH (bark), ment^{d}. (case of Wm. Johnson) 242
JAMET, JAQUES, &c., confession by, ment^{d}. (libel &c., ag^{t}. ship Marquis of Royan) 355

JARVIS, ZECHARIAH, Edwards ag^{t}., ... 331

JEFFERYES or JEFFRY
David, Mr., (Petit jury) 323
David, (Special jury) 363

JEFFRYS (or JEOFFERYS) CREEK, John Knights of, ... 252

JEMPSON
John, (Indian), Sarah wife of, ment^{d}. (case of Tom Indian) . . 22
Sarah, wife of John Jempson (Indian), ment^{d}. (case of Tom Indian) . 22

JENKINS
Henry, Mr., answer to pet. of, ... 200, 201
Joell, ag^{t}. Waldron 78
ment^{d}. (case of Mr. Isaac Waldron) 89

PAGE

JENNER
Thomas, (Grand Jury) 53, 94, 151, 298
(1st. Jury of trials &c.) 140
Mr., (Jury) 176
(Jury for attaints) 181, 267
Mr., (2d. Jury for trials &c.) 224
Capt., (Grand Jury) 243
JENNISON
Samuel, (Jury) 210, 300
(Jury of trials) 299
JEOFFERYS CREEK. (*See* JEFFRYS CREEK.)
JERSEY (ISLAND OF)
ship Martha of, ... 230
John Blaine of, ... 292
Jacob Seale of, ... 333
JESSON
Jacob, (2d. Jury for trials &c.) 45
case of, (obstructing the jury) 55
Mr., agent &c., (libel &c.) 76
JETHRO, OLD, (Indian), case of, (abusive speeches) 54
JEWELL, NATHANLL., of Boston, mariner, Clay agt., ... 341
JEWETT
Maximillian, &c., case referred to, (Hooke agt. Pike) 154
Nehemiah, Shatswell agt., ... 205, 214
JOANES. (*See* JONES.)
JOHN (Indian)
of Marlborough, case of, (murder) 53
(alias Anusquenut), case of, (murder) 54
(alias Mucksumquenut), case of, (murder) 54
JOHN & BENJAMIN (ketch)
mariners of, (libel &c.) 117
(execn.) 373, 374
JOHN & MARY (ship) of London, mate &c. of, (libel &c.) 40
JOHNS ADVENTURE (ketch &c.)
master of, Noyse agt., ... 106
Angier agt., ... 106
mariners of, agt. Craty &c. 147
JOHNSON
Abigail, (case of Darby Bryan) 114
of Boston, case of, (adultery) 115
Bethya, daughter of John Johnson, (case of Thos. Waters) . . . 158
Francis, (Grand Jury) 78, 202
Isaack, " 53
John, of Woburn (case of Thos. Waters) 158
Senr., Mills agt., ... 258
Joseph, of Boston, butcher, (case of James Morgan) 294
Marmaduke, execr. of his admx. agt. Commrs. of the United Colonies . 95
Mathew, &c., for owners of ship Dove, agt. Cannon 52

PAGE

JOHNSON, *continued.*
Mathew, atty., ag^{t}. Gardiner 100
Michael, &c., mariners of ship Herron, (libel &c.) 159, 160
Ruth, adm^{x}., her exec^{r}. ag^{t}. Comm^{rs}. of the United Colonies, . . . 95
Samuel, &c., atty^{s}., ag^{t}. Apleton 279
Thomas, &c., Davis ag^{t}., ... 195
Stoddard ag^{t}., ... 196
Townsend ag^{t}., ... 204, 205
adventurer in ship Resolution, ag^{t}. Phipps &c. 212
William, (Grand Jury) 32, 56, 59
case of, (piratically assaulting &c.) 241, 242
Esqr., present at Court, 251, 255, 266, 273, 287, 296, 297, 298, 300, 302, 305, 320–322, 327, 336, 345
Zachariah, (1st. Jury for trials &c.) 70
(Petit Jury) 323
Zachary, (1st. Jury of trials) 66
(2^{d}. " " ") 215
JOHNSTON, THOMAS, of Boston, mariner, case of, (piracy &c.) 309, 310, 320, 322
JOLLS, THOMAS, (Jury) 176
JONES or JOANES
David, (1st. Jury for trials &c.) 120
(2^{d}. " " " ") 215
(Jury of trials) 336
Dorothy, case of, (murder) 51
Isaac, (Grand Jury) 151, 230, 266, 302, 305, 336
John, Crispe ag^{t}., ... 18
mariner of ship Treble Crowne, (libel &c.) 119
Josiah (Jury for appeals) 233
(Jury for attaints) 233
Morgan, house of, (case of Maurice Bret &c.) 51
JOSEPH (Indian)
of Martins Vineyard, case of, (murder) 295
found guilty of cruelty to his wife 296
Spoonhaut, case of, (murder) 53
JOY
Ann, widow, Atkins ag^{t}., ... 21
Joseph, assignee, Wharton ag^{t}., ... 48
&c. ag^{t}. Leveret 185, 186
principal on bond of attaint (Joy &c., ag^{t}. Leveret) . . 186
&c. ag^{t}. Addams 191
Thomas, Woodmansey ag^{t}., ... 45
his assignee, Wharton ag^{t}., ... 48
(Woodmansey ag^{t}. Frost) 59
ag^{t}. Church 96
JOYLIFF or JOYLIFFE
John, Mr., &c. chosen comm^{rs}. for Boston & oath &c., 67, 96, 168, 199, 214, 357
John, surety on bond of attaint (Gifford ag^{t}. Read) 185

PAGE

JUDGMENT, entry of, declared null &c. (Porter & Apleton) 159
(*See also* MAGISTRATES.)

JUDSON
Randall, (libel ag^t. Rodriego &c.) 34
&c., order for execution of, 1 July [1675] 39
Randolph, Englishman, case of, (piratically seizing vessels) . . 38

JURY
of trials, or petit jury, for appeals &c. and for admiralty cases, list of, 3, 17, 18, 22, 25, 32, 33, 35, 36, 37, 44, 45, 53, 56, 57, 59, 60, 65, 66, 70, 71, 78, 79, 95, 96, 108, 120, 121, 135, 140, 141, 149, 150–152, 153, 160, 161, 170, 171, 176, 181, 182, 192, 193, 203, 210, 215, 223, 224, 228, 230, 231, 233, 242, 244, 245, 252, 256, 257, (266, 267?), 274, 275, 288, 289, 298, 299, 300, 302, 306, 308, 311, 319, 322, 323, 336, 337, 345, 346, 360, 362, 363
attaint of, (*See* ATTAINT.)
law as to damage &c. (Bonner ag^t. Heyman) 1
ment^d. (case of Amy Wellen) 14
(case of John Winsland) 117
(case of Ellinor May) 138
(libel ag^t. pink Expectation) 149
(order as to charges) 170
(case of Robin (Negro) &c.) 304
(case of Richard Lillie) 359
obstructing of, (case of Jacob Jesson) 55
allowance to, ... 171
of trials of attaint, list of, 2, 3, 134, 180, 181, 191, 192, 203, 215, 232, 233, 244, 255, 256, 266, 267, 288, 289
of inquest ment^d. (inquisition on body of Bickford) 33

JURY (GRAND). (*See* GRAND JURY.)

KATORE. (*See* KETORE.)

KEECH or KEETCH
John, of Boston (libel &c.) 105, 106
&c., sureties on bond of attaint, (Homes ag^t. Checkly), 282
merchant, (libel &c.) 298, 300
(petit jury) in room of Tim^o. Clarke 323
&c., sale to, (libel &c. ag^t. Long) (exec^n.) 375, 376

KEENE or KEINE, KEYNE
John, ag^t. Piper 9
Oxe ag^t., ... 124
Wisewall ag^t., ... 144
Dafforne ag^t., ... 156
Mathews ag^t., ... 181
Wm., &c., costs granted to, ... 87

KEETCH. (*See* KEECH.)

KEINE. (*See* KEENE.)

KEITH
George, &c., motion of, for a Court of Admiralty 63
libel ag^t. Davis 64

PAGE
KELLY, JOHN, prisoner debtor, sale of, (order on pet. of Sparrey) . . . 146
KELSEY, JOHN, &c., mariners of pink Endeavor, (libel &c.) . . . 117, 118
KELSO, WM., chirurgeon of ship Ann & Hesther, (libel &c.) . . . 174, 177
KEMBLE. (*See* KIMBALL.)
KEMP, ROBERT, carpenter of ship John & Mary, &c. (libel &c.) 40
KENNEBEC, EASTWARD, &c., inhab^ts^. of, (appointment of constables) . . 11, 12
KENNY, THO., negro to Francis Wyman, case of 126-7
KENT
John, master of brigantine Merrimack, (case of Pound &c.) . 308-313
Rich^d^., Dole &c. ag^t^., ... 207
William, order for Treasurer to pay to, ... 36
&c., atty^s^., trustees &c. of Emery ag^t^., ... 122
taverner, granted a license 208
KETLE. (*See* KETTLE.)
KETORE (or KATORE), JACOB, &c., mariners of ship Apollow, ag^t^. Hollaway &c. 132-3
KETTLE or KETLE, KITLE
Joseph, (Jury for trials &c.) 228, 362
(Grand Jury) 287
Samuel, (Grand Jury) 255
(Jury for attaints &c.) 191, 289
(2^d^. Jury for trials) 192, 337, 362
KEYNE. (*See* KEENE.)
KEYS, SOLOMON, &c., sureties, bond by, (case of Crispe &c.) 57
KILCUP or KILCUPP
Roger, (Jury of trials) 362
Wm., assignee of Hoare ag^t^., ... 219
KIMBALL or KEMBLE
Benja., (certificate & order for payment for service under Capt. Hathorn) 104
Henry, (2^d^. Jury for trials &c.) 25
his adm^x^. &c., owners of ship Salamander, Woodman ag^t^., . 61
Mary, adm^x^., &c., owners of ship Salamander, Woodman ag^t^., . . . 61
Thomas, &c., Barnes ag^t^., ... 120
KING
Abigaile, cart driven over, (case of James Foord) 60
Daniel, &c., guardians, Blainy ag^t^., ... 111
Elisabeth, exec^x^., &c., Blainy ag^t^., ... 111
Hezekiah, of Weymouth, bond by, ... 250
James, mariner of ship John & Mary, &c. (libel &c.) 40
Ralph, &c., guardians, Blainy ag^t^., ... 111
Junr., of Lynn, murder of, (case of Jno. Newhall &c.) . . 306-7
Samuel, his daughter Abigail ment^d^. (case of Foord) 60
Wm., case of, (blasphemy) 201
KINSLEY, ENOS, Mekins ag^t^., ... 221
KIRBEE or KIRBY
George, plaintiff, (appeal) 288

PAGE

KIRBY, etc., *continued.*
Wm., &c., seamen &c. of ship Lixborn merchant, (libel &c.) . . . 92–3
case of, (mutinous carriage) 93
KITLE. (*See* KETTLE.)
KITTERY (Town of), money due from, (order on complaint &c. of Foster) . 104
KNAPS, THOMAS, adventurer in ship Resolution, ag^{t}. Phipps &c. . . 212, 213
KNELL, PHILLIP, (Jury) 149
KNIGHT or KNIGHTS
Christopher, &c., mariners, case of, (piracy) 319, 320
Ezekel, Mr., who married widow of Valentine Hill, order for dower . 147
John, (1st. Jury for trials &c.) 44
&c., Dumer ag^{t}., ... 44
atty^{s}., ag^{t}. Dummer 108
(Jury) 176
indictment as to, ... 202
(Jury for trials &c.) 228, 252
of Jeofferys Creek, (case of Phillip Darland &c.) . . . 252–3
(Jury for attaints) 267
(Grand Jury) 345
Joseph, ag^{t}. Peacocke 135
Griffin ag^{t}., ... 267
Mary, wife of John Knights (case of Phillip Darland) 252
case of, (adultery) 252–3
prisoner, order on pet. of, ... 254
Phillip, ag^{t}. Cave 163
Richard, ag^{t}. Cutt 8
Mr., (2^{d}. Jury for trials &c.) 18
(Jury) 22, 37
adm^{r}., &c., Brattle ag^{t}., ... 100–1
ag^{t}. Heath 113
&c., atty^{s}., trustees &c. of Emery ag^{t}., ... 122
Robert, ag^{t}. Leach &c. 184, 194
Leach &c. ag^{t}., ... 202
Samuel, Blood ag^{t}., ... 279, 280
KNOWLTON, THOMAS, Fairefeild ag^{t}., ... 181

LACY
Thomas, ag^{t}. Melot 124
by atty., ag^{t}. Melott 124
in behalf of Oxe, ag^{t}. Keene 124
LAGOONE OF [TERMINOS?] in Bay of Campeachy ment^{d}. 132
LAKE
Jno., (Jury of Inquest) inquisition on body of Beckford 34
Lancelott, of Boston, Somes ag^{t}., ... 364
Mary, Mrs., widow exec^{x}. &c., adm^{r}. of Batt ag^{t}., ... 269
Tho., (Grand Jury) 53
LAKIN, WM., (Grand Jury) 78

PAGE

LAMB or LAMBE
——, &c., houses of, in Roxbury, burning of, (case of Cheffaleer, negro) 197
Abiel, for his wife late widow of Buckminster, order on est. . . . 103
&c., case of, as to, ... 158
ag[t]. Clarke 165
ag[t]. Hill 187
Clark ag[t]., ... 345
&c. ag[t]. Winthrop, Treas[r]. &c., ... 366
Caleb, (2[d]. Jury for trials &c.) 121
Joshua, of Roxbury, case of his negro servant Maria, ... 198
(Jury) 231

LAMBERT
John, master, (case of Wm. Johnson) 242
constable, " 242

LAMOIGNE. (*See* LEMOIGNE.)

LAMPSON, JOSEPH, constable of Malden, ag[t]. Green 329

LANCASTER (Town of), &c., Indians &c. of, ... 52–3

LANDER or LAUNDER
Daniel, case of, (piracy &c.) 315, 316, 320
John, &c., adm[r]. of Corwin ag[t]., ... 288

LANG
James, master of pink Endeavor, (libel &c.) 118
ment[d]. (memento) 118

LANGHORNE or LONGHORNE
Thomas, (Jury for trial of attaint) 2, 233
(2[d]. Jury for trials &c.) 3, 79, 108, 141, 153
(Jury of trials) 35, 37
(1st. Jury of trials &c.) 59, 135, 203
(Jury for appeals) 233

LARGIN, JN[o]., &c., case of, (killing of Indians) 57

LARKIN, THO., (1st Jury of trials &c.) 95

LASCIVIOUS ACTIONS. (*See* CRIMES.)

LASON, GEORGE, commander of pink Two Brothers, ag[t]. Brenton, Coll[r]. &c., 349

LATTIMORE, CHRISTOPHER, ag[t]. James &c. (Marblehead Commons) . . 20

LAUGHTON or LAUTON, LAWTON
[———, Lawton] & Bonner 1
Henry, Pecke ag[t]., ... 8
liberty granted to, (answer to motion of Leatherland) . . 21
answer to pet. of, ... 75
(case of Wm. Waldron) 86
Thomas, Mr., &c., of Lynn, cases referred to, (Lattimore ag[t]. James &c.) 20
&c., Selectmen of Lynn, Olliver &c. ag[t]., ... 111
Mr., Sen[r]., &c. ag[t]. Broune 195
Mr., &c., atty[s]., ag[t]. Browne 225

LAUNDER. (*See* LANDER.)

LAURENC
LAURENCE (*See* LAWRENCE.)

PAGE

LAUTER, ZACKERIAH, carpenter of ship Ann & Hesther, &c. (libel &c.) . . 172

LAUTON. (*See* LAUGHTON.)

LAW

as to jury (Bonner agt. Heyman) 1

point of, for the bench to determine (admr. of Coggan and wife agt. Clarke) 4

title appeals, sect. 1, mentd. in special verdict (Greely agt. Young) . 81

title conveyances, sect. 3d., mentd. in special verdict (Woodbridge agt. Williams) 83

question as to power of clerk to grant summons for another town, . 112

page 95, sect. 9, mentd. (Martin agt. Briggs &c.) 152

title firing of houses, p. 52, mentd. (case of Jack, negro,) . . . 199

title rape, p. 15, mentd. (case of Wm. Cheny) 199

anno 1674, title judgments frustrated &c., mentd. (order on pet. of John Gyfford) 231

maritime, page 93, sect. second, mentd. (Gretian agt. Torrey) . . 232

title innkeepers, mentd. (case of George Moncke) 250

title murder, mentd. (case of John Dounton) 272

title Courts, sect. 6, mentd. (case of Saml. Shrimpton) . . . 299

(*See also* MAGISTRATES, BENCH, and SPECIAL VERDICT.)

LAWRENCE or LAURENC, LAURENCE

——, Capt., case of, (affronting the Governor's warrant &c.) . . 170

——, Capt., carrying goods on board his sloop mentd. (case of Josiah Cobbham) 171

John, Junr., of Sudbury, case of, (bestiality) 87

Nicholas, master of ketch Salisbury, (information &c.) 343–4

commander, (appointment of appraisers) 356

master of ketch Salisbury, order as to appeal . . . 360

Peter, order on petn. of, ... 172

LAWTON. (*See* LAUGHTON.)

LAYTON. (*See* LEIGHTON.)

L'CORDIER, ROMAIN, master, (libel &c. agt. ship Gift of God) . . . 332

LEACH

Samuel, &c., Knight agt., ... 184, 194

agt. Knight 202

LEADBETTER

Henry, (Jury for trial of attaint) 134, 181

(1st. Jury of trials &c.) 135

(2d. " " " ") 181

(Grand Jury) 255, 287

(Jury of trials) 57

LEATHERLAND, LETHERLAND or LYTHERLAND

William, answer to motion of, ... 21

Broune agt., ... 25

agt. Porter, ... 195

LEAVER, THO., Senr., agt. Nelson 134

LE BRUNN, EDWARD, Mr., master &c. of ship Martha of Jersey, (information &c.) 230

PAGE

LECTURE
mentd. (case of Benjn. Goad) 14
(order as to execn. of Driver &c.) 33
(order for execn. of Roads &c.) 39
in Boston mentd. (case of Darby Bryan) 115
mentd. (case of Joshua Rice &c.) 240
(case of Phillip Darland) 252
(case of James Morgan) 295
(case of Saml. Shrimpton) 297

LECTURE DAY
mentd. (case of Ruth Read) 10
(case of Anna Negro) 30
at Charlestown, mentd. (case of Thomas Davis) 70
(case of Elisth. Broune) 71
mentd. (case of Peter Cole &c.) 74
(order as to warrants &c.) 200
at Salem mentd. (case of John Dounton) 272
in Boston mentd. (case of Martin Williams) 360
mentd. (case of Hannah Owen) 361

LEE
John, Gifford agt., ... 110, 124
agt. Leveret, ... 239
Joseph, agt. Heynes 194
agt. Waingright 274

LEEDS
Joseph, (2d. Jury for trials &c.) 153
(1st. " " " ") 203
(Jury for attaints) 266
(Jury for trials) 302, 311, 319, 345
(Jury) 360
Richd., (Grand Jury) 56, 59, 94

LEGG
John, &c. (Marblehead Commons), Lattimore agt., ... 20
Bartlet agt., ... 20
Nathaniel, mariner of ship Merchants Adventure, agt. Stone . . . 213
Samuel, agt. Davis 27
Flood agt., ... 110
agt. Flood 142
Mr., (1st. Jury of trials &c.) 161
(Jury) 230
agt. Lilly 247
of Boston, mariner, guardian of Gatliff agt., ... 362

LEIGHTON OR LAYTON
Thomas, Mr., &c., attys., agt. Browne 225
Tho., (Grand Jury) 273

LEMOIGNE OR LAMOIGNE
———, mentd. (case of Peter Lorphelin) 146
Barnard, Capt., by attys. agt. White &c. 129

PAGE

LETHERLAND. (*See* LEATHERLAND.)
LEUIS. (*See* LEWIS.)
LEVERET
Hudson, Captain Hudson agt., ... 48
agt. assignee of Gifford 50
atty., agt. Watts &c. 112
admr., Bullis agt., ... 113
Joy &c. agt., ... 185–6
costs agt. granted to Foule 188
atty., Joy &c. agt., ... 191
Symonds agt., ... 216, 217
Lee agt., ... 230
agt. Randolph, Collr. &c., ... 223
John, Esqr. or Govr.,
present at Court, 1, 15, 16, 23, 24, 32–34, 36, 43, 52, 55, 58, 61, 91–94, 105–107, 117, 119, 128, 133, 373
&c., petition to, ... 89
present at meeting of the Council in Boston 1 Nov. 1677 . . . 104
Fox agt., ... 125
LEVERMORE. (*See* LIVERMORE.)
LEWIS OR LEUIS
Edward, murder of, (case of Dorothy Jones &c.) 51
Samuel, Wayte agt., ... 165
LEXBON. (*See* LISBON.)
LIDGED / LIDGET / LIDGETT } OR LYDGET, LYDGETT
———, Mrs., & Co. agt. Poole &c., execution respited &c. 92
Mr. (or Mrs.), farm of, (Phips &c. agt. Bowers) 224–5
Charles, surety for Roope, agt. Hughson 112
&c., execrs., agt. Eyres 324
Elizabeth, Mrs., execx., &c. (libel &c.) 64
& Co. (answer to pet. of Jno. Poole) 94
execx. &c., Poole agt., ... 105
Mrs., Smith agt., ... 113
Peter, Mr., &c., award of, (Newman agt. Smith) 25
his execx., &c., (libel &c.) 64
of Boston, merchant & owner of ketch Content, his execx. &c., Poole agt., 105
LIFE, LIMB &c., Jury for. (*See* JURY FOR TRIALS.)
LILLIE OR / LILLY }
Edward, agt. Payne 280
of Boston, cooper, case of his son Richard 358
&c., appraisers, (libel &c. agt. Checkly & wife) (execn.) . 385–6
Richard, son of Edward Lillie, case of, (manslaughter) 358–9
Samuel, Legg agt., ... 247
(Jury of trials) 302, 311

PAGE

LIME. (*See* LYME.)
LIME HOUSE in Boston (case of Joseph Indian) 296
LINCOLNE
Sam., (case of Wm. Clapp &c.) 287
Stephen, (Grand Jury) 287
LINDE. (*See* LYNDE.)
LINDS, SAMUELL, &c. chosen constables in Boston & oath 206
LISBON or LEXBON, LIZBORNE
merchants in, (answer to pet. of Alvin Child) 12
ship Antonio of, ... 13
LISBON MERCHANT, (ship)
seamen &c. of, (libel &c.) 92–3
ment[d]. (case of Wm. Kirby) 93
LISLEY
Elizabeth, wife of Robert, pet. for divorce 131
Robert, pet. for divorce by his wife Elizabeth 132
LITTLEFIELD, JOSIAH, case of, (uttering false statements) 356
LITTLE JOHN (Indian), case of, (murder) 53
LIVERMORE or LEVERMORE
John, (Jury for attaints) 233
(Jury for trials &c.) 233
Sam., (1st. Jury of trials &c.) 161
LIXBORN MERCHANT (ship). (*See* LISBON MERCHANT (ship).)
LIZBORNE. (*See* LISBON.)
LLOYD. (*See* LOYD.)
LOBDELL, NICOLAS, (2[d]. Jury of trials &c.) 346
LOCK, WM., chirurgeon of ship John & Mary, &c. (libel &c.) 40
LODER
John, trustee of his wife Mary, Foy ag[t]., ... 368
Mary, late wife of John Loder, Foy ag[t]. her trustee 368
LOFT
Elizabeth, exec[x]., ag[t]. Oliver 337
Oliver ag[t]., ... 350
Richard, his exec[x]. ag[t]. Oliver 337
Oliver ag[t]., ... 350
LONDON (City of)
ment[d]. (answer to pet. of Mary Sanders) 31
ship John & Mary of, ... 40
Jn[o]. Sweeting of, ... 122
Sam[l]. Sheaffe of, ... 123
Mr. Edward Bass, merchant in, ... 132
voyage to, ment[d]. (libel ag[t]. Loyd &c.) 151
ship Batchellors Delight of, ... 170
ship Ann & Hester of, ... 172, 174–5
ship Resolution of, ... 173
ship Merchants Adventure of, ... 213
ship Richard of Boston bound from New England to, ... 335
Frederick Clutterbuck of, ... 335

PAGE

LONDONDERRY in Ireland ment^d. (complaint &c. ag^t. Newton &c.) . . . 41–2

LONG

Hannah, atty., Harris ag^t., ... 193

John, (Grand Jury) 35

Mr., (Jury for trial of attaint) 134

(2^d. Jury of trials &c.) 135

(Grand Jury) 151

William, master of ketch John & Benjamin, (libel &c. & exec^n.) 117, 373–5

Harris ag^t., ... 193

Zachariah, (1st. Jury for trials &c.) 44

(Jury for attaints) 255

(1st. Jury for appeal) 257

Zachary, (2^d. Jury for trials &c.) 18, 215

(Jury) 22

LONGFELLOW

Jno. (cancelled), Pickard &c. ag^t., ... 134

William, &c. ag^t. Child 112

ag^t. Oxe 112

Pickard &c. ag^t., ... 134, 143

LONGHORNE. (*See* LANGHORNE.)

LONGWORTH, THOMAS, mariner of ship George, &c. (libel &c.) 173

LORD

Richard, &c., merchants, (libel &c.) 63

Mr., &c., motion for a Court of Admiralty 63

Robert, marshal of Ipswich, Gifford ag^t., ... 155

marshal, Bishop ag^t., ... 238, 248

Samuel, ag^t. Addams 197

(Jury of trials) 337

Thomas, (1st. Jury of trials) 25

(Jury for attaints) 267

Senr., (Jury of trials) 323

Wm., his relict (Abigaile Whight) &c., Manning ag^t., ... 154

LORD COMMISSIONERS

ment^d. (libel &c. ag^t. ship Gift of God) 332

(libel &c. ag^t. ship William &c.) 333–4

of the High Court of Admiralty, appeal to, (Information ag^t. Lawrence) 344

ment^d. (libel &c. ag^t. ship St. John Frigott) 353

LORD HIGH ADMIRAL

office of, ment^d. (libel &c. ag^t. ship Gift of God &c.) 332–4

(libel &c. ag^t. ship St. John Frigott) 353

LORPHELIN or LORPHLYIN

Peeter, Frenchman, case of, (incendiarism) 145–6

LOUDEN / LOUDON (*See* LOWDEN.)

LOW, JOHN, Terti[us], atty., Cross ag^t., ... 348

PAGE

LOWDEN OR LOUDEN, LOUDON
James, (2d. Jury of trials &c.) 161
(Jury for attaints) 255
(2d. Jury for appeals) 256
case of, (slander) 363
Richard, (Jury for trial of attaint) 2
(2d. Jury for trials &c.) 3, 153
(1st. Jury for appeals &c.) 108
(Grand Jury) 190, 214, 230, 244, 266, 302, 305, 361
LOWELL OR LOWLE
Benjamin, agt. Gerrish 82
Lowle &c. agt., ... 139
John, case of, (holding a correspondency with the Dutch) 15
(2d. Jury for trials &c.) 79
Joseph, agt. Skinner 3
Richard, &c., by atty., agt. Lowle 139
LOWLE. (*See* LOWELL.)
LOYD OR LLOYD
Abraham, master &c. of ship Michael, &c., Tucker &c. agt., . 150, 151
James, assignee, &c., (libel &c.) 58
owner of pink Hopewell, (libel &c.) 92
(Jury) 160, 176
(1st. Jury of trials &c.) 203
Toy agt., ... 257
Mr., &c., appointed to appraise ketch Salisbury 356
merchant, Belchar agt., ... 362
assignee, &c., (libel &c.) (execn.) 372
LUDDEN, JOSEPH, &c., case of, ... 5
LUDKIN, ARON, (Grand Jury) 133
LUGG, SAMUEL, master of ship Expedition, &c. (libel &c.) 177
LUGGER, JNO., "clarke" of his Majesties Customs, (information &c.) . 296, 297
LUIST, ROBERT, mariner &c. of ship Providence, Waterhouse agt., . . 350
LUMAS OR LUMMAS
——— (Lord?), Bishop agt., (in margin) 238
Edward, Farley agt., ... 193
Samuell, agt. Quarles 239
LUXFORD, REUBEN, (Jury of trials) 362
LYDGET / LYDGETT (*See* LIDGET.)
LYDSTON, WM., &c., mariners of pink Endeavor, (libel &c.) . . . 117, 118
LYING. (*See* CRIMES.)
LYME OR LIME
ship Providence of, ... 40
in New England, Wm. Measure of, ... 39
LYNCH, NICHOLAS, complaint of Smith agt., ... 240, 241

PAGE

LYND } or LINDE
LYNDE }
Joseph, (Grand Jury) 24, 44
Mr., (2d. Jury for trials &c.) 203
&c., committee, (order on est. of Savage) 229
Rebeckah, Mrs., of Charlestown, (case of Anna Negro) 29
Samuel, (2d. Jury for trials &c.) 96
(Grand Jury) 305
Symon, Mr., (Grand Jury) 17, 35, 255, 287
(1st. Jury for trials &c.) 78
Wardell agt., ... 280
land of, (Hundlocke agt. Baker &c.) (execn.) 389, 390
Thomas, &c., answer to pet. of, ... 62
master of ketch Pellican, &c. (libel &c.) 62
LYNDON, AUGUSTIN, (case of Ruth Read) 10
LYNES, THOMAS, (Jury) 150
LYNN (Town of)
Mr. Thos. Laughton of, ... 20
&c., Capt. James Olliver &c. agt., ... 111, 135
by attys., agt. Browne 225
Jno. Fuller of, ... 274
by attys., agt. Apleton 279
John Newhall, tertius, &c., of, ... 306, 321, 360
John Paul of, ... 345
LYON
Jno., (Jury for attaints) 233
Peter, (2d. Jury for trials &c.) 45
(1st. " " " ") 95
(1st. Jury for appeals &c.) 274
Samuel, (Jury of attaints) 244
(2d. Jury of trials &c.) 245
LYTHERLAND. (*See* LEATHERLAND.)

MACKEE (or MAKEE), DANIEL, surety of Maze agt., ... 97
MACKLISH, JNO., carpenter's mate of ship Herron, &c. (libel &c.) 159
MACKQUINIS. (*See* MAGUINIS.)
MACOLLY, JOHN, &c., complaint of Bisco agt., ... 286
MAGISTRATE trying title of land, special verdict as to (Apleton agt. Roads), 276, 277
MAGISTRATES
declaration, order or vote by,
Bonner agt. Heyman &c. 1
case of Benanuel Bowers 3
Admr. of Coggan & wife agt. Clarke 4
Atkinson agt. Williams 5
case of Benja. Goad 10
As to constables of Kennebec 12
mentd. in margin 16
Crispe agt. Joanes 18

PAGE

MAGISTRATES, *continued.*

declaration, order or vote by,

Colcord agt. Redman 18
Complaint of Isaac Griffin 19
case of Tom Indian 22
Griffyn agt. Gove 99
case of Mary Drury 101
case of Walter Gendall 102
Dixe agt. Morse 108
Nurse agt. Endecot 120
Waldron agt. Tare 120
Hull agt. Wincoll 122
Complaint of Thomas Walters 169
Petition of George Hutchinson 175
Wharton agt. Reynolds 202
As to costs agt. Mr. Randolph 220
Phips &c. agt. Bowers 224, 225
Gretian agt. Torrey 232
case of Wm. Johnson 242
Ingolls agt. Bishop 262
Admr. of Batt agt. Lake 269
Marret agt. Cutter 275
Foy agt. trustee of Loder 368
Stanbury agt. Harris 368

&c., notice to be given by, (case of Wm. Darvall &c.) 14
&c., reflections on, (case of Bozoone Allen) 29
&c. in Boston, special Court of Assistants called by, ... 32
at a Court of Admiralty 9 Apr. 1674 (order for the Treasurer to pay Kent &c.) 36
&c. present at Court 22 Aug. [1676] 63
present at Court 7 Sept. 1677 105
&c. present at Court 17 April 1686 299
&c., pĕtition to, ... 89
&c., case referred to, (case of Wm. Pope) 104
mentd. (case of Ellinor May) 138
(Wisewall agt. Keene) 144
(Greene agt. Baker) 162
(answer to petn. of Ellinor Redding) 223
(complaint of Smith agt. Lynch) 240
(libel agt. Andreason &c.) 263
(Hundlock agt. Hubbard &c.) 294
former judgment made null (Porter & Apleton) 159
&c., confession before, (case of Geo. Russell) 169
&c., license granted to Wm. Kent 208
&c., special Court of Assistants called by, ... 251
&c. assembled in County Court, Boston, (case of Saml. Shrimpton) . 297
at Boston mentd. (Usher agt. Frizell) 302
(*See also* BENCH and SPECIAL VERDICT.)

PAGE

MAGUINIS or MACKQUINIS, DANIEL, Bacon ag^{t}., ... 291
MAINE, PROVINCE OF, (libel &c. ag^{t}. bark Gift of God &c.) 176
MAIOR } (See MAYRS.)
MAIRES }
MAJESTIES or }
MAJESTY }
proclamation ment^{d}. (libel ag^{t}. Andreason &c.) 264
plantations, sale to, (case of Joseph Indian) 296
in Council, order from, 26 Sept. 1689 ment^{d}. (Usher ag^{t}. Frizell) . 302
colors, sloop Mary sailing under, ment^{d}. (case of Thos. Pound &c.)
308, 309, 311–314, 316–318
MAKEE. (See MACKEE.)
MALDEN, (Town of), Joseph Lampson, constable of, ... 329
MAMPAUS NACKOSUT (Indian), case of (murder) 53
MAN
John, (2^{d}. Jury of trials &c.) 135
ag^{t}. Savage 137
ag^{t}. Bratle 250
MANDER, THOMAS, &c., mariners of ship Apollow, ag^{t}. Hollaway &c. . . 132–3
MANING. (See MANNING.)
MANLY, WM., Webb (marshal) ag^{t}., ... 235, 244
MANNING or MANING
Elisabeth, wife of Nicholas Maning, pet. for divorce 240
George, master of bark Phillip, (case of Rodriego &c.) 35–39
Nicholas, Capt., ag^{t}. Whight & wife 153
Whight ag^{t}., ... 162
ag^{t}. Broune &c. 164
pet. for divorce by his wife Elisabeth 240
overseers &c. of children of Grey ag^{t}., (exec^{n}.) 376
ag^{t}. overseers &c. of children of Grey (exec^{n}.) 376–7
William, Mr., (Jury for trial of attaint) 2
(2^{d}. Jury of trials &c.) 25
(Grand Jury) 78, 120, 140, 190, 214, 255
MANSFEILD
Andrew, &c. ag^{t}. Broune 195
&c. atty^{s}., ag^{t}. Browne 225
MANSLAUGHTER. (See CRIMES.)
MARBELL or }
MARBLE }
Wm., Marshall ag^{t}., ... 289
MARBLEHEAD (Town of)
Jno. Buttery of, ... 103
ment^{d}. (information ag^{t}. Boury &c.) 210
Joseph Gatchell of, ... 253
Selectmen of, Stilson ag^{t}., ... 328
MARBLEHEAD COMMONS (Bartlet ag^{t}. James &c.) 20
MARCH
Dorcas, & husband Hugh, case of, as to lawfully living as man & wife, 127

PAGE

MARCH, *continued.*
Hugh & his wife Dorcas, case of, as to lawfully living as man & wife, 127
Senr., Fletcher for John March & wife ag^t^., ... 214
Jemima, & husband John ag^t^. March 214
John, & wife Jemima, ag^t^. March 214
Capt., of Newbury, ag^t^. Carr 367
MAREA, Spanish Indian, servant to French, case of (infanticide) . . . 115
MARIA (Negro)
ment^d^. (case of Cheffaleer (negro)) 197
(case of Jack (negro)) 199
servant to Joshua Lambe, case of, (arson) 198
MARIAN } MARION } or MARRIAN, MARRION
Isack (Jury for attaints) 266
John (Jury of inquest) (inquisition on body of Bickford) 34
(Jury for attaints) 255
adm^r^., ag^t^. Lake 269
Senr., (Grand Jury) 302, 305
MARITIME
case excepted from order for caution money for court charges . . 171
law, page 93, sect. second, ment^d^. (Gretian ag^t^. Torrey) 232
MARLBOROUGH (Town of)
Indians sent from, ... 52
ment^d^. (case of Reup (Indian)) 53
John Indian of, ... 53
Samuel Newton of, ... 342
MARQUIS OF ROYAN (ship) (libel &c.) 354
MARRET or } MARRETT }
Amos, ag^t^. Cutter 275
ag^t^. Holland 347
MARRIAGE
joining persons in, Capt. Danl. Fisher empowered for, on pet^n^. from Dedham 87
case of Dorcas & Hugh March 127
MARRIAN } MARRION } (*See* MARION.)
MARSH, ALLEXANDER, (Grand Jury) 287
MARSHAL. (*See* MARSHALL.)
MARSHAL
the, allowance to, (Courts order as to officers fees) 62
verdict as to levying execution &c. (Colcord ag^t^. Drake) . . 81
ment^d^. in memento as to Lang 118
order to, (case of Saml. Shrimpton) 297
MARSHAL GENERAL
ment^d^. (case of Benj^a^. Goad) 11
(answer to pet^n^. of Benj^a^. Goad) 14
(Governors declaration as to case of Goad &c.) 14

PAGE

MARSHAL GENERAL, *continued.*
mentd. (case of Anna Negro &c.) 30, 70, 71, 74, 76, 91
(case of Darby Bryan &c.) 115
(case of Ephraim Beamis) 116
(courts order as to warrants) 200
(order on petn. of Jno. Gyfford) 231
(case of Joshua Rice &c.) 240
(case of Phillip Darland) 252
(case of Joseph Gatchell) 254
(case of James Morgan) 295
(case of Saml. Shrimpton) 297, 299
return of warrant as to Saml. Shrimpton 301
(order as to execution of Hugh Stone &c.) 304, 306, 309, 310, 311, 320, 322
appointment of Samuel Gookin as, ... 342

MARSHALL OF MARSHAL
Benjamin, Daniel agt., ... 84
Pepen agt., ... 143
agt. Cogswell 274
Edmund, Daniel agt., ... 84
Samuel (Jury of trials) 322
(Petit jury) 323
Thomas, Capt., agt. Waldron 78
(case of Mr. Isaac Waldron) 89
Apleton agt., ... 261
William, commander, (Wharton agt. Reynolds) 202
(1st. Jury for trials &c.) 215
agt. Marbell 289
agt. Moore 290
agt. Soley 290
&c., libel of Wharton &c. agt., ... 297
MARSTON, WILLIAM, mate of ship Apollow, &c. agt. Hollaway &c. . . . 132–3
MARTHA OF JERSEY (ship) master &c. of, (information &c.) 230
MARTHAS VINEYARD. (*See* MARTINS VINEYARD.)
MARTIN OF MARTYN
Benjamin, &c., Martin agt., ... 152
George, & wife Susannah agt. Winsly & wife 5
Winsly agt., ... 6
Richard, (2d. Jury of trials &c.) 45
agt. Briggs &c. 152
Mr., agt. Rost 217
Susannah, & husband George agt. Winsly & wife 5
MARTINS VINEYARD
mentd. (Poole agt. Phipps &c.) 211
(Johnson agt. Phipps &c.) 212
(Aires agt. Phipps &c.) 212
(Knaps agt. Phipps &c.) 213
Joseph Indian of, ... 295

PAGE

MARTINS VINEYARD SOUND (case of Thomas Pound &c.) . 307–314, 316–318
MARTYN. (*See* MARTIN.)
MARTYNS VINEYARD. (*See* MARTINS VINEYARD.)
MARY (ketch, sloop, &c.)
of Salem, (case of Thomas Hawkins &c.) . . 305, 307, 309–313, 315–318
of Boston (case of Thomas Pound &c.) . . 308, 309, 311–314, 316–318
&c., Black agt., ... 324
Black, master of, agt. Bronsdon &c. 324
of Boston, commander of, libel agt. bark Speedwell 352
owner of, agt. Brenton, Collr., ... 366

MASON
Arthur, bond by 51
Trumble agt., ... 97
(Grand Jury) 214, 251, 302, 305, 336
agt. Tight 234
Tyte agt., ... 255
guardian, agt. Legg 362
Joseph, (Jury of attaints &c.) 289
of Watertown, agt. Stone &c., Selectmen, ... 346
Samuel, stealing from, mentd. (case of Thos. Davis &c.) 189

MASSACHUSETTS (or MASSACHUSETTS BAY, COLONY OF.)
Seal of, mentd. (case of John Weaver) 23
Hampshire County in, ... 33
money, clippings of, (case of Peeter Lorphelin) 146
Josiah Chickatabut, sachem of, ... 208
commrs. for the United Colonies, Rawson &c. agt., . . . 208, 209
mentd. (case of Wm. Johnson) 242
Governor &c. of, Court of Assistants held by, 1 Sept. 1685 273
mentd. (case of Samuel Shrimpton) 299
Court of Assistants for, at Boston 24 Dec. 1689 301
mentioned 322, 327
Rowley Woods in, ... 336
Governor &c. of, (libel agt. bark Speedwell) 352
of, (libel &c. agt. ship Marquis of Royan) 354
mentd. (case of Martin Williams) 360

MASSACHUSETTS BAY
Half way rock in, ... 305, 307, 309, 310, 312, 313, 315–317
Nantasket Road in, ... 319
MASSACHUSETTS BAY, COLONY OF. (*See* MASSACHUSETTS.)
MASSEY, SAMUEL, late prison keeper of Boston, agt. Robie 303
MATANZAS, BAY OF, in Cuba, mentd. 129

MATHER
Timothy, (Grand Jury) 17, 44, 94, 202, 251
(1st. Jury for trials &c.) 224

MATHEW or MATHEWS
Daniel, case of, ... 167
&c., warrant "signed to," 171

PAGE

MATHEWS, etc., *continued*,
Daniel, Barton agt., ... 195, 222
James, of New York, by atty., agt. Keene 181
MATSON, THOMAS, agt. Dispaw 100
MATTOCK, STEVEN, &c., costs granted to, ... 87
MAXFEILD
Clement, (Cleomen) (1st. Jury for trials &c.) 78
(2d. Jury for trials &c.) 203
(Grand Jury) 298
Wm., mariner of ship George, &c. (complaint &c.) 41
MAY
[ ]ge, (1st. Jury for trials &c.) 3
Ellinor, case of, (whoredom &c.) 138
Hugh, &c., mariners of ship Apollow, agt. Hollaway &c. . . . 132, 133
John, (Jury for trial of attaint) 134
(Grand Jury) 151
Wm., master of pink Supply, (libel &c.) 41
MAYDENHEAD (ship), master of, &c., (libel &c.) 176
MAYHO or MAYO
[George], (1st. Jury for trials &c.) 3
Jno., (Grand Jury) 273
MAYRS or MAIOR, MAIRES
Robert, case of, ... 84
Sam., (Jury of trials &c.) 33
MAZE, WM., his surety, agt. Mackee 97
MAZURE, BENJAMIN, English agt., ... 109
MEAD or MEADE
Nicho: (1st. Jury of trials &c.) 161
Richd., Alcock agt., ... 121
Wm., (Jury for trials &c.) 228
MEARES or MEERES
James, (2d. Jury for trials &c.) 203
(Jury of trials &c.) 252
MEASURE
William, of Lyme in New England, merchant, libel &c. agt. Haughton, 39
merchant, libel of Haughton agt., ... 42
MEDFORD (Town of), land &c. within bounds of, (Prout agt. Brooks &c.) . 349
MEDLECOTT. (*See* MIDLECOT.)
MEERES. (*See* MEARES.)
MEETING HOUSE, (THIRD), in Boston, disturbance in, (case of Allexander Colman) 127
MEKINS, THOMAS, agt. Kinsley 221
MELINES or MELYNES
———, Mr., &c. agt. Dudsson &c. 15
———, & Co., mentd. (Dudson & Co., ship Expectation,) 16
Isaac, Mr., &c., answer to pet. of, ... 13, 14

PAGE

MELINES OR MELYNES, *continued.*
Isaack, commander, (Dudson & Co., ship Expectation,) 16
MELLOWES
James, (Jury for attaints) 255
(2d. Jury for appeals) 256
MELOT } or MILOTT
MELOTT }
Augustin, Lacy agt., ... 124
Oxe agt., ... 124
MELYN or }
MELYNE }
Jacob, (Jury of trials) 302, 306
" in room of Thayer 310
(Petit Jury) 323
Mr., foreman, (Jury of trials) 362
MELYNES. (*See* MELINES.)
MERCHANTS ADVENTURE (ship) of London, carpenter &c. of, agt. Stone . 213
MERRILL
Abraham, Perkins agt., ... 244
Jno., son of Nathl. Merrill, (Cleoments agt. Merrill) 221
Nathaniel, Cleoments agt., ... 221
MERRIMACK (brigantine) of Newbury (case of Thos. Pound &c.) . 308, 309, 310, 312, 313
MERRIMACK RIVER (case of John Weaver) 23
MERRIT, AMOS, (2d. Jury of trials) 362
MESSENGER
Henry, shop of, mentd. (libel &c. agt. Checkly & wife) (execn.) . . 385
John, Hudson agt., ... 84
Symeon, &c., execr. of Clarke agt., ... 153
MESSMAKER, ——, Mr., (case of John Lowell) 15
METANSIS (MATANZAS), Bay of, in Cuba, mentd. 129
MICARTER, THADDEUS, Turner agt., ... 187
MICHAEL (ship) of Bristol, mariners &c. of, agt. Loyd &c. 150
MICHAEL, PEETER, &c., mariners of ketch Ollive Branch, (libel &c.) . . 131
MICHARD, ABRAHAM, Monsr., merchant in Rochell, (libel &c. agt. ship Marquis of Royan) 355
MICHELSON. (*See* MITCHELSON.)
MIDDLESEX, COUNTY OF,
mentioned 71, 72, 73, 87
Treasurer of, bond to, (case of Tho. Kenny (negro)) 127
MIDDLESEX COUNTY COURT. (*See* COUNTY COURT MIDDLESEX.)
MIDDLETON or MIDLETON
John, carpenter of ship Endeavor, &c. agt. Smith, ... 130, 131
&c., libel of Smith &c. agt., ... 132
MIDGLEY. (*See* MIGELEY.)
MIDLECOT or MEDLECOTT
Richard, &c., attys., Shakeley &c. agt., ... 29
(Jury of trials, &c.) 32

PAGE

MIDLECOT or MEDLECOTT, *continued.*
Richard, atty., Endecott &c. agt., ... 96
Mr., (Jury) 171
&c., Gifford agt., ... 218
MIDLETON. (*See* MIDDLETON.)
MIGELEY or MIDGLEY
Thomas, agt. Smith 195
Goulding agt., ... 204
MIGHILL
Elisabeth, & husband Samuel agt. Toppan &c. 29
Samuel, & wife Elisabeth agt. Toppan &c. 29
MILES, EXPERIENCE, agt. Heyden 6
MILITARY COMPANIES in Boston (case of Walter Gendall &c.) 102-3
MILITIA of Wenham, certificate presented by order of, ... 104
MILLER, MATHEW, Atkinson agt., ... 270
MILLEVASHE (or Thousand Cow) commander, (libel &c. agt. ship St. John Frigott) 353
MILLS, JNO., agt. Johnson 258
MILNER, NATHANIEL, mariner, agt. Wing 367
MILOTT. (*See* MELOT.)
MILSON, RICHARD, gunner of ship George, &c. (libel &c.) 173
MILTON (Town of)
Peter Addams of, ... 230
Mr. Peter Thatcher of, ... 369
MINISTER &c. mentd. (answer to pet. of Wm. Morse) 190
MINOT or MYNOT, MYNOTT
James, (Grand Jury) 1
John, (1st Jury of trials &c.) 25
(Jury for attaints) 255
(1st. Jury for appeal) 257
MIRRICK, JAMES, Atkinson agt., ... 223
MISDEMEANOR. (*See* CRIMES.)
MITCHELL, THOMAS, &c., case of, (concurrence with pirates) 42
MITCHELSON or MICHELSON
———, Holman &c. agt., ... 218
Edward, marshal general,
execution (Admr. of Dinely agt. est. of Stenwicke) . 371, 372
(Skinner &c. agt. Ship Dove &c.) 372, 373
(Bromehall &c. agt. Long) 374, 375
(Overseers &c. of children of Grey agt. Manning) 376, 377
(Hollowell &c. agt. Butler) 381
(Wheeler &c. agt. Checkly & wife) 383
MIXTER, ISACK, (1st Jury for trials &c.) 215
MONCK / MONCKE / MONCKS or MONKS
George, case of, ... 250
taverner, case of, ... 351

PAGE

Monhegin, appointment of constable at, ... 12
Monks. (*See* Moncks.)
Moor or More
Moore
Benj., (Jury of trials) 35
Enoch, (Jury) 160
Marshall agt., ... 290
&c., libel of Wharton &c. agt., ... 297
Francis, (Grand Jury) 35, 244
(Jury of trials) 299
(Jury) 300
John, costs agt., granted to Heyman 188
(1st. Jury for trials &c.) 203
(Jury of trials) 298
(Jury) 300
Thomas, master of pink Supply, &c. (libel &c.) 41
(1st. Jury for trials &c.) 44
master of ship Phoenix, &c. (libel &c.) 76
instead of Jno. Swett (1st. Jury for trials) 120
(2d. Jury of trials &c.) 141, 203
(Jury) 150, 176
(Grand Jury) 230
agt. Porter 246
Mr., &c., appraisers, (libel &c. agt. Schinking) (execn.) . 378–9
Wm., &c. agt. Wilson 136
More. (*See* Moore.)
Morey, Thomas, (Jury of trials) 362
Morgan
James, of Boston, case of, (murder) 294, 295
Wm., Chocke agt., ... 157
Morrell, Jacob, of Salisbury, Dolbery agt., ... 348
Morrey, John, his marriage at Jamaica to Hannah Goss mentd. (order on pet. of Phillip Goss) 326
Morrice or
Morris
Edward, (Grand Jury) 24
Isaac, (2d. Jury of trials) 337
Morrison, James, &c., privateers, (order as to account of Earl) . . . 250
Morse or Mosse
Elisabeth, wife of Wm. Morse, case of, (familiarity with the devil) . 159
answer to pet. of her husband Wm. Morse, ... 189, 190
Jerremiah, Dixie agt., ... 108
John, (Jury of inquisition on body of Bickford) 34
(1st. Jury of trials &c.) 65, 70, 140
(2d. Jury for appeals) 256
(Jury for attaints) 256
Joseph, &c., mariners, agt. ketch Friendship (execn.) 391–2
William, case of his wife Elisabeth, ... 159

PAGE

MORSE or MOSSE, *continued.*
William, answer to pet. of, in behalf of his wife Elisabeth, . . . 189
MOSELY
———, Capt., Indians sent from Marlborough and letter by, ment^{d}. . 52
Samuel, Capt., (libel ag^{t}. Rodriego) 34
MOSSE. (*See* MORSE.)
MOULDER
Christian, & husband Nicholas ment^{d}. (case of George Cole &c.) . 12
Nicholas, & wife Christian ment^{d}. " " " . . 12
part owner of ship Dove, &c. (libel &c.) 58
(exec^{n}.) . . . 372–3
MOUNTFORT, HENRY, of Boston, merchant, Adams, adm^{x}., ag^{t}., ... 330
MOUNTJOY
George, of Boston, mariner, ag^{t}. Hemlock 325
Hemlock ag^{t}., ... 341
MUCKSCUMPEY (Indian), case of, (murder) 54
MUCKSUMQUENUT (alias Jno.) (Indian), case of, (murder) 54
MUDDY RIVER, Andrew Gardner of, ... 304
MULLEN, JAMES, cooper of ship Herron, &c. (libel &c.) 159, 160
MULLIGAN, HUGH, case of, ... 280
MUMFORD
Benjamin, Peirse ag^{t}., ... 225, 246
William, of Boston, slater, ag^{t}. Wyllys 351
MUMUCKSUNCASUSUCQUATER (alias Thomas) (Indian), case of, (murder) . 54
MURDER. (*See* CRIMES.)
MUSSEY. (*See* MUZZEY.)
MUTINOUS CARRIAGE. (*See* CRIMES.)
MUZEY / MUZZEY } or MUSSEY
Benjamin, ag^{t}. Waldron 79
Brookes ag^{t}., ... 268
MYNOT / MYNOTT } (*See* MINOT.)

NACKOSUT, MAMPAUS, (Indian), case of, (murder) 53
NAGGS or / NAGS }
Richard, &c., mariners of ship Jno. Adventure, ag^{t}. Craty &c., . . 147
case of, (lying) 147
NANAPATU, JAMES (Indian), case of, (murder) 54
NANNY
Katherin, late wife of Edwd. Naylor, (case of Edwd. Naylor) . . 32
Robert, trustee of his wife & children, Chase ag^{t}., ... 17
NANTASKET ROAD in Massachusetts Bay ment^{d}. 319
NANTUCKET (Island of)
ment^{d}. (Dudson & Co., ship Expectation,) 16
(Lemoigne ag^{t}. White &c.) 129

PAGE

NASH, JOSEPH, of Boston, mariner, Smith agt., ... 365
NASHUA (Town of), inhabitants of, murder of, ... 52
NASSAW (Dutch prize) mentd. (Lemoigne agt. White &c.) 129
NATICK (Town of), Ruler at, (case of old Jethro (Indian)) 54
NATOW (Indian), (Jury) 22
NAYLER or }
NAYLOR }
Edward, case of, (intruding on his late wife Katherin Nanny) . . . 32
mentd. (Phipps agt. Bronsdon) 337
NECKE
——, master of bark Beginning, (libel &c. agt. Brimsden) . . . 128
John, of Boston, master of bark Beginning, Bodkin agt., ... 128
NEEDHAM or }
NEEDOM }
Ezekiel, agt. Farr 247
Wm., (Grand Jury) 43
NEELAND, EDWARD, Senr., husbandman, agt. Foster 345
NEFFE, WILLIAM, case of, (deserting the garrison at Falmouth &c.) . . . 321
NEGRO
Anna, &c., presentments &c. agt., mentd. in margin 25
Basto, case of, (rape) 74
Jack, servant to Faireweather, case of, (bestiality) 74
Hannah, case of, ... 151, 152
Cheffaleer, case of, (arson) 197
Maria, mentd. (case of Cheffaleer, negro, &c.) 197, 199
of James Pemberton, case of, ... 198
Maria, case of, (arson) 198
Jack, servant to Woolcot, case of, (arson) 199
Robin, case of, (murder) 304, 305, 321
Jno. Cream, replevin for, (Stanbridge agt. Goffe) 330
Nathanael Force, sale of, (Hall agt. Backway) 350
named Hector mentd. (libel &c. agt. Checkly & wife) (execn.) . . . 384
NEGUS, BENJA, (Grand Jury) 65, 94
NELSON, PHILLIP, Leaver agt., ... 134
NEPONET, JNO. (Indian), trial of, mentd. 214
NEVARS, RICHARD, by atty., agt. Gardiner 100
NEVERSON or NEVISON, NEVISSON
——, (complaint of Bisco agt. Farrell &c.) 286
Jno., (Jury for trial of attaint) 134
John, Mr., (1st. Jury of trials &c.) 135
NEVIS mentd. (case of Allexander Colman) 127
NEVIS FACTOR (ship)
mentd. (libel of Hodsdall agt. Davis &c.) 63
(libel of Hooper agt. Davis &c.) 64
libel &c. of Davis agt., ... 76
NEVISON }
NEVISSON } (*See* NEVERSON.)

PAGE

NEWBURY (Town of)
men of, witnesses, allowance for the Treasurer to pay, ... 50
by atty[s]., ag[t]. Dummer 108
meeting house in, ment[d]. (answer to pet. of Wm. Morse) 190
brigantine Merrimack of, ... 308–310, 312, 313
Henry Toltwood of, ... 336
Peter Toppam &c. of 338
Joseph Downer of, ... 357
Capt. John March of, ... 367
NEWBURY (ketch), complaint of Randolph, Coll[r]. &c., ag[t]., ... 220
NEWBY
Georg, ag[t]. Hinchman 226
Dawes ag[t]., ... 270
NEWCOMB, ANDREW, plaintiff, (appeal) 65
NEWELL
Isaac, (1st. Jury for trials &c.) 17
(2[d]. " " " ") 79, 153, 274, 337
Sen[r]., (Jury of trials) 323
(Jury of trials) 362
Jacob, (2[d]. Jury of trials) 362
John, (Jury of trials) 56
(Jury for trials of attaint) 191
(1st. Jury for trials &c.) 192
Joseph, (Jury) 176
NEW ENGLAND
Boston in, ... 1, 172–175, 179, 251, 302, 303, 372
Roxbury in, ... 10
Lyme in, ... 39
ment[d]. (libel &c. ag[t]. Bull) 40
(Martin ag[t]. Briggs &c.) 152
(libel &c. ag[t]. Isaac &c.) 174
(libel &c. ag[t]. Branson &c.) 175
(Poole ag[t]. Phipps &c.) 211
(Aires ag[t]. Phipps &c.) 212
(Johnson ag[t]. Phipps &c.) 212
(Knaps ag[t]. Phipps &c.) 213
(case of Martin Williams) 359, 360
County of Middlesex in, ... 71–73
Sudbury in, ... 86
Edw[d]. Randolph, Collector of his Majesties customs in, . 150, 176, 210
County of Suffolk in, ... 188, 198, 199, 234, 295, 298, 300
Mr. Barnard Randolph, Dep[ty]. Coll[r]. &c. of his Majesties customs in, . 230
Massachusetts Bay in, ... 273, 352
money of, ... 330, 392
ship Richard of Boston bound from, ... 335
Jahleel Brenton, Coll[r]. &c. of his Majesties customs in, 342–344, 349, 355, 356, 360, 366
Ipswich in, ... 352
statement dated at, 27 Aug. 1681 379

PAGE

NEWFOUNDLAND
mentd. (libel &c. agt. ship Gift of God &c.) 332-334
Scilly Cove in, ... 334
Bonavista Road in, ... 335
cruising on banks of, mentd. (libel &c. agt. ship Marquis of Royan) . 354

NEWHALL
John, tertius, of Lynn, yeoman, &c., case of (murder) . 306, 307, 321
found guilty of manslaughter, . . 307, 321
&c. order as to, ... 360
Thomas, &c., agt. Broune 195
Waite agt., ... 363, 364

NEWITCHAWANNICK in Yorkshire, garrison at, ... 104

NEWMAN
Thomas, agt. Smith 25
(1st. Jury for trials &c.) 152
agt. Palmer 227

NEWMARCH or NEWMARSH
John, of Ipswich, Berry agt., ... 331
agt. Berry 331

NEWTON
Charls, part owner of ship George, &c. (complaint &c.) 41
Isaac, his widow mentd. (case of Saml. Newton & wife) . . . 342
Rebekah, (widow of Isaac Newton) & husband Samuel, case of, (forbidden to cohabit) 342
Samuel, of Marlborough, & wife Rebekah, case of, (forbidden to cohabit) 342

NEW YORK
mentd. (libel &c. agt. Shice) 56
James Mathews of, ... 181

NICCOLLS or NICHOLLS
John, Clark agt., ... 47
Nathaniel, (Jury of attaints) 244
(2d. Jury of trials &c.) 245
Randall, (Grand Jury) 1, 133, 202, 242, 273
Randolph, (Grand Jury) 251

NIGHTINGALE or NIGHTINGALL
ketch Hopewell formerly so called (libel &c. agt. Shice) 56

NODLES ISLAND, mentd. (case of Saml. Shrimpton) 297

NON SUIT
for non-appearance (Bryan agt. Soames) 98
(Egerton agt. Smith) 166
(Atkinson agt. Mirrick) 223
(Baker agt. Addams) 266
(Wardell agt. Lynde) 280
(March agt. Carr) 367

PAGE

NON SUIT, *continued.*
granted
(libel ag^{t}. pink Expectation) 149
(Farr ag^{t}. Witter) 269
for reasons of appeal not being signed
(est. of Wm. Snelling) . . 153
(Williams ag^{t}. Townsend) . 155
(Holman &c. ag^{t}. Michelson) . 218
(Peasley ag^{t}. Clark) . . 221
(Wright &c. ag^{t}. Sparrey) . 235
declared by the Court
(ass^{nee}. of Wayte ag^{t}. exec^{r}. &c. of Cooke) . 164
(Hoare ag^{t}. Cooke &c.) 166
(case of Daniel Mathew) 167
(libel &c. ag^{t}. Turell) 174
(Gifford ag^{t}. Walter &c.) 218
judgment as to, (Hundlock ag^{t}. Hubbard &c.) 294
for reasons of appeal not being seasonably brought in
(Wing ag^{t}. Halsey) . . 206
(Fosket ag^{t}. Foskett) . . 328
(Gookin &c. ag^{t}. Savage &c.) 329
(Savage ag^{t}. Savage &c.) . 329
(Francis &c. ag^{t}. Danforth) 330
desired (Rawson &c. ag^{t}. Stoughton &c., comm^{rs}.,) 209
plea for,
(assignee of Hoare ag^{t}. Kilcup) 219
(Raymond ag^{t}. Orchard) 224
(Torrey ag^{t}. Gretian) 226
(Exec^{rs}. of Usher ag^{t}. assignee &c. of Harwood) . . . 237
because time of Court "was missed" in reasons of appeal (Wright ag^{t}. Sparrey) 235
as to, (Bishop ag^{t}. Lord, marshal) 248
(Wisewall &c. ag^{t}. Paige &c.) 256

NORCRAS or NORCROSS NORCROSSE
Richard, (1st. Jury for trials &c.) 44
(2^{d}. " " " ") 141
(Grand Jury) 361

NORDEN
Nathaniel, Capt., &c., selectmen of Marblehead, Stilson ag^{t}., . . . 328
(Jury) 360
Samuel, ag^{t}. Scottow 292

NORFOLK COUNTY COURT. (*See* COUNTY COURT NORFOLK.)

NORMAN
———, Mr., atty., exec^{n}. delivered to, (Batt ag^{t}. Severans) . . . 9
———, Mr., exec^{n}. delivered to, (Waldron ag^{t}. Henderson) . . 119
John, ag^{t}. Orne 267, 273

PAGE

NORMAN, *continued.*
Richard, &c., sureties on bond of attaint, (Knight ag^{t}. Leach &c.) . 194
Thomas, atty., (libel ag^{t}. fifty hogsheads of tobacco &c.) 168
NORTH
Edward, master of ketch Betty, (libel &c.) 118
&c., mariners of ship Apollow, ag^{t}. Hollaway &c., . . . 132
Richard, legal proof of will of, (Martyn &c. ag^{t}. Winsly &c.) . . 6
NORTHEN or NORTHEND
Ezekiel, &c., lot layers &c., ag^{t}. Longfellow, ... 134, 143
NORTH HAMPTON
County Court at, (case of Mary Parsons) 31
Joseph Parsons of, ... 33
Samuel Holten of, ... 197
house of Lieut. Clark in, ... 198
County Court at, (Mekins ag^{t}. Kinsley) 221
Samuel Stebbins of, ... 342
NORTON
——, Mr., of Piscataqua, exec^{n}. delivered to, (Colcord ag^{t}. Palmer), 19
George, Playsted ag^{t}., ... 184
ag^{t}. Plaisted 271
John, &c. appraisers, (Manning ag^{t}. overseers &c.) (exec^{n}.) . . 377
NOTARY PUBLIC, ment^{d}. (case of John Weaver) 23
NOVA SCOTIA ment^{d}. (Belchar ag^{t}. Lloyd) 362
NOWEL or NOWELL
Michael, case of, ... 84
Samuel, Mr. or Esqr.,
present at Court, 178, 179, 190, 202, 208, 209, 211, 213, 214, 223, 228–232, 241, 243, 251, 266, 273, 287, 300
&c., exec^{rs}., Usher ag^{t}., ... 203
ag^{t}. assignee &c. of Harwood 237
ag^{t}. Goddard 293
NOYCE or NOYES NOYSE
——, Mrs., house of, (case of Wm. Clapp &c.) 285–287
John, (1st. Jury for trials &c.) 17
ag^{t}. Winslow 106
Sarah, of Boston, widow, house of, (case of Uriah Cleoments) . . 283
NURSE, FRANCIS, ag^{t}. Endicot 120, 235
NUTTER, HATEEVILL, Elder, &c., comm^{rs}., (order for dower) . . . 147

OATH
by Maj^{r}. Genl. Daniel Dennison 22
of a freeman taken by Barnard Capen 78
by constables of Boston 80, 206
by commissioners, Boston, ... 96, 168, 199, 214
by Samuel Gookin, mar^{l}. gen^{l}., ... 342

PAGE

OBBINSON
William, ag^{t}. Gilbert 79
Hill ag^{t}., ... 151, 161, 180
ODLING, RICHARD, &c., mariners of ship Ann & Hesther, (libel &c.) . . 172
OLDHAM, SAM^{LL}., (Jury of trials) 336
OLIVER or OLLIVER
James, Capt., &c. ag^{t}. Town of Lynn &c. 111, 135
exec^{x}. &c. of Cooke ag^{t}., ... 165, 166
Capt., Cooke, exec^{x}., &c. ag^{t}., ... 179
accusation by, (case of Uriah Cleoments) 283
Mr., (case of Wm. Clapp &c.) 285, 286
John, (Jury) 171
Nathaniel, Homes ag^{t}., ... 290
of Boston, Merch^{t}., exec^{x}. of Loft ag^{t}., ... 337
ag^{t}. exec^{x}. of Loft 350
Mr., land of, (Butler ag^{t}. Hollowell &c.) (exec^{n}.) . . 381
Thomas, (2^{d}. Jury for trials &c.) 79, 215
(Grand Jury) 244
(Jury of attaints &c.) 289
OLLIVE BRANCH (ketch), mariners of, libel &c. ag^{t}. Barnes &c., ... 131
OLLIVER. (*See* OLIVER.)
ORCHARD
Robert, surety & atty., ag^{t}. Winslow 29
searcher, (libel &c.) 75
ag^{t}. Pollard 109
Sandford ag^{t}., ... 196
Raymond ag^{t}., ... 224
ORDINANCES OF CHRIST in Boston (answer to motion of Wm. Leatherland), 21
ORNE, BENJ^{A}., Norman ag^{t}., ... 267, 273
OSGOOD, JN^{O}., Left., &c., Selectmen of Andover, ag^{t}. Fuller 108
OTTO (or HAWTO) PEETER, Capt., &c., atty^{s}., ag^{t}. White &c. 129
OUGHTRED
Charles, atty., ag^{t}. Hawkins 68
Poole ag^{t}., ... 81
atty., ag^{t}. Blackleach &c. 85
Palmer &c. 123
OWEN
Hannah, of Braintree, case of, (forbidden to cohabit with her husband Josiah) 361
Josiah, case of his wife Hannah, (forbidden to cohabit) 61
Phillip, mariner of ship George, &c. (complaint &c.) 41
OXE
Robert, Longfellow &c., ag^{t}., ... 112
by atty. ag^{t}. Melott 124
ag^{t}. Keene 124
OXENBRIDGE, JN ., Mr., &c., trustees &c., Rice ag^{t}., ... 24
OYES, proclamation by an, (case of Elizth. Fanning) 358
OYNES, JN^{O}., under name of Mr. Woodman, ment^{d}. (case of Ephraim Beamis) 116
OYSTER RIVER, Ensigne Jno. Davis of, ... 147

PAGE

PADDY, THO., &c., Bennet agt., ... 184

PAGE or PAIGE
- ——, Mr., &c., Melynes &c. agt., ... 15
- Anna, Mrs., &c., Wisewall, agt., ... 249
  - & husband Nicholas, agt. Wisewall 255
  - Wisewall &c. 256
- Nicholas, merchant, &c., libel &c. of Davenport agt., ... 77
  - libel &c. of Wilkins agt., ... 92
  - Mr., &c. agt. Dudley &c. 155
  - atty., West agt., ... 157
  - agt. Brimsden 168
  - Mr., (order as to ship Edward & Ann) 170
  - Capt., Carr agt., ... 181
  - of Boston, merchant, &c., bond by, ... 210
  - &c., Wisewall agt., ... 249
  - bond by, (Wisewall agt. Paige &c.) 249
  - Capt., & wife Ann agt. Wisewall 255
    - &c., Wisewall &c. agt., ... 256
  - Mr., & wife Anna agt. Wisewall &c. 256
  - Col., surety on bond of appeal, (information agt. Lawrence) 344
    - atty., agt. Morrell 348

PAGUSKMENUT (alias PETER) (Indian) case of, (murder) 54

PAIGE. (*See* PAGE.)

PAINE or PAYNE
- Elisabeth, spinster, case of, (infanticide) 228
- John, Hutchinson agt., ... 28
  - Mr., est. of, mentd. (Brattle agt. Knight, admr., &c.) . . . 101
  - est. of mentd. (case of Capt. Thos. Bratle) 103
- Moses, (Grand Jury) 78, 94, 133, 244, 301, 305
- Steeven, (1st. Jury of appeals &c.) 274
- William, &c., sureties on bond of attaint, (Perkins agt. Fenno) . . 257
- Wm., blacksmith, Lilly agt., ... 280

PALMER
- Christopher, Colcord agt., ... 19
  - Barefoot agt., ... 98
- John, &c., Sheaffe agt., ... 123
  - est. of Windor in hands of, &c., Baskerville agt., ... 141
- Lesly, Newman agt., ... 227
- Sarah, wife of John Palmer, (Sheaffe agt. Palmer &c.) 123
- Tho., Sheaffe agt., ... 98

PAPER, wearing of, as a badge. (*See* PUNISHMENT.)

PARKE, THO., (Jury of trials) 56

PARKEMAN, ELIAS, Townsend agt., ... 24

PARKER
- John, bond by, ... 57
  - &c., order as to rendezvous & marching "with the forces," . 58
- Tho., &c., sureties, bond by, (case of Jno. Parker) 57

PARKES. (*See* PARKS.)

PAGE

PARKHURST, JNO., (Jury for attaints) . . . 267
PARKS or PARKES
Tho., (2d. Jury for trials &c.) . . . 203
William, Mr., (Grand Jury) . . . 43, 59, 94, 119, 133, 202, 232
(2d. Jury for trials &c.) . . . 224
Deacon, (order on est. of Savage) . . . 229
Mr., &c., comtee., (order on est. of Savage) . . . 229
PARLIAMENT
Act of, (case of Josiah Cobbham) . . . 171
for encouragement of trade &c. (information agt. Lawrence) 343
preventing fraud &c. (information agt. Lawrence) . . 343
PARMITER
John, Mr., &c., chosen constable of Boston & oath . . . 80
(Jury) . . . 171
(1st. Jury for trials &c.) . . . 181
plaintiff, (appeal) . . . 196
(Jury for attaints) . . . 232
(Jury for trials &c.) . . . 233
PARRECK or PARRICK
John, master of ketch Brothers Adventure, (libel &c.) . . . 91
PARRIS
Owen, of Barbadoes, agt. Fletcher . . . 202, 203
Samuel, agt. Harris . . . 250
Mr., (Jury for attaints) . . . 255
(1st. Jury for appeal) . . . 256
foreman, (Perkins agt. Fenno) . . . 257
(Thomas ?) Mr., " " . . . 257
Thomas, Jacklin agt., . . . 274
PARRY, WM., (1st. Jury for trials &c.) . . . 120
PARSON or PARSONS
Joseph, of Northampton, case of his wife Mary, (witchcraft) . . 31, 33
(Jury for attaints) . . . 255
(1st. Jury for appeal) . . . 256
&c., of Boston, merchants, Bulkley agt., . . . 338
Mary (Courts order to send for witnesses) . . . 31
wife of Joseph Parsons, case of, (witchcraft) . . . 31, 33
William, &c., mariners, (libel &c.) . . . 40
mentd. (Hundlocke agt. Baker &c.) (execn.) . . 389, 390
PASON
Ephraim, (2d. Jury of trials) . . . 346
Giles, (Grand Jury) . . . 44, 65, 232, 244, 251
(1st. Jury for appeals &c.) . . . 108
John, (2d. Jury for trials &c.) . . . 25
Samuel, (Jury for attaints) . . . 255
(1st. Jury for appeal) . . . 257
PATCH, ———, Davenport agt., . . . 166

PAGE

PATRICK, MOSES, mariner of ship John & Mary, &c. (libel &c.) 40

PATRIDG or PATRIDGE

Nehemiah, agt. Waynwright 46

PATTEN or PATTYN

John, by atty., agt. Dyer 4

agt. Winsley 4

Mr., agent &c., (libel &c.) 55

Thomas, atty., agt. Dyer 4

agt. Winsley 4

of Boston, merchant, (libel &c.) 43

PATTESHALL

Richard, Checkly agt., ... 227

agt. Heskett 292

PATTYN. (*See* PATTEN.)

PAUL

John, of Lynn, agt. Barrow 345

Samuel, (Jury of trials &c.) 33

(2d. Jury for appeals &c.) 108

(2d. Jury for trials &c.) 153

(Jury of attaints) 244

(1st. Jury for trials &c.) 245

PAYNE. (*See* PAINE.)

PAYTON, BAZALEELL, his admr., Bullis agt., ... 113

PEACOCK or PEACOCKE PEACOKE

Mary, wife & atty. to Saml. Peacock, agt. Pen 273

Samuel, Knight agt., ... 135

his wife & atty. agt. Pen 273

PEAKE, JONATHAN, (1st Jury for trials &c.) 224

PEARCE PEARS PEARSE (*See* PEIRCE.)

PEASE

Gurtrude, widow of Henry Pease, (case of Ellacot) 252

Henry, murder of, mentioned " 251

Jno., agt. Freake 80

Samuel, commander of sloop Mary, (case of Pound &c.) 308, 309, 311–318

PEASLEY, JOSEPH, agt. Clark 221

PECK or PECKE

Thomas, agt. Lauton 8

Trumble agt., ... 219

PECKER

James, (Grand Jury) 266

of Boston, housewright, (case of Uriah Cleoments) . . . 284

order as to, (case of Wm. Clapp) 286, 287

PAGE

PEETERS
Richard, &c., mariners of ketch John & Benjamin, (libel &c.) . . 117
(execn.) 373–4

PEGGEY or PEGGY
Edward, of Boston, agt. Crisp 365

PEIRCE or PEARCE, PEARS, PEARSE, PEIRSE
Antho., (Grand Jury) 94
Elizabeth, (case of Benjn. Symons) 73
Joseph, declaration by, (case of Sara Bradbrook) 145
[Boston] (Jury) 210
[Watertown] (Jury) 210
Moses, agt. Mumford 225, 246
Nathaniel, Chocke agt., ... 141
Nehemiah, plaintiff, (appeal) 167
fine remitted 170
Samuel, (1st. Jury of trials &c.) 66, 70, 245
(Jury of attaints) 244
agt. Haward 279
Thomas, (Jury for trial of attaint) 3
(1st. Jury for trials &c.) 3
William, of Woburn, Read agt., ... 351

PEIRPOINT. (*See* PIERPONT.)

PEIRSE. (*See* PEIRCE.)

PELLICAN (ketch), master of, &c. (libel &c.) 62

PELTON
John, Senr., (Grand Jury) 17
(Grand Jury) 120
Robert, late mate of bark Hope, (libel &c.) 148
Samuel, agt. Thompson 162

PEMAQUID, appointment of constables at, ... 12

PEMBERTON
James, (Grand Jury) 179, 214
case of his negro 198
Baker agt., ... 259
Joseph, &c., Baker agt., ... 267
Mary, (case of Geo. Russell) 169
Thomas, &c., Baker agt., ... 267
Jacklin agt., ... 268

PEN, WM., Peacock agt., ... 273

PENTECOST or PENTICOST
Jno., (Grand Jury) 32, 140

PEPEN, SAMUEL, agt. Marshall 143

PEPPER, ROBT., (2d. Jury for trials &c.) 18

PERKINS
Abraham, Atkinson agt. 123, 136
Hovey agt., ... 363

PAGE

PERKINS, *continued.*
David, of Beverly, (case of Phillip Darland, &c.) 252–3
Edmond, ag^{t}. Smith 239
ag^{t}. Merrill 244
ag^{t}. Fenno 257, 258, 266
of Boston, shipwright, ag^{t}. Winslow 323
PERRIN, JOHN, &c., mariners of ship Apollow, ag^{t}. Hollaway &c. . . . 132–3
PERRY
Ann, case of, (scandalous offence) 197
pet. for divorce 229
(alias Ann Sheffeild), Homes ag^{t}., ... 261, 266
ag^{t}. Homes (exec^{n}.) 386–388
Samuel, Jury of attaints 244
(2^{d}. Jury of trials &c.) 245
Seth, (Jury of inquest) (inquisition on body of Bickford) 34
ag^{t}. Deane 80
Turnor ag^{t}., ... 122
ag^{t}. Hurd 215, 216
Waterhouse ag^{t}., ... 325
(Grand Jury) 345
of Boston, ag^{t}. Alford 352, 363
PERSY, ISLE OF, ment^{d}. (libel &c. ag^{t}. ship St. John Frigott) 353
PETER (alias Paguskmenut) (Indian), case of, (murder) 54
PETIT, HENRY, Dawes ag^{t}., ... 268
PETIT GUANARE or
PETIT GUAUARE
ment^{d}. (Lemoigne ag^{t}. White &c.) 129
PETIT JURY. (*See* JURY.)
PETTEE, JAMES, &c., seamen &c. of ship Lixborn merchant (libel &c.) . . 92–3
PHILLIP (bark) belonging to Freake (case of Rodriego &c.) 35–39
PHILLIP (Indian?), his man & David Indian ordered to be sent away . . 54
PHILLIP, SAMUEL, &c., ag^{t}. Holliock 248
PHILLIPS
Henry, (Grand Jury) 251
John, (1st. Jury for trials &c.) 17
(Grand Jury) 32, 94
&c., of Charlestown, merchants, (libel &c.) 55
Mr., (2^{d}. Jury for trials &c.) 59
Esqr., present at Court . . 302, 305, 320–322, 327, 345, 359, 361
Jnothan, (2^{d}. Jury for trials &c.) 275
Samuel, &c., ag^{t}. Holliock 248
Wm., (Petit jury) 323
Zachary, case of, ... 84
PHIPPS or
PHIPS
Samuel, (Jury for attaints &c.) 255, 288
Mr., (1st. Jury for appeals &c.) 289
(Special jury) 363

PAGE

PHIPS OR PHIPPS, *continued.*
Solomon, (Jury) 160
(1st. Jury for trials &c.) 181
&c., agt. Bowers 224
drivers of Charlestown common, Bowers agt., . . 232
(Grand Jury) 336
William, agt. Dudson 102
agt. Hamond 113
commander of ship Resolution, &c., Poole &c. agt., . 211–213
Sr., commander of frigott Golden Rose agt. Bronsdon . . 337–8
PHOENIX (ship) master of, &c. (libel &c.) 76
PICKARD, JNO., &c., lot layers, agt. Longfellow 134, 143
PICKERING
John, Waynwright agt., ... 46
agt. Frost 69
PICKMAN, NATHANIEL, Senr., &c., appraisers, (Manning agt. overseers &c.) 377
PICKMAND, BENJA., Archer &c. agt., ... 275
PIERPONT OR PEIRPOINT
John (Grand Jury) 56, 202, 214
Robert, (Jury for attaints) 266
(Grand Jury) 302, 305
PIETERSON, CLOICE, mate of ship Salamander, &c. (libel &c.) 179
PIGGET, ROBERT, &c., finding of jury for, (case of Ludden &c.) 5
PIKE OR PYKE
Robert, Major, agt. Gove 6
Gove agt., ... 16
Hooke agt., ... 154
Mr. or Esqr., present at Court . 209, 214, 241, 243, 255, 266, 287, 298, 300, 326
Esqr., agt. Winsley 279
PILLORY. (*See* PUNISHMENT, Miscellaneous.)
PINCHON. (*See* PYNCHON.)
PINNOCK, THOMAS, murder of, (case of Leonard Pomery) 242–3
PIPER, NATHANIEL, Keine agt., ... 9
PIRACY &c. (*See* CRIMES.)
PIRATES mentd. (case of Thos. Mitchell &c.) 42
PISCATAGE OR PISCATAQUA
Mr. Norton of, ... 19
Robert Williams of, ... 30
PITCHER, JNO., &c., Randolph, Collr., agt., ... 219
PITE, GEORGE, &c., Dauson agt., ... 289
PITMAN
William, plaintiff, (appeal) 109
bond declared forfeited 110
PITTAM OR PITTOM
John, &c., sureties on bond of attaint, (Thaier agt. Savage) . . . 186
Wardell agt., ... 260

PAGE

PITTS, WM., agt. Badcock 166
PITTYMEE, ANDREW, Indian interpreter, sworn to interpret court declarations &c. 296
PLACE
John, master of ship Hope of Boston (libel &c.) 210
mentd. (bond by Shrimpton &c.) . . . 211
PLAISTED or PLAYSTED
John, agt. Norton 184
Norton agt., ... 271
PLATTS
Thomas, Harrison agt., ... 237, 238, 245, 254, 255
of Boston, his widow & admx. &c., Brentnal agt., ... 326
PLAYSTED. (*See* PLAISTED.)
PLIMOUTH, COLONY. (*See* PLYMOUTH COLONY.)
PLUM or PLUMBE
Jno., Wayte agt., ... 227
PLUMER, SAM., &c., Dumer agt., ... 44
PLYMOUTH COLONY Jurisdiction mentd. (Dudson & Co., ship Expectation,) . 16
POLE. (*See* POOLE.)
POLLARD, SAMUEL, Orchard agt., ... 109
POMERY, LEONARD, case of, (manslaughter) 242
POND
William, (Grand Jury) 56, 78, 230
deed of, mentd. (Heinshaw agt. Voss) 185
PONSAW, LE [SEU], M[ONSEER], Governor for the french king at Tortudoes, &c. (Lemoigne agt. White &c.) 129
POOLE or POLE
John, &c., owners of ship Salamander, Woodman agt., ... 61
merchant, &c. (libel &c.) 64
agt. Oughtred 81
merchant, &c., Sheaffe agt., ... 85
&c., Lydgett & Co. agt., execution respitted &c. 92
Mr., answer to petition &c. of, ... 94
merchant, agt. execx. of Lydget &c. 105
Mr., &c., agt. Dudley &c. 155
Theophilus, of ship Resolution, agt. Phipps &c. 211
POPE, WM., Mr., case of, (cursing authority) 104
PORCUPINE (ship)
commander of, libel &c. agt. ship Gift of God &c. 332
William of Weymouth, . . . 333–4
St. John Frigott of Quebec, . . 353
PORDIDGE, GEORG, (Jury of trials &c.) 252
PORTER
——, Mr., & Mr. Apleton, case between, ... 159
Abel, (Grand Jury) 1, 24, 56, 232, 273
agt. Cater. 137, 138
Apleton agt., ... 154, 159, 167

PAGE

PORTER, *continued.*
Abel, Senr., Lytherland ag^{t}., ... 195
Junr., Moore ag^{t}., ... 246
Joseph, ag^{t}. Flood 196
PORTINGALL, CHRISTOPHER, case of, (rape) 230
PORT ROYAL ment^{d}. (libel ag^{t}. bark Speedwell) 352
PORTSMOUTH (Town of)
Jno. Cutt of, ... 8
County Court at, (Sevy ag^{t}. Deering) 18
(Barefoote ag^{t}. Shackford) 67
(Pickering ag^{t}. Frost) 69
(Waldron ag^{t}. Tare) 120
and Dover, Courts at, June [1676] (libel &c. ag^{t}. Thornhull) . . 75
Court of Associates at, (Porter ag^{t}. Cater) 138
30 Sept. 1679 (Waldron ag^{t}. Walton) . . 153
PORTUGAL FRIGOTT of the Harbor of St. Mallo ment^{d}. (libel &c. ag^{t}. ship William) 333
POTTER
Edmond, of Ipswich, Davison ag^{t}., ... 364
Robert, Senr., &c., atty^{s}., ag^{t}. Apleton 279
POTTS, JOHN, &c., mariners of pink Endeavor (libel &c.) 117, 118
POUND
Thomas, of Boston, mariner, case of, (piracy &c.) . 307, 308, 320, 322
&c., confederating with, (case of Wm. Neffe) 321
POWEL or POWELL
Ralph, ag^{t}. Cotton 167
PRATT, WILLIAM, (2^{d}. Jury of trials) 346
PRENTICE
James, (1st. Jury for trials &c.) 120
Thomas, Senr., (1st. Jury for appeals &c.) 108
(1st. Jury for trials &c.) 215
PRESTON
Daniel, (Jury for attaints) 181
(2^{d}. Jury for trials &c.) 181, 215
(Grand Jury) 202, 273
Jnothan (1st. Jury for appeals &c.) 274
PRICE
Elizabeth, Mrs., her exec^{r}. ag^{t}. exec^{r}. of Price 328
John, Capt., exec^{r}., exec^{r}. of Price ag^{t}., ... 328
case of Croad ag^{t}., ment^{d}. (pet^{n}. of Croad & decree) 356
Walter, Capt., his exec^{r}., exec^{r}. of Price ag^{t}., ... 328
case of Croad ag^{t}., ment^{d}. (pet^{n}. of Croad & decree) 356
PRISON
commitment to, (case of Ruth Read &c.) 10, 29, 30, 50, 51
(case of Richard Scott) 60

PAGE

PRISON, *continued.*
commitment to, (answer to pet. of Rebeckah Cooly) 116
(case of Morris Conway) 144
(case of Thomas Waters) 158
(case of Capt. Laurence) 170
(case of Cheffaleer, negro, &c.) 197, 198
(case of George Fairfax) 200
(case of Mary Webster) 229
(case of Joshua Rice) 234
(case of Samuel Bayly) 251
(case of Wm. Clapp) 284
(case of James Morgan) 295
(case of Joseph Indian) 296
(Butler agt. Hollowell &c.) (execn.) 382
in Boston, commitment to, (case of Mary Parsons) 31
(case of Hannah Owen) 361
keeper of, Walter Gendall sent by mittimus to, ... 90
order on pet. of, ... 114
(Sheffeild agt. Homes) (execn.) 387
(Hundlocke agt. Baker &c.) (execn.) . . 389
mentd. (answer to pet. of Wm. Morse) 190
breaking of, (case of Robert Dendy) 115
(order on bill of charges of Bell &c.) 116
prisoner brought from, (case of Allexander Colman) 127
(case of Joshua Rice &c.) 240
(case of Joseph Gatchell) 253
(case of Uriah Cleoments &c.) 283-4
release from, est. being rendered, (order on complaint of Walters) . 169
paying charges, (order on petn. of Warner) 146
prisoner returned to, (case of Tho. Davis &c.) 189
(case of Phillip Darland &c.) 252, 254
(case of Wm. Clapp &c.) 285
(case of Hugh Stone) 303
mentd. (order as to account of Earl) 250
(order as to Gardiner) 281
(case of Bridget Denmarke) 358
(case of Richard Lillie) 359
prisoner discharged from, (order on pet. of Haukins) 31
(" " " " Knights) 254
at Cambridge, (order on complaint of Bernard) 283
PRISONER DEBTOR, sale of, (order on pet. of Jno. Sparrey) 146
PRIVATEER in Boston Harbor, (case of Peeter Lorphelin) 146
PRIVATEERS &c. mentd. (libel &c. agt. ship William) 333
PROCLAMATION of his Majesty mentd. (libel agt. Andreason &c.) 264
PROUT
Ebenezer, Dunster &c. agt., ... 143
Capt., agt. Brooks &c. 349
Timothy, Mr., Senr., (Jury) 149

PAGE

PROUT, *continued.*

Timothy, Mr., Sen[r]., &c., appraisers, (libel &c. ag[t]. Schinking) (exec[n].) 378–9

Wm., exec[r]. of Scarlet ag[t]., ... 95

PROVIDENCE, goods &c. sold at, (Bulkley ag[t]. Thayre &c.) 338

PROVIDENCE (ship)

of Lime, master of, libel &c. of Bacon &c. ag[t]., ... 40

mariner &c. of, Waterhouse ag[t]., ... 350

PUBLIC NOTARY ment[d]. (case of John Weaver) 23

PUBLIC WORSHIP, disturbance at, (case of Alex[dr]. Colman) 127

PUDNEY, JN[o]., Gardiner ag[t]., ... 110

PUNISHMENT

Capital

case of Benj[a]. Goad 11, 14

Tom Indian 22

Rob[t]. Driver 30

Nicholas Faevor 32

Peter Rodriego 35

John Roads &c. 37

Rich[d]. Fouler 37

Peeter Grant 38

Randolph Judson 38

Samuel Guile 50

Little Jn[o]. Indian 53

Stephen Goble 71

Daniel Goble, &c. 72–3

Basto, negro. 74

Caleb, Indian, &c. 76

Maria, negro, (sentenced to be burned to death) . . 198

Jack, negro, ... 199

Wm. Cheny 199

James Morgan 295

Hugh Stone 303–4

Thomas Hawkins 306, 320, 322

Thomas Pound 308, 320, 322

Thomas Johnston 310, 320, 322

Eleazer Buck 311, 320, 322

John Sickterdam 312, 320

Wm. Dun 314, 320

Richard Griffin 315, 320

Daniel Lander 316, 320

William Warren 318

Samuel Watts 319, 320

William Coward, &c. 320, 322

Elizabeth Emmerson 357

Banishment

case of Walter Gendall 102

Ellinor May 138

Thomas Waters 158

PAGE

PUNISHMENT, *continued.*

Banishment

case of Thomas Davis &c. 189

complaint of Boston Comm[rs]., &c. ag[t]. Sherlot 197

case of Cheffaleer, negro, &c. 197, 198

Miscellaneous

by pinning paper on the breast with inscription, & whipping (case of Ruth Read) 10

by fining (case of John & Sam[l]. Bennet) 11

by admonishing (case of George Cole, &c.) 12

by censuring (case of Nicholas Shapleigh) 12

by whipping (case of John Weaver, &c.) 23

(case of Edward Thomas) 24

by fining (case of Bozoone Allen) 29

by admonishing (case of Paul Batt) 29

by standing on the gallows with a rope about her neck &c. (case of Anna Negro) 30

second punishment remitted (case of Mary Haukins) . . 31

by whipping (case of Thomas Mitchell &c.) 42

by fining (case of Mr. Ting) 52

(case of the Deputy Governor &c.) 52

by whipping (case of old Jethro, Indian) 54

by fining (case of Jn[o]. Foster) 54

(case of Jacob Jesson) 55

by standing on the gallows with rope about the neck & whipping (case of Maurice Brett, &c.) 56–7

by standing in the pillory with ear nailed to it, ear to be cut off, fining & whipping (case of Maurice Brett) 57

by fining (case of James Foord) 60

(case of Ezekiel Fogg) 61

(case of Richard Scott) 61

(case of Jonathan Woodman) 62

by standing on the gallows with a rope about the neck, and whipping (case of Tho[s]. Davis &c.) 70

by standing on the gallows with a halter thrown over it, and whipping (case of Peter Cole &c.) 74

by fining (case of Jn[o]. Flynt) 85

(case of Peeter Bent, Jun[r].) 86

(case of Jn[o]. Haughton) 87

(case of Mr. Isaack Waldron) 89, 90

(case of Sam[l]. Symonds, Esq. Dep[ty] Gov. &c.) . . 90

by running the gantlet, rope about the neck, forfeiture of lands & banishment (case of Walter Gendall) 102

by running the gantlet (case of Jn[o]. Watts) 103

discharge as commissioner & fined (case of Capt. Thomas Bratle) 103

by fining (case of Wm. Bowdish) 103

by whipping & fining (case of Wm. Pope) 104

PAGE

PUNISHMENT, *continued.*
Miscellaneous
by fining (case of Sam[l]. Hunting) 114
by standing on the gallows with a rope about his neck & whipping (case of Darby Bryan &c.) 115
by whipping or fining (case of Robert Dendy) 115
by standing on the gallows with a rope about his neck and whipping (case of Ephraim Beamis) 116
by whipping (case of Allexander Colman) 127
(case of Ellinor May) 138
(case of George Shepardson) 144
(case of Morris Conway) 144
by admonishing (case of Rich[d]. Chamberlain) 145
by whipping (case of Sara Bradbrooke &c.) 145
by standing in the pillory and having both ears cut off (case of Peter Lorphelin) 146
by fining (case of Nicholas Shapleigh &c.) 147
(information ag[t]. Armitage) 176
(case of Jn[o]. Dyar) 188
by whipping &c. (case of Thomas Davis &c.) 189
(case of Ann Perry) 197
by branding in the forehead with the letter B, and whipping &c. (case of George Fairfax) 200
by whipping (case of Wm. King) 201
(case of Elisabeth Payne) 228
(case of James Fuller) 229
by standing on the gallows with a rope about the neck & whipping (case of Joshua Rice &c.) 240
by burning the hand &c. (case of Leonard Pomery) 243
by standing on the gallows with rope about the neck & whipping (case of Phillip Darland &c.) 252–3
by placing head & hand in the pillory & having tongue pierced with a hot iron (case of Joseph Gatchell) 254
by fining & whipping (case of John Dounton) 272
by branding on forehead with letter B, and having both ears cut off, &c. (case of Uriah Cleoments) 284
by fining (case of Wm. Clapp &c.) 285–6
by whipping &c. (case of Joseph Indian) 296
by fining (case of Mr. Edward Thomas) 305
by payment of court charges (case of Jn[o]. Newhall, tertius, &c.) 307, 321
by paying charges of prosecution &c. (case of Robin, negro) . 321
by fining (case of Josiah Littlefield) 356
(case of Bridget Denmarke) 358
(case of Richard Lillie) 359
by standing in the pillory with a paper signifying his crime &c. (case of Martin Williams) 360

PAGE

Purchis or Purkis
George, substitute, (Sheaffe agt. Palmer &c.) 123
atty., agt. est. of Windor &c. 141
Olliver, Mr., (Hutchinson agt. Payne) 28
&c., Brattle agt., ... 100, 101
Putman. (See Putnam.)
Putnam or Putman
John, &c. plaintiffs, (appeal) 123
Left., Baker agt., ... 214
agt. Baker 256
Capt., of Salem, Rea agt., ... 329
Nathaniel, Sandford agt., ... 19, 44
for owners of the iron works, Gold &c. agt., ... 27
Gold agt., ... 45
&c., plaintiffs, (appeal) 123
Nathani[el], Allin agt., ... 192
Thomas, Left., Richards agt., ... 44
Pyke. (See Pike.)
Pynchon or Pinchon
———, Major, (courts order to send for witnesses) 31
John, Senr., Esqr., his assignee, Collecot agt., ... 8
Junr., assignee, Collecot agt., ... 8
Esqr., present at Court, 16, 23, 33, 34, 65, 70, 76, 92, 94, 119, 128, 130–132, 149, 150, 190, 209, 223, 229
(Grand Jury) 255
of Boston, merchant, agt. Forster &c. 328

Quarles, Wm., Lummas agt., ... 239
Quebec, ship St. John Frigott of, ... 353
Question as to power of clerk of the writs (Olliver &c. agt. Town of Lynn &c.) 111
Quilter
Francis, agt. Quilter 156
Joseph, Quilter agt., ... 156
Quinsey, Daniel, (1st. Jury for trials &c.) 224

Ragland
John, &c., mariners of ketch John & Benjamin, (libel &c.) 117
(execn.) . 373–4
Rainsford. (See Raynsford.)
Rand
Isaac, mate of ship John & Mary, &c. (libel &c.) 40, 41
& Co., Smith agt., ... 46
Nathaniel, (Jury for trial of attaint) 134
(1st. Jury of trials &c.) 135
Randolph
———, Mr., &c., warrant "signed to," 171

PAGE

RANDOLPH, *continued*.
——, Mr., bill of costs ag[t]., vote by Magistrates &c. as to, . . . 220
Barnard, Mr., Dep[ty]. Coll[r]., (information &c.) 230
Edward, Esq[r]., Coll[r]. &c. ag[t]. pink Expectation 149
Gretian &c. 150
Jackson &c. 160
fifty hogsheads of tobacco &c. . . . 168
Clay 170, 171
Cobbham to answer to charge of, ... 171
allowance to, ... 171
ag[t]. Armitage &c. 175, 176
bark Gift of God &c. 176
Huling &c. 176
two hogsheads of Irish yarn in hands of Harding 177
ship Expedition &c. 177
Hutchinson 209
Boury &c. 210
Place 210
Armitage ag[t]., ... 210
ag[t]. Place ment[d]. (bond by Shrimpton &c.) . 211
Pitcher &c. 219
Wallis 219
Willet 220
ketch Newbery &c. 220
Leveret ag[t]., ... 223
RAPE. (*See* CRIMES.)
RASTER, LUKE, merchant, &c., case of, ... 107
RATES, neglecting to gather, (Mason ag[t]. Stone &c.) 346
RAUSON. (*See* RAWSON.)
RAVENSCROFT, SAMUEL, Mr., &c., Lemoigne ag[t]., ... 129
RAWSON or RAUSON
Edward, Secretary &c., record &c. attested &c. by, 19, 26, 39, 46, 62, 75, 85, 101, 104, 106, 121, 124, 127, 130, 132, 139, 147, 166, 169–172, 190, 206, 208, 211, 214, 216, 224, 229, 231, 240, 249, 250, 253, 263, 264, 265, 271, 272, 282, 293, 294, 301, 371, 372, 373, 376, 378, 380, 382, 383, 386, 387, 388, 390, 391, 393
memo. by, ... 19, 21, 25
ment[d]. in margin, 85, 121, 146, 147, 154, 157, 203, 296
execution certified by, 371, 372, 374, 377–379, 381, 383, 388, 389, 392
&c. ag[t]. Stoughton &c., comm[rs]., ... 208, 209

PAGE

Rawson or Rauson, *continued.*
William, ag^t. Glover &c. . . . 26, 65
ag^t. Billing or (Billings) . . . 26, 96
&c., securities on bond of attaint, (Woodmansy ag^t. Joy) . 45
ag^t. Briggs . . . 65
atty., ag^t. Baker . . . 162
&c. ag^t. Stoughton &c., comm^{rs}., . . . 208, 209
ag^t. Gilbert . . . 245, 255
&c., sureties on bond of attaint, (Baker ag^t. Wharton) . 248
(2^d. Jury for trials &c.) . . . 274

Raymond
——, ment^d. (order on pet. of Dwight) . . . 200
——, " (case of George Fairfax) . . . 200
Daniel, by atty., ag^t., Orchard . . . 224

Raynsford or Rainsford
Solomon, &c., Greene ag^t., . . . 109
ag^t. Winthrop, Treasurer, &c., . . . 366

Rea, Daniel, of Salem, ag^t. Putnam . . . 329

Read or Reade
Christopher, (Jury for appeals) . . . 233
(Jury for attaints) . . . 233
Gibson ag^t., . . . 271
George, of Woburn, ag^t. Pearse . . . 351
Phillip, &c., sureties, ag^t. Williams . . . 68
Dr., Gifford ag^t., . . . 185, 192
ag^t. Bacon . . . 281
Robert, mariner of ship Merchants Adventure, &c., ag^t. Stone . . 213
Ruth, case of, (adulterous carriage) . . . 10
Wm., case of his wife Ruth . . . 10

Reasons of appeal
not signed (Martyn ag^t. Winsley) . . . 5
non suit for, (estate of Wm. Snelling) . . . 153
(Williams ag^t. Townsend) . . . 155
(Holman &c. ag^t. Michelson) . . . 218
(Peasley ag^t. Clark) . . . 221
(Wright &c. ag^t. Sparrey) . . . 235
reflections declared in, (case of Paul Batt) . . . 31
(case of Mr. Isaac Waldron) . . . 89
&c. to be delivered up (Woodbridge ag^t. Gerrish) . . . 68
not being seasonably brought in, non suit for, (Wing ag^t. Halsey) . 206
(Fosket ag^t. Foskett) . 328
(Gookin &c. ag^t. Savage &c.) . . . 329
(Savage ag^t. Savage &c.) . . . 329
(Francis ag^t. Danforth), 330
time of Court being missed in, non suit for, (Wright ag^t. Sparrey) . 235

PAGE

RECORDS
"second book" of, (Court of Assistants, beginning 3 Mar. 1673) . 1
"day book" ment[d]. in margin (Court of Assistants or Admiralty), 16, 231
for executions, book of, (Court of Assistants) 371, 379, 382, 386, 388, 391
book of, (Court of Admiralty), ment[d]. 376
RECOVERY (ship)
master of, libel of Gibbs ag[t]., ... 75
&c., libel &c. ag[t]. Gibbs 76
libel &c. ag[t]. Woodmansey 118, 119
&c., libel &c. ag[t]. Checkly & wife 130
(exec[n].) 382–3
REDDING, ELLINOR, answer to pet. of, ... 223
RED FLAG, sailing under, ment[d]. (case of Thomas Pound &c.), 308, 309, 311, 312, 317, 318
REDMAN
John, Colcord ag[t]., ... 18
atty., ag[t]. Town of Hampton 19
REETCH or (KEETCH), JN[o]., of Boston, (libel &c.) 105
REFLECTIONS. (*See* CRIMES.)
RELIGION, scoffing at. (*See* CRIMES.)
REMINGTON or RIMINGTON
———, Mr., foreman, (Wisewall ag[t]. Paige &c.) 250
Jonathan, (Mr.) (2[d]. Jury for trials &c.) 71, 192, 362
(Jury for trials of attaint) 192, 244
(Grand Jury) 242
(1st. Jury for trials &c.) 245
Lt., foreman, (Jury of trials) 302
Mr. " " 311, 315, 317, 319
REPROACHFUL WORDS ag[t]. authority. (*See* CRIMES.)
RESOLUTION (ship)
of London, seamen of, libel &c. ag[t]. Cobb &c. 173
&c., libel &c. of Tompkins ag[t]., ... 173
ment[d]. in margin 174
(Poole &c. ag[t]. Phipps &c.) 211–213
REUP (Indian), of Marlborough, case of, (murder) 53
REYNOLD or REYNOLDS
———, Left., as to being a legal officer (Wharton ag[t]. Reynold) . 193
Nathaniel, Wharton ag[t]., ... 192
Left., Wharton ag[t]., ... 202
RICE or RISE
Benj[a]., ag[t]. Avery 273
Joseph (Jury for attaints) 181
(1st. Jury for trials &c.) 181
Joshua, of Boston, cordwainer, case of, (adultery) 234, 240
(case of Elizabeth Crockett) 234
Nicholas, by atty[s]., ag[t]. trustees &c. of Bellingham 24
RICHARD (alias Frederick) (ship), of Boston, libel &c. of Southack agt., . 334–5

PAGE

RICHARD, PETER, commander, (libel &c. ag^t. ship Marquis of Royan) . . 354
RICHARD & Mary (ship)
of Swansey (case of John Weaver) 23
(case of Edward Thomas) 24
RICHARDS
——, Mr., to appoint time &c. (Newman ag^t. Smith) 25
Arthur, mariner of ship George, &c. (complaint &c.) 41
Edward, ag^t. Putman 44
&c., sureties on bond of attaint, (Apelton, &c. ag^t. Hawkes &c.) 236
atty^s., ag^t. Apleton 279
probate of will of, (Bullard, &c. ag^t. judgment of County Court) 291
James, Esqr., present at Court 22 Apr. 1686 300
John, Mr., &c., award of, ment^d. (Newman ag^t. Smith) 25
Capt., &c., comm^{rs}., chosen by freeman of Boston, allowed &c. by the Court 67, 96
Esqr., present at Court, 149–151, 161, 169, 172, 173, 176, 178, 179, 190, 202, 208, 241, 243, 251, 255, 266, 273, 287, 296, 297, 298, (300?) 302, 305, 320–322
John, ag^t. Witter 187
(Grand Jury) 298
RIMINGTON. (*See* REMINGTON.)
RING.
Robert, ag^t. Worcester 82
ag^t. Buswell 82
RISE. (*See* RICE.)
ROADES, or
ROADS
Henry, Apleton, ag^t., ... 276–7
ag^t. Apleton 281
John, & Co., &c., libel of Freake &c. ag^t., ... 34
&c., case of, (Piracy) 36
of Boston, case of, (Piratically seizing vessels &c.) 36
(case of Peter Grant) 38
&c., order for execution of, ... 39
pirates, (case of Thomas Mitchell, &c.) 42
Josiah, Hauthorn &c. ag^t., ... 215
Theophilus, (Grand Jury) 361
ROBBERY. (*See* CRIMES.)
ROBBINS
Georg. &c., case of, (Killing of Indians) 57
Richard, (Grand Jury) 59, 78, 242
William, house &c. of, (Butler ag^t. Hollowell &c.) (exec^n.) . . 381
ROBBINSON. (*See* ROBINSON.)
ROBERTS
John (Joseph ?), by atty., ag^t. Coleman 269
Tho., ship built by, (Smith ag^t. Hiskett) 339

PAGE

ROBIE. (*See* ROBY.)
ROBIN (Negro).
servant of Andrew Gardner, case of, (murder) 304
servant, found guilty of manslaughter 305, 321
ROBINEAU, Stephen, mariner &c. of ketch Amitie ag[t]. Assailly 324
ROBINSON or ROBBINSON
John, master of brigantine Samuel (case of Lillie) 358
Nathaniel, Freake agt., ... 102
Samuel (2[d]. Jury for trials &c.) 79
Thomas, his guardian, admr. of Coggan & wife ag[t]., ... 17
ROBY or ROBIE
Henry &c., ag[t]. Evins 6, 136
ag[t]. Colcord 7
atty., ment[d]. (Waldron ag[t]. Walton) 153
William, instead of Jacklin (1st Jury for trials &c.) 192
of Boston, merchant, Massey ag[t]., ... 303
feofee &c., Foy ag[t]., ... 368
ROCHELL
Jn[o]. Toton of, chirurgeon, ... 43
in France, Jn[o]. Bayly of, ... 55
Mons[r]. Abraham Michard, merchant in, ... 355
ROCHFORD, SAMUEL, &c., mariners of ship Ann & Hesther (libel &c.) . . 172
ROCK or ROCKE
Joseph, adm[r]., ag[t]. Clarke 3, 4
ag[t]. guardian of Robbinson 17
(Mr.), ag[t]. Francks 142, 143, 180
Mr., (libel &c., ag[t]. Schinchinke) 178
RODRIEGO
Peter, &c., libel of Freake &c. ag[t]., ... 34
Dutchman, case of, (piratically seizing vessels, &c.) 35
ROGERS
Gamaliel, ag[t]. Tite 234
John, (case of Ruth Read) 10
Rebeckah " 10
ROOPE, ANTHONY, his surety ag[t]. Hughson 112
ROSE
Rob[t]., ment[d]. (case of Wm. Pitman) 110
Roger, Thayer ag[t]., ... 5
complaint of Griffyn ag[t]., ... 19
ag[t]. Stowell 121
Yeales ag[t]., ... 184
ROST, THOMAS, Martyn ag[t]., ... 217
ROULAND (or ROWLAND), SAMUELL, ag[t]. Hobbs 27
ROW or ROWE
Elias (Grand Jury) 17, 120, 202, 230, 232
(2[d]. Jury of trials &c.) 141

PAGE

Rowe &c., *continued.*
El[i]jah, (Grand Jury) 273
Rowland (or Rouland), Samuell, ag[t]. Hobbs 27
Rowley (Town of), Elizabeth Horsely of, ... 336
Rowley Woods in Massachusetts (case of Henry Toltwood) 336
Roxbury (Town of)
Benjamin Goad of, ... 10
ment[d]. (answer to pet. of Benj[n]. Goad) 14
house of Dr. Swan in, ... 198
Thomas Swann of, ... 198
Joshua Lambe of, ... 198
Jn[o]. Baker of, ... 260
John Hayward of, merchant, ... 352
Rucke ———, Mr., (libel ag[t]. Bartholmew &c.) 76
Ruggels or / Ruggles / Rugles
John, ag[t]. Hudson 64–5
(Jury for trial of attaint) 134
(1st. Jury of trials &c.) 135
(2[d]. " " " ") 203
Sen[r]., (Jury of trials) 302, 311, 319
Samuel, (1st. Jury of trials &c.) 65, 95
Left., (1st. Jury for trials &c.) 120
(Jury for trials of attaint) 192, 233
(2[d]. Jury for trials &c.) 193
Left., (Grand Jury) 266
Ruming or / Rumings
Jn[o]., Captain Hudson ag[t]., ... 101
Rumley Marsh or / Rumney Marsh
John Floyd of, ... 271
Thomas Brentnal formerly of, ... 326
Rusell or / Russell
———, Mr., (order on complaint of Walters) 169
present at Court 12 Oct. 1683 241
George, Hon[ble]. Esq[r]., case of, (fornication) 169
James, Mr. or Esq[r]., present at Court, 58, 149, 150, 151, 159, 161, 173, 176, 178, 179, 190, 202, 208, 209, 211, 213, 214, 223, 228–232, 241, 243, 251, 266, 273, 287, 296–298, 300,302, 305, 320, 321, 322, 327, 336,345, 359, 361
Bellingham, ag[t]., ... 164
Treasurer &c., Cobbham bound to, ... 171
&c. appointed to keep County Court at Essex . 253
Homes ag[t]., ... 270

PAGE

RUSSELL OR RUSELL, *continued.*
James, Mr. or Esq[r]., Treasurer &c. (bond by Wharton &c.) . . . 272
slandering of, (case of James Lowden) . . . 363
(Grand Jury) 78
exec[r]., Golding ag[t]., ... 98
Jason, (2[d]. Jury of trials) 362
Joseph, (Jury of trials) 323
Richard, Esq[r]., present at Court, 1, 15, 16, 23, 24, 32–36, 41, 43, 52, 55, 58, 61
Treas[r]. &c., bond to, (case of Blandchard &c.) . . . 22
(Woodmansey ag[t]. Joy) . . . 46
his exec[r]., Golding ag[t]., ... 98
Thomas, (Grand Jury) 35
Mr. &c., of Charlestown, merchants, (libel &c.) 55
William, (Jury of trials) 345
(Jury) 360

RYALL
Isaac, (Jury for trials of attaint) 192, 256
(1st. Jury for trials &c.) 192
(1st. Jury for appeal) 257
Joseph, (1st. Jury of trials &c.) 135
(2[d] " " " ") 362
William, (Jury of attaints) 244
(2[d]. Jury of trials) 245
(Jury of trials) 299
(Jury) 300

RYDER, JOHN, ag[t]. Sharp 7

SABBATH, Court of Assistants sitting every day except the, ... 305
SABIN, BENJA., (Jury for attaints) 267
SAFFIN or SAFFYN
———, Mr., (Phips &c. ag[t]. Bowers) 224
John, Mr., (Grand Jury) 53
&c. chosen constables for Boston & oath 80
atty., ag[t]. Walley 99, 100
Mr., (Jury) 150
&c. chosen comm[rs]. for Boston & oath &c. 168, 199, 214
ag[t]. Holt 187
Mr. &c. on behalf of Bowers ag[t]. Phipps &c. 232
ag[t]. Burton 281
Thomas, case of, ... 249
&c., bond by, (case of Thomas Saffin) 249
ag[t]. Baxter 282

ST. CHARLES (bark) (case of Wm. Johnson) 242
ST. CHRISTOPHERS, ISLAND OF,
Mr. Wm. Woodrope, &c. of, ... 298, 300
Sanctillo Heynes of, ... 300, 301

PAGE

St. John (ship) of Dublin (Randolph agt. Jackson &c.) 160
St. John Frigott (ship or bark) of Quebec (libel &c.) 353, 354
St. Mallo
mentd. (libel agt. ship William &c.) 333, 335
Frederick Clutterbuck, merchant in, ... 335
St. Tobin, (libel agt. bark Speedwell) 352
Salamander (ship)
owners of, Woodman agt., ... 61, 62
(a prize belonging to the Duke of Brandenburgh) mate &c. of, (libel &c.) 179

Sale
Ephraim, (2d. jury for trials &c.) 96
(Grand Jury) 305
Salem (Town of)
County Court at, 19, 27, 44, 45, 47, 66, 67, 83, 100, 107, 109, 110, 111, 112, 120, 123, 134, 135, 136, 137, 143, 154, 155, 163, 164, 181, 192–195, 214, 215, 222, 223, 225, 233, 235, 236, 248, 258, 259, 261-263, 267, 270, 274, 275–279, 288, 327, 328, 329, 331, 339, 340, 345, 346, 356, 357, 376. (*See also* County Court — Essex.)
Selectmen of, mentd. (Lattimore agt. James &c.) 20
Jno. Flynt of, ... 85
Wm. Bowdish of, ... 103
port of, ketch belonging to, (case of Wm. Johnson) 242
County Court, reference from, mentd. (order on est. of Wade) . . 250
clerk of, (order on pet. of Jona. Wade) 265
Wm. Dounton of, ... 271
Jno. Henderson &c. of, ... 272
ketch Mary of, ... 305, 307, 309–313, 315–318
Phillip English of, ... 326, 341, 346
John Crode of, ... 328
Capt. John Putnam of, ... 329
Daniel Rea of, ... 329
Stephen Small of, ... 339
John Blaney, Senr., of, ... 340
Wm. Dunton of, gaolkeeper, ... 340
Philip Cromwell of, ... 341
Capt. Walter Price of, ... 356
Martin Williams of, bricklayer, ... 359
church of, John Broune, Senr., Ruling Elder of, ... 376
Wm. Broune of, Assistant, ... 377
Henry Skerry of, marshal, ... 388
Salisbury (Town of).
County Court at, ... 16–19, 46, 81, 82, 98, 99, 140, 142, 154, 156 (*See also* County Court — Norfolk.)
and Hampton Courts, Major Hauthorne appointed to keep, . . . 127
Abraham Broune of, ... 140
Jacob Morrell of, shipwright, ... 348
Richard Carr of, ... 367

PAGE

SALISBURY (ketch)
master of, (information &c.) 343–4
Burroughs &c. appointed to apprize, ... 356
ment^{d}. (order as to appeal of Lawrence) 360
SALTER
Jabez, Cheeckley ag^{t}., ... 47
(2^{d}. jury for appeals &c.) 108
(Jury of trials) 362
SALTONSTAL or SALTONSTALL
——, Mr. (order on complaint of Walters) 169
——, Maj^{r}., ment^{d}. (March ag^{t}. Carr) 367
Nathaniel, Mr., judgment confirmed (Griffyn ag^{t}. Gove) 99
Esqr., present at Court, 128, 130, 131, 133, 139, 148, 149, 150, 151, 161, 179, 190, 202, 209, 214, 241, 243, 255, 273, 302
Richard, Esqr., present at Court, ... 170, 175, 179, 190, 202
SAMBORN or SAMBORNE
John, &c., atty^{s}., ag^{t}. Tilton 7
SAMUEL (brigantine) ment^{d}. (case of Richard Lillie) 358
SANDERS
Mary, wife of William, petition for divorce 30
Robert, (Grand Jury) 32
Wm., pet. for divorce by his wife Mary, ... 30, 31
SANDEY, WINSOR, of Boston, mariner, Ball ag^{t}., ... 351
SANDFORD SANDIFORD (See SANFORD.)
SANDS
John, ag^{t}. Hutchinson 17
his exec^{n}. ag^{t}. Hutchinson respited 32
SANFORD or SANDFORD, SANDIFORD
——, land of, (Sandford ag^{t}. Putman) 45
Abraham, &c., mariners, (libel &c.) 40
Elisha, &c., owners of ship Salamander, Woodman ag^{t}., ... 61
Henry, libel &c. of Parrick ag^{t}., ... 91
(Jury) 150
Robert, ag^{t}. Putman 19, 44
ag^{t}. Orchard 196
Tho., Mr., (1st. Jury for trials &c.) 215
SARGEANT or SARJANT
——, Mr., ment^{d}. (case of Saml. Shrimpton) 298, 299
Elisabeth, & husband Peter ag^{t}. Shrimpton, exec^{r}., &c. 276
Peter, Mr., & wife Elisabeth " " " " 276
SARL. (See SEARLE.)
SATLE or SETLE
Richard, (2^{d}. Jury for trials &c.) 121
(Grand Jury) 255

PAGE

SAVAG or SAVAGE
——, Major, letter to, ment[d]. (case of Rich[d]. Scott) 60
Speaker, (Alden ag[t]. Clarke, as to bill of costs) . . 158
Ephraim, Capt., (Jury for attaints) 266
Willis ag[t]., ... 268
&c., Savage ag[t]., ... 329
Gookin & wife ag[t]., ... 329
appraisers, (libel &c. ag[t]. Checkly & wife) (exec[n].) . 384–5
Jn[o]., &c., mariners of ship Herron, (libel &c.) 159, 160
Mary, Mrs., relict of Tho[s]. Savage, Esq[r]., order on estate . . . 229
spinster, ag[t]. Savage &c. 329
Thomas, Major, &c., com[rs]., chosen by freeman of Boston and oath &c. 67, 96
Jun[r]., (2[d]. Jury of trials &c.) 96
(Jury) 149
Major, Apleton ag[t]., ... 123
Man ag[t]., ... 137
Esq[r]. or Major, present at Court, 150, 151, 159–161, 169, 170, 172, 176, 178, 179, 190
Thaier ag[t]., ... 186, 191
relict of, order on estate of, ... 229

SAWIN
John, (2[d]. Jury for trials &c.) 60
(1st. Jury for appeals &c.) 274

SCANDALOUS OFFENCE. (*See* CRIMES.)

SCARBOROUGH or SCARBOROW
Samuel, (Jury for trials of attaint) 192, 267
(1st. Jury for trials &c.) 192

SCARLET or SCARLETT
John, (2[d]. Jury for trials &c.) 25
exec[r]., ag[t]. Prout 95
(Grand Jury) 139
(1st. Jury for trials &c.) 192
(2[d]. Jury for appeals) "in behalf of" Incr. Sumner . . 256
(Grand Jury) 266
Samuel, Capt., &c., award of, ment[d]. (Newman ag[t]. Smith) . . 25
his exec[r]. ag[t]. Prout 95

SCATE, JN[O]. (Jury for attaints) 180

SCATES, JOHN, (1st. Jury for trials &c.) 181

SCHENKING, SCHINKING, SCHINKINK or SHINCHINK, SHINCHINKE
Barnard, merchant, libel &c. of Gretian ag[t]., ... 178
(exec[n].) . . . 378–380

SCILLY COVE in Newfoundland, ship William seized at, ... 334

SCIRE FACIAS, judgment on, (Stebbins ag[t]. English) 346

PAGE

SCOFFING &c. (*See* CRIMES.)
SCOTT
John, (Jury of trials) . . . 345
(Jury) . . . 360
Richard, case of, (writing untruths &c.) . . . 60, 61
SCOTTO or SCOTTOW
Jn°., &c., ag^{t}. Calley . . . 96
Joshua, Left., (Grand Jury) . . . 17
Capt., (2^{d}. Jury for trials &c.) . . . 79
ag^{t}. Wheelewright . . . 152
Capt., by atty., ag^{t}. Hutchinson . . . 186
Norden ag^{t}., . . . 292
deed by, ment^{d}. (libel &c. ag^{t}. Checkly & wife) (exec^{n}.) . 385
Tho., &c., exec^{rs}., ag^{t}. Sweeting . . . 79
SCRIPTURE, "Math. the 12th 32" and "Luke 17. 3." ment^{d}. (pet^{n}. of Isaac Waldron) 90
SCRIPTURE, SAMUEL, testimony by, ment^{d}. (case of Joseph Spoonhaut (Indian)) 53
SEAL OF THE COLONY ment^{d}. (case of John Weaver) . . . 23
SEALE, JACOB, of the Island of Jersey (libel &c. ag^{t}. ship William) . . 333
SEARLE, or SARL, SERLL
Ephraim, (Jury of trials) . . . 299
(Jury) . . . 300
Phillip, (1st. Jury for trials &c.) . . . 59
(2^{d}. " " " ") . . . 60
Robt., (2^{d}. Jury for trials &c.) . . . 96
SEARS or SERES
Giles, of Ipswich (libel ag^{t}. bark Speedwell) . . . 352
Jn°., Collicot &c. ag^{t}., . . . 219
SEAVER or SEAVOR or SEVER
Caleb, (2^{d}. Jury for trials &c.) . . . 215
Nath., (1st. " " " ") . . . 59
Robert, (Jury for trial of attaint) . . . 2
(2^{d}. Jury for trials &c.) . . . 3
(Grand Jury) . . . 78
Senr., (Jury) . . . 210
Suball, (1st. Jury for trials &c.) . . . 78, 152
SEAWALL. (*See* SEWALL.)
SECRETARY
ment^{d}. (case of Benj^{a}. Goad) . . . 11, 14
(answer to pet. of Alvin Child) . . . 12
(case of Wm. Darvall &c.) . . . 14
in margin . . . 16
(Courts order as to witnesses &c.) . . . 31
(order for execution of Robt. Driver &c.) . . . 33
(libel &c. ag^{t}. Page) . . . 92

PAGE

SECRETARY, *continued.*
ment[d]. (order on pet. of Elisabeth Bowers) 104
(order as to ten pounds caution money for court charges) . 171
(order on pet. of John Gyfford) 231
(order on est. of Mr. Wade) 250
(libel ag[t]. Andreason &c.) 264
(order on pet. of Mr. Jon[a]. Wade) 265, 266
(Hitchins ag[t]. Browne) 276
(order as to Jon[a]. Gardiner) 281
(order on complaint by Sam[l]. Bernard) 283
(case of James Morgan) 295
(case of Samuel Shrimpton) 297–299
(libel ag[t]. Keech &c.) 298
(case of Hugh Stone) 304
(case of Thomas Hawkins) 306
(case of Thomas Pound &c.) 309–311, 320, 322
&c. to allow of bill of costs 31
ordered to put bond in suit (case of Edw[d]. Naylor) 32
allowance to, (order as to officers fees) 62
letter to, ment[d]. (case of Peter Lorphelin) 146
warrants to be issued by, ... 199
present at Court 18 Mar. 1681 208
SEDGWICK or SEDGWICKE
Robert, ag[t]. Willis 101
&c., appraisers, (libel &c. ag[t]. Checkly & wife) (exec[n].) . 384–5
SEDITION. (*See* CRIMES.)
SEIZING INDIANS (case of Wm. Waldron &c.) 86–88, 91
SELECTMEN
of Salem &c., cases referred to, (Lattimore ag[t]. James &c.) . . 20
of Andover ag[t]. Fuller 108
of Lynn &c., Olliver &c. ag[t]., ... 111
ment[d]. (answer to pet. of Wm. Morse) 190
&c. for Boston, complaint ag[t]. Sherlot 197
ment[d]. (answer to pet. of Ellinor Redding) 223
of Charlestown (Phips &c. ag[t]. Bowers) 224
of Cambridge ag[t]. the drummers of Cambridge 289
of Marblehead, Vincent Stilson ag[t]., ... 328
of Watertown, Joseph Mason ag[t]., ... 346
SELLING INDIANS (case of Wm. Waldron &c.) 86–88, 91
SENDALL
Samuel, (Grand Jury) 43
&c., ag[t]. judgment &c. of Stoddard, comm[r]., ... 66
SERES. (*See* SEARS.)
SERLL. (*See* SEARLE.)
SETLE. (*See* SATLE.)
SEVER. (*See* SEAVER.)
SEVERANS, JOSEPH, Batt ag[t]., ... 9

PAGE

[SEVERICK], WM., (Jury of inquest) (inquisition on body of Bickford) . 34
SEVY, THOMAS, agt. Deering 18
SEWALL or SEAWALL
Samuel, Mr., (2d. Jury for appeals &c.) 108
Esqr., present at Court, 255, 266, 273, 287, 296–298, 300, 302, 305, 321, 322, 327, 336, 345, 359, 361
SEXTON
Thomas, by atty., agt. Winslow 68
master of ship Elizabeth, dep. by, 14 June 1679 . . . 132
SHACKFORD, WM., Barefoote agt., ... 67
SHADDOCK
William, (Jury of trials &c.) 252
(1st. Jury for appeals &c.) 289
(Jury of attaints &c.) 289
Inglesby agt., ... 291
SHAKELEY, JOHN, &c., by atty., agt. Winslow 29
SHAPLEIGH
———, Major, (answer to pet. of Edward Colcord) 24
Nicholas, Major, mentd. (answer to pet. of Alvin Child) . . . 12
case of, (concealing goods &c.) 12, 13
answer to pet. of, ... 14, 16
&c., mariners of ship Jno. Adventure, agt. Craty &c., . . 147
case of, (lying) 147
SHARP or SHARPE
John, Ryder agt., ... 7
(2d. Jury of trials) 337
Richard, (Jury for trial of attaint) 3
(1st. Jury for trials &c.) 3
SHARROT (or STARAST) PAUL, Left., of ship Salamander, &c. (libel &c.) . 179
SHATSWEL or SHATSWELL
Richard, agt. Jewet 205, 214
principal, &c., bond by, (Shatswel agt. Jewet) 205
SHATTOCK, PHILLIP, (2d. Jury of trials) 337
SHEAFF or SHEAFFE
Sampson, agt. Hunkin 45
by atty., agt. Hawkins 68
Mr., by atty., agt. Blackleach &c. 85
agt. Palmer 98
Mr., surety, &c., bond by, (Wharton agt. Reynold) . . 193
(Jury of trials &c.) 252
Samuell, of London, by atty., agt. Palmer &c. 123
SHEFFEILD
(alias Perry) Ann, Homes agt., ... 261, 266
agt. Homes (execn.) 386–388
SHELLY, RALFE, master of ship Speedwell, &c., case of, ... 107

PAGE

SHELSTON, ROBERT, of Boston, laborer, Devaulx ag^t., ... 327
SHEPARDSON, GEORGE, case of, (inciting to theft) 144
SHEPHEARD, ANDREW, his exec^rs. ag^t. Sweeting 79
SHERLOT or SHERLOTT
Henry, Mr., (Frenchman), dancing master &c., complaint of Boston comm^rs. &c. ag^t., 197

SHERMAN
Jno., Mr., (Grand Jury) 35
Joseph, (Jury for attaints) 181
(2^d Jury for trials &c.) 181
Mr., his servant &c., complaint of Bisco ag^t., ... 286
SHICE, LAWRENC ZACKARIAH, (Dutchman), master of ketch Hopewell, (libel &c.) 55, 56

SHINCHINK / SHINCHINKE (*See* SCHINKING.)
SHIPPEN
Edward, (Jury for trial of attaint) 2
(2^d. Jury for trials &c.) 3
relict & adm^x. of Davenport ag^t., ... 99
atty., ag^t. Sprague 222
Mr., wharf of, ment^d. (libel &c. ag^t. Checkly & wife) (exec^n.) 386

SHIPPING
Act for encouraging &c. of, (Lason ag^t. Brenton, Coll^r.,) 349
(libel ag^t. pink Three Brothers &c.) . 355
(Shrimpton ag^t. Brenton, Coll^r.,) . . 366

SHOARE
Jonathan, ag^t. Yale 9
Sampson, ag^t. Gibbs 68
SHORTRIGGS, WM., master of ketch Elinor (case of Coward &c.) 319
SHO SHANNOUGH (Jury for trial of Tom Indian) 22
SHRIMPTON
Epaphras, Mr., testimony by, ment^d. (Stanbury ag^t. Harris) . . 367
Henry, Mr., exec^r., &c., Sarjant & wife ag^t., ... 276
Samuel, Mr., merchant, &c. (libel &c.) 34
(Grand Jury) 56, 255
Mr., (Case of Sarah Bradbrooke) 145
declaration by, (libel ag^t. pink Expectation) 149
of Boston, merchant, &c., bond by, ... 210, 211
Mr., &c., Webb ag^t., ... 215
(Jury of trials, &c.) 228
of Boston, merchant, case of, (seditious actions) . 297–299
as to indictment of, ... 301
Esqr., present at Court 20 Jan. 1689 321
23 " " 322
owner of brigantine Mary, ag^t. Brenton, Coll^r., &c. . 366
SHUITE, MICAELL, &c., appraisers, (Elliot &c. ag^t. ketch Friendship) (exec^n) 392
SICKTERDAM, JOHN, case of, (piracy &c.) 311, 312, 320

PAGE

SIMONS. (*See* SYMONDS.)

SIMPSON } or SYMSON
SIMSON

John (Jury of trials) 302, 311, 319, 362

Saml. (Jury for attaints) 266

SKEATS, JOHN, (Petit jury) 323

SKELTON, ———, land of, ment^d^. (Sandford ag^t^. Putman) 45

SKERRY

———, ment^d^. (case of Bethyah Gatchel) 138

Henry, marshal generals deputy, return of exec^n^. by, (overseers &c. ag^t^. Manning.) 377

of Salem, marshal, return of exec^n^. by, (Boober & wife ag^t^. Downing), 388

SKINNER

James, Waldron ag^t^., ... 96

Nicholas, master of ship Dove, &c. (libel, &c.) 58

late master of pink Hopewell, (libel, &c.) 92

master of pink Dove, &c. (libel, &c.) (exec^n^.) 372–3

Thomas, Lowle ag^t^., ... 3

&c., sureties on bond of attaint, (Apleton &c. ag^t^. Hawkes &c.) 236

SLANDER. (*See* CRIMES.)

SMALEBONES, JN^o^., &c., mariners of ship James Frygott, (libel, &c.) . . 128

SMALL, STEPHEN, of Salem, ag^t^. Bullock 339

SMALLPOX, order as to, ment^d^. (case of Wm. Pope) 104

SMART, JOHN, quartermaster of ship John & Mary, &c., (libel &c.) . . 40

SMIT or }
SMITH }

———, Mrs., widow, Egerton, ag^t^., ... 166

———, ag^t^. Wharton &c., execution respited 286

———, Mr., Wharton ag^t^., ... 286

Arthur, Perkins ag^t^., ... 239

Christopher, pet. for divorce by his wife Dorcas 200

Daniel (2^d^ Jury of appeals &c.) 108

(1st Jury for trials &c.) 203

(1st Jury for appeal) 256

(Jury for attaints) 255

Dorcas, wife of Christopher, pet. for divorce 200

Edward (1st Jury for trials &c.) 203

Elisabeth, widow relict of Francis Smith, ag^t^. Hudson 44

Francis, his widow relict Elisabeth ag^t^. Hudson 44

George, merchant, Newman, ag^t^., ... 25

James (2^d^. Jury for appeals &c.) 108

ag^t^. Bouden 134

John, his assignee, ag^t^. Aglin 7

&c., capital offenders, (case of Nicholas Shapleigh) . . . 13

merchant, atty., Newman ag^t^., ... 25

merchant, (libel &c., ag^t^. Bull) 40

PAGE

SMITH OR SMIT, *continued.*

John, merchant, and part owner of ship John & Mary (libel &c.) . 41
(Grand Jury) 44, 202
merchant, agt. Rand & Co. 46
(Jury of trials) 57
Mr., agt. Lydget 113
(2d. Jury for trials &c.) 121
Clarke agt., ... 236
Esqr., present at Court, ... 302, 305, 320, 322, 336, 359
Jonathan (2d. Jury of trials) 362
Joseph, plaintiff, (appeal) 9
Golding & wife agt., ... 193
acknowledgment by, (Golding & wife agt. Smith) 194
Migeley agt., ... 195
atty., Goulding agt., ... 204
Wharton, &c., agt., ... 271, 282, 293
as to bond of, (order on pet. of Richd. Wharton &c.) . . 272
Katherin, costs granted to, (Egerton agt. Smith) 166
for her son John, Clarke agt., ... 236
Launcellot, complaint agt. Lynch 240, 241
Michael, killing &c. of, mentd. (case of Mary Hale) 189
Nicholas, &c., mariners, (libel &c.) 40
Richard, his surety agt. Swift, &c. 69
Everden agt., ... 164
Robert, agt. Batchiler 110
Samuel, commander of ship Endeavor, Francis &c. agt., ... 130
&c., libel agt. Francis &c., . 132
Thomas, (Grand Jury) 24
&c., mariners of ketch Ollive Branch (libel &c.) 131
(Jury of trials &c.) 252
of Boston, blacksmith, agt. Hiskett 339
smith, agt. Nash 365
shop of, mentd. (Butler agt. Hollowell &c.) (execn.) . . 381

SNELLING, WM., estate of, appeal from settlement of, by attorney of Francis Davenport, 153

SNOW, SAM., by atty., &c. agt. Sparrey 235

SOAMES OR SOMES

John, (case of George Cole, &c.) 12
agt. Bryant 97
Bryan agt., ... 98
of Boston, agt. Lake 364

SOLEY OR SOLLE SOLLY

Mathew, (1st. Jury for trials &c.) 120
(2d. " " " ") 215
Sarah, widow, Marshall agt., ... 290
widow, &c., libel of Wharton &c. agt., ... 297

PAGE

SOMES. (*See* SOAMES.)

SOUTHACK

Cyprian, Capt., commander of ship Porcupine,
libel &c. agt. ship Gift of God 332
agt. ship Wm. of Waymouth . . . 333–4
agt. ship Richard of Boston . . . 334
agt. ship St. John Frigott of Quebec . 353

SPANISH INDIAN SERVANT (Marea), case of, (infanticide) 115

SPANISH MONEY mentd. (case of Martin Williams) 359

SPANISH WITNESSES mentd. (libel agt. Andreason &c.) 264

SPARHAUKE, NATHANIEL, (Grand Jury) 180, 214

SPARREY

John, order on pet. of, ... 146
Wright &c. agt., ... 235

SPECIAL JURY, list of, ... 363

SPECIAL VERDICT

(on attaint) as to right to give damage (Bonner agt. Heyman &c.) . 1
as to deed being authentic (Atkinson agt. Williams) 5
as to disposal of estate where no legal proof of will (Martyn &c. agt. Winsley &c.) 5–6
as to confession and one evidence being sufficient (case of Benj. Goad) 10
as to evidence (Crispe agt. Joanes) (See Court Files No. 1324, 5th. paper) 18
as to costs when no damage is proved (Gold &c. agt. Putnam &c.) . 27
as to contract (Hutchinson agt. Payne) 28
as to the judgment of Court of Assistants being a legal foundation (Cogswell agt. Cogswell) 66
as to a marshal levying execution on person & estate and releasing the person (Colcord agt. Drake) 81
(as to law of appeal) (Greely agt. Young) 81
as to attachment constituting duress (Woodbridge agt. Williams) . 83
as to power to impress (Griffyn agt. Gove) 99
as to attorney suing for his own use &c. (Hull agt. Wincoll) . . 122
(subject not stated) (Pickard &c. agt. Longfellow) 134
lessors non-performance does not release the lessee (Hill agt. Obbinson) 151
as to attachment of bill of exchange (West agt. Barter) 157
as to re-entry &c. (Hill agt. Obbinson) 161
as to action by surety agt. the principal &c. (Pelton agt. Thompson) . 162
as to validity of a prior deed (Heinshaw agt. Voss) 185
as to officer attaching being a legal officer (Wharton agt. Reynold) . 192
as to affirmation by constable being a legal evidence (answer to pet. of Jenkins) 201
as to goods on board ship, legally seized, being forfeited (Wharton agt. Reynolds) 202
as to legacy to wife, whether to be her husband's after her death (Chapman agt. Barry) 205
as to acquittance from promise upon marriage (Fletcher for March & wife agt. March) 214

PAGE

SPECIAL VERDICT, *continued.*

as to power of Selectmen to limit number of cattle &c. (Phips &c. agt. Bowers) (Wood &c. agt. Bowers) 224

as to legality of account under maritime law (Gretian agt. Torrey) . 232

as to liability of administrator (Allen agt. Elliot) . . . 260–261

as to evidence and as to parties joining in suit (Ingolls agt. Bishop) . 262–3

as to books of deceased party being legal evidence (admr. of Batt agt. Lake) 269

as to evidence, whether not denying is owning (Rice agt. Avery) . . 273–4

as to evidence (Marret agt. Cutter) 275

as to Magistrate trying title of land (Apleton agt. Roads) . . . 276–7

as to obligation of receiver of goods to deliver to assignee (Stanbury agt. Harris) 367

whether possession given under a levy on a ship gives power as trustee (Foy agt. trustee of Loder) 368

(*See also* MAGISTRATES and BENCH.)

SPEEDWELL (ship or bark)

&c., case of, ... 107

libel of Alden agt., ... 352, 353

SPEERE

George, Wooddey agt., ... 81

agt. Bracket 182

SPENCER, ABRAHAM, (Allen agt. Elliot) 260

SPOONHAUT, JOSEPH (Indian), case of, (murder) 53

SPRAGUE

Antho., (2d. Jury for trials &c.) 274

Phineas, (1st. Jury for appeals &c.) 274

Richard, (Grand Jury) 17

(Jury) 149

Capt., (Jury for attaints) 180

(1st. Jury for trials &c.) 181

foreman, mentd. (Gretian agt. Sweathy) . 182, 183, 190

(Sweatie agt. Greatian) 182–3

(Gretian agt. Stainer) 191

(Joy &c. agt. Adams) 191

(Thaier agt. Savage) 191

Goffreigh agt., ... 222

SPRING

Henry, (Jury of trials &c.) 33, 242

(2d. Jury of trials &c.) 203

(Jury) 231

(Grand Jury) 302, 305

John, (2d. Jury for trials &c.) 45

(Jury for attaints) 256

(1st. Jury for appeal) 257

SPRINGFIELD (Town of), James Fuller of, ... 228

SPURR, ROBERT, (2d. Jury of trials) 362

PAGE

SQUIRE
Ellinor, (case of John Bennet &c.) 11
John, (Jury of trials) 336
STAINER or STAYNOR
Roger, Gretian agt., ... 183, 191
by atty., agt. Gretian 206
STAINTOR (or STAYNOR) Roger, Gretian agt., ... 183
STANBRIDGE, JOHN, agt. Goffe 330
STANBURY
Thomas, (2d. Jury for trials &c.) 121
&c., chosen constables for Boston & oath 206
(Jury of trials) 345
(Jury) 360
of Boston agt. Harris 367
STANION, JNO., &c. agt. Colcord 7
STANLEY, GEORGE, of Beverly, White agt., ... 348
STARAST (or SHARROT), Paul, Left., of ship Salamander, &c. (libel &c.) . 179
STARNES. (*See* STEARNES.)
STARR, RICHARD, &c., (libel &c.) 23
STAUGHTON. (*See* STOUGHTON.)
STAYNOR. (*See* STAINER.)
STEALING. (*See* CRIMES.)
STEALING AND SELLING INDIANS (case of Wm. Waldron &c.) . . . 86–88, 91
STEARNES or STARNES, STERNES
Nath., (Grand Jury) 288
Samuel, " 53
(1st. Jury for trials &c.) 95, 181
(2d " " " ") 153
(Jury for attaints) 181
STEBBINS
John, (Jury of trials) 56
(Grand Jury) 190
Mary, wife of Saml. Stebbins, pet. for divorce 342
Rebecca, of Boston, widow, English agt., ... 326
agt. English 346
Samuel, of North Hampton, pet. for divorce by his wife Mary, . . 342
STEDMAN, JOHN, (Grand Jury) 232, 255
STEEPHENS, STEEVENS } (*See* STEVENS.)
STENWICKE, CORNELIUS, est. of, in hands of Davis, admr. of Dinely agt., (execn.) 371
STEPNEY, FRANCIS, plaintiff, (appeal) 294
STERNES. (*See* STEARNES.)
STERRY, WM., master of ship Treble Croune, (libel &c.) 119
STEVENS or STEEPHENS, STEEVENS.
Erasmus, quartermaster of ship Resolution, &c., Poole &c. agt., . 211–213
Thomas, boatswain of ship George of Bristol, &c. (libel &c.) . 173–4
Timothy, (Jury for trials of attaint) 192

PAGE

STEVENS, &c., *continued.*
Timothy, (1st. Jury for trials &c.) 192
(Grand Jury) 266
STILSON, VINCENT, of Marblehead, agt. Norden &c., Selectmen 328
STOAKES, MICHAELL, Harris agt., ... 196
STODDARD
——, Mr., &c., comrs. sentence of, appealed from, (case of Maior) . 84
(case of Phillips), 84
(case of Nowell), 84
(answer to pet. of Jenkins) 201
Anthony, guardian, admr. of Coggan & wife agt., ... 17
&c., trustees &c., Rice agt., ... 24
commr. in Boston, judgment &c. of, Conney &c. agt., . . 66
Mr., &c., chosen commrs. for Boston, allowed &c. by the Court & oath, 67, 96, 168, 199, 214
agt. Davy 280
Symeon, agt. Johnson 196
STONE
——, Mr., foreman, (Webb (marshal) agt. Manly) 235
(Homes agt. Sweathy) 238
Hannah, case of her husband Hugh 303, 304
Hugh, of Andover, husbandman, case of, (murder) 303–4
John, (Jury of trials) 35
(Grand Jury) 65, 108, 151, 242
&c., Selectmen of Watertown, Mason agt., ... 346
Samuel, (2d. Jury of trials &c.) 45
(Jury for attaints) 233
Mr., (Jury for trials &c.) 233
Senr., (Grand Jury) 302
(Grand Jury) 345
Symon, (Grand Jury) 53
(1st. Jury for trials &c.) 95
Wm., Capt., commander of ship Merchants Adventure, Daniel &c. agt., 213
STONINGTON (Town of), Thomas Bell &c. of, ... 116
STOREY or STORY
Rouland, (Jury of attaints) 244
(1st. Jury for trials &c.) 245
Thomas, &c. mariners, case of, (piracy) 319, 320
STOUGHTON or STAUGHTON
William, Esqr., present at Court, 1, 15, 16, 23, 24, 32–36, 41, 43, 52, 53, 55, 58, 61, 62, 63, 65, 70, 76, 148–151, 161, 169, 170, 172, 173, 176, 177, 179, 190, 202, 208, 209, 211, 213, 214, 223, 228–232, 240, 241, 243, 273, 287, 296, 297, 298, 300, 345, 361
&c., Commrs. for the United Colonies, Rawson &c. agt., 208
chosen as guardians by Chickatabut, ... 208

PAGE

STOWARD (?), ANTHONY, Mr., &c. chosen constables at Boston & oath, . 80
STOWELL, SAMUEL, Rose ag[t]., ... 121
STOWERS
  Richard, (1st. Jury of trials &c.) 161
    Welch ag[t]., ... 246
    (1st. Jury for appeals &c.) 274
STRAITE (or STREIGHT), THOMAS, (2[d]. Jury of trials &c.) . . 141, 161, 362
STRANGER (Mr. Henry Jenkins) granted a hearing 200
STRATTEN or STRATTON
  Bartholmew, &c., owners of ship Salamander, Woodman ag[t]., . . 61
  Eliplam, (case of George Cole &c.) 12
  Richard, ag[t]. Gidley 369
STRAWBRIDGE, JAMES, (Grand Jury) 179
STREET or STRET
  Elizabeth, wife of Robert Street, pet. for divorce 227
  Robert pet. for divorce by his wife Elizabeth 227
STREIGHT. (*See* STRAITE.)
STRET. (*See* STREET.)
STRETTENS, JN[O]., (Grand Jury) 242
STROUT, RICHARD, mariner of ship Merchants Adventure, &c. ag[t]. Stone . 213
STUART, JAMES, &c., case of, ... 5
SUDBURY (Town of)
  Peeter Bent, Jun[r]., of, ... 86
  Jn[o]. Lawrence of, ... 87
SUFFOLK (County of)
  Boston in, ... 86, 234, 295, 298, 300
  Braintree in, ... 188
  Roxbury in, ... 198
  Dorchester in, ... 199
  Marshal of, ment[d]. (case of ship Speedwell &c.) 107
    ag[t]. Manly 235
    ment[d]. 378, 383
    writ of exec[n]. directed to, ... 383, 384
  Treasurer of, ment[d]. (order on pet. of Earle) 114
    Lambe &c. ag[t]., ... 366
  ment[d]. (case of Hon[ble]. George Russell, Esq[r].) 169
SUFFOLK COUNTY COURT. (*See* COUNTY COURT — SUFFOLK.)
SUGARS, GREGORY, commander of ship Concord, (Bulkley ag[t]. Thayre &c.) 338
SUIT, as to parties joining, (Ingolls ag[t]. Bishop) 262, 263
SUMER. (*See* SUMMER.)
SUMERS, HENRY, Wyman ag[t]., ... 267
SUMMER or SUMER
  (or Sumner) Increase, (Jury for attaints) 255
    Roger, (Grand Jury) 108
SUMMONS, question as to power of clerk of writs to grant, (Olliver &c. ag[t]. Town of Lynn &c.) 112

PAGE

Sumner
Increase, (Jury for attaints) 255
(2d. Jury for appeal) 256
(Jury of trials) 362
Roger, (2d. Jury for trials &c.) 71
(Grand Jury) 108
(1st. Jury for trials &c.) 152
William, (Grand Jury) 59
(Jury for attaints) 232
(Jury for appeals) 233
Supply (pink), master of, &c. (libel &c.) 41
Surety
freed if no execution within a month (Sheaffe agt. Blackleach &c.) . 85
action by, agt. the principal, judgment as to, (Pelton agt. Thompson) . 162
Swallow (sloop), &c., Randolph, Collr., agt., ... 219, 220
Swan or Swann
——, Dr., &c., houses of, in Roxbury, burning of, (case of Cheffaleer, negro) 197
Robert, agt. Browne &c., attys. for Town of Haverhill, ... 156
Senr., of Haverhill agt. Wainwright 327
Thomas, of Roxbury, house of, burning of, (case of Maria, negro,) . 198
Swansey (Town of), ship Richard & Mary of, ... 23, 24
Swasy, Stephen, evidence by, mentd. (answer to petn. of Mary Sanders) . 31
Swayne or Sweyne
Jeremiah, Esqr., present at Court 24 Dec. 1689 302
7 Jan. " 305
17 " " 320
Sweathy or Sweatie
Stephen, agt. Greatian 182
Gretian agt., ... 182, 190
Wayt agt., ... 207, 208, 226
Homes agt., ... 238, 244
Sweete, John, &c., Gibbs agt., ... 77
Sweeting
John, execrs. of Shepheard agt., ... 79
of London, admr., trustees &c. of Emery &c. agt., ... 122
his admr., trustees &c. of Emery &c. agt., ... 122
Swett
John, (Jury) 37
(1st. Jury for trials &c.) 120
Tho. Moore instead of, (1st Jury for trials &c.) 120
(Jury for attaints) 233
(Jury for trials &c.) 233
Joseph, (2d. Jury for trials &c.) 18
Sweyne. (*See* Swayne.)

PAGE

SWIFT
Obadiah, &c., surety of Smith agt., ... 69
(1st. Jury of trials &c.) 161

SYMES or }
SYMMS }
Timo., (2d. Jury for trials &c.) 79
Wm., (Jury of trials &c.) 33

SYMOND or }
SYMONDS } or SIMONS
SYMONS }
Benjamin, of Woburn, case of, (rape) 73
Herlakinden, Bennet agt., ... 83
Mr., agt. Leveret 216, 217
Joseph, &c., sureties, (case of Benja. Symons) 73
(2d. Jury of trials) 346
Samuel, Esqr. or Depty. Govr., present at Court, 1, 15, 16, 23, 24, 33, 34, 36, 43, 52, 58, 91–94, 107, 119
&c., fined 90

SYMSON. (*See* SIMPSON.)

TAFT
Robert, Bateman agt., ... 161
plaintiff (appeal) 206, 207

TAINTER } or TAYNTOR
TAINTOR }
Joseph, (Grand Jury) 1, 202
(2d. Jury for trials &c.) 18
(Jury) 22
&c., attys., agt. Chenery 26
(Jury for trials &c.) 228

TALBOT, LANCELLOT, mentd. (Clary &c. agt. ketch Elisabeth & Margaret) . 106
TANNER, ARTHUR, (Jury) 160
TAPPIN, JOHN, (Grand Jury) 53, 78

TARE
Thomas, Waldron agt., ... 120
agt. Hinderson 206

TARPOLIN COVE in Martins Vineyard Sound (case of Wm. Dun &c.), 313, 314, 316–318
TATMAN, JABEZ, (2d. Jury of trials &c.) 25, 161
TAY. (*See* TOY.)

TAYLOR,
JAMES, (2d. Jury for trials &c.) 60
(1st. " " " ") 161
Mr., (Jury for attaints) 232
(Jury for appeals) 233
foreman, mentd. in margin 236, 237
master, (case of Wm. Johnson) 242
John, &c., execr. of Clarke agt., ... 153

PAGE

TAYLOR, *continued.*
William, (Grand Jury) 17
murder of, (case of John Winsland) 117
Mr., &c., atty[s]., ag[t]. White &c. 129
TAYNTOR. (*See* TAINTOR.)
TEUDOR. (*See* TUDOR.)
THAIER / THAIRE } (*See* THAYER.)
THANKSGIVING, public day of, (24 Sept. 1674), appointed by Council . 23
THATCHER
Mary, of Boston, widow, ag[t]. Thatcher 369
Peter, Mr., of Milton, Thatcher ag[t]., ... 369
Thomas, (Jury) 160
Mr., ag[t]. Davy 217
THAXTER, JN[o]. (1st. Jury for trials &c.) 44
THAYER / THAYRE } or THAIER, THAIRE
Nathaniel, (2[d]. Jury for trials &c.) 60
(1st. " " " ") 161
&c. sureties on bond of attaint, (Thaier ag[t]. Savage) . . 186
(1st. Jury for appeals, &c.) 274
(Jury of trials) 302, 304, 308, 310, 311, 319
&c., of Boston, merchants, Bulkley ag[t]., ... 338
of Boston, ag[t]. Townsend 362
Richard, ag[t]. Rose 5
ag[t]. Clap 186
ag[t]. Savage 186
principal on bond of attaint (Thaier ag[t]. Savage) . . . 186
Sen[r]., ag[t]. Savage 191
Zackery, Arnold ag[t]., ... 247
THEFT. (*See* CRIMES.)
THIRSTON
Benjamin, (Jury of inquest) (Inquisition on body of Bickford) . . 84
(2[d]. Jury for trials &c.) in room of Rob[t]. Searle . . 96
THOMAS (alias MUMUCKSUNCASUSUCQUATER) (Indian), case of, (murder) . 54
THOMAS
Edward, mariner of ship Richard & Mary, case of, (false oath) . . 24
(Jury of trials) 302, 304
Mr., (Juror), case of, (default in appearance) 305
of Boston, merchant, Wylly ag[t]., ... 361
John, case of, (piratically seizing small vessels &c.) 39
&c., mariners of ship Herron, (libel &c.) 159, 160
Symon, &c., mariners of ship Ann & Hesther, (libel &c.) 172
THOMPSON / THOMSON } or TOMPSON
Benjamin, ag[t]. Emmery 80, 97
John, &c., atty[s]., Pelton ag[t]., ... 162
Sam., " " " " 162
Wm., Pelton ag[t]. 162

PAGE

THORNHILL, TIMOTHY, Sr., of Barbados, Barrt., Tippet agt., ... 340
THORN HULL, WALTER, Mr., (libel &c.) 75
THORNTON
Timothy, (Jury for attaints) 180
(2d. Jury for trials &c.) 182
&c. chosen constables in Boston & oath 206
Cowell agt., ... 238
Mr., of Boston, merchant (libel &c.) 298, 300, 301
&c. chosen commrs. for Boston & sworn 358
THOUSAND COW (or Millevashe), commander, mentd. (libel &c. agt. ship St. John Frigott) 353
THREE BROTHERS (pink), (libel &c.) 355, 356
THURTON, THOMAS, of Boston, his admr. agt. Colman 336, 337
THWING, EDWARD, &c. agt. Holliock 248
TICKNER, HENRY, &c., for owners of ship Dove, agt. Cannon 52
TIDD or TYD, TYDD
John, (Grand Jury) 345
Joshua, " 24, 108
TIGHT. (*See* TITE.)
TILESTON / TILESTONE } or TYLESTON
Thomas, (Grand Jury) 140, 190, 255, 345
Senr., (Grand Jury) 180
Timothy, (1st. Jury for trials &c.) 44, 140
(2d. " " " " 71, 182
(2d. Jury for appeals &c.) 108
(Jury for attaints) 181
(Jury of trials &c.) 228
TILTON or TYLTON
Daniel, Town of Hampton agt., ... 7
Peter, Esqr., present at Court 1 June 1680 149
8 " " 150
16 Oct. " 169
1 June 1681 190
6 Sept. " 190
1 June 1682 209
22 May 1683 229
4 Sept. " 232
12 Oct. " 241
TIMBERLEG, WM., &c., testimony by, mentd. (case of Mrs. Hope Ambrose) . 127
TING / TINGE } (*See* TYNG.)
TIPPET, NICOLAS, of Boston, merchant, agt. Thornhill 340
TITE or TIGHT, TYTE
Henry, Rogers agt., ... 234
Mason agt., ... 234
agt. Mason 255

PAGE

TODD
John, &c., mariners of ship Endeavor, ag[t]. Smith 130, 131
libel of Smith &c. ag[t]., ... 132

TOLEMAN or / TOLLMAN / TOLMAN
John, (2[d]. Jury for trials &c.) 79, 181
(Jury for attaints &c.) 181, 288
(1st. Jury for appeals &c.) 289
Thomas, Jun[r]., (1st. Jury for trials &c.) 17
(2[d]. Jury for trials &c.) 71, 224
(Grand Jury) 133, 190, 232
Sen[r]., (Grand Jury) 214

TOLTWOOD, HENRY, of Newbury, case of, (felonious assault) 336
TOM INDIAN, case of, (rape) 21
TOMLIN, WM., Allin & Co. ag[t]., ... 141

TOMPKINS
John, &c., seamen of ship Resolution, (libel &c.) 173
Thomas, boatswain of " " &c., (libel) 173

TOMPSON. (*See* THOMPSON.)

TOPPAM or / TOPPAN
Jacob, Mighill & wife ag[t]., ... 29
of Newbury, Toppam ag[t]., ... 338
Peter, Heynes ag[t]., ... 66
of Newbury, ag[t]. Toppam 338

TORREY or / TORRY
———, constable, order as to bill of charges 251
Josiah, libel &c. of Gretian ag[t]., ... 178
ag[t]. Gretian 180, 193, 226, 246
Gretian ag[t]., ... 232
(Jury for attaints) 266
Phillip, (Grand Jury) 120, 180, 214, 230
Wm., Jun[r]., (Grand Jury) 287

TOTMAN, JABEZ, (Grand Jury) 287
TOTON, JN[o]., of Rochell, chirurgeon, (libel &c.) 43
TOUNESEND / TOUNSEND (*See* TOWNSEND.)
TOUT SAINTS, LE SONT, late mate of ship Gift of God, (libel &c.) . . . 332
TOWN, clerk of writs of, question as to power of, (Olliver &c. ag[t]. Town of Lynn &c.) 111, 112

TOWNE
Peter, (1st. Jury for trials &c.) 152, 224, 245
(Jury of attaints) 244

TOWNESEND / TOWNSEND or TOUNESEND, TOUNSEND
Elizabeth, relict of James Townsend, Thaire ag[t]., ... 362

PAGE

TOWNSEND, etc., *continued.*
James, Williams ag^{t}., . . . 155
(2^{d}. Jury of trials &c.) . . . 224
ag^{t}. Edwards . . . 259, 260
(Grand Jury) . . . 298
his relict, Elizabeth, Thaire ag^{t}., . . . 362
Joseph, (1st. Jury of trials &c.). . . . 17
&c., libel of Clarke ag^{t}., . . . 23
ag^{t}. Parkeman . . . 24
Mr., (Jury of trials) . . . 242
&c., appraisers, (Hundlocke ag^{t}. Baker &c.) (exec^{n}.) 390, 391
Penn, (2^{d}. Jury for trials &c.) . . . 153
Capt., ag^{t}. Johnson . . . 204, 205
(Jury) . . . 210
&c., Webb ag^{t}., . . . 215
&c. committee, (order on est. of Savage) . . . 229
(Grand Jury) . . . 298
foreman, (case of Saml. Shrimpton) . . . 299
&c. ag^{t}. Fyfield &c. . . . 325
Capt., &c. chosen comm^{rs}. for Boston & sworn . . . 357
Samuel, execution issued out for, ment^{d}. in margin . . . 11
TOY or TAY
Isaiah, (2^{d}. Jury for trials &c.) . . . 203
(Jury of attaints &c.) . . . 244, 288
(1st. Jury for trials &c.) . . . 245
(1st. Jury for appeals &c.) . . . 289
juryman, objections ag^{t}., (case of James Morgan) . . . 295
(Jury of trials) . . . 302, 306, 308
Jeremiah, Harwood ag^{t}., . . . 257
ag^{t}. Loyd . . . 257
of Boston, mariner, ag^{t}. Harwood & wife . . . 369
TRADE
act of parliament for encouragement of, &c. (information ag^{t}. Lawrence) 343
&c., act for encouragement of, (libel ag^{t}. pink Three Brothers, &c.) . 355
TRAINE or TRAYNE
John, (Jury for trial of attaint) . . . 134
(1st. Jury of trials &c.) . . . 135
ag^{t}. Barnard . . . 275
suit of, ment^{d}. (order on complaint of Bernard) . . . 283
TRAMPEUZ (ship). (*See* TRIUMPUEZ (ship).)
TRAYNE. (*See* TRAINE.)
TREAKE (or FREAKE), ELISABETH, ag^{t}. Robbinson . . . 102
TREASON, &c. (*See* CRIMES.)
TREASURER ment^{d}. 12, 14, 22, 24, 36, 45, 50, 54, 56, 57, 61, 62, 73, 86, 87, 88, 90, 104, 107, 114, 116, 123, 124, 127, 166, 171, 172, 178, 182, 183, 185, 186, 188, 189, 193, 194, 198, 200, 205, 223, 224, 225, 226, 229, 235, 236, 238, 248, 250, 251, 254, 258, 260, 261, 272, 282, 293, 296, 366

PAGE

TREBLE CROUNE (ship), mariner of, (libel &c.) 119
TRESCOTT, WM., (Grand Jury) 244
TRESPASS proved and no damage, judgment as to costs, (Gold, &c., ag[t]. Putman) 27
TRIUMPUEZ (ship), commander of, &c., libel of Dyre ag[t]., ... 263-4
TROT or } TROTT }
Barnard, (2[d]. Jury of trials, &c.) 25
ag[t]. Gourdon 165
Bernard, foreman, (Grand Jury) 301
Mr., foreman, (Grand Jury) 305
Thomas, (Grand Jury) 133, 180
Sen[r]. (Grand Jury) 214, 361
(1st. Jury for trials &c.) 224
William, mariner, &c., (libel, &c.) 64
(Poole ag[t]. exec[x]. of Lydgett) 105
TROWBRIDGE, JAMES, (Grand Jury) 244
TRUMBALL or } TRUMBLE }
John, (Grand Jury) 53
ag[t]. Mason 97
(Jury for trial of attaint) 134
Broune ag[t]., ... 156
ag[t]. Peck 219
TUCKE, THOMAS, (1st. Jury for trials &c.) 152
TUCKER
Benjamin, (Jury of attaints) 244
(1st. Jury for trials &c.) 245
(Grand Jury) 336
Edw[d]., &c., mariners &c. of ship Michael, ag[t]. Loyd &c. . . . 150, 151
Jn[o]. " " " " " " " " " . . . 150, 151
Robert, carpenter's mate of ship Merchants Adventure, &c. ag[t]. Stone . 213
Walter, one of the owners of ship Providence, (libel &c. ag[t]. Bull) . 40
TUDOR (or TEUDOR), JN[o]., assignee, ag[t]. Aglin 7
TUFFTS
Peter, (Jury for trial of attaint) 2
(2[d]. Jury for trials &c.) 3
TUREL } TURELL } or TURRILL TURILL }
Colburn, &c., case of, (default) 315
Daniel, (Jury for trial of attaint) 3
(1st. Jury for trials &c.) 3
(Grand Jury) 119
Jun[r]., (2[d]. Jury of trials &c.) 135
Mr., Sen[r]., libel &c. of Clay ag[t]., ... 174
Jun[r]., &c., ag[t]. Smith 271
order on pet. of, ... 272

PAGE

TURILL, etc., *continued.*
Daniel, Junr., &c., bond by, ... 272
ag^t^. Smith 282
atty., ag^t^. Shaddock 291
blacksmith, &c. ag^t^. Smith 293
John, &c., sale to, (libel &c. ag^t^. Long) (exec^n^.) 375, 376
Samuel, (1st. Jury for trials &c.) 224
Thomas, &c., privateers, (order as to account of Earle) 250
TURNER or TURNOR
Ephraim, (2^d^. Jury for trials &c) 18
(Jury) 22
(Jury of inquest) (inquisition on body of Bickford) . . 34
ag^t^. Harris 83
by atty., ag^t^. Micarter 187
John, ag^t^. Perry 122
atty., ag^t^. Micarter 187
TURRILL. (*See* TURELL.)
TURTUDOES &c., gov^r^. for the French king at, (Lemoigne ag^t^. White &c.) . 129
TWO BROTHERS (pink or buss), commander of, Brenton, Coll^r^. &c., ag^t^., . 349
TWO HOGSHEADS of Irish yarn in hands of Harding, (libel &c.) . . . 177
TWO SISTERS (ship), of Boston, master of, (information &c.) 176
TYD / TYDD (*See* TIDD.
TYLER, John, of Charlestown, ag^t^. Wright 350, 351
TYLESTON. (*See* TILESTON.)
TYLTON. (*See* TILTON.)
TYNG / TYNGE or TING, TINGE
Edward, Mr. or Esqr., present at Court, 1, 12, 15, 16, 23, 24, 32–36, 41, 43, 52, 53, 55, 58, 61–63, 65, 70, 76, 77, 91, 92, 94, 105–107, 117, 119, 128, 130, 131–133, 139, 148–150, 159, 160, 161, 169, 170, 172, 173, 373
(Courts order as to witnesses &c.) 31
fined for his absence from Court, ... 52
ag^t^. Davis 67
dep. sworn before, ... 139
oath before, ... 385
Capt., &c., Paige &c. ag^t^., ... 155
Jonathan, Mr., ag^t^. Chadwell 137
TYTE. (*See* TITE.)

UNITED COLONIES
comm^rs^. for, est. of Johnson ag^t^., ... 95
Rawson &c. ag^t^., ... 208, 209

PAGE

URIN OR }
URING }
Edward, &c., case of, (concurrence with pirates) 42
USHER
Hezekiah, Mr., bond by, ... 51
agt. Usher 111
Mr., agt. Usher 137–139
Mr., Junr., (Usher agt. Usher) 139
Mr., (depn. by Maudet Engis) 139
case of his servant (stealing) 145
goods stolen from, (case of Sara Bradbrooke) 145
his execrs., Usher agt. 203
&c., execrs., " " 203
Mr., &c., execrs., agt. assignee &c. of Harwood 237
agt. assignee &c. of Harwood 237
his execrs. agt. assignee &c. of Harwood 237
agt. Bulkley 243
&c., sureties on bond of attaint, (Baker agt. Wharton) 248
agt. Smith 271, 282, 293
order on pet. of, ... 272
&c., bond by, ... 272
Walker agt., ... 325
Mr., agt. admrs. of Wharton, case of, mentd. (petn. of Usher & decree) 356
petition and decree 356
John, (Mr.), Usher agt., ... 111, 137, 139
Mr., of Boston (depn. by Maudet Engis) 139
agt. execrs. of Usher 203
Mr., principal on bond of attaint, (Phips &c. agt. Bowers) . 224–5
&c. on behalf of Bowers agt. Phipps &c. 232
Esqr., agt. Frizell 302
order of his Majesty in Council that he be not molested (Usher agt. Frizell) 303
UTTERING FALSE STATEMENTS &c. (*See* CRIMES.)

VALLENTINE, THOMAS, Accorman agt., ... 135
VAUGHAN, WM., Left., &c. libel &c. agt. Thornhull 75
VAULX, PETER DE, of Boston, merchant, agt. Shelston 327
VEREN
Hilliard, cler., copy attested by, ... 376
John, agt. Frost 141
VICKERS
Joseph, agt. Walker 278
Roger, Walker agt., ... 277, 278
VINCENT, WM., Sr., of Bas sa blous, burgess & merchant dwelling in St. Malo, (libel &c. agt. ship William) 333
VINER, ANTHONY, &c., mariners of ship James Frygot, (libel &c.) . . . 128

PAGE

VIRGINIA
voyage to, (Bacon &c. ag[t]. Bull) 40
ment[d]. (case of Mary Hare) 126
(libel &c. ag[t]. Brimsden) 128
(Apleton ag[t]., Porter) 154

VOSS or / VOSSE
Robert, by atty., ag[t]. Glover 204
Thomas, Henshaw ag[t]., ... 185
ag[t]. Heinshaw 187
atty., ag[t]. Glover 204

VYALL
John, Sen[r]., (Grand Jury) 65
(Grand Jury) 108
(1st. Jury for trials &c.) 120

WABAN, Ruler of Natick, (case of old Jethro (Indian)) 54

WADE
——, Capt., (order on est. of Mr. Wade) 250
——, Mr., est. of, order as to, ... 250
Jonathan, Capt., Gookin ag[t]., ... 225
Mr., answer to complaint of his son Jonathan, ... 265
order on pet. of, ... 265
Capt., answer to complaint of, ... 265
Nathaniel, Mr., &c., order as to, (est. of Jon[a]. Wade) 265
Thomas, Mr., &c., order as to, (est. of Jon[a]. Wade) 265

WADEING RIVER, Thomas Brentnal now of, ... 326

WAINEWRIGHT / WAINGRIGHT / WAINWRIGHT or WAYNWRIGHT
Fr——, Swan ag[t]., ... 327
Francis, ag[t]. Pickering 46
Patridge ag[t]., ... 46
exec[r]. &c. of Bishop ag[t]., ... 60
John, Lee ag[t]., ... 274
of Ipswich, Dennis ag[t]., ... 347
Simon, atty., Swan ag[t]., ... 327

WAIT / WAITE or WAYT, WAYTE
Gamaliel, (Grand jury) 214, 251
John, Mr., ment[d]. (dep[n]. by Thomas Sexton) 132
(Jury for trial of attaint) 134
(1st. Jury of trials &c.) 135
(Jury of trials) 319
ag[t]. Newhall 363
Return, &c. ag[t]. exec[x]. of Dickinson 26
by atty., ag[t]. Walley 99
(case of Robert Dendy) 116

PAGE

WAITE, etc., *continued.*
Return, ag^t. Leuis . . . 165
case of, ment^d. in margin . . . 203
marshal, ag^t. Sweathy . . . 207, 208, 226
Fisher ag^t., . . . 218
ag^t. Plumbe . . . 227
&c., sureties on bond of attaint, (Webb ag^t. Manly) . . . 235
marshal gen^ls. dep^ty., return of exec^n. by, . . . 381–2
Richard, &c. ag^t. exec^x. of Dickinson . . . 26
marshal, his assignee ag^t. exec^x. &c. of Cook . . . 164
WAKEFEILD, SAMUEL, Apleton ag^t., . . . 277
WALDRON
Isaac, plaintiff, (appeal) . . . 77
Basset ag^t., . . . 78
Marshall agt., . . . 78
Jenkins ag^t., . . . 78
Muzey ag^t., . . . 79
Edmonds ag^t., . . . 79
Mr., of Boston, Apothecary, case of, (injurious speeches &c.) . 88
petition of, . . . 89
acknowledgment of, . . . 90
ag^t. Henderson . . . 119
ag^t. Tare . . . 120
ag^t. Walton . . . 153
ag^t. Wisewall . . . 216
ag^t. Frary &c. . . . 216
Gilbert ag^t., . . . 227
Ri———, sarj. major, statement by, (certificate as to Bilson &c.) . 104
William, &c., seizing vessels &c. of, (case of Andreson) . . . 36
now resident in Boston, &c., case of, (stealing of Indians), 86, 88, 91
(Isaac?), fined (case of Mr. Isaac Waldron) . . . 89
ag^t. Skinner . . . 96
WALES
ment^d. (libel &c. ag^t. ship Richard) . . . 335
(information ag^t. Lawrence) . . . 343, 344
WALES, JOHN, (1st. Jury for appeals &c.) . . . 108
WALKER
Benjamin, (Jury) . . . 149
Mr., in room of Faning (2^d. Jury for trials &c.) . . . 215
(Jury of trials) . . . 242
(2^d. Jury for trials &c.) . . . 274
of Boston, merchant, ag^t. Hawkins . . . 347
Isaac, (2^d. Jury for appeals &c.) . . . 108
(2^d. Jury for trials &c.) . . . 161
&c., sureties, (case of Thomas Saffin) . . . 249
Obadiah, bond given by, . . . 51
Robert, (Grand jury) . . . 1, 214
Samuel, (1st. Jury for trials &c.) . . . 44

PAGE

WALKER, *continued.*
Samuel, ag^{t}. Vickers 277, 278
Vickers ag^{t}., ... 278
Susanna, ag^{t}. Usher 325
Thomas, (1st. Jury of trials &c.) 25
(2^{d}. Jury of trials &c.) 79, 245
(Jury for trial of attaint) 134, 244
brick maker, case of his negro servant (arson) 197–8

WALLEY
John, Wayte ag^{t}., ... 99, 100
Mr., (1st. Jury for appeals &c.) 108
(Jury) 149
Capt., &c., chosen comm^{rs}. for Boston & oath &c., . 168, 199, 214
(Jury for trials of attaint) 191
(1st. Jury for trials &c.) 192
foreman, (Knight ag^{t}. Leach &c.) 194

WALLICE or WALLIS
Robert, master of pink Good Hope (libel &c.) 219

WALTER or WALTERS
Thomas, ag^{t}. Gifford 163
order on complaint of, ... 169
&c., Gifford ag^{t}., ... 218, 247
Mr., (order on pet. of Jno. Gyfford) 231

WALTON
George, Waldron ag^{t}., ... 153
Nathaniel, &c. (Marblehead Commons), Bartlet ag^{t}., ... 20

WAR
with the Indians ment^{d}. (case of Walter Gendall &c.) 102
proclamation of, ment^{d}. (libel &c. ag^{t}. ship Richard) 334–5

WARD
Benjamin, est. of, ment^{d}. (Butler ag^{t}. Hollowell &c.) 140
ment^{d}. (Hollowell &c. agt. Butler) (exec^{n}.) . . . 380–382
John, (2^{d}. Jury for trials &c.) 108
Mary, wife of Benja. Ward (Hollowell &c. ag^{t}. Buler) (exec^{n}.) . 380

WARDELL
———, widow, ag^{t}. Lynde 280
Elizabeth, ag^{t}. Pittam 260

WARNER
John, ag^{t}. Francklin 144
&c., case of, execution in, suspended 146
order on pet. of, ... 146

WARREN
Daniel (Jury of trials) 302, 311, 319
Humphry (Jury for trial of attaint) 3
Mr., of Boston, merchant, &c. (libel &c.) 34
John, (Grand Jury) 120

PAGE

WARREN, *continued*.
John, Senr., (Grand Jury) 336
William, witness, (case of Edward Browne) 315
case of, (piracy &c.) 317, 318, 320
of Boston, ag^t^. Callender 347
WAT[ ], STEPHEN, (Petit Jury) 323
WATCHHOUSE in Boston (case of Joseph Indian) 296
WATERHOUSE
David, of Boston, merchant, ag^t^. Perry 325
&c., merchants, Pynchon ag^t^., ... 328
of Boston, merchant, ag^t^. Luist 350
WATERS or WATTERS
Joseph, his assignee, Gibbs ag^t^., ... 50
Sampson, (2^d^. Jury for trials &c.) 121
Stephen, (Grand Jury) 242
Thomas, case of, (rape) 158
Wm., case of, ... 180
WATERTOWN (Town of)
Ephraim Beamis of, ... 116
Cardin Drabston of, ... 125
Christopher Grant, Junr. of, ... 125
Selectmen of, Mason ag^t^., ... 346
Joseph Mason of, ... 346
WATKINS
John, (Jury of trials) 345
Tho., (Grand Jury) 59
WATSON
John, (1st. Jury for trials &c.) 3, 78, 152
(2^d^. " " " ") 18
(Jury) 22
warrant issued out to, (case of old Jethro (Indian)) . . . 54
(Grand Jury) 230, 298, 361
(Jury of trials) 302, 311, 319
WATTERS. (*See* WATERS.)
WATTS
Jno., mariner, case of, (treachery) 102, 103
Michael, &c., Ballard ag^t^., ... 100, 112
Samuel, witness, (case of Edward Browne) 315
case of, (piracy &c.) 318–320
WAY
———, Left., &c., atty^s^., (case of James Nanapatu, Indian) . . . 54
R———, ment^d^. in margin 93
Richard, (Jury of inquest) (inquisition on body of Bickford) . . . 34
Left., (Jury of trials) 56
(Grand Jury) 65, 190, 202, 243, 287
atty., Pease ag^t^., ... 80
&c., trustees &c., ag^t^. adm^r^. of Sweeting 122
ag^t^. Hauford 122

PAGE

WAY, *continued.*
Richard, (Jury of trials) 311, 319
Lt., (Grand Jury) 361
(Special Jury) 363
WAYMOUTH (Town of). (*See* WEYMOUTH (Town of).)
WAYNWRIGHT. (*See* WAINWRIGHT.)
WAYT }
WAYTE } (*See* WAITE.)
WEARING A BADGE. (*See* PUNISHMENT.)
WEATHERSFIELD (Town of), Mr. Samuel Woolcot of, ... 198
WEAVER
John, mariner, &c., case of, (lying &c.) 23
case of, (wounding Cole) 57
WEB or }
WEBB }
———, Marshal, (case of Darby Bryan) 115
ment^d. in margin 147
Christopher, &c., sureties on bond of attaint, (Homes ag^t. Sweathy) . 238
atty., (Basse ag^t. Crosby) 258
(Griffyn ag^t. Knight) 267
Mr., atty., (Blaney ag^t. Dunton) 340
Daniel, &c., evidence by, ment^d. (answer to pet. of Mary Sanders) . 31
J——, Cler., record signed by, ... 367
Joseph, ag^t. Burton 203
marshal, surety of Gretian ag^t., ... 207
ag^t. Shrimpton &c. 215
marshal, principal on bond of attaint, (Webb ag^t. Manly) . 235
marshal of Suffolk, ag^t. Manly 235
&c., sureties on bond of attaint, (Homes ag^t. Sweathy) . . 238
ag^t. Manly 244
surety on bond of attaint, (Basse ag^t. Crosby) 258
&c., bond by, (Homes ag^t. Sheffeild) 261
Cler., record attested by, ... 359
marshal of Suffolk ment^d. (libel &c. ag^t. Schinking) . . 378–9
(libel &c. ag^t. Checkly and wife) 383, 384, 386
WEBSTER
James, Bagly ag^t., ... 259
Mary, wife of Wm. Webster, case of, (witchcraft) 229, 233
Wm. of Hadly, case of his wife Mary, " 229, 233
WEEDEN, JOSEPH, Wright ag^t., ... 204
WEEKES or }
WEEKS }
Amiel, (Grand Jury) 24
(Jury of trials &c.) 32
Joseph, (Jury of trials) 302, 306, 308
Samuell, (Grand Jury) 78

PAGE

WELCH or WELSH
Phillip, &c., mariners of ketch Ollive Branch, (libel &c.) 131
Thomas, (1st. Jury of trials) 66, 70
agt. Stowers 246

WELD
John, (Grand Jury) 53
(Jury for appeals) 233
(Jury for attaints) 233
Thomas, (Grand Jury) 17, 35, 59, 108, 190
Mr., &c., committee, (order on est. of Lambe) 103
Hall & wife agt., ... 163

WELLEN
Amy, wife of Richard Wellen, case of, (adultery) 14, 15
mentd. (case of Jno. Glandfeild) 15
Richard, case of his wife Amy, (adultery) 14

WELLINGTON
Richd., (Grand Jury) 35
Roger, (1st. Jury of trials &c.) 25

WELLS
John, (Grand Jury) 24
Thomas, agt. Batt 48
agt. Allin 155

WELSH. (*See* WELCH.)

WELSTED or WELSTEED
William, Senr., (Jury of trials) 302, 306, 308
(Special Jury) 363

WENHAM (Town of)
militia of, certificate presented by order of, ... 104
Wm. Fairfield of, ... 348

WEST, WM., agt. Barter 157

WEYMOUTH (Town of)
Marea (Spanish Indian) of, ... 115
Hezekiah King of, ... 250
Samuel Bayly of, ... 251
ship William of, ... 333–4
in England, Jacob Chubb of, ... 333

WHARTON
——, Mr., &c., Melynes &c. agt., ... 15
agt. Smith, execution respited 286
&c., Smith agt., " " 286
Richard, &c., agt. Darvall 5
attys., agt. trustees &c. of Bellingham 24
agt. assignee of Joy 48
Mr., libel &c. of Elson &c. agt., ... 58
&c., Elson agt., ... 59
& Co., libel of Lord &c. agt., ... 63
surety, agt. Swift &c. 69

PAGE

WHARTON, *continued.*
Richard, Mr., &c., atty^{s}., ag^{t}. White &c. 129
ag^{t}. Reynold 192
principal, &c., bond by, (Wharton ag^{t}. Reynold) . . 193
ag^{t}. Reynolds 202
surety on bond of attaint, (Phips &c., ag^{t}. Bowers) . 224–5
Baker ag^{t}., ... 248
principal on bond of attaint, (Baker ag^{t}. Wharton) . . 248
& Co., ag^{t}. Baker 249
(Grand Jury) 255
Mr., &c. ag^{t}. Smith 271, 282, 293
order on pet. of, ... 272
bond by, ... 272
of Boston, merchants, (libel &c.) 297
his adm^{rs}., case of Usher ag^{t}., ment^{d}. (pet^{n}. by Usher & decree) 356
WHEATLY, JN^{o}., &c., mariners of ship James Frygott, (libel &c.) . . . 128
WHEELER
Henry, master of ship Recovery, libel of Gibbs ag^{t}., ... 75
&c., libel &c. ag^{t}. Gibbs . . . 76
libel &c. ag^{t}. Checkly & wife . 130
libel &c. ag^{t}. Checkly & wife (exec^{n}.) 382–384, 386
WHEELEWRIGHT
John, Mr., feofee in trust for wife &c. of Nanny, Chase ag^{t}., . . 17
Samuel, Scottow ag^{t}., ... 152
WHETCOMB or WHETCOMBE
James, &c., sureties, bond by, (case of Rich^{d}. Scott) 61
Mr., surety, (Oxe ag^{t}. Melott) 124
est. of, &c., Baskervill ag^{t}., ... 141
(Mr.), (Jury) 149, 160
(Grand Jury) 229, 273
Josiah, assignee, Gibbs ag^{t}., ... 50
WHIGHT. (*See* WHITE.)
WHIPLE
Jennet, Mrs., Allen ag^{t}., ... 26
exec^{x}., Wayte &c. ag^{t}., ... 26
John, Capt., &c., case referred to, (Hooke ag^{t}. Pike) 154
WHIPPING. (*See* PUNISHMENT.)
WHITE or WHIGHT
Abigaile, (relict of Wm. Lord), and husband Resolved, Manning ag^{t}., 153–4
Ebenezer, (Jury of trials) 299
(Jury) 300
George, Bishop ag^{t}., ... 20
James, (2^{d}. Jury of trials &c.) 25
(Jury for trial of attaint) 134
(1st. Jury of trials &c.) 135

PAGE

WHITE OR WHIGHT, *continued.*
John, joyner, (2d. Jury for trials &c.) 121
(Grand Jury) 202
(Jury of attaints) 244
(2d. Jury of trials &c.) 245
&c., agt. Smith 271, 282
order on pet. of, ... 272
bond by, ... 272
joyner, &c. agt. Smith 293
(Jury of trials) 311, 319
Joseph, pet. for divorce by his wife Mary 147
Mary, wife of Joseph, pet. for divorce 147
Paul, Capt., by atty., agt. Hendrick 142
agt. Heath 142
Philip, of Beverly, agt. Stanley 348
Resolved, & wife Abigaile, Manning agt., ... 153, 154
agt. Maning 162
Thomas, (1st. Jury for trials &c.) 78
Capt., &c., Lemoigne agt. 129
&c., agt. Bowers 224
drivers of Charlestown common, Bowers agt., . . . 232
(Jury of attaints) 244
(1st. Jury for trials &c.) 245
WHITMORE, JOHN, &c., Prout agt., ... 349
WHITNEY
John, Senr., (Jury for trial of attaint) 2
(2d. Jury for trials &c.) 3
(1st. Jury for trials &c.) 152
(Grand Jury) 214, 244, 345
Richard, (1st. Jury for trials &c.) 70
(Jury for trials of attaint) 192
(2d. Jury for trials &c.) 193
WHITTACRE, JNO., &c., attys., agt. Chenery 26
WHITTENHALL, BENJAMIN, &c., mariners of ship Ann & Hesther, (libel &c.) . 172
WHITWELL
William, (Jury) 37
(Jury for trial of attaint) 134
WHOREDOM. (*See* CRIMES.)
WILDER
Jno., &c., costs granted to, ... 87
[Nathaniel], &c., objections agt. Remington as juryman, ... 71
Nathaniel, of Concord, case of, (murder of Indians) 72
&c., examination &c. of, mentd. (costs granted to Keene &c.) 87
Tho., &c., costs granted to, ... 87
WILKINS
John, master of bark Flower, &c. (libel &c.) 92
agt. Helgerson 215

PAGE

WILKINSON
Jacob, ment^d. (Butler ag^t. Hollowell &c.) (exec^n.) 382
Thomas, commander of pink Three Brothers, &c. (libel &c.) . . 355–6
WILKY, JOHN, his admr. ag^t. Clarke 245
WILL, legal proof of (Martyn &c. ag^t. Winsly &c.) 6
WILLARD or WILLURD
———, Mr., ment^d. (case of old Jethro, Indian,) 54
Mary, ment^d. (case of Ephraim Beamis) 116
Symon, Esqr., present at Court [28 May 1674] 15
1 Sept. 1674 16
9 & 21 Oct. 1674 23
13 May 1675 33
24 " " 35
17 June " 36
17 Mar. 1675–6 58
29 Mar. 1676 61

WILLET
Andrew, &c., Randolph, Esqr., Coll^r. &c., ag^t., ... 219
owner of sloop Swallow, Randolph, Esqr., ag^t., ... 220
WILLEY or WILLY, WYLLY
Edward, Mr., (2^d. Jury for trials of appeal) 256
foreman, (Homes ag^t. Sheffeild) 261
Mr., ag^t. Savage 268
(Jury of trials) 298
(Jury) 300
Capt., foreman, (Grand Jury) 345
of Boston, shopkeeper, ag^t. Thomas 361

WILLIAM (ship)
of Bristol, master of, &c. (information &c.) 210
of Waymouth (libel &c.) 333–4
WILLIAMS
———, Mr., (case of Joseph Homes, Senr., &c.) 285
An, &c., finding of jury for, (case of Joseph Ludden, &c.) 5
Edw., mariner, (libel &c. ag^t. ship Nevis factor) 76
Isack, (1st. Jury for trials &c.) 152
John, Atkinson ag^t., ... 4
&c., atty^s., Shakeley &c. ag^t., ... 29
(Jury of inquest) (inquisition on body of Bickford) . . 34
Englishman, case of, (piratically seizing vessels &c.) . . 38
sureties of Fog ag^t., ... 68
ag^t. Townsend 155
ag^t. Brookings 217
Martin, of Salem, bricklayer, case of, (uttering of false counterfeit money) 359, 360
Nathaniel, Woodbridge ag^t., ... 83
ag^t. Calley 95
&c., sureties on bond of attaint, (Gretian ag^t. Sweathy) . 182
(Sweatie ag^t. Gretian) . 182–3

PAGE

WILLIAMS, *continued.*
Nathaniel, &c., sureties on bond of attaint, (Gretian ag[t]. Staynor) . 183
(2[d]. Jury for trials &c.) 274
Richard, &c., Barnes ag[t]., ... 201
Robert, (Grand Jury) 1, 17, 32, 65, 94, 244, 255
of Piscataqua, fisherman, (case of Rob[t]. Driver) 30
(case of Nicholas Faevor) 32
Samuel, (Sen[r]), (Grand Jury) 108, 151, 244, 255, 298
Stephen, (2[d]. Jury for appeals &c.) 108
(Jury for attaints) 255
(2[d]. Jury for appeals) 256
WILLINGTON
Benja., Clary ag[t]., ... 121
Roger, (Jury) 230
WILLIS OF WYLLYS
Edward, Leiut., &c., chosen constables at Boston & oath 80
Mr., (2[d]. Jury of trials &c.) 141
(Jury) 150
Haugh ag[t]., ... 223
Left., &c., sureties on bond of attaint, (Torry ag[t]. Gretian), 226
Mr., (Jury) 230
(2[d]. Jury for appeal) 256
foreman (2[d]. Jury) (Homes ag[t]. Sheffeild) 261
Mr., ag[t]. Savage 268
of Boston, merchant, Mumford ag[t]., ... 351
Capt., (Special Jury) 363
Henry, &c., of Stonington, order on bill of charges 116
Rebeckah, Sedgwick ag[t]., ... 101
WILLOWBY, FRANCIS, Esq[r]., his exec[x]. &c., Bellingham ag[t]., ... 157
WILLURD. (*See* WILLARD.)
WILLY. (*See* WILLEY.)
WILSON
Alexander, seaman, (case of Nicholas Shapleigh) 12, 13
Alice & son, neglect of, (case of John & Sam[l]. Bennet) 11
Edward, (2[d]. Jury of trials &c.) 25
(Jury of trials) 299
(Jury) 300
Humphry, Boulter &c. ag[t]., ... 136
Nath, (2[d]. Jury for trials &c.) 96
Thomas, (Jury for trials of attaints) 192, 267
(1st. Jury for trials &c.) 192
WINCHIP, EDWARD, (Jury of trials) 302, 306, 308
WINCOLL
——, Capt., ment[d]. (order for dower to widow of Hill) 147
Jn[o]., Capt., Hull ag[t]., ... 122
WINDOR
John, his relict & adm[x]. men[d]. (Sheaffe ag[t]. Palmer &c.) 123
merchant, est. of, in hands of Palmer, &c., Baskervill ag[t]., . 141

PAGE

WINDOR, *continued.*
Sarah, (relict &c. of John Windor), wife of Jn°. Palmer, (Sheaffe agt. Palmer) 123
WINDSOR, JOSHUA, &c., sureties, bond by, (Shatswell agt. Jewet) . . . 205
WING
John, agt. Halsey 206
&c., Waldron agt., ... 216
Capt., Dauson agt., ... 288
Danson agt., ... 366
of Boston, Milner agt., ... 367
WING LANE (or Hudsons Lane) in Boston 389, 390
WINSLAND, JOHN, case of, (murder) 117
WINSLEY or WINSLY
John, (2d. Jury for trials &c.) 3
Pattyn agt., ... 4
Davis agt., ... 111
Mary, & husband Nathaniel, Martyn & wife agt., ... 5
Nathaniel, & wife Mary, Martyn & wife agt., ... 5
agt. Martyn 6
Pike agt., ... 279
WINSLOW
Edward, master of ketch Johns Adventure, Angier agt., ... 106
Noyse agt., ... 106
John, (Jury) 171
of Boston, merchant, Perkins agt., ... 323
Natha., Sexton agt., ... 68
Samuel, Shakeley &c., agt., ... 29
WINSLY. (*See* WINSLEY.)
WINTHROP
Adam, (Jury for attaints) 180
atty., agt. Stoakes 196
(Jury) 230
Mr., Treasurer of Suffolk County, Lambe &c. agt., ... 366
Wait, Esqr. or Majr. Genll., present at Court 20 Jan. 1689 321
23 " " 322
8 Apr. 1690 322
2 Sept. " 327
3 Mar. 1690-1 . . . 336
1 Mar. 1691-2 . . . 361
WISE, JOSEPH, (1st. Jury for trials &c.) 59
WISEWALL / WISEWALLE / WISEWELL / WISWALL
Ebenezer, (Jury for attaints) 267
Enoch, (Grand Jury) 24, 32, 108, 244
John, agt. Keene 144
&c., case of, execution in, suspended 146

PAGE

WISWALL, etc., *continued.*
John, Junr., Waldron ag^t^., ... 216
ag^t^. Paige &c. 249
Paige & wife ag^t^., ... 255
Senr., &c., Paige & wife ag^t^., ... 256
ag^t^. Paige &c. 256
Noah, (1st. Jury for trials &c.) 44, 140
(2^d^. " " " ") 71
(Grand Jury) 94
(Jury for attaints) 233, 289
(Jury for trials &c.) 233
(1st. Jury for appeals &c.) 289
WITCHCRAFT. (*See* CRIMES.)
WITHERETT, WILLIAM, of Boston, merchant, Dunclin ag^t^., ... 365
WITHINGTON, RICHARD, (Grand Jury) 1
WITHRINGTON
Ebenezer, (Jury for attaints) 232
(Jury for appeals) 233
John, (Jury for attaint) 192
(2^d^. Jury for trials &c.) 192
(1st. " " ") 215
WITT
Thomas, of Lynn, yeoman, &c., case of, (murder) 306, 307
found guilty of being an accessory to manslaughter . 307, 321
WITTER
Josiah, Richards ag^t^., ... 187
Farr ag^t^., ... 269
WOBURN (Town of)
Benjamin Symons of, ... 73
John Johnson of, ... 158
Thomas Waters of, ... 158
Thomas Fuller of, ... 274
Seth Wyman of, ... 341
George Read &c., of, ... 351
WOOD
Ellice, (2^d^. Jury of trials &c.) 141
George, &c., mariners of ship Apollow, ag^t^. Hollaway &c. . . . 132–3
Josiah, &c., ag^t^. Bowers 224
drivers of Charlestown common, Bowers ag^t^., ... 232
WOODBRIDGE
John, Esqr., present at Court, 4 Sept. 1683 232
12 Nov. 1683 241
2 Sept. 1684 255
Thomas, ag^t^. Gerrish 67
atty, ag^t^. Winslow 68
ag^t^. Williams 83
atty. & surety, ag^t^. Heath and ag^t^. Hendrick 142
Greely ag^t^., ... 165

PAGE

WOODDEY, WOODDIE, WOODDY, or WOODY, WOODEE

Isaack, ag[t]. Speere 81
Richard, (Jury of trials &c.) 33
(Jury of inquest) (inquisition on body of Bickford) . . 34
(Grand Jury) 56, 94, 139
ag[t]. Harrison 60
Left., &c., guardians, plaintiffs, (estate of children of Ann Hitt), 153
Capt., (2[d]. Jury for trials &c.) 181
foreman, (Gifford ag[t]. Read) 192

WOODEE. (*See* WOODDEY.)

WOODMAN

——, Jn[o]. Oynes under name of, (case of Ephraim Beamis) . . 116
Jonathan, ag[t]. Stratten &c. 61

WOODMANCY, WOODMANSEY, WOODMANSY

John, (1st. Jury for trials) 3
(Grand Jury) 35
bond of attaint (Woodmansey ag[t]. Joy) 45
ag[t]. Joy 45
Mr., ag[t]. Frost 58, 59
libel &c. of Culpepper ag[t]., ... 118, 119
&c., sureties on bond of attaint, (Rauson ag[t]. Gilbert) . . 245
appraisers, (libel &c. ag[t]. Checkly & wife) (exec[n].) . . 384-5

WOODROPE, WILLIAM, Mr., of Island of St. Christophers now resident in Boston, owner &c. (libel &c.), 298, 300, 301

WOODWARD

George, (Jury for trial of attaint) 3
(1st. Jury for trials &c.) 3
(2[d]. " " " ") 45

WOODY. (*See* WOODDEY.)

WOOLCOT

John, (Sen[r].), Atkinson ag[t]., ... 220, 233
Samuel, Mr., of Weathersfield, case of his negro servant Jack . . 198

WORCESTER

Constante, widow, house of, in Boston (case of James Morgan) . . 294
Samuel, Ring ag[t]., ... 82

WORDEN, SAMUEL, ag[t]. Addams 239

WOT BIOMPANOW (Indian), (Jury) 22

WOUNDING &c. (*See* CRIMES.)

WRIGHT

George, (Phipps ag[t]. Bronsdon) 337
Henry, by atty., &c. ag[t]. Sparrey 235
of Boston, carpenter, Tyler ag[t]., ... 350-1
W ——, (Jury of inquest) (inquisition on body of Bickford) . . 34
William, (1st. Jury for trials &c.) 70

PAGE

WRIGHT, *continued.*
William, Junr., by atty., ag^t^. Weeden 204
Senr., atty., ag^t^. Weeden 204
WRITING UNTRUTHS &c. (*See* CRIMES.)
WYLLY. (*See* WILLEY.)
WYLLYS. (*See* WILLIS.)
WYMAN
Francis, case of his negro Tho. Kenny 126
ag^t^. Sumers 267
Seth, of Woburn, Clarke ag^t^., ... 341

YALE, TIMOTHY, Shoare ag^t^., ... 9
YEALES, TIMOTHY, ag^t^. Rose 184
YORK (Town of)
County Court at, complaint &c. of Foster referred to, ... 104
Samuel Banks of, ... 325
YORK COUNTY COURT. (*See* COUNTY COURT — YORK.)
YORKSHIRE, Newitchawannick in, garrison at, ... 104
YOUNG or }
YOUNGE }
Jno., Greely ag^t^., ... 81
YOUNGLOVE, SAM^LL^., Cross ag^t^., ... 348

www.ingramcontent.com/pod-product-compliance
Lightning Source LLC
Chambersburg PA
CBHW030536080526
44585CB00012B/181

* 9 7 8 1 6 3 9 1 4 6 5 4 3 *